UNDERSTANDING NONPROFIT AND TAX EXEMPT ORGANIZATIONS
Second Edition

UNDERSTANDING NONPROFIT AND TAX EXEMPT ORGANIZATIONS

Second Edition

Nicholas P. Cafardi
Dean Emeritus and Professor of Law
Duquesne University School of Law

Jaclyn Fabean Cherry
Assistant Professor of Law
University of South Carolina School of Law

ISBN: 978-1-4224-9757-9

Library of Congress Cataloging-in-Publication Data

Cafardi, Nicholas P.

Understanding nonprofit and tax exempt organizations / Nicholas P. Cafardi, Jaclyn Fabean Cherry. -- 2nd ed.

p. cm. -- (Understanding series (New York, N.Y.))

Includes index.

ISBN 978-1-4224-9757-9 (softbound)

1. Nonprofit organizations--Taxation--Law and legislation--United States. 2. Charitable uses, trusts, and foundations--Taxation--United States. 3. Nonprofit organizations--Law and legislation--United States. 4. Charitable uses, trusts, and foundations--United States. I. Cherry, Jaclyn Fabean. II. Title.

KF6449.C345 2012

343.7306'6--dc23

2011048439

This publication is designed to provide authoritative information in regard to the subject matter covered. It is sold with the understanding that the publisher is not engaged in rendering legal, accounting, or other professional services. If legal advice or other expert assistance is required, the services of a competent professional should be sought.

NOTE TO USERS

To ensure that you are using the latest materials available in this area, please be sure to periodically check the LexisNexis Law School web site for downloadable updates and supplements at www.lexisnexis.com/lawschool.

Editorial Offices

121 Chanlon Rd., New Providence, NJ 07974 (908) 464-6800

201 Mission St., San Francisco, CA 94105-1831 (415) 908-3200

www.lexisnexis.com

MATTHEW◊BENDER

To the memory of Nicholas P. Cafardi, Sr.
& Antoinette R. Cafardi

-NPC

To my parents, Jack and Ann Fabean.

-JFC

PREFACE

Understanding Nonprofit and Tax Exempt Organizations (Second Edition) is a guide for the law student or practitioner who is looking to understand the law governing the nonprofit, tax exempt sector. This text deals with the many types of tax exempt organizations; the rules, regulations and limitations imposed on tax exempt organizations by the courts, the Internal Revenue Code (IRS) and the Treasury Regulations (the Regulations); the charitable contribution and fundraising issues affecting tax exempt organizations; the unrelated business income tax, excise taxes and intermediate sanctions imposed on tax exempt organizations; and the rules regarding private foundations. In particular, this second edition reflects recent changes in the law made by the Pension Protection Act of 2006 and the Patient Protection and Affordable Care Act of 2010.

The text begins with an introduction to nonprofit organizations by discussing the relevant law in general, as nonprofits are governed by state law. Next, tax exempt organizations are discussed, by first giving the reader the background on where such organizations fit in the nonprofit sector; why the organizations are given preferential tax treatment; what form these organizations take; and how such organizations are governed and dissolved.

An analysis of tax exempt organizations would not be complete without detailed information on the various rules, regulations and tests they must follow in order to obtain or retain their tax exempt status. This text provides detailed explanations of these, as well as the consequences for failure to comply.

The tax exempt sector is populated with numerous types of organizations. This text explains the major types of tax exempt organizations. Highlighted are the primary categories of IRC Section 501(c)(3) organizations: religious organizations, educational organizations, healthcare organizations and arts organizations. Also treated are all the other types of Section 501(c)(3) organizations: charitable, scientific, public safety testing, literary, organizations that foster amateur sports and organizations for the prevention of cruelty to children and animals. After explaining Section 501(c)(3) organizations in a comprehensive manner, the text turns to the other areas of major tax exempt activity: Section 501(c)(4) social welfare organizations, Section 501(c)(5) labor organizations, Section 501(c)(6) trade associations, Section 501(c)(7) social clubs and Section 501(c)(8) fraternal benefit organizations. There is also a chapter on Section 527 political organizations.

Finally the text ends with explanations of charitable solicitation, fundraising, the unrelated business income tax, and private foundations. The final chapter is a guide to the IRS procedures for obtaining and maintaining tax exempt status. We believe that all of these topics together provide a reasonably complete overview of the nonprofit, tax exempt sector.

Cases, the IRC, and the Regulations are used to discuss and explain the issues relevant to tax exempt organizations. When the IRC and the Regulations are cited, very often the language used is a paraphrase or a direct quote; however, for the ease of reading, quotations have been omitted. Also unless stated otherwise, the statutory and regulatory cites are from the current (as of the date of publication) version of these documents.

While it is important to remember that Revenue Rulings, Revenue Procedures, General

PREFACE

Counsel Memoranda, Technical Advice Memoranda and Private Letter Rulings may not be used as legal precedent, they are useful to illustrate the IRS's position and have been used as such in this text.

The authors would like to thank the law school students and practitioners who have chosen this book in their study of nonprofit and tax exempt organizations. It is an exciting and growing area of the law that has a tremendous impact on our society. The expanding interest in this field of study in law schools is manifested by the fine casebooks that have been published on this subject in recent years: our own *Tax Exempt Organizations*, published by Lexis/Nexis; *The Tax Law of Charities and Other Tax Exempt Organizations* by Professors Jones, Willis, Brennen and Moran, published by Thompson West; *Non Profit Organizations Law and Policy* by Professors Phelan and Desiderio, also published by Thompson West; and *Taxation of Nonprofit Organizations* by Professors Fishman and Schwarz, published by Foundation Press.

The authors would like to thank Erin Powers, Esquire, without whom the first edition of this text would not have been completed. Erin's unending enthusiasm, professionalism, patience, attention to detail and unwillingness to accept anything but the best is greatly appreciated. We would also like to acknowledge her assistance on the rough drafts of several of the chapters in the first edition. We would also like to thank our student research assistants for their help on this second edition: Matthew Orie (Dean Cafardi) and Amanda Bleu Turner, Katherine Stanton, and Courtney Grosenick (Professor Cherry).

Thank you to all of our students in our "tax exempt organizations", "nonprofit organizations", and "nonprofit organizations clinic" classes, for their continuing input on the subject matter. Your enthusiasm has kept us going all these years.

Thank you to Heather Dean, Cristina Gegenschatz, and Elisabeth Roszmann Ebben of LexisNexis Law School Publications, Matthew Bender & Co., Inc.

Thank you to our families for their love and support.

TABLE OF CONTENTS

TABLE OF CONTENTS

TABLE OF CONTENTS

TABLE OF CONTENTS

TABLE OF CONTENTS

TABLE OF CONTENTS

TABLE OF CONTENTS

TABLE OF CONTENTS

TABLE OF CONTENTS

TABLE OF CONTENTS

TABLE OF CONTENTS

TABLE OF CONTENTS

Chapter 1

INTRODUCTION TO TAX EXEMPT ORGANIZATIONS

§ 1.01 INTRODUCTION

The idea that certain types of organizations should not pay taxes is an ancient one, long predating the American legal system or the Internal Revenue Code (I.R.C.). The notion that the income of a favored sector ought not be taxed goes back to biblical times[1] and has continued to develop through the ages. The *Elizabethan Statute of Charitable Uses* of 1601[2] listed various types of charitable activities whose income was not to be taxed. Basically, the statute summarized activities that had been previously recognized as charitable under the common law. The first federal income tax statute included an exemption for "corporations, companies, or associations organized and operated solely for charitable, religious, or educational purposes."[3] Similar language has been in every successive version of the federal income tax law and today is enshrined in Section 501(c)(3) of the I.R.C.[4]

§ 1.02 CATEGORIES OF ORGANIZATIONS IN THIRD SECTOR

In order to develop an overview of the tax exempt sector, it is necessary to understand the relationship between the four basic categories of organizations that comprise it: (1) nonprofit organizations, (2) tax exempt organizations, (3) charitable organizations, and (4) private foundations. The following chart illustrates this relationship:

---

[1] Genesis 47:24.

[2] 43 Elizabeth I, ch. IV (1601).

[3] The Revenue Act of 1894, ch. 349 § 32, 28 Stat. 509, 556. This version of the federal income tax was declared unconstitutional in Pollock v. Farmers' Loan & Trust Company, 157 U.S. 429 (1895). After the adoption of the Sixteenth Amendment, the federal income tax was restored by the Tariff Act of 1913, ch. 16, § II(G)(a), 38 Stat. 114, which repeated the language exempting charitable, religious or educational organizations.

[4] I.R.C. § 501(c)(3).

Note that "non-profit organizations" is the broadest of the four categories, and that it also includes all of the other terms. In other words, all tax exempt organizations are nonprofit, all charitable organizations are nonprofit, and all private foundations are nonprofit. In addition, starting with the largest category, nonprofit organizations, each following category is a subgroup of the preceding category. Tax exempt organizations are a type of nonprofit organization. Charitable organizations are a type of tax exempt organization. Private foundations are a type of charitable organization. The lines between the different types of organizations are often not clearly defined, thus the dotted line.[5]

As the circle gets tighter, so do the rules. The rules governing tax exempt organizations are more demanding than the rules for nonprofits. The rules governing charitable organizations are more stringent than the rules for tax exempt organizations. Finally, the rules for private foundations are the strictest of all. Much of what is discussed in this book concerns these rules.

[A]   Nonprofit Organizations

The instinctive definition that a nonprofit organization is an organization that does not make a profit is incorrect. Organizations that do not make a profit would not last very long before they drowned in a sea of red ink. Nonprofit organizations can make a profit, but it is not referred to as a "profit." Rather, it is referred to as an excess of revenues over expenses.[6] In order to survive, even nonprofit organizations must end the year with an excess of revenues over expenses. What makes nonprofits into nonprofits is what they do with their excess revenues. Unlike for-profits, which distribute annual earnings to the owners or shareholders, nonprofits do not distribute their excess revenues. Because a nonprofit has no owners to whom excess revenues can be distributed, these excess revenues remain with the nonprofit enterprise to be used to further the nonprofit's activities. This is referred to as the "non-distribution constraint,"[7] and it is what separates nonprofit enterprises from for-profit enterprises.[8]

---

[5] The chart was developed from John Simon's "Taxonomy Chart," published in THE TAX TREATMENT OF NONPROFIT ORGANIZATIONS (Walter W. Powell ed., 1987). Note that the broad term "organization" is used here because the organizations in these categories can take various forms, as discussed in Chapter 2.

[6] See Hansmann, The Role of Nonprofit Enterprise, 89 YALE L.J. 835 (1980).

[7] Id. The term "non-distribution constraint" originated with Professor Henry Hansmann.

[8] See §§ 2.01 et seq., 3.01 et seq. and 4.01 et seq. for further information on what it means to be a nonprofit organization.

There are three basic types of nonprofit organizations: the unincorporated association, the charitable trust, and the nonprofit corporation. These entities are all creatures of state law, and the legal formalities and powers of each will vary from state to state.[9]

[B] Tax Exempt Organizations

A tax exempt organization is a type of nonprofit organization not subject to the federal income tax. There are many different types of tax exempt organizations according to the I.R.C. Section 501(c) has 29 subcategories of exempt organizations, not to mention Section 501(d) apostolic organizations, Section 501(e) nonprofit hospital cooperatives, Section 501(f) nonprofit educational common investment funds, Section 527 political organizations, and Section 528 homeowners' associations.[10]

The major type of tax exempt organization is the Section 501(c)(3) organization. There are more organizations in this category of tax exempt organization than there are in any other category. Section 501(c)(3) of the I.R.C. exempts from federal income taxation:

> Corporations, and any community chest, fund, or foundation, organized and operated exclusively for religious, charitable, scientific, testing for public safety, literary, or educational purposes, or to foster national or international amateur sports competition (but only if no part of its activities involve the provision of athletic facilities or equipment), or for the prevention of cruelty to children or animals, no part of the net earnings of which inures to the benefit of any private shareholder or individual, no substantial part of the activities of which is carrying on propaganda, or otherwise attempting, to influence legislation (except as otherwise provided in subsection (h)), and which does not participate in, or intervene in (including the publishing or distributing of statements), any political campaign on behalf of (or in opposition to) any candidate for public office.

A major part of this text will be spent parsing and applying Section 501(c)(3). The language from the very first federal income tax statute is still there, granting exemption from federal income taxation to charitable, religious, and educational organizations. But there have been additions over the years so that now the full list covers the following types of organizations:

- religious[11]

- charitable[12]

---

[9] See § 2.01 *et seq.* for further information on the forms nonprofit organizations can take.

[10] See Appendix E for a Chart summarizing various tax exempt organizations. 26 U.S.C. § 501(c); Affordable Care Act, Pub. L. No. 111-148, § 1322(h)(1), 124 Stat. 119 (2010) (to be codified at 26 U.S.C. § 501(c)) (adding the twenty ninth subcategory, CO-OP health insurance issuers).

[11] *See* § 8.01 *et seq.*

[12] *See* § 1.04.

- scientific[13]

- public safety testing[14]

- literary[15]

- educational[16]

- foster national amateur sports competitions[17]

- foster international amateur sports competitions[18]

- prevention of cruelty to children[19]

- prevention of cruelty to animals[20]

Note that all of these must be conducted as a nonprofit organization, and according to the statute, that means that no part of its net earnings can inure to the benefit of any private shareholder or individual.[21] There is also language in the statute limiting the political activities of Section 501(c)(3) organizations.[22]

While Section 501(c)(3) organizations may constitute the largest category of tax exempt organizations, there are other types of tax exempt organizations that are just as important. They include: Section 501(c)(4) social welfare organizations, Section 501(c)(5) labor organizations, Section 501(c)(6) trade associations, Section 501(c)(7) social clubs, Section 501(c)(8) fraternal benefit organizations, Section 501(d) apostolic organizations, Section 501(e) nonprofit hospital co-ops, Section 527 political organizations, and Section 528 homeowners' associations.[23]

None of the above organizations are obliged to pay the federal income tax on what the I.R.C. refers to as their "exempt function income."[24] This does not mean, however, that they completely escape federal taxes. All of these organizations are subject to the unrelated business income tax imposed by Section 511 and defined in

---

[13] *See* § 12.06.

[14] *See* § 12.07.

[15] *See* § 12.08.

[16] *See* § 9.01 *et seq.*

[17] *See* § 12.09.

[18] *Id.*

[19] *See* § 12.10.

[20] *Id.*

[21] I.R.C. § 501(c)(3).

[22] *Id.* (stating that an organization must not participate in or intervene in any political campaign on behalf of (or in opposition to) any candidate for public office).

[23] See § 13.01 *et seq.* for further information on § 501(c)(4) organizations. See § 14.04 for further information on § 501(c)(5) labor organizations. See § 14.05 for further information on § 501(c)(6) trade associations. See § 14.06 for further information on § 501(c)(7) social clubs. See § 14.07 for further information on § 501(c)(8) fraternal benefit organizations. See § 8.07 for further information on § 501(d) apostolic organizations. See § 10.05[E] for further information on § 501(e) nonprofit hospital co-ops. See § 15.01 *et seq.* for further information on § 527 political organizations. See § 13.04[B][2] for further information on § 528 homeowners' associations.

[24] I.R.C. § 512.

Sections 512 through 514.[25] Section 501(c)(3) organizations that fit into a subcategory called "private foundations" must also pay the federal excise tax on investment income imposed by Section 4940 and, if the circumstances warrant, the other private foundation taxes specified in Sections 4941–4945.[26]

It is not enough for an organization to say it is tax exempt. The organization must normally apply for recognition of tax exempt status with the Internal Revenue Service (IRS).[27] If the organization provides sufficient information to demonstrate its eligibility for tax exemption, the IRS will recognize it as exempt. Once recognized by the IRS as exempt, the organization must maintain this status by completing various yearly filings. Failure to comply with these requirements will result in the IRS revoking the organization's tax exemption.[28]

[C]   Charitable Organizations

The meaning of the term "charitable" has been long debated, and the Regulations provide little clarification, stating only that the term "charitable" should be broadly applied in its generally accepted legal sense.[29] Further complicating the term is that it has also become common to speak of all those types of organizations listed in Section 501(c)(3) as charitable, with the exception of public safety testing organizations. This is because Section 170 of the I.R.C., which creates the income tax deduction for charitable contributions, defines charitable contributions as gifts to organizations "operated exclusively for religious, charitable, scientific, literary, or educational purposes, or to foster national or international sports competitions, . . . or for the prevention of cruelty to children or animals."[30] With the notable exception of public safety testing organizations, the language of I.R.C. Section 170 tracks the language of I.R.C. Section 501(c)(3), thus explaining why the term "charitable" has attached to Section 501(c)(3) organizations in general.

As the United States Supreme Court said in *Bob Jones University v. United States:*[31]

> This 'charitable' concept appears explicitly in Section 170 of the Code. That section contains lists of organizations virtually identical to that contained in Section 501(c)(3). It is apparent that Congress intended that list to have the same meaning in both sections. In Section 170, Congress used the list of organizations in defining the term 'charitable contributions.' On its face,

---

[25] Generally, income is subject to the unrelated business income tax to the extent it is from a trade or business, regularly carried on, not related to their exempt purposes. See § 16.01 *et seq.* for further information on unrelated business income.

[26] See § 19.04 for further information on excise taxes.

[27] Churches, their integrated auxiliaries, and conventions or associations of churches are exempt from the requirement to apply to the IRS for recognition of tax exempt status. *See* § 508(c)(1)(A).

[28] See § 20.01 *et seq.* for further information on the requirements for qualifying and maintaining tax exempt status.

[29] 26 C.F.R. § 1.501(c)(3)–1(d)(2).

[30] I.R.C. § 170(c)(2)(B).

[31] 461 U.S. 574 (1983).

therefore, Section 170 reveals that Congress' intention was to provide tax benefits to organizations serving charitable purposes. The form of Section 170 simply makes plain what common sense and history tell us: in enacting both Section 170 and Section 501(c)(3), Congress sought to provide tax benefits to charitable organizations. . . .[32]

It is the overlap of Section 170 and Section 501(c)(3) that accounts for the term charitable being applied to all Section 501(c)(3) organizations, with the exception of public safety testing organizations. All Section 501(c)(3) organizations, except for public safety testing organizations, can receive tax deductible charitable gifts. Donors to Section 501(c)(3) organizations can deduct those contributions on their personal income taxes. This ability to attract tax deductible gifts, combined with the exemption from federal income taxes, provides substantial economic benefits to charitable organizations. But in exchange for these benefits, charitable organizations are required to surrender their political voice. Section 501(c)(3) organizations can only lobby the government to an insubstantial degree,[33] and they may not participate at all in campaigns for electoral office.[34] And, of course, because charities are, by definition, nonprofit organizations, none of their income can inure to the benefit of any private shareholder or individual.[35]

[D] Private Foundations

There are two types of Section 501(c)(3) charitable organizations: those that are private foundations and those that are not. Private foundations are Section 501(c)(3) organizations that are susceptible to the control of one or a small group of donors, and for that reason are subject to a special statutory regimen.[36] Private foundation status, as a subdivision of Section 501(c)(3) charitable organizations, was created by Congress in the Tax Reform Act of 1969.[37] Following extensive public hearings that focused on the misuse of Section 501(c)(3) organizations by major donors who, in effect, controlled the charity, and used their control to benefit themselves, Congress added Sections 507–509 on private foundations to the I.R.C.[38]

Section 508(b) creates the presumption that every Section 501(c)(3) organization is a private foundation unless it can demonstrate to the IRS that it is not. The ways

---

[32] *Id.* at 585.

[33] They may elect a "safe harbor" lobbying expenditure formula under I.R.C. § 501(h). The words of § 501(c)(3) are: "no substantial part of the activities of which is carrying on propaganda or otherwise attempting to influence legislation."

[34] The words of I.R.C. § 501(c)(3) are: "not participate in, or intervene in (including the publishing or distributing of statements) any political campaign on behalf of (or in opposition to) any candidate for political office."

[35] I.R.C. § 501(c)(3). This is, of course, the nondistribution constraint. See § 17.01 *et seq.* for further information on charitable gifts and income tax deductions.

[36] I.R.C. §§ 4940–4945. See § 19.04 for further information.

[37] Tax Reform Act of 1969, Pub. L. No. 91-172, 83 Stat. 487 (1969).

[38] See § 19.01 *et seq.* for further information on private foundations.

that this can be done are listed in Section 509(a)(1)-(4).[39] An organization demonstrates that it is not a private foundation by (1) fitting into a well-established category of publicly supported charity, such as a church, college, university, or hospital; (2) receiving a large enough level of public support to merit public attention and monitoring; or (3) linking itself closely to a publicly supported charity so that it qualifies as a "supporting organization."[40] If it cannot demonstrate (1), (2) or (3), it is a private foundation. Thus, there are two basic categories of Section 501(c)(3) charitable organizations: charities that are publicly supported in one of the ways outlined in I.R.C. § 509(a)(1)–(4)[41] and "private foundations." Section 501(c)(3) organizations are either one or the other, and the burden is on them to demonstrate their "non-private foundation" status[42] (i.e., public charity status) to the IRS or be bound by the extensive statutory limitations on private foundations.[43]

As stated above, private foundations are subject to a special statutory regimen that public charities do not have to worry about.[44] These include: an excise tax on the investment income of private foundations;[45] a self-dealing tax when insiders benefit from transactions with the private foundation;[46] a tax if they fail to distribute a minimum amount of their income every year to other charitable organizations;[47] a tax if they accumulate too large an ownership share in for-profit businesses;[48] a tax if they make high-risk investments;[49] and a catch-all tax on all other misuse of the private foundation's tax exempt status.[50]

§ 1.03   CONCLUSION

Understanding the rules, regulations, and legal complexities of tax exempt organizations has never been more important as the sector continues to prosper, accounting for more than $303 billion in annual charitable giving alone.[51] It is one of the most vibrant and interesting sectors of our nation's economic, social, and

---

[39] *Id.*

[40] These are the categories of I.R.C. § 509(a)(1), (2) and (3). Section 509(a)(4) decrees that public safety testing organizations (the only type of § 501(c)(3) organization that does not qualify as "charitable" since it cannot receive tax deductible charitable gifts) are, by definition, not private foundations. They are the only type of § 501(c)(3) organization that is neither a private foundation nor a public charity.

[41] Generally referred to as "public charities."

[42] "Non-private foundations" is the IRS's name for those § 501(c)(3) organizations that most of us simply call "public charities" or, better, "publicly supported charities."

[43] See § 19.01 *et seq.* for further information on public charities and private foundation status.

[44] *Id.*

[45] I.R.C. § 4940.

[46] I.R.C. § 4941.

[47] I.R.C. § 4942.

[48] I.R.C. § 4943.

[49] I.R.C. § 4944.

[50] I.R.C. § 4945.

[51] *See Giving to Charities in 2009*, CHRON. PHILANTHROPY (June 9, 2010), *available at* http://philanthropy.com/article/Giving-to-Charities-in-2009-A/65835/.

political life — encompassing such diverse groups as Planned Parenthood, the Roman Catholic Church, the Boy Scouts, and the AIDS Coalition.[52] Understanding tax exempt organizations is well worth the effort as they wield tremendous influence on society today.

---

[52] See Appendix E for a Chart outlining various tax exempt organizations.

Chapter 2

STRUCTURING A NONPROFIT ORGANIZATION

§ 2.01 INTRODUCTION

Nonprofit groups may choose to be structured in one of three different ways: (1) as unincorporated associations, (2) charitable trusts, or (3) nonprofit corporations. This chapter will begin by considering the rationales for why an organization would choose to structure itself as a nonprofit entity. There are a number of reasons given in the scholarly literature.

§ 2.02 RATIONALES

[A] Historical

First, there is the historical rationale.[1] Some types of organizations began their existence as nonprofits and they remain so to this day. To a large extent, this happened in the history of the United States because the frontier extended beyond the area of the country where there was an effective government. For their protection and common good, the settlers formed voluntary, nonprofit associations that provided services such as fire protection and security from attack. Volunteer fire companies that exist in much of America today are a prime example of nonprofit organizations that have, historically, always been nonprofit.

[B] Contract Failure

A second rationale is Professor Henry Hansmann's contract failure theory.[2] According to Professor Hansmann, contract failure (sometimes also called market failure) occurs in three distinct situations: (1) where those paying for goods are not the same as those who receive them, e.g., the donors to CARE or the Red Cross, and those who actually benefit from those organizations; (2) where the cost of providing the goods is the same no matter how many people enjoy the goods, e.g., clean air and water; and (3) where the services being delivered are so complex there is no way to put an actual price on them, e.g. health care, nursing care. In each of these three situations, a contract failure has occurred. The market is unable to fairly establish the price of the goods, so society relies on nonprofits to provide them because nonprofits, without a need to make a profit for their investors, have

---

[1] *See* LESTER M. SALAMON, AMERICA'S NONPROFIT SECTOR: A PRIMER (2d ed. 1999).

[2] *See* Henry Hansmann, *The Role of Nonprofit Enterprise*, 89 YALE L.J. 835 (1980); Hansmann, *Reforming Nonprofit Corporation Law*, 129 U. PA. L. REV. 497 (1981).

no reason to overprice these goods and will therefore price them fairly.[3]

Professor Hansmann explains this rationale as the "nondistribution constraint." Nonprofits, he says, are constrained to keep any excess of revenues over expenses within the nonprofit enterprise itself, to be used for the purposes of the enterprise, and for no other purpose. They may not distribute them to officers, members, directors, or shareholders. Because of the nondistribution constraint, nonprofits have no reason to gouge those who pay for services and can be trusted to price them fairly. They are fiduciaries for their donors or patrons of the money that they receive from them, to be used for the nonprofit purposes of the organization.[4]

[C]   Government's Inability to Respond

There are certain things that government cannot do — for example, participate in religious activity; or will not do — for example, acting as a check or balance on itself. These areas of activity are left, respectively, to religious organizations and to public interest groups such as Common Cause.[5] In some of the literature, the inability of the government to engage in activities performed by the nonprofit sector is also referred to as "government failure,"[6] to create a parallel with the previous category of "market failure." It is often said that, what the government cannot do, and what the market chooses not to do, the nonprofit sector should do.

[D]   Societal & Political Innovation

This area is closely related to Section 1.01[C]. As the Filer Commission stated, "[Nonprofit] organizations, precisely because they are nongovernmental and need not be attuned to a broad and diverse constituency, can take chances and experiment in areas where legislators and government agencies are hesitant to tread."[7] Once these ideas are proven to be worthwhile, often the government does become involved. The Filer Commission gives the example of HMOs, physician's assistant training programs, and birth control technology, all of which were originally undertaken by the nonprofit sector, shown to be viable societal options, and then were either absorbed by or funded by the government.[8] The same is true

---

[3] Hansmann, *The Role of Nonprofit Enterprise, supra* note 2, at 846–68. Hansmann's work in nonprofit theory was groundbreaking. Not everyone is in complete agreement with him. For some differing views, see Rob Atkinson, *Altruism in Nonprofit Organizations*, 31 B.C. L. Rev. 501 (1990), holding that all nonprofit organizations (other than "mutual commercial nonprofits") operate under a form of altruism and because altruism is highly valued by society the exemption is deserved; Richard Steinberg & Bradford Gray, *"The Role of Nonprofit Enterprise" in 1993: Hansmann Revisited*, 22 Nonprofit & Voluntary Sector Q. 297 (1993), which reviews Hansmann's contract failure theory. *See also* Avner Ben-Ner, *Nonprofit Organizations: Why do They Exist in Market Economies? in* The Economics of Nonprofit Institutions: Studies In Structure And Policy (Susan Rose-Ackerman ed., 1986); Estelle James & Susan Rose-Ackerman, The Nonprofit Enterprise In Market Economics (1986).

[4] Hansmann, *The Role of Nonprofit Enterprise, supra* note 2, at 838–845.

[5] *See* The Commission On Private Philanthropy And Public Needs (The Filer Commission), Giving In America: Towards A Stronger Voluntary Sector 43–44 (Report of the Commission, 1975).

[6] *See* Salamon, America's Nonprofit Sector, *supra* note 1.

[7] The Commission on Private Philanthropy and Public Needs, *supra* note 5, at 60.

[8] *See* Lester M. Salamon, *Partners in Public Service: The Scope and Theory of Government-*

in the creation of new governmental policies. Because it must deal with vested interests, government is slow to adopt new ways of operating. The nonprofit sector is more able to perform public policy analysis that can lead to governmental reform than the government itself, as for example, regional planning agencies.[9] In addition, the government is slow to move in the area of social or political innovation because it is responsible to a larger constituency. Nonprofit organizations are not so constrained and have, therefore, taken the lead in this area while the government is left to follow.

[E]   Protection of Freedom

Sections 2.02[C] and [D] explained the almost paragovernmental role that some nonprofits play. The role described in this section is not so much paragovernmental as it is contra-governmental. The nonprofit sector can also serve as a balancing force in society to the strength of the government and the marketplace.[10] In society, both government and the for-profit sector are very powerful forces. When their interests overlap, there is very little breathing space for those who would contradict or even question them. The nonprofit sector often provides a contrary voice to these powerful forces. For example, in the public policy debate on various health care issues, from prescription drug benefits to the end-of-life care of the elderly, it has been the nonprofit sector that has spoken for the elderly poor who could not speak for themselves.

[F]   Creation of Cultural Goods

The costs of creating great works of art, literature, or drama for public use and enjoyment do not vary based on the size of the audience. Once the original cost is borne, there may be as many or as few partakers as the work merits. This was discussed in Hansmann's contract failure theory in Section 2.02[B]. Because of the significant "free rider" problem, i.e., where persons are free to enjoy the work without paying for its creation or who pay significantly less than what their pro-rated cost for the work would be, the creation of cultural goods falls largely, but not completely, to nonprofit organizations.[11] Aside from the economic argument, it has always been a role of nonprofit organizations to encourage and protect the kind of free speech and freedom of expression that the arts require. This is yet another reason why organizations that create cultural goods, often called arts organizations, use the nonprofit model.

Nonprofit Relations, in THE NONPROFIT SECTOR: A RESEARCH HANDBOOK 90 (Walter W. Powell ed., 1987).

   [9] *See* Bazil Facchina et al., *Privileges and Exemptions Enjoyed By Nonprofit Organizations: A Catalog and Some Thoughts on Nonprofit Policymaking,* NYU PROGRAM ON PHILANTHROPY AND THE LAW (1993).

   [10] JAMES DOUGLAS, *Political Theories of Nonprofit Organization, in* THE NONPROFIT SECTOR, *supra note* 8, at 43. *See also* SALAMON, AMERICA'S NONPROFIT SECTOR, *supra* note 1.

   [11] WILLIAM J. BAUMOL & WILLIAM G. BOWEN, PERFORMING ARTS — THE ECONOMIC DILEMMA (1966).

[G] Social & Ethnic Associations

Nonprofits are also the place in society where individuals of a like mind come to form social and ethnic associations. For example, most organizations that own and operate a private golf course are structured as nonprofit social organizations.[12] Social organizations also run athletic competitions, train people to play chess, operate private airplane clubs and facilities, and comprise the many ethnic and fraternal organizations such as the Daughters of the American Revolution, Elks, Moose, Oddfellows, Knights of Columbus, the Slovak Union, the Polish Falcons, the Sons of Italy, the Ancient Order of Hibernians, and so on. Very often the purpose of these organizations is the protection and preservation of their ethnic or religious roots.[13]

§ 2.03 STRUCTURE CHOICES

Nonprofit organizations that seek to qualify for tax exempt status are structured in one of three ways: they are organized as unincorporated associations, charitable trusts, or nonprofit corporations. Tax exempt organizations may not be operated as a group of individuals or by a partnership.[14] Individuals choosing their structure look to governing state law and often to their legal advisors for assistance because the choice of form that the organization chooses has a great deal to do with the ultimate mission of the organization, what the incorporators hope to accomplish, and an understanding that choice of form does make a difference for operational, governance, and dissolution purposes. Liability and tax concerns also influence the form an organization chooses before seeking tax exempt status.

The terms in the IRC regarding structure are basically very clear, although when discussing a trust, the IRC uses the words "fund" or "foundation."[15] While tax exemption is primarily a matter of federal law, choice of structure will be governed primarily by state law governing unincorporated associations, charitable trusts, and nonprofit corporations.

[A] Unincorporated Associations

Unincorporated associations are the least structured form of nonprofit organization. Many nonprofit organizations start out as unincorporated associations, before putting a plan together and assessing the organizational options available. An unincorporated association is just that — an association of individuals without a formal legal structure. It is simply a group of people who have come together for a common purpose (in this case, a charitable purpose) and who are not interested in the legal details and structure and paperwork required by incorporation or other more formal legal structure. What many do not know is that

---

[12] I.R.C. § 501(c)(7).

[13] *See* SALAMON, AMERICA'S NONPROFIT SECTOR, *supra* note 1.

[14] *See* IRS EXEMPT ORGANIZATIONS HANDBOOK § 321.1 (1977); Emerson Inst. v. United States, 356 F.2d 824 (D.C. Cir. 1966).

[15] Fifth-Third Union Trust Co. v. Comm'r, 56 F.2d 767 (6th Cir. 1932); G.C.M. 15778, XIV-2 C.B. 118 (1935).

although there is little paperwork required of this form (needing only a constitution or bylaws if seeking 501(c)(3) tax exempt status),[16] there is also little protection afforded to this group or association by law.

There are few statutory rules and little case law to govern unincorporated associations. The law of agency governs liability within the organization, and although Section Six of the Uniform Unincorporated Association Act[17] grants limited liability to individuals involved in these organizations, it has not been widely followed. An unincorporated association has no legal existence apart from the individuals that comprise it; as a result, individual members can be held personally liable for the debts and legal injuries of the association. Under common law, a member can not sue the association for injuries alleged to have been caused by the association, because this is regarded as an individual suing himself. Unless there is an enabling statute within the state, the organization cannot hold or receive property in its name, it cannot contract in its name, and banks and creditors may be reluctant to do business with such an association.[18]

[B] Charitable Trusts

A second form of nonprofit organization is the charitable trust.[19] Charitable trusts exist at common law and there are few formalities involved in creating them. A donor, sometimes also called a settlor or trustor, gives property, the trust corpus or trust res, to a trustee, with instructions to hold the property in trust for the charitable purposes stated by the donor. Charitable trusts, unlike other forms of trust, do not have individual, named beneficiaries. Rather, the beneficiaries of a charitable trust are an indefinite group of people, sometimes simply identified as "the public," who are the proper objects of charity. For this reason, charitable trusts are held to provide a public, as opposed to a private, benefit. The founding document, the declaration of trust, will identify the donor, the trustee, the trust property or trust corpus, the trust's charitable purposes, policies for trust administration and distribution of assets and dissolution, successor trustees or method of selection, and the duration of the trust.

While a written declaration is not required to create a trust at common law, one is required for purposes of the federal income tax exemption. In order to qualify for IRC Section 501(c)(3) tax exempt status, the declaration of trust must limit its purpose to one or more exempt purposes provided by the IRC.[20] The declaration

---

[16] IRS EXEMPT ORGANIZATIONS HANDBOOK, *supra* note 14, at § 321.4.

[17] Uniform Unincorporated Association Act § 8.

[18] BRUCE R. HOPKINS, THE LAW OF TAX EXEMPT ORGANIZATIONS (7th ed. 1998).

[19] See RESTATEMENT (SECOND) OF TRUSTS § 348 (revised 2d ed. 1977), which states:

"A charitable trust is a fiduciary relationship with respect to property arising as a result of a manifestation of an intention to create it, and subjecting the person by whom the property is held to equitable duties to deal with the property for a charitable purpose." The Restatement further states that often there are no definitely ascertainable beneficiaries of a charitable trust. If a charitable trust does not designate a particular charity or charities as its beneficiary, the public is the beneficiary. However, if a charitable trust is created to support a particular charity, the named charity would be the designated beneficiary.

[20] I.R.C. § 501(c)(3); Matter of Troy, 364 Mass. 15, 57, 306 N.E.2d 203, 227 (1973). The court

must also provide that, upon dissolution of the trust, all of its remaining assets will be distributed for similar charitable purposes to one or more charitable organizations. Additional IRC Section 501(c)(3) requirements prohibiting private inurement and limiting political activities must also be included in the declaration. If the trust will function as a private foundation,[21] it must include a statement that it will refrain from activities that would violate specific excise tax requirements found in the IRC.[22]

Creating a charitable trust is generally easier than creating a nonprofit corporation and allows for more privacy, as the founding documents are not required to be filed with the state.[23] Those holding the trust property are subject to equitable duties to use the property for charitable purposes. Charitable trusts are enforced by the attorney general and not the trust beneficiaries, who by definition are an indeterminate class and therefore cannot act.[24] Because a trust is not a statutory organization, it does not generally report to the state. It typically does so only in cases where there are mandatory reporting requirements by certain states regarding the trust's charitable activity or charitable fundraising.[25]

[C] Nonprofit Corporations

[1] Historical Development

Nonprofit corporations have existed longer than for-profit corporations. A good case can be made that historically the roots of nonprofit corporations are in the ancient Roman law's *collegium*, which were groups of people, like burial societies or artisans' guilds or religious societies, that were recognized by the state as having a separate legal existence apart from the individual members who comprised them.[26] This idea that there could be an organization doing work and having rights different from the individuals who owned it made its way into the canon law of the Roman Catholic Church, the major legal system of medieval Europe. In the 1200s, when Europe's first universities arose, they were granted legal existence by the Church as *universitas*, which is simply the Latin term for corporation. Not until the 1600s, with the need to capitalize the high-risk sea voyages to the Americas and the East Indies, did the Western legal tradition create the idea of the joint stock or business corporation.[27]

---

concluded that though an organization is formed under a nonprofit corporate statute, it does not in and of itself, guarantee that a charitable corporation has been formed. Courts will look to the organizational documents, including bylaws, to make this determination.

[21] See § 19.01 *et seq.* on private foundations.

[22] I.R.C. §§ 4941–4945. *See* IRS Publication 557, Forming a Tax Exempt Organization (Rev. Dec. 2004).

[23] *See* Restatement (Second) of Trusts § 348.

[24] See generally state statutes concerning the powers and duties of the state's attorney general.

[25] *See, e.g.*, Illinois Charitable Trust Act, 14 Ill. Adm. Code 480.10].

[26] Nicholas P. Cafardi & Jaclyn Fabean Cherry, Tax Exempt Organizations: Cases and Materials 3 (2d ed. 2008).

[27] *Id.*

[2] Defining Nonprofit Corporations

Although the self-evident definition of a nonprofit corporation is that it is a corporation that does not make a profit, it is more accurate to say that a nonprofit corporation is one that does not distribute any excess of revenues over expenses.[28] What the organization does with the excess revenue (or profit) is what distinguishes it from for-profit organizations.[29]

> A nonprofit organization is, in essence, an organization that is barred from distributing its net earnings, if any, to individuals who exercise control over it, such as members, officers, directors, or trustees. . . . Net earnings, if any, must be retained and devoted in their entirety to financing further production of the services that the organization was formed to provide.[30]

The term coined by Professor Hansmann for this prohibition on the distribution of excess revenues by nonprofit corporations is the "nondistribution constraint."[31]

Most nonprofit organizations choose to operate under the nonprofit corporate form. "For these organizations, the nondistribution constraint is imposed, either explicitly or implicitly, as a condition under which the organization receives its corporate charter."[32]

> [A] nonprofit corporation is distinguished from a for-profit . . . corporation primarily by the absence of stock or other indicia of ownership that gives the owners a simultaneous share in both profits and control.[33]

Many of the state statutes governing nonprofit corporations are similar to business corporations law. This may or may not be an advantage. The similarity often offers a familiar model as well as a body of analogous case law that can be transported to the nonprofit context.[34] On the other hand, because of the similarities, the many important differences between business corporations and nonprofit corporations are often overlooked or misunderstood. Because these questions are state-specific, it is important to be familiar with the individual nonprofit corporations law of the state of operation.

[3] Formalities of a Nonprofit Corporation

A nonprofit corporation must conform to more formalities in its creation, operation, and dissolution than either the unincorporated association or the charitable trust. On the other hand, internal governance is generally more flexible in nonprofit corporations, which makes it easier for nonprofit corporations to react to changed circumstances than unincorporated associations or charitable trusts. For example, a nonprofit corporation can more easily amend its corporate govern-

---

[28] Hansmann, *The Role of Nonprofit Enterprise, supra* note 2, at 835–901.

[29] *Id.*

[30] *Id.*

[31] *Id.*

[32] *Id.; see also* MODEL NONPROFIT CORP. ACT (2008).

[33] Hansmann, *The Role of Nonprofit Enterprise, supra* note 2, at 838.

[34] *See* MODEL NONPROFIT CORP. ACT (2008).

ing instruments (by a vote of the Board of Directors in accordance with the corporate bylaws) than can unincorporated associations or charitable trusts, although this flexibility is not unlimited.[35]

A nonprofit corporation is a "legal" as opposed to a "physical" person. As a legal person, it can sue and be sued, enter into contracts, and hold property in its own name.[36] It has an indefinite existence and is managed by a board of directors, who serve specific terms throughout the corporate existence. The powers of the board of directors are specified in state law and in the nonprofit corporation's bylaws. Directors of a nonprofit corporation are held to a high standard of care and have fiduciary duties of care, loyalty, and of mission (or obedience) to the nonprofit corporation.[37]

[4]   Model Nonprofit Corporation Act

There are widely differing approaches among the states regarding the law that governs nonprofit corporations and that have been adopted as nonprofit corporation statutes. Some states follow the original Model Nonprofit Corporation Act, drafted in 1952 by the Committee on Corporate Laws of the Section of Corporation, Banking and Business Law of the American Bar Association, and revised in 1957 and 1964 to more closely follow the Model Business Corporation Act.[38] The drafters believed that the body of law that had developed to interpret the Model Business Corporation Act could be a resource in interpreting provisions of the Nonprofit Act,[39] which proved true in some cases. A very few states have no separate nonprofit corporate statute, but use their for-profit corporate statute in resolving issues that are nonprofit in nature. Other states have adopted, in whole or in part, the Revised Model Nonprofit Corporation Act, which was approved by the American Bar Association in 1987.[40]

In August 2008, the Third Edition of The Model Nonprofit Corporation Act (MNCA) was approved by the American Bar Association. In drafting the Third Edition, the committee decided three things: "(1) [to]follow the Model Business Corporation Act provisions to the extent possible, considering certain differences that distinguish nonprofit corporations from for profit corporations; (2) [to] eliminate the classification scheme included in the Revised MNCA; and (3) [to] make the provisions pertaining to the role of the attorney general optional, if desired, with a suggestion to adopting states that provisions regarding the supervision of nonprofit organizations would be better located in a different place in

---

[35] *See* Alco Gravure, Inc. v. Knapp Found., 64 N.Y.2d 458 (1985); Carolyn C. Clark & Glenn M. Trost, *Forming a Foundation: Trusts vs. Corporations*, 3 Prob. & Prop. Rev. 32 (May/June 1989).

[36] *See also* James F. Fishman & Stephen Shwarz, Taxation of Nonprofit Organizations: Cases And Materials 48 (2003).

[37] See § 3.01 *et seq.* for further information on the duty of directors to nonprofit corporations.

[38] ABA, Model Nonprofit Corp. Act (1952); ABA, Rev. Model Nonprofit Corp. Act (1964).

[39] Model Nonprofit Corp. Act; Rev. Model Nonprofit Corp. Act 3; Marilyn Phelan, Nonprofit Enterprises: Corporations, Trusts And Associations, Apps. D & E (2000).

[40] See individual state nonprofit corporation statutes.

a state's statutory scheme."[41] The decision to eliminate the classification system, which is considered a big change, stems from much disagreement among adopting states regarding this provision. The 1987 Revised Model Nonprofit Corporation Act distinguishes between two types of nonprofit organizations, the *public benefit* organization and the *mutual benefit* organization. A public benefit organization is one that serves a public or charitable purpose. Its mission is generally charitable, educational, or religious, and it operates to serve a community need. It is usually open to the public and receives its support from the general public. Mutual benefit organizations are formed to serve the common needs of their members. The interests served are generally limited.[42] These organizations include chambers of commerce, labor unions, and social clubs.[43] States that adopted this component ran into serious issues because the classifications did not match those in the Internal Revenue Code for tax exemption, turning the decision to follow this classification system "into a trap for the unwary."

Two other restrictions included in the 2008 Act provide that "a fundamental transaction property held in trust or otherwise dedicated to a charitable purpose may not be diverted from that purpose without an appropriate order" and "in transactions such as mergers" private inurement is prohibited.[44]

Becoming familiar with the individual statutory law of the state of incorporation must be a part of all decisions made by or for nonprofit organizations.[45] This may include a review of the Model Nonprofit Corporate Act version that the statute is based on as well as a review of the statute itself.

[5] Formation

An organization that chooses the nonprofit corporate form generally incorporates the organization in the jurisdiction where it is located, although for many other reasons, including taxes, additional sites of operation, etc., it may choose another state. Because incorporation is governed by state statute, choice and knowledge of the state law becomes critical.

[a] Filing Articles of Incorporation

The first step in forming a nonprofit corporation is the filing of Articles of Incorporation, usually with the Department of State of the state of incorporation.[46] Most incorporation statutes require that the applicant provide the following information: name of the corporation; corporate address; purpose;[47] name and address of incorporators; date of incorporation; date of end of fiscal year; whether

---

[41] Rev. Model Nonprofit Corp. Act Introduction xxix (1988).

[42] *Id.*; *See* Rev. Model Nonprofit Corp. Act § 17.07 (1988).

[43] See Ga. Code Ann. § 53-12-110; Okla. Stat. Ann. tit. 60 § 601; Fla. Stat. § 496.404 as examples of states that have not adopted the classification system.

[44] Model Nonprofit Corp. Act Intro. xxii (2008).

[45] *Id.*

[46] *See* 15 Pa. Cons. Stat. Ann. §§ 5301–5311 for one example of requirements. Although similar in most states, California offers some different requirements. *See* Cal. Corp. Code §§ 5130, 7130.

[47] The act of incorporation is governed by state law and the purpose listed for incorporation should

the corporation intends to have members; and the names and addresses of the original board of directors.[48]

If the nonprofit corporation intends to seek IRC Section 501(c)(3) tax exempt status, then its corporate articles must limit its purpose to one or more exempt purposes provided by the IRC.[49] The articles must also provide that, upon dissolution of the corporation, all assets of the corporation will be distributed for similar charitable purposes to one or more charitable organizations. Assets may not be distributed to corporate members upon dissolution. Additional IRC Section 501(c)(3) requirements prohibiting private inurement and limiting political activities must also be included in the corporate articles. If the nonprofit corporation is a private foundation,[50] it must include a statement that it will refrain from activities that would violate specific excise tax requirements[51] found in the IRC. The IRS makes this all very easy on the incorporators by providing sample language for the corporate articles of a nonprofit corporation that seeks to qualify as tax exempt in IRS Publication 557, "Forming a Tax Exempt Organization."[52]

If the nonprofit corporate articles comply with the requirements of state law, then the secretary of state will record the documents and send a date-stamped copy back to the original incorporators.[53] At this point, incorporation has been accomplished. Most states also have advertising requirements to put the community on notice that the organization has incorporated.

[b]   Drafting Bylaws

The nonprofit corporation must draft a set of bylaws. The bylaws are the internal document that sets forth the rules and procedures for governing the corporation. Bylaws are more flexible than the Articles of Incorporation as they can easily be amended to address the needs of the organization by a vote of the Board of Directors in accordance with the bylaws. The procedures for making amendments should always be included in the bylaws.[54]

---

conform to state law; however, it is important to remember that the purpose for state incorporation should be compatible with the purpose required for federal tax exemption. I.R.C. § 501(c)(3). For further information on qualified organizations for federal tax exemption, see §§ 8.01 *et seq.*; 9.01 *et seq.*; 10.01 *et seq.*; 11.01 *et seq.*; 12.01 *et seq.*; 13.01 *et seq.*; and 14.01 *et seq.*

[48] See particular state law for exact requirements.

[49] I.R.C. § 501(c)(3); *Matter of Troy*, 364 Mass. 15 (court concluded the fact that an organization was formed under a nonprofit corporate statute does not in and of itself guarantee a charitable corporation has been formed). Courts will look to the organizational documents, including bylaws, to make this determination.

[50] See § 19.01 *et seq.* on private foundations.

[51] I.R.C. §§ 4941–4945.

[52] IRS Publication 557, *supra* note 22.

[53] Some states issue a *Certificate of Incorporation* and others a *Charter*, but they all serve as documentation of the incorporation for the organization.

[54] Bylaws include such things as: meeting times, number and terms of board members, what constitutes a quorum; what officer responsibilities are; what committees will be established; what powers and responsibilities committees will have; election procedures; removal procedures; notice requirements; and amendment procedures.

Although much of the document begins as boilerplate, an organization usually tailors the document to the organization's needs, being very specific about roles and duties of Board Members, as this is a working document of some importance.[55] Typically, nonprofit corporate bylaws, unlike nonprofit corporate articles, do not need to be filed with the state.

[6] Purpose and Powers

[a]   Conforming to State Public Policy

As discussed above, nonprofit corporations are governed by state law. The individual states decide which types of organizations can be organized as nonprofit corporations under their state law. Normally, this does not create issues of great legal moment. There is, however, a body of case law that discusses what qualifies as a charitable or nonprofit purpose under state law.[56]

> The rationale for such oversight was that the incorporated status was a privilege initially granted by the legislature by special act rather than a right. Later, incorporation became available for corporations with specified purposes, but the legislature retained some control over chartering non-profit groups which they vested in a state official or judge.[57]

This same type of oversight can be seen in the public policy requirement for federal tax exempt status,[58] which finds its roots as far back as the Elizabethan *Statute of Charitable Uses.*[59]

The *Statute of Charitable Uses* created a list of public purposes which qualified as charitable. This list is reflected in later statutes dealing with the topic of what qualifies as a public charity.[60] The courts interpreted the *Statute* to mean that activities not serving a public purpose are not charitable. An activity that is illegal does not serve a public purpose, and therefore, is not charitable. For example, in *DeCosta v. DePaz,*[61] a case decided in 1754, a will that directed that a sum of money be applied to the maintenance of a *yeshiva*, or assembly for reading Jewish law, and for advancing the Jewish religion was declared invalid because it was not charitable

---

[55] *See* Barbara L. Kirshten, Nonprofit Corporation Forms Handbook (1993); *Matter of Troy*, 364 Mass. 15.

[56] *See* Hansmann, *Reforming Nonprofit Corporation Law,* supra note 2.

[57] Note, *Judicial Approval as a Prerequisite to Incorporation of Nonprofit Organizations in New York and Pennsylvania,* 55 Colum. L. Rev. 380, 382 (1955), cited in Fishman & Schwarz, Nonprofit Organizations, *supra* note 36. See *Ass'n for Preservation of Freedom of Choice v. Shapiro,* 9 N.Y.S.2d 376, 214 N.Y.S.2d 388, 174 N.E.2d 487 (1961) where the court stated that since the purposes set forth in the Certificate of Incorporation were not contrary to state law, there was no basis for rejection even though the lower court found such purposes (including promoting ways for those in our multicultural society to find their fullest development) violated public policy and were injurious to the community.

[58] See § 7.02[B] for further information on public policy.

[59] 43 Elizabeth I ch. IV (1601).

[60] Statute of Charitable Uses, 43 Elizabeth I ch. IV (1601) includes the following (among others) as charitable uses: "maintenance of sick and maimed soldiers and mariners, schools . . . , repair of bridges, ports, havens, causeways, churches . . . orphans, . . . marriages of poor maids. . . ."

[61] 2 Swans 487 (Chancery 1754).

and was against public policy. At the time, in England, the practice of the Jewish faith was outlawed. Therefore, any support of the Jewish faith was an illegal act. The court decided that the money should be directed to an Anglican hospital more in keeping with "Christian religion." A similar fate befell trusts established for Catholic purposes because, at that time, the practice of the Catholic faith was considered illegal.[62]

Despite its rather unfortunate genesis in religious discrimination, the doctrine that a charitable organization or a trust could not be created for a purpose that was illegal and therefore violative of public policy became accepted in the common law and now applies to nonprofit corporations. "A purpose is illegal if the trust or charity's object is in violation of a statute, tends to induce the commission of a crime, or if the accomplishment of the purpose violates public policy."[63] As demonstrated in numerous cases throughout this text, the standard of what violates public policy evolves over time and changes as society's standards change; therefore, those interpreting what meets with the current standard are given some discretion.[64] While activities that are illegal clearly violate public policy, the category is broader than that. For example, the "segregation" academies denied tax exempt charitable status in *McGlotten v. Connally*[65] and its progeny were not acting illegally, although they were violating public policy.

What is considered lawful or proper or within public policy has not always been easy to discern. In *State ex rel. Church v. Brown*,[66] the Ohio secretary of state refused to accept articles of incorporation for a nonprofit corporation formed to provide facilities for coeds to practice nudism. The secretary determined that although technically formed correctly, the purpose violated a state statute that prohibited anyone over the age of 18 from willfully exposing his private parts in the presence of two or more persons of the opposite sex.[67]

The secretary of state of Ohio also refused to accept articles of a nonprofit corporation because the "office [found] . . . that acceptance of the proposed articles of incorporation for Greater Cincinnati Gay Society, Inc. appear[ed] to be contrary to public policy since homosexuality as a 'valid life style' [was] . . . defined by statute as a criminal act."[68] The decision was based on a statute that the secretary claimed authorized him to decide if a corporation's purpose was lawful. The Ohio Supreme Court agreed that "the promotion of homosexuality as a valid life style is contrary to the public policy of the state."[69] Such decisions are a reminder that the

---

[62] *See* Nicholas Cafardi, *Bequests for Masses: Doctrine, History & Legal Status*, 20 Duq. L. Rev. 403 (1982).

[63] Austin Wakeman Scott et al., 6 Scott and Ascher on Trusts § 38.11, at 2630 (5th ed. 2006 & Supp. 2009).

[64] See § 7.02[B] for further information on tax exempt organizations and public policy.

[65] 338 F. Supp. 448 (D.D.C. 1972).

[66] 133 N.E.2d 333 (Ohio 1956).

[67] *Id.* at 335.

[68] State *ex rel.* Grant v. Brown, 313 N.E.2d 847 (Ohio 1974), *appeal dismissed and cert. denied sub nom.*, 420 U.S. 916 (1975).

[69] *Id.* at 849.

common law source of the "public policy" requirement was a prior form of discrimination (religious).

[b]   Conforming to State Non-Commercial Purposes

Aside from public policy considerations, states also consider whether a nonprofit corporation is organized for a commercial purpose (which is not considered acceptable) and whether the purpose is truly charitable. In *People ex rel. Groman v. Sinai Temple*,[70] the California Court of Appeals held that a nonprofit corporation originally organized as a religious organization, which later began operating a cemetery in conformity with its doctrines, did not violate a state statute that prohibited a nonprofit corporation from distributing gains, profits, or dividends to its members. "Carrying on business at a profit as an incident to the main purposes of the corporation and the distribution of assets to members on dissolution are not forbidden to nonprofit corporations. . . ."[71]

When a nonprofit corporation participates in commercial activities or has a commercial purpose, apart from the problems it will have with federal tax exempt status, it may also violate state statutes that prohibit nonprofits from engaging in commercial activity and it may make it more difficult for the nonprofit corporation to qualify for state income or property tax exemption. Property tax exemption, which is governed by state law, is very important to most nonprofits. Because most nonprofits operate very close to the line, their federal income tax (and state income tax) burden is often slight if it exists at all. Being exempt from the federal income tax, then, is not a substantial economic benefit for many nonprofit organizations. On the other hand, exemption from state property taxes usually provides a very substantial economic benefit and offers the greatest dollar value to the nonprofit, together with the ability to receive tax deductible gifts that accompanies federal tax exempt status. Though an organization has qualified for federal tax exemption, it still must meet the requirements of the state where it owns property in order to qualify for property tax exemption. Basically, if an organization qualifies as a "purely public charity" as defined by the state constitution, it must then meet legislative or court requirements to qualify for property tax exemption.[72]

---

[70] 20 Cal. App. 3d 614, 99 Cal. Rptr. 603 (1971).

[71] *Id.*

[72] See State v. North Star Research and Development Inst., 294 Minn. 56, 200 N.W.2d 410 (1972), where the court set forth 6 factors to be met by an organization in order to qualify as a "purely public charity" and therefore, become exempt from property tax. And later, in North Star Research Institute v. County of Hennepin, 306 Minn. 1, 236 N.W.2d 754 (1975), where the court concluded North Star was not a "purely public charity." See also Under the Rainbow Child Care Center, Inc. v. County of Goodhue, 741 N.W.2d 880, 886 (Minn. 2007), where the court determined that the organization was not a "purely public charity" because it did not provide "charity" to recipients free of charge or at considerably reduced rates, and in reviewing the multi-part test of North Star stated that while ". . . not all of the North Star factors must be satisfied in order to qualify for exemption, some of the factors are, indeed, essential."

[c]   Conforming to State Definitions of Charity

The definition of charity varies from state to state and although the term is used in the I.R.C., it is never fully defined. Some state statutes attempt to define charity by mimicking the I.R.C. and referencing terms such as educational, philanthropic, humane, artistic, etc., while others simply state that the organization's purpose must be charitable and lawful. In one case, a trust that chose to support research into the proof of the human soul was deemed charitable,[73] although the study of the occult was found not charitable.[74] The IRC defines charity by using its generally accepted legal definition as broadly developed and outlined in the common law.[75] Other states, such as Pennsylvania, have elaborate tests to determine what is charitable.[76]

The questions surrounding what is and is not charitable will be revisited in sections on federal tax exemption and the requirements of the I.R.C.[77] It is enough to know, at this point, that decision makers have broad power to interpret the meaning of what is charitable according to state law and that these powers include the power to tax (property and other taxes) which is crucial to the existence of most nonprofits.

§ 2.04   TAX EXEMPT STATUS

Once the organization has formed as an unincorporated association, trust or nonprofit corporation, federal tax exempt status can be sought, if desired. For example, once a nonprofit corporation has filed articles of incorporation (and had them accepted by the state), given notice, drafted bylaws, and held the first organizational meeting of the Board of Directors to ratify the bylaws, then federal tax exempt status can be sought. For most Section 501(c)(3) organizations this is done by filing Form 1023 with the IRS. Other types of Section 501(c) organizations file Form 1024.[78]

§ 2.05   STATES' ROLE IN CHOICE OF STRUCTURE

Choice of structure affects the role of the state in a nonprofit organization's affairs. Several lawsuits have been brought in state courts to determine the powers and reach of attorney generals in the nonprofit area.[79] Most of the decisions turn on

---

[73] *In re* Estate of Kidd, 106 Ariz. 554, 479 P.2d 697 (1971).

[74] *In re* Matter of Carpenter, 163 Misc. 474, 297 N.Y.S. 649 (1937).

[75] 26 C.F.R. § 1.501(c)(3)-1(d)(2).

[76] *See* Hosp. Utilization Project v. Commonwealth, 487 A.2d 1306 (Pa. 1985). *See also* Shaw Public Trust v. Day and Others, 1 All. ER 745 (Chauncery 1957), where the English courts concluded that the will of Bernard Shaw did not propose a charitable purpose (the study and statistical analysis of the alphabet with the purpose of adding letters and sounds and applying such methodology to one of his plays), and therefore, held the trust invalid.

[77] See §§ 6.01 *et seq.* and 7.01 *et seq.* for further information.

[78] See § 20.01 *et seq.* for further information.

[79] *See, e.g.*, Rev. Model Nonprofit Corp. Act §§ 1.7, 3.04, 8.10, 14.03-14-04; Cal. Corp. Code §§ 5142,

the structure and choice of form of the organization.[80] When the choice of form is an unincorporated association, the role of the state attorney general is minimal.[81] When an organization is structured as a nonprofit corporation, the attorney general only has the powers specified in the state's nonprofit corporation statute or other statutes. Normally these statutes involve the attorney general only in egregious or criminal behavior by the organization or its board or in some instances during the dissolution process. When the nonprofit organization is structured as a charitable trust, however, the role of the state attorney general is greater. Because the beneficiaries of a charitable trust are considered to be indefinite and unable to speak for themselves, the state attorney general has the common law power, under the doctrine of *parens patriae*, to bring suit to enforce the terms of a charitable trust and to see that charitable trust assets are in fact used for charitable purposes.

Attorneys general in many states often find themselves challenging organizations over their duties to the state and the community based on their choice of structure.[82] It can happen that a nonprofit corporation also embodies a charitable trust, in which case the attorney general will follow the *parens patriae* role of greater involvement, rather than the lesser statutory role he or she has with regard to nonprofit corporations. The question turns on whether the nonprofit corporation functions as a charitable trust. When a charitable trust is involved, the public is the beneficiary, and the property in such a trust, even if held by a nonprofit corporation, must be devoted to purposes beneficial to the public that can be policed by the attorney general. Whether or not a nonprofit corporation embodies a charitable trust is a question of fact. The court in *Younger v. Wisdom Society*[83] stated that "in determining whether a corporation was organized exclusively for charitable purposes . . . the trial court . . . was not bound either by the articles of incorporation or by the particular code sections that the corporation was formed under, but the court could consider the corporation's actual conduct and method of operation."[84]

In *People v. George F. Harding Museum*,[85] the Attorney General of Illinois brought suit against a nonprofit corporation under the Illinois Charitable Trust Act in order to enforce the terms of a charitable trust, maintaining that the organization no longer operated a museum open to the public, which was one of its stated charitable purposes. The court reviewed the purposes of the organization as set

---

5250, 6511, 9230; N.Y. NOT-FOR-PROFIT CORP. LAW. § 112; Brown v. Memorial Nat'l Home Found., 329 P.2d 118, 132–133 (1958).

[80] *See, e.g.*, MODEL NONPROFIT CORP. ACT §§ 1.70, 3.04 (2008); CAL. CORP. CODE §§ 5142, 5250, 6511, 9230; N.Y. NOT-FOR-PROFIT CORP. LAW § 112; *Brown v. Memorial Nat'l Home Found.*, 329 P.2d at 132–133.

[81] As discussed here and in § 3.01 *et seq.*, the laws pertaining to the structure and governance of nonprofit organizations is governed by state law. Where applicable, examples have been provided; however, individual state law should be consulted in dealing with nonprofit organization issues.

[82] *See* Rob Atkinson, *Unsettled Standing: Who (Else) Should Enforce the Duties of Charitable Fiduciaries?* 23 J. CORP. L. 655 (1998); A UNIFORM SUPERVISION OF TRUSTEES FOR CHARITABLE PURPOSES ACT, 7B U.L.A. 727 (1978); REV. MODEL NONPROFIT CORP. ACT §§ 1.7, 3.04, 8.10, 14.03-14-04; CAL. CORP. CODE §§ 5142, 5250, 6511, 9230; N.Y. NOT-FOR-PROFIT CORP. L. § 112; Brown v. Memorial Nat'l Home Found., 329 P.2d at 132–33.

[83] 121 Cal. App. 3d 683 (1981).

[84] *Id.* at 690; *see also* Cal. Employment Comm'n v. Bethesda Found., 54 Cal. App. 2d 348 (1942).

[85] 374 N.E.2d 756 (Ill. App. 1978).

forth in the Articles of Incorporation, and determined that the nonprofit corporation was in fact organized and operated as a charitable trust. The court then reviewed charitable trust law and the definition of a charitable purpose.[86] The court cited Bogert in defining a charitable trust as "one which is for the public benefit,"[87] and the RESTATEMENT OF THE LAW OF TRUSTS, which defines the nature of a charitable purpose as follows: "A purpose is charitable if its accomplishment is of such social interest to the community as to justify permitting the property to be devoted to the purpose in perpetuity."[88] In this case, the court held that the attorney general had the common law power to enforce the terms of a charitable trust and to guarantee that the funds of the nonprofit corporation were being used for the intended charitable trust purposes.[89]

In *Commonwealth of Virginia v. The Joco Foundation*,[90] on the other hand, the Supreme Court of Virginia determined that the state attorney general could not intervene in the disposition of assets of nonprofit corporations devoted to charitable purposes without a specific grant of power by the state legislature. The court decided that the State Corporate Commission was the proper forum for determining issues regarding the management of charitable assets held by nonprofit corporations. It determined that the attorney general did not have inherent powers to act on behalf of the public in these matters. The court disagreed with the attorney general's position that a nonprofit corporation devoted to charitable purposes was a charitable trust.[91]

---

[86] *Id.* at 759.

[87] *Id.* at 761, *citing* BOGERT, TRUSTS AND TRUSTEES § 369 at 62 (revised 2d ed. 1977).

[88] *George F. Harding Museum*, 374 N.E.2d at 761, *citing* RESTATEMENT (SECOND) OF TRUSTS § 368, comment b, at 248.

[89] *Id.* at 760.

[90] 558 S.E.2d 280 (Va. 2002).

[91] *Id.* at 284.

Chapter 3

GOVERNANCE OF NONPROFIT ORGANIZATIONS

§ 3.01 INTRODUCTION TO GOVERNANCE

This chapter concentrates on the governance issues of nonprofit corporations, though first touching briefly on the governance issues of unincorporated associations and trusts.[1]

[A] Unincorporated Association Governance

The governance structure of an unincorporated association is determined by the articles of association, or bylaws. The authority of those governing (usually members in good standing) comes from the law of agency.[2]

[B] Trust Governance

Trusts are governed by trustees who receive their legal authority generally from the terms of the trust instrument and by statute.[3] There are different standards or duties of care for trustees of trusts compared to boards of directors of nonprofit corporations, with the duty being somewhat higher for trustees.[4] Trustees are self-perpetuating, unless the trust instrument states differently. Their governance does not include elections, quorums, membership, or other such issues. Trustees hold the title to trust property in their names, are permitted to contract in the name of the trust, and can be removed by court order.[5]

---

[1] *See* Henry B. Hansmann, *Reforming Nonprofit Corporation Law*, 129 U. Pa. L. Rev. 497, 509–538 (1981); 3 Austin Wakeman Scott et al., Scott and Ascher on Trusts § 18.1, at 1266 (5th ed. 2006 & Supp. 2009); 5 *id.* § 37.3.2 at 2410; Harry G. Henn & Michael George Pfeiffer, *Nonprofit Groups: Factors Influencing Choice of Form*, 11 Wake Forest L. Rev. 181, 194 (1975).

[2] *See* Hansmann, *supra* note 1; 3 Scott, *supra* note 1, § 18.1 at 1266; 5 Scott, *supra* note 1, § 37.3.2 at 2410; Henn & Pfeiffer, *supra* note 1.

[3] *See* 3 Scott, *supra* note 1, § 18.1 at 1266; 5 Scott, *supra* note 1, § 37.3.2 at 2410.

[4] Henn & Pfeiffer, *supra* note 1, at 193–196.

[5] *Id.*

[C]   Nonprofit Corporation Governance

Groups organized as nonprofit corporations are governed by a Board of Directors, which is also self-perpetuating.[6] The Board of Directors is governed by state statute (nonprofit corporation),[7] the Model Nonprofit Corporation Act, and or case law. Some statutes are fashioned on the Model Nonprofit Corporation Act while others have their genesis in the for-profit corporate statutes of their state.[8] Although this does seem to work, it is a relatively careless way for lawmakers to have addressed this area of the law. A board of directors of a nonprofit corporation is responsible for overseeing the corporation and is bound to the corporation through its fiduciary duties. A board member serves a designated term and is governed by the bylaws of the organization and by state law. Nonprofit directors are selected because they are sources of funding, have a certain prominence in the community and can bring recognition to the organization, or have skills which would benefit the organization (business management, legal, or mission related).[9] Nonprofit boards are committed to ensuring that the organization remains true to its mission. Boards are responsible for fundraising and organizing volunteers of the organization. "Management of nonprofit organizations normally is vested in its senior employees. A basic function of the board is to select these executives and to oversee their performance. The model that an organization adopts will depend upon the size and scope of its activities, needs and characteristics, and the board environment."[10]

§ 3.02   MANAGING THE NONPROFIT

As stated above, boards of directors are generally governed by the terms of the organization's bylaws, and the nonprofit laws of the state of incorporation. Board members are appointed and removed in accordance with the terms of the bylaws. The actions of board members are interpreted in conjunction with the organization's bylaws. Other board members, high-level employees, and members who question board action do so in accordance with the terms of the bylaws.[11] For example, in a New York case from 1953,[12] members of a nonprofit organization brought suit questioning whether the bylaws were illegally adopted or were against the law of the land. Plaintiffs claimed that certain of the organization's bylaw provisions conflicted with the state statute. They believed that the board "unlawfully usurped

---

[6] See Hansmann, *supra* note 1, at 509–538 (1981). Self-perpetuating boards appoint their own members.

[7] See 15 Pa. C.S.A. § 5301 *et seq.* as an example of a nonprofit corporation statute based on the for-profit statute of the state.

[8] See individual state law and case law for approach used. See also Louisiana World Exposition v. Federal Insur. Co., 864 F. 2d 1147 (5th Cir. 1989); John v. John, 153 Wis. 2d 343 (Ct. App. 1989); Grace v. Grace Institute, 19 N.Y. 2d 307 (1967).

[9] *See generally* Section of Business Law, Guidebook for Directors of Nonprofit Corporations (George W. Overton ed., 1993).

[10] See Bayless Manning, *The Business Judgment Rule and the Director's Duty of Attention: Time for Reality*, 39 Bus. Law 1477, 1484 (1984), for more information on the duties of nonprofit boards.

[11] *See* Barbara L. Kirschten, Nonprofit Corporation Forms Handbook (1993).

[12] Bailey v. American Soc. for Prevention of Cruelty to Animals, 282 A.D. 502 (N.Y. App. Div. 1953).

too much power to itself with respect to acceptance of new members and expulsion of present members. . . ."[13] The plaintiffs also questioned the self-perpetuating powers of the board. The court found neither to be a violation because the self-perpetuation of the board was included in the terms of the bylaws, and there was no improper or unlawful action in adopting the bylaws.[14] Although permitting the self-perpetuating nature of boards of nonprofit corporations, courts are somewhat more careful with regard to self-perpetuating roles for specific board members or employees.[15]

§ 3.03   FIDUCIARY DUTIES

The boards of directors of nonprofit corporations are bound by fiduciary duties. The fiduciary duty requires that the individual members and the board collectively act unselfishly and give to the organization its highest level of care. Having its genesis in trust law, *fiducia*, meaning trust, the relationship between a board and the organization it serves is similar to the relationship between a trustee and the trust's beneficiary. The fiduciary obligation serves as an "alternative to direct monitoring" of a board's behavior.[16]

[A]   Duty of Care

The duty of care asks a director: (1) to be reasonably informed; (2) to participate in decisions; and (3) to do so in good faith. Though many statutes continue to require the additional responsibility of acting with the care of an ordinarily prudent person in similar circumstances, the Model Nonprofit Corporation Act of 2008 has removed this standard.[17] The duty of care requires a director to be informed and to exercise independent judgment. To fulfill this requirement, the director should monitor the organization's activities by attending meetings, exercising his or her own independent judgment in making decisions, and reading materials supplied by the staff of the organization. A director should request further information if he or she believes the information is not adequate.[18] For

---

[13] *Id.* at 505.

[14] The court also stated that no question as to the bylaws and their ratification had occurred in the 50 years since their adoption and that a claim at this time seemed untenable. *Bailey*, 282 A.D. at 504. *See also* Fitzgerald v. Nat'l Rifle Ass'n, 383 F. Supp. 162 (D.N.J. 1974).

[15] See Solomon v. Hall-Brooke Found., Inc., 619 A.2d 863 (Conn. App. Ct. 1993), where the founder and employee of an organization who was fired under her lifetime contract was given no relief. The court cited that ". . . directors have no power to hire an employee on a lifetime basis . . ." as this is seen as a device to hamstring future boards. *See also* Osborne v. Locke Steel Chain Co., 153 Conn. 527, 537, 218 A.2d 526 (1966).

[16] Louisiana World Exposition v. Federal Ins. Co., 864 F.2d 1147 (5th Cir. 1989); Grace v. Grace Inst., 19 N.Y.2d 307 (1967); DEBORAH A. DEMOTT, FIDUCIARY OBLIGATION, AGENCY AND PARTNERSHIP 12 (1991); *see also* Litwin v. Allen, 25 N.Y.S.2d 667 (1940); Dana Brakman Reiser, *Enron.org: Why Sarbanes-Oxley Will Not Ensure Comprehensive Nonprofit Accountability*, 38 U.C. DAVIS L. REV. 205 (2004).

[17] SECTION OF BUSINESS LAW, GUIDEBOOK FOR DIRECTORS OF NONPROFIT CORPORATIONS 19 (George W. Overton & Jeannie Carmedelle Frey, eds., 2003). *See* MODEL NONPROFIT CORP. ACT § 8.30, 8.33, 8.41–42 (2008).

[18] SECTION OF BUSINESS LAW, *supra* note 17, at 19–22.

example, if a director notes a shortcoming in an auditor's report, but ignores the shortcoming, then that director may be in violation of the duty of care.

[1] Relying on Information

A director may rely on information provided by another director, committee, officer, employee, or agent of the organization as long as the director believes the source to be reliable and competent. A director may not rely blindly on others. The director must comply with general standards of care in the selection and monitoring of those on whom he or she has relied for information. If a director has a reasonable basis to be suspicious, he should make further inquiry. However, "a director need not exhaustively research every issue personally to comply with the legal requisites."[19] The board of directors generally does not manage the corporation, but delegates this function to others. As with the reliance on information from others, the board may not blindly rely on those to whom they have delegated authority; thus, the board should set policies and oversee those to whom authority has been delegated.[20]

[2] Business Judgment Rule

The obligation for directors to exercise due care does not mean that the directors will incur liability for honest mistakes of judgment.[21] The business judgment rule provides that decisions by boards about business matters are presumed correct. The rule provides complete protection from liability for business judgments as long as the judgment is rational, involves no conflict of interest, and the director acted in a manner he believes is reasonably informed.[22]

A Delaware case, *Smith v. Van Gorkom*,[23] interprets the business judgment rule as requiring a board to:

- Decide issues only after proper deliberation, absent any undue haste or pressure;

- Be prepared prior to any decision making; study, read, request materials;

- Participate in the discussions leading up to the decision;

- Maintain proper written records of all discussions and keep all material relied on to make decisions;

- If the transaction is a major one, ask for and review expert opinions (accounting, legal, etc.); and

---

[19] DANIEL L. KURTZ, BOARD LIABILITY: GUIDE FOR NONPROFIT DIRECTORS 29 (1988).

[20] DEMOTT, *supra* note 16, at 12.

[21] *See* KURTZ, *supra* note 19.

[22] DEMOTT, *supra* note 16, at 12; *Corporate Control Transactions, supra,* at 700–703.

[23] 488 A. 2d 858, 874–75 (Del. 1985). See Sarah Helene Duggin & Stephen M. Goldman, *Restoring Trust in Corporate Directors: The Disney Standard and the "New" Good Faith*, 56 AM. U. L. REV. 211 (2006) for a discussion of the "new" good faith standard included in the Delaware legislation which passed following the Van Gorkom decision.

- If the information being relied on is prepared in-house, make sure it is independent and reliable.[24]

The purpose of the business judgment rule is to protect rational, informed, business decisions and to permit risk taking, innovation, and creative entrepreneurial activities that are characteristic of nonprofit corporate enterprises.[25]

In *George Pepperdine Foundation v. Pepperdine*,[26] a nonprofit brought suit against its former directors for damages that resulted from "dissipation of its assets through illegal and speculative transactions and mismanagement of its affairs."[27] The court did not hold the board members liable, stating that the board made decisions based on the leadership of the founder. Further, the court continued, although the directors are held to the highest degree of honor and integrity, they should not be held liable for honest mistakes of judgment. The case was later overruled by *Holt v. College of Osteopathic Physicians and Surgeons*.[28] Directors of nonprofit organizations are generally given the benefit of the doubt where the business judgment rule is concerned.[29]

[3] Trust Standard

The California Court of Appeals held the directors of the John M. Redfield Foundation in violation of their fiduciary duty by failing to make investment decisions and holding the organization's income in a regular account during a five-year period.[30] The court agreed with the attorney general that "[a]ll three directors in concentrating on their feud left the foundation in a state of suspended animation for several years ignoring their obligations to carry on its charitable purposes and to manage its assets with the degree of care and diligence which a prudent man would exercise in the management of his own affairs."[31]

Directors in *In re Estate of Donner*,[32] were found to have breached their duty of care by not fulfilling their unique duties to preserve the assets of the estate. The court ordered much of the loss to be repaid by the directors.

---

[24] Kurtz, *supra* note 19, at 49–51.

[25] *Id.*

[26] 126 Cal. App. 2d 154 (1954).

[27] *Id.* at 155.

[28] 394 P.2d 932 (Cal. 1964).

[29] *See* Linda Sugin, *Resisting the Corporatization of Nonprofit Governance: Transforming Obedience Into Fidelity*, 76 Fordham L. Rev. 893 (2007); Denise Ping Lee, Note, *The Business Judgment Rule: Should It Protect Nonprofit Directors?*, 103 Colum. L. Rev. 925 (2003); James J. Fishman, *Improving Charitable Accountability*, 62 Md. L. Rev. 218 (2003); Reiser, *supra* note 16.

[30] Lynch v. John M. Redfield Found., 9 Cal. App. 3d 293, 88 Cal. Rptr. 86 (1970).

[31] *Id.* at 302; *see also* Holt v. College of Osteopathic Physicians & Surgeons, 394 P.2d at 937; Cal Corp. Code §§ 5231(a), 7231(a).

[32] 82 N.Y.2d 574, 626 N.E.2d 922 (1993).

[4] Corporate Standard

Directors who are perceived as overseeing a nonprofit that is akin to a for-profit corporation (hospitals), are held to what the courts label a corporate standard of care.[33] The court found in *Stern v. Lucy Webb Hayes National Training School for Deaconesses* (Sibley Hospital case) that several directors had breached their duty of care because they failed to meet the standards set forth for board members who were managing the fiscal and investment affairs of this nonprofit. The standards require a board member: (1) to use due diligence in supervising the actions of those making day-to-day financial decisions for the organizations when assigned to such a committee; (2) to disclose benefits to the board member when an organization enters a business or financial transaction that will benefit him or her; (3) to abstain from participating in a vote that will substantially benefit him or her; and (4) to perform duties "honestly, in good faith, and with a reasonable amount of diligence and care."[34] A court will generally punish directors for self-dealing transactions, as this court did, even if the financial injuries to the organization are not substantial. Board fiduciary responsibilities are taken seriously by the courts. Approximately 20 states have codified this corporate standard of care.[35]

It has also been adopted by the Model Nonprofit Corporate Act.[36]

Included in a board's duty of care is the responsibility not to alter the corporation's structure in order to fulfill the corporation's purposes "unless and until the fulfillment of those charitable purposes has become impossible or impractical" for the corporation as initially structured.[37] In *Zehner v. Alexander*, the board of directors planned to close a college for women based on declining enrollment, various in-depth studies, and expert advice. The board planned to form a foundation out of the remains of the corporation in an attempt to fulfill the corporate objective of fostering the liberal education of women. The court found that the board of a nonprofit corporation must seek Orphan's Court approval before changing the nature of an institution.[38] Here, as in many governance cases, directors were in turmoil amongst themselves. Many bad decisions for an organization have their genesis in conflicts of the board.

[B] Duty of Loyalty

[1] Generally

The duty of loyalty requires directors to exercise their powers in good faith and in the best interests of the corporation, rather than in their own interests or the interests of another entity or person.[39]

---

[33] Stern v. Lucy Webb Hayes Nat'l Training School for Deaconesses, 381 F. Supp. 1003 (D.D.C. 1974).

[34] *Id.* at 1015.

[35] KURTZ, *supra* note 19, at 23.

[36] MODEL NONPROFIT CORP. ACT §§ 8.30–8.31 (2008).

[37] Zehner v. Alexander, Pa. Ct. Common Pleas, Orphans Court Division (1979).

[38] *Id.*

[39] SECTION OF BUSINESS LAW, *supra* note 17, at 29.

Several examples of conflict of interest situations are listed throughout individual state statutes and the Model Nonprofit Corporate Act,[40] and include: "improperly using an organization's property or assets on a more favorable basis than available to outsiders; usurping a corporate opportunity; improperly using material nonpublic organizational information; taking insider advantages; engaging in corporate waste; and competing with an organization."[41]

[2] Conflicts of Interest

Directors may have interests that conflict with those of the corporation.[42] A conflict of interest may occur either directly or indirectly. A director may have an investment relationship with an entity with which the corporation is dealing or a conflict may arise from some family relationship. The duty of loyalty requires a director to be sensitive to potential conflict, to disclose the conflict before the board takes any action and, upon disclosure, to have a disinterested board review the matter. The disclosure should address the existence of the interest and its nature. The disclosure, especially if related to a material conflict of interest, should be in writing and be fully recorded in the minutes.[43]

[3] Corporate Opportunity Doctrine

A corporate opportunity arises when a director knows of a transaction that may fall within the corporation's future activities. Before a director engages in a transaction on his or her own behalf that may be of interest to the nonprofit, the director should disclose the transaction to enable the board to act or decline to act regarding the transaction.[44]

A director should maintain confidentiality of all matters involving the organization "until there has been a general public disclosure or unless the information is a matter of public record or common knowledge."[45] Nonprofit organizations, along with tax exempt organizations, are prohibited from allowing individuals who have control over the organization, through service on the board or through the donation of large sums of money, to benefit. This is a prohibition against "private inurement."[46] The prohibition against inurement means, among other things, that a private individual should not receive organization funds except as reasonable compensation for providing goods or services. Proscribed private inurement involves transactions including unreasonable compensation, unreasonable rental charges, and unreasonable borrowing arrangements.[47]

---

[40] MODEL NONPROFIT CORP. ACT §§ 8.32, 8.33, 8.60 (2008); CAL. CORP. CODE §§ 5227, 5233–37, 7233, 7236; N.Y. NOT-FOR-PROFIT CORP. LAW §§ 715–16.

[41] MODEL NONPROFIT CORP. ACT §§ 88.32, 8.33, 8.60 (2008).

[42] Jordan v. Duff & Phelps, Inc., 815 F.2d 429 (7th Cir. 1987), cert. denied, 485 U.S. 901 (1988).

[43] See id. at 440.

[44] See id. at 442; American Baptist Churches v. Galloway, 271 A.D.2d 92 (N.Y. App. Div. 2000) (discussing the corporate opportunity doctrine as it relates to public benefit organizations).

[45] SECTION OF BUSINESS LAW, supra note 17, at 34.

[46] I.R.C. § 501(c)(3).

[47] 26 C.F.R. § 1.501(c)(3)-1(c)(2).

If the board chooses to deal with an inside supplier of goods or services, then the corporate records must reflect that any payments were reasonable and that the best interests of the corporation were the overriding consideration in deciding to use such a supplier.[48]

A breach of the corporate opportunity doctrine will also be punished as a breach of fiduciary duty. In *Northeast Harbor Golf Club Inc. v. Harris*,[49] the Supreme Judicial Court of Maine vacated a judgment entered in the Superior Court. The Northeast Harbor Golf Club maintained that the trial court erred in finding that Nancy Harris, the club President, did not breach her fiduciary duty by purchasing and developing property abutting the golf course. Because the Maine Supreme Judicial Court adopted the ALI approach to corporate opportunity, stating that there is a clear procedure "whereby a corporate officer may insulate herself through prompt and complete disclosure from the possibility of a legal challenge," it remanded the case for further proceedings.[50]

[4] Applying the Duty of Loyalty

Courts generally focus on the facts of each case when considering duty of loyalty issues. A transaction that is inappropriate in one circumstance may be acceptable given another factual situation.[51]

The court in *Nixon v. Lichtenstein*,[52] found that the board engaged in self-dealing and did not act in good faith or in the best interests of the organization.[53] The board violated its own self-dealing clause and exceeded its own gross income cap for board members. It improperly paid legal fees for individuals involved in a lawsuit not related to the organization, and expended money for personal telephone systems and expenses.[54]

Directors of a charitable hospital were held to have a continuing duty of loyalty and care in the management of a hospital's fiscal and investment affairs in *Stern v. Lucy Webb Hayes National Training School for Deaconesses*.[55] The court went so far as to require the directors to read the court's opinion and sign off on it within a specified period to be sure that its mandates would be understood and followed.[56]

In *The Committee to Save Adelphi*,[57] the trustees of the organization were removed by the New York Board of Regents and then by the court. The New York

---

[48] See § 6.04 for further information on private inurement.

[49] 661 A.2d 1146 (Me. 1995).

[50] *Id.* at 1152.

[51] *Id.*

[52] 959 S.W.2d 854 (Mo. Ct. App. 1997).

[53] *Id.* at 862.

[54] *Id.* at 856.

[55] 381 F. Supp. 1003 (D.D.C. 1974).

[56] *Id.*

[57] The Committee to Save Adelphi v. Diamandopoulos, Board of Regents of the University of the State of New York, www.regents.nysed.gov/adelphi.html (Feb. 5, 1997) (website inactive, report on file with author).

Board of Regents, an independent body appointed by the legislature to five-year terms, possessed the authority to regulate all aspects of education in New York State. The Board of Regents was granted the power to remove trustees for neglect of duty through state statute. Some of the reasons cited for the removal of the trustees were "the excessive compensation paid to the university's president, a failure to review his job performance, refusal to abide by the university's bylaws relating to faculty governance, as well as board misconduct, neglect of duties and impermissible conflicts of interest."[58] In a settlement of the attorney general's lawsuit the ousted Adelphi trustees paid the University $1.23 million from their personal funds, and assumed an additional $400,000 in legal fees. Adelphi received an additional $1.45 million from the board's directors' and officers' liability insurance policy.[59]

[C] Duty of Obedience

Boards of Directors are bound through the duty of obedience (or mission) by the founding documents of a corporation (corporate articles and bylaws) in carrying out the corporation's actions and in the expenditure of funds gifted to the corporation.

For example, in the New York Supreme Court case, *In the Matter of Manhattan Eye, Ear and Throat Hospital*,[60] the court explained that the board of directors is charged with the duty to ensure that the mission of the corporation is carried out. The duty of obedience requires the "director of a not-for-profit corporation to be faithful to the purposes and goals of the organization, since [u]nlike business corporations, whose ultimate objective is to make money, nonprofit corporations are defined by their specific objectives: perpetuation of particular activities are central to the *raison d'etre* of the organization."[61]

The board of the Eye, Ear and Throat Hospital decided to sell the assets of the organization, abandoning the original mission. The decision was made following a great deal of review with the assistance of financial and other experts, yet the court found a breach of the duty of obedience (or duty to mission). It stated that "[a] charitable board is essentially a caretaker of the not-for-profit corporation and its assets. As caretaker, the board has the fiduciary obligation to act on behalf of the corporation . . . and advance its interests."[62] Generally, it is the state attorney

---

[58] *Id.*

[59] *See* David M. Halbfinger, *Lawsuits Over Ouster of Adelphi Chief Are Settled*, N.Y. TIMES, Nov. 18, 1998, at B1.

[60] Manhattan Eye, Ear & Throat Hospital v. Spitzer, 186 Misc. 2d 126, 715 N.Y.S.2d 575 (1999). *See* Peter D. Jacobson & Soniya Keskar Mathur, *Health Law 2010: It's Not All About the Money*, 36 AM. J. L. & MED. 389 (2010), discussing the duty of obedience in the context of the cases *Manhattan Eye, Ear and Throat Hospital* and Littauer v. Spitzer, 287 A.D.2d 202 (2001) which "have generated an unclear outline of director obligations with respect to an organization's mission," and continuing that "the *Littauer* decision appears to limit the [*Manhattan Eye, Ear and Throat Hospital*] court's reliance on the duty of obedience to preserve board obligations to health care organization's mission."

[61] *Id.* at 152. *See also* BJORKLUND, FISHMAN & KURTZ, NEW YORK NONPROFIT LAW AND PRACTICE: WITH TAX ANALYSIS § 11-4[a], at 414.

[62] *Manhattan Eye, Ear and Throat Hospital*, 186 Misc. 2d at 151.

general who raises the question of fiduciary responsibility, but the court did not find that such action had been taken and therefore addressed this issue itself. The state attorney general eventually did act, alleging that the board of directors had breached its fiduciary duty of obedience.

The state attorneys general also acted in the following cases, where it was alleged that the boards of directors breached their fiduciary duty of obedience.

In *Attorney General v. Hahnemann Hospital*,[63] the court disagreed with the attorney general and held that there had been no breach of the duty of obedience. The trustees had amended the articles of organization to allow for the sale of the hospital's assets. The court found this to be enough.[64]

In *Brown v. Memorial National Home*,[65] where the original mission was the operation of an organization for needy parents of World War II servicemen, the court found a breach of the duty of obedience where the board reorganized to allow uses different from the original patriotic mission.

The duty of obedience requires that the board of directors operate the organization for exempt purposes. The board is responsible for knowing the content of the articles of incorporation, the bylaws, and all other founding documents and for assuring compliance. Procedures should be put in place so that the expectations are clear to those overseeing and those operating the organization. Maintaining nonprofit and tax exempt status is the duty of the board, as well as assuring that the proper tax and other required documents are filed (e.g., Form 990).[66]

The board of directors of a nonprofit is also responsible for setting the compensation for the executive director[67] and for directing investments for the organization. Because of the complexity of finances and investments, the board is required to meet the "prudent person"[68] standard when making investment decisions. Although both of these duties have been under scrutiny lately, as the for-profit corporate world has been barraged with unethical practices by many of their boards, it is recklessness in awarding executive compensation in the nonprofit world that has caused great concern. The Chronicle of Philanthropy continues to print stories of excessive compensation. Intermediate sanctions have been established as a deterrent and as punishment for a breach of fiduciary duty by boards.[69] Reasonable compensation can be determined by boards in many different ways. Mostly, they must look to similar positions in similar organizations (same size, general mission, number of employees, etc.). The board is responsible for

---

[63] 397 Mass. 820, 494 N.E.2d 1011 (1986).

[64] *Id.*

[65] 162 Cal. App. 2d 513, 329 P.2d 118 (1958).

[66] See § 20.01 *et seq.* for further information on establishing and maintaining a tax exempt organization.

[67] *See The Committee to Save Adelphi, supra* note 57.

[68] *See* RESTATEMENT (THIRD) TRUSTS § 90; Uniform Management of Institutional Funds Act § 5.

[69] *See* General Accounting Office, *Briefing Report to Congressional Requesters on Tax Exempt Organizations, reprinted in* 11 EXEMPT ORG. TAX REV. 739 (1995); Towers Perrin, 1998 MANAGEMENT COMPENSATION REPORT FOR NOT-FOR-PROFIT ORGANIZATIONS (1998); *see also* § 6.06.

conducting this fair market value type of analysis before setting compensation and giving raises.

§ 3.04 ENFORCEMENT

Typically, the state attorney general is responsible for overseeing charitable organizations in order to protect the public's interest. He or she is responsible for assuring the proper distribution of charitable trusts, and can bring appropriate action when there is a perceived violation. The attorney general is responsible for the enforcement of charitable solicitation laws and for overseeing mergers and acquisitions between charities. It is only the attorney general who can institute a legal proceeding because the general public lacks standing.[70]

In *People v. Grasso*,[71] the role of the Attorney General of New York with regard to a nonprofit organization board's decisions was called into question. In an appeal brought by the former Chairman and Chief Executive Officer (Richard Grasso) of the New York Stock Exchange (NYSE), which is a New York nonprofit regulated by nonprofit corporate law, Grasso challenged the authority of the Attorney General to investigate his compensation as excessive. In part, he claimed that the New York statute provided that the Attorney General's role was as an overseer of nonprofit organizations and that he must prove fault with regard to a nonprofit board of director's decisions and not make the decisions himself. He argued that the Attorney General had no statutory authority to decide himself whether the compensation was excessive. The court agreed that the Attorney General cannot "tread on the Legislature's policy-making authority."[72]

---

[70] Rob Atkinson, *Unsettled Standing: Who (Else) Should Enforce the Duties of Charitable Fiduciaries?*, 23 Iowa J. Corp. L. 655 (1998).

[71] People v. Grasso, 11 N.Y.3d 64 (2008).

[72] *Id.* at 72.

Chapter 4

DISSOLVING A NONPROFIT ORGANIZATION

§ 4.01 INTRODUCTION

Nonprofit organizations dissolve for many different reasons. They may outlive their purpose and no longer be needed by the constituents they were formed to assist. This happens when the need was of limited duration and the nonprofit organization was able to provide services during the time of need. Many times the community itself, government, or other sources, such as for-profit corporations, take over the role of providing the services so that the nonprofit's services are no longer needed. Other times, nonprofits run into financial trouble and can no longer remain viable organizations, while at other times a merger may occur, leaving the original organization to dissolve.[1]

A nonprofit board may choose to liquidate voluntarily or it may be forced to close by creditors. Some organizations quit operations and become defunct without ever going through the legal dissolution process. Dissolution is a procedure that is regulated by state statute.[2] Issues such as where the remaining assets should go when an organization dissolves, and whether the board of directors can distribute these assets to themselves not only depend upon the particular statute, but also on the structure of the organization itself.

Nonprofits generally resist dissolution more often than their for-profit counterparts. Nonprofits with greater assets will more likely resist dissolution than those with less.[3] Boards often feel pressure to keep these nonprofit, mission-driven organizations in existence and may be embarrassed to initiate this process. A for-profit board would not usually have these misgivings.[4]

---

[1] *See* Evelyn Brody, *Whose Public? Parochialism and Paternalism in State Charity Law Enforcement*, 79 IND. L.J. 937, 947 (2004); James J. Fishman, *Checkpoints on the Conversion Highway: Some Trouble Spots in the Conversion of Nonprofit Health Care Organizations to For-Profit Status*, 23 IOWA J. CORP. L. 701, 705 (1998).

[2] *See, e.g.*, 15 PA. CONS. STAT. §§ 5101–6162; N.Y. NOT-FOR-PROFIT CORP. LAW arts. 10–11; Kara A. Gilmore, *Missouri Focus: House Bill 1095: The New Nonprofit Corporation Law for Missouri*, 63 UMKC L. REV. 633, 658 (1995).

[3] *See* WILLIAM G. BOWEN ET AL., THE CHARITABLE NONPROFITS 96 (1994).

[4] *See* Denise Ping Lee, *The Business Judgment Rule: Should It Protect Nonprofit Directors?*, 103 COLUM. L. REV. 925 (2003); Evelyn Brody, *The Limits of Charity Fiduciary Law*, 57 MD. L. REV. 1400, 1401 (1998).

§ 4.02   DISPOSITION OF ASSETS

Nonprofit organizations can dissolve voluntarily or involuntarily by judicial order. Voluntary dissolution occurs as a result of different events. Events such as bankruptcy, the loss of corporate members, or a mission limited to a specific purpose will trigger dissolution. Board members, organization members, and/or the Attorney General generally have the power to initiate a voluntary dissolution, depending on the various state statutes.[5]

Various reasons are given for an involuntary dissolution by state statutes. These include: abandonment of the organization's mission and activities; insufficient assets to discharge liabilities; deadlock among the board of directors; dissension among members; fraudulent mismanagement; failure to carry out the organization's purpose; waste of corporate assets; failure to pay creditors; violation of statutes; failure to pay taxes; and failure to adhere to filing and record keeping requirements.[6]

A nonprofit organization can voluntarily seek liquidation under the bankruptcy code but cannot be forced into involuntary liquidation.[7] The dissolution process varies by state, but generally follows a similar procedure. The board of directors must vote by formal resolution to dissolve. A plan of dissolution must be drafted and accepted by the board and members (if the organization has any). Creditors must be notified of the dissolution with time allotted for the payment of any outstanding liabilities. Once an organization has dissolved, it carries on no activities except those required to wind up its affairs.[8]

When dissolving a Section 501(c)(3) organization, the organizational test[9] requires that the articles of organization include a clause stating that upon dissolution the organization distribute its assets to an organization with the same or similar mission.[10]

All of the formal requirements for dissolution must be met beginning with a formal plan of dissolution.

---

[5] See 26 C.F.R. § 1.501(c)(3)-1(b)(4); 805 ILL. COMP. STAT. ANN. § 105/112.05–105/112.15; CAL. CORP. CODE §§ 6610, 8610; OR. REV. STAT. ANN. § 65.621–65.624; N.Y. NOT-FOR-PROFIT CORP. LAW art. 10.

[6] See MODEL NONPROFIT CORP. ACT § 14.20 (2008); N.Y. TAX LAW § 203-a(1); 15 PA. CONS. STAT. ANN. §§ 5981–5989.

[7] 11 U.S.C. § 303(a).

[8] See the following examples for state statutes addressing the dissolution process: MODEL NONPROFIT CORP. ACT § 14.20 (2008); N.Y. TAX LAW § 203-a(1); 15 PA. CONS. STAT. ANN. §§ 5971–5989; 805 ILL. COMP. STAT. ANN. § 105/112.16; CAL. CORP. CODE §§ 6610, 8610; OR. REV. STAT. ANN. § 65.637; N.Y. NOT-FOR-PROFIT CORP. LAW § 1002-a(c)(2). See also 26 C.F.R. § 1.501(c)(3)-1(b)(4).

[9] See § 6.01 et seq. for further information on the IRS tests for tax exemption.

[10] 26 C.F.R. § 1.501(c)(3)-1(b)(4).

[A] Public Benefit vs. Mutual Benefit

Oftentimes the method for distribution of assets depends on whether the organization is a public benefit or mutual benefit nonprofit organization. In *In re Los Angeles County Pioneer Society*,[11] the court held that a nonprofit that exists for the private benefit of its members is permitted to distribute its assets among its members upon dissolution. In *Pioneer*, the organization's aim was to promote the social life of its members through their "common interest in California history."[12] The recipients of the benefits were the members in good standing and not the general public.[13]

Pioneer states that public benefit organizations must transfer their assets to other charitable or similar organizations; upon dissolution,[14] however, mutual benefit organizations can distribute their assets to either their members or in accordance with a plan provided for in their founding documents such as articles of incorporation or bylaws.[15] Public benefit organizations must transfer assets upon dissolution to one or more organizations described in IRC Section 501(c)(3) or to one or more public benefit corporations.[16] The original Model Nonprofit Corporation Act has been criticized for placing "no meaningful restrictions on distributions."[17]

Although not always clear, the test to determine how to distribute the remaining assets in a dissolving organization has been determined to be a variation of trust law. The standard is less strict than the *cy pres* doctrine of charitable trust law.[18] In *Matter of Multiple Sclerosis Service Organization of New York, Inc.* (MSSO),[19] MSSO was an organization that broke off from a national organization and existed separately for 17 years, operating a recreational center for individuals with multiple sclerosis. MSSO provided "transportation, specialized equipment, and counseling services."[20] The court determined that the assets of a dissolving nonprofit organization should be distributed in keeping with the corporation's purpose.[21]

Because no organizations were specified, a committee was formed to find qualified distributees — that is, organizations engaged in similar activities. Four

---

[11] 257 P.2d 1 (Cal. 1953). The organization had as its purpose the social interaction and preservation and perpetuation of pioneer history in California.

[12] *Id.* at 13.

[13] *Id.*

[14] *Id.*; *see also* MODEL NONPROFIT CORP. ACT § 14.05(a)(4)(2008).

[15] *Los Angeles County Pioneer Society*, 257 P.2d at 13; *see also* CAL. CORP. CODE § 8717(b); N.Y. NOT-FOR-PROFIT CORP. LAW § 1002-a(c)(2).

[16] *Los Angeles County Pioneer Society*, 257 P.2d at 13.

[17] *See* Henry Hansmann, *Reforming Nonprofit Corporation Law*, 129 U. PA. L. REV. 497, 575–579 (1981).

[18] *See* RESTATEMENT (THIRD) OF TRUSTS § 67 (2003).

[19] 68 N.Y.2d 32 (Ct. App. 1986) (relying on later repealed N.Y. NOT-FOR-PROFIT CORP. LAW § 1005(a)(3)(a). The current statute is N.Y. NOT-FOR-PROFIT CORP. LAW § 1002-a(c)(2)).

[20] *Id.* at 36.

[21] *Id.* at 36–37.

organizations were selected by the committee. The committee sought the court's approval and the Attorney General's office was notified of the selection. The national organization then intervened, claiming that its purposes were more like the dissolving organization than the four organizations that were chosen. The question became "not whether principles of a *cy pres* nature apply to the distribution of the assets of a dissolving charitable corporation but what the governing principle is."[22] A changed standard for governing distribution,[23] has been adopted which includes a change from the phrase "best accomplish the general purposes" to "engage in activities substantially similar to those of the dissolved corporation."[24] "Substantially similar" is broader in scope and less limiting than the previous phrase.[25]

The court in *Matter of Multiple Sclerosis Service Organization* stated that the courts followed the original common law rule dealing with the original purpose of the testator,[26] but that it is the activities of the dissolving corporation[27] that govern the "choice of recipient charities."[28] This does not mean, however, that the corporation is not limited by the purposes of its founding documents, but that to the extent that the activities are more limited, the latter must be taken into consideration.[29] Statutes concerned with the distribution of assets upon dissolution require that funds be transferred to an organization with a similar purpose. Although a *cy pres* concept is involved, it is not the strict common law standard.[30]

[B]   Charitable Trusts

Courts will apply the doctrine of *cy pres* to save a trust and assure that its general purpose is being honored. Equity permits a trustee to substitute another charitable object that is as similar as possible to the original object, when the original purpose becomes impossible or impractical.[31] Therefore, a court is permitted to direct the trust property to a different charitable purpose from the one designated in the trust instrument.[32]

A three-part test to determine whether it is proper to modify a trust under the *cy pres* doctrine is set out by the RESTATEMENT OF TRUSTS and is often used by courts. Applicants must show: (1) a valid charitable trust exists; (2) the settlor's

---

[22] *Id.* at 38.

[23] *See* N.Y. NOT-FOR-PROFIT CORP. LAW § 1005(a)(3)(a) (as discussed in *Matter of Multiple Sclerosis Service Organization*, 68 N.Y.2d 32).

[24] *Matter of Multiple Sclerosis Service Organization*, 68 N.Y.2d at 40.

[25] *Id.*

[26] GEORGE GLEASON BOGERT ET AL., THE LAW OF TRUSTS AND TRUSTEES § 431, at 114 (3d ed. 2005); RESTATEMENT (THIRD) OF TRUSTS § 67 cmt. a (2003); 6 AUSTIN WAKEMAN SCOTT ET AL., SCOTT AND ASCHER ON TRUSTS § 39.5, at 2697 (5th ed. 2006 & Supp. 2009).

[27] N.Y. NOT-FOR-PROFIT CORP. LAW § 1002-a(c)(2).

[28] *Matter of Multiple Sclerosis Service Organization*, 68 N.Y.2d at 43–44.

[29] *Id.* at 44; *see also* Alco Gravure, Inc. v. Knapp Foundation, 479 N.E.2d 752 (1985).

[30] *Matter of Multiple Sclerosis Service Organization*, 68 N.Y.2d at 44.

[31] BOGERT, *supra* note 26, § 431, at 114.

[32] 6 SCOTT, *supra* note 26, § 39.5.2, at 2709 n.2.

specific charitable obligation is frustrated, necessitating *cy pres* modification to carry out the settlor's wishes; and (3) the settlor's general charitable intent is not restricted to the precise purpose identified in the trust instrument.[33]

The deviation doctrine allows a court to alter the administrative or procedural provisions of a trust. The doctrine is applied when "it appears to the court that compliance is impossible or illegal, or that owing to circumstances not known to the settlor and not anticipated by him, compliance would defeat or substantially impair the accomplishment of the purposes of the trust."[34] The court in *In re the Barnes Foundation*,[35] stated that for there to be deviation from the administrative provisions of a trust, a court must generally find the presence of two elements: "(1) unforeseen and unforeseeable change in circumstances, and (2) a frustration of the settlor's main objectives by this change, if strict obedience to the settlor directions were required."[36] *Cy pres* is the modification of the trust purpose while deviation is the modification of its administration.[37]

In *Jackson v. Phillips*,[38] the testator left a $10,000 bequest "for the preparation and circulation of books, newspapers, the delivery of speeches, lectures and other means as [in] their judgment will create a public sentiment that will put an end to . . . slavery in this country."[39] He went on to leave other funds for similar purposes. Slavery was abolished in 1865 when the Thirteenth Amendment was ratified. The court carried out the testator's intentions "as nearly as possible" by assigning the first bequest to an established organization to promote the education and to support the interests of former slaves.[40]

Courts may reform an offending clause of a charitable trust if its provisions violate the Constitution or statutes.[41] In *Shannon v. Eno*,[42] funds bequeathed to fund a home for cats was insufficient; therefore, the court ordered the money go to the Connecticut Humane Society, whose purpose was to care for abandoned animals.[43]

---

[33] Alex M. Johnson, Jr. & Ross D. Taylor, *Revolutionizing Judicial Interpretation of Charitable Trusts: Applying Relational Contracts and Dynamic Interpretation to Cy Pres and America's Cup Litigation*, 74 Iowa L. Rev. 545, 561 (1989). *See also* United States v. Cerio, 831 F. Supp. 530 (E.D. Va. 1993); Sharpless v. Religious Society of Friends, 548 A.2d 1157 (N.J. Super. Ct. App. Div. 1988).

[34] Restatement (Second) of Trusts § 381 (1959).

[35] 683 A.2d 894 (Pa. Super Ct. 1996).

[36] *Id.* (quoting Bogert, *supra* note 26, § 561, at 230; *see also* Niemann v. Vaughn Community Church, 113 P.3d 463 (Wash. 2005).

[37] *See* Restatement (Second) of Trusts § 381; Restatement (Third) of Trusts § 67 (2003).

[38] 96 Mass. 539 (1867).

[39] *Id.*

[40] *Id.*

[41] See Trustees of Univ. of Delaware v. Gebelein, 420 A.2d 1191 (Del. Ch. 1980), where the court eliminated the word "white" but allowed scholarship to females to remain; Wooten v. Fitz-Gerald, 440 S.W.2d 719 (Tex. App. 1969), where trust for "aged white men" was changed to "aged men"; and Bob Jones Univ. v. United States, 461 U.S. 574 (1983), where the Supreme Court found that racial discrimination in the admission policy was not compatible with tax exempt status.

[42] 179 A. 479 (Conn. 1935).

[43] *Id.*

Courts are less inclined to apply the *cy pres* doctrine to cases where gender discrimination is involved and more likely to apply it where there is race discrimination. Courts will not apply *cy pres* to religious restricted trusts unless there is state action involved. Courts will deny the application of the *cy pres* doctrine where it is invoked on grounds that a trust would be more fair or equitable if the doctrine were applied. In *In re Estate of Buck*,[44] Beryl H. Buck left an estate valued between $7 million and $10 million for the "care for the needy in Marin County and for other nonprofit charitable, religious or educational purposes in that County."[45] The primary asset in the trust was a block of stock in the Belridge Oil Company, which was later purchased by Shell Oil Company. The trust assets grew to almost $400 million dollars by 1985, which generated $23 million dollars each year for distribution by the trustees of the Buck estate. Because Marin County did not have a large population in the 1980s, and because its per capita income was high and there was a low incidence of poverty and unemployment, the trustees petitioned to have the trust modified under the *cy pres* doctrine. It wished to relax the geographic limitations allowing it to use the funds in the four neighboring counties. The case was settled out of court with the geographic limitation to Marin County remaining. The court found that the *cy pres* doctrine was inapplicable when denying a petition for modification.[46]

§ 4.03 CONVERSIONS OF NONPROFIT ORGANIZATIONS

In some cases, it is in an organization's best interest to convert its assets to a for-profit entity. When an organization is doing so well or a particular industry has changed so much that the organizations operating in the area begin to see potential for great financial growth, it is often the decision of the board of directors to convert the organization to a for-profit entity. In doing so, funds can be shared by investors and shareholders alike. The conversions have occurred most often with Health Maintenance Organizations (HMOs), hospitals, and Blue Cross insurance companies.[47]

[A] Health Maintenance Organizations

HMOs, or health maintenance organizations, provide their members or subscribers with all of their healthcare needs, from doctor's visits to diagnostic tests to hospitalization, in return for a monthly charge. HMO members have a primary care physician in the HMO who serves as the "gatekeeper" and who basically decides what medical services a member needs. Using its members as a bargaining base, an HMO can contract with primary care physicians and hospitals in bulk, driving down health care costs. Or at least that is the theory.[48] Physicians

---

[44] No. 23259 (Cal. Super. Ct., Marin County, Aug. 15, 1986).

[45] *Id.*

[46] *Id.*

[47] See § 10.01 *et seq.* for further information on healthcare organizations.

[48] *See* Amanda N. Hill, *Tax-Exempt Status Denied to HMOs Owned by Tax-Exempt Corporation*, 30 J.L. Med. & Ethics 118 (2002); Theresa McMahon, *Fair Value? The Conversion of Nonprofit HMOs*, 30 U.S.F. L. Rev. 355 (1996).

choose to participate in HMOs as either employees or partners because it is a cost-efficient way to engage in services on a prepaid fee contract.[49] The arrangement of services between the HMO and the physicians is entered into to hold down increasing medical care costs.[50] Although these organizations were originally founded by physicians, they ended up being run by professional managers.[51] The federal government provided loans and financing in the early stages but eventually ceased to do so. HMOs began to convert to for-profit status and "at least two-thirds of all HMOs in the United States are now profit-seeking businesses, compared to fewer than 20 percent in 1981."[52]

[B] Hospitals

"Only one percent of all nonprofit hospitals have converted to for-profit status,"[53] according to a 1996 study presented at the National Center on Philanthropy and the Law. Among the reasons that are given is that hospitals have a long-standing presence in most communities and strong relationships with most members of the community. Local control remains important, and therefore conversions are not as readily acceptable by those in control.[54]

[C] Blue Cross

Blue Cross plans were established in the 1930s so that patients would have the means to pay for healthcare. These plans were tax exempt because of their social mission. Blue Cross has become very successful with approximately 50 independent Blue Cross plans serving nearly 70 million people.[55] Competitive pressures have caused these plans to merge and convert to for-profit status.[56] As Blue Cross has converted, the question has become: to whom are the assets of the nonprofit organization owed; if to anyone at all, and because these plans were tax exempt, having lost federal tax exemption in 1986 with the enactment of IRC Section 501(m), how should the charitable assets be valued?[57] These questions are continuing to be addressed on a case-by-case basis.

---

[49] *See* Health Maintenance Organization Act of 1973, 42 U.S.C. §§ 300e-300e-14; MICH. COMP. LAWS § 500.3501 (2010).

[50] *Id.*; *see also* Colombo & Hall, *The Future of Tax-Exemption for Nonprofit Hospitals and other Health Care Providers*, 2 HEALTH MATRIX 1 (1992).

[51] *Id.*

[52] Bailey, *Charities Win, Lose in Health Shuffle*, CHRON. PHILANTHROPY 1, 11 (June 14, 1994).

[53] Bradford Gray, *Conversions of Nonprofit Health Plans & Hospitals, in* AN OVERVIEW OF THE ISSUES AND THE EVIDENCE IN CONVERSION TRANSACTIONS: CHANGING BETWEEN NONPROFIT AND FOR-PROFIT FORM (National Center on Philanthropy & the Law 1996).

[54] *Id.*

[55] Louise Kertesz, *Not Your Father's Blue Cross*, MOD. HEALTHCARE 14 (Oct. 14, 1996).

[56] *Id.* See also I.R.C. § 501(m) which, when enacted, cost Blue Cross its federal tax exemption.

[57] See Lawrence E. Singer, *The Conversion Conundrum: The State and Federal Response to Hospitals' Changes in Charitable Status*, 23 AM. J.L. & MED. 221 (1997); Phillip P. Bisesi, *Conversion of Nonprofit Health Care Entities to For-Profit Status*, 26 CAP. U.L. REV. 805 (1997), for further discussion of these issues.

[D] Structure

Conversions to for-profit status can be structured in several different ways, including: (1) conversions in place; (2) sale of assets; (3) merger with a for-profit; or (4) drop-down conversions.[58]

A conversion in place requires only an amendment to the articles of incorporation and the bylaws converting the nonprofit to a for-profit entity. The organization itself remains in existence as do its contracts, but as a for-profit it has the power to issue stock. This type of conversion is only permitted in a limited number of states.[59]

An asset sale requires that a nonprofit organization sell its assets to a for-profit for fair market value.[60] "After the sale, the for-profit corporation owns the business assets formerly owned by the charitable corporation."[61] This is the structure that is used when a nonprofit hospital sells its assets to a for-profit organization. Proceeds of the sale are required to be used for charitable purposes, so that the creation of foundations is a typical component of these sales.[62] An organization can either form a new for-profit organization into which it merges its for-profit or it can merge its nonprofit with another nonprofit, becoming a new for-profit organization. A foundation is usually created to acquire the assets of the nonprofit.[63]

The drop-down conversion involves the transfer of operating assets and liabilities to a wholly or partially owned subsidiary in exchange for stock.[64] There may be three organizations as a result of this type of transaction: (1) a newly formed for-profit; (2) a private foundation; and (3) an IRC Section 501(c)(4) organization.[65]

§ 4.04 OTHER RESTRUCTURING

Instead of dissolving or converting their organizations, many nonprofits are choosing to reorganize in order to take advantage of certain laws in the changing tax exempt environment. Reorganization permits flexibility in operations, improved balance sheets, and more efficient delivery of services. Hospitals have taken advantage of restructuring more than other charitable organizations.[66]

The most common restructuring is a parent-subsidiary holding company model whereby a parent company is organized under the nonprofit statute of the state of

---

[58] *See* Thomas Silk, *Conversions of Tax- Exempt Nonprofit Organizations: Federal Tax Law and State Charitable Law Issues*, 13 EXEMPT ORG. TAX REV. 745, 746 (1996); Gray, *supra* note 53.

[59] Gray, *supra* note 53.

[60] Silk, *supra* note 58, at 745.

[61] Gray, *supra* note 53.

[62] Silk, *supra* note 58, at 745; *see also* 26 C.F.R. § 1.501(c)(3)-1(b)(4).

[63] Gray, *supra* note 53.

[64] *Id.*

[65] Silk, *supra* note 58, at 746.

[66] Melvin Horwitz, *Corporate Reorganization: The Last Gasp or Last Clear Chance for the Tax-Exempt, Nonprofit Hospital?*, 13 AM. J.L. & MED. 527, 543 (1988).

incorporation. The nonprofit hospital becomes a subsidiary or subdivision of the parent.[67] The parent company can have other nonprofit and for-profit entities under its corporate umbrella, including long-term care facilities, data processing organizations, and commercial cleaning groups.[68]

Another way that a nonprofit can restructure is by forming a joint venture.[69] The nonprofit's assets can be leased to a new entity that is managed by a for-profit. A joint venture agreement is entered into that provides for a board that has equal representation by the nonprofit and the for-profit.[70] Joint ventures provide advantages for hospitals through the integration of resources. Those who would argue against these joint ventures believe that the economic benefits derived by the for-profit far outweigh the community benefit.[71]

§ 4.05 ANTITRUST AND NONPROFITS

[A] Generally

The United States Supreme Court, in *Northern Pacific Railroad v. United States*,[72] stated that "[t]he Sherman Act[73] was designed to be a comprehensive charter of economic liberty aimed at preserving free and unfettered competition as the rule of trade. . . . [U]nrestrained interaction of competitive forces will yield the best allocation of our economic resources, the lowest prices, the highest quality and the greatest material progress. . . . [T]he policy unequivocally laid down by the act is competition."[74] The consumer is to be the primary beneficiary of the Act.[75]

The two main provisions of the Sherman Act are sections one and two. Section one states that every contract, combination, or conspiracy that unreasonably restrains trade or commerce is illegal.[76] Section two states that every person who monopolizes trade, or attempts to monopolize or conspires to do so, shall have committed a felony.[77]

---

[67] *Id.* at 544–45.

[68] *Id.*

[69] See § 10.05 for further information on joint ventures.

[70] Bruce Japsen, *For Sale or Lease: More For-Profits Opt for Leasing Route in Hospital Deals*, MOD. HEALTHCARE 42 (Jan. 27, 1997).

[71] See Rev. Rul. 98-15, 1998-1 C.B. 718, for analysis by the IRS.

[72] 356 U.S. 1 (1958).

[73] 15 U.S.C. §§ 1–3.

[74] *Id.*; *Northern Pacific*, 356 U.S. at 4.

[75] Jefferson Parish Hospital Dist. No. 2 v. Hyde, 466 U.S. 2 (1984).

[76] 15 U.S.C. § 1.

[77] 15 U.S.C. § 2.

The Clayton Act,[78] another antitrust statute, states that price discrimination is illegal.[79] Under this Act, corporations cannot sell the same product to similarly situated buyers for different prices, and must be careful of certain mergers and exclusive buying arrangements.[80] Section one of the Sherman Act and section seven of the Clayton Act should be reviewed when analyzing a nonprofit merger.[81]

Courts use either the *per se* doctrine or the rule of reason when analyzing restraints on trade under the Sherman Act.[82] Under the *per se* doctrine, anything that falls within the Act is a violation regardless of the reasons or the effect. Under the rule of reason, the court will conduct an inquiry into why a certain business practice has been changed. A quick look rule is also used by the courts when an in-depth inquiry is not justified. It is the rule of reason that is most used when courts analyze nonprofits.[83] The Federal Trade Commission Act[84] gives the Federal Trade Commission the authority to enforce the antitrust statutes. It prohibits unfair competition and any deceptive practices or acts.[85]

These statutes apply to nonprofits and are analyzed in several ways. "All of the possible objectives of antitrust law — from efficient resource allocation, minimum production costs, and maximum innovation to equal access to the market and fair distribution according to competitive standards — can implicate the activities of nonprofit organizations."[86] It does not matter whether the organization is for-profit and pays dividends to its owners and board members or whether it is a nonprofit organization that uses its resources to further its mission; if the behavior is anti-competitive, the statutes apply. The antitrust laws have been applied to trade associations, labor organizations, medical regulatory organizations, and amateur athletic groups.[87] Not many cases involve mutual benefit organizations.[88]

In *Apex Hosiery Co. v. Leader,*[89] the United States Supreme Court held that the union monopolization set forth in the case did not violate antitrust laws. The Court looked to the purpose of the antitrust statutes in analyzing the facts of the case.[90] In *Goldfarb v. Virginia State Bar,*[91] the United States Supreme Court stated that nonprofit status does not protect an organization from the antitrust statutes. The case involved a challenge to the minimum fees that were established by the county

---

[78] 15 U.S.C. §§ 12–19, 21–27, 44; 29 U.S.C. § 52.

[79] *Id.*

[80] *Id.*

[81] *See* United States v. General Dynamics Corp., 415 U.S. 486 (1974); United States v. Columbia Steel Co., 334 U.S. 495 (1948).

[82] *General Dynamics Corp.,* 415 U.S. 486; *Columbia Steel Co.,* 334 U.S. 495.

[83] *General Dynamics Corp.,* 415 U.S. 486; *Columbia Steel Co.,* 334 U.S. 495.

[84] 15 U.S.C. § 45.

[85] *Id.; see also* FTC v. Indiana Federation of Dentists, 476 U.S. 447 (1986).

[86] 1B Phillip Areeda & Herbert Hovenkamp, Antitrust Law § 261 a (3d ed. 2006 & Supp. 2008).

[87] Note, *Antitrust and Nonprofit Entities,* 94 Harv. L. Rev. 802 (1981).

[88] *Id.*

[89] 310 U.S. 469 (1940).

[90] *Id.*

[91] 421 U.S. 773 (1975).

bar association. The bar challenged the appropriateness of using these statutes when the goal of the organization was not profit, but the Court stated that the Sherman Act was to be applied broadly and included the activities of an organization like the bar association.[92]

[B]   Health Care Organizations

The healthcare industry has unique dimensions that affect normal supply and demand and consumer awareness of certain activities. These include: "third party payment which makes consumers of services less sensitive to the true costs of care; the absence of information and ability to monitor quality, which forces patients to follow the recommendations of their doctors, reducing the consumer incentive to 'shop' for medical care; barriers to entry for new healthcare providers, such as certificates of need and licensing requirements; and ethical considerations in favor of creating available healthcare services to the largest number of people regardless of their ability to pay, causing demand to flow from need rather than from price or supply."[93]

In their writings on healthcare organizations and finance, Furrow et al.,[94] discuss the changes in healthcare and the application of antitrust laws in this area of nonprofit law. Although published in 1991, their work remains relevant in explaining the important aspects of healthcare that call antitrust laws into play. The uniqueness of these organizations and their operation and financing create difficulties for applying antitrust laws.[95]

Furrow et al. review section one of the Sherman Act and ask how "contracts, combinations and conspiracies" should be applied to hospitals. Are a hospital and its medical staff capable of conspiring? Does the proscription on interstate commerce reach to the denial of staff privileges by a single hospital or doctor? What kind of agreements are prohibited?[96]

The several defenses to antitrust liability include: the state action doctrine (exempts from antitrust liability actions taken pursuant to a clearly expressed state policy to restrict free competition); the exercise of the First Amendment right to petition the government (relevant in lobbying); and the Health Care Quality Improvement Act (limiting immunity for peer review activities).[97]

The application of antitrust laws has become more prevalent as hospital mergers have become more common. The development of new technologies, insurance, Medicare and Medicaid changes, along with societal changes, has prompted hospitals to transform themselves structurally.[98]

---

[92] *Id.* at 786.

[93] Health Care Committee, Section of Antitrust Law, THE ANTITRUST HEALTH CARE HANDBOOK II 2–3 (1993).

[94] BARRY R. FURROW ET AL., THE LAW OF HEALTH CARE ORGANIZATIONS AND FINANCE 448–452 (1991).

[95] *Id.*

[96] *Id.*

[97] *Id.*

[98] Jonathan Baker, *The Antitrust Analysis of Hospital Mergers and the Transformation of the*

The most recent edition of the Department of Justice Merger Guidelines was issued in 1992 with the Federal Trade Commission.[99] A five-step analysis is used to determine whether there has been impermissible competition. These are: (1) the definition, measurement, and concentration of the relevant market in which the merging firms operate; (2) the potential adverse competitive effects flowing from the merger; (3) whether entry into the relevant market by new firms would be timely, likely, and sufficient to counteract any adverse effects of the merger on competition; (4) whether the merger would result in significant net efficiencies; and (5) whether either merging party qualifies as a failing firm.[100]

In *In re Hospital Corporation of America (HCA)*,[101] HCA acquired Hospital Affiliates International for $650 million in stock. Ultimately, HCA became the owner of seven of the 14 hospitals in the Chattanooga area. HCA was required to divest itself of two of the hospitals and was enjoined from further acquisitions without FTC approval by the court.[102]

In *United States v. Rockford Memorial Corporation*,[103] the United States attempted to enjoin the merger of the two largest hospitals in Rockford based on section one of the Sherman Act and section seven of the Clayton Act. The district judge held the merger violated section seven of the Clayton Act and issued an injunction, but never addressed concerns with section one of the Sherman Act.[104]

Section seven provides that "no person . . . shall acquire . . . the whole or any part of the stock or other share capital and . . . no person subject to the jurisdiction of the Federal Trade Commission shall acquire the whole or any part of the assets of another person," where the effect may be to lessen competition or create a monopoly.[105] Under Illinois law, nonprofits are forbidden from having stock and, in this case, the organization did not have any. The court held, after a lengthy discussion, that the district court's subordinate findings demonstrating a violation of section one would be upheld (the District Judge never reached the issue). The court made this decision without reviewing the section seven determination.

The court believed that the government provided facts that indicated the market conditions, while the defendants only provided conjecture about the effect these

---

Hospital Industry, 51 Law & Contemp. Probs. 93 (1988).

[99] Department of Justice & Federal Trade Commission Horizontal Merger Guidelines, 57 Fed. Reg. 41552 (Apr. 2, 1992), 4 Trade Reg. Rep. (CCH) 13,104 (Apr. 2 1992), as amended May 5, 1992 and April 8, 1997.

[100] Health Care Committee, *supra* note 94, at 56–57.

[101] 106 F.T.C. 361 (1985), *aff'd*, Hospital Corp. of Am. v. FTC, 807 F.2d 1381 (7th Cir. 1986), *cert. denied*, 481 U.S. 1038 (1987).

[102] *Id.*

[103] 898 F.2d 1278, 1280, *cert. denied*, 498 U.S. 920 (1990). The suit was brought under the Sherman Act, 15 U.S.C. § 1, and the Clayton Act, 15 U.S.C. § 7.

[104] *Id.*

[105] *Id.*

nonprofits would have on competition.[106]

[C] Educational Organizations

The activities of higher educational institutions have sometimes led to antitrust scrutiny. Areas such as athletics, financial aid, tuition pricing, and joint ventures for research purposes have attracted scrutiny in this regard.[107]

In *NCAA v. Board of Regents*,[108] the United States Supreme Court held that the NCAA's television plan, to promote and regulate intercollegiate athletics, violated the Sherman Act. Although horizontal price fixing and output limitations are ordinarily condemned as a matter of law under the *per se* approach because the probability that such practices are anticompetitive is so high, the Court applied the rule of reason, as some horizontal restraints on competition were essential if the product was to be available at all.[109] Because the television plan restrained price and output, there was a potential for anticompetitive effects.

Potential antitrust liability also can arise where colleges and universities compete or partner with for-profit entities such as bookstores. In *Sunshine Books v. Temple University*,[110] a private book seller alleged that the University attempted to monopolize the sale of undergraduate textbooks through predatory pricing. The Third Circuit held that the book seller's submissions on questions of payroll allocation raised a genuine issue of material fact with respect to the University's cost against which the prices were to be measured.[111]

Another case that addressed the potential antitrust liability where colleges and universities compete or partner with other entities is *American National Bank & Trust Company of Chicago v. Board of Regents*.[112] This case dealt with competition for housing between a university and private dormitory owners. Here, the court denied a motion for summary judgment by the owners of the private dormitories based on the Sherman Act.[113]

In *United States v. Brown University*,[114] the Antitrust Division of the Department of Justice filed a complaint against M.I.T. and the eight Ivy League Schools. The Division alleged that the institutions colluded by "agreeing to award

---

[106] *Id.* at 1286. *See also* United States v. Dakota Hospital Association, 640 F. Supp. 1028 (D.N.D. 1986).

[107] Douglas R. Richmond, *Antitrust and Higher Education: An Overview*, 61 UMKC L. Rev. 417, 446 (1993). See also Marjorie Webster Junior College v. Middle States Ass'n, 432 F.2d 650 (D.C. Cir. 1970), *cert. denied*, 400 U.S. 965 (1970), where the court held that the Sherman Act did not extend to the "noncommercial aspects of the liberal arts"; Arizona v. Maricopa County Med. Soc'y, 457 U.S. 332 (1982); and § 9.01 *et seq.* for more information on tax exempt educational organizations.

[108] 468 U.S. 85 (1984).

[109] *Id.* at 101.

[110] 697 F.2d 90 (3d Cir. 1982).

[111] *Id.* at 96.

[112] 607 F. Supp. 845 (N.D. Ill. 1984); *see also* Campus Ctr. Disc. Den, Inc. v. Miami Univ., 114 F.3d 1186 (6th Cir. 1997).

[113] *American National Bank & Trust Company*, 607 F. Supp. at 851.

[114] 5 F.3d 658 (3d Cir. 1993).

financial aid exclusively on the basis of need, agreeing to utilize a common formula to calculate need, and collectively setting each commonly admitted students' family contribution toward the price of tuition" in violation of section one of the Sherman Act.[115] Although the other Ivy League schools settled, M.I.T. refused to do so. The district court found that the Ivy Overlap Group's conduct constituted trade or commerce under section one of the Sherman Act. The court issued a permanent injunction against the conduct because the Agreement set "a selective discount off the price of educational services" that constituted price fixing.[116] The court of appeals discussed at length whether the Agreement qualified as a conspiracy restraining "trade or commerce." It also discussed whether the Agreement was a "necessary ingredient" to achieve the social welfare objectives of M.I.T. to promote equality of access to higher education and economic and cultural diversity. The court remanded to the district court where it expected a review of these alternate theories.[117] M.I.T. eventually settled. The settlement restored some aspects of the collaborative overlap process that the schools had been using. The cooperating schools could set financial aid policies and share some information; however, they could not compare aid packages of individuals.[118]

[D] Damages & Liability

In *American Society of Mechanical Engineers, Inc. v. Hydrolevel Corporation*,[119] the United States Supreme Court held that American Society of Mechanical Engineers, Inc. (ASME), through its agents who committed certain acts with apparent authority, had violated the antitrust laws. ASME was a nonprofit organization with more than 90,000 members drawn from all fields of engineering. It promulgated codes for engineers. Much of the work was done by volunteers. These volunteers, the Court stated, acted as ASME's agents and affected large numbers of individuals and competitive fortunes of businesses. The Court in its ruling hoped to ensure that standard-setting organizations, like this one, would act with care in the future when permitting their agents to speak for them.[120] The Court continued that "since treble damages serve as a means of deterring antitrust violations and of compensating victims, it is in accord with both the purposes of the antitrust laws and principles of agency law to hold [ASME] liable for the acts of agents committed with apparent authority."[121]

---

[115] *Id.* at 659.

[116] *Id.* at 664–66.

[117] *Id.* at 679; *See also* 15 U.S.C. § 1.

[118] Matthew Brelis, *MIT, US Revolve Suit on Aid Data to Let Ivy Schools Share Info on Need*, BOSTON GLOBE, Dec. 23, 1993, at 21.

[119] 456 U.S. 556 (1982).

[120] *Id.* at 577.

[121] *Id.* at 575. See also the Volunteer Protection Act of 1997, Pub. L. 105-19, 111 Stat. 26, 42 U.S.C. § 14501, which protects volunteers from individual liability for ordinary negligence.

Chapter 5

RATIONALES FOR TAX EXEMPTION

§ 5.01 INTRODUCTION

There is no one uniform rationale for the existence of tax exempt organizations. Neither the case law nor the work of legal scholars converges on one, widely agreed upon theory that supports the exemption of these organizations from paying the federal income tax. It is not enough simply to say that they are exempt because Congress chose to exempt them and wrote the tax IRC to say so, though in a certain basic sense, that is exactly the case. A rationale is important for the tax exempt sector, if for no other reason than that, absent a cogent rationale for its existence, the tax exempt sector depends simply on legislative grace, which can support, restrict, or abolish it as Congress wishes. Given the many, often controversial, activities that tax exempt organizations are involved in, some coherent rationale is necessary to support their existence. This chapter will look at the rationales that have been used to justify the existence of tax exempt organizations, focusing first on those rationales suggested by the case law and then turning to the theories of the various scholars on this topic.

§ 5.02 PUBLIC BENEFIT THEORY

One of the earliest United States Supreme Court cases on tax exempt organizations, *Trinidad v. Sagrada Orden*,[1] states the Court's understanding of the basis for tax exemption: "Evidently the exemption is made in recognition of the benefit which the public derives from the corporate activities of the class named, and is intended to aid them when not conducted for private gain."[2] In the case of *McGlotten v. Connally*,[3] the district court, citing the legislative history, gave the following explanation of the public benefit theory:

> The rationale for allowing [the tax exempt sector] has been that by doing so, the government relieves itself of the burden of meeting public needs which, in the absence of charitable activity would fall on the shoulders of the Government. The Government is compensated for its loss of revenue by its relief from financial burdens which would otherwise have to be met by appropriations from public funds.[4]

---

[1] 263 U.S. 578 (1924).

[2] *Id.* at 581.

[3] 338 F. Supp. 448 (D.D.C. 1972).

[4] *Id.* at 456 (citing H.R. Rep. No. 1860 (1938)). The opinion in *McGlotten* focused more specifically on the constitutionality of allowing individual taxpayers to deduct gifts made to certain § 501(c)(8)

The United States Supreme Court, in the case of *Bob Jones University v. United States*,[5] which closely followed the legal reasoning of *McGlotten*, also cited this legislative history, as supporting the proposition that "charities were to be given preferential treatment because they provided a benefit to society."[6] The Court of Claims took a similar view in *Founding Church of Scientology v. United States*,[7] where it said that: "Implicit in Section 501 is the recognition that certain institutions and organizations exist and function for purposes which Congress deems beneficial to society as a whole. In order to foster these aims, funds which would otherwise be acquired and expended for public good by the government are left by Congress in the hands of those organizations to be used in furtherance of their beneficial ends."[8] Another version of the public benefit theory was offered by Chief Justice Burger in *Walz v. Tax Commissioner of the City of New York*:[9]

New York, in common with the other States, has determined that certain entities that exist in a harmonious relationship to the community at large, and that foster its 'moral or mental improvement,' should not be inhibited in their activities by . . . taxation . . .[10]

Justice Brennan echoed this rationale in his concurrence in *Walz*, writing that, "[T]hese organizations are exempted because they, among a range of other private, nonprofit organizations contribute to the well-being of the community . . ."[11]

As these cases indicate, the public benefit theory is a very basic rationale supporting the existence of the tax exempt sector simply because tax exempt organizations perform activities (education, health care, social welfare, moral or mental improvement, etc.) that benefit the common good, and therefore their existence should be encouraged by the government in the nature of a tax exemption.[12] As one commentator has written, "[t]he basic motive for these tax favors has been a wish to encourage activities that were recognized as inherently meritorious and conducive to the general welfare."[13] It is also sometimes said, as in the *McGlotten* case, that by performing these types of community benefit activities, the tax exempt sector is relieving the government of a burden that would otherwise have to be supported by tax dollars, thus in effect saving the government money.[14]

---

organizations; however, the opinion also discusses the public benefit theory in relation to exempt status and charitable deduction for gifts to such organizations.

[5] 461 U.S. 574 (1983).

[6] *Id.* at 589.

[7] 412 F.2d 1197 (Ct. Cl. 1969).

[8] *Id.* at 1199 (citing Duffy v. Birmingham, 190 F.2d 738, 740 (8th Cir. 1951)).

[9] 397 U.S. 664 (1970).

[10] *Id.* at 672. *Walz* involved the constitutionality of a state statute exempting from taxation the real property of religious organizations, and was not a federal income tax exemption case.

[11] *Id.* at 687 (Brennan, J., concurring).

[12] *Cf.* Tank Truck Rentals, Inc. v. Comm'r, 356 U.S. 30 (1958) (tax benefits such as deductions and exclusions generally are subject to limitation on public policy grounds).

[13] Chauncey Belknap, *The Federal Income Tax Exemption of Charitable Organizations: Its History and Underlying Policy*, IV RESEARCH PAPERS SPONSORED BY THE COMMISSION ON PRIVATE PHILANTHROPY AND PUBLIC NEEDS 2025, 2039 (1977).

[14] *McGlotten*, 338 F. Supp. at 456.

Relieving the government of a burden is not really a separate rationale, then, but merely a way of providing a public benefit.

§ 5.03   PLURALISM THEORY

While the pluralism theory has been cited approvingly in the case law, it has unfortunately never appeared in a majority opinion. The theory first appeared in Justice Brennan's concurrence in the *Walz* case.[15] He wrote, "government grants exemptions to religious organizations because they uniquely contribute to the pluralism of American society by their religious activity. Government may properly include religious institutions among the variety of private, nonprofit groups that receive tax exemptions, for each group contributes to the diversity of association, viewpoint, and enterprise essential to a vigorous, pluralistic society."[16] Citing Justice Brennan, Justice Powell, in his concurrence in *Bob Jones University v. United States*, wrote:

> In my opinion, such a [restrictive] view of [tax exemption] ignores the important role played by tax exemptions in encouraging diverse, indeed often sharply conflicting activities and viewpoints. As Justice Brennan has observed, private, nonprofit groups receive tax exemptions because "each group contributes to the diversity of association, viewpoint and enterprise essential to a vigorous, pluralistic society." Far from representing an effort to reinforce any perceived "common community conscience," the provision of tax exemption to nonprofit groups is one indispensable means of limiting the influence of governmental orthodoxy on important areas of community life.[17]

In essence, the pluralism theory supports the existence of tax exemption because nonprofit, tax exempt organizations provide a counterweight to government control in essential areas of our lives (e.g., healthcare, education, literature, and the arts), and they are an important and necessary part of our political society.[18] Tax exempt organizations serve as "mediating structures," creating a protective interface between an encroaching government and the individual, thus helping to protect the freedom of the individual.[19] By fostering the expression of diverse viewpoints, they help to create the type of vibrant political discourse that is necessary in a free

---

[15] *Walz*, 397 U.S. 664.

[16] *Id.* at 689; *see also* Wash. Ethical Soc'y v. D.C., 249 F.2d 127, 129 (D.C. Cir. 1957).

[17] *Bob Jones Univ.*, 461 U.S. at 609 (Powell, J., concurring); *see also* David Horton Smith, *The Impact of the Volunteer Sector on Society, in* THE NONPROFIT ORGANIZATION: ESSENTIAL READINGS (D.L. Gies et al., eds., 1990). Smith describes the voluntary sector as, "that part of society which, collectively, is most likely to say that, 'the emperor has no clothes.'"

[18] Necessary in the sense contemplated by the First Amendment's guarantees of freedom of association and freedom to petition the government for grievances. *See* U.S. CONST. amend. I.; *see also* Nicholas P. Cafardi, *The Third Sector, in* NICHOLAS P. CAFARDI & JACLYN FABEAN CHERRY, TAX EXEMPT ORGANIZATIONS: CASES AND MATERIALS 120–124 (2d ed. 2008).

[19] PETER L. BERGER & RICHARD JOHN NEUHAUS, TO EMPOWER PEOPLE: THE ROLE OF MEDIATING STRUCTURES IN PUBLIC POLICY 1–15 (1977).

society.[20] Because they provide this strong underpinning for our political freedoms, government has chosen to encourage these types of institutions by granting them tax exempt status.[21]

§ 5.04 SUBSIDY THEORY

The subsidy theory holds that tax exemption is a form of government grant or subsidy to organizations that qualify as tax exempt.[22] In other words, by not taxing the organization's income, and allowing the organization to keep its income, the government is, to the extent of the taxes that would have been paid, subsidizing the organization.[23] In his dissent in *Walz*, Justice Douglas cited a report of the Brookings Institute (on the Iowa tax system): "Tax exemption, no matter what its form, is essentially a government grant or subsidy. Such grants would seem to be justified only if the purpose for which are made is one for which the legislative body *would be equally willing to make* a direct appropriation from public funds equal to the amount of the exemption . . ."[24] In his majority opinion in that same case, Chief Justice Burger went out of his way to reject the subsidy theory, writing that: "[t]ax exemptions . . . constitute mere passive state involvement with religion and not the affirmative involvement characteristic of outright governmental subsidy."[25] In *Regan v. Taxation with Representation*,[26] Justice Rehnquist delivered the unanimous opinion writing that, "[b]oth tax exemptions and tax deductibility are a form of subsidy that is administered through the tax system. A tax exemption has much the same effect as a cash grant to the organization of the amount of tax it would have to pay on its income."[27]

---

[20] *See, e.g.*, ALEXIS DE TOQUEVILLE, DEMOCRACY IN AMERICA (J.P. Mayer, ed. and George Lawrence, trans., 1969).

[21] *See also* Barbara Bucholtz, *Reflections on the Role of Nonprofit Associations in a Representative Democracy*, 7 CORNELL J. L. & PUB. POL'Y 555, 571–83 (1998); JAMES DOUGLAS, WHY CHARITY?: THE CASE FOR A THIRD SECTOR (1983). See Green v. Connally, 330 F. Supp. 1150, 1162 (D.D.C.), *aff'd sub nom.* Coit v. Green, 404 U.S. 997 (1971), for further discussion of the pluralism theory.

[22] See Nina J. Crimm, *An Explanation of the Federal Income Tax Exemption for Charitable Organizations: A Theory of Risk Compensation*, 50 FLA. L. REV. 419 (1998), in which she states that the subsidy theory "is based upon the notion that charitable organizations relieve the government of burdens by providing essential goods and services that the government otherwise would be responsible for delivering." *See also* H.R. Rep. No. 75-1860, 19 (3d Sess. 1938).

[23] In McCulloch v. Maryland, 17 U.S. 316, 431 (1819), Chief Justice Marshall noted "[t]hat the power to tax involves the power to destroy; that the power to destroy may defeat and render useless the power to create"; however, in Panhandle Oil Co. v. Mississippi *ex rel.* Knox, 277 U.S. 218, 223 (1928), Justice Holmes stated in his dissent that "the power to tax is not the power to destroy while this Court sits . . ."

[24] *Walz*, 397 U.S. at 709 (Douglas, J., dissenting).

[25] *Id.* at 691.

[26] 461 U.S. 540 (1983).

[27] *Id.* at 544. Justice Blackmun filed a concurring opinion, in which Justices Brennan and Marshall joined. *Id.* at 551.

§ 5.05   INCOME MEASUREMENT THEORY

Another theory offered to support the tax exemption of "public service organizations" is based on the difficulty or inappropriateness of using the traditional categories of taxable revenues and deductible expenses that apply to for-profit organizations to categorize the revenue and expenses of public service organizations.[28] This theory is sometimes referred to as the "Income Measurement Theory,"[29] although a more apt description might be the "difficulty of income measurement theory."

The following are examples highlighting the difficulty in determining taxable revenues and deductible expenses to public service organizations. First, should the dues, endowment income, gifts, and bequests paid or given to a public service organization all be categorized as taxable income? Or should dues and gifts be excluded from taxable income, because they are really only a type of "pass-through income" to these organizations on which income tax was already paid by the dues payor or donor? Second, IRC Section 102 allows donees to exclude gifts from their gross income. Should not the same be true for public service organizations? Should the staff salaries of public service organizations be allowable deductions? What about the prohibition of IRC Section 162 that expenditures that are not motivated by a desire for profit cannot be deducted? By definition, no non-profit, public service organization seeks to turn a profit. As a result, its expenditures for salaries and its benefactions are not motivated by a profit motive. How, then, are they deductible?

Even if one could arrive at a fair and workable formula to determine what the "taxable income" of a public service organization might be, one would still need to determine what a fair tax rate would be. Based on current tax structures, the government would deprive public service organizations of their ability to perform public services, and in effect thereby tax — not the public service organization — but the beneficiaries who are deprived of these benefits.

Due to these serious difficulties in the practical administration of an income tax on public service organizations, the proponents of this theory hold that the status quo, i.e., the exemption of public service organizations from paying the federal income tax, should prevail. They are better left untaxed, "allowing their resources to pass intact to the beneficiaries."[30] Critics of this theory would hold that the difficulties in ascertaining the taxable income of a public service organization or what its deductible expenses should be are overstated by its proponents.[31] Certainly, the IRC has never been averse to dealing with complexities, and while practical difficulties may exist in ascertaining the taxable income or deductible

---

[28] Boris I. Bittker & George K. Rahdert, *The Exemption of Nonprofit Organizations from Federal Income Taxation*, 85 Yale L.J. 299, 301 (1976).

[29] *Id.* at 304; *see also* Nina J. Crimm, *Evolutionary Forces: Changes in For-Profit and Not-for-Profit Health Care Delivery Structures; a Regeneration of Tax Exemption Standards*, 37 B.C. L. Rev. 1, 2–3 (1995); John Colombo, *Why Is Harvard Tax Exempt?*, 35 Ariz. L. Rev. 841, 857 (1993).

[30] Bittker & Rahdert, *supra* note 28, at 301.

[31] *See* Rob Atkinson, *Altruism in Nonprofit Organizations*, 31 B.C. L. Rev. 501, 610–16 (1990); Mark A. Hall & John D. Colombo, *The Charitable Status of Nonprofit Hospitals: Toward a Donative Theory of Tax Exemption*, 66 Wash. L. Rev. 307, 385–87 (1991); Henry Hansmann, *The Rationale for Exempting Nonprofit Organizations from Corporate Income Taxation*, 91 Yale L.J. 54, 58–62 (1981).

expenses of a public service organization, they would appear to be nothing that the IRC could not define, and thus, in itself, the "Income Measurement" rationale provides a rather weak basis for exemption.

§ 5.06 CAPITAL SUBSIDY THEORY

Yet another theory, the capital subsidy theory, has been offered by Professor Henry Hansmann for the tax exemption of nonprofit organizations. Professor Hansmann writes that "the exemption serves to compensate for difficulties that nonprofits have in raising capital, and that such a capital subsidy can promote efficiency when employed in those industries in which nonprofit firms serve consumers better than their for-profit counterparts."[32] Because of what Hansmann has termed the "nondistribution constraint,"[33] nonprofit corporations cannot sell equity shares to shareholders who would then be entitled to the earnings of the nonprofit corporation. Nor, according to Professor Hansmann, is the sale of debt (bonds) a viable way for nonprofits to raise capital. As a result of being foreclosed from the two most common ways by which a corporation raises capital (the sale of debt or equity), nonprofit corporations need another viable source of capital. That is accomplished by allowing nonprofit corporations to retain their earnings to build capital reserves to replace the capital funding that they could not otherwise achieve.[34] As Professor Hansmann writes, "[a] case therefore can be made against an income tax on nonprofits on the ground that such a tax would (at current corporate rates) cut retaining earnings roughly in half, and hence would further cripple a group of organizations that is already capital-constrained. Or, put differently, the exemption can be understood as a subsidy to capital formation."[35]

Professor Hansmann himself realizes that "this argument is not without difficulties."[36] It seems not to fit those industries affected by contract failure, and therefore does not cover all nonprofits. It is, he writes, "a crude mechanism for subsidizing capital formation in the nonprofit sector."[37] Professors Mark A. Hall and John D. Colombo explicitly challenge its application to the hospital industry, where many nonprofit hospitals have had adequate access to capital markets through the issuance of tax-exempt bonds.[38]

---

[32] Hansmann, *supra* note 31 at 72.

[33] *Id.* at 69–70.

[34] *Id.* at 54–75.

[35] *Id.* at 74.

[36] *Id.*

[37] Hansmann, *supra* note 31, at 75.

[38] Hall & Colombo, *supra* note 31. For further examples of critiques on Professor Hansmann's work, see Atkinson, *supra* note 31; Ira Mark Ellman, *Another Theory of Nonprofit Corporations*, 80 MICH. L. REV. 999 (1982); Richard Steinberg & Bradford Gray, *The Role of Nonprofit Enterprise in 1993: Hansmann Revisited*, 22 NONPROFIT & VOLUNTARY SECTOR Q. 297 (1993).

§ 5.07 DONATIVE THEORY

Professors Mark Hall and John Colombo articulate another theory to support federal tax exemption of certain nonprofit organizations. Writing about the federal income tax exemption for nonprofit hospitals, they said that "the primary rationale for the charitable tax exemption is to subsidize those organizations capable of attracting a substantial level of donative support from the public."[39] In a subsequent article, they broadened this rationale to fit not just nonprofit hospitals, but the entire tax exempt sector.[40] There, they wrote: "It [the donative theory] reasons that donative institutions deserve a tax subsidy because the willingness of the public to contribute demonstrates both worthiness and neediness."[41] Donations to these organizations are a sign that, in the public's eye, they merit public support, but because donations rarely meet the entire list of a worthy nonprofit's needs, a "shadow subsidy" in the form of a tax exemption is necessary as well.[42]

In analyzing why this "shadow subsidy" takes the form of tax exemption, as opposed to a direct government subsidy, Hall and Colombo fall back on the government failure theory: "The political stalemate that prevents a direct government subsidy means that, however flawed, an implicit subsidy through the tax system is the only available mechanism for subsidy."[43]

Finally, in assessing the universality and the historical consistency of their "donative theory," Hall and Colombo argue as follows: The donative theory [supporting charities that have demonstrated their worthiness for support] is the only theory that is able to justify all of the various types of tax exemptions and benefits that charities can enjoy. They are the exemptions from federal income tax, from local tax, and the ability to attract tax deductible gifts under IRC Section 170. The donative theory thus meets the universality requirement because "those institutions that receive donative support deserve subsidy through all available tax mechanisms: income, property, and sales tax exemptions as well as the charitable deduction."[44] Hall and Colombo also find that the donative theory is uniquely capable of "reconciling the charitable exemption's historical connection with the law of charitable trusts,"[45] which the courts have held to be the source of the tax exemption.[46]

---

[39] Hall & Colombo, *supra* note 31, at 390.

[40] Mark A. Hall & John D. Colombo, *The Donative Theory of the Charitable Tax Exemption*, 52 Ohio St. L.J. 1379 (1991).

[41] *Id.* at 1385.

[42] *Id.* at 1385–1432.

[43] *Id.* at 1386.

[44] *Id.* at 1387.

[45] Hall & Colombo, *supra* note 40, at 1387.

[46] *See McGlotten*, 338 F. Supp. 448; *Bob Jones Univ.*, 461 U.S. 574; *see also* Atkinson, *Theories of the Special Tax Treatment of Nonprofit Organizations*, Federal And State Taxation of Exempt Organizations Chapter 15 (1994).

§ 5.08 RATIONALES FOR TRADE ASSOCIATIONS, SOCIAL CLUBS & FRATERNAL BENEFIT ORGANIZATIONS

The preceding sections dealt with the more common rationales offered to justify the existence of the types of tax exempt organizations deemed to be "charitable," i.e., performing some public benefit. These "charitable" organizations predominate in Section 501(c)(3) of the IRC. There are many other types of tax exempt organizations in Section 501(c) of the IRC, however, and the differing rationales have been proposed to support their exemption from federal income taxation.

[A] Labor & Trade Associations

It has been suggested that Section 501(c)(5) labor unions and Section 501(c)(6) trade associations or business leagues should be exempt from federal income taxation on the grounds that a healthy business climate, which such associations promote, advances the public welfare.[47] Another rationale for the federal tax exemption of labor unions and trade associations is that, in order to make up for the contract and market failure in the areas of society represented by trade associations and labor unions, nonprofit alternatives such as trade associations and labor unions should be encouraged by being afforded tax exempt status.[48]

[B] Social Clubs & Fraternal Benefit Organizations

Another theory has been used to justify the exemption from federal income taxation of Section 501(c)(7) social clubs and Section 501(c)(8) fraternal benefit organizations. This theory has been referred to as the "cooperative" theory. As first proposed by Professors Bittker and Rahdert, this theory states that:

> in such organizations individuals are simply banding together to provide services to themselves collectively. Since individuals are not taxed on household production that they use directly for their personal consumption, such as leisure activity and home-grown vegetables, it is inconsistent to levy a tax on the proceeds resulting when individuals band together, in a nonprofit or a cooperative corporation, to produce services for themselves. In other words, if an individual is not taxed on the [imputed] return he receives from his private backyard tennis court, why should a tax be levied on the proceeds from a tennis club that he and his neighbors form?[49]

Professor Hansmann criticized this rationale on the grounds that it favors an activity solely based on its structure as a member-controlled nonprofit, returning benefits to members and not investors, as its for-profit counterpart might.[50]

---

[47] CAFARDI & CHERRY, *supra* note 18, at 142.

[48] *Id.*; *see also* LESTER M. SALAMON, AMERICA'S NONPROFIT SECTOR: A PRIMER 11–13 (2d ed. 1999).

[49] Bittker & Rahdert, *supra* note 28, at 301.

[50] *See* Hansmann, *supra* note 31.

§ 5.09 ADDITIONAL THEORIES

[A] Historical Theory

The chapter began by saying that the most basic rationale for the existence of the tax exempt sector is simply that Congress has written the tax law that way. Because, from the very beginning of the tax law, certain types of organizations have always been excluded from the federal income tax, a rationale based on this *ipse dixit* of Congress can be stated thusly: Some types of organizations are exempt from the federal income tax because they always have been. This would include "charitable, religious, or educational" organizations because words excluding them were in the original federal income taxation statute and have been in every succeeding statute.[51]

[B] Double Taxation or Immorality Theory

This justification for the federal income taxation refers to the many types of Section 501(c) organizations that simply represent a pooling of their members' income to perform certain services for them. It covers the many types of cooperative organizations recognized as tax exempt. "Congress has generally been willing to exempt the income of the organizations formed for the mutual benefit of members so long as they are primarily financed by members."[52] Of the different types of Section 501(c) organizations, by far the largest number of them could be characterized as a type of mutual organization whose main income is from its members. This would include such major 501(c) organizations as labor unions, business leagues, social clubs, and fraternal benefit organizations. Because this income was already taxed once, in the hands of the members, to tax it again when they pay dues to an organization who only does collectively what the individual members could not, as individuals, do, seemed improper. This is, in effect, a double taxation or an immorality characterization.[53]

[C] Lobbying Theory

This theory is rather straightforward. Some types of organizations are tax exempt because they had the political clout to convince Congress to grant them tax exempt status. Such examples as the National Football League (a Section 501(c)(6) organization) and the Masons (a Section 501(c)(1) organization) spring to mind.[54]

---

[51] *See* James J. McGovern, *The Exemption Provisions of Subchapter F*, 29 TAX LAW. 523 (1976); *see also* WILLIAM LANGLAND, THE BOOK CONCERNING PIERS THE PLOWMAN (Rachel Atwater ed., Donald and Rachel Attwater trans., 1957); Statute of Charitable Uses, 43 Elizabeth I ch. IV; Tariff of 1894, ch. 349, § 32, 28 Stat. 556.

[52] McGovern, *supra* note 51, at 526.

[53] *Id.* 523–528.

[54] *Id.*

[D]   The Failure Theories: Market, Government, Contract

There are certain things that the market will not do, usually because there is no profit in them, as for example, providing what are called public goods, e.g., unpolluted air to breathe, clean rivers and lakes to recreate in, and so forth; that is to say, goods that we all share without paying for them. In the provision of such public goods, there is no truly effective way to deal with the "free rider" problem — making everybody pay to enjoy them so as to derive a profit from them. This is called "market failure."[55]

There are certain things that government cannot do, as for example, provide places to perform sacramental or other religious acts; or provide oversight for media fairness, or oversee the effectiveness of government programs.[56] And there are things that government can do, but lacks the political will to do, as for example, provide adequate care for the poor or the criminal or the drug addict. These are called "government failure."

There are certain services (and it is almost always services and not goods) that, due to their nature, or due to the fact that the person receiving the services is not the person paying for the services, where it is impossible for the person paying for the services to ascertain whether the price being charged for the services is a fair price. This is frequently the case in regard to health care or care of the elderly or even education. This is called "contract failure."[57] The parties to the transaction do not have the ability to contract at market rates for the services because they lack a way to truly establish what that contract price should be.

It has been posited that the nonprofit, tax-exempt sector provides a solution to these types of failures. Nonprofit, tax-exempt organizations can, through charitable support, as opposed to fee-charging, help to overcome the free-rider problem in the provision of public goods. Because nonprofit, tax exempt organizations are not restricted by the government's need not to offend the strictures of the First Amendment, they can, of course, perform religious activities or report on media fairness or even watchdog the government itself. They can also do those things that there is no governmental consensus to do, in regard to providing for the poor, elderly, ill, or outcast. Finally, because of what Professor Hansmann calls the "nondistribution constraint," nonprofit tax exempt organizations that provide health care or educational services are posited as more likely than not to charge a fair price for them. Because they have no obligation to distribute profits to shareholders, but rather are compelled to keep all excess revenues to improve the enterprise (the nondistribution constraint), nonprofit, tax-exempt organizations have no reason to "gouge" those they serve with their prices.[58]

---

[55] Salamon, *supra* note 48, at 11–13.

[56] Giving in America, Report of the Commission on Private Philanthropy and Public Needs, 44–45 (1975).

[57] Henry Hansmann, *Reforming Nonprofit Corporation Law*, 129 U. Pa. L. Rev. 497 (1981).

[58] Henry Hansmann, *The Role of Nonprofit Enterprise*, 89 Yale L.J. 835 (1980).

§ 5.10   ADDITIONAL BENEFITS OF FEDERAL TAX EXEMPTION

Organizations that qualify as exempt from the federal income tax also receive a number of additional benefits as a result of that status.[59]

[A]   Tax Deductible Gifts

The major benefit for Section 501(c)(3) organizations is that, with the exception of public safety testing organizations, they can receive gifts that the donors may deduct from their federal income taxes.[60] Donations for charitable purposes to Section 501(c)(8) organizations are also deductible as are donations to Section 501(c)(19) veterans organizations.[61]

[B]   State & Local Income Tax Exemption

As a matter of individual state law, organizations that qualify for federal income tax exemption can also usually qualify for exemption from state and local income taxes on their exempt function income.[62]

[C]   Property Tax Exemption

Also as a matter of state law, tax exempt organizations may escape the obligation to pay state and local taxes on real estate that they own and that they use for their exempt activities. This tends to be a narrower exemption than the state income tax exemption in that it applies primarily to Section 501(c)(3) organizations and not to the other types of federally tax exempt organizations. Each state will have its own criteria for whether or not the real estate of an exempt organization qualifies for this exemption. In Pennsylvania, which has been a hotbed of litigation in this area,[63] the exemption from local real estate taxes of "purely public charities" is written into the state constitution.[64] The tax exemption by New

---

[59] For a comprehensive list of federal, state, and local government benefits accorded to nonprofit organizations, see BAZIL FACCHINA, EVAN SHOWELL & JAN E. STONE, PRIVILEGES AND EXEMPTIONS ENJOYED BY NONPROFIT ORGANIZATIONS: A CATALOG AND SOME THOUGHTS ON NONPROFIT POLICYMAKING, N.Y.U. School of Law, Program on Philanthropy and the Law (1993).

[60] I.R.C. § 170(c) (2004). See also § 17.01 *et seq.* for further discussion of charitable contributions.

[61] I.R.C. § 170(c)(3), (4).

[62] See § 2.05 for further information on state involvement in tax exemption.

[63] *See* City of Wash. v. Bd. of Assessment, 704 A.2d 120 (Pa. 1997); Hosp. Utilization Project v. Commonwealth, 487 A.2d 1306 (Pa. 1985); Bd. of Revision of Taxes of the City of Phila. v. Am. Board of Internal Med., 623 A.2d 418 (Pa. Commw. Ct. 1993); Sch. Dist. of Erie v. Hamot Med. Ctr., 602 A.2d 407 (Pa. Commw. Ct. 1992); City of Pittsburgh v. Bd. of Prop. Assessment Appeals, 564 A.2d 1026 (Pa. Commw. Ct. 1989).

For litigation in other states, see Camps Newfound/Owatonna v. Town of Harrison, 520 U.S. 564 (1997); Rideout Hosp. Found. v. Cnty. of Yuba, 10 Cal. Rptr. 2d 141 (Cal. App. 1992); Howell v. Cnty. Board of Cache Cnty., 881 P.2d 880 (Utah 1994); Utah Cnty. v. Intermountain Health Care, 709 P.2d 265 (Utah 1985); Med. Ctr. Hosp. of Vt., Inc. v. City of Burlington, 566 A.2d 1352 (Vt. 1989).

[64] PA. CONST. art. VIII, § 2(a)(v); *see also* Bruce Ledewitz & Joel Fishman, THE PENNSYLVANIA CONSTITUTION WEB PAGE, available at http://www.duq.edu/law/pa-constitution/ (last visited May 27, 2005);

York of church property was the subject of an unsuccessful constitutional challenge.[65]

At a time when many state and local governments are strapped for income, many questions have been raised about the continuing need for the local property tax exemption for charitable organizations.[66] Creative devices, such as "PILOTs" (payments in lieu of taxes) by which a charity reimburses the local municipality for the police, fire, and other municipal services it receives, are becoming popular. This is a slippery slope, however, that threatens the viability of the tax exempt sector.[67]

THE PENNSYLVANIA CONSTITUTION: A TREATISE ON RIGHTS AND LIBERTIES (Ken Gormley, et al. eds., 2004).

[65] *Walz*, 397 U.S. 664.

[66] PROPERTY TAX EXEMPTION FOR CHARITIES: MAPPING THE BATTLEFIELD (Evelyn Brody ed., 2002); Robert T. Bennett, *Real Property Tax Exemptions of Non-Profit Organizations*, 16 CLEV. MAR. L. REV. 150 (1967); Janne Gallagher, *Sales Tax Exemptions for Charitable, Educational, and Religious Nonprofit Organizations*, 7 EXEMPT ORG. TAX REV. 429 (1993); William R. Ginsberg, *The Real Property Tax Exemption of Nonprofit Organizations: A Perspective*, 53 TEMPLE L.Q. 291 (1980); Margaret A. Potter & Beaufort B. Longest, Jr., *The Divergence of Federal and State Policies on the Charitable Tax Exemption of Nonprofit Hospitals*, 19 J. HEALTH POL. POL'Y & L. 393 (1994); Rebecca S. Rudnich, *State and Local Taxes on Nonprofit Organizations*, 22 CAP. U. L. REV. 321 (1993).

[67] CAFARDI & CHERRY, *supra* note 18, at 120–24.

Chapter 6

IRS TESTS FOR TAX EXEMPTION

§ 6.01   INTRODUCTION

There are four tests that an organization must meet in order to be recognized as tax exempt by the IRS. These tests are the organizational test, the operational test, the private inurement test, and the political activities test.

§ 6.02   ORGANIZATIONAL TEST

The organizational test is met within the four corners of the organization's founding document. The founding document can be the articles of incorporation of a nonprofit corporation, the trust indenture of a charitable trust, or the articles of association of a voluntary association.[1] It is the basic document that commences the legal existence of the organization, and for that reason is sometimes called the "creating document" or the "founding document." Bylaws are not, typically, considered to be a founding document, and cannot normally be used to help an organization meet the organizational test.[2]

In order to meet the organizational test, the founding document must:

- Specify the exempt purposes of the organization. Exempt purposes are those purposes defined as exempt in the IRC. Section 501(c)(3) specifies that religious, charitable, scientific, testing for public safety, literary, educational, fostering national or international amateur sports competition, and preventing cruelty to children or animals are exempt purposes.[3]

- Specify that the organization will perform only exempt function activities, and not authorize the organization to engage, except to an insubstantial degree, in any non-exempt activities.[4]

- Prohibit any lobbying, except to an insubstantial degree; the founding document may, however, allow the organization to make an election under IRC Section 501(h) regarding the calculation of allowable lobbying expenses.[5]

---

[1]   26 C.F.R. § 1.501(c)(3)-1(b)(2).

[2]   *See* Elisian Guild, Inc. v. United States, 412 F.2d 121 (1st Cir. 1969); John Danz Charitable Trust v. Comm'r, 32 T.C. 469 (1959); Santa Cruz Bldg. Ass'n v. U.S., 411 F. Supp. 871 (E.D. Mo. 1976).

[3]   I.R.C. § 501(c)(3).

[4]   26 C.F.R. § 1.501(c)(3)-1(b).

[5]   26 C.F.R. § 1.501(c)(3)-1(b)(3).

- Prohibit any participation in a political campaign, either in favor of or against a candidate.[6]

- Dedicate the assets of the organization to continued exempt uses upon the organization's termination.[7]

Organizations that are private foundations, as opposed to public charities, must also include in their founding document additional requirements, specified in IRC Section 508(e) on the restrictions that apply to private foundations.[8]

An organization will not be regarded as meeting the organizational test if its founding document expressly empowers it, except insubstantially, to carry on non-exempt activities or if its purposes as stated are broader than the exempt purposes stated in the statute, even when the articles themselves otherwise disallow such non-exempt activities or purposes.[9]

In the case of *Amend 16 Robert Wirengard v. Commissioner*,[10] the Tax Court was faced with corporate articles that were vague in their description of potential activities in which the corporation was empowered to engage. Language elsewhere in the articles that the corporation was organized "exclusively for educational, welfare and charitable purposes," did not remedy this defect. In looking to the administrative record in the case, the Tax Court found that it referenced the organization's website, which described the organization as offering what appeared to be commercial banking services. That was enough. The Tax Court found that the organizational test had not been met.

In the case of *Columbia Park and Recreation Association v. Commissioner*,[11] it was held that the presence in the founding document of language committing the organization to the "recreation, comfort or convenience" of the residents of a private development and boiler-plate language authorizing the organization "to perform all of the duties and obligations of the corporation" was evidence of substantially non-exempt purposes.[12]

While the IRS takes the position that the organizational test must be met within the terms of the founding document itself, some courts have declared that the

---

[6] *Id.*

[7] *See* Rev. Proc. 82-2, 1982-1 C.B. 367; 26 C.F.R. § 1.501(c)(3)-1(b)(4); Chief Steward of the Ecumenical Temples and Worldwide Peace Movement and His Successors v. Comm'r, 49 T.C.M. (CCH) 640 (1985); Bethel Conservative Mennonite Church v. Comm'r, 746 F.2d 388 (7th Cir. 1984).

[8] I.R.C. § 508(e)(1) states that "[a] private foundation shall not be exempt from taxation . . . unless its governing instrument includes provisions the effects of which are (A) to require its income for each taxable year to be distributed at such time and in such manner as not to subject the foundation to tax . . . , and (B) to prohibit the foundation from engaging in any act of self-dealing . . . from retaining any excess business holdings . . . from making any investments in such manner as to subject the foundation to tax . . . and from making any taxable expenditures."

[9] 26 C.F.R. § 1.501(c)(3)-1(b).

[10] T.C. Memo. 2005-30.

[11] 88 T.C. 1 (1987).

[12] *Id.* at 17.

corporate articles must be read, not by themselves, but "in context."[13] Part of this context can be supplied by the applicable state law, which controls in terms of construing the articles of an organization.[14] Courts have considered additional factors to determine whether this test is met. As the court said in *Peoples Translation Service v. Commissioner*:[15]

> [t]he issue of 'organized' . . . is primarily a question of fact not to be determined merely by an examination of the certificate of incorporation but by the actual objects motivating the organization and the subsequent conduct of the organization.[16]

Some courts, then, have disregarded the IRS's focus on the founding document alone, and have held that the mere existence in the founding document of the possibility of non-exempt activities does not, in itself, disqualify the organization from exempt status.[17] Rather, these courts have held that an examination of the organization's by-laws[18] or actual activities is proper to meet the organizational test.[19] This is not the position of the IRS. The IRS continues to determine the organizational test from the founding document. The majority of court opinions support the IRS on this point.[20]

In effect, the organizational test is a magic words test. The IRS wishes to see, in the founding document, the language that it is used to seeing, authorizing only exempt activities by the organization, prohibiting private inurement, limiting the organization's political activities, and committing the organization's assets irretrievably to exempt purposes. That any organization would fail the organizational test is difficult to understand, especially because the IRS has itself created and published templates for the founding document.[21] As a result, an attorney who drafts non-conforming founding documents for a client seeking tax exempt status has no defense against the inevitable malpractice claim.

---

[13] *See* Christian Manner Int'l Inc. v. Comm'r, 71 T.C. 661 (1979); Elisian Guild, Inc. v. U.S., 412 F.2d 121 (1st Cir. 1969).

[14] *See* Holden Hosp. Corp. v. S. Ill. Hosp. Corp., 174 N.E.2d 793 (Ill. 1961).

[15] 72 T.C. 42 (1979).

[16] *Id.* at 48. Cited by the court in *Peoples Translation Serv.* were Taxation with Representation v. U.S., 585 F.2d 1219, 1222 (4th Cir. 1978) and Samuel Friedland Found. v. U.S., 144 F. Supp. 74, 85 (D.N.J. 1956).

[17] Gen. Conference of the Free Church of America v. Comm'r, 71 T.C. 920 (1979); John Danz Charitable Trust v. Comm'r, 32 T.C. 469, 477 (1959), *aff'd*, 284 F.2d 726 (9th Cir. 1960).

[18] The court in *Colo. St. Chiropractic Soc'y v. Comm'r*, 93 T.C. 487, 495 (1989), viewed the organizational test as entailing a "purely . . . factual inquiry," writing that the court was not required to "myopically consider *only*" articles of incorporation or other creating documents. It then found suitable language in the bylaws limiting the corporation to exempt purposes.

[19] Dillingham Transp. v. U.S., 146 F. Supp. 953 (Ct. Cl. 1957); *Colo. St. Chiropractic Soc'y*, 93 T.C. 487; Blake v. Comm'r, 30 T.C.M. (CCH) 781 (1971).

[20] *See, e.g.*, Santa Cruz Bldg. Ass'n v. United States, 411 F. Supp. 871 (E.D. Mo. 1976), which found a corporate charter too broad to meet the organizational test because it included one non-exempt purpose.

[21] *See* I.R.S. Publication 557 *Tax-Exempt Status for Your Org.* (Rev. Oct. 2010).

§ 6.03   OPERATIONAL TEST

In addition to being organized for exempt purposes, an organization must also be operated "exclusively" for exempt purposes according to the wording in the statute.[22] In construing the statute, the IRS has not insisted that "exclusively" have the common dictionary meaning of "solely" or to the exclusion of all other purposes.[23] Rather, the IRS has interpreted the statute's exclusivity requirement to mean that an organization must be operated *primarily* (but not exclusively) for exempt purposes.[24] This is sometimes referred to as the "primary purpose" test. In IRS-speak, "exclusively" means "primarily."[25]

[A]   Primary Purpose

Under the primary purpose test, an organization is not operated for exempt purposes if any of its primary activities are in furtherance of a non-exempt purpose.[26] It may, however, have insubstantial activities that are not in furtherance of its exempt purposes and still meet the operational test.[27] In the case of *Better Business Bureau v. United States*,[28] the organization sought exempt status as a Section 501(c)(3) educational organization on the basis that it educated business people to act honestly and consumers to avoid being victimized.[29] The Supreme Court refused to accept this self-characterization of the organization, looking rather to its activities, saying that, "in order to fall within the claimed exemption, an organization must be devoted to educational purposes exclusively. This plainly means that the presence of a single non-educational purpose, if substantial in nature, will destroy the exemption . . ."[30] Because the Bureau's activities were primarily commercial, rather than educational, it was found not to meet the operational test.[31]

In applying the operational test, the IRS uses an organization's activities to evaluate its purposes. Therefore, when an organization's primary activity benefits a private rather than a public interest, the organization will fail the operational test.[32] While an organization's purposes may be stated in the founding document in

---

[22] I.R.C. § 501(c)(3) states that a tax exempt organization be organized and operated exclusively for an exempt purpose. *See also* 26 C.F.R. § 1.501(c)(3)-1(c)(1), -1(a)(1).

[23] *See* Orange Cnty. Agric. Soc'y, Inc. v. Comm'r, 55 T.C.M. (CCH) 1602 (1988), *aff'd*, 893 F.2d 529 (2d Cir. 1990).

[24] *See* Better Bus. Bureau of Wash., D.C. v. United States, 326 U.S. 279 (1945); Universal Church of Jesus Christ, Inc. v. Comm'r, 55 T.C.M. (CCH) 144 (1988).

[25] 26 C.F.R. § 1.501(c)(3)-1(a)(1), -1(c)(1).

[26] Universal Life Church v. United States, 13 Cl. Ct. 567 (1987), *aff'd without opinion*, 862 F.2d 321 (Fed. Cir. 1988); Church by Mail, Inc. v. Comm'r, 765 F.2d 1387 (9th Cir. 1985).

[27] *Better Bus. Bureau of Wash., D.C.*, 326 U.S. 279.

[28] *Id.*

[29] *Id.*

[30] *Id.* at 283.

[31] *Id.*

[32] For example, in Columbia Park and Recreation Ass'n v. Comm'r, 88 T.C. 1 (1987), a large private development, acting in many ways like a municipality, was denied exempt status, essentially because all

such a way as to meet the organizational test, the way the organization carries out those purposes (its activities) may demonstrate to the IRS that it is operated for substantial non-exempt purposes. Thus, in applying the operational test, the IRS focuses on the organization's operations — that is, its activities.[33]

In the case of the *American Campaign Academy v. Commissioner*,[34] the court said that it had to examine more than the "four corners of the organization's charter" in order "to discover the actual objects motivating the organization."[35] Based on the Academy's focus on training Republican political operatives, the court held that its primary activities were non-exempt, because they benefited private (i.e., Republican), as opposed to public, interests. In the case of *B.S.W. Group, Inc. v. Commissioner*,[36] exempt status was denied to an organization that was organized to provide support services to disadvantaged clients in the areas of health, housing, vocational skills, and cooperative management.[37] While the statement of these purposes in the organization's founding document met the organizational test, the organization's activities were carried out in a manner similar to for-profit consulting services, including the charging of above-cost fees to clients. In such a situation, the organization will meet the organizational test, but fail the operational test.[38] Under the operational test, the purposes toward which an organization's activities are directed, and not the nature of the activities themselves, is ultimately dispositive of the organization's right to be classified as a Section 501(c)(3) organization.[39] In applying the operational test, the IRS has determined that the presence of even one non-exempt activity, if substantial in nature, violates the operational test. Such an organization is not operated exclusively (i.e., primarily) for exempt purposes.[40] Determining the purposes of an organization is a factual question that concerns "both the actual as well as the stated purpose for the existence of the organization and the activities it engages in to accomplish those purposes."[41]

---

of its activities, which clearly resembled municipal services, benefited the private development; on the other hand, a group of business people who created an organization which built and maintained a parking garage did qualify for exempt status because the garage was open to the public, and did not only benefit the business peoples' interests. Monterey Pub. Parking Co. v. United States, 481 F.2d 175 (9th Cir. 1973), *aff'd*, 321 F. Supp. 972 (N.D. Cal. 1970). The IRS does not accept the holding in *Monterey.* Rev. Rul. 78-86, 1978-1 C.B. 151.

[33] *See* 26 C.F.R. § 1.501(c)(3)-1(c)(1), -1(a)(1).

[34] 92 T.C. 1053 (1989).

[35] *Id.* at 1064 (quoting *Taxation with Representation*, 585 F.2d at 1222).

[36] 70 T.C. 352 (1978).

[37] *Id.* at 360. See also Rev. Rul. 72-369, 1972-2 C.B. 245, denying exemption to an organization providing managerial and consulting services "at cost" to unrelated exempt organizations, and contrast it with Rev. Rul. 71-529, 1971-2 C.B. 234, granting exemption to an organization providing investment management services to unrelated exempt organizations substantially below cost.

[38] *B.S.W. Group*, 70 T.C. at 360.

[39] Golden Rule Church Ass'n v. Comm'r, 41 T.C. 719, 728 (1964).

[40] *See also* Am. Campaign Acad. v. Comm'r, 92 T.C. 1053 (1989).

[41] Christian Manner Int'l, Inc. v. Comm'r, 71 T.C. 661, 668 (1979).

[B]   Commercial Activities

One way in which the IRS and the courts apply the operational test to an organization's activities is by comparing the exempt organization's activities to similar activities carried out by non-exempt, for-profit entities. It is not correct to think that operating a commercial business automatically makes the organization fail the operational test. That is not the law. Numerous exempt organizations operate commercial businesses — for example, religious publishing houses.[42] The operational test simply requires that these otherwise commercial activities be substantially in furtherance of the organization's exempt purposes.[43] In making its comparison to the for-profit sector, the IRS will look to the particular manner in which the commercial activities of an exempt organization are carried out, their commercial hue, the presence of a profit-making motive — in effect, any characteristic that admits of a non-exempt purpose for these activities.[44] For example, in the case of *Federation Pharmacy Services, Inc. v. Commissioner*,[45] an organization that provided prescription medicine to senior citizens at below market rates, but that still operated with a profit motive, was denied exemption because it was functioning in a manner similar to regular prescription drug stores.[46]

To the extent the IRS can determine that the commercial activities of an exempt organization are too commercial to be in furtherance of its exempt purposes, the organization will fail the operational test. Some authors and courts have referred to this as a separate test of exempt status, calling it the "commerciality" test.[47] Basically, it is simply an application of the operational test, and any exempt organization that carries on substantial, commercial activities, unrelated to its exempt purposes, will fail the operational test.

In addition to the "commerciality" test, which may be viewed as simply a version of the operational test,[48] in recent years, the IRS has also begun to apply yet another adumbration of the operational test, which it calls the "commensurate" test. This test simply asks whether the exempt organization is performing adequate exempt activities commensurate with its resources.[49] If the organization is paying too much to outside consultants, e.g., fundraisers, and spending too little on actual charitable work, then it is not performing exempt activities commensurate with its ability. In other words, it has a primary activity (funding the fund-raisers) that is not exempt, thereby disqualifying itself under the

---

[42] 26 C.F.R. § 1.501(c)(3)-1(c)(1), -1(e)(1); S.F. Infant Sch. v. Comm'r, 69 T.C. 957 (1978); Monterey Pub. Parking Co. v. United States, 481 F.2d 175 (9th Cir. 1973), *aff'd*, 321 F. Supp. 972 (N.D. Cal. 1970).

[43] Edward Orton, Jr., Ceramic Found. v. Comm'r, 56 T.C. 147 (1971); *Golden Rule Church Ass'n*, 41 T.C. at 728–29.

[44] *B.S.W. Group*, 70 T.C. at 357; Am. Inst. for Econ. Research v. U.S., 302 F.2d 934, 938 (1962); Scripture Press Found. v. U.S., 285 F.2d 800, 803–04 (1961).

[45] 72 T.C. 687 (1979).

[46] *Id.* at 692–93.

[47] See § 7.01 *et seq.* for further information on the commerciality test.

[48] *See* § 7.03[B].

[49] Rev. Rul. 64-182, 1964-1 C.B. 186; United Cancer Council, Inc. v. Comm'r, 109 T.C. 326 (1997), *rev'd and remanded*, 165 F.3d 1173 (7th Cir. 1999).

operational test. In the one major case that the IRS brought, asserting this commensurate doctrine, the courts did not agree with it, refusing to revoke the exempt status of an organization that the IRS deemed to be paying too much to its outside fundraisers.[50]

[C]   Private Benefit

An organization is not "operated" for exempt purposes unless it serves a public rather than a private interest. Private benefit is an application of the operational test where there are benefits to private (as opposed to public) interests.[51]

To determine if there is private benefit, the courts examine the facts to establish whether the individuals benefiting from the activities of an exempt organization are too narrow, too small, or too limited a group. For example, in *American Campaign Academy v. Commissioner*,[52] it was determined that a school that trained individuals to manage and work in political campaigns and that would otherwise have qualified as an exempt educational institution, did not qualify because the only political operatives it ever trained were Republican. Because it benefited only Republican interests, the American Campaign Academy was found to have served private as opposed to public interests.[53]

The seminal case of *Aid to Artisans, Inc. v. Commissioner*[54] involved a charity that aided disadvantaged artisans by purchasing their handicrafts. In examining whether a private benefit existed in that case, the Tax Court said that, "[t]he questions [of whether an organization serves private interests] . . . may be resolved by examining the definiteness and charitable nature of the class to be benefited and the overall purpose for which the organization is operated."[55] Upon finding that the disadvantaged artisans were legitimate objects of charity, that they did not comprise too narrow a group, and that the benefits provided by Aid to Artisans were distributed to the group without selectivity, the court declared Aid to Artisans an exempt organization.[56]

In two cases involving organizations that ran games of chance (lottery ticket sales and bingo games) as part of a larger for-profit lounge operation, *P.L.L. Scholarship Fund v. Commissioner*[57] and *K.J.'s Fund Raisers, Inc. v. Commissioner*,[58] the IRS and the courts had no trouble finding that such intertwined activities benefited a private and not a public interest.

---

[50] *United Cancer Council*, 109 T.C. 326.

[51] Redlands Surgical Servs. v. Comm'r, 113 T.C. 47 (1999), *aff'd*, 242 F.3d 904 (9th Cir. 2001). Private benefit should not be confused with private inurement; see § 6.04[D] for further information.

[52] 92 T.C. 1053.

[53] *Id.* See also I.R.S. Gen. Couns. Mem. 39,862 (Nov. 21, 1991) and I.R.S. Gen. Couns. Mem. 37,789 (Dec. 18, 1978) for two variations on how the IRS defines "private interest" before and after *Am. Campaign Acad.*

[54] 71 T.C. 202 (1978).

[55] *Id.* at 215.

[56] *Id.* at 215–16.

[57] 82 T.C. 196 (1984).

[58] 74 T.C.M. (CCH) 669 (1997).

§ 6.04   PRIVATE INUREMENT TEST

[A]   Overlap of Control and Benefit

The third test that an organization must pass to be recognized as an exempt 501(c)(3) organization is the private inurement test. This test states that an organization does not qualify as exempt if its net earnings inure, in whole or in part, to the benefit of private shareholders or individuals.[59] Private shareholders and individuals are the "insiders" of an exempt organization, its board members, officers and managers, the ones who control the organization. As one court has said, "A charity is not to siphon its earnings to its founder, or the members of the board, or their families, or anyone else fairly to be described as an insider, that is, as the equivalent of an owner or manager. The test is functional. It looks to the reality of control rather than to the insider's place in a formal table of organization."[60] The private inurement test prohibits those who control an exempt organization (no matter what their nominal role in the organization may be) from benefiting from the organization's activities.[61] Any time there is overlap of control and benefit in an exempt organization, the chances are very strong that impermissible private inurement is occurring, and that the organization will not qualify as tax exempt.

For some reason, the vast majority of cases in which the IRS has refused to grant or has revoked exempt status on the basis of private inurement involve independent, usually newly established churches.[62] A rather typical case of this type is the *Church of Modern Enlightenment v. Commissioner*,[63] in which a New York City Transit Authority bus driver started a new church with his sister and co-worker as fellow trustees and members of the church. The church's purpose was to foster a "theological synthesis of Christianity and Buddhism."[64] The bus driver was "head of the Church and Order"[65] in whom final authority over the church was vested. The church's only income was the bus driver's salary, which he contributed to the church and which the church in turn used to support the bus driver as its sole minister. The IRS had no trouble finding that the church's payments to the founding minister, which he controlled, were a disqualifying form of private

---

[59] 26 C.F.R. § 1.501(c)(3)-1(c)(2). A similar restriction applies to 501(c)(4) and 501(c)(6) organizations as well.

[60] *United Cancer Council*, 165 F.3d at 1176.

[61] *Id.* at 1178.

[62] This is not to suggest that all cases involving private inurement involve churches. For further examples of courts discussing the private inurement issue with non-church related organizations, see Westward Ho v. Comm'r, 63 T.C.M. (CCH) 2617 (1992), where the court found private inurement to business owners when they established an organization to "relocate" an indigent person who had disrupted their businesses; *American Campaign Acad.*, 92 T.C. 1053; Goldsboro Art League, Inc. v. Comm'r, 75 T.C. 337 (1980) (discussed *infra* § 11.02[C]). *See also* Retired Teachers Legal Def. Fund v. Comm'r, 78 T.C. 280 (1982).

[63] 55 T.C.M. (CCH) 1304 (1988).

[64] *Id.*

[65] *Id.*

inurement.[66] There is also a whole line of cases in which the IRS has had to deal with "mail order" ministries that claimed exempt status as churches.[67]

In analyzing these churches under a private inurement rubric, the IRS is seeking the weak underbelly of these "church" organizations, and rather than litigate with them about whether or not they are bona fide churches, with all the First Amendment difficulties that would entail, it is simply easier for the IRS to say that these organizations function to benefit the founding preacher or controlling minister and his or her family.[68] Private inurement is a lot easier to prove than whether or not the "Church of Believe Anything You Want As Long As You Put Your Money In The Collection Plate" is a real church, entitled to 501(c)(3) status.[69] And speaking of the collection plate, in *People of God Community v. Commissioner*, the IRS, upheld by the Tax Court, had no trouble finding that where a minister's compensation was based on a fixed percentage of the gross tithes and offerings received by the church, private inurement had occurred.[70]

[B]   How Inurement Occurs

One of the most famous private inurement cases involves the Church of Scientology.[71] In that case, L. Ron Hubbard, the founder of Scientology, was taking a straight commission on all "auditing and training" sessions for church initiates, for which there was a set, non-negotiable fee. He was receiving royalty payments and setting the rates for the church's sale of his literature. He had received, for himself and family members, undocumented "loans" from church funds, and had had the church reimburse him and family members for unspecified personal expenditures."[72] The IRS and the courts held that Hubbard's control of the church, which he used for his personal benefit, constituted impermissible private inurement.[73]

In a similar case, the restaurant owners of Burlington, Vermont incorporated "Westward Ho," and sought tax exempt status as an organization that provided grants and loans "to certain indigent and antisocial persons who may have a strong desire or need to leave the Burlington area, but who lack the means to pay for transportation to their destination of choice.[74] The only beneficiary of this organization was a homeless person who had disrupted business at the restaurants

---

[66] *Id.*

[67] "Mail-order ministries" are churches which obtain their charter from a mail-order "parent" ministry. *See* Universal Life Church v. U.S, 372 F. Supp. 770 (E.D. Cal. 1974) (mail-order ministries were allowed to enjoy tax exempt status).

[68] Unitary Mission Church of Long Island v. Comm'r, 74 T.C. 507 (1980); Bubbling Well Church of Universal Love v. Comm'r, 74 T.C. 531 (1980), *aff'd*, 670 F.2d 104 (9th Cir. 1981).

[69] See § 8.01 *et seq.* for further information on churches and tax exemption.

[70] 75 T.C. 127 (1980).

[71] Founding Church of Scientology v. United States, 412 F.2d 1197 (Ct. Cl. 1969).

[72] *Id.* at 1200–01.

[73] *Id.* at 1202; *see also* Church of Scientology of Cal. v. Comm'r, 823 F.2d 1310 (9th Cir. 1987).

[74] *Westward Ho*, 63 T.C.M. (CCH) 2617.

owned by Westward Ho's founders.[75] Despite its similarity to the operations of those charities which provide indigent children with a chance to spend the summer in the country such as "The Fresh Air Fund,"[76] the Tax Court had no trouble upholding the IRS's position in this case that Westward Ho really operated for the benefit of its founders and not the general public, thereby failing the private inurement test.[77]

[C] Improper Valuation

It is not always the case that private inurement will be as blatant as it was in the *Scientology* case or the *Westward Ho* case, where the overlap of control and benefit of those who controlled the organization and those who benefited from it was so obvious. Real skullduggery is usually better disguised, and while the paradigm of the overlap of control and benefit is always the means by which private inurement is determined,[78] it is more often the case that the benefit, while present, is far from obvious. For example, it can occur in situations where the tax exempt organization has business dealings with its officers, members, or directors (or their family members) and makes below or no interest loans to them or pays them vastly inflated sums for goods or services. Business transactions between an insider to the exempt organization, one who exercises some degree of control over it such as an officer, member, director, or key employee, are not per se prohibited.[79] When they occur, however, they must be transacted at arm's length, using a reasonableness standard such as would apply in the marketplace for whatever goods or services are being exchanged.[80]

In the case of *John Marshall Law School and John Marshall University v. United States*,[81] a tax exempt law school and university were operated by two brothers, Theo and Martin Fenster, and their relatives. The exempt status of these organizations was revoked by the IRS on the basis of no interest, unsecured, loans made to the Fensters, scholarships granted to their children, and payment of various personal, non-business-related expenses on their behalf.[82] Another case to touch on this point was *Harding Hospital, Inc. v. United States*,[83] which involved a situation in which physicians sold the assets of a private hospital to a newly-formed tax exempt organization for an inflated purchase price.

Because of their interaction with hospital-based physicians, tax exempt hospitals must be very careful in their financial dealings with these physicians, especially

---

[75] *Id.*

[76] "The Fresh Air Fund" is a nonprofit agency providing free summer vacations to disadvantaged children. Information on this group is available at www.freshair.org (last visited May 27, 2005).

[77] *Westward Ho*, 63 T.C.M. (CCH) 2617.

[78] *See* 26 C.F.R. § 1.501(c)(3)-1(c)(2).

[79] Nixon v. Lichtenstein, 959 S.W.2d 854 (Mo. Ct. App. 1997).

[80] This is the rule for public charities as opposed to private foundations. Private foundations are prevented from engaging in self-dealing which is explained in § 6.06.

[81] 228 Ct. Cl. 902 (1981).

[82] *Id.* at 903.

[83] 505 F.2d 1068 (6th Cir. 1974).

when they or parties related to them, in business dealings or otherwise, are on the hospital board. Hospitals have been found not to be operating as charities when they are "operated so that there is prohibited inurement of earnings to the benefit of private shareholders or individuals."[84] In a similar vein, *Anclote Psychiatric Center, Inc. v. Commissioner*[85] held that the sale of the assets of a tax exempt hospital to a private corporation controlled by the hospital's board members at $1,200,000 less than fair market value constituted prohibited private inurement.[86] It may also happen in cases involving business transactions between a tax exempt organization and its officers, members, or employees that the tax exempt organization has failed to keep adequate records on these business transactions, thus making it impossible to determine whether the business transaction was, in fact, a permissible arm's length transaction or whether it constituted a form of impermissible private inurement.[87] Because the burden of keeping proper records is on the taxpayer, failure to keep adequate records has allowed the IRS to successfully assert that an exempt organization that fails to keep adequate business records of its dealings with related parties cannot meet the burden of demonstrating that it has not engaged in private inurement, and therefore does not merit tax exempt status.[88]

[D] Private Inurement vs. Private Benefit

Because they sound alike, it often happens that there is confusion between private inurement and private benefit. They may sound alike, but they are completely different concepts. The absence of private inurement is one of the IRS's four major tests for exempt status (the organizational, operational, private inurement, and political activities tests). Private benefit is an application of the operational test.[89]

Private inurement involves an overlap of control and benefit. The ones who are benefited are the insiders in the organization, those who control it. Private benefit does not involve a benefit to insiders; rather it involves a benefit to private as opposed to public interests. An organization is not operated for exempt purposes unless it serves a public rather than a private interest.

In *United Cancer Council, Inc. v. Commissioner*,[90] the IRS found that the United Cancer Council (UCC) was not operated exclusively for charitable purposes but was operated for the private benefit of its fundraising company, Watson and Hughey. This finding of the IRS was upheld by the Tax Court as a form of private inurement, and not as a form of private benefit. The Tax Court accepted the IRS's finding that the fundraising contract that UCC had with Watson and Hughey, which required Watson and Hughey to advance fundraising costs and which gave

---

[84] I.R.S. Tech. Adv. Mem. 9451001 (Dec. 23, 1994).

[85] T.C. Memo 1998-273.

[86] *Id.*

[87] New Life Tabernacle v. Comm'r, 44 T.C.M. (CCH) 309 (1982).

[88] *Id.*

[89] Redlands Surgical Servs. v. Comm'r, 113 T.C. 47 (1999), *aff'd*, 242 F.3d 904 (9th Cir. 2001).

[90] 165 F.3d 1173 (7th Cir. 1999).

the fundraiser control over UCC's fundraising operations, made Watson and Hughey an insider of UCC. The Seventh Circuit reversed.[91] It held that, because Hughey and Watson was an outside contractor, the private inurement analysis was inapplicable. According to the Seventh Circuit, a private inurement analysis is appropriate only when the party is a "founder, or the members of its board, or their families, or anyone else fairly to be described as an insider, that is, as the equivalent of an owner or manager."[92]

A good case could be made that a different result would have been obtained under a private benefit analysis, because Watson and Hughey had received 90 percent of UCC's total donations as its fee. These numbers make a strong case that UCC was operated for a private and not a public interest because its income primarily benefited the fundraising company. Although the IRS had argued private benefit, this issue was not a part of the Tax Court's decision and was, therefore, not considered by the Seventh Circuit Court.

§ 6.05   EXCESS BENEFIT TRANSACTIONS & INTERMEDIATE SANCTIONS

Prior to 1996, if a Section 501(c)(3) organization engaged in acts that resulted in private inurement or private benefit, referred to as excess benefit transactions, the IRS's only remedy was to revoke the organization's tax exempt status.[93] The harsh consequences of this remedy neither punished the wrongdoers in the organization, nor did it protect the true beneficiaries of the tax exempt organization's charity. Its harshness also meant that it was seldom invoked. To address this problem, IRC Section 4958 was added to the IRC in 1996. This new section creates what are termed "intermediate sanctions." Intermediate sanctions allow the IRS to punish the true wrong-doers in an excess benefit situation without jeopardizing the organization's tax exempt status. The rules on intermediate sanctions apply equally to Section 501(c)(3) and 501(c)(4) organizations.

Intermediate sanctions focus on transactions between the tax exempt organization and the "disqualified persons" who benefited from the improper transaction. A disqualified person is basically any person who was in a position to exercise substantial influence over the affairs of the organization within the last five years (referred to as the look-back period).[94]

The Pension Protection Act of 2006 broadened the definition of "disqualified person" as to Section 509(a)(3) supporting organizations. For them, a "disqualified person" is any person who: (1) was in a position of substantial influence during the period five years before the transaction or (2) was a family member or (3) was a 35 percent controlled entity.[95] The PPA also redefines "excess benefit" for Section 509(a)(3) organizations to include "any grant, loan, compensation or similar

---

[91] *Id.*

[92] *Id.* at 1176.

[93] Rev. Proc. 90-27, 1990-1 C.B. 514.

[94] 26 C.F.R. § 53.4958-3(a).

[95] I.R.C. § 4958(f)(1)(A), (B), (C).

payment provided by [a supporting] organization to a [substantial contributor, family member of a substantial contributor or a 35% controlled entity]."[96] As examples of a disqualified person, the Regulations cite voting members of the organization's governing body, its officers,[97] and their family members.[98] The Pension Protection Act of 2006 added to the definition of disqualified persons, for excess benefit transactions, donors, donor advisors, investment advisors to donor advised funds, and their family members.[99] An entity that is 35 percent controlled by a disqualified person is also considered a disqualified person.[100] An excess benefit transaction is any transaction in which an economic benefit is provided by the tax exempt organization, directly or indirectly, to or for the use of a disqualified person if the value of the benefit exceeds any consideration provided for it.[101]

. The prime area for excess benefit transactions is in regard to compensation payments made by exempt organizations to individuals or to other organizations. The Regulations create some safe harbors in this respect. Fixed payments made to persons pursuant to an initial contract are not covered by the intermediate sanctions rules.[102] An initial contract is a written agreement between the organization and a person who is not a disqualified person as to the organization prior to entering into the contract.[103] Executive compensation is rebuttably presumed not to confer an excess benefit as long as it was approved in advance by an authorized body or committee of the organization, which had no conflicts of interest, which had obtained and relied upon outside data as to comparability and reasonableness, and which properly documented the basis for its decision.[104]

A disqualified person who receives an excess benefit is initially taxed at the rate of 25 percent of the excess benefit. If the excess benefit is not properly remedied within the taxable period by repayment or other action necessary to restore the exempt organization to the status quo, then an additional tax equivalent to 200 percent of the excess benefit is levied on the recipient.[105] There is also a tax equal to 10 percent of the excess benefit levied on the exempt organization manager who knowingly participated in the excess benefit transaction, unless the manager's

---

[96] I.R.C. § 4958(c)(3)(A).

[97] For example, the president, CEO, COO, CFO, treasurer, 26 C.F.R. § 53.4958-3(c), those with financial interests in exempt provider-sponsored health care organizations are also disqualified persons. 26 C.F.R. § 53.4958-3(c)(4). *See* 15 THE NONPROFIT COUNSEL: THE LAW OF TAX EXEMPT ORGANIZATIONS MONTHLY1, 1–5 (1998).

[98] This term includes spouses, siblings (whole and half), siblings' spouses, ancestors, children, grandchildren, great grandchildren and the spouses of children, grandchildren and great-grandchildren. 26 C.F.R. § 53.4958-3(b).

[99] I.R.C. § 4958(f).

[100] I.R.C. § 4958(f)(1)(C).

[101] I.R.C. § 4958(c)(1)(A).

[102] 26 C.F.R. § 53.4958-4(a)(3)(i). This reflects the holding in *United Cancer Council v. Comm'r*, 165 F.3d 1173 (7th Cir. 1999).

[103] 26 C.F.R. § 53.4958-4(a)(3)(iii).

[104] 26 C.F.R. § 53.4958-6(a)(1), (2), (3).

[105] I.R.C. § 4958(a)(1), (b).

participation was not willful or was due to reasonable cause.[106]

The first intermediate sanctions case filed by the IRS involved excess compensation paid to the trustees of the famous Bishop Estate of Hawaii. That case was settled by the trustees repaying $14 million to the exempt organization. The first case to proceed to full litigation was *Caracci v. Commissioner*,[107] in which the IRS challenged the sale of nursing home assets by an exempt organization to disqualified persons for less than fair market value. Under the Medicare reimbursement program, the nursing homes were being paid at cost, and so were not generating a profit, but they were generating an income stream, including enough to pay executive-level compensation. Two accounting firms, working for lawyers for the disqualified persons, issued appraisals stating that the value of the exempt organization's assets was in the negative, being less that the organization's liabilities. The exempt organization's assets were transferred to the disqualified parties in consideration of their assumption of liabilities and nothing more. The Tax Court agreed with the IRS that negative book value does not mean that the organization's assets had no value. Based on the income stream alone, the court found that the fair market value of the assets transferred to the disqualified parties, minus liabilities, was in excess of $5 million. It upheld the excess benefit taxes on the disqualified parties based on that amount. The Tax Court did not agree, however, with the IRS's revocation of the tax exempt status of the nursing home organization, pointing out that an exempt organization had to remain there for the disqualified persons to reimburse.[108] On appeal, the Fifth Circuit reversed the Tax Court and found for the taxpayers.[109] In overturning the decision, the Fifth Circuit Court of Appeals held that the Tax Court committed a "cascade of errors" in its determination of the Caraccis' liability. The Court of Appeals held that the Tax Court erred in issuing deficiency notices based on an intermediate analysis, holding that an intermediate analysis, as opposed to a final economic study, allowed the IRS to prevent the Caraccis from correcting the allegedly prohibited transaction before the IRS could issue sanctions. The Court further held that as a matter of law the Tax Court erred in its choice of method for determining the fair market value of the non-profit corporation and it also erred in its findings of fact regarding the value of the corporation, by ignoring the expert testimony offered by the Caraccis.

§ 6.06   POLITICAL ACTIVITIES TEST

There are two types of political activity that are prohibited by the political activities test: lobbying and electioneering. Lobbying is attempting to influence the passage of legislation, and there are two types of lobbying: direct lobbying and grassroots lobbying. Direct lobbying is actually contacting legislators in an attempt to influence the passage of legislation. Grassroots lobbying is indirect; it involves urging the public to contact legislators in regard to certain legislation. Electioneering is the participation in a political campaign for elective office, either by endorsing

---

[106] I.R.C. § 4958(a)(2).

[107] 118 T.C. 379 (2002).

[108] *Id.*

[109] Caracci v. Comm'r, 456 F.3d 444 (5th Cir. 2006).

and working on behalf of a candidate or by campaigning against a particular candidate.[110] The distinction between electioneering (participating in an election) and lobbying (attempting to influence legislation) is critical because Section 501(c)(3) organizations cannot electioneer at all, but they may lobby to an insubstantial degree. These restrictions come directly from the words of the statute itself, which specify that no substantial part of the activities of a 501(c)(3) organization can consist of carrying on propaganda, or otherwise attempting to influence legislation,[111] nor can it participate in, or intervene in (including the publishing or distributing of statements), any political campaign on behalf of (or in opposition to) any candidate for public office.[112]

In fleshing out the words of the statute, the Regulations speak in terms of an action organization.[113] As happens elsewhere in the IRC and the Regulations, e.g., in the sections on private foundations, the IRS defines an organization by saying what it is not. An action organization cannot qualify as an exempt organization, and an exempt organization cannot be an action organization.[114]

An organization is an action organization if a substantial part of its activities is attempting to influence legislation by propaganda, or otherwise, or if it participates or intervenes, directly or indirectly, in any political campaign on behalf of or in opposition to any candidate for public office.[115] If a putative 501(c)(3) organization functions as an action organization, then it flunks the political activities test and does not qualify as exempt.[116]

[A]　Limitations on Lobbying

In 1919, the IRS issued the first prohibition on lobbying by charitable organizations when it adopted a regulation that stated that "associations formed to disseminate controversial or partisan propaganda" did not qualify as charitable.[117] The first major case in this area was *Slee v. Commissioner.*[118] In that case, the Second Circuit upheld the IRS's position that the American Birth Control league

---

[110]　Roberts Dairy Co. v. Comm'r, 195 F.2d 948 (8th Cir. 1952); Am. Hardware & Equip. Co. v. Comm'r, 202 F.2d 126 (4th Cir. 1953).

[111]　I.R.C. § 501(c)(3). This language was added to the Tax Code in 1934, after the Second Circuit had already found that political activity did not qualify as an exempt purpose in Slee v. Comm'r, 42 F.2d 184 (2d Cir. 1930).

[112]　The ban on electioneering activity was made part of the 1954 Tax Code at the motion of then Senator Lyndon Johnson of Texas during the floor debate on the bill in the Senate. Johnson evidently believed that a Texas-based charitable organization had aided his opponent in the 1954 primary election. The "no political campaigning" language has no other legislative history. It has been part of § 501(c)(3) ever since. *See* Colleen Sealander, *Standing Behind Government-Subsidized Bipartisanship*, 60 Geo. Wash. L. Rev. 1580 (1992), and Anne Berrill Carroll, *Religion, Politics and the IRS: Defining the Limits of Tax Law Controls on Political Expression by Churches*, 76 Marq. L. Rev. 217, 228 (1992).

[113]　26 C.F.R. § 1.501(c)(3)-1(c)(3).

[114]　*Id.*

[115]　*Id.*

[116]　See § 15.01 *et seq.* for further information on action organizations.

[117]　26 C.F.R. § 45 art. 517 (1919).

[118]　42 F.2d 184.

did not qualify for exemption because it was disseminating propaganda to both legislators (direct lobbying) and the voting public (grassroots lobbying) in an attempt to overturn laws prohibiting birth control. While he did not agree with the IRS's use of the polemic "propaganda" characterization, Judge Learned Hand did accept that "political agitation is outside the statute."[119]

While the first restriction on lobbying by charitable organizations came from an IRS Regulation, Congress soon modified the statute itself to prohibit exempt organizations from doing substantial lobbying.[120]

[1] Defining Legislation

The Regulations define "legislation" as action by Congress, any state legislature, any local council or similar governing body or the public in a referendum, initiative, constitutional amendment, or similar procedure.[121] Administrative rules, promulgated by the executive, and not the legislative branch, are not considered to be legislation. But organizations that attempt to influence the United States Senate, or a similar state legislative body, in the approval process of an executive nomination, e.g., of federal or state judges, are considered to be lobbying.[122]

If an organization's goals can only be achieved through changes in legislation, it will be denied exemption even when it never explicitly targets any specific legislation.[123] Even the League of Women Voters was denied exempt status because its voter educational activities were found to involve the influencing of legislation.[124] However, when all an organization does is engage in non-partisan analysis of prospective or present legislation, even when it provides that analysis to the legislature, it is not lobbying.[125] It also is not lobbying when an organization responds to a legislature's request to provide it with information in the organization's area of expertise.[126] Nor is it lobbying when an organization contacts its members in regard to organizational interests, even when those interests may involve present or proposed legislation.[127] Urging its members to then contact their legislators in regard to these matters, however, would cross the line into grassroots lobbying.[128]

---

[119] *Id.* at 185.

[120] I.R.C. § 103(6) (1934).

[121] 26 C.F.R. § 1.501(c)(3)-1(c)(3)(ii).

[122] I.R.C. § 4911(c)(2).

[123] Fund for the Study of Econ. Growth and Tax Reform v. IRS, 161 F.3d 755 (D.C. Cir. 1998).

[124] League of Women Voters v. U.S., 180 F. Supp. 379 (Ct. Cl.), *cert. denied*, 364 U.S. 822 (1960).

[125] Rev. Rul. 70-79, 1970-1 C.B. 127.

[126] Rev. Rul. 70-449, 1970-2 C.B. 111.

[127] *See, e.g., League of Women Voters*, 180 F. Supp. 379; *Fund for the Study of Econ. Growth*, 161 F.3d 755.

[128] *See, e.g.*, cases cited *supra* note 126.

[2] Defining Substantial Part

Before Congress provided a "safe harbor" definition of what would constitute substantial lobbying in the statute,[129] the litigation was over whether an organization's lobbying was or was not substantial.[130] In the case of *Seasongood v. Commissioner*,[131] the court applied a numerical test, holding that an organization that devoted less than five percent of its time and effort to lobbying was not lobbying substantially.[132] Other courts attempted a broader balancing test.

A major case in this field involved Christian Echoes National Ministry, the newspaper, radio, and television ministry of Dr. Billy James Hargis.[133] Dr. Hargis was an ordained minister of a rather conservative political nature. Christian Echoes engaged in grassroots lobbying by directing its adherents to contact their members of Congress on a plethora of issues (immigration, the liberal press, the need to maintain the House Unamerican Activities Committee, the World Court, federal aid to education, socialized medicine, public housing, and many other issues). Christian Echoes also endorsed Senator Goldwater in the 1964 presidential election and campaigned for him and against President Johnson. In a kind of a balancing test, the IRS found that these political activities were of a substantial nature.[134] The Tenth Circuit, disavowing a strict percentage test, had no trouble finding that "balanced in the context of the [organization's] objectives and circumstances," Christian Echoes' many political activities disqualified it as an exempt organization.[135] The circuit court also dismissed an argument by Christian Echoes that the political activities limitation on Section 501(c)(3) organizations was an unconstitutional violation of its free speech rights.[136]

On the heels of the *Christian Echoes* case, the Court of Claims, in *Haswell v. United States*,[137] adopted much of the same language, holding that "[t]he political efforts of an organization must be balanced in the context of the objectives and circumstances of the organization to determine whether a substantial part of its activities is to influence, or is an attempt to influence, legislation. A percentage test to determine whether the activities are substantial is not appropriate. Such a test obscures the complexity of balancing the organization's activities in relation to its objectives and circumstances in the context of the totality of the organization."[138]

---

[129] I.R.C. § 501(h).

[130] Nationalist Movement v. Comm'r, 102 T.C. 558, 589 (1994), stated that "[w]hether an activity is substantial is a facts-and-circumstances inquiry not always dependent upon time or expenditure percentages." (citing Manning Ass'n v. Comm'r, 93 T.C. 596, 610–11 (1989)).

[131] 227 F.2d 907 (6th Cir. 1955).

[132] *Id.* at 912.

[133] Christian Echoes Nat'l Ministry v. Comm'r, 470 F.2d 849 (10th Cir. 1972).

[134] *Id.; see also* Krohn v. U.S., 246 F. Supp. 341 (D. Colo. 1965); *Seasongood*, 227 F.2d 907; Kuper v. Comm'r, 332 F.2d 562 (3d Cir. 1964).

[135] *Christian Echoes*, 470 F.2d at 857–58.

[136] *Id.* at 856–57.

[137] 500 F.2d 1133 (Ct. Cl. 1974).

[138] *Id.* at 1142.

Normally in determining whether an organization devoted a substantial part of its activities to lobbying, the courts examined factors such as how much employee time or member time was spent on legislative activities and what part of the organization's revenues was spent on legislative activities, but there was no bright-line rule on what percentage of time, efforts, or revenue constituted a "substantial part."[139]

[3] Section 501(h) Election

In 1976, to clarify matters as to what was and was not "substantial lobbying," Congress adopted Section 501(h) of the IRC. Section 501(h) allows all 501(c)(3) organizations (except churches, their integrated auxiliary organizations, and private foundations) to elect to be governed by an expenditure formula that provides a safe harbor for their lobbying expenditures.

Section 501(h) deals with both direct lobbying expenditures and indirect or grassroots lobbying expenditures. Together, these two expenditure amounts are weighed against a sliding scale. Total lobbying expenditures cannot exceed 20 percent of the first $500,000 of an organization's exempt purpose expenditures for the tax year, 15 percent of the next $500,000, 10 percent of the third $500,000, and five percent of any exempt purpose expenditure amount beyond that. Within these limits total lobbying expenditures can never exceed $1,000,000 and grassroots lobbying cannot exceed 25 percent of total lobbying expenditures.[140]

In determining whether these percentages are met, an organization's exempt purposes expenditures are the total amounts paid or incurred by such organization to accomplish its exempt purposes.[141] This would include salaries, overhead, and all lobbying costs. It also includes straight-line depreciation expenses. It does not include fundraising expenses paid to a third party, nor does it include capital expenditures.[142] Fundraising expenditures within the organization, i.e., salaries of fundraisers employed by the organization, are exempt purpose expenditures.[143]

Lobbying expenses are expenditures for the purpose of influencing legislation as defined in Section 4911(d).[144] That section defines influencing legislation in two ways: as direct lobbying and as grassroots lobbying. Direct lobbying is any attempt to influence legislation through communication with any member or employee of a legislative body, or with any government official or employee who may participate in the formulation of the legislation when the principal purpose of the communication is to influence legislation.[145]

---

[139] *Nationalist Movement*, 102 T.C. at 589, stated that "whether an activity is substantial is a facts-and-circumstances inquiry not always dependent upon time or expenditure percentages," (citing *Manning Ass'n*, 93 T.C. at 610–11).

[140] I.R.C. § 4911(c)(2).

[141] I.R.C. § 4911(e).

[142] *Id.*; 26 C.F.R. § 56.4911-4.

[143] I.R.C. § 501(h).

[144] I.R.C. § 501(h)(2)(A).

[145] 26 C.F.R. § 56.4911-2(b)(i).

Grassroots lobbying is any attempt to influence legislation through an attempt to affect the opinions of the general public or any segment thereof.[146] Grassroots lobbying refers to specific (i.e., pending) legislation, reflects a view on the legislation, and encourages the recipient to take action with respect to the legislation.[147] This last requirement is sometimes referred to as the "call to action" requirement. A communication to the public about pending legislation is not grassroots lobbying unless it includes a request to the recipient to do something about the legislation, such as contacting a legislator, or provides the address of the legislature, or uses a petition or tear-off postcard to communicate with the legislature or specifically identifies a legislator who will be voting on the proposed legislation and his or her position on it.[148]

The IRS has a special rule for certain mass media advertisements that would not ordinarily qualify as grassroots lobbying because they lack a call to action. If within two weeks before a vote by a legislative body, or a committee (but not a subcommittee) thereof, on a highly publicized piece of legislation, an organization's paid advertisement appears in the mass media, the paid advertisement will be presumed to be a grassroots lobbying communication when it reflects a view on the general subject of such legislation and either refers to the highly publicized legislation or encourages the public to communicate with legislators on the general subject of such legislation.[149] This presumption can be rebutted by the organization if it can show that the paid advertisement is a type of communication regularly made by the organization in the mass media without regard to the timing of legislation (that is, a customary course of business exception) or that the timing of the paid advertisement was unrelated to the upcoming legislative action.[150]

When the public is the legislator itself, as for example, in referenda, ballot initiatives, or similar procedures, any communication by an exempt organization to the public regarding the referenda, ballot initiative, or similar procedure is direct and not grassroots lobbying.[151]

In order to provide additional guidance to charities in their determination of what is and what is not a lobbying expenditure, the IRC specifies a number of actions that will not be considered as influencing legislation. These are: (1) making available the results of nonpartisan analysis or study; (2) providing technical advice or assistance to a government body or to a committee or other subdivision thereof in response to a written request by such body or subdivision; (3) appearances before, or communications to, any legislative body with respect to a possible decision of such body which might affect the existence of the organization, its

---

[146] 26 C.F.R. § 56-4911-2(b)(2)(i).

[147] 26 C.F.R. § 56-4911-2(b)(2)(ii).

[148] 26 C.F.R. § 56.4911-2(b)(2)(iii). The last category, identifying a legislator who will be voting on the legislation and his or her position on it, does not qualify as "directly encouraging" a legislator, but rather only as "encouraging" a legislator. 26 C.F.R. § 56.4911-2(b)(2)(iv). The difference is subtle, but important in as much as nonpartisan analysis by an exempt organization, which is not considered lobbying, may also include what would otherwise qualify as "encouraging" a legislator.

[149] 26 C.F.R. § 56.4911-2(b)(5)(ii).

[150] *Id.*

[151] 26 C.F.R. § 56.4911-2(b)(1)(iii).

powers and duties, tax exempt status, or the deductions of contributions to the organization; (4) communications between the organization and its bona fide members with respect to the legislation or proposed legislation of direct interest to the organization and its members, except where the communication includes a call to action; and (5) communications with a government official or employee, other than a lawmaker (i.e., a member of the executive branch) unless the principal purpose of the communication is to influence legislation.[152] Charities can do any or all of the above and not be considered to be engaged in attempting to influence legislation.

In addition to these exceptions specified in the statute, the Regulations also provide that examinations and discussions of broad social, economic, and similar problems are neither direct lobbying communications nor grassroots lobbying communications even if the problems are of the type with which the government would be expected to deal ultimately.[153]

A charity can elect to be covered by Section 501(h) by filing Form 5768 with the IRS.[154] Once filed, the election is good for every tax year that follows, until the election is revoked.[155] If a revocation is made during a tax year, it becomes effective starting with the next tax year.

Once a charity makes this election, it must report its direct and grassroots lobbying expenditures to the IRS annually on its Form 990 informational filing.[156] Should the charity have expenditures in excess of those allowed by Section 501(h), then it must pay an excise tax of 25 percent of the excess amount.[157] In situations in which a Section 501(c)(3) organization has lobbying expenditures of 50 percent or more in excess of the amounts permitted by Section 501(h) over a period of four years, it will no longer qualify as tax exempt, because this would mean that the organization was now lobbying to a substantial degree and would be in violation of the political activities test.[158] In such situations, not only would the organization lose its Section 501(c)(3) status, it would also have to pay an excise tax of five percent on its lobbying expenses in the year it ceased to qualify as a Section 501(c)(3) organization.[159] This five percent tax is also applicable to the excessive (more than insubstantial) lobbying expenses of Section 501(c)(3) organizations that are not covered by Section 501(h); and just as organizations that elect to be covered by Section 501(h) rules on their lobbying expenses can lose their tax exempt status by

---

[152] I.R.C. § 4911(d)(2).

[153] 26 C.F.R. § 56.4911-2(c)(2).

[154] The election, re-election or revocation is made by filing Form 5768 with the IRS. 26 C.F.R. § 1.501(h)-2(a), -2(c), -2(d).

[155] I.R.C. § 501(h).

[156] I.R.S. Form 990; 26 C.F.R. § 56.4911-10(c). See Appendix D for a sample Form 990.

[157] 26 C.F.R. § 1.501(h).

[158] *Id.*

[159] I.R.C. § 4912 (a). Under I.R.C. § 4912(b), the organization manager who agreed to the excessive lobbying is also responsible for a five percent tax, "unless such agreement was not willful and is due to reasonable cause."

repeated, excessive lobbying, so too can Section 501(c)(3) organizations not covered by a Section 501(h) election.[160]

[B] Restrictions on Electioneering

While Section 501(c)(3) organizations may, under the statute, lobby to an insubstantial degree, they may not participate in an electoral campaign, for or against a candidate, in any way.[161] The prohibition is absolute. A Section 501(c)(3) organization that does intervene in an election will be considered to be an action organization,[162] and if the violation is egregious enough, it will fail the political activities test, and no longer qualify for exempt status.[163] A major case in this regard is *Branch Ministries v. Rossotti*,[164] where the electioneering activities of the Church at Pierce Creek caused the loss of its tax exempt status. There, the church placed full-page ads in national newspapers asking voters to reject the Democratic candidate for President, Bill Clinton, because his positions "concerning abortion, homosexuality, and the distribution of condoms to teenagers in schools violated Biblical precepts."[165] The IRS had no trouble finding this to be a clear violation of the restrictions on electioneering, meriting loss of exempt status, and the court agreed. Similarly in *Association of the Bar of the City of New York v. Commissioner*, a Section 501(c)(3) bar association that ranked candidates for elective judicial office was found not to merit tax exempt status.[166] Recognizing that some violations of the "no electioneering" prohibition may not be as serious as others, Congress has added Section 4955 to the IRC, which allows the imposition of intermediate sanctions on the prohibited electioneering activities of Section 501(c)(3) organizations.[167]

Because the prohibition on electioneering is so clear, most of the law in this area deals with the "voter education" activities of Section 501(c)(3) organizations, and whether those activities are generally permissible educational activities allowable to a Section 501(c)(3) organization, or whether they cross the line into impermissible participation in an electoral campaign.

This will always be a question of the facts and circumstances of each case, but the IRS has provided some examples as guidance. A compilation of the voting records of all members of Congress on major legislative issues involving a wide range of subjects, with no editorial comment and no express or implied approval or disapproval is permissible voter education.[168] Publication of the responses of all the candidates in a given race in response to a questionnaire sent by the organization which the questionnaire dealt with issues solely on the basis of their importance

---

[160] I.R.C. § 4912.

[161] 26 C.F.R. § 1.501(c)(3)-1(c)(3)(i).

[162] 26 C.F.R. § 1.501(c)(3)-1(c)(3)(iii).

[163] 26 C.F.R. § 1.501(c)(3)-1(c)(3)(i).

[164] 211 F.3d 137 (D.C. Cir. 2000).

[165] *Id.* at 140.

[166] 858 F.2d 876 (2d Cir. 1988), *cert. denied*, 109 S. Ct. 1768 (1989).

[167] See § 6.06 for further information on Intermediate sanctions.

[168] Rev. Rul. 78-248, 1978-1 C.B. 154 (Situation 1).

and interest to the electorate as a whole, with no express or implied approval or disapproval, is permissible voter education;[169] however, should the questionnaire indicate a bias on certain issues, publication of those results is impermissible electoral activity.[170] An organization devoted to land conservation that publishes a voter guide of incumbent's voting records on selected land conservation issues, even with no express statements for or in opposition to any candidate has, by its emphasis on one area of concern, crossed the line into impermissible electioneering.[171]

An organization that summarizes the voting records of all members of Congress in a monthly newsletter mailed only to a few thousand nationwide members, who are not concentrated in any one voting district, whose content did indicate whether or not those votes were in accord with the organization's position, but did not contain any reference to an election or impliedly endorse or reject an incumbent as a candidate for office, nor deal with an individual's overall qualification for office, nor compare candidates, and further pointed out the limitations of judging the qualifications of an incumbent on the basis or a few selected votes, was considered permissible non-partisan voter education.[172]

Public forums or debates operated by Section 501(c)(3) organizations are a recognized and permissible educational activity.[173] Providing a forum for candidates during an election campaign can also be a permissible educational activity.[174] Problems occur, however, when the forum manifests a bias for or against one of the candidates. Forums where all legally qualified candidates are invited, where the questions are prepared and presented by a non-partisan, independent panel, where the topics cover a broad range of issues, where each candidate is treated equally and where there is no editorial comment by the moderator, have all been held to qualify as a permissible voter education activity.[175]

In 2007, IRS issued an omnibus revenue ruling, 2007-41, covering 21 different situations in which Section 501(c)(3) organizations become involved in political activity.[176] The first two situations deal with voter education, voter registration, and get-out-the-vote activities, which, if conducted in a non-partisan manner, are a permissible activity of an exempt organization. In Situation 1, a neutral voter registration booth at a state fair was permissible; in Situation 2, a get-out-the-vote drive targeted at one candidate's supporters was not.

The next four examples in Revenue Ruling 2007-41 deal with individual activity by organizational leaders. In Situation 3, a newspaper ad listing the CEO of an exempt hospital as one of the supporters of a candidate that was paid for by the

---

[169] *Id.* at Situation 2.

[170] *Id.* at Situation 3.

[171] *Id.* at Situation 4.

[172] Rev. Rul. 80-282, 1980-2 C.B. 178 (in which Situations 3 and 4 of Rev. Rul. 78-248 were distinguished).

[173] Rev. Rul. 66-256, 1966-2 C.B. 210.

[174] Rev. Rul. 74-574, 1974-2 C.B. 160.

[175] Rev. Rul. 86-95, 1986-2 C.B. 73.

[176] Rev. Rul. 2007-41, 2007-1 C.B. 1421.

candidate's campaign was permissible in that the ad was not paid for nor was it an official publication of the hospital, and the endorsement was in the CEO's personal and not hospital official capacity. In Situation 4, the endorsement of a candidate by a university president in the university's alumni newsletter was not permissible. In Situation 5, a church minister's endorsement of a candidate at a press conference for the candidate that was reported in the local paper was permissible in that the minister did not do so at a church function, in a church publication or using church assets, and did not identify himself as speaking for the church. In Situation 6, the endorsement of a candidate by the chairman of the board of an exempt organization at a meeting of the board was impermissible.

The next three examples in Revenue Ruling 2007-41 involve a candidate for political office speaking at forums or events organized by exempt organizations. In such situations, IRS says that it looks at "whether the organization provides an equal opportunity to participate to political candidates seeking the same office; whether the organization indicates any support for or opposition to the candidate; and whether any political fundraising occurs." When several candidates appear at public forum organized by an exempt organization, the IRS says that it is a question of whether the questioners are nonpartisan, whether the topics cover a broad range, whether each candidate has the same opportunity to express his or her views, whether questions require the candidates to state their agreement or not with the organization's positions, and whether the moderator of the event makes statements implying approval or disapproval of the candidates.

To illustrate these rules, Situation 7 deals with an exempt historical society that on three successive occasions invites all three candidates for a public office to address its members on purely neutral terms. The historical society itself makes no comments on the candidates' qualifications or positions. This is a permissible political activity. Situation 8 involves a similar situation, but there are four candidates and one declines the historical society's invitation. In the public announcements of the candidates' appearances, and again at the events, the society makes it clear that the order of the speakers was determined randomly and that the fourth candidate was invited but declined to appear. This, too, is permissible political activity. In Situation 9, a church minister invites only one candidate to address the congregation during services, and at that service the minister encourages a high voter turnout, but does not specifically endorse the candidate. The minister's selectivity in inviting only one candidate makes this impermissible intervention in a political campaign.

The next four examples involve the appearance of candidates for public office at events organized by exempt organizations, not in their capacity as candidates, but rather as "public figures." Such public figures might include someone who does hold political office, someone who is an expert in a field outside of politics, or someone who is a "celebrity or has led a distinguished military, legal, or public service career." In such situations, IRS says it will look at whether "the individual is chosen to speak solely for reasons other than candidacy for public office; whether the individual speaks solely in a non-candidate capacity; whether any campaign activity occurs in connection with the candidate's attendance; whether the organization maintains a nonpartisan atmosphere on the premises or at the event where the candidate is present; and whether the organization clearly indicates the capacity in which the candidate is appearing and does not mention the individual's political candidacy or the upcoming election."

To apply these rules, IRS, in Situation 10, posits an exempt historical society meeting at which a candidate, in attendance, who is also the Lieutenant Governor, is identified only as the Lieutenant Governor, but not as a candidate, from the podium by the society's president. This is permissible. In Situation 11, a congressman running for re-election is invited to attend a groundbreaking ceremony for an exempt hospital in his district. The chair of the hospital's board introduces the congressman, with no reference to the election or the congressman's candidacy. Similarly, in his remarks, the congressman makes no reference to the election or his candidacy, and no campaign fundraising occurs either. This is permissible. In Situation 12, in an exempt university's regular alumni newsletter, it mentions the fact that an alumnus is running for mayor of a certain city. Other than this bare statement, there is no reference to the election or the alumnus's candidacy. This is permissible. In Situation 13, a mayor who is running for re-election attends a performance by an exempt symphony orchestra in a city park. The chair of the symphony's board, in her remarks, identifies the mayor in the audience, thanks him for his past support of the orchestra and asks the crowd to support the mayor for re-election. This is impermissible intervention by the exempt symphony in a campaign for public office.

In the next part of Revenue Ruling 2007-41, which covers three examples, IRS attempts to distinguish issue advocacy statements, which may be permissible, from intervention by a tax exempt 501(c)(3) organization in a political campaign, which never is. The factors that IRS says it will consider in making this determination include: "whether the statement identifies one or more candidates for public office; whether the statement expresses approval or disapproval for one or more candidates' positions and/or actions; whether the statement is delivered close in time to the elections; whether the issue addressed in the communication has been raised as an issue distinguishing candidates for a given office; whether the communication is a part of an ongoing series of communications by the organization on the same issue that are made independent of the timing of any election; and whether the timing of the communication and identification of the candidate are related to a non-electoral event such as a scheduled vote on specific legislation by an officeholder who also happens to be a candidate for public office."

In Situation 14, an exempt university places ads in the major newspapers of a state urging people to contact the state's U.S. Senator to urge her to support a Senate bill that would provide needed funds to the university. A vote on this bill is scheduled soon after the ad appears, but this is also during the time that the Senator is running for re-nomination. Even so, the ad does not mention the election or the Senator's candidacy. The ad is a permissible issue advocacy statement because it is tied to the Senate vote on a bill affecting the university, and not to the election campaign, and nothing in the facts indicates that education is an issue that would distinguish the Senator from her opponents.

In Situation 15, an exempt educational organization runs a series of radio ads throughout the state urging increased state spending on education. The ads are not part of any kind of ongoing public awareness series by the organization, and they end with a request that the listener tell the state's governor what you think about "under-funded schools." When the ads are heard, there is no concurrent legislative action pending on the school funding issue, and the ads are broadcast during an electoral campaign in which the governor's opponent has made school funding an election issue. These ads are a type of impermissible intervention in a campaign for public office by the exempt organization.

In Situation 16, there is a state senate election in which the candidates are clearly divided on their support for public funding of mass transit, one pro, the other con. At the annual fundraising dinner of an exempt community development organization, held in this senatorial district, the organization's executive director gives a stemwinder urging public support of mass transit and in particular, the use of the vote in the upcoming state senate election to elect a supporter of public funding for mass transit. Although no candidate is identified by name, the implication is clear, this occurs during an election at an official event of the exempt organization and is not permitted.

IRS is also concerned that the business activities of an exempt organization, the provision of goods, services or facilities, could be used for impermissible intervention in a campaign for public office. To this end, IRS says it will consider whether the goods, services, or facilities are "available to candidates in the same election on an equal basis . . . are available only to candidates and not to the general public; whether the fees charged to candidates are the organization's customary and usual rates; and whether the activity is an ongoing activity of the organization or whether it is conducted only for a particular candidate." Situation 17 posits an exempt museum that rents a historic hall that it owns to a candidate on the same, first-come, first-served, terms on which it is available, on a regular basis, to the general public and for the standard fee. This activity is permitted. Situation 18 describes an exempt theater organization that rents its mailing list, at market rates, to a candidate for public office who is favorable to the organization's interests, refusing requests from the other candidates to do the same. This is also the only time that the organization has rented out its mailing list. This is not a permitted activity.

IRS ends Revenue Ruling 2007-41 with three examples involving the use of the web sites of exempt organizations for political purposes. Situation 19 involves an exempt organization whose web site posts an unbiased, nonpartisan voter's guide, with links to each candidate's own web site on a neutral basis. This is permissible voter education. Situation 20 describes an exempt hospital that has educational links on its web site to other web sites, one of which belongs to a national newspaper and contains an article praising the hospital's treatment program for a particular disease. On another part of its website, not the page where the article regarding the hospital appears, the newspaper site provides links to its politically oriented editorials, some of which endorse candidates in an upcoming election. The exempt hospital's link to the newspaper web site is permissible inasmuch as it is for educational and not political purposes, given the context. In Situation 21, the web site of an exempt church organization lists the biographies of its ministers, its services schedule, its community outreach programs and the activities of the church's members, one of whom is running for political office. On the site, the church posts a message that encourages people to vote for this church member in the upcoming election. This is an impermissible political campaign activity.

[C]   Section 4955 Excise Taxes

There is an excise tax, levied by IRC Section 4955, on the improper political expenditures of a Section 501(c)(3) organization. These improper political expenditures are: (1) any amount paid or incurred by a Section 501(c)(3) organization in any participation in, or intervention in (including the publication or distribution of statements), any political campaign on behalf of (or in opposition to) any candidate for public office[177] and (2) expenditures for speeches or services of a candidate, their travel expenses, conducting polls or preparing papers or other materials for them, advertising or fundraising for them and, in general, any expense that has the primary effect of promoting public recognition of a candidate.[178]

The Section 4955 excise tax is two-tiered. The initial tax is 10 percent of the political expenditure, payable by the organization, and a tax of 2½ percent of the political expenditure, payable by the organization's manager who authorized the expenditure, unless it was not willfully done or was due to a reasonable cause.[179] An additional tax of 100 percent of the political expenditure falls on the organization, and a 50 percent tax falls on the management when the organization fails to correct (i.e., retrieve the amount improperly expended) within the taxable period.[180]

The IRS may go to court to enjoin the "flagrant" political expenditures of a Section 501(c)(3) organization.[181] In such flagrant abuse situations, the IRS may also immediately end the organization's tax year and demand the immediate payment of any income or excise taxes due.[182] The ultimate penalty for political abuses by a Section 501(c)(3) organization is, of course, the revocation of its tax exempt status by the IRS. A Section 501(c)(3) organization that loses its exempt status for this reason may not seek tax exemption as a 501(c)(4) social welfare organization, which is allowed certain limited political activities.[183]

[D]   Additional Regulations of Political Activity

In addition to the limits on political activity inherent in Section 501(c)(3) and related sections of the IRC dealing with the political activities of charitable organizations, it is also the case that Section 501(c)(3) organizations are subject to

---

[177] I.R.C. § 4955(d)(1).

[178] I.R.C. § 4955 (d)(2). The IRC attaches these activities to "an organization which is formed primarily for purposes of promoting the candidacy or prospective candidacy of an individual for public office." A fortiori, they also describe the type of political activity that is clearly prohibited to all Section 501(c)(3) organizations.

[179] I.R.C. § 4955(a).

[180] I.R.C. § 4955(b).

[181] I.R.C. § 7409; 26 C.F.R. § 301.7409-1.

[182] I.R.C. § 6852; 26 C.F.R. § 301.6852-1.

[183] I.R.C. § 504. See also § 13.01 et seq. discussing 501(c)(4) organizations.

general legislation affecting the political activities of all citizens. For example, a Section 501(c)(3) organization is also subject to the Bipartisan Campaign Reform Act,[184] which amended the Federal Election Campaign Act.

The BCRA limits the participation of corporations in the federal electoral process. *Citizens United v. FEC*[185] overturned many restrictions on corporate spending in elections, but the restrictions on nonprofit tax-exempt corporations' electioneering derive from Section 501(c)(3) itself, and therefore are still in place.

[E] Constitutional Issues

Because the restrictions on the political activities of a Section 501(c)(3) organization effectively deprive these organizations of a political voice, there has been some concern that this limitation on political activity may violate an organization's free speech rights or its rights to petition the government. As to churches, the issue presents itself as whether the government is using Section 501(c)(3) to control their political activities in a way that penalizes their free exercise rights. None of these challenges have had much success in the courts, however.[186] After the United States Supreme Court's decision in *Regan v. Taxation with Representation of Wash.*,[187] the law is reasonably clear that "Congress has not violated [Taxation with Representation of Washington's] First Amendment rights by declining to subsidize its First Amendment activities."[188] In a concurring opinion, Justice Blackmun, joined by Justice Brennan and Justice Marshall, opined that what made the political restrictions on Section 501(c)(3) organizations constitutionally acceptable was that the IRC allowed them to have related Section 501(c)(4) organizations that could be politically active on the 501(c)(3) organization's behalf. As long as no charitable dollars passed from the 501(c)(3) to the 501(c)(4), the law's purpose, of prohibiting tax deductible dollars from being used for political purposes, was met. The concurring Justices found this legislative scheme to be constitutionally acceptable.[189]

---

[184] 2 U.S.C. § 431 *et seq.*

[185] 130 S. Ct. 876 (2010).

[186] *See, e.g.,* Christian Echoes Nat'l Ministry v. Comm'r, 470 F.2d 849 (10th Cir. 1972).

[187] 461 U.S. 540 (1983).

[188] *Id.* at 548.

[189] *Id.* at 551 (Blackmun, J., concurring).

Chapter 7

COURT IMPOSED LIMITS ON TAX EXEMPT ORGANIZATIONS

§ 7.01 INTRODUCTION

In addition to the four tests for tax exempt status contained in the IRC and defined in the Tax Regulations,[1] there are also judicially crafted limitations or doctrines that must be considered when establishing and maintaining tax exempt status. The court-crafted requirements discussed in this chapter are the Illegality, Public Policy, and Commerciality Doctrines. Although these doctrines do not have their basis in the IRC or the Tax Regulations, they do have the force of law and give extended powers to the IRS in determining whether organizations are eligible for tax exemption.[2]

§ 7.02 ILLEGALITY & PUBLIC POLICY DOCTRINES

The illegality and public policy doctrines are closely related. Obviously, illegal activity is contrary to public policy. These doctrines are from the historic law of charitable trusts stating that charitable purposes do not encompass the support of illegal acts (illegality doctrine) or acts contrary to public policy (public policy doctrine).[3] The Supreme Court in *Ould v. Washington Hospital for Foundlings*[4] alluded to these concepts well over a hundred years ago. In *Ould*, the Court stated, "[a] charitable use, where neither law nor public policy forbids, may be applied to almost anything that tends to promote the well-doing and well-being of social man."[5] The illegality doctrine is the most straightforward of the doctrines discussed in this section and will be addressed first. The public policy doctrine is a bit more

---

[1] See § 6.01 *et seq.* for further information on the IRC tests for tax exemption.

[2] Legal scholars have engaged in heated debates regarding these doctrines because they are generally loosely defined and give powers to the IRS that are not specifically outlined in the IRC. *See* David A. Brennen, *The Power of the Treasury: Racial Discrimination, Public Policy, and "Charity" in Contemporary Society*, 33 U.C. Davis L. Rev. 389 (2000); John K. McNulty, *Public Policy and Private Charity: A Tax Policy Perspective*, 3 Va. Tax Rev. 229 (Winter 1984); Bruce R. Hopkins, *The Most Important Concept in the Law of Tax-Exempt Organizations Today: The Commerciality Doctrine*, 5 Exempt Org. Tax Rev. 459 (1992); Paul J. Streer, *Obtaining and Preserving Tax-Exempt Status Under § 501(c)(3): Judicially Developed Factors for Detecting the Presence of Substantial Nonexempt Activities*, J. Am. Tax Ass'n 63 (Spring 1985).

[3] Restatement of Trusts § 377 (2d ed. 1959).

[4] 95 U.S. 303 (1877).

[5] *Id.* at 311.

amorphous and the lack of supporting case law has left its interpretation open for debate by legal scholars.[6]

[A]   Illegality Doctrine

The illegality doctrine dates back to the common law of England. As a part of the English Reformation, the Roman Catholic mass was declared an illegal activity. As a result, bequests for masses in England were readily voided by the courts as gifts in support of illegal acts.[7] In the United States, the concept of denying tax benefits for illegal activity was first introduced in *Tank Truck Rentals, Inc. v. Commissioner.*[8] In this case, the United States Supreme Court determined that fines paid for violation of state maximum vehicle weight laws were not deductible as a business expense.[9] Though this entity was for-profit, the Court determined that a business deduction for these illegal activities would flout the statutes that made the punished acts illegal to begin with.[10]

The illegality doctrine was first applied in the realm of tax exemption in *Revenue Ruling* 75-384, in which the IRS held that an advocacy organization that was founded to promote world peace and disarmament did not qualify for tax exemption either as a 501(c)(3) charitable or 501(c)(4) social welfare organization because it engaged in illegal activities. The organization's primary activities were staging antiwar demonstrations where the demonstrators broke local laws and breached public order.[11] In that ruling, the IRS said that "[i]llegal activities, which violate the minimum standards of acceptable conduct necessary to the preservation of an orderly society, are contrary to the common good and the general welfare of the people in a community and thus are not permissible means of promoting [exempt] purposes. . . ."[12]

Any organization whose activities are in violation of the law will therefore fail to qualify as a tax exempt organization as a result of the illegality doctrine. Illegal activities cannot be valid exempt activities. Note, however, that organizations whose purpose is simply to change the law, and not violate it, can usually qualify as a Section 501(c)(4) social welfare organization, but they would not qualify as a Section 501(c)(3) organization because of their lobbying activity.

---

[6] *See* Brennen, *supra* note 2; McNulty, *supra* note 2; Richard S. Myers, *Same-Sex "Marriage" and the Public Policy Doctrine*, 32 CREIGHTON L. REV. 45 (1998).

[7] *See* Nicholas P. Cafardi, *Bequests for Masses: Doctrine, History and Legal Status*, 20 DUQ. L. REV. 403 (1982).

[8] 356 U.S. 30 (1958).

[9] *Id.* at 34–35.

[10] *Id.* at 33–34; *see also* Charles A. Borek, *The Public Policy Doctrine and Tax Logic: The Need for Consistency in Denying Deductions Arising from Illegal Activities*, U. BALT. L. REV. 45 (1992).

[11] Rev. Rul. 75-384, 1975-2 C.B. 204.

[12] *Id.*

[B] Public Policy Doctrine

The public policy doctrine is a requirement, superimposed over the operational test, that an exempt organization serve a public purpose.[13] Organizations that engage in activities contrary to a clearly established public policy are not serving public purposes and so do not qualify for tax exemption.

The public policy doctrine has primarily developed in regard to the tax exempt status of segregated private schools. Following the 1964 Civil Rights Act and the integration of public schools, parents in a number of communities pulled their children from the public schools and sent them to racially segregated private schools instead. Because nonprofit educational organizations normally qualify for tax exempt status, these schools, called "segregation academies," were able to attract, as a major form of support, tax deductible gifts and grants. They also were not taxed on their exempt function income.

The tax exempt status of these segregated private schools was challenged, not by the IRS, but by taxpayer parents of minority children arguing that the grant of tax exempt status to these schools violated their constitutional rights.[14] The courts agreed, holding that schools that violated public policy by discriminating on a racial basis did not qualify for tax exemption. The IRS then issued a news release indicating that it could not "legally justify" granting charitable status to private schools that racially discriminate, nor could it allow tax deductions for contributions to such schools.[15] Based on the IRS's position, the tax exemptions for several schools were denied or revoked because they engaged in discriminatory practices.[16]

The issue of whether racially discriminatory private schools qualified for tax exempt status reached the United States Supreme Court in *Bob Jones University v. United States.*[17] In analyzing the tax exempt status and the ability to attract tax deductible gifts of the organizations described in IRC Section 501(c)(3) and 170(c)(2), the Court found a requirement that such organizations must meet the common law standards of charity, as found in the law of charitable trusts. Such organizations deemed charitable by the IRC, the Court said, must serve a public purpose and not be contrary to established public policy.[18] The Court went on to hold that, based on the Constitution, congressional statutes, executive orders, and

---

[13] RESTATEMENT OF TRUSTS § 377.

[14] Green v. Kennedy, 309 F. Supp. 1127 (D.D.C. 1970), *cont'd sub nom.* Green v. Connally, 330 F. Supp. 1150 (D.D.C.), *aff'd sub nom.* Coit v. Green, 404 U.S. 997 (1971). See also Rev. Rul. 67-235, 1967-2 C.B. 79, which stated that the IRS would deny exempt status to schools which discriminated on the basis of race.

[15] IRS News Release (July 10, 1970), *reprinted in* 7 STAND. FED. TAX REP. (CCH) § 6,790.

[16] See Bob Jones Univ. v. United States, 461 U.S. 574 (1983), where both Bob Jones University and Goldsboro Christian School's exemptions were revoked. See Calhoun Acad. v. Comm'r, 94 T.C. 284 (1990), for an example of another school whose exemption was revoked based on racially discriminatory reasons.

[17] 461 U.S. 574. This case contains an analysis for both *Bob Jones Univ.* and *Goldsboro Christian Schs, Inc.*, decided in the same opinion. Both situations were analyzed on the same principles.

[18] *Id.* at 586. This was actually the rationale used by the lower courts in the *Green* line of cases. *See* cases cited *supra* note 14.

court decisions, there existed a clear national public policy, which the IRS was able to interpret and apply, against racial discrimination in education.[19] The Court accepted the IRS's position that Bob Jones University was not charitable, and therefore could not qualify for Section 501(c)(3) status because its discriminatory dating policy violated this clearly defined public policy against racial discrimination.[20]

The IRS has a rather intense regimen to guarantee that tax exempt schools do not discriminate on a racial basis.[21] After the *Bob Jones* case was decided, several other racial discrimination cases in private schools addressed the same issue. In *Calhoun Academy v. Commissioner*,[22] the Tax Court found that although the school had a nondiscriminatory policy, the lack of African American students, applicants, and teachers gave the inference of discrimination.[23] The Tax Court denied exemption on public policy grounds because the Academy lacked a good faith nondiscriminatory admissions policy.[24]

The Public Policy Doctrine is different from the Illegality Doctrine because acts that violate public policy are not always illegal. The segregation academies whose charitable status was undone by the public policy doctrine were not illegal enterprises. But their racially discriminatory policies did violate public policy. To date, the public policy doctrine has applied primarily to racial discrimination in private schools. The *Bob Jones* decision has not resulted in a glut of litigation over the scope of the public policy doctrine.

The extent to which the public policy doctrine applies to issues beyond racial discrimination in private education remains unclear. One of the few cases discussing public policy in another context is the *Church of Scientology of California v. Commissioner*,[25] where the court revoked the tax exemption of the Church of Scientology based partially on the grounds that the organization violated "well defined standards of public policy by conspiring to prevent the IRS from assessing and collecting taxes owed by the church."[26]

---

[19] "An unbroken line of cases following *Brown v. Board of Education* establishes beyond doubt this Court's view that racial discrimination in education violates a most fundamental national public policy, as well as rights of individuals." *Id.* at 593.

[20] *Id.* at 605.

[21] 26 C.F.R. § 1.501(c)(3)-1(d)(3).

[22] 94 T.C. 284 (1990).

[23] *Id.* at 304.

[24] *Id.* at 305.

[25] 83 T.C. 381 (1984), *aff'd*, 823 F.2d 1310 (9th Cir. 1987), *cert. denied*, 486 U.S. 1015 (1988).

[26] *Church of Scientology of Cal.*, 823 F.2d at 1313. In addition to public policy, the court found two other reasons to deny exemption: the Church was operated for a substantial commercial purpose, and its earnings inured to the benefit of L. Ron Hubbard. *Id.* at 1312–13.

§ 7.03 THE COMMERCIALITY DOCTRINE

[A] Origins of the Doctrine

In determining whether an organization is operated for an exempt purpose, courts have detoured into an area known as the commerciality doctrine.[27] More specifically, the courts have developed this doctrine in applying the IRC's requirement of an exclusively charitable purpose[28] to organizations that engage in activities such as the sale of goods and services that could be described as commercial in nature. The basis of this court-made doctrine is the proposition that organizations that act in a commercial manner have a primary purpose, namely their commercial activities, which is a non-exempt purpose, thereby disqualifying them from exempt status.

The IRC and Tax Regulations provide no reference to the commerciality doctrine as a requirement for exempt status and are virtually silent on commercial activity as it relates to tax exempt organizations.[29] The commerciality doctrine is a creation of the courts without a clear basis in the IRC or the underlying Regulations. Even without justification in the IRC or Regulations, the doctrine has developed through the weight of judicial decision, and the IRS has begun to use this concept as a justification for denial of tax exemption.[30] Because the development of the doctrine is based on less than clear language in a number of cases, its application has been a bit uneven.[31]

A further problem with the commerciality doctrine is that it has long been settled law that exempt organizations are not barred from commercial activities, but only commercial activities that are not in furtherance of their exempt purposes.[32] As a result, the mere performance of commercial activities by an exempt organization, even highly successful commercial activities, is not determinative of exempt status. Commercial activities must be unrelated to exempt purposes to be disqualifying.

---

[27] *See* John D. Colombo, *Why is Harvard Tax-Exempt?* 35 ARIZ. L. REV. 841, 848 (Winter 1993). The commerciality doctrine is sometimes referred to as the business activity doctrine. *Id.*

[28] 26 C.F.R. § 1.501(c)(3)-1(e).

[29] I.R.C. § 501(m) was added to the I.R.C. in 1986 and deals with the denial of tax exemption to commercial-type insurance companies. While the Tax Regulations do not refer to the commerciality doctrine, they do refer to commercial activities as they relate to the imposition of unrelated business income tax (UBIT). See 26 C.F.R. § 1.513-1(b), which states that the use of commercial advertising can be considered in determining trade or business; 26 C.F.R. § 1.513-1(c)(1) and (2)(ii) state that the frequency and continuity of commercial activities can be considered in determining whether an activity is regularly carried on; 26 C.F.R. § 1.501(c)(3)-1(e) discusses trade or business as it applies to unrelated business income; and 26 C.F.R. § 1.501(c)(3)-1(e)(1) states that an organization's primary purpose shall be determined by all the facts and circumstances, including the size and extent of the trade or business and the size or extent of the activities which are in furtherance of one or more exempt purposes.

[30] *See, e.g.*, Scripture Press Found. v. United States, 285 F.2d 800, 802 (Ct. Cl. 1961).

[31] *See, e.g.*, Manning Ass'n v. Comm'r, 93 T.C. 596 (1989); Am. Inst. for Econ. Research v. United States, 302 F.2d 934, 938 (Ct. Cl. 1962); B.S.W. Group, Inc. v. Comm'r, 70 T.C. 352, 357–58 (1978); Fed'n Pharmacy Serv., Inc. v. Comm'r, 625 F.2d 804 (8th Cir. 1980).

[32] 26 C.F.R. § 1.501(c)(3)-1(c)(1), -1(e)(1); S. F. Infant Sch., Inc. v. Comm'r, 69 T.C. 957 (1978); Monterey Pub. Parking Co. v. United States, 481 F.2d 175 (9th Cir. 1973).

The case of *Trinidad v. Sagrada Orden de Predicadores*[33] is often credited as the source of the commerciality doctrine. In discussing the activities of a tax exempt religious order, the United States Supreme Court focused, in part, on the commercial purposes of the order.[34] The religious order realized income from rents, dividends, and interest as well as profits from the occasional sale of wine, chocolate, and other articles supplied for use in its churches, schools, and other agencies. The Court rejected the IRS argument that the order was "operated for business and commercial purposes." Instead, the Court held that the organization was organized and operated exclusively for exempt purposes even though it had commercial income. It further held that there was no competition with for-profit commercial business, and while the religious order did realize some profits, these profits were a negligible factor and incidental to the religious purposes for which the corporation was created and conducted.[35]

The commerciality doctrine further evolved in *Better Business Bureau of Washington, D.C. v. United States.*[36] The Better Business Bureau (the Bureau) sought tax exemption as an educational organization that focused on teaching merchants to conduct their businesses honestly and teaching consumers to avoid being victimized and to purchase goods intelligently.[37] The Court denied tax exemption to the Bureau, finding that it engaged in the nonexempt purpose[38] of promoting a profitable business community, thereby basing their holding on the presence of a substantial, non-exempt commercial purpose.[39]

The analysis in *Trinidad* and *Better Business Bureau* should sound very familiar. It is basically the operational test. The operational test requires both that an organization engage primarily in activities that accomplish its exempt purpose and that not more than an insubstantial part of its activities further a non-exempt purpose.[40] In applying the operational test in these cases, the courts have asked whether the organizations' activities are commercial in nature. These questions spawned the beginning of the commerciality doctrine. Considering its source, a good argument can be made that the commerciality doctrine is really nothing more than a version of the operational test. If an organization is operated for commercial purposes or the commercial purposes are substantial in nature, then the inference can be made that it is not operated for exempt purposes.

---

[33] Trinidad v. Sagrada Orden de Predicadores de law Provincia del Santisimo Rosario de Filipinas, 263 U.S. 578 (1924). See § 6.01 *et seq.* for further information on the test for tax exemption.

[34] *Sagrada Orden de Predicadores*, 263 U.S. at 581.

[35] *Id.* at 582.

[36] 326 U.S. 279 (1945).

[37] *Id.* at 282–83.

[38] *Id.* at 283. "The presence of a noneducational purpose, if substantial in nature, will destroy the exemption regardless of the number or importance of truly educational purposes." *Id.*; *see also* 26 C.F.R. § 1.501(c)(3)-1(c)(1).

[39] *Id.*

[40] 26 C.F.R. § 1.501(c)(3)-1(c)(1). See § 6.03 for further discussion of the operational test.

In *Better Business Bureau*, the Court did apply an operational test analysis,[41] but instead of stopping the analysis there, the Court went on to discuss the commercial hue[42] of the organization.[43] The Court determined that this commercial hue was "directed fundamentally to ends other than that of education [and that a]ny claim that education is the sole aim of [the Bureau's] organization is thereby destroyed."[44]

[B] Applying the Doctrine

In stating that the existence of a substantial commercial purpose will preclude tax exemption, *Trinidad* and *Better Business Bureau* started the line of cases that turned what should have been merely an application of the operational test into the murky depths of the commerciality doctrine.[45] Determining whether a substantial non-exempt commercial purpose is present in an organization is considerably more difficult than determining whether the organization is operated for non-exempt purposes. Different courts have taken different approaches in determining what constitutes substantial non-exempt commercial purposes, based on the facts and circumstances of each case.

Some cases have tried to determine what constitutes substantial non-exempt activities quantitatively. In *Church in Boston v. Commissioner*,[46] the Tax Court determined that spending 20 percent of revenues on a non-exempt purpose[47] was substantial. In *World Family Corporation v. Commissioner*,[48] the Tax Court found that less than 10 percent of revenues spent on non-exempt purposes was not substantial and therefore did not preclude tax exemption.[49] However, in *Manning Association v. Commissioner*,[50] the Tax Court specifically rejected the idea that *World Family Corporation* created a safe-harbor 10 percent ceiling on substantial non-exempt activities. Basing its decision in *Manning Association* on facts and circumstances that included the non-exempt activity of renting a historical site for

---

[41] *See* 26 C.F.R. § 1.501(c)(3)-1(c)(1).

[42] *Better Bus. Bureau*, 326 U.S. at 283.

[43] The Bureau's charter, which the Court claimed was commercial in nature and only incidentally educational, provided for five activities including: (1) prevention of fraud by informing and warning merchants and the general public; (2) fighting fraud by bringing fraudulent practices to the public's attention; (3) elevating business standards by convincing businesses that *caveat emptor* misleading advertising, extravagant claims and price comparisons are not good business; (4) educating consumers to be intelligent buyers; and (5) cooperating with various governmental agencies. *Id.* at 281–82.

[44] *Id.* at 284.

[45] It is the authors' belief that the cases herein cited as being commerciality doctrine cases should be operational test cases. The analysis should begin with whether an organization engages primarily in activities that accomplish its exempt purpose, and continue with whether the activity is a substantial or insubstantial part of the organization's activity.

[46] 71 T.C. 102 (1978).

[47] *Id.* at 107–08. See also Copyright Clearance Ctr. v. Comm'r, where the court recognized that "a nonexempt purpose even perhaps somewhat beyond a de minimis level has been permitted without loss of exemption." 79 T.C. 793, 805 (1982).

[48] 81 T.C. 958 (1983).

[49] *Id.* at 967.

[50] 93 T.C. 596 (1989).

use as a restaurant, the Tax Court determined that it did not qualify for tax exemption.[51]

Some courts have focused on a qualitative approach to determining whether commercial activity is substantial.[52] Yet others have considered whether there is: (1) competition with for-profit commercial entities;[53] (2) provision of below-cost services;[54] (3) pricing policies;[55] (4) reasonableness of financial reserves;[56] (5) use of commercial promotional methods (i.e., advertising);[57] (6) an appropriate level of charitable donations;[58] and (7) an excessive amount of profits.[59] On this last point, courts are inconsistent on whether financial success can be detrimental to obtaining or maintaining tax exempt status.[60]

[C]   For-Profit Comparison Standard

In applying the commerciality doctrine, courts disfavor exempt organizations that appear to be competing with for-profit companies that provide similar goods or services.[61] When dealing with cases focusing on the commercial nature of a nonprofit organization, courts often refer to the "unfair competition" it poses to its for-profit counterparts.[62] With the underlying premise that tax exempt organizations ought not to be competing with for-profits, the courts compare the commercial activity of the exempt organization to that of the for-profit, and if the similarity is too great, they find that the commerciality doctrine has been

---

[51]   *Id.* at 610–11.

[52]   *See, e.g., Manning Ass'n*, 93 T.C. 596 (1989).

[53]   *See, e.g.*, American Inst. for Econ. Research v. United States, 302 F.2d 934, 938 (Ct. Cl. 1962); Easter House v. United States, 12 Cl. Ct. 476, 486 (1987) (court held that the plaintiff's competition with other commercial organizations gives its activities an impermissible commercial hue); *B.S.W. Group, Inc.*, 70 T.C. 352 (court determined that competition with commercial firms is strong evidence of a nonexempt commercial purpose). Courts may engage in a counterparts test to determine if there is unfair competition between a for-profit business and a tax exempt organization. *See* HOPKINS, THE LAW OF TAX-EXEMPT ORGANIZATIONS (8th ed. 2003).

[54]   *See, e.g.*, Fed'n Pharmacy Serv., Inc v. Comm'r, 625 F.2d 804 (8th Cir. 1980); *B.S.W. Group, Inc.*, 70 T.C. 352; *Easter House*, 12 Cl. Ct. 476.

[55]   *See, e.g.*, Living Faith, Inc. v. Comm'r, 950 F.2d 365 (7th Cir. 1991) (use of retail pricing methods was used as a factor in finding the organization operated in a commercial manner).

[56]   *See, e.g.*, Presbyterian & Reformed Publ'g Co. v. Comm'r, 743 F.2d 148 (3d Cir. 1984).

[57]   *See, e.g., Living Faith, Inc.*, 950 F.2d 365 (use of advertising and promotional materials was used as a factor in finding the organization operated in a commercial manner).

[58]   *See, e.g., Am. Inst. for Econ. Research*, 302 F.2d 934.

[59]   *See Scripture Press Found.*, 285 F.2d 800, 803 (Ct. Cl. 1961) (court rejected the notion that large profits automatically preclude tax exemption, but added that "[profits are] at least some evidence indicative of a commercial character . . .").

[60]   *Id.* at 803; *see also* JONES ET AL., THE TAX LAW OF CHARITIES AND OTHER EXEMPT ORGANIZATIONS 166–167 (1999); Hopkins, *The Most Important Concept in the Law of Tax Exempt Organizations Today, supra* note 2; Streer, *supra* note 2; Colombo, *supra* note 27 at 848.

[61]   *See B.S.W. Group, Inc.*, 70 T.C. 352.

[62]   *See Scripture Press Found.*, 285 F.2d 800; *Fed'n Pharmacy Serv., Inc.*, 625 F.2d 804; *Living Faith, Inc.*, 950 F.2d 365.

violated.[63]

In *Federation Pharmacy Services*,[64] the organization provided prescription drugs to the elderly and disabled persons. Qualified persons were able to receive five percent off the cost of the drugs, while others were charged market rates. The court found: (1) the organization relied financially on the sale of prescription drugs to the public; and (2) there was no accommodation made for those unable to pay, therefore it operated for a substantial commercial purpose.[65] The court also found that granting tax exemption to Federated would "necessarily disadvantage other for-profit drug stores with which Federated competes."[66]

In *Living Faith, Inc.*,[67] the organization operated vegetarian restaurants and health food stores in furtherance of the Seventh Day Adventist Church's doctrine that healthful eating promoted virtuous conduct. In determining that the organization operated in a commercial manner, the court looked at factors that indicated the activities the organization engaged in were commercial in nature. They were: (1) the organization sold goods and services to the public, which made the operations presumptively commercial;[68] (2) there was direct competition with similar for-profit organizations in the area; (3) there was no below-cost pricing (all prices were retail); (4) the organization advertised and used promotional materials; (5) the restaurants and stores had hours of operation similar to their for-profit counterparts; (6) the organization had salaried employees instead of relying on volunteers; and (8) the organization solicited no charitable contributions.[69]

[D] Publishing Houses

It is amazing how many cases using the commerciality doctrine involve publishing houses, especially religious publishing houses. In these cases the commerciality doctrine arises in connection with the issue of whether the act of publishing materials (educational or otherwise) can be considered an exempt activity or if it is a nonexempt commercial purpose.[70] Although these cases deal with similar types of organizations, the analyses of how those activities affect exemption differ greatly.

In *Scripture Press Foundation*,[71] the Foundation generated substantial profits by publishing and selling religious literature for the purposes of upgrading the

---

[63] *See Presbyterian and Reformed Publ'g Co.*, 743 F.2d 148 (where the court made this comparison, but came down on the side of exemption anyway).

[64] 625 F.2d 804.

[65] *Id.* at 809.

[66] *Id.* at 808.

[67] 950 F.2d 365.

[68] *Id.* at 373.

[69] *Id.* at 372–75.

[70] See, e.g., Elisian Guild, Inc. v. United States, 412 F.2d 121, 125 (1st Cir. 1969), where a publishing house was granted exemption because there was no operational profits.

[71] 285 F.2d 800. It is important to note that Forest Press and St. Germain engaged in non-publishing activities which were related to their exempt purpose, while Scripture Press' sole activity was publishing.

quality of teaching materials for Bible instruction in Sunday schools.[72] The Tax Court found the sale of religious materials which, although religiously inspired, amounted to its primary purpose being a trade or business for profit and therefore non-exempt.[73] The court went on to state that "there are many commercial [businesses] which sell Bibles, scrolls, and other religious and semi-religious literature which have not been granted exemption as to that part of their businesses."[74] The court in *Scripture Press* took into consideration net profits, surplus revenue, and amounts expended on tax exempt functions in making their decision.

In *Scripture Press*, the court distinguished the facts from two other publishing house cases, *Forest Press Inc. v. Commissioner*[75] and *St. Germain v. Commissioner*,[76] stating that there was a difference between organizations that have commercial activities as a part of their overall activities (St. Germain and Forest Press) and those that have commercial activities as their sole activity (Scripture Press).[77] *Forest Press* involved an educational organization that promoted and published the Dewey Decimal library codification system. The IRS denied exemption because, it said, Forest Press engaged in a commercial publishing enterprise and was not organized or operated for exempt purposes.[78] The court disagreed with the IRS and found Forest Press to merit exemption, explaining that, "[b]y its charter, this corporation might lawfully have been used as the means of increasing the wealth of its founders and stockholders. But the evidence is all to the effect that this was never the purpose or intent and has not been the effect."[79] In *St. Germain*, the organization sold religious literature in connection with its religious activities. The IRS argued that the organization derived profits from the sale of these publications, evidencing a non-exempt commercial purpose. The court rejected this contention stating that, "[t]he sale of religious literature . . . held to propagate the precepts of the [organization] are activities closely associated with, and incidental to, the religious purposes of the [organization]. Such activities bear an intimate relationship to the proper functioning of the [organization], and we do not believe that income received from these activities prevents . . . [it] from being an organization organized and operated 'exclusively' for religious purposes . . . ."[80]

---

[72] *Id.* at 803.

[73] *Id.* at 806. The court in this case specifically avoided the issue of unrelated business income by finding that Scripture Press' activities did not "warrant tax exemption." *Id.* at 807.

[74] *Id.* at 806. When the court engages in a comparison of the activities of an exempt organization with those of for-profit businesses, they are said to be engaging in a counterparts test to determine if there is unfair competition between a for-profit business and a tax exempt organization. *See* HOPKINS, *supra* note 53.

[75] 22 T.C. 265 (1954).

[76] 26 T.C. 648 (1956).

[77] *Scripture Press*, 285 F.2d at 803–06.

[78] *Forest Press*, 22 T.C. at 266–67.

[79] *Id.* at 269.

[80] *St. Germain*, 26 T.C. at 658.

Imbedded within the above decisions are rather interesting views on the effect of financial success with regard to maintaining an organization's exempt status. In *Scripture Press*, the IRS tried to distinguish the *Forest Press* and *St. Germain* cases by arguing that exemption was allowed in those cases partially based on the small profits realized by those organizations. The difference in the *Scripture Press* case was the substantial profits it realized. The Tax Court rejected this argument stating that, "if the . . . [IRS] seeks . . . to suggest that where an organization's profits are very large a conclusion that the organization is noncharitable must follow, we reject such a suggestion."[81] But the court added that, "if, however, [IRS] means only to suggest that . . . [profits] are at least some evidence indicative of a commercial character we are inclined to agree."[82] This left the door open for future courts to consider an organization's financial success in denying or granting exemption.

The court in *The Golden Rule Church Association v. Commissioner*[83] stated that it "regard[s] consistent nonprofitability as evidence of the absence of commercial purposes."[84] In addition, a case decided in 1969 found a religious publisher exempt because the organization did not have operational profits,[85] and the court concluded that the "deficit operation reflects not poor business planning nor ill fortune but rather the fact that profits were not the goal of the operation."[86]

In *Presbyterian and Reformed Publishing Company*,[87] another religious publishing house was initially denied exemption because of the "commercial hue" it generated by virtue of its profits, professional staff, and competition with commercial publishers.[88] The Circuit Court, however, determined that the Company should be given exemption because it maintained its religious affiliation in accordance with Section 501(c)(3). Even in granting exemption, the Circuit Court remained concerned about the commercial aspect of the company quoting the Tax Court's statement that when "an organization's management decisions replicate those of commercial enterprises, it is a fair inference that at least one purpose is commercial . . . ."[89] But the Circuit Court also stated that "success in terms of audience reached and influence exerted, in and of itself, should not jeopardize the tax-exempt status of organizations which remain true to their stated goals."[90]

The analysis in the *Presbyterian* case highlights the "Catch 22"[91] created by the courts' decisions when they attempt to apply the commerciality doctrine based on an organization's profits. If an organization is successful and generates a profit it

---

[81] *Scripture Press*, 285 F.2d at 803.

[82] *Id.*

[83] 41 T.C. 719 (1964), *nonacq.* 1964-2 C.B. 8.

[84] *Id.* at 731.

[85] Elisian Guild, Inc. v. U.S., 412 F.2d 121 (1st Cir. 1969).

[86] *Id.* at 125.

[87] 743 F.2d 148 (3d Cir. 1984).

[88] *Id.* at 151–54.

[89] *Id.* at 155.

[90] *Id.* at 158.

[91] JONES ET AL., *supra* note 60.

"attacks one of the economic justifications for [its] tax exemption."[92] Yet if it operates at a loss, the organization jeopardizes its very existence because no organization can long survive operating consistently in the red.

In a non-religious publishing house case, *American Institute for Economic Research v. United States*,[93] an organization that disseminated publications containing investment advice was denied tax exemption. The court rejected the notion that the Institute was engaged in educational activities and held that the organization's exemption should be denied because "its purpose is primarily a business one."[94]

[E]   Conclusion

In 2003, the court in *Airlie Foundation v. IRS*[95] finally attempted to define the commerciality doctrine. The court determined that the Foundation, which operated a conference center, engaged in conduct of both a commercial and exempt nature. The court's analysis focused on the operational test with emphasis on whether the activities conducted by the Foundation were conducted for a commercial purpose. While certain factors, including the Foundation's fee structure and subsidization practice were indicative of non-commercial purpose, other factors, such as the nature of its clients, competition with for-profits, advertising expenditures, and substantial revenues, strongly suggested a commercial purpose. The court denied exemption finding a "distinctive 'commercial hue'" to the way the foundation carried out its business.[96] It stated that "in applying the operational test, courts have relied on what has come to be termed the 'commerciality doctrine'. . . . [i]n many instances, courts have found that, due to the 'commercial' manner in which an organization conducts its activities, that organization is operated for nonexempt commercial purposes rather than for exempt purposes."[97] Although there have not been any recent cases on the commerciality doctrine, IRS continues to apply it in private letter rulings. In Priv. Ltr. Rul. 201109029, IRS denied exempt status to an organization that collected, processed, and sold rainwater.[98] In Priv. Ltr. Rul. 201044018, it denied exempt status to an organization that provided paratransit for the elderly on a fee basis.[99] In Priv. Ltr. Rul. 201008050, it denied exempt status to an organization that sold life coaching programming, alternative and integrative

---

[92]   *Id.* at 193.

[93]   302 F.2d 934 (Ct. Cl. 1962).

[94]   *Id.* at 938. Compare with Fides Publishers Assoc'n v. United States, 263 F. Supp. 924, 934 (N.D. Ind. 1967), where the court determined that a nonprofit organization is operated for a charitable purpose even if it engages in a commercial activity, so long as it is in furtherance of its exempt purpose.

[95]   283 F. Supp. 2d 58, 63 (D.D.C. 2003). This is the first case to actually use the term commerciality doctrine in a court opinion.

[96]   *Id.* at 65.

[97]   *Id.* at 63. *See also* Trinidad v. Sagrada Orden de Predicadores, 263 U.S. 578; Colombo, *supra* note 27, at 848; Nina J. Crimm, *An Explanation of the Federal Income Tax Exemption for Charitable Organizations: A Theory of Risk Compensation*, 50 FLA. L. REV. 419 (1998); Carolyn Wright, *Commerciality Doctrine Poses Substantial Threat to EOs*, TAX NOTES TODAY, Nov. 15, 1996.

[98]   I.R.S. Priv. Ltr. Rul. 201109029 (Mar. 4, 2011).

[99]   I.R.S. Priv. Ltr. Rul. 201044018 (Nov. 5, 2010).

healing products, including nutritional supplements.[100] In Priv. Ltr. Rul. 200944053, it denied exempt status to an organization that, for a fee, analyzed performance data for its member healthcare organizations.[101]

---

[100] IRS Priv. Ltr. Rul. 201008050 (Nov. 30, 2007).

[101] I.R.S. Priv. Ltr. Rul. 200944053 (Oct. 30, 2009); *See also* I.R.S. Priv. Ltr. Rul. 200849017 (Dec. 5, 2008); I.R.S. Priv. Ltr. Rul. 200847019 (Nov. 21, 2008); I.R.S. Priv. Ltr. Rul. 200847018 (Nov. 21, 2008); I.R.S. Priv. Ltr. Rul. 200845053 (Nov. 7, 2008).

Chapter 8

RELIGIOUS ORGANIZATIONS & CHURCHES

§ 8.01 INTRODUCTION

Churches and religious organizations are not the same thing. They are both Section 501(c)(3) organizations, but while all churches could qualify as religious organizations, not all religious organizations can qualify as churches.[1] A more limited concept is intended by the IRC for the term "church" than is intended by the term "religious organization."[2] Churches receive a number of tax benefits that religious organizations, which are not churches, do not receive.

§ 8.02 RELIGIOUS ORGANIZATIONS

[A] Defining Religion

"Religious organizations" is the broader of the two categories. The tax exemption for religious organizations has been in every version of the federal income tax law.[3] In 1890, the United States Supreme Court observed that the term religion has "reference to one's views of his relations to his Creator, and to the obligations they impose of reverence for his being and character, and of obedience to his will."[4] The Court has also noted that the "essence of religion is belief in a relation to God involving duties superior to those arising from any human relation."[5]

---

[1] Chapman v. Comm'r, 48 T.C. 358, 363 (1967).

[2] *Id.*

[3] The Tariff Act of 1894, Congress' first attempt to tax corporate income, specifically exempted religious organizations from the law's reach. This act was declared unconstitutional in Pollock v. Farmers' Loan and Trust Co., 157 U.S. 429 (1895), and Congress' inability to tax incomes was remedied by the 16th Amendment (1913). The Revenue Act of 1913, which re-instituted the federal income tax, again exempted religious organizations. The exemption was repeated in the 1954 and the 1986 IRCs.

[4] Davis v. Beason, 133 U.S. 333, 342 (1890).

[5] United States v. Macintosh, 283 U.S. 605, 633 (1931). In equally older cases, state courts have also attempted to define religion. Some noteworthy examples follow: McMasters v. State, 29 A.L.R. 292, 294 Okla. Crim. App. 1922), where the Oklahoma Criminal Appeals Court opined that religion has "reference to man's relation to Divinity; to reverence, worship, obedience, and submission to the mandates and precepts of supernatural or superior beings"; Nikulnikoff v. Archbishop, 255 N.Y.S. 653, 663 (Sup. Ct. 1932), where the Superior Court of New York City stated that, "Religion as generally accepted may be defined as a bond uniting man to God and a virtue whose purpose is to render God the worship due him as the source of all being . . ."; Taylor v. State, 11 So. 2d 663, 673 (Miss. 1943), where the Mississippi Supreme Court said that, "[T]he Christian religion, in its most important ultimate aspect, recognizes, has faith in and worships a Divine Being or Spirit-one Father of all mankind-who has the power to and will

In more recent times, however, the courts and the IRS have shied away from attempting to define religion or religious content. As the IRS has said, "An analysis of the First Amendment to the Constitution of the United States indicates that it is logically impossible to define 'religion.'[6] The Eighth Circuit, in *Teterud v. Burns*,[7] stated that "[i]t is not the province of government officials or courts to determine religious orthodoxy."[8] Rather than determine whether an organization is religious, based on its beliefs, the IRS looks to the sincerity with which those beliefs are held. "[T]he proper rule . . . is that in the absence of a clear showing that the beliefs and doctrines under consideration are not sincerely held by those professing or claiming them as a religion, the Service cannot question the 'religious' nature of those beliefs."[9] Whether or not beliefs are sincerely held is determined by an objective criterion: do the beliefs inform the lives of those professing them?

Once a showing has been made that the beliefs are sincerely held, the analysis proceeds to determine whether the beliefs are religious in nature.[10] In *Africa v. Commonwealth of Pennsylvania*,[11] the Third Circuit created a three-part test to determine whether beliefs are religious in nature. That test looks at: (1) whether the beliefs address fundamental and ultimate questions concerning the human condition, (2) whether the beliefs are comprehensive in nature and constitute an entire system of belief instead of merely an isolated teaching, and (3) whether the beliefs are manifested in external forms.[12]

These two elements are combined by the IRS and the courts in determining whether an organization is religious, namely: are the beliefs sincerely held and are they religious in nature? This analysis was applied by the court in *Church of the Chosen People v. United States.*[13] In that case, the court did not come to a clear determination of whether the organization's beliefs, which consisted primarily of a preference for a gay lifestyle, could be considered "sincerely held." But on the question of whether these beliefs were religious in nature, the court found that the organization's beliefs were not comprehensive in nature, but instead focused on only one aspect of human existence, namely sexual preference.[14] As a result, the

---

forgive the transgressions of repentants and care for the immortal souls of the believers, and which belief brings earthly solace and comfort to and tends to induce right living in such believers"; Minersville School District v. Gobitis, 108 F.2d 683, 685 (3d Cir. 1939), where the Third Circuit said that "[r]eligion is squaring human life with superhuman life . . . [w]hat is common to all religions is belief in a superhuman power and an adjustment of human activities to the requirements of that power . . . ."

[6] I.R.S. Gen. Couns. Mem. 36993 (Feb. 3, 1977); *see also Unity Sch. of Christianity*, 4 B.T.A. 61 (1926); United States v. Ballard, 322 U.S. 78 (1944); United States v. Seeger, 380 U.S. 163 (1965). Note that these cases were attempting to apply the term "religious" outside of a tax context.

[7] 522 F.2d 357 (8th Cir. 1975).

[8] *Id.* at 360.

[9] I.R.S. Gen. Couns. Mem. 36993 (Feb. 3, 1977).

[10] Church of the Chosen People v. United States, 548 F. Supp. 1247, 1252 (D. Minn. 1982).

[11] 662 F.2d 1025, 1032 (3d Cir. 1981), *cert. denied*, 456 U.S. 908 (1982) (as amended January 6, 1982).

[12] *Id.*

[13] 548 F. Supp. 1247.

[14] *Id.* at 1253.

organization clearly did not meet the test for religious organizations.[15]

[B] Applying the Operational Test

Of the four IRS tests for tax exemption — organizational, operational, political activities and private inurement — the operational test focuses on the purpose and not the nature of the activity.[16] In order for an organization to meet the operational test, the IRS has said, the resources of an organization "must be devoted to purposes that qualify as exclusively charitable. . . ."[17] This means that organizations that print and publish religious tracts can qualify as exempt religious organizations as long as they are doing so for religious purposes and they meet the other three IRS tests.[18] Religious publishing houses where the primary purpose appeared to be too commercial in nature, i.e., turning more than a modest profit, have not been found to be tax exempt, despite the fact that their publications were limited to religious texts.[19] The religious publishing houses that were denied exemption, or had it revoked, were seen as too commercial to qualify as exempt organizations. Indeed, it is mostly in the area of religious publishing houses that the so-called "commerciality test" was born.[20]

Outside of the publishing area, there are other types of activities that organizations have attempted to characterize as fulfilling a religious purpose in order to obtain or keep their exempt status. Organizations that operate what they characterize as religious retreat centers, for example, have sought exemption as religious organizations. Whether the exemption is granted to such organizations as genuinely religious, as in the area of publishing, will depend on whether the organizations are perceived as too commercial in their operations to qualify as operating primarily for exempt religious purposes. In the case of *Junaluska Assembly House, Inc. v. Commissioner*,[21] the operation of a religious retreat center was found not to be so commercial as to deprive the organization of

---

[15] *Id.* In a case applying the New York Real Property Tax Law to the Holy Spirit Association (also known as the "Unification Church" and sometimes more commonly referred to as the "Moonies" after their founder Reverend Sun Myung Moon), the New York Court of Appeals applied a very similar, non-content-based test: Does the religious organization assert the challenged purposes and activities are religious, and is that assertion bona fide? Answering "yes" to both, the court reversed a lower court holding denying the property tax exemption to the Unification Church. Holy Spirit Assoc'n v. Tax Comm'n, 435 N.E.2d 662 (N.Y. 1982).

[16] *See* Fed'n Pharmacy Serv. v. Comm'r, 72 T.C. 687 (1979), *aff'd*, 625 F.2d 804 (8th Cir. 1980); Est. of Haw. v. Comm'r, 71 T.C. 1067 (1979); B.S.W. Group, Inc. v. Comm'r, 70 T.C. 352 (1978).

[17] Rev. Rul. 72-369, 1972-2 C.B. 245.

[18] *See* A. A. Allen Revivals, Inc. v. Comm'r, 22 T.C.M. (CCH) 1435 (1963); The Golden Rule Church Assoc'n v. Comm'r, 41 T.C. 719 (1964); Elisian Guild, Inc. v. United States, 412 F.2d 121 (1st Cir. 1969); Pulpit Res. v. Comm'r, 70 T.C. 594 (1978); Presbyterian and Reformed Publ'g Co. v. Comm'r, 743 F.2d 148 (3d Cir. 1984).

[19] *See* Scripture Press Found. v. United States, 285 F.2d 800 (Ct. Cl. 1961); Fides Publishers Assoc'n v. United States, 263 F. Supp. 924 (N.D. Ind. 1967); Christian Manner Int'l v. Comm'r, 71 T.C. 661 (1979); Inc. Trustees of Gospel Worker Soc'y v. United States, 510 F. Supp. 374, *aff'd*, 672 F.2d 894 (D.C. Cir. 1981), *cert. denied*, 456 U.S. 994 (1982); Presbyterian and Reformed Publ'g Co., 743 F.2d 148.

[20] *See* cases cited *supra* note 19; see also § 7.01 *et seq.* for further information on commerciality.

[21] 86 T.C. 1114 (1986).

exemption,[22] while in the *Schoger Foundation v. Commissioner*,[23] the operation of a religious retreat center was found to be too recreational and social to qualify for exemption.[24]

Yet another area that religious groups have attempted to baptize as qualifying for the religious exemption is the job training area. In *The Golden Rule Association v. Commissioner*,[25] a religious organization taught that God's laws applied not just in the personal, but also in the economic sphere. In order to persuade people to apply God's laws to their business activities, the Church ran several model businesses, staffed by "student ministers." These businesses included a redwood processing company, a laundry and dry cleaner, a manufacturing company, a hotel, a restaurant, a sawmill, and a plant nursery, all of which operated at a net loss. The student ministers attended morning devotional services daily and in the evenings attended classes or religious discussion groups. Approximately 25 to 30 percent of their training time was spent on applying the organization's religious teachings in relationships with the public.[26] In upholding the organization's tax exempt status, the court said that, "the training projects operated by the [organization] and its student ministers were carried on exclusively for religious purposes."[27]

A contrary example is found in *Tony and Susan Alamo Foundation v. Commissioner*,[28] where the Foundation claimed that it was rehabilitating physically, mentally, and spiritually downtrodden people through religious training, counseling, and industrial education. The Foundation operated a restaurant, gas stations, thrift and grocery stores and an auto repair shop. All of these endeavors were staffed by adherents of the Foundation who participated in active prayer and devotional life operated by the Foundation. The profits from these businesses were used to support the staff and the opulent life style of the organization's founders, Tony and Susan Alamo.[29] In revoking the Foundation's exempt status, the Tax Court applied the rule outlined above, namely that the existence of a substantial nonexempt purpose, regardless of the coexistence of an exempt purpose, precludes an organization from qualifying under Section 501(c)(3). Rather than being a communal group only tangentially engaged in unrelated trades or businesses, the court held that the Foundation "was akin to a city of full-time workers, who also happen to pray together. Any sincerely held religious beliefs were secondary to the [Foundation's] main purpose, i.e., the operation of the businesses to provide subsistence to foundation members and economic wealth to [the founders]."[30]

---

[22] *Id.* at 1128.

[23] 76 T.C. 380 (1981).

[24] *Id.* at 388–89.

[25] 41 T.C. 719.

[26] *Id.* at 723–25.

[27] *Id.* at 729.

[28] 63 T.C.M. (CCH) 2422 (1992).

[29] *Id.*

[30] *Id.*

[C]   Communal Living

The religious exemption, as the *Alamo Foundation* case mentions, has been used effectively by religious groups who do adopt a communal lifestyle that supports its members. Primary among these are what are often referred to as religious orders of priests, monks, or nuns who work for their religious order and who are, in turn, supported by that order. Such groups exist in the Catholic, Orthodox, and some mainstream Protestant faiths. The IRS has ruled that these groups do qualify for exempt status, even though their income is used to support their members, as long as the members of the organization live under a strict set of rules requiring moral and spiritual self-sacrifice and dedication to the goals of the organization at the expense of their material well-being; the members make a long-term commitment to the organization; the organization is part of a larger church body; the members' common life requires a significantly stricter level of moral and religious discipline than is required of other church members; the members work full-time to serve the larger church and they regularly participate in public or private prayer, religious study, teaching, care of the aged, missionary work, or church reform or renewal.[31]

Other communal living organizations that have tried to take advantage of the religious order exemption to qualify for exempt status have not been successful. One example is the case of *New Life Tabernacle v. Commissioner*,[32] which involved a commune that collected the income from its members and in turn used this income to support them and their families. The commune had weekly worship services and Bible study four nights a week. It also operated its own religious school. Because it could not demonstrate that the benefits provided to members were not a form of private inurement, the organization was denied exemption.[33]

§ 8.03   CHURCHES

[A]   Defining Churches

The same definitional problems that typify the IRS's handling of religious organizations occur even more so in the IRS's attempts to define a church, for the same constitutional reasons.[34] In the early case of *De La Salle Institute v. United States*,[35] the issue was whether a religious order, such as those discussed in the previous section, could qualify as a church. The order operated a novitiate that trained novices and operated Catholic high schools, homes for its members, a winery, and a distillery. It also operated chapels at its schools and at the novitiate.[36] The court said that the tail (i.e., doing "churchy" things like operating chapels)

---

[31]   Rev. Proc. 91-20, 1991-1 C.B. 524.

[32]   44 T.C.M. (CCH) 309 (1982).

[33]   *Id.*

[34]   *See* C. Whelan, *"Church" in the Internal Revenue Code: The Definitional Problems*, 45 FORDHAM L. REV. 885 (1977).

[35]   195 F. Supp. 891 (N.D. Cal. 1961).

[36]   *Id.*

could not wag the dog. The term "church" had been used by Congress in the IRC, the court said, in the "common meaning and usage of the word."[37] It went on to find that the religious order did not qualify as its own church.[38]

In *Chapman v. Commissioner*,[39] the issue was whether an interdenominational group of missionaries who came from a number of different churches, none of which controlled the group, could qualify as their own church. The Tax Court denied the group status as a church, reasoning that the word "church" in the IRC referred to denominations or sects, and was not used in any universal sense such as that suggested by the missionaries. While the decision did not require that a church have a hierarchy, or even a building, the concurring opinion did emphasize that a church has to at least have a congregation of its own.[40]

[B] Churches versus Religious Associations

How is a church different from a religious organization? The courts that have looked at this question center their analysis on three points. First, Congress intended that "churches" be more restrictively defined than "religious organizations." You can, for example, teach a religious message and not be a church.[41] Second, "[t]he means by which an avowedly religious purpose is accomplished [is what] separates a 'church' from other forms of religious enterprise."[42] Third, the courts look mainly to the 14-points test and the associational test to make a determination between a religious organization and a church.[43] A discussion of these two tests follows.

[1] Fourteen-Point Test

In 1980, the IRS announced the criteria that it would use to determine whether an organization qualified as a church.[44] Rather than attempt a definition that might run afoul of the First Amendment, the IRS has resorted to a checklist of 14 points, or operational characteristics, that it would use to help determine if an organization

---

[37] *Id.* at 903, 1961 U.S. Dist. LEXIS 5592, at *34. More recent decisions have said that "common meaning and usage" must take into account the 1st Amendment's protection of diverse religious beliefs. *See* Found. of Human Understanding v. Comm'r, 88 T.C. 1341 (1987).

[38] *Id.* at 905.

[39] 48 T.C. 358 (1967).

[40] *Id.* at 367.

[41] Church of the Visible Intelligence that Governs the Universe v. United States, 4 Cl. Ct. 55, 64 (1983); *see also* Am. Guidance Found. v. United States, 490 F. Supp. 304, 306 (D.D.C. 1980); Chapman v. Comm'r, 48 T.C. 358, 363 (1967) ("[E]very religious organization is not per se a church.").

[42] Spiritual Outreach Soc'y v. Comm'r, 927 F.2d 335, 339 (8th Cir. 1991); *see also American Guidance Found.*, 490 F. Supp. at 306; First Church of In Theo v. Comm'r, 56 T.C.M. (CCH) 1045 (1989); United States v. Jeffries, 854 F.2d 254, 258 (7th Cir. 1988) (an established congregation, regular religious services, and dissemination of a doctrinal code "help distinguish a church from some other form of religious enterprise.").

[43] Found. of Human Understanding v. United States, 614 F.3d 1383 (Fed. Cir. 2010).

[44] Speech of Jerome Kurtz, IRS Commissioner, 7th Biennial PLI Conference on Tax Planning, *reprinted in* FEDERAL TAXES ¶ 54,820 (1978) (also published at IR-1930 as a news release); *see also Am. Guidance Found.*, 490 F. Supp. at 306 n.2.

qualifies as a church. These 14 points ask if the organization has a(n):

- Distinct legal existence.

- Recognized creed and form of worship.

- Definite and distinct ecclesiastical government.

- Formal code of doctrine and discipline.

- Distinct religious history.

- Membership not associated with any other church or denomination.

- Organization of ordained ministers.

- Ordained ministers selected after completing prescribed studies.

- Literature of its own.

- Established places of worship.

- Regular congregations.

- Regular religious services.

- Sunday school for the religious youth instruction.

- School for the preparation of its ministers.

The origin of this 14-point test was a speech given by the IRS Commissioner in 1978,[45] but it was adopted by the federal courts in *American Guidance Foundation v. United States*.[46] In that case, the District Court held that a family that worshiped together at a relative's apartment did not qualify as a church. The court found the lack of a real congregation that assembled regularly to worship together and that was open to and sought others to join them in their worship and in study of their doctrine was determinative. The court thought that these elements were minimally necessary for a church to exist.[47] In *Church of the Visible Intelligence that Governs the Universe*,[48] the court denied status as a church to an organization that met few of the 14 criteria. The organization had only three members and it did not appear to have any ministerial activities or underlying dogma.[49] The court also noted that the organization did not perform any of the charitable activities typical of a church, although "charitable activities" is not one of the 14 points.[50] In *Universal Bible Church, Inc. v. Commissioner*,[51] an organization without its own religious history, that did not have a membership greater than its officers, that met in an officer's

---

[45] Kurtz, *supra* note 44.

[46] 490 F. Supp. 304 (D.D.C. 1980); *see also* Church of the Visible Intelligence that Governs the Universe v. United States, 4 Cl. Ct. 55 (1983); Williams Home, Inc. v. United States, 540 F. Supp. 310 (W.D. Va. 1982); Lutheran Soc. Serv. of Minn. v. United States, 758 F.2d 1283 (8th Cir. 1985).

[47] *Am. Guidance Found.*, 490 F. Supp. at 307.

[48] 4 Cl. Ct. 55.

[49] *Id.* at 58.

[50] *Id.* at 65.

[51] 51 T.C.M. (CCH) 936 (1986).

home, and that did no instruction of the young was held not to be a church. In fact, the organization's main activity was its religious broadcasts.[52]

As the above cases demonstrate, the 14-point test is heavily slanted toward mainstream churches, which will meet all 14 criteria, and away from less traditional ministries that might have trouble meeting even a few of the criteria. While not all of the points must be met to qualify as a church, the IRS gives greater import to some points than others, e.g., the existence of an established congregation served by an organized ministry; the provision of regular religious services and religious education for the young; and the dissemination of a doctrinal code, are of central importance.[53]

[2] Associational Test

It is perhaps for this reason that the Tax Court does not favor the 14-point test, but prefers to use a test that is labeled variously as the spiritual coherence test or the associational test. In *Church of Eternal Life v. Commissioner*,[54] the Tax Court stated that the spiritual coherence test as whether the organization was "a coherent group of individuals and families that join together to accomplish the religious purposes of mutually held beliefs. In other words, a church's principal means of accomplishing its religious purposes must be to assemble regularly a group of individuals related by common worship and faith."[55] In *Foundation of Human Understanding v. Commissioner*,[56] the Tax Court cites the associational test found in *American Guidance Foundation*,[57] where the court said that, "[a]t a minimum, a church includes a body of believers or communicants that assembles regularly in order to worship."[58] In seeking a core group, bound by common beliefs, that has regular meetings, available to the public, where the group worships together and provides instruction in the faith to others, the two tests, spiritual coherence and associational, despite their diverse names, are looking for the same things, and a group that meets one test will meet the other.[59]

---

[52] *Id.*

[53] See First Church of In Theo v. Comm'r, 56 T.C.M. (CCH) 1045 (1989), where an organization with no creed of its own, no real membership or congregation, no ministerial functions or organized ministry, no instruction of the young, and whose main activity was religious publishing did not qualify as a church; and Spiritual Outreach Soc'y v. Comm'r, 927 F.2d 335 (8th Cir. 1991), where a group with no congregation or ministers of its own and no instruction of the young, but whose main activity was interdenominational gospel sings and retreats, did not qualify. *See also* CAFARDI & CHERRY, TAX EXEMPT ORGANIZATIONS: CASES AND MATERIALS 249 (2d ed. 2008).

[54] 86 T.C. 916, 924 (1986).

[55] *Id.*

[56] 88 T.C. 1341 (1987).

[57] 490 F. Supp. 304 (D.D.C. 1980). The opinion in *Am. Guidance Found.* continues, "Unless the organization is reasonably available to the public in its conduct of worship, its educational instruction, and its promulgation of doctrine, it cannot fulfill this associational role." *Id.* at 306. It is from this second part of the quote that the associational test takes its name.

[58] *Id.*

[59] *Id.*; *see also* Craig A. Mason, Comment, *"Secular Humanism" and the Definition of Religion*, 63 WASH. L. REV. 445 (1988).

The Tax Court in *Foundation of Human Understanding* stated that it is not using the fourteen point test.[60] The court points out that the organization does have a distinct legal existence; does have a recognized creed; does have regular services open to the public at an established place of worship; and does have ordained ministers with a course of prescribed studies for them. The court goes on to describe what the organization lacks: a discrete membership (people don't have to leave their church to join this one); a formal school for ministers; a Sunday school for the young; and a definite ecclesiastical government apart from the role and rule of its founding minister.[61] In fact, the Foundation of Human Understanding was basically a radio ministry, reaching thousands of persons through the weekly broadcasts of its services, but also reaching 50 to 350 persons at regularly held services. As pointed out above, the IRS's 14 points work well in analyzing the criteria for mainstream churches, and not so well with newer forms of ministry. It was perhaps for this reason that the Tax Court in *Foundation of Human Understanding*, eschewed the 14-point test, because it sensed that, on the 14-point scale, the Foundation met fewer of the criteria than it lacked, but was still a church. Using the associational test, it found it to be so.[62]

Unfortunately, things did not remain that way for the Foundation of Human Understanding. It moved more of its activities to the broadcasting and Internet arenas, and stopped having regular services. Because of these changes IRS determined that while the Foundation did still qualify as a Section 501(c)(3) religious organization, it was no longer a church. The Court of Claims, in a decision that discussed the 14 points at length, but that finally relied on the associational test, agreed with the IRS.[63] The U.S. Court of Appeals for the Federal Circuit upheld the Court of Claims, saying that "[c]ourts have been more receptive to the associational test as a means of determining church status . . ."[64] Without at least a regular congregation that met to hold regular services, and despite its extensive electronic ministry, the Foundation could not qualify as a church.[65] In terms of which test to use — the IRS's 14 points or the "associational" test — it should be

---

[60] 88 T.C. at 1358.

[61] *Id.*

[62] *Id.* at 1360–61.

[63] Found. of Human Understanding v. United States, 88 Fed. Cl. 203 (2009).

[64] Found. of Human Understanding v. United States, 614 F.3d 1383, 1388 (Fed. Cir. 2010) (citing Church of Eternal Life & Liberty, Inc. v. Comm'r, 86 T.C. 916, 924 (1986) ("To qualify as a church an organization must serve an associational role in accomplishing its religious purposes."); *Am. Guidance*, 490 F. Supp. at 306 ("At a minimum, a church includes a body of believers or communicants that assembles regularly in order to worship."); *Visible Intelligence*, 4 Cl. Ct. at 65; VIA v. Comm'r, 68 T.C.M. (CCH) 212 (1994); *Found. of Human Understanding*, 88 T.C. at 1357; Church of Spiritual Tech. v. United States, 26 Cl. Ct. 713, 730–31 n.36 (1992); Spiritual Outreach Soc'y v. Comm'r, 58 T.C.M. (CCH) 1284 (1990), *aff'd*, 927 F.2d 335 (8th Cir. 1991) ("[A] church is a cohesive group of individuals who join together to accomplish the religious purposes of mutually held beliefs."); *Chapman*, 48 T.C. at 367 (Tannenwald, J., concurring) ("In my opinion, the word 'church' implies that an otherwise qualified organization bring[s] people together as the principal means of accomplishing its purpose."); *see also Spiritual Outreach*, 927 F.2d at 338 (noting the Tax Court's holding that the organization "failed to fulfill an associational requirement" but resolving the case without reaching "the associational requirement issue.").

[65] *Found. of Human Understanding*, 614 F.3d 1383 (Fed. Cir. 2010).

noted, as the appeals court did in *Foundation*, "[W]e recognize that the associational test and the '14 criteria test' substantially overlap; as courts have pointed out, among the most important of the 14 criteria are the requirements of 'regular congregations' and 'regular religious services.' "[66] And those two criteria are, of course, the essence of the associational test.

In *VIA v. Commissioner*,[67] the Tax Court was again asked to look at a non-conformist type of church, one whose purpose was to promote wellness, and whose infrequent and irregular meetings, when they did take place, were exchanges of information about exercise, nutrition, and stress management, accompanied by group meditation.[68] Here, too, the Tax Court eschewed the IRS's 14-point test, while admitting that the test was helpful in deciding what was essentially a question of fact, i.e., whether an organization is a church. Rather than rely on the 14-point test, the Tax Court said that it preferred to look at the religious purposes of the organization and the ways by which these purposes were accomplished. The court also cited the associational test, whether the organization had "a body of believers or communicants that assembles regularly in order to worship."[69] Referencing, but evidently not relying on the 14-point test, the Tax Court found that VIA met only two of the 14 points, it had a distinct legal existence and a literature of its own. It then went on to hold that VIA did not qualify as a church, evidently because it failed the associational test.[70]

[C]   Qualifying as a Church for IRS Purposes

Whether it is the IRS using its 14-point test or the Tax Court using the spiritual coherence or associational test, deciding whether an organization can qualify as a church still can cause significant First Amendment problems. It is probably for this reason that, when organizations seek to qualify as a church by filing Form 1023,[71] the IRS focuses primarily on the private inurement test.[72]

Although churches need not file tax returns, not even the informational Form 990 required of all other 501(c)(3) organizations,[73] they are not relieved of the obligation to keep records of the money they take in and how it is spent.[74] This money must be used for bona fide church purposes, such as reasonable (i.e., negotiated at arm's length, in line with market rates) support of the clergy, maintenance of worship space, religious education, and works of charity and religion. Church dollars that go directly to the minister's pocket, without the

---

[66] *Id.* at 1389.

[67] 68 T.C.M. (CCH) 212 (1994).

[68] *Id.*

[69] *Id.*

[70] *Id.*

[71] See § 20.02[B] for further information on IRS Form 1023.

[72] *See* W. Catholic Church v. Comm'r, 73 T.C. 196 (1979); Synanon Church v. United States, 820 F.2d 421 (D.C. Cir. 1987).

[73] I.R.C. § 6033(a)(2)(A). See § 20.04 for more information on IRS Form 990.

[74] 26 C.F.R. § 1.6033-2(i). Tax exempt churches, not required to file annual tax returns, are not exempted from other record keeping requirements.

intervening judgment of any church agency on the value of the minister's services, especially in situations where the minister is in control of the church organization, will invariably be considered by the IRS to violate the private inurement test, thereby depriving the church of tax exempt status. This practice is also subject to the IRC Section 4958 tax on excess benefit transactions and can trigger a Section 7611 church tax inquiry by the IRS.[75]

The Church of Gospel Ministry was a mail-order ministry. It placed ads offering "ordination" in newspapers across the country. It ordained those who sent back a completed application form, which requested the applicant's name, address, and signature, certifying that the applicant was truly sincere in his or her will to serve the Lord. Ordination was conferred without charge; however, ordination certificates were offered for a fee, as were Honorary Doctors of Divinity. For a monthly fee, ministers could form independent churches chartered as branches of the Church of Gospel Ministry, but the central church exercised no authority over these branches. The church did take steps to see that its ministers were able to perform marriages, memorial services, baptisms, and other ministerial functions under the laws of all 50 states. The church also sold Bibles, marriage manuals, baptismal certificates, and marriage certificates through the mail. The church had no doctrine or statement of beliefs beyond belief in the existence of God, the divinity of Christ, and the power of prayer. With the revenues and donations that it sought, the central church supported an orphanage in Mexico.[76]

The IRS revoked the tax exempt status of the church and the church appealed under 26 U.S.C. Section 7428, seeking review in federal district court.[77] The district court agreed that the Church of Gospel Ministry was organized and operated for religious and charitable purposes, but found that the church, due to its sloppy record keeping, could not sustain its burden in regard to the private inurement test. Because it did not keep exact records for numerous checks issued to cash, it could not show who received these funds or for what purpose, nor could it account for numerous gifts by donors directly to its president. Because an organization must qualify as a 501(c)(3) organization in order to qualify as a church, the court held that the Church of Gospel Ministry could not be a church, because, in failing the private inurement test, it did not qualify as a 501(c)(3) organization.[78]

Perhaps the most egregious case of mail order ministries has been the IRS's litigation with the Universal Life Church, founded specifically to exploit the tax laws in the hope that Congress would eliminate all religious tax exemptions. Ordination in the Universal Life Church and the formation of branch churches, as in Gospel Ministries, was by mail order. The "church," once founded, then received as "donations" the salary of its "minister" from the minister's day job. These donations were sought to be deducted by the minister as charitable donations to a church under IRC Section 170(b)(1)(a)(I), thus relieving the "minister" of a large

---

[75] *See* Church of Gospel Ministry, Inc. v. United States, 640 F. Supp. 96 (D.D.C. 1986); *see also* I.R.C. § 4958.

[76] *Church of Gospel Ministry*, 640 F. Supp. at 97–98.

[77] *Id.* at 96.

[78] *Id.* at 98–100.

share of his or her individual income tax burden. This is clearly a tax avoidance situation and not a bona fide church, and there is a long list of cases holding that such "churches" are not tax exempt and gifts to them are not deductible, on private inurement grounds.[79]

Even bona fide churches, when they are getting started, can run afoul of the tax exemption requirements of the IRC. In its earliest days, the Church of Scientology, founded by L. Ron Hubbard, was denied tax exempt status because Hubbard, through his control of the church, was using church funds to make payments to himself and relatives, without adequate information or documentation, giving rise to the "logical inference . . . that these payments were disguised and unjustified distributions of plaintiff's earnings."[80] Without proper documentation, the church failed to meet the requirements of a 501(c)(3) organization on private inurement grounds.[81]

[D] Benefits of Church Status for IRS Purposes

Churches enjoy numerous special rules in their dealings with the IRS. For example, under Section 508(a), churches do not have to formally apply to the IRS for recognition of their tax exempt status. If they do choose to apply, Sections 508(b) and 508(c)(1)(A) exempts churches from having to notify the IRS that they are non-private foundations.[82] Churches are automatically considered to be non-private foundations, so they do not have to worry about this notification requirement.[83] Religious organizations that are not churches do not enjoy this presumption and they must provide the non-private foundation notification to the IRS.

Gifts to churches are also given special treatment. Gifts to churches are deductible at the rate of 50 percent of the donor's contribution base (normally the donor's adjusted gross income), whereas gifts to religious organizations, unless they qualify as non-private foundations, are only deductible up to 30 percent of the donor's contribution base.[84] Additionally, under Section 514(b)(3)(E), churches enjoy a longer period (15 years versus 10) than other types of exempt organizations

---

[79] *See* Universal Life Church v. United States, 14 Cl. Ct. 343 (1988); *see also* Davis v. Comm'r, 81 T.C. 806 (1983), *aff'd*, 767 F.2d 931 (9th Cir. 1985). Oddly enough, there is a case holding that the parent Church of Universal Life does qualify for exemption, Universal Life Church v. United States, 372 F. Supp. 770 (E.D. Cal. 1974), so reluctant are courts to get involved in defining religion.

[80] Founding Church of Scientology v. United States, 412 F.2d 1197, 1201 (Ct. Cl. 1969), *cert. denied*, 397 U.S. 1009 (1970); Church of Scientology of Cal. v. Comm'r, 83 T.C. 381 (1984), *aff'd*, 823 F.2d 1310 (9th Cir. 1987), *cert. denied*, 486 U.S. 1015 (1988).

[81] *See* cases cited *supra* note 80; *see also* I.R.C. § 170(b)(1)(A)(i). In 1993, after years of litigation with the IRS, the Service granted the Church of Scientology tax exempt status in a settlement agreement. *See Scientologists in $12.5 Million IRS Pact: Other Developments*, FACTS ON FILE WORLD NEWS DIGEST (Dec. 31, 1997).

[82] The advantage to churches in applying for IRS recognition of their tax exempt status, even though they do not have to, is that the IRS recognition assures donors of the tax deductibility of their contributions.

[83] I.R.C. §§ 509(a)(1), 170(b)(1)(A)(i).

[84] I.R.C. § 170(b)(1)(A)(i), (B)(i).

do to classify income from debt-financed property that they plan to use for their exempt purposes as related (actually as not unrelated) income; and unlike other types of tax exempt organizations, the property need not be in the church's neighborhood.

There are several special rules that apply specifically to churches and their informational filings to the IRS. Under Section 6033(a)(2)(A), churches need not file the informational Form 990 annually with the IRS.[85] Religious organizations that do not qualify as churches, on the other hand, must file the Form 990 annually with the IRS.[86]

Under Section 6043(b), churches need not file returns with the IRS with respect to their liquidation, dissolution, termination, or substantial contraction; non-church religious organizations must file returns on these matters.[87]

Other rules that apply specifically to churches include Section 7611, which entitles churches (but not religious organizations) to procedural safeguards with respect to the IRS examinations or inquiries. Sections 410(c)(1)(B), 411(e)(1)(B), 412(h)(4) and 414(e) state that the qualified retirement plan for a church is exempt from the participation, vesting, and funding requirements that apply to non-church plans.[88] Section 1402 (e) exempts certain ministers from the self-employment tax.[89] Section 3121 (b)(8) exempts qualified churches from the Social Security tax and Section 3401(a)(9) exempts churches from the withholding tax requirements.[90]

§ 8.04 CONVENTIONS OR ASSOCIATIONS OF CHURCHES

The IRC states that "a church or a convention or association of churches" is eligible to receive tax deductible gifts.[91] The previous section explained what a church was; this section will explain what is meant by "a convention or association of churches." In defining a convention or association of churches the Regulations are no help. The IRS has stated that "[a]n organization is described in [this] section if it is a church or a convention or association of churches."[92] The term "convention or association of churches" normally means a central organization of independent churches of the same denomination where the church is organized on a congregational, as opposed to a hierarchical, basis.[93] For example, the Southern Baptist Convention is a voluntary association or convention of individual Southern Baptist churches or congregations that, while belonging to the convention, retain their

---

[85] See § 20.04 for further information on IRS Form 990.

[86] Religious organizations that qualify as "integrated auxiliaries" of a church need not file the Form 990. I.R.C. § 6033(a)(2)(A)(I). See this chapter for a definition of integrated auxiliaries of churches.

[87] I.R.C. § 6043(b).

[88] See I.R.C. §§ 410(c)(1)(B), 411(e)(1)(B), 412(h)(4), 414(e).

[89] See I.R.C. § 1402(e). See also I.R.C. § 1402(a)(8) for information on the computation requirements for ministers subject to any tax on self-employment.

[90] I.R.C. §§ 3121(b)(8), 3401(a)(9).

[91] See 26 C.F.R. §§ 1.170-2, 1.170A-9.

[92] 26 C.F.R. § 1.170A-9(b).

[93] See Lutheran Soc. Serv. of Minn., 758 F.2d at 1288.

independence as individual congregations. This language in the IRC allows the central organization itself to qualify as a charitable organization, although it technically is not a church itself. But the term does not have to refer to a central grouping of independent churches of the same denomination. It can also refer to an ecumenical grouping of churches that are not of the same denomination if they have formed their own association for religious purposes.[94] The Pension Protection Act of 2006 amended the definition of a "convention or association of churches" to say that "any organization which is otherwise a convention or association of churches shall not fail to so qualify merely because the membership of such organization includes individuals as well as churches or because individuals have voting rights in such organization."[95]

§ 8.05   GROUP RULING

Both hierarchically organized and congregationally organized churches may ask the IRS to be covered by a group ruling that recognizes the tax exempt status of the church's central organization and all of its hierarchical or congregational affiliates. This process requires the church's central organization to certify to the IRS annually a list of its affiliates (the group) and to further certify that these affiliates individually meet the requirements for tax exempt status.[96] This group ruling for a church can also cover the church's integrated auxiliaries. Based on the central organization's certification, the IRS will recognize the individual tax exempt status of each affiliate. Although churches are not formally required to seek tax exempt status,[97] the benefit in seeking a group ruling is not just the ease of proceeding as a group, but also the fact that the group ruling allows donors to donate to individual churches or church affiliates, knowing that they are giving to a bona fide Section 501(c)(3) organization.[98]

§ 8.06   INTEGRATED AUXILIARIES OF CHURCHES

Churches do more than simply offer religious services in their sanctuaries on their weekly day of worship. Many churches operate schools, seminaries, men's groups, women's groups, children's groups, or social service agencies, very often doing so without ever establishing any separate legal existence for this activity. Unincorporated church organizations are simply programs of the church that operates them. As such, they remain a part of the legal entity of the church, sharing its tax exempt status, until a separate legal existence, usually through incorporation as a separate nonprofit corporation, is obtained for them, usually for liability or administrative reasons.[99]

---

[94] Rev. Rul. 74-224, 1974-1 C.B. 61.

[95] Pension Protection Act of 2006, Pub. L. No. 109-280, § 1222, 120 Stat. 780 (2006).

[96] Rev. Proc. 80-27, 1980-1 C.B. 677.

[97] I.R.C. § 508(c)(1)(A).

[98] Rev. Proc. 80-27, 1980-1 C.B. 677.

[99] *See* Lutheran Soc. Serv. of Minn. v. United States, 583 F. Supp. 1298 (D. Minn. 1984), *rev'd*, 758 F.2d 1283 (8th Cir. 1985); Reka Potgieter Hoff, *The Financial Accountability of Churches for Federal*

Under the IRC, these church-related entities, once they are separately incorporated, need a basis for their own tax exempt status. It is through their relationship to their founding church that this may occur, in a category that the IRC labels "integrated auxiliaries" of churches. The original Regulations on integrated auxiliaries required their activity to be "exclusively religious,"[100] and defined "exclusively religious" in such a way that, if the organization had any basis for tax exempt status other than its religious activity, it was not "exclusively religious."[101] This was an obvious difficulty for schools and social service agencies, both of which could easily qualify as 501(c)(3) educational or social welfare organizations.[102]

Many churches did not agree with the IRS's definition of integrated auxiliaries, primarily on the grounds that the IRS appeared to be limiting religious activity to what went on in the sanctuary, unwilling to admit that religiously motivated activity, outside the sanctuary, even when it had its own basis for tax exemption, was still considered by the church to be an exercise of its religion.[103] Because there were significant benefits to being an integrated auxiliary of a church, namely tax exempt status and exemption from filing the annual informational tax return, the Form 990, required of all 501(c)(3) organizations except churches and their integrated auxiliaries, it was worth fighting over this highly restrictive definition of integrated auxiliaries.

Lutheran Social Services of Minnesota is a separately incorporated agency of the Lutheran Church that provides child care and adoption services, counseling services, residential treatment services for emotionally disturbed individuals, mentally disabled individuals and young male felons, a nutrition program for the elderly, a camp for mentally and physically impaired persons, and a chaplaincy program. It challenged the IRS's definition of "integrated auxiliary."[104] Because Lutheran Social Services could have qualified for tax exempt status on other than religious grounds, the IRS determined that it was not an integrated auxiliary and had to file Form 990. While the district court agreed with the IRS, the Eighth Circuit did not. It looked at the fact that Congress had, in the statute, required the auxiliary activities of religious orders to be "exclusively religious" in order to qualify for the filing exemption, but had not used similar language in the section on the integrated auxiliaries of churches. Because Congress obviously knew how to require "exclusively religious" activity when it wanted to, the court ruled that the Service had exceeded the statutory language in imposing an "exclusively religious" requirement in the Regulations regarding the integrated auxiliaries of churches. The "exclusively religious" requirement is no longer in the Regulations.[105]

Income Tax Purposes: Establishment or Free Exercise?, 11 VA. TAX REV. 71 (1991); Wendy Gerzog Shaller, *Churches and Their Enviable Tax Status*, 51 U. PITT. L. REV. 345 (1990).

[100] Former Reg. § 1.6033-2(g)(5)(i).

[101] Former Reg. § 1.6033-2(g)(5)(ii).

[102] *See* Western Catholic Church v. Comm'r, 73 T.C. 196 (1979); United States v. Whitney Land Co., 324 F.2d 33 (8th Cir. 1963).

[103] Reed, *Integrated Auxiliaries, Regulations and Implications*, 23 CATH. LAW. 211 (1978).

[104] *Lutheran Soc. Serv. of Minn.*, 583 F. Supp. at 1300.

[105] *Lutheran Soc. Serv. of Minn.*, 758 F.2d at 1289–90.

Today, in order to qualify as an integrated auxiliary of a church, an organization must do the following: (1) qualify under Section 501(c)(3) as tax exempt; (2) qualify as a non-private foundation or public charity under Section 509(a)(1), 509(a)(2) or 509(a)(3); (3) affiliate itself with a church or convention or association of churches in the sense that there is some legal or financial link between the two; and (4) obtain its support internally, i.e. it must be supported by the church. Because of the above requirements for qualification, an integrated auxiliary of a church cannot do both of the following: receive payments for admissions, goods, services, or the sale of facilities to the general public (excluding those sold at a nominal or disproportion-ately low cost) and receive more than 50 percent of its support from the government, public contributions, the sale of admissions or goods, the performance of services or the furnishing of facilities in activities that do not qualify as unrelated business activities.[106]

§ 8.07 APOSTOLIC ORGANIZATIONS

In addition to Section 501(c)(3) religious organizations and churches, there is another type of religious organization that is exempt from federal income tax under Section 501(d) of the IRC. These are "Apostolic Organizations." Section 501(d) states that religious or apostolic associations or corporations are exempt from federal income tax if they have a common treasury or community treasury, even if such associations or corporations engage in business for the common benefit of the members, but only if the members thereof include (at the time of filing their returns) in their gross income their entire pro rata shares, whether distributed or not, of the taxable income of the association or corporation for such year. Any amounts included in the gross income of a member shall be treated as a dividend received.[107]

The idea of a common treasury and common work to sustain the believing community goes back to the earliest days of the Christian era. Today, this work is carried on by religious orders.[108] Section 501 (d) apostolic organizations differ from religious orders in that their members do not take a vow of poverty, and they are not prohibited from owning property outside of the organization.[109] Apostolic organizations have a long history in the United States, and the origins of Section 501(d) trace back to the Shakers.[110] When this section was introduced into the IRC, the rationale given in the legislative history was that this section would exempt apostolic organizations from the corporate tax and the undistributed profits tax, as long as each member reported their share of organizational income on their own tax

---

[106] 26 C.F.R. § 1.6033-2(h)(4).

[107] *Id.*

[108] *See also* JACOB MERTENS JR., LAW OF FEDERAL INCOME TAXATION §§ 34.01-171 (1991) (discussing various categories of exempt organizations).

[109] See Twin Oaks Cmty., Inc. v. Comm'r, 87 T.C. 1233 (1986), where the Tax Court overturned the IRS revocation of tax exempt status for Twin Oaks finding that Twin Oaks was a religious apostolic organization that had a common or community treasury. The court also stated that I.R.C. § 501(d) does *not* require the taking of vows of poverty or the restriction on owning property outside of the organization.

[110] 80 CONG. REC. 9074 (1936).

returns. Seen in this way, it is evident that Section 501(d) apostolic organizations were made exempt by Congress to avoid a double taxation.[111]

§ 8.08   CHURCHES & POLITICAL ACTIVITY

Churches, like all other Section 501(c)(3) organizations, are subject to the political activities test, which means that they may not participate in any electoral campaigns, for or against a candidate, and they may not lobby, except insubstantially. The only difference between churches and other 501(c)(3) organizations in the political sphere is that churches were, at their own request, omitted from those Section 501(c)(3) organizations that could opt, under Section 501(h), for safe harbor rules on their lobbying expenses.[112] This does not mean that churches cannot lobby. It simply means that they are left with the language of Section 501(c)(3), which says that "no substantial part" of their activities can consist in lobbying.[113] The organizations should also be aware of the requirements referenced in the formulae of Section 4911 that implement Section 501(h).[114]

There is a significant overlap of moral and political issues.[115] Churches may, indeed it is their job to, opine on moral issues. This causes a problem; when does a church's opining on moral issues crosses over into impermissible political activity?

The easy answer is that any church activity directed for or against a particular candidate or political party will be considered impermissible electioneering and violative of the political activities test. A church can teach that certain activity is immoral. A church can even say that it is immoral to vote for unidentified candidates who support that activity. The problem occurs when the church identifies candidates or specific political parties and indicates an electoral preference for or against them either at a church function, or in an official church publication or using church assets.[116] If the church applies its teachings for or against a candidate for public office, it has crossed the line from permissible preaching, which is not limited by its tax exempt status, to impermissible electioneering, which is totally prohibited by Section 501(c)(3).[117] But if all the church does is to elucidate its teachings in the moral realm, without reference to candidates or political parties, that will cause no problems. Similarly, if a church's minister, speaking in a personal and not an official capacity, at a non-church related event, endorses a particular candidate, that is not considered electioneering by the church but rather private, personal political

---

[111] See § 5.09[B] for an analysis of avoidance of double taxation as a rationale for tax exemption.

[112] I.R.C. § 501(h)(5)(A).

[113] *See* Douglas Cook, *The Politically Active Church*, 35 Loy. U. Chi. L.J. 457 (2004).

[114] I.R.C. §§ 501(h)(7), 4911.

[115] For example, is the death penalty moral? Is abortion on demand moral? Is a preventive war moral? Is failing to provide an adequate safety net for the poor, the aged, the infirm, moral? The list goes on.

[116] Rev. Rul. 2007-41, 2007-1 C.B. 1421, Situation 5.

[117] See Christian Echoes Nat'l Ministry, Inc. v. United States, 470 F.2d 849 (10th Cir. 1972), where the organization addressed the general public through broadcasts; and Branch Ministries, Inc. v. Rossotti, 40 F. Supp. 2d 15 (D.D.C. 1999), where the organization addressed the general public through newspaper ads.

activity by the minister.[118] If the church campaigns for or against a candidate with the general public, it has crossed the line from permissible preaching, protected by the First Amendment, to impermissible electioneering, prohibited by Section 501(c)(3). But if all the church does is to elucidate its teachings in the moral realm, even when it applies these teachings to the positions of identified candidates, even if it asks its members, as opposed to the general public, to vote for or against candidates according to these moral precepts, this is protected First Amendment activity and is not electioneering.[119]

The law on lobbying is more lenient. While Section 501(c)(3) organizations may not electioneer at all, they may lobby insubstantially.[120] So churches may lobby against laws they consider to be immoral, and they may publicly say so, and they will be within the area of political activity allowed by Section 501(c)(3) as long as the amount of the lobbying does not become substantial. There is no bright-line rule on what is substantial lobbying, no automatic percentage of annual organization expenditure that crosses the line. In comparison, Section 4911(c) establishes the safe harbor formula for Section 501(c)(3) organizations that can elect under Section 501(h), where the line appears to fall somewhere between 15 and 20 percent of exempt purpose expenditures, with grassroots (direct to the public) lobbying being only 25 percent of overall lobbying expenses.[121]

Churches have fallen afoul of the political activities test, and as a result, have lost their tax exempt status. In the case of *Christian Echoes National Ministry, Inc. v. United States*,[122] the church, at the direction of its founder and president, Dr. Billy James Hargis, was found to have both lobbied substantially and electioneered. The Christian Crusade magazine, published by Christian Echoes, was found to contain numerous articles appealing to the public to contact their congressperson on a number of issues, from immigration law to the House Committee on Un-American Activities, to stopping federal aid to education, socialized medicine and public housing to the Nuclear Test Ban Treaty, the Panama Canal Treaty, and firearms control legislation. These appeals to the public to contact their legislators consti- tuted grassroots lobbying, and were found to be so numerous as to be substantial. On the question of electioneering, while it had criticized President Kennedy outside of a campaign context, the organization had urged the defeat of Senator Fulbright of Arkansas, and had attacked President Johnson and Senator Humphrey, the Democratic candidates in the 1964 presidential election. That year, the Christian Echoes convention endorsed Senator Goldwater of Arizona, the Republican candi- date for president. This was clearly electioneering, which is entirely prohibited by Section 501(c)(3). Christian Echoes tried to argue that the political restrictions of

---

[118] Rev. Rul. 2007-41, 2007-1 C.B. 1421, Situation 5.

[119] *See* cases cited *supra* note 117.

[120] 26 C.F.R. § 1.501(c)(3)-1(c)(3).

[121] *See* I.R.C. §§ 501(h), 4911(c). Note, however, that I.R.C. § 501(h)(7) states: "nothing in this subsection or in § 4911 shall be construed to affect the interpretation of the phrase "no substantial part of the activities of which is carrying on propaganda, or otherwise attempting to influence legislation," under [501](c)(3)." *See also Christian Echoes Nat'l Ministry*, 470 F.2d 849 (organization addressed the general public through broadcasts); *Branch Ministries, Inc.*, 40 F. Supp. 2d 15 (organization addressed the general public through newspaper ads).

[122] 470 F.2d 849 (10th Cir. 1972).

Section 501(c)(3) were violative of the First Amendment's free exercise guarantee, but the court disagreed, stating that tax exemption was a privilege, not a right, and that Congress was free to place reasonable restrictions on the activity of tax exempt organizations.[123]

In a more recent case, *Branch Ministries, Inc. v. Rossotti*,[124] the Branch Ministries Church at Pierce Creek had placed full-page advertisements in the *Washington Times* and *USA Today* on October 30, 1992, four days before the presidential election, attacking Democratic candidate, Bill Clinton, for supporting abortion on demand, homosexuality, and the distribution of condoms in public schools. The ad cited various Biblical passages that condemned such practices, stating that "Bill Clinton is promoting policies that are in rebellion to God's laws," and ending with the question, "How then can we vote for Bill Clinton?" The ad was clearly identified as being placed by The Church at Pierce Creek, its pastor, and various other co-sponsors.[125]

Branch Ministries' first defense was that, unless it could show that it was not a bona fide church, the IRS had no statutory authority to revoke its tax exempt status. The IRS responded to Branch Ministries by stating that while it may be a church, it may not electioneer as an organization defined in Section 501(c)(3).[126]

Next, Branch Ministries argued selective prosecution, but in order to sustain that they had to show discriminatory effect or discriminatory motive. They were unable to show this.[127]

Branch Ministries then argued that its free exercise rights were being violated.[128] The court found that the only burden placed on the church as a result of the revocation of their tax exempt status was that they would have less money to expend on religious activities as a result of their electioneering. That burden was found to be insubstantial, but the court went on to add that, even if this were a substantial burden, there is a countervailing compelling interest by the government, namely maintaining the integrity of the tax system and not subsidizing partisan political activity.[129]

Finally, Branch Ministries argued that the IRS had engaged in content-based viewpoint discrimination in violation of Branch Ministries' Fifth Amendment right to equal protection and in violation of their First Amendment right to free speech. The court found that the IRS was not seeking to control any speech in the church's precincts, which may or may not have qualified as an open forum, but rather was acting because the church took out nationwide, full-page ads attacking a candidate four days before an election. There was no doubt in the court's mind that the IRS's

---

[123] *Id.*

[124] 40 F. Supp. 2d 15 (D.D.C. 1999).

[125] *Id.* at 17.

[126] *Id.* at 20.

[127] *Id.* at 21.

[128] *Id.* at 24.

[129] *Id.* at 25–6.

revocation of Branch Ministries' tax exempt status was justified.[130]

§ 8.09   CHURCH AUDIT PROCEDURES ACT

Congress has created special rules governing how the IRS may audit churches.[131] The Church Audit Procedures Act (CAPA) is meant to protect churches from unnecessary IRS intrusion into their affairs by creating certain safeguards for churches in an audit situation. First of all, only an appropriate high-level Treasury official can order a church audit, and to do so must reasonably believe that the church may not be exempt under Section 501(c)(3) or may be carrying on an unrelated trade or business. The church must be fully notified in writing of the concerns that triggered the inquiry, the general subject matter of the inquiry, and its administrative, constitutional, and statutory rights. The IRS can only physically examine church records if it gives a 15-day advance written notice to the church and to the IRS regional counsel. Regional counsel then has 15 days to object to the audit, which is to be taken into account by the IRS in deciding whether to proceed. The IRS must provide the church with the opportunity to meet to try to resolve the issues to be dealt with in the proposed audit. No physical examination of records is allowed until 15 days after the initial notice to the church. The IRS can only look at church records or examine church activities to the extent necessary to determine any tax liability or whether the organization is operated as a church. The IRS has two years after the initial notice to the church to conclude its investigation, unless prolonged by litigation. The IRS regional counsel must approve in advance any determination made by the IRS in a church audit as to the church's tax exempt status, ability to receive tax-deductible gifts, or any tax liability.[132]

The protections of CAPA were litigated in the case of *United States v. C.E. Hobbs Foundation for Religious Training and Education, Inc.*[133] There the court held that the IRS had to show more than relevance in regard to the church records it was requesting in its inquiry. Rather, the court held that the IRS had to show that: (1) the purpose of its investigation was proper, and (2) explain how the particular documents, or categories of documents (a) fall directly and logically within the scope of those purposes, and (b) will help significantly to further an investigation within the scope of those purposes.[134]

The question of who was a "an appropriate high level Treasury official" capable of ordering a church audit was litigated in *United States v. Living Word Christian Center.*[135] The IRS was initially investigating the Living Word Christian Center for allegations of inappropriate political activity when it stumbled on evidence of possible improper financial dealings between the church and the minister. The CAPA required notice of audit was signed by the IRS Director, Exempt Organiza-

---

[130] *Id.* at 26.

[131] Church Audit Procedures Act, 26 U.S.C. § 7611.

[132] *Id.*

[133] 7 F.3d 169 (9th Cir. 1993).

[134] *Id.*; *see also* United States v. Church of Scientology of Boston, 933 F.2d 1074 (1st Cir. 1991); United States v. Church of Scientology Western U.S., 973 F.2d 715 (9th Cir. 1992).

[135] 2009 U.S. Dist. LEXIS 6902 (D. Minn. Jan. 30, 2009).

tions, Examination (DEOE). The church argued that the notice was defective because it was not signed by "an appropriate high level Treasury official." The federal magistrate agreed with the church and so did the district court.

The problem was actually caused by the Internal Revenue Service Restructuring and Reform Act of 1998. Originally the regulations to CAPA had defined a high-level Treasury official as a "Regional Commissioner (or higher Treasury official)"[136] but the RRA had eliminated the position of Regional Commissioner, leaving the meaning of "high-level Treasury official" ambiguous, and the regulations had not been revised. The magistrate determined that the Director of Exempt Organizations, Examination, who was four management levels below the Commissioner of the IRS did not qualify as high-level enough.[137] The district court upheld the magistrate and dismissed the IRS's administrative summons to make the church comply with the audit. The same issue was almost litigated in *Southern Faith Ministries, Inc. v. Geithner*,[138] where the church sought a writ of mandamus against the Secretary of Treasury, to challenge an audit authorized by the Director of Exempt Organizations, Examination (DEOE), but because IRS had not issued a summons in that case, the court said the church's request was premature.

IRS has since proposed changes to the regulations that would identify the Director, Exempt Organizations or the Commissioner or Deputy Commissioner, Tax Exempt and Government Entities, as this high-level official.[139] Amendments to the Regulations Regarding Questions and Answers Relating to Church Tax Inquiries and Examinations, 74 Fed. Reg. 149 (proposed July 31, 2009) (to be codified at 26 C.F.R. part 301).

§ 8.10   SPECIAL ISSUES FOR CHURCHES

[A]   Legal Structure

Even for established churches, there is no uniform legal structure. For example, in the Roman Catholic Church in the United States, some parishes are incorporated under state law, some parishes function under charitable trust law, and some parishes are simply restricted assets of the diocesan corporation. The important thing for the more established churches, when they are pursuing a legal structure, is to make sure that the structure they choose conforms to the internal law of the church.

With newly organized churches, it is rare that any thought is given to what legal structure the church should take. Initially, the church consists of a founding minister and a flock. Title to property is not an issue because the church rents its sanctuary space. Once the congregation grows and becomes more established, and wishes to own its own church building, issues like legal capacity and legal structure

---

[136]   26 C.F.R. § 301.7611-1 Q&A (1).

[137]   United States v. Living Word Christian Ctr., 2008 U.S. Dist. LEXIS 106639 (D. Minn. Nov. 18, 2008).

[138]   660 F. Supp. 2d 54 (D.D.C. 2009).

[139]   Prop. Treas. Reg. § 301.7611-1, 74 Fed. Reg. 39003 (Aug. 5, 2009).

come to the forefront. Unless it has a larger ecclesiastical polity to fall back on, then the church is free to choose its own legal structure. Because the church will want to qualify as a 501(c)(3) organization, it would be wise to use the nonprofit structures that the IRS is comfortable with in determining tax exempt status.[140] There is a question of state law as well, because some states limit a church's ability to incorporate,[141] and some state laws specify that unincorporated associations (which is how many churches begin) cannot own property at all.[142] If a church does not plan its legal structure properly, it can be forced into a default structure in liability litigation that it would not have chosen itself.[143]

[B] Liability in Church Organizations

[1] Church Practices

The nature of churches is such that it is their business to promulgate and to enforce certain rules of conduct, usually derived from their interpretation of scripture or other founding documents of the church. Some churches practice a shunning or marking ceremony in which a member is publicly identified as a sinner.[144] Such conduct by the shunning or marking church often leads to litigation by the shunned or marked member for invasion of privacy, intentional infliction of emotional distress, and outrageous conduct. Some courts have accepted a First Amendment defense on such suits, at least as to their members.[145]

Sometimes a church will offer a "bylaws" defense to lawsuits involving their practices. In other words, shunning or marking is provided for in scripture, the founding document or other church polity, to which the shunned or marked member consented when he or she joined the church.[146] While some courts have accepted this defense, others have not.[147] In the case of *Guinn v. Church of Christ of Collinsville*,[148] a church member was admonished for her extramarital sexual activity by church elders, being warned that if she did not cease, she risked being publicly identified as a sinner. When the activity did not cease, the church member was publicly denounced from the pulpit. She filed suit, alleging outrageous conduct and invasion of privacy. The Oklahoma Supreme Court held that the member was free to leave the church, making the church's actions after her departure actionable; however, while she was a member, the court said that she had consented to the

---

[140] See § 2.01 *et seq.* for further information on nonprofit structures.

[141] VA. CONST. art. IV, § 14.

[142] Murphy v. Traylor, 289 So. 2d 584 (Ala. 1974). *See generally* Kauper & Ellis, *Religious Corporations and the Law*, 71 MICH. L. REV. 1499 (1973).

[143] Cox v. Thee Evergreen Church, 836 S.W.2d 167 (Tex. 1992).

[144] *See* Paul T. Hayden, *Religiously "Motivated" Outrageous Conduct: Intentional Infliction of Emotional Distress as a Weapon Against "Other People's Faiths,"* 34 WM. & MARY L. REV. 580 (1993).

[145] Paul v. Watchtower Bible & Tract Soc'y of N.Y., Inc., 819 F.2d 875 (9th Cir. 1987), *cert. denied*, 484 U.S. 926 (1987); *see also* Hadnot v. Shaw, 826 P.2d 978 (Okla. 1992).

[146] Smith v. Calvary Christian Church, 614 N.W.2d 590 (Mich. 2000).

[147] *Id.*

[148] 775 P.2d 766 (Okla. 1989).

church's disciplinary rules, which constituted a form of waiver as to the discipline imposed while she was still a member.[149]

[2] Parent & Subordinate Liability

Another liability issue with churches is whether a parent body can be held responsible for the tortious actions of a subordinate church body.[150] For example, can a diocese be held responsible for the torts of a parish employee? The issue is even more complicated when the tort is the action or omission not of an employee, but of a volunteer.[151] Because, very often, the parent body has more assets available to judgment creditors, plaintiff's lawyers will want to include it as a defendant in any suit against the subordinate body. Ascending liability in church organizations can present very difficult issues of fact.

Plaintiffs often argue that higher church bodies or adjudicatories are automatically responsible for the actions of lower bodies. In one case, plaintiffs sued a national church body for the torts of a minister who had served in two different regional organizations in two different states. They based their claims of liability against the national body on a theological statement in the church's Book of Order, which stated that the actions of one member are the actions of all members.[152] The trial court recognized this as an attempt to use theology to hold the national church liable for the torts of the minister, and dismissed the case on First Amendment grounds.[153]

In any assessment of liability in a multi-tiered church organization, the analysis must be fact-specific and it must start with an analysis of which church entity was responsible for the tortious acts. This will require identifying the religious body that has actual control over the matter that caused the litigation and had the ability to do something about it.[154] It is rare that national church bodies have any meaningful legal control over local operations, even though those local operations are under the national church's theological jurisdiction. Even in churches organized on a more regional basis, it is rare that the region actually can or does control local units, again despite the fact that these local units operate within the regional authority's theological jurisdiction. Statements of theological jurisdiction are not proof of control.

The liability of a higher church body for the torts committed at a local level will normally depend on whether it can be established that the parent body controls the subordinate body in the area of operations where the tort occurred, because in the

---

[149] *Id.*

[150] *See* Mark Chopko, *Ascending Liability of Religious Entities for the Actions of Others*, 17 Am. J. Trial Adv. 289 (1993); William Bassett, *The Churches in Court: Fundamentals of Litigation*, in Religious Organizations and The Law Vol. II, Chapter 7 (1997).

[151] *See* Folwell v. Bernard, 477 So. 2d 1060 (Fla. Dist. Ct. App. 1985); Malloy v. Fong, 37 Cal. 2d 356, 232 P.2d 241 (1951).

[152] N.H. v. Presbyterian Church (U.S.A.), Petition No. Cj 97-7006-61, para. V, I-K (Oklahoma County, Okla. 1997).

[153] N.H. v. Presbyterian Church (U.S.A.), 998 P.2d 592 (Okla. 1999).

[154] Chopko, *Stating Claims Against Religious Institutions*, 44 B.C. L. Rev. 1089 (2003).

legal system, liability travels pathways of control. Problems of this nature occur more often in hierarchically structured churches, because the congregational structure of other churches militates against control by a higher church body.[155]

[C] Church Property Issues

A not-infrequent problem with church organizations that has generated substantial litigation, is who owns the church property in a schism? Schisms occur in a hierarchical church when a lower church body attempts to break away from the parent body, and take the church structure and the attendant land with it, usually alleging that the parent has adopted beliefs or practices that are antithetical to what the parent church had originally believed or practiced.[156] Due to the First Amendment issues involved in litigating church property ownership between parent body and breakaway congregations, there has developed a significant body of United States Supreme Court decisions on this issue.[157]

The United States Supreme Court first turned aside the possibility of state courts awarding church property to one group or another by the court's deciding which group had kept the church's original teachings and which group had departed from the original doctrine. Under this approach, church property was considered, by implied trust, to remain with those who had not departed from the original doctrines of the church. Once a court determined which group was which, it could, under trust law, award the property to the original doctrine group. This approach was rejected by the United States Supreme Court because it allowed courts to determine who had and who had not departed from doctrine, a purely religious determination that was protected by the First Amendment from judicial involvement.[158]

In order to keep courts from determining matters of religious doctrine in church property disputes, the United States Supreme Court applied a "deference" approach. Under this approach, courts were required to give "deference" on First Amendment grounds to "the decisions of the highest judicatories of a religious organization of hierarchical polity on matters of discipline, faith, internal organization, or ecclesiastical rule, custom or law,"[159] even when the effect of such deference is to award the property to one side or the other. For example, when the

---

[155] *See* Chopko, *Ascending Liability of Religious Entities, supra* note 150; Bassett, *Fundamentals of Litigation, supra* note 150; *see also* Gaffney & Sorensen, ASCENDING LIABILITY IN RELIGIOUS AND OTHER NONPROFIT ORGANIZATIONS (1984); *see also* Wood v. Benedictine Soc'y of Ala., 530 So. 2d 801 (Ala. 1988) where the court failed to find a master/servant or principal/agency relationship between a Benedictine monk, who had allegedly vandalized an abortion clinic and harmed a person there, and the local abbot and bishop.

[156] The local denomination can also argue that it has evolved away from its relationship with the hierarchical church. *See* From the Heart Church Ministries, Inc. v. A.M.E. Zion Church, 803 A.2d 548 (Md. 2002), *cert. denied*, 537 U.S. 1171 (2003).

[157] *See* MAIDA & CAFARDI, CHURCH PROPERTY, CHURCH FINANCES AND CHURCH-RELATED CORPORATIONS 105–111 (1984).

[158] Watson v. Jones, 80 U.S. 679 (1872); *see also* Presbyterian Church in U.S. v. Hull Presbyterian Church, 393 U.S. 440 (1969).

[159] Serbian E. Orthodox Diocese v. Milivojevich, 426 U.S. 696, 713 (1976).

highest church judicatory decides who the proper bishop is, and that person, as bishop, is the legal title holder to the property, the effect of the courts deferring to this ecclesiastical ruling is to award the property to the judicatory-designated bishop.

While the deference approach is one way to handle church property disputes, it is not the only one. The United States Supreme Court has ruled that a judge may read church deeds, church rules, corporate articles, and bylaws or church contracts and apply neutral principles of law to the documents to make a property award.[160] This has come to be called the "neutral principles" approach, and courts are free to use this or the "deference" approach in adjudicating church property disputes. Obviously the neutral principles approach gets the courts much more involved in religious affairs than the deference approach. The United States Supreme Court's response to that was that church bodies themselves, by putting the appropriate language in deeds, trusts, contracts, and so forth, could themselves govern where their property went.[161]

While the "deference" approach works well in highly organized hierarchical churches, where there are well-established internal legal systems,[162] it is less clear how the approach works when dealing with congregational churches (i.e., non-hierarchical churches). When reviewing congregational church documents under the deference approach, some courts have attempted to create an exception to the general rule (that the majority vote of the members controls) by finding that a majority vote is determinative "unless there has been 'such an abrupt departure from congregational principles' as to discredit the ruling group."[163]

§ 8.11   CONSTITUTIONAL CONSIDERATIONS

As noted at the beginning of this chapter, the tax exemption for religious organizations has been in every version of the federal income tax law from the very start. Nonetheless, it has been criticized as an impermissible form of government aid to religion, prohibited by the First Amendment's Establishment Clause. For those who would accept the "subsidy" theory of federal tax exemptions, in which federal tax exemptions are analogized to federal grants or subsidies of the dollars that would otherwise be payable as federal income tax, then the exemption amounts

---

[160] Jones v. Wolf, 443 U.S. 595 (1979).

[161] Justice Blackmun, who wrote the decision, practically pled with church groups to do so. "Through appropriate reversionary clauses and trust provisions, religious societies can specify what is to happen to church property in the event of a particular contingency, or what religious body will determine ownership in the event of a schism or doctrinal controversy." *Id.* at 603–04.

[162] In Mills v. Baldwin, 362 So. 2d 2 (Fla. 1978), the Supreme Court of Florida overturned a lower court decision which had allowed a Presbyterian congregation to walk away from its parent group, taking the church building with it, arguably on a "neutral principles" of law approach. The Florida Supreme Court instead deferred to a decision by the appropriate church adjudicatory, the Presbytery, as to who the rightful owner of the property was. On the other hand, the Maryland Court of Appeals did allow a local church to leave the national church body with its property on facts indicating that the national church had no ownership interest in the same. *See From the Heart Church Ministries, Inc.*, 803 A.2d 548.

[163] Holiman v. Dovers, 366 S.W.2d 197, 209 (Ark. 1963) (citing Ables v. Garner, 220 Ark. 211, 246 S.W.2d 732 (1952)).

to an improper government subsidization of religion.

This was basically the argument of the plaintiff in *Walz v. Tax Commission*,[164] in which the property tax exemption of churches was challenged by a taxpayer who argued that the exemption was a way of forcing him to make a grant or contribution of his tax payments to a religious organization. The United States Supreme Court refused to see tax exemption as a form of subsidy. It held that the New York state property tax exemption for religious organizations was part of a larger legislative scheme to foster organizations that exist in a harmonious relationship to the community at large, and that foster the community's moral or mental improvement, which was a valid secular purpose for such a law. In addition, the Court saw the effect of the law as not excessively entangling government with religion. The Court opined that the opposite, the taxation of religious organizations, would actually have a more entangling effect.[165]

Although *Walz* dealt with a state property tax exemption, the constitutional analysis would be the same for Section 501(c)(3)'s exemption of religious organizations from the federal income tax.

In the recent case of *Arizona Christian School Tuition Organization v. Winn*,[166] which involved a taxpayer Establishment Clause challenge to an Arizona state law allowing the use of state income tax credits of up to $500 for contributions to school tuition organizations, which in turn give the money to private, mostly religious, schools, the Court applied the rule on standing from *Flast v. Cohen*,[167] which says that "individuals suffer a particular injury for standing purposes when, in violation of the Establishment Clause and by means of the taxing and spending power, their property is transferred through the Government's Treasury to a sectarian entity."[168] Because there was no government expenditure in this case, but rather the grant of a tax credit, the Court held that, "The distinction between governmental expenditures and tax credits refutes respondents' assertion of standing."[169]

This case basically says that when there is a transfer of what otherwise would be tax dollars without the intervention of the government in taking those dollars through taxes and then turning them over to the religious organization, but through the device of tax credits, in which the money does not pass through the government's hands, there is no taxpayer injury and therefore no standing.

Even more interesting, this decision, like *Walz*, also rejects the idea that tax exemptions granted to a religious organization (or to any other exempted party for that matter) are a form of government subsidy. The basis of the subsidy theory of tax exemption is the premise that the government, in allowing the taxpayer not to pay taxes, i.e., to keep its own money, is subsidizing the taxpayer, but the Court in Arizona Christian School Tuition Organization said, "Respondents' . . . position

---

[164] 397 U.S. 664 (1970).

[165] *Id.*

[166] 131 S. Ct. 1436 (2011).

[167] 392 U.S. 83 (1968).

[168] *Id.* at 105–06.

[169] *Ariz. Christian Sch. Tuition Org.*, 131 S. Ct. at 1447.

assumes that income should be treated as if it were government property even if it has not come into the tax collector's hands. That premise finds no basis in standing jurisprudence. Private bank accounts cannot be equated with the Arizona State Treasury."[170]

So is the subsidy theory dead?

---

[170] *Id.* at 1448.

Chapter 9

EDUCATIONAL ORGANIZATIONS

§ 9.01 INTRODUCTION

Section 501(c)(3) of the IRC provides that an organization may be exempt from federal income tax if it is organized and operated exclusively for an educational purpose.[1] Regulation Section 1.501(c)(3)-1(d)(ii)(3) defines the term *educational*, as used in Section 501(c)(3), as relating to either of the following:

- The instruction or training of the individual for the purpose of improving or developing his capabilities.

- The instruction of the public on subjects useful to the individual and beneficial to the community.[2]

The term "educational" is interpreted broadly and includes more than the formal schooling received at primary and secondary schools or at universities.[3] It also includes, for example, the informal educational activities provided by publishing books, newspapers, and pamphlets.

Some scholars have questioned the rationale for exempting the larger, formal educational institutions under the umbrella of charitable organizations.[4] In his article, *Why is Harvard Tax-Exempt? (And Other Mysteries of Tax Exemption for Private Educational Institutions)*,[5] John D. Colombo, "examines the exemption for private educational institutions in light of the rationales advanced to justify tax exemption for charitable institutions."[6] He finds that tax exemption "for private educational institutions extends to the beginning of Colonial America,"[7] with the

---

[1] I.R.C. § 501(c)(3).

[2] 26 C.F.R. § 1.501(c)(3)-1(d)(3).

[3] *Id.*

[4] *See* Risa L. Lieberwitz, *The Corporatization of the University: Distance Learning at the Cost of Academic Freedom?* 12 B.U. Pub. Int. L.J. 73 (2002); Lynn Lu, *Flunking the Methodology Test: A Flawed Tax-Exemption Standard for Educational Organizations That "Advocate a Particular Position or Viewpoint"*, 29 N.Y.U. Rev. L. & Soc. Change 377 (2004); John D. Colombo, *Why Is Harvard Tax-Exempt?*, 35 Ariz. L. Rev. 841 (Winter 1993); John Bello, *Economics 101: A Study of the Tax-Exempt Status of Colleges and Universities*, 34 Suffolk U. L. Rev. 615 (2001).

[5] Colombo, *supra* note 4.

[6] *Id.* at 843.

[7] *Id.* at 844; *see also* John F. Persons et al., *Criteria for Exemption Under 501(c)(3)*, *in* Research Papers Sponsored by the Commission on Private Philanthropy and Public Needs 1909, 1923 (U.S. Dept. of Treas. 1977).

seeds for this tax exemption actually beginning in the fourteenth century.[8] In colonial times, the exemption for educational organizations was connected to the exemption for churches and religious institutions because educational organizations at that time trained ministers as a primary objective.[9] Many of these organizations began as quasi public schools, such as Harvard, Yale, and William and Mary, which "were chartered with a grant of public funds."[10] The exemptions survived as the United States was formed and most states have constitutional or statutory provisions that exempt educational organizations from "state and local property and income taxes."[11] The exemption at the federal level was a recognition of the universal application of exemption at the local and state level.[12] The exemption was incorporated into the 1894 federal income tax act, which act was declared unconstitutional in 1895. The same exemption for educational institutions was included in every subsequent federal income tax statute.[13]

Professor Colombo goes on to discuss the federal standards for the tax exemption of private educational organizations. The general standards under Section 501(c)(3) of the IRC require that the entity be organized and operated for exempt purposes, one of the stated exempt purposes being education, and that it not engage in any private inurement or political activity.[14] Defining the term *education* has been the challenge for IRS and the courts. Statutory language has never defined *educational* and Treasury has never confined education to traditional schools. Early on, the "educational exemption applied to activities as diverse as studying ruffled grouse,"[15] to more recent application to museums, zoos, and symphony orchestras.[16]

The IRS and the courts have had to apply some limitations when applying the tax exemption requirements to "educational" institutions. Even though a for-profit organization operates a school for training individuals (which could qualify as an exempt educational activity under the IRC), the IRS and courts have not granted exemption to for-profit educational providers. Such organizations obviously cannot pass the private inurement test. Nor do the IRS and the courts permit exemption for educational organizations involved in "propaganda;" and they are careful to deny exemption where there is discrimination in the educational organization's admission policies. Although IRS and the courts have tried to apply the commerciality doctrine as a reason for denying tax exempt status to some educational organizations, the application has proven difficult as there are no clear guidelines for when an

---

[8]   *See* WILLIAM LANGLAND, THE VISION OF PIERS THE PLOWMAN (1362).

[9]   Colombo, *supra* note 4, at 845.

[10]   *Id.*

[11]   *Id.* at 846.

[12]   RESEARCH PAPERS SPONSORED BY THE COMMISSION ON PRIVATE PHILANTHROPY, *supra*, at 1924.

[13]   *Id.*

[14]   I.R.C. § 501(c)(3).

[15]   I.T. 228, 5-1 C.B. 80 (1926).

[16]   *See* 26 C.F.R. § 1.501(c)(3)-1(d)(3)(ii), Exs. 2-4; *see also* Ann Arbor Dog Training Club, Inc. v. Comm'r, 74 T.C. 207 (1980); San Francisco Infant School, Inc. v. Comm'r, 69 T.C. 957 (1978); Rev. Rul. 60-143, 1960-1 C.B. 192; Rev. Rul. 65-271, 1965-2 C.B. 161; Rev. Rul. 65-298, 1965-2 C.B. 163; Rev. Rul. 69-538, 1969-2 C.B. 116.

educational organization crosses the line and becomes too commercial.[17] All of the tax exempt colleges and universities charge market rate (and above) tuition for their educational services. As long as these revenues remain with the organization, however, there is no difficulty. On the other hand, an educational organization that does not pass the "private benefit" version of the operational test (the organizations' benefits must primarily flow to the general public and not to a narrow group) will be denied exemption.[18] Because the federal and state tax definitions of education are broad and grounded in common and trust law (for exemption purposes), Professor Colombo believes that there is a great deal of discretion in this area as to what can and cannot qualify as an exempt educational organization.

§ 9.02   FORMAL VERSUS INFORMAL EDUCATIONAL ORGANIZATIONS

Although neither the IRC nor the courts actually split their decisions in these cases between "formal" and "informal" educational organizations, it is a helpful distinction. The two prongs of Regulation Section 1.501(c)(3)-1(d)(ii)(3), cited earlier, easily break down into these two categories. The first prong speaks of the training of an individual for his own benefit, as would take place in a school environment. This is the area of the formal educational organization. The second prong speaks of instructing the public in ways beneficial to the community. This can happen in any way that information can be provided to an individual, and so is called informal educational activity. It needs no schoolhouse to take place. A formal educational organization has specific requirements designated by Revenue Rulings and followed by the courts, whereas informal educational organizations have less specific requirements.[19]

[A]   Formal Educational Organizations

[1]   Introduction

In Revenue Ruling 73-434,[20] the IRS elaborates the test, as stated in IRC Section 170(b)(1)(A)(2), which qualifies an organization as a formal educational organization. The organization in question was a survival school seeking Section 501(c)(3) tax exemption as an educational organization. The organization had "full-time instructors who regularly conducted a 26-day survival course, mostly out-of-doors, to teach young people how to survive in a natural environment."[21] This was the only activity of the organization. The purpose was to "develop an individual's

---

[17] *See* Big Mama Rag, Inc. v. United States, 631 F.2d 1030 (D.C. Cir. 1980).

[18] *See* American Campaign Acad. v. Comm'r, 92 T.C. 1053 (1989).

[19] See the following revenue rulings for examples of types of informal educational organizations: Rev. Rul. 65-271, 1965-2 C.B. 161; Rev. Rul. 65-298, 1965-2 C.B. 163; Rev. Rul. 67-4, 1967-1 C.B. 121; Rev. Rul. 67-342, 1967-2 C.B. 187; Rev. Rul. 68-504, 1968-2 C.B. 211; Rev. Rul. 69-441, 1969-2 C.B. 115; Rev. Rul. 70-640, 1970-2 C.B. 117; Rev. Rul. 71-421, 1971-2 C.B. 229; Rev. Rul. 73-569, 1973-2 C.B. 178; Rev. Rul. 74-16, 1974-1 C.B. 126; Rev. Rul. 74-595, 1974-2 C.B. 164; Rev. Rul. 78-99, 1978-1 C.B. 152.

[20] 1973-2 C.B. 71.

[21] *Id.*

knowledge and skills so that he may cope with the hazards of nature in situations where the usual sources of help or support are not available."[22] Subjects included "water survival, seamanship, first aid, firefighting, climbing, and rescue operations."[23] Income was derived from tuition payments and contributions. The organization was granted tax exempt status under Section 501(c)(3) because it met the requirements set forth for a formal educational organization:

- Its primary function is the presentation of formal instruction;

- Its courses are interrelated and are given in a regular and continuous manner, thereby constituting a regular curriculum;

- It normally maintains a regular faculty; and

- It has a regularly enrolled body of students in attendance at a place where its educational activities are carried on.[24]

The requirements of a formal educational institution are sometimes referred to as: (1) regular curriculum; (2) regular faculty; (3) regular student body; (4) in regular attendance; (5) at a regular campus.

[2] Guidelines & Recordkeeping Requirements

After the United States Supreme Court decision in *Brown v. Board of Education*,[25] and the passage of the 1964 Civil Rights Act by Congress, some communities opened "private schools" that qualified as 501(c)(3) organizations and were supported by tax deductible gifts. These private schools discriminated in their admission policies and were sometimes called "segregation academies." Many times their stated purposes were to provide a segregated alternative to the newly integrated public schools. This led to Revenue Procedure 75-50.[26] The Revenue Procedure sets forth guidelines and record keeping requirements for determining whether organizations that are applying for 501(c)(3) tax exempt status, and those already recognized as such, have a racially nondiscriminatory policy as to students.

This Revenue Procedure based its policies and procedures on the rulings which stated that a school that does not have a racially nondiscriminatory policy: as to students did not qualify for federal tax exemption.[27] Accordingly, a school must show the following:

- It has adopted a racially nondiscriminatory policy as to students;

- The policy is made known to the general public; and

---

[22] *Id.*

[23] *Id.*

[24] *Id.*; *see also* Rev. Rul. 72-101, 1972-1 C.B. 144; Rev. Rul. 69-492, 1969-2 C.B. 36.

[25] 347 U.S. 483 (1954).

[26] 1975-2 C.B. 587.

[27] Rev. Proc. 75-50 cites Rev. Rul. 71-447, 1971-2 C.B. 230, as an example of a school being denied tax exemption because it did not have a racially nondiscriminatory policy.

- Since the adoption of the policy: that it has operated in a bona fide manner in accordance therewith.[28]

Revenue Ruling 71-447, upon which Revenue Procedure 75-50 is based, states that "a racially nondiscriminatory policy as to students means: the school admits the students of any race to all the rights, privileges, programs, and activities generally accorded or made available to students at that school and that the school does not discriminate on the basis of race in administration of its educational policies, admissions policies, scholarship and loan programs, and athletic and other school-administered programs."[29] Discrimination on the basis of race includes discrimination on the basis of color and national or ethnic origin.[30]

The procedures set forth include an examination of the school's guidelines (organizational requirements, statement of policy,[31] publicity,[32] facilities and programs, scholarship and loan programs, certification, faculty and staff, failure to comply), application for tax exempt status,[33] public complaints of racial discrimination, and record keeping requirements (exceptions, failure to maintain records).[34] The above Revenue Ruling and Revenue Procedure make it clear that the IRS will not grant tax exempt status or allow an organization to continue as exempt once it has gained such status, if it practices racial discrimination of any kind. Racial discrimination is clearly contrary to the public policy of the United States and cannot be sanctioned with exempt status.[35] On the other hand, single-sex formal educational institutions still thrive and enjoy the benefits of 501(c)(3) tax exempt status.[36]

---

[28] Rev. Proc. 75-50, 1975-2 C.B. 587. Note, however, that Rev. Proc. 75-50 and Rev. Rul. 71-447 deal with private schools and do not apply to public schools.

[29] Rev. Proc. 75-50, 1975-2 C.B. 587 (citing Rev. Rul. 71-447).

[30] *Id.*

[31] A racially nondiscriminatory policy as to students must be included in all brochures and catalogues dealing with student admissions, programs, and scholarships.

[32] The racially nondiscriminatory policy must be known to all segments of the general community served by the school.

[33] The application for tax exempt status must include the racial composition of the student body and faculty and administrative staff for the year of filing and for as many years as is feasible to project.

[34] The U.S. District Court for the District of Columbia also ordered specific guidelines and recordkeeping requirements for Mississippi private schools in *Green v. Connally*, 330 F. Supp. 1150 (D.D.C.), *aff'd. sub nom. Coit v. Green*, 404 U.S. 997 (1971).

[35] *See* Bob Jones University v. United States, 461 U.S. 574 (1983).

[36] See United States v. Virginia, 518 U.S. 515 (1996), where the Supreme Court addressed whether the Constitution permits public sponsorship of single sex education at the college level. The Supreme Court concluded that the publicly funded Virginia Military Institute could not exclude women from its cadet corps, however the Court refused to rule more broadly on the constitutionality of single gender educational institutions. *See also* Anita K. Blair, *The Equal Protection Clause and Single-Sex Public Education: United States v. Virginia and Virginia Military Institute*, 6 SETON HALL CONST. L.J. 999 (1996); Jolee Land, *Not Dead Yet: The Future of Single-Sex Education After* United States v. Virginia, 27 STETSON L. REV. 297 (1997).

[3] Applying Tests for Tax Exemption

Formal educational organizations must always be mindful that all four tests for 501(c)(3) status are applicable. In *American Campaign Academy v. Commissioner*,[37] the American Campaign Academy, a Virginia corporation incorporated by the General Counsel of the National Republican Congressional Committee, sought a declaratory judgment stating that it was exempt under IRC Section 501(c)(3).[38] The Academy's purposes were to organize and operate a school to train individuals for careers as political campaign managers or other campaign professionals, sponsor research and publication relating to conducting a political campaign, sponsor research including public opinion toward certain political issues, and elevate the standards of professionalism in the conduct of political campaigns.[39] Its primary activity was to operate a school to train individuals for careers as political campaign professionals. The organization was the outgrowth of a course of instruction run by the National Republican Congressional Committee (NRCC).[40] NRCC contributed furniture and computer hardware to the Academy, two of six full-time Academy faculty were previously involved with NRCC's training program, and one of the Academy's three directors was a member of the Republican National Committee.[41] Exemption was denied based on the IRS's contention that the Academy failed to "operate" exclusively for an exempt purpose.[42]

To demonstrate that it met the "operational" test, the Academy was required to show that its primary activities accomplished an exempt purpose. It had to establish "that no more than an insubstantial part of its activities" did not further an exempt purpose.[43] Organizations that operate for the benefit of private, as opposed to public, interests do not operate exclusively for exempt purposes.[44] Private interests include those of private individuals, a founder or his family, shareholders or persons controlled directly or indirectly by these private interests.[45] The IRS contended that the Academy's activities substantially benefited the private interests of the Republican party, and did not serve a public purpose.

The Academy argued that because no insider benefited from the Academy's activities, it did not violate the private inurement test, and that therefore it did not provide any private benefit, because the requirements of private inurement and private benefit are similar. The Tax Court disagreed. It determined that although the prohibitions against private inurement and private benefit share common and

---

[37] 92 T.C. 1053 (1989).

[38] *Id.* at 1054.

[39] *Id.* at 1055.

[40] *Id.*

[41] *Id.* at 1056.

[42] *Id.* at 1078.

[43] *Id.* at 1065; *see also* 26 C.F.R. § 1.501(c)(3)-1(c)(1); Better Business Bureau v. United States, 326 U.S. 279, 283 (1945); Copyright Clearance Center v. Comm'r, 79 T.C. 793, 804 (1982).

[44] 26 C.F.R. § 1.501(c)(3)-1(d)(1)(ii). *See also* Retired Teachers Legal Fund v. Comm'r, 78 T.C. 280, 286 (1982), where prohibited private benefits included an "advantage; profit; fruit; privilege; gain; [or] interest."

[45] *American Campaign Academy*, 92 T.C. at 1065.

overlapping elements, they are two distinct tests and must be evaluated independently. An organization must satisfy the private inurement test, but it must also satisfy the private benefit aspect of the operational test, i.e., it must not operate in such a way as to confer a private, as opposed to a public, benefit. This court determined that non-incidental benefits conferred on disinterested parties may serve private interests and, in fact, did so here, as private benefits flowed to the Republican party.[46] The Academy, therefore, failed to establish that it operated exclusively for exempt purposes under Section 501(c)(3). The court determined that the Academy was not entitled to exemption from tax under Section 501(a).[47]

[4]   Private Schools

Questions regarding the rights of the state to require the public education of children and the rights of parents to educate their children at whatever institution they choose (public or private) have raised constitutional issues, as seen in *Pierce v. Society of the Sisters of Holy Names of Jesus and Mary.*[48] In that case, appellants were restrained from threatening or attempting to enforce the state's Compulsory Education Act.[49]

The act required "every parent, guardian, or other person having control or charge or custody of a child between eight and sixteen years to send him 'to a public school for the period of time a public school shall be held during the current year' in the district where the child resides; and failure to do so is declared a misdemeanor."[50] Several private schools (one religious and one military) challenged the act's constitutionality. They alleged that the bill conflicted with parental rights regarding the education of their children. The United States Supreme Court stated that it was plain that the Act unreasonably interfered with the liberty of parents and guardians to "direct the upbringing and education of children under their control."[51] It stated, further, that "rights guaranteed by the Constitution may not be abridged by legislation which has no reasonable relation to a purpose within the competency of the State."[52]

In *New Life Baptist Church Academy v. East Longmeadow,*[53] another constitutional question was raised concerning educational requirements imposed by the state. This case questioned "the extent to which the First Amendment permits a religious group to refuse to comply with state rules and procedures for determining the adequacy of the secular education that the religious group provides to

---

[46] *Id.* at 1068; *see* Church of Ethereal Joy v. Comm'r, 83 T.C. 20, 21 (1984); Goldsboro Art League, Inc. v. Comm'r, 75 T.C. 337, 345 n.10 (1980); *see also* 26 C.F.R. § 1.501(c)(3)-1(d)(1)(ii). *But see* Rev. Rul. 76-456, 1976-2 C.B. 151 (informal educational organization formed to advance ethics and morality in political campaigns was found to be organized and operated exclusively for exempt purposes).

[47] *American Campaign Academy*, 92 T.C. at 1078.

[48] 268 U.S. 510 (1925).

[49] *Id.* at 530.

[50] *Id.*

[51] *Id.* at 534–35.

[52] *Id.* at 535.

[53] 885 F.2d 940 (1st Cir. 1989).

children."[54] Massachusetts compulsory school attendance laws required that the local school committee "approve" the education that private schools provided. The New Life Baptist Church Academy brought suit to prevent the school committee from carrying out its approval process. The process required the committee to gather written information about the Academy; review the credentials of the teachers; and to visit the school, more than once, to observe the quality of teaching.[55] Although the Academy suggested a less intrusive method for the state to use (requiring standardized testing with specific results), this court did not find free exercise or establishment clause violations. It stated that the school committee's gathering of information for "approval" decision making did not pose any "reasonable likelihood" of excessive entanglement.[56]

In *Zelman v. Simmons-Harris*,[57] the state of Ohio established a pilot program to provide educational choice to families with children who reside in the Cleveland City School District. The majority of the children enrolled in this school district were from low-income and minority families. The issue was whether the program offended the Establishment Clause of the United States Constitution by funding education at religious schools. The Court held that it did not.[58]

After the state auditor found that the Cleveland public schools were in "crisis," and failed to meet any of the 18 state standards for minimal acceptance performance, Ohio enacted the Pilot Project Scholarship Program.[59] The program provided financial assistance to families in any Ohio school district "under federal court order requiring supervision and operational management of the district by the state superintendent."[60] Cleveland was the only school district to fall within the category.[61]

The program provided two types of assistance: (1) tuition aid for students in kindergarten through eighth grade to attend a participating public or private school, and (2) tutorial aid for students choosing to remain in public school. The Court believed this program to be neutral "in all respects toward religion."[62] It stated that, as in *Witters*, there was no financial incentive[s] skewing the program toward religious schools.[63] The program "provides benefit directly to a wide spectrum of individuals, defined only by financial need and residence in a particular

---

[54] *Id.* at 941.

[55] *Id.* at 942.

[56] *Id.* at 954. *Compare* Surinach v. Pesquera de Busquets, 604 F.2d 73 (1st Cir. 1979), where the court found the power to regulate, fix, control, freeze, and review the school's prices were a continuing involvement, which led to impermissible entanglement.

[57] 536 U.S. 639 (2002).

[58] *Id.*

[59] *Id.* at 644.

[60] *Id.* at 644–45; *see also* Ohio Rev. Code Ann. § 3313.975(A) (Anderson 1999 & Supp. 2000).

[61] *Zelman*, 536 U.S. at 645.

[62] *Id.* at 653.

[63] *Id.* at 650; *see also* Witters v. Washington Dept. of Servs. for the Blind, 474 U.S. 481, 487–488 (1986).

school district. . . . The program is therefore a program of true private choice."[64]

As indicated above, an important issue that private schools must be aware of is the IRS requirement that private schools have racially nondiscriminatory admission policies.[65] This was addressed in the well-known United States Supreme Court case, *Bob Jones University v. United States* and its companion case, *Goldsboro Christian Schools, Inc. v. United States*.[66] The Court granted certiorari to decide whether Bob Jones University and Goldsboro Christian Schools qualified as 501(c)(3) tax exempt organizations based on the fact that their admission policy (*Goldsboro*) and dating standards (*Bob Jones University*) enforced racial discrimination on the basis of religious doctrine.[67]

The Court found that these organizations did not qualify under Section 501(c)(3) because they violated the public policy of the United States against racial discrimination. It stated "It has now become an established principle of American law, that courts of chancery will sustain and protect . . . a gift . . . to public charitable uses, provided the same is consistent with local laws and public policy. . . ."[68]

The Circuit Court in *Doe v. Kamehameha Schools*,[69] considered "whether a private, nonprofit K-12 school that receives no federal funds violates § 1981 by preferring Native Hawaiians in its admissions policy."[70] The court answered no, affirming the District Court decision. The private school was created through a charitable testamentary trust which was established by the "last direct descendent of King Kamehameha I, Princess Bernice Pauahi Bishop, who left her property in trust for a school dedicated to the education and upbringing of Native Hawaiians."[71] This case was decided differently from *Bob Jones University* or *Goldsboro Christian Schools*[72] because the court believed that under the special relationship doctrine, Congress has the power to treat "Native Hawaiians" as a political classification to which exclusive educational benefits can be provided.[73] Because the admissions policy was designed in response to the educational deficits as to native Hawaiian children in Hawaii, the court concluded it was a valid policy.[74]

---

[64] *Zelman*, 536 U.S. at 662.

[65] Rev. Rul. 71-447, 1971-2 C.B. 230.

[66] 461 U.S. 574 (1983).

[67] *Id.* at 577. See also § 6.01 *et seq.* on the tests for tax exemption.

[68] *Bob Jones*, 461 U.S. at 591; *see also* Perin v. Carey, 16 L. Ed. 701, 24 How. 465, 501 (1861).

[69] 470 F.3d 827 (9th Cir. 2006).

[70] *Id.* at 829.

[71] *Id.* at 831.

[72] 461 U.S. 574.

[73] 470 F.3d at 856.

[74] *Id.*

[B] Informal Educational Organizations

The term educational, as discussed early on in this chapter, includes "instruction of the public on subjects useful to the individual and beneficial to the community."[75]

Informal educational institutions do not need a regular faculty, curriculum, or student body. They must only provide instruction or training for a general purpose or regarding a particular subject. When dealing with informal organizational institutions, the IRS is often more concerned with whether the organization is truly educational or whether it is merely disseminating propaganda.

Perhaps the best example of the IRS and the courts wrestling with this distinction is in *Big Mama Rag, Inc. v. United States*.[76] In this case, the IRS rejected Big Mama Rag's (BMR) application for tax exemption finding that it was not entitled to tax exemption as an educational or charitable organization under Section 501(c)(3). BMR was "a nonprofit organization with a feminist orientation."[77] Its purpose was "to create a channel of communication for women that would educate and inform them on general issues of concern to them."[78] The organization's primary activity was the production of a newspaper but it also spent time promoting women's rights through seminars, lectures, and a free library. After a protest by BMR, a hearing was held in the IRS National Office.[79] The denial of tax exempt status was affirmed. The grounds were: (1) the commercial nature of BMR's newspaper; (2) the political and legislative commentary found throughout; and (3) the articles, lectures, editorials, etc., promoting lesbianism.[80] On appeal, the district court found no violation of the commerciality doctrine but did find that BMR did not satisfy the requirements for an educational or charitable organization.[81]

The definition of "educational" provides that: "[A]n organization may be educational even though it advocates a particular position or viewpoint so long as it presents a *sufficiently full and fair exposition* of the pertinent facts as to permit an individual or the public to form an independent opinion or conclusion." (emphasis added)[82] This is referred to as the "full and fair exposition" test. It is based on IRS's premise that organizations that propagandize are not truly educating anyone. The district court found that BMR did not meet this test.[83] The appeals court did not agree. It found that the Regulations defining "educational" did not clearly indicate which organizations were subject to the "full and fair exposition" test, and further that the test itself was unconstitutionally vague.[84] The

---

[75] 26 C.F.R. § 1.501(c)(3)-1(d)(3)(i).

[76] 631 F.2d 1030 (D.C. Cir. 1980).

[77] *Id.* at 1032.

[78] *Id.*

[79] *Id.*

[80] *Id.* at 1038; *see also* 26 C.F.R. § 1.501(c)(3)-1(d)(2), (3), -1(d)(3)(i).

[81] *Big Mama Rag*, 631 F.2d at 1040.

[82] 26 C.F.R. § 1.501(c)(3)-1(d)(3)(i).

[83] *Big Mama Rag*, 631 F.2d at 1040.

[84] *Id.* at 1035.

court concluded that the definition of "educational" lacked "sufficient specificity to pass constitutional muster."[85] After the court's decision in *Big Mama Rag*, IRS attempted to remedy the alleged "vagueness" of the "full and fair exposition" test by putting the gloss of a "methodology" test on it. The methodology test examines the following:

- Whether the presentation of viewpoints unsupported by a relevant factual basis constitutes a significant portion of the organization's communications;

- To the extent viewpoints purport to be supported by a factual basis, are the facts distorted;

- Whether the organization makes substantial use of particularly inflammatory and disparaging terms, expressing conclusions based more on strong emotional feelings than objective factual evaluations; and

- Whether the approach to a subject matter is aimed at developing an understanding on the part of the addressees, by reflecting consideration on the extent to which they have prior background or training.[86]

In order to address First Amendment concerns that IRS was not simply censoring an organization's unpopular speech by denying it exempt status, the focus of the IRS was now to be on the method and not the truth or accuracy of the content of an informal educational organization's publications.

The first case to consider the new "methodology test" revision of the "full and fair exposition" test was *National Alliance v. United States*.[87] National Alliance was denied tax exempt status by the IRS District Director, who stated that the organization was neither "charitable" nor "educational."[88] National Alliance published a monthly newsletter, organized lectures and meetings, and distributed books "all for the stated purpose of arousing in white Americans of European Ancestry an understanding of and a pride in their racial and cultural heritage and an awareness of the present dangers to that heritage."[89] The IRS argued that National Alliance was not educational under the methodology test. The district court concluded that the methodology test was also unconstitutionally vague and remanded the matter to the IRS. This appeal ensued.[90]

The appeals court determined that the first step was to decide whether the National Alliance materials could qualify as educational under any use of that term, before it would consider the IRS's "full and fair exposition" test as modified by the

---

[85] *Id.* at 1039.

[86] *Id.* at 1035; *see also* I.R.C. § 501(c)(3); 26 C.F.R. § 1.501(c)(3)-1(d)(3); Rev. Proc. 86-43, 1986-2 C.B. 729. *See also* Families Against Government Slavery v. Comm'r, T.C. Memo 2007-49 where the court denied tax exempt status to an organization that carried on public protests to educate the public on the alleged slavery and entrapment of Hollywood celebrities by government officials, based on Rev. Proc. 86-43. Petitioners activities were primarily presentations of unsupported opinion, which did not further an educational purpose.

[87] 710 F.2d 868 (D.C. Cir. 1983).

[88] *Id* at 869.

[89] *Id.*; *see also* 26 C.F.R. § 1.501(c)(3)-(1)(d)(2), (3).

[90] *National Alliance*, 710 F.2d at 869–70.

methodology test.[91] A look at the National Alliance publications determined that the materials where "appeals for action, including violence, to put to disadvantage or to injure persons who are members of named racial, religious, or ethnic groups."[92] Although the appeals court did not attempt to define *educational*, it found that New Alliance's publications were far outside the range that Congress "intended to subsidize in the public interest"[93] by granting tax exempt status for educational purposes.[94] The appeals court found nothing that would suggest that National Alliance was an educational organization after reviewing its activities. It went on to state, though, that it was not deciding whether the methodology test, in fact, cured the vagueness of the full and fair exposition test.[95] In the subsequent case of *Nationalist Movement v. Commissioner*,[96] the Tax Court did apply the methodology test, finding that it was not unconstitutionally vague or overbroad.

While social clubs are normally exempt under IRC Section 501(c)(7), some clubs that teach their members certain skills have attempted to qualify as Section 501(c)(3) educational organizations. In *Minnesota Kingsmen Chess Association, Inc. v. Commissioner*,[97] the issue was whether the organization was organized and operated exclusively for educational purposes under Section 501(c)(3). In its original Articles of Incorporation the organization included 'recreation' as one of its purposes. The IRS denied 501(c)(3) status and the organization amended its Articles to exclude the word "recreation." An adverse determination letter was again issued by the IRS. The Minnesota Kingsmen was, at the time, affiliated with the United States Chess Federation (501(c)(4)) and the Minnesota State Chess Association (501(c)(7)).[98]

Minnesota Kingsmen's activities included the following: organizing chess tournaments for its members; providing instruction; and publishing a bulletin and newsletter notifying members of future tournaments. The court concluded that Minnesota Kingsmen did not meet the operational test. It found that at least half of the organization's time was spent promoting and conducting tournaments. It stated that "[T]he presence of a single noneducational purpose, if substantial in nature, will make the organization ineligible for the exemption, regardless of the number or importance of truly educational purposes."[99]

---

[91] *Id.* at 870.

[92] *Id.* at 873.

[93] *Id.*

[94] *Id.*

[95] *Id.* at 874.

[96] 102 T.C. 558, *aff'd*, 37 F.3d 216 (5th Cir. 1994).

[97] 46 T.C.M. (CCH) 1133 (1983).

[98] *Id.*

[99] *Id.*; *see also* I.R.C. § 501(c)(3); 26 C.F.R. § 1.501(c)(3)-1(a); Better Business Bureau v. United States, 326 U.S. 279, 283 (1945). *See also* St. Louis Science Fiction Limited v. Comm'r, T.C. Memo 1985-162, where the IRS denied tax exempt status to a club which stated an educational purpose in its incorporation documents but operated in a commercial manner.

§ 9.03 FUNDING

[A] New Funding Sources

The funding of formal educational organizations occurs primarily through payment for services (tuition) and through gifts, grants, and membership fees. In Michael Goldstein's 1999 article, "Capital Ideas,"[100] the various ways of raising capital for formal educational organizations are discussed. Of the many ways to raise money, Goldstein suggests that the stock market, where "you get other people's money by selling them an ownership interest-equity" in the entity you are seeking to capitalize, is one of the best. The problem with nonprofit tax exempt educational organizations is that there is no equity interest to sell because no one has actual ownership in the organization. Although no one owns the educational organization, the organization owns things, such as buildings, books, machinery, laboratories and, even, sometimes, for-profit subsidiary entities that Goldstein says can be used to create capital. In this article, he discusses several examples for capitalization of nonprofit organizations. He begins by reminding the reader that research institutions have long created for-profit spinoffs to commercialize technology that is developed on campus, and some universities spin off their hospitals as for-profits.[101]

In Service Model One (Renting a Room with a View), an exempt educational organization provides the content and a for-profit entity provides the delivery facility. This model is employed by the Caliber Learning Network, which is "a public company that has created a network of electronic classrooms."[102] The classrooms provided computer access and live video. A university partner, Johns Hopkins University, created the content: a graduate curriculum in business administration for practicing physicians. "The University sets admissions standards, enrolls the students, delivers the curriculum in Caliber's classrooms through a combination of recorded and live video and the Internet, evaluates student performance, and issued directly and through the services agreement."[103] The proceeds of the sale of these educational services support the institution's exempt activities and the value of the stock adds to its endowment. If the venture does not succeed, it does not matter as much, for the university's own money was not at risk.[104]

In the Bifurcation Model, the functions of the exempt educational organization are divided into academic and non-academic. The institution itself continues to perform the academic functions, while a for-profit subsidiary, which it creates, handles all of the other functions such as marketing, maintenance of technology and back office matters.[105]

---

[100] Michael B. Goldstein, Dow, Lohnes & Albertson, PLLC, *Capital Ideas, U. Bus.* 46 (Oct. 1999).

[101] *Id.*

[102] *Id.* at 48.

[103] *Id.*

[104] *Id.* at 49.

[105] *Id.* at 48–50.

In the Operating Subsidiary Model, the institution not only spins off its non-academic functions, but some of its academic functions as well. New York University did this when it created NYUonline. The purpose was to bring NYU's noncredit and professional programs to a national and international audience.[106]

The Joint Venture Model involves the creation of a new for-profit entity with a for-profit partner. These types of ventures are created to market technology mediated learning courses to a wider audience. One partnership was created between the Public Broadcasting Service (PBS) and the Williams Companies. PBS had created the satellite-based Adult Learning Service (ALS), enrolling more than 100,000 students each year. Through ALS, The Business Channel, designed to provide executive training, was created. Williams was a technology company with an extensive fiber-optic network and emerging desktop video delivery system. The two partnered, through a new for-profit company, PBS The Business Channel. PBS contributed its name, logo, and content. Williams provided capital and access to its technology.[107]

In a Common Enterprise Model, the same kind of combinations can be developed but with two or more exempt educational institutions working together. In this model, there would be the creation of an intervening nonprofit entity between the institutions and the for-profit entity.[108]

Goldstein believes that tax exempt academic institutions must consider three things when contemplating these various structures as capital investments. First, colleges and universities must remember that these partnerships take time and the benefits are not immediate. Second, institutions must think about not only buying things, but also buying time through these ventures. Third, they must remember that creating a for-profit can add speed and efficiency to an otherwise slow academic process.[109]

These are all new and used ideas that Goldstein believes need to be considered when balancing the needs and value of academia with the need to compete in a highly technology-driven world.

[B]   Investment Vehicles

The Common Fund is a pooled investment vehicle for a number of colleges and universities. In an attempt to professionalize the investments of formal educational organizations, a prominent private foundation suggested the creation of a common investment fund to a number of colleges and universities and paid the original management and administrative expenses. As the fund prospered, it began to depend on fees from its member colleges and universities, leading IRS to suggest that it was no longer tax exempt, because many for-profit investment management firms functioned in much the same way. Thanks to the lobbying clout of the colleges and universities involved, Section 501(f) was added to the IRC. That section

---

[106] *Id.* at 50.

[107] *Id.* at 50–51.

[108] *Id.* at 51.

[109] *Id.*

exempts from taxation organizations "organized and operated solely to hold, commingle, and collectively invest and reinvest . . . in stocks and securities, the moneys contributed thereto by each of the members of such organizations, and to collect income therefrom and turn over the entire amount thereof, less expenses, to such members," when the organization is organized and controlled by its members, all of whom are tax exempt formal educational organizations.[110]

§ 9.04   RIGHTS OF STUDENTS

The following is a brief overview of the rights of the students within educational organizations. Students are subject to disciplinary measures and academic determinations by schools. The law that governs these situations is discussed below.

[A]   Suspension

If a student is disciplined through a suspension, the courts will generally not get involved unless the state was somehow involved in the situation. A private school may be the subject of litigation through contract law, and courts will become involved for reasons of bad faith, or arbitrary or unreasonable behavior on the part of the school.[111] Courts will generally not review cases involving students dismissed for academic reasons except when bad faith or arbitrary behavior is suspected. Generally, courts hold that school authorities are best qualified to resolve disputes concerning grades and degrees.[112]

In *Harris v. Trustees of Columbia University*,[113] several student rights matters were at issue. Originally, Mr. Harris was affiliated with Columbia University as an employee and was therefore entitled to lease an apartment at a reduced fee. He was asked, after some time, to provide a letter showing his continued affiliation with the University so that his lease arrangement could continue. He provided a letter, which later was alleged to be fraudulent. This became an issue when he enrolled as a student and wished to remain in his apartment. Because a department Dean believed the letter to be fraudulent from years earlier, he expelled Mr. Harris from school.[114]

The court found few cases "dealing with judicial review of university expulsion of a student for non-academic discipline."[115] In most of the cases that were found, the university action was upheld.[116] In this case, the court found that the actions of the

---

[110] I.R.C § 501(f). *See also* Hunt v. McNair, 413 U.S. 734 (1973) for an example of the use of tax exempt bonds by a religiously affiliated educational organization.

[111] *See* Marilyn E. Phelan & Robert J. Desiderio, Nonprofit Organizations Law and Policy 648 (3d ed. 2010) (2003).

[112] *Id.*

[113] 98 A.D.2d 58, 470 N.Y.S.2d 368 (1983).

[114] *Id.* at 369–70.

[115] *Id.* at 372.

[116] *Id. See also* Goldstein v. New York Univ., 76 A.D. 80, 78 N.Y.S. 739 (1902), where a student was expelled from NYU Law School for the indiscretion of passing a letter to another student expressing a desire to make her acquaintance; Samson v. Trustees of Columbia Univ., 101 Misc. 146, 167 N.Y.S. 202

university were not consistent with the law or the disciplinary procedures of the university. They stated that "the submission of an allegedly fraudulent letter concerning his apartment was not 'immoral or unconscionable' conduct related to his status as a student."[117] The court ordered that Mr. Harris be reinstated.

[B] Privacy

The privacy rights of students regarding educational records are governed by The Family Educational Rights and Privacy Act.[118] The United States Supreme Court held that this Act did not create a private right for students to sue in *Gonzaga University v. Doe*,[119] and dismissed a claim for an alleged violation of the Family Educational Rights and Privacy Act (FERPA). The Supreme Court said that FERPA only provided an administrative review procedure for the enforcement of its nondisclosure provisions.[120]

The procedures under the Act include the following: they permit inspection, review, and amendment of the educational records by a student and require prior consent for disclosure of records to third parties.[121] The Act denies federal funds to institutions with policies permitting the release of personal records to third parties. A student may have a formal or informal hearing to challenge the information in his record and may insert information explaining matters in his file. There are certain persons or organizations that the information may be released to without the permission of the student or parent.[122] In all other cases, the consent of the student is required for the release of student file information.

(Sup. Ct. 1917), *aff'd without opin.*, 181 A.D. 936, 167 N.Y.S. 1125 (1917), where a student making an anti draft speech was not permitted to register on grounds of moral unfitness; and Anthony v. Syracuse Univ., 224 A.D. 487, 489, 231 N.Y.S. 435 (1928), where a student was expelled because of rumors about her life style.

[117] *Harris*, 470 N.Y.S.2d at 373.

[118] 42 U.S.C. § 1232g.

[119] 536 U.S. 273 (2002).

[120] *Id.* at 290; *see also* 42 U.S.C. § 1983.

[121] These rights pertain to the student's parents if the student is under 18. *See* 42 U.S.C. § 1232g.

[122] These include other school officials, officials of other schools for transfer purposes, and certain authorized representatives of the government for educational purposes. *See Gonzaga Univ.*, 536 U.S. at 289; 42 U.S.C. § 1232g.

Chapter 10

HEALTHCARE ORGANIZATIONS

§ 10.01 INTRODUCTION TO HOSPITALS

Healthcare organizations are not mentioned at all in Section 501(c)(3) of the IRC. Initially, hospitals were found to be tax exempt because they provided health care to the poor, and the relief of poverty was the classic definition of charitable.[1] Because Section 501(c)(3) exempts from the federal income tax organizations operated exclusively for religious, charitable, scientific, testing for public safety, literary or educational purposes, hospitals easily fell into the charitable category.[2] This policy was set forth in Revenue Ruling 56-185,[3] which said that a hospital was tax exempt only if it was "operated to the extent of its financial ability for those not able to pay for the services rendered and not exclusively for those who are able and expected to pay."[4]

Some hospitals associated with university medical schools can also qualify as educational organizations because they are considered teaching hospitals: hospitals where doctors are trained, or even as scientific organizations, if they are research hospitals. It is also important to note that while Section 501(c)(3) does not specifically mention healthcare as an exempt activity, Section 170(b)(1)(A)(iii), on the deduction of charitable gifts, expressly states that gifts to an organization, the principal purpose or functions of which are to provide medical or hospital care or medical education or medical research, are deductible.[5]

[A] Indigent Care & Charity Standard

While organized healthcare started out in the United States as the provision of healthcare to the poor, by the late twentieth century that situation had changed dramatically. Patient care revenue increased along with healthcare costs. The

---

[1] *See* 26 C.F.R. § 1.501(c)(3)-1(d)(2); Restatement (Third) of Trusts § 28 (2003); *see also* Kathleen Boozang, *Mission, Margin, and Trust in the Nonprofit Health Care Enterprise*, 5 Yale J. Health Pol'y L. & Ethics 1 (2005).

[2] *See* I.R.C. § 501(c)(3).

[3] 1956-1 C.B. 202.

[4] *Id.* The position of the IRS in this Revenue Ruling has also been upheld in litigation. *See, e.g.,* Comm'r v. Battle Creek, Inc., 126 F.2d 405 (5th Cir. 1942); Davis Hosp. Inc. v. Comm'r, T.C.M. (P-H) ¶ 45,097 (1945); Intercity Hospital Ass'n v. Squire, 56 F. Supp. 472 (W.D. Wash. 1944); Goldsby King Mem'l v. Comm'r, T.C.M. (P-H) ¶ 44,233 (1944); Lorain Ave. Clinic v. Comm'r, 31 T.C. 141 (1958); Olney v. Comm'r, 17 T.C.M. (CCH) 982 (1958); Sonora Cmty. Hosp. v. Comm'r, 46 T.C. 519 (1966), *aff'd*, 397 F.2d 814 (9th Cir. 1968).

[5] I.R.C. § 170(b)(1)(A)(iii).

federal government became a major purchaser of healthcare services through the Medicare and Medicaid programs, which funded healthcare for those who were not able to pay. Employer-provided insurance programs covered working people. As a result of the entry of these third-party payors into the healthcare market, the need to provide healthcare to the poor, or those who could not pay for it, while not entirely alleviated, was no longer the primary focus of tax exempt hospitals.[6]

[B] Community Benefit Standard

In 1969, the IRS realized that the promotion of the health of the community, apart from the provision of below cost or no cost healthcare for relief of the poor, and even apart from the fact that all or part of the cost of services was born by patients or third-party payors, was itself a valid charitable activity.[7] The focus now was on the community benefit that a tax exempt hospital provided, and that community benefit still forms the basis of the tax exempt status of hospitals. In Revenue Ruling 69-545,[8] the IRS said:

> [t]he promotion of health, like the relief of poverty, and the advancement of education and religion, is one of the purposes in the general law of charity that is deemed beneficial to the community as a whole even though the class of beneficiaries eligible to receive a direct benefit from its activities does not include all members of the community, such as indigent members of the community, provided that the class is not so small that its relief is not of benefit to the community. . . . [B]y operating an emergency room open to all persons and by providing hospital care for all those persons in the community able to pay the cost thereof either directly or through third party reimbursement, Hospital A is promoting the health of a class of persons that is broad enough to benefit the community.[9]

After this revenue ruling, provided a hospital met the other tests for tax exemption, it qualified as exempt as long as it had an emergency room open to all, regardless of the patient's ability to pay.

This change by the IRS, from requiring tax exempt hospitals to provide indigent care under Revenue Ruling 56-185,[10] to requiring only that a tax exempt hospital maintain an emergency room open to all under Revenue Ruling 69-545,[11] was

---

[6] There are critics who say that these developments have so changed the nature of healthcare that even nonprofit hospitals are no longer truly performing charity. *See* Utah Cnty. Bd. of Equalization v. Intermountain Health Care, Inc., 709 P.2d 265 (Utah 1985); *see also* Nina Crimm, *Evolutionary Forces: Changes in For-Profit and Not-For-Profit Health Care Delivery Structures; A Regeneration of Tax Exemption Standards*, 37 B.C. L. REV. 1 (1995); Gabriel Aitsebaomo, *The Nonprofit Hospital: A Call for New National Guidance Requiring Minimum Annual Charity Care to Qualify for Federal Tax Exemption*, 26 CAMPBELL L. REV. 75 (2004); John D. Colombo & Mark A. Hall, *The Future of Tax-Exemption for Nonprofit Hospitals and Other Health Care Providers*, 2 HEALTH MATRIX 1 (1992).

[7] Rev. Rul. 69-545, 1969-2 C.B. 117.

[8] 1969-2 C.B. 117.

[9] *Id.*

[10] Rev. Rul. 69-545, 1969-2 C.B. 117.

[11] *Id.*

challenged in the courts. An indigent rights group, in *Eastern Kentucky Welfare Rights Organization v. Shultz*,[12] filed suit claiming that the IRS's change in the requirements for tax exempt hospitals had harmed them, and they sought to have Revenue Ruling 69-545 declared invalid. They won a summary judgment in the district court, but on appeal to the D.C. Circuit, the IRS position was upheld.[13] The circuit court relied on the legal history of the term *charitable* in Section 501(c)(3).[14] Citing specifically to the historical law of charitable trusts (as the IRS had itself done in the challenged ruling), the court found that the concept of *charitable* was much broader than simply relief of the poor, and that the promotion of health was a valid charitable purpose.[15] The court reasoned that the term *charitable* could not be frozen in time, but must recognize the changing economic, social, and technological circumstances of society. In that regard, the court cited the movement of third-party payors into health care, explaining that this had "greatly reduced the number of poor people requiring free or below cost hospital services."[16]

In 1983, the IRS addressed the issue of whether hospitals without emergency rooms could qualify for tax exempt status, because the 1969 ruling seemed to imply that, without an emergency room open to all, there was not enough of a community benefit to sustain exempt status.[17] The question arose for two reasons. First, there are a number of specialty hospitals, treating specific diseases or ailments, that do not have emergency rooms. For example, a hospital dedicated to cancer treatment, or treatment of diseases of the eye, or a psychiatric hospital, by its specialty nature would not typically have an emergency room. Second, centralized health care management agencies, very often agencies of state or local government, in an effort to lower healthcare costs through the closing of duplicative services, had caused the closing of a number of hospital emergency rooms in areas where other hospitals were already meeting this need.

The IRS's answer came in Revenue Ruling 83-157. Under this Revenue Ruling, the IRS states that hospitals without emergency rooms open to all could still qualify as tax exempt based on other factors. These factors include: (1) a board of directors drawn from the community, (2) an open medical staff policy, (3) the treatment of

---

[12] 370 F. Supp. 325 (D.D.C. 1973), *rev'd*, 506 F.2d 1278 (D.C. Cir. 1974), *dismissed for lack of standing*, 426 U.S. 26 (1976).

[13] *Id.*

[14] *Id.* at 1287; *see also* I.R.C. § 501(c)(3).

[15] *E. Ky. Welfare Rights Org.*, 506 F.2d at 1287; *see also* RESTATEMENT (THIRD) OF TRUSTS § 28 (2003); 6 AUSTIN WAKEMAN SCOTT ET AL., SCOTT AND ASCHER ON TRUSTS §§ 38.1, 38.5 (5th ed. 2006 & Supp. 2009).

[16] *E. Ky. Welfare Rights Org.*, 506 F.2d at 1288. Courts consistently reject the contention that exempt hospitals have an affirmative duty to provide free or under-cost care to indigents, or that indigents have a right to sue on such duty. They also reject the contention that indigents are third party beneficiaries of a hospital's exempt status. *See* Burton v. William Beaumont Hosp., 347 F. Supp. 2d 486 (E.D. Mich. 2004); Kizzire v. Baptist Health Sys., 343 F. Supp. 2d 1074 (N.D. Ala. 2004); Peterson v. Fairview Health Servs., 95 A.F.T.R.2d (RIA) 1005 (D. Minn. 2005); Jellison v. Fla. Hosp. Healthcare Sys., 2005 U.S. Dist. LEXIS 8036 (M.D. Fla. Mar. 14, 2005); Wright v. St. Dominic Health Servs., 95 A.F.T.R.2d (RIA) 1383 (S.D. Miss. 2005); Hagedorn v. St. Thomas Hosp., Inc., 2005 U.S. Dist. LEXIS 7259 (M.D. Tenn. Feb. 7, 2005); Sabeta v. Baptist Hosp. of Miami, Inc., 410 F. Supp. 2d 1224 (S.D. Fla. 2005); Quinn v. BJC Health Sys., 364 F. Supp. 2d 1046 (E.D. Mo. 2005).

[17] Rev. Rul. 83-157, 1983-2 C.B. 94.

persons paying their bills with the aid of public programs like Medicare and Medicaid, and (4) the application of any surplus to improving facilities, equipment, patient care, and medical training, education, and research.[18] The factors indicate that, despite the absence of an emergency room, the hospital is operating exclusively to benefit the community.

§ 10.02   MULTI-CORPORATE FORM

Very few tax exempt hospitals function as just one healthcare corporation today. Originally, most tax exempt hospitals were stand-alone operations; one hospital corporation serving a local community. Beginning in the 1970s, tax exempt hospitals began to restructure into the multi-corporate format, primarily for re-imbursement reasons. These early restructurings involved the separate incorporation of the exempt hospital's profit centers so that their income did not show up on the hospital's bottom line, adversely affecting the hospital's Medicare, Medicaid, and third-party payments, which reimbursed the hospital on a cost basis.[19]

What resulted was a tax exempt parent holding corporation and several subsidiary corporations, some tax exempt, some not. For example, under the parent corporation, which did nothing except hold interests in its subsidiaries,[20] there would be the actual hospital corporation, which still delivered healthcare in a way that benefited the community and was tax exempt;[21] a fund-raising foundation that supported the healthcare delivery services of the hospital, and was also tax exempt,[22] perhaps some separately incorporated departments of the hospital, such as the emergency room, or the radiology department, which could also qualify for tax exemption;[23] and some for-profit organizations, such as a real estate development corporation, the income of which was taxable.

Since hospitals are no longer reimbursed on a cost basis, the rationale that originally drove the multi-corporate health care delivery system is no longer applicable. Other reasons have intervened, however, such as the need to segregate unrelated business income, the need to have a flexible structure that allows joint venturing, the need to meet state laws on certificates of need for various healthcare-related undertakings, and the need to have a separate, non-exempt arm capable of extensive lobbying, that make multi-corporate healthcare delivery systems attractive, if not necessary.[24]

---

[18] *Id.*

[19] For further background information on the history of hospital structures, see Douglas M. Mancino, *Income Tax Exemption of the Contemporary Nonprofit Hospital*, 32 ST. Louis U. L.J. 1015 (1988); Robert Charles Clark, *Does the Nonprofit Form Fit the Hospital Industry?*, 93 HARV. L. REV. 1416 (1980); Crimm, *supra* note 6; Aitsebaomo, *supra* note 6; Colombo & Hall, *supra* note 6.

[20] Since the parent holding corporation is not itself doing any charity, its own tax exempt status must be based on the integral part test. 26 C.F.R. § 1.502-1(b). The leading case is *Northwestern Medical Corporation*, TAX NOTES, Sept. 9, 1993. *See also* § 10.03 for further information on the integral parts test.

[21] I.R.C. § 501(c)(3).

[22] I.R.C. § 509(a)(3), as a supporting organization.

[23] 26 C.F.R. § 1.502-1(b) (the integral part test).

[24] *See* Crimm, *supra* note 6; Aitsebaomo, *supra* note 6; Clark, *supra* note 19.

§ 10.03   INTEGRAL PART TEST

The integral part test is basically a derivative form of tax exemption. Under this test, an organization that provides services to a tax exempt organization can qualify for its own exempt status, as long as the services it provides are in furtherance of the first organization's exempt purposes. The regulations specify that an organization that provides services to an affiliated exempt organization is itself exempt if the services would not constitute an unrelated trade or business if performed by the affiliate.[25] Under the integral part test, two conditions must be met: (1) the two organizations must be related, and (2) the subordinate organization's activities must be in furtherance of the exempt purposes of the parent organization.[26]

The physicians who worked in the anesthesiology department of the Boston Hospital for Women, all of whom were also faculty members of the Harvard University Medical School, incorporated as the B.H.W. Anesthesia Foundation, Inc. The Boston Hospital for Women was a bona fide 501(c)(3) organization, and served as a teaching hospital for the Harvard University Medical School. The reason behind this incorporation was to create an entity that would bill for the member physicians' anesthesiology services. This organization then used this revenue to pay salaries to the anesthesiologist-physicians, but such payments were governed by Harvard's System of Titles and Appointments policy, which resulted in below-market remuneration to the physician members, even when combined with their teaching salaries from the Harvard medical school. In fact, less than half (40 percent) of organization revenues were paid out as physicians' salaries. The rest paid for other costs associated with operating the anesthesiology department, such as accounting costs, office costs, library costs, and supply costs. The organization treated all of BHW's patients, without regard to ability to pay, resulting in free services to more than 10 percent of those treated. In addition, the organization both conducted research activities and instructed Harvard medical students.[27]

When this organization applied for tax exempt status and was not given a timely decision by the IRS, the issue of its status was brought before the Tax Court in *B.H.W. Anesthesia Foundation, Inc. v. Commissioner.*[28] The Tax Court had to determine whether the private benefit aspects of the organization, namely the physicians' remuneration, meant that the organization served private as opposed to public interests. Because the organization's members were the ones receiving the salaries, there were also control-benefit issues; in other words, the court was asking whether it failed the private inurement test. There is no doubt that if this organization had simply been an incorporated medical practice, it would fail both the operational and private inurement tests. But the court found that B.H.W. Anesthesia Foundation was an integral part of the hospital and Harvard University Medical School, both of which are Section 501(c)(3) organizations. It was only doing, as a separate corporation, what the hospital's anesthesiology department had done, and even though it was now a separate corporation, it still served the hospital's

---

[25] 26 C.F.R. § 1.502-1(b).

[26] *Id.*

[27] B.H.W. Anesthesia Found., Inc. v. Comm'r, 72 T.C. 681, 682 (1979), *nonacq.*, 1980-2 C.B. 2.

[28] *Id.*

patients and applied all of its operating revenues for the benefit of the hospital.[29]

That there were payments to the physician members of the organization was neither a private benefit, in violation of the operational test, nor was it private inurement, because the salaries were reasonable in the market. Further, salaries were not determined by the physician members, but by the Harvard formula.[30]

In a similar case involving the University of Maryland Medical School and the incorporation of its medical staff, the members of which both provided services at a teaching hospital affiliated with the medical school and taught in the medical school, the IRS argued that, because the organization was delivering general medical services and remunerating its physicians, it was a non-exempt organization.[31] As in *B.H.W. Anesthesia Foundation*, the Tax Court found that the organization was simply doing the work of the medical school and the hospital, and because they were tax exempt, so should the organization be tax exempt. The Tax Court brushed aside the IRS's concern that the organization was structured as a professional corporation, not typical of tax exempt structures, on the ground that state law required this form for the delivery of medical services. Nor did the presence of stockholders trouble the court, because, in the event of a dissolution, they would only receive the $1 par value of their shares, and the assets of the organization would be distributed to other charities.[32]

The Tax Court in *Redlands Surgical Services v. Commissioner*[33] determined that when an otherwise tax exempt hospital separately incorporates one of its departments, or its whole medical staff, which then form an integral part of the larger tax exempt organization, these separately incorporated organizations are entitled to their own tax exempt status so long as they are under the supervision or control of the larger entity and so long as they expressly limit their purposes to advancing the interests of the larger entity and serve no private interests. Unfortunately, this was not the case for Redland Surgery Center, which served the commercial interests of its for-profit partners more than the interests of its exempt affiliates.[34]

In *Geisinger Health Plan v. Commissioner*,[35] a health maintenance organization (HMO)[36] that did not qualify for tax exempt status on its own argued that it should still qualify for exempt status because it was an integral part of the multi-corporate Geisinger System, which did enjoy tax exempt status.[37] This is a slightly different use of the integral part test from that discussed in *B.H.W.*, *Redlands*, and *University of Maryland Physicians*. In previous cases, a department of a tax

---

[29] *Id* at 685.

[30] *Id.* at 686.

[31] Univ. of Md. Physicians, P.A. v. Comm'r, 41 T.C.M. (CCH) 732 (1981).

[32] *Id.*; *see also* Univ. of Mass. Med. Sch. Grp. Practice v. Comm'r, 74 T.C. 1299 (1980).

[33] 113 T.C. 47 (1999), *review denied*, 242 F.3d 904 (9th Cir. 2001) (per curiam).

[34] *Id.* at 92–93.

[35] 985 F.2d 1210 (3d Cir.) (*Geisinger II*), remanded, 100 T.C. 394 (1993) (*Geisinger III*), aff'd, 30 F.3d 494 (3d Cir. 1994) (*Geisinger IV*).

[36] See § 10.07 for further information on HMOs.

[37] *Geisinger II*, 985 F.2d 1210.

exempt hospital was separately incorporated by the hospital, and because it continued to do the work of the tax exempt hospital, of which it was an integral part, it qualified for its own tax exempt status.[38]

In *Geisinger*, the HMO was not a pre-existing part of the exempt healthcare provider. Rather, it was created as a part of the multi-corporate hospital to serve the healthcare needs of those in the Geisinger service area, and it did so by contracting for these services from other divisions of the exempt healthcare provider, and charging for them, arguably at discounted rates, to its subscribers. It provided no services itself, and 20 percent of its subscribers were not patients of the Geisinger System Hospitals.[39]

The test applied by the Tax Court was a simple one: did the HMO (the part), further the exempt purposes of the healthcare organization (the exempt whole)? Because approximately 20 percent of the HMO's patients were not patients of the System hospitals, the Tax Court concluded that, in providing these services, the HMO was not furthering the exempt purposes of the Geisinger system and could not claim integral part status.[40]

The Third Circuit, on review, applied a slightly different version of the integral part test. It said that the integral part test had two requirements: (1) the subordinate organization must not engage in activities that would constitute an unrelated trade or business if performed by the parent, and (2) the subordinate organization's relationship to the parent organization must boost or enhance the subordinate organization's ability to accomplish exempt purposes to such an extent that the subordinate organization could, on its own, qualify for exempt status. The Third Circuit found that the HMO's relationship with the hospital system did nothing to enhance the HMO's exempt activities, because the patients it served with the Geisinger relationship were the same patients it would serve without the Geisinger relationship. Without this boost to the HMO's ability to accomplish exempt purposes through its relationship with the Geisinger System, the Third Circuit concluded that the integral part test was not met, and denied it exempt status as an integral part of the larger exempt system.[41]

§ 10.04   HOSPITAL CONVERSIONS & PRIVATE INUREMENT

The non-profit, tax exempt hospital has obvious tax advantages that make it a preferable means for the delivery of healthcare services. In the case of *Harding Hospital v. United States*,[42] a for-profit, physician-owned psychiatric hospital wished to convert the enterprise into a non-profit, tax exempt hospital. The hospital's corporate articles were amended to make it a non-profit corporation,

---

[38] *B.H.W. Anesthesia Found.*, 72 T.C. 681; *Univ. of Md. Physicians*, 41 T.C.M. (CCH) 732; *Redlands Surgical Servs.*, 113 T.C. 47.

[39] *Geisinger IV*, 30 F.3d at 496.

[40] *Geisinger III*, 100 T.C. at 395.

[41] *Geisinger IV*, 30 F.3d at 498.

[42] 358 F. Supp. 805 (S.D. Ohio 1973), *aff'd*, 505 F.2d 1068 (6th Cir. 1974).

application was filed and granted for 501(c)(3) status, only to be later challenged by the IRS.[43]

By contract with the hospital, the former physician owners, the Harding-Evans Medical Associates, provided medical supervision, teaching, and supervision in the residency and other training programs, and also indigent patient treatment. Between 90 and 95 percent of the patients admitted to the hospital were patients of the Associates. The hospital also had a sweetheart rental arrangement with the Associates for office space, equipment and business office services, under which the Associates were paying vastly under market rates. The Board of Trustees of the hospital, while it had some connections with the former physician owners, was evidently not controlled by them.[44]

The district court and the Sixth Circuit had no trouble agreeing with the IRS that Harding Hospital did not merit tax exempt status on several grounds.[45] Indigent care was provided only after a patient's resources were exhausted. The fact that the overwhelming majority of patients were patients of the Associates indicated that the hospital was primarily benefiting the Associates, a private versus a public benefit. There was also a clear private benefit in the hospital's rental agreement with the Associates, and in the agreement for supervisory services. Under these circumstances, the operational test was clearly not met.[46]

While for-profit to non-profit tax exempt status conversions are possible in the hospital field, it is essential that all four tests (organizational, operational, private inurement, political activities) be complied with in the transformance.[47] Otherwise, the attempted transformation will not pass muster.[48]

Conversion of a tax exempt, nonprofit hospital to a for-profit, non-exempt organization is a much more difficult proposition.[49] The almost insurmountable difficulty will be the private inurement test, which requires that, upon dissolution of a tax exempt organization, the assets must go to another tax exempt organization. Apparently in order to avoid this dissolution requirement, the corporate directors of the Anclote Psychiatric Center, a 501(c)(3) hospital, sold the operating assets of the hospital to a for-profit corporation in which the directors owned all of the stock. The sale was for a modest amount, and left the tax exempt hospital corporation still in existence, holding a bag of cash, but basically without any operating assets. Two years later, the for-profit corporation sold the same assets to another for-profit

---

[43] *Id.* at 1070.

[44] *Id.*

[45] *Id.*

[46] *Id.*

[47] See § 6.01 *et seq.* for further information on the tests for tax exemption.

[48] *See Harding Hosp.*, 358 F. Supp. 805.

[49] *See* Fla. v. Anclote Manor Hosp., 566 So. 2d 296 (Fla. Dist. Ct. App. 1990). *See also* Queen of Angels Hosp. v. Younger, 66 Cal. App. 3d 359, 136 Cal. Rptr. 36 (1977), in which assets from the sale of a tax exempt hospital were not able to be distributed to the founding religious order, which also controlled the hospital corporation, but were held in trust for the corporation's exempt purposes; and *In re* Manhattan Eye, Ear & Throat Hosp. v. Spitzer, 715 N.Y.S.2d 575 (Sup. Ct. 1999), preventing the sale of a non-profit, tax exempt hospital on grounds that the sales price did not take into account goodwill for the hospital's name, or its business value.

corporation for five times what they had paid for them.[50] The attorney general of Florida was unsuccessful in seeking a disgorgement of profits by the directors, but the IRS did revoke the tax exempt status of the original hospital corporation on grounds that the first sale to the director-controlled for-profit caused a private benefit.[51] The IRS could have, but apparently did not, seek an excess benefit tax against the directors under IRC Section 4958.

The sale of tax exempt hospitals to for-profit operating corporations has become more and more common. There are various reasons why a tax exempt hospital would sell itself to a for-profit. Sometimes, it is simply that the tax exempt hospital is losing money and can no longer sustain its operations. Sometimes, the local healthcare market is such that small, stand-alone hospitals, facing a predatory competitive environment that they never had to face before, cannot compete effectively. Or tax exempt hospitals may take this route because it gives them access to capital through the for-profit that they would not otherwise have.[52] Whatever the reasons, the tax exempt issues will always be the same. The sale must be for fair market value or better, otherwise an impermissible private benefit has occurred. The proceeds of the sale must continue to be used for exempt purposes, otherwise the operational test and possibly the private inurement test will not be met.[53] For this last reason, there now exist a number of tax exempt foundations that use the income from the investment of tax exempt hospital sales proceeds to continue to provide some form of community benefit, such as operating neighborhood clinics or funding healthcare for those who cannot do so themselves.[54]

§ 10.05   HOSPITAL JOINT VENTURES

[A]   Hospital-Physician Joint Ventures

Even before the entry of for-profit providers into the hospital market, which was largely accelerated by the availability to providers of guaranteed governmental or third-party payments, hospitals were joint venturing with the physicians on their medical staffs. Because hospitals need patients, and because the source of patients is the admitting physician on the hospital medical staff, there was an obvious hospital self-interest in keeping these physicians happy.

In Revenue Ruling 69-383,[55] the IRS approved a hospital's payments to a hospital-based radiologist of a percentage of the hospital's radiology revenues in

---

[50] *Anclote Manor Hosp.*, 566 So. 2d at 297.

[51] *Id.*

[52] *See* Mancino, *supra* note 19; Crimm, *supra* note 6; Colombo & Hall, *supra* note 6; Gary J. Young, *Federal Tax-Exemption Requirements for Joint Ventures Between Nonprofit Hospital Providers and For-Profit Entities: Form over Substance?*, 13 ANN. HEALTH. L. 327 (2004).

[53] *See Anclote Manor Hosp.*, 556 So. 2d 296; *Queen of Angels Hosp.*, 66 Cal. App. 3d 359, 136 Cal. Rptr. 36; *In re Manhattan Eye, Ear and Throat Hosp.*, 715 N.Y.S.2d 575.

[54] *See* Att'y Gen. v. Hahnemann Hosp., 494 N.E.2d 1011 (Mass. 1986) (proceeds from the sale of an exempt hospital could be used to support other exempt health care providers, but not generalized health education or research).

[55] 1969-2 C.B. 113.

exchange for the radiologist's management and professional services.[56] In approving this arrangement, the IRS warned that percentage forms of compensation by a tax exempt organization were not acceptable when they had the effect of transforming the organization into a joint venture with the percentage-payees or where they were disguised forms of distributing profits. The IRS also pointed out that, if such percentage arrangements resulted in unreasonable compensation they would be impermissible forms of private inurement.[57]

In General Counsel Memorandum 37789, the IRS again took up hospital-physician joint ventures.[58] A tax exempt hospital wished to lease some land adjacent to the hospital to members of its medical staff, on which they would build a physicians' office building. The lease amount was nominal, $1 a year, and the hospital was planning on lending the physicians some of the construction costs at market rates. The IRS found that this arrangement provided a private benefit to the physicians in the form of the nominal rental amount, and warned that the hospital could not maintain its tax exempt status if it went ahead with the transaction.[59]

In General Counsel Memorandum 39732, the IRS approved an exempt hospital participating as a general partner with physicians from its medical staff to establish: "(1) a free-standing physical therapy center, (2) a free standing ambulatory surgery center, and (3) a magnetic resonance imaging facility."[60] None of these facilities was currently in existence, so their creation would improve the health of the community, and the joint venture would be the owner of these endeavors, subject to all the risks, responsibilities, and rewards.[61]

In General Counsel Memorandum 39862,[62] the IRS took up a much more complicated form of hospital-physician joint venture in which the tax exempt hospital sought to establish a for-profit corporation, the stock of which would be jointly owned by the hospital and staff physicians. This for-profit would then be a general partner in four limited partnerships, also formed with staff physicians, that would operate the hospital's outpatient surgery department; its outpatient diagnostic department; its ophthalmology department; and its cardiac nuclear medicine department; and the for-profit would share in the partnerships' revenue streams to the extent those streams exceeded current levels. The hospital claimed that this arrangement was in furtherance of its exempt purpose because it would make the partnered departments more efficient. In this situation, the IRS said, "these arrangements, despite their joint venture cloak, are merely an arrangement between an exempt hospital and its medical staff physicians through which the

---

[56] *Id.* Due to changes in reimbursement formulas, such income splits are no longer feasible.

[57] *Id.*

[58] I.R.S. Gen. Couns. Mem. 37789 (Dec. 18, 1978).

[59] *Id.*

[60] I.R.S. Gen. Couns. Mem. 39732 (May 19, 1988).

[61] *Id.* I.R.S. Gen. Couns. Mem. 37789 followed the ruling in *Plumstead Theatre Society, Inc. v. Commissioner,* 74 T.C. 1324 (1980), in which The Tax Court overturned IRS's position that participation by an exempt organization in a general partnership was inconsistent with exempt status.

[62] I.R.S. Gen. Couns. Mem. 39862 (Nov. 22, 1991).

hospital shares its net profits from the designated activities with the physicians. The partnership's only true function is to purchase, receive, and distribute the net revenue stream from the activity. A hospital's participation in this type of partnership does not clearly further any exempt purpose."[63]

From the development of the law in this area, it seems that hospital-physician joint ventures are possible where they create new methods of delivering healthcare to the community, but not where they simply repackage existing realities in a way that rewards the physicians through the use of the hospital's exempt status. And obviously, the operational test, in the form of no private benefit and the private inurement test, are always applicable to these transactions.[64]

[B] Physician Recruitment & Acquisition of Physician Practices

Although they are not joint ventures, strictly speaking, very often the agreements that hospitals strike in their attempt to recruit certain physicians to their medical staffs involve the hospital subsidizing the physician's private practice. While it did not involve a recruiting hospital, Revenue Ruling 73-313[65] did establish that a community organization founded to raise funds and build a medical office building in order to attract physicians to an area where there were none could qualify for tax exempt status. As long as there was a demonstrable community need, evidence that lack of an office building had frustrated physician recruitment efforts, negotiations with the physician were at arm's length, and the physician was not in any way connected with persons in the organization, the IRS agreed that such an organization was helping to promote and protect the health of the community.[66]

In a rather extensive Revenue Ruling[67] on the physician recruitment practices of tax exempt hospitals, the IRS approved such hospital practices as providing signing bonuses, below-market office rental rates for a limited number of years, mortgage guarantees, loans at reasonable terms to start a practice, reimbursement for tail coverage at the physician's prior practice, or other personal liability insurance, and income guarantees (within fair market ranges) for a limited number of years.[68] The facts of the various situations described in the ruling seem to indicate that as long as there is a true need for the physician's services in the hospital's service area, the negotiations are at arm's length and are overseen by the hospital board or are pursued according to clear board-established policies and do not result in unreasonable compensation to the physician, then such recruitment policies do not jeopardize the hospital's tax exempt status.[69]

---

[63] *Id.*

[64] See §§ 6.03 and 6.04 for further information on the operational and private inurement tests.

[65] 1973-2 C.B. 147.

[66] *Id.*

[67] Rev. Rul. 97-21, 1997-1 C.B. 121.

[68] *Id.*

[69] *Id.*

In an attempt to guarantee that they will continue to receive patients from physician practices, exempt hospitals have also engaged in the purchase of physician's private practices, in which they pay the physician for the practice, the patients of the practice become patients of a hospital-based practice, and the physician becomes the employee of the hospital, and continues to see patients much as before. Under the Medicare and Medicaid anti-kickback statute, however, hospitals may not pay physicians for future referrals to the hospital.[70]

[C] Integrated Delivery Systems

Buying practices seems to be a permissible way around the anti-kickback law, but it is still not without peril to the hospital's exempt status.[71] When tax exempt hospitals purchase and then continue to operate physician practices as a part of their overall charitable purpose, namely to benefit the community through the promotion of health, they are creating an integrated delivery system, which simply means that the diagnostic and other types of primary care that were delivered by for-profit physicians operating their own practices are now integrated into the tax exempt hospital's own healthcare operations, so that the hospital is the provider of all healthcare from the office visit to any necessary hospital follow-up. Because the physicians' practices have been integrated into the hospital's healthcare delivery system, these arrangements are called integrated delivery systems.[72]

Normally such integrated delivery systems do not jeopardize the hospital's tax exempt status. There are dangers in such arrangements, in the private benefit and private inurement areas.[73] The tests for tax exempt status still apply to these integrated delivery systems, and physician practice acquisitions by a tax exempt hospital must be at arm's length, for market rates, and in furtherance of the hospital's exempt purposes. The salaries that the physician-employees are paid by the hospital for operating these hospital-based practices cannot exceed market rates. When hospitals overpay for practices or for physicians' services, they are engaging in private benefit transactions that can, if egregious enough, deprive them of their exempt status[74] or result in the lesser penalty of intermediate sanctions.[75]

---

[70] 42 U.S.C. § 1320a-7b(b) outlines the criminal penalties for acts involving federal healthcare programs.

[71] See the following law review articles for further information on the current state of tax exempt hospitals: Aitsebaomo, *supra* note 6; Crimm, *supra* note 6; Colombo & Hall, *supra* note 6; Mancino, *supra* note 19; and Clark, *supra* note 19.

[72] *See* Carl H. Hitchner et al., *Integrated Delivery Systems: A Survey of Organizational Models*, 29 WAKE FOREST L. REV. 273 (1994). *See also* Spencer Rich, *U.S. Hospitals Aren't Waiting for Congress*, WASH. POST, June 21, 1994, at A4, which cites an accounting firm survey where seventy one percent of all hospitals are developing integrated delivery systems.

[73] See § 6.04[D] for further information on private benefit and private inurement.

[74] Tech. Adv. Mem. 9451001 (Dec. 23, 1994).

[75] 26 U.S.C. § 4958. See § 6.06 for further information on intermediate sanctions.

[D] Hospital-Hospital Joint Ventures

Some tax exempt hospitals have sought partnerships with for-profit health care providers, usually the large for-profit hospital chains, in order to survive in the highly competitive health care market.[76] Revenue Ruling 98-15[77] outlines the circumstances under which the IRS will recognize that a tax exempt hospital can enter a joint venture with a for-profit healthcare provider and still maintain its tax exempt status.

Revenue Ruling 98-15 contrasts two different joint venture situations, involving a tax exempt hospital and a for-profit health care provider. In the first situation, the tax exempt hospital facility would be operated by the joint venture between the tax exempt hospital and the for-profit partner. The tax exempt hospital controlled the board of directors of the joint venture, and the board had extensive oversight powers. The governing documents could not be altered without the direct action of the exempt hospital, and the documents committed the joint venture to the charitable mission of the exempt hospital. Also, in the first situation, there was an arm's-length management contract, at market rates, for a fixed term, renewable only by mutual consent, and an independent management company ran the day-to-day affairs of the joint venture. None of the key people in the tax exempt partner accepted inducements from the for-profit to agree to the joint venture, and the tax exempt partner used the income from the joint venture to carry on charitable, health-care-related activities.[78]

What the IRS was setting up in the first situation was a tax exempt organization that was in control of the joint venture and that had sufficient corporate power in the joint venture to ensure that it was going to continue to deliver healthcare that would benefit the community. All of the details supplied by the IRS in its description of this first situation, the structure and binding priorities of the new company's governing board, the arm's length management agreement with a third party, the lack of financial inducements to the tax exempt organization's officers and key employees, and what the tax exempt will do with its earnings, have that purpose: to demonstrate that the joint venture is effectively controlled by the tax exempt partner and that it will continue to provide a public, as opposed to a private, benefit that advances the health of the community. In the first situation, the tax exempt partner retains its tax exempt status.[79]

In the second situation, the tax exempt hospital did not have control or oversight powers for the joint venture. The tax exempt partner only had a reactive role on founding document changes, and the documents did not commit the joint venture to any specific charitable mission. There also was a management agreement in the second situation presented in Revenue Ruling 98-15, but it was with a subsidiary of

---

[76] *See* Young, *supra* note 52.

[77] 1998-1 C.B. 718.

[78] *Id.*

[79] *Id.*; *see also* Young, *supra* note 52; Eileen M. Newell, *Healthcare Joint Ventures: Pushing Tax-Exempt Law to the Limits?*, 18 J. CONTEMP. HEALTH L. & POL'Y 467 (2002); Darryll K. Jones, *Special Allocations and Preferential Distributions in Joint Ventures Involving Taxable and Tax Exempt Entities*, 31 OHIO N.U.L. REV. 13 (2005).

the for-profit partner, it did not have a fixed term, and the rates were merely a percentage of the joint venture's income. Additionally, the tax exempt partner had agreed in advance to approve as CEO and CFO of the joint venture persons with ties to the for-profit partner, and the tax exempt partner used the income from the joint venture for charitable, health-care-related purposes.[80]

In this second situation, the tax exempt organization is not in control in the joint venture, and there is no guarantee the contributed assets will be used by the new company for exempt purposes. In fact, they appear to be being used for the benefit of the for-profit partner, which of course is a private use. The management contract favors the for-profit partner, and is basically non-terminable by the new company, which is another private benefit. The joint venture will be led by individuals whose first loyalty is to the for-profit partner. As a result, the tax exempt hospital that participates in this joint venture will lose its tax exempt status, because it clearly fails the operational test.[81]

The applicable law is that a tax exempt organization may enter a partnership or joint venture and still meet the operational test if participation in the joint venture furthers an exempt charitable purpose, and the structure permits the tax exempt organization to act exclusively in furtherance of its exempt purposes and only incidentally for the benefit of for-profit partners. The tax exempt partner in the first situation in Revenue Ruling 98-15 certainly met this burden; the tax exempt partner in the second did not.[82]

Tax exempt organizations can also engage management companies to conduct activities on behalf of the tax exempt organization and even to direct the use of the tax exempt's assets, as long as the tax exempt organization keeps ultimate authority over the assets and activities being managed. This is the case in the first situation; it is not the case in the second.[83]

Revenue Ruling 98-15 was long awaited to clear up what tax exempt hospitals could do in joint ventures with for-profits. The revenue ruling is clearly based on a contrast of control. In the first situation, the tax exempt partner is in control. In the second, it is not. The problem with it, however, is that it describes two extreme examples, leaving the middle ground unexplored. The answers to questions such as where does a tax exempt organization cross the line in ceding power in the new company to the for-profit partner; how much power is too much power to give the for-profit partner; and how many governance powers must the tax exempt organization maintain so that the joint venture acts exclusively in pursuit of its exempt purposes remain unclear.

In *Redlands Surgical Services v. Commissioner*,[84] a tax exempt hospital, through a complicated corporate and partnership structure, operated an ambulatory surgical center with for-profit partners. Nothing in the structure of the

---

[80] Rev. Rul. 98-15, 1998-1 C.B. 718.

[81] *Id.*

[82] *Id.*

[83] *Id.*; *see also Plumstead Theatre Soc'y*, 74 T.C. 1324.

[84] 113 T.C. 47 (1999).

partnership agreement expressly or impliedly obliged the for-profit parties to put charitable objectives first. The tax exempt partner did not have formal voting control in the partnership, nor did it have any other formal or informal control that would allow it to ensure furtherance of its charitable purposes. A management contract actually gave the for-profit parties control over day-to-day affairs and an incentive to maximize profits. The overall effect of the partnership was to give the for-profit parties market advantages and competitive benefits. These factors were enough for the court to find that the tax exempt partner was furthering private, as opposed to public, interests by entering into this partnership, and that it no longer qualified as tax exempt.[85]

In *St. David's Health Care System, Inc. v. United States*,[86] a tax exempt hospital in Austin, Texas, entered a joint venture with Columbia/HCA, a for-profit healthcare corporation that also operated hospitals in the Austin area. The joint venture controlled and jointly operated both St. David's and HCA's Austin-area hospitals. The IRS concluded that, as a result of its partnership with HCA, St. David's no longer qualified as tax exempt. St. David's appealed to the Federal District Court, which ruled in St. David's favor, holding that, in a complex corporate arrangement, St. David's had maintained control of the joint enterprise.[87] The IRS appealed.[88]

The Fifth Circuit focused on whether or not St. David's continued to meet the operational test.[89] It cited the well-known statement of that test: "The presence of a single non-exempt purpose, if substantial in nature, will destroy the exemption regardless of the number or importance of truly exempt purposes."[90] The Circuit then focused on the control of the joint venture, saying, "when the non-profit organization cedes control over the partnership to the for-profit entity, we assume that the partnership's activities substantially further the for-profit's interests. . . . Conversely, if the non-profit organization . . . retains control, we presume that the non-profit's activities via the partnership primarily further exempt purposes."[91] This statement of the standard by the Fifth Circuit was a subtle, but important shift. The question was now whether the exempt hospital had ceded control to its for-profit partner, and not whether it had maintained control.

The circuit court then performed a detailed analysis of the corporate structure of the joint venture. It did not agree with the district court that St. David's controlled the joint venture, but it did not find that it had ceded control to the for-profit partner, either. Rather, holding that the district court had been too quick to find that St. David's had maintained control, it said that material questions of fact still existed and it vacated the lower court's ruling in St. David's favor and sent the

[85] *Id.* at 93.

[86] 2002-2 U.S. Tax Cas. (CCH) ¶ 50,745, 90 A.F.T.R.2d (RIA) 6878, *vacated and remanded*, 349 F.3d 232 (5th Cir. 2003).

[87] *Id.*

[88] 349 F.3d 232.

[89] *Id.* at 235.

[90] Better Bus. Bureau of D.C. v. United States, 326 U.S. 279, 283 (1945).

[91] *St. David's Health Care Sys.*, 349 F.3d at 238.

case back for further fact-finding proceedings. In a jury trial, it was found that St. David's had not ceded control and was entitled to keep its exemption.

Due to the current economic climate in healthcare, it is reasonable to expect that joint ventures between tax exempt hospitals and for-profit chains will continue to be created. It is important that the professionals who structure such joint ventures have a clear legal standard to guide their efforts in maintaining the tax exempt status of the tax exempt partner. Because the for-profit partner has an ownership interest in the joint venture, there is no question that the joint venture itself cannot qualify as tax exempt. But the joint venture will be providing an income stream to the tax exempt organization, and that income may qualify as tax exempt under certain circumstances.[92]

At the present time, the standard is: Who controls the joint venture? Does it primarily further the exempt purposes of the tax exempt partner or the non-exempt purposes of the for-profit partner? If the answers to these questions are that the tax exempt organization is in control, or at least that it has not ceded control, and that the joint venture primarily furthers exempt purposes, then the tax exempt partner may maintain its tax exempt status, even though it is participating with a for-profit partner in a non-tax exempt joint venture.[93]

In Revenue Ruling 2004-51,[94] in a non-hospital joint venture, the IRS dealt with a university that had contributed not all, but a part, of its assets to a joint venture formed with a for-profit that produced interactive videos for teacher training.[95] The joint venture had a 50-50 board, but the university controlled the academic portion of the joint venture's activities, while the for-profit provided and controlled production expertise. The IRS held that the joint venture did not change the university's exempt status, implying that 50-50 control of the joint venture is acceptable as long as the exempt partner controls the charitable aspects of the joint venture.[96] The effect that this revenue ruling will have on hospital joint ventures is not clear, but it certainly opens a door to an analysis that bifurcates the activities of a joint venture between nonprofit (i.e., exempt) and for-profit (i.e., non-exempt) activities. It would also look at which partner controls the exempt activities. If the exempt partner controls the exempt activities, evidently the joint venture will not endanger the tax exemption of the nonprofit partner.

[E]   Shared Services Organizations

Prior to 1968, the law on the tax exempt status of shared hospital services organizations was unclear. It was the IRS's position that if two or more hospitals created an organization to perform shared services for them in the same way that a commercial organization would provide those services, the organization did not

---

[92] Rev. Rul. 98-15, 1998-1 C.B. 718; *Plumstead Theatre Soc'y*, 74 T.C. 1324; *Redlands Surgical Servs.*, 113 T.C. 47; *St. David's Health Care Sys.*, 349 F.3d 232.

[93] *Id.*

[94] 2004-22 I.R.B. 974.

[95] *Id.*

[96] *Id.*

qualify for its own tax exemption.[97] The Court of Claims rejected the IRS's position in *Hospital Bureau of Standards and Supplies, Inc. v. United States*.[98] Because of this uncertainty in the law, Congress enacted Section 501(e) of the IRC. Under Section 501(e), two or more tax exempt hospitals or other types of tax exempt healthcare providers, such as the outpatient section of a county health department,[99] can form cooperative service providers, and those cooperative service providers will qualify for tax exempt status under certain circumstances. First, the organization must be a cooperative, i.e., owned by the participating tax exempt healthcare organizations and paying all net earnings to them. Second, it must perform services for its member hospitals, which, if the hospitals performed them, would be considered services in furtherance of their exempt purposes. Third, the shared services must consist of either data processing, purchasing (including group purchasing), warehousing, billing and collection, food, clinical, industrial engineering, laboratory, printing, communications, record center, or personnel (including selection, testing, training, and education) services.[100]

After some initial confusion, this statutory list has been held to be exhaustive, and not illustrative, by the courts.[101] A hospital cooperative laundry service argued that it could still qualify as a tax exempt organization on its own, under the general charitable language of Section 501(c)(3), regardless of Section 501(e)'s failure to mention laundry services. Using this argument, a shared hospital laundry services cooperative sought tax exemption under Section 501(e), and was denied exemption by the IRS. The district court ruled in the laundry's favor.[102] The Third Circuit reversed,[103] holding that Section 501(e) was the exclusive means by which a cooperative hospital service organization could qualify as tax exempt, and that the omission of shared laundry services from 501(e)'s list was determinative. The United States Supreme Court adopted the Third Circuit's reasoning.[104] Its opinion relied heavily on the fact that, in the legislative history of Section 501(e), laundries had been proposed for inclusion, but that Congress had specifically chosen not to place them on the list of 501(e) organizations. In effect, the United States Supreme Court's opinion holds that, as to cooperative services performed for tax exempt healthcare organizations, the language of Section 501(e) limits the more general language of Section 501(c)(3).[105]

---

[97] Rev. Rul. 54-305, 1954-2 C.B. 127.

[98] 158 F. Supp. 560 (Ct. Cl. 1958). In this case several member hospitals worked together to provide the service of procuring supplies and researching the most efficient use and maintenance of hospital supplies. The court found that the hospitals did not operate for a pecuniary profit and that the hospitals were not operating for the primary purpose of carrying on a trade or business for profit. *Id.* at 564.

[99] I.R.S. GCM 39692 (Jan. 19, 1988).

[100] I.R.C. § 501(e).

[101] *See* Hosp. Cent. Servs. Ass'n v. United States, 623 F.2d 611 (9th Cir. 1980) (holding that a shared laundry services organizations do not did qualify for tax exemption). *But see* N. Cal. Cent. Servs., Inc. v. United States, 591 F.2d 620 (Ct. Cl. 1979); United Hosp. Servs., Inc. v. United States, 384 F. Supp. 776 (S.D. Ind. 1974) (holding that they do).

[102] HCSC-Laundry v. United States, 473 F. Supp. 250 (E.D. Pa. 1979).

[103] 624 F.2d 428 (3d Cir. 1980).

[104] 450 U.S. 1 (1981).

[105] *Id*; *see also* I.R.C. § 501(c)(3), (e).

§ 10.06   HOMES FOR THE AGED

Much as with hospitals, the IRS's first approach to homes for the aged was that only those that provided care to the elderly for free or below cost could qualify as charitable institutions.[106] This approach was modified slightly a few years later, when the IRS ruled in Revenue Ruling 61-72[107] that a home for the aged was exempt from federal income tax if it provided residential care to the elderly who could not do so for themselves, at substantially below cost, and whose services ministered to the needs and the relief of hardship or distress of aged individuals.[108] In 1964, Revenue Ruling 64-231[109] dealt with the fact that many homes for the elderly charged entrance fees and life-care fees, and the IRS ruled that such fees had to be taken into account to determine whether homes for the aged met the below-cost requirements of tax exempt status.[110]

There was a significant change in the IRS's position in 1972. The IRS no longer relied on the availability of free or below-cost care for the elderly as a basis for tax exempt status. Rather, the IRS recognized in Revenue Ruling 72-124[111] that the elderly, completely apart from considerations of financial need, were a bona fide recipient of charity simply because of their advanced years. In this regard, the IRS said that the elderly had three primary needs: (1) the need for housing, (2) the need for health care, and (3) the need for financial security, and that an organization that met these needs was operating for tax exempt, charitable purposes.[112]

The need for housing was met, the IRS said, if the organization provided residential facilities for the elderly that met their physical, emotional, recreational, social, religious, or similar needs. The need for healthcare was met if the organization either itself provided some form of health care, or if it had some continuing arrangement with another facility or health professionals that would help to maintain the physical and mental health of its residents. The need for financial security, which the IRS described as "the aged person's need for protection against the financial risks associated with the later years of life,"[113] was met if the organization met two conditions. The first condition is that the organization have an established policy of maintaining in residence any persons who become unable to pay their regular charges. The second condition is that the organization operate so as to provide its services to the elderly at the lowest feasible cost, taking into account the organization's financial resources and requirements. Organizations that provide discounted rates for persons of limited means, who they do not evict when they are unable to pay, are presumed to be meeting the need for financial security. If an organization meets the three needs of the aged, for housing, for healthcare,

---

[106] Rev. Rul. 57-467, 1957-2 C.B. 313. A home for the aged which did not accept charity cases and discharged patients who failed to meet monthly payments did not qualify as tax exempt.

[107] 1961-1 C.B. 188.

[108] *Id.*

[109] 1964-2 C.B. 139.

[110] *Id.*

[111] 1972-1 C.B. 145.

[112] *Id.*

[113] *Id.*

and for financial security, it merits tax exempt status even though it charges for its services.[114]

Since 1972, organizations that provide residential care for the elderly have seen the same changes in healthcare delivery that tax exempt hospitals have experienced, including the proliferation of for-profit nursing homes. One way that tax exempt nursing homes have tried to cope with this increasingly competitive market is by expanding their own services, beyond residential care, to include assisted living facilities, which then serve as feeder programs for their residential care facilities. Assisted living facilities typically provide assistance with the normal aspects of daily life, usually in separate, but connected, living units, where some communal activities also take place. As long as these assisted living facilities meet the three needs of the elderly for housing, health care, and financial security, they may qualify for exempt status.[115]

In Revenue Ruling 79-18,[116] the IRS recognized the exempt status of an organization that constructed and operated apartment units that were specially designed for the needs of elderly residents. The apartments had entry ramps, wide doorways, railings, special grab bars in the restrooms, and other safety features. There was 24-hour-a-day emergency medical coverage and transportation for medical visits. The apartment manager ran social and recreational programs for residents. Residents were 65 or older and did pay a rental charge. Admission was limited to those who could pay, but once a person was admitted to an apartment unit, the organization was committed to maintaining them, regardless of their ability to pay, to the extent possible. Charges were set at the lowest feasible cost, keeping in mind the need for some reserve funds. The organization was governed by a community board, consisting of civic leaders and others with a specialized interest in the elderly.[117]

The IRS found that this organization did meet the special needs of the elderly by providing safe housing, specially designed for the elderly, at a cost that was affordable to a large number of elderly in the area, and by its commitment not to evict elderly residents once they could no longer pay its fees.[118] Skilled nursing homes that serve not just an aged population, but anyone with round-the-clock healthcare needs not requiring hospitalization are generally considered exempt organizations on the basis that they are promoting the health of the community,

---

[114] *Id.* After this 1972 classification of the elderly as bona fide objects of charity, a spate of other, non-healthcare related rulings followed: Rev. Rul. 75-198, 1975-1 C.B. 157 (recognizes the exempt status of senior centers that operated recreational centers for the elderly and provided counseling service to the elderly for their special needs); Rev. Rul. 75-385, 1975-2 C.B. 205 (recognizes the exempt status of a rural retreat that provided, for a nominal charge, two week vacations for the elderly in the country); Rev. Rul. 76-244, 1976-1 C.B. 155 (recognizes the exempt status of a home meal delivery service for the elderly and handicapped that operated at or below cost); Rev. Rul. 77-42, 1977-1 C.B. 141 (recognizes the exempt status of an organization that provides free, non-commercial and educational closed circuit radio broadcasts to the elderly); Rev. Rul. 77-246, 1977-2 C.B. 190 (recognizes the exempt status of an organization that provides bus transportation for the elderly and handicapped).

[115] Rev. Rul. 72-124, 1972-1 C.B. 145.

[116] 1979-1 C.B. 194.

[117] *Id.*

[118] *Id.*

much as non-profit hospitals qualify. They provide their patients not just with a place to live, but with 24/7 nursing and medical care. Very often they serve as a step-down facility for patients recovering from hospital-based surgery and serve those with chronic illnesses or serious medical needs who are incapable of caring for themselves.[119]

Recent years have seen the development of community care retirement communities to serve the elderly. These organizations engage in the selling or rental of apartments or condominiums (usually on a revolving basis, i.e., the organization retains a right of repurchase and may participate in the unit's appreciation) on a planned campus that gives older individuals the freedom of their own residence but with a sense of community. The campus may include golf, tennis, swimming pool, or other recreational opportunities. When the health of a resident is at a point where they require it, the community care retirement community can provide them with assisted living services, such as prepared meals, in-home medical care, on-site physicians, preventive health and wellness programs, physical therapy, and transportation services to their apartments or condominiums. If and when elderly residents are physically unable to maintain their own residences any longer, they are eligible for residential care in an on-site skilled nursing home, operated by the organization. At that point, their original unit is sold, and the sale proceeds from their original apartments or condominiums are used to support this residential care. It is possible, of course, for such community care retirement communities to meet the same three needs of the elderly: housing, healthcare, and financial security, and qualify residential care facilities for tax exemption. This will even be the case when the facilities consist of condominiums or apartments that are sold or rented to the elderly at market rates.[120]

§ 10.07   HEALTH MAINTENANCE ORGANIZATIONS

Health maintenance organizations (HMOs) provide their members or subscribers with all of their healthcare needs, from doctor's visits to diagnostic tests to hospitalization, in return for a monthly charge. HMO members have a primary care physician in the HMO who serves as the "gatekeeper" and who basically decides what medical services a member needs. Using its members as a bargaining base, an HMO can contract with primary care physicians and hospitals in bulk, driving down health care costs. Or at least that is the theory.[121]

Originally, the IRS was reluctant to grant HMOs status as Section 501(c)(3) organizations because they typically benefit only their members which constitutes a private, and not a public, benefit and because their insurance activities appeared to be more commercial than charitable. The IRS did agree that the HMOs might qualify for Section 501(c)(4) status as social welfare organizations.[122]

---

[119] *Id.*

[120] P.L.R. 9540067 (May 19, 1995).

[121] *See* Amanda N. Hill, *Tax-Exempt Status Denied to HMOs Owned by Tax-Exempt Corporation,* 30 J.L. MED. & ETHICS 118 (2002); Theresa McMahon, *Fair Value? The Conversion of Nonprofit HMOs,* 30 U.S.F. L. REV. 355 (1996).

[122] *See* Sound Health Assn. v. Comm'r, 71 T.C. 158, 159 (1978), *acq.* 1981-2 C.B. 2.

But then, the IRS agreed in Revenue Ruling 69-545[123] that the promotion of health was "one of the purposes in the general law of charity that is deemed beneficial to the community as a whole even though the class of beneficiaries eligible to receive a direct benefit from its activities does not include all members of the community, such as indigent members of the community, provided that the class is not so small that its relief is not of benefit to the community."[124] This appeared to open the door to Section 501(c)(3) status for HMOs.

There are two basic types of HMOs: the staff model and the network model. In the staff model, the HMO has its own medical staff consisting of physicians whom it employs to care for its members. In the network model, the HMO does not employ any physicians, but rather contracts with them, usually at discounted or volume rates, to provide healthcare to its members. The medical staff model HMO is more analogous to a hospital than the network model, which more resembles an insurance carrier.[125]

The IRS does recognize some staff model HMOs as tax exempt 501(c)(3) organizations, provided that they serve a public rather than a private interest. To serve a public interest, the HMO must satisfy the same community benefit requirement that the IRS imposes on hospitals seeking exemption. The IRS will examine the HMO's operations in their entirety to make this determination.[126]

In *Sound Health Association v. Commissioner*,[127] the Tax Court applied the law pertaining to tax exempt hospitals in deciding an HMO's exempt status. Sound Health was structured as a tax exempt organization. Its articles of incorporation committed it to the promotion of the health of the community. But the major questions were: (1) was it operated as a tax exempt organization? (2) did it promote the health of the community? or (3) did it serve the private interests of its members? Sound Health qualified because it employed doctors, healthcare providers, and medical personnel who were not affiliated with the HMO to provide healthcare to its subscribers. The court found it significant that Sound Health provided healthcare services both to subscribers and to members of the general public through its outpatient clinic where both subscribers and all emergency patients were treated, regardless of their ability to pay. It also provided some free healthcare to non-subscribers, subsidized the dues of some needy subscribers, conducted research and ran programs to educate the general public on health matters. This is the staff model HMO, which operates very much like a tax exempt hospital, and the fact situation is very close to that of Revenue Ruling 69-545,[128] which formed the obvious basis for the Tax Court's finding that Sound Health qualified as a tax exempt charitable organization in that it provided a benefit to the whole community,

---

[123] 1969-2 C.B. 117.

[124] *Id.*

[125] See Tech. Adv. Mem. 9451001 (Dec. 23, 1994) for a discussion of how the IRS classifies staff physicians in these situations.

[126] *See* Rev. Rul. 83-157, 1983-2 C.B. 94.

[127] 71 T.C. 158 (1978).

[128] 1969-2 C.B. 117.

and not just its subscribers.[129]

In *Geisinger Health Plan v. Commissioner*,[130] the HMO was the network model.[131] Geisinger did not employ its own physicians, rather it contracted for their services; and in effect, repackaged these services to its subscribers at the reduced rate it had negotiated with the physicians. This seemed very much like a simple insurance plan to the IRS, and the IRS ruled that the Geisinger HMO did not qualify for tax exempt status. Geisinger appealed and the Tax Court reversed the Commissioner's decision.[132] The IRS appealed to the Third Circuit, which reversed the Tax Court and upheld the IRS's decision that Geisinger did not qualify for tax exempt status. The Third Circuit saw, in Geisinger's limitation of benefits to subscribers only, a fatal flaw. That meant that the HMO was operating for a private, not a public, interest, and did not pass the operational test. While Geisinger did have a plan to eventually benefit some needy non-subscribers, the court dismissed this effort as minuscule.[133]

As the law develops, the distinction that is being drawn by the IRS and the courts is that staff model HMOs, found to promote the health of the general public, can qualify for tax exempt status because of their similarities to tax exempt hospitals. Network model HMOs, on the other hand, are more similar to a form of health insurance that benefits only subscribers, and such health insurance plans do not qualify for exempt status. In fact, Congress added Section 501(m) to the IRC in 1986 specifically to take away the tax exempt status of Blue Cross-Blue Shield-type organizations that provided commercial-type insurance.[134]

This distinction was affirmed in the case of *IHC Health Plans, Inc. v. Commissioner*,[135] where the Tax Court upheld the IRS's position that an HMO that contracted for physicians' services for its subscribers, from a hospital system that was tax exempt, did not itself qualify for exempt status.[136]

§ 10.08 MEDICAL RESEARCH ORGANIZATIONS

Under Section 170(b)(1)(A)(iii), medical research organizations are a type of charitable health care organization. An organization qualifies as a tax exempt medical research organization if it has medical research as its principal purpose or function and is directly engaged in the continuous, active conduct of medical

---

[129] *Sound Health Ass'n*, 71 T.C. at 186.

[130] *Geisinger II*, 985 F.2d 1210. While it denied the HMO tax exempt status in its own right, the Third Circuit remanded to the Tax Court for a determination of whether the HMO could qualify for exemption under the integral part test. See § 10.03 for further information on the integral parts test.

[131] See § 10.03 for an analysis of *Geisinger Health Plan v. Commissioner* under the integral parts doctrine. In this case, Geisinger used an integral parts doctrine argument only after it was found not to qualify as a tax exempt HMO organization.

[132] *Geisinger II*, 985 F.2d 1210.

[133] *Id.*

[134] *See* I.R.C. § 501(m); IHC Health Plans, Inc. v. Comm'r, T.C. Memo 2001-246, *aff'd*, 325 F.3d 1188 (10th Cir. 2003).

[135] *Id.*

[136] *Id.* at 1202.

research in conjunction with a tax exempt hospital.[137] Medical research organizations at for-profit hospitals do not qualify.[138] Joint efforts with a tax exempt hospital mean that the medical research organization conducts research at a space within or adjacent to the hospital, is allowed to regularly use hospital facilities, and that its researchers closely cooperate with the medical staff of the exempt hospital.[139]

Medical research involves the conduct of investigations, experiments, and studies to discover, develop, or verify knowledge regarding the causes, diagnosis, treatment, prevention, or control of both physical and mental illnesses.[140] An organization meets the principal purpose or function requirement if it either devotes a substantial part of its assets or expends a significant percentage of its endowment for medical research.[141] An organization that simply pays for medical research to be done by other organizations but does not do any medical research itself does not qualify.[142]

Devoting a substantial part of its assets to medical research means that the organization uses more than one-half of its assets for that purpose.[143] Devoting a significant percentage of its endowment for medical research means that the organization expends at least 3.5 percent of the fair market value of its endowment annually for that purpose.[144]

---

[137] 26 C.F.R. § 1.170A-9(d)(2)(ii).

[138] Rev. Rul. 66-245, 1966-2 C.B. 71.

[139] 26 C.F.R. § 1.170A-9(d)(2)(vii).

[140] 26 C.F.R. § 1.170A-9(d)(2)(iii).

[141] 26 C.F.R. § 1.170A-9(d)(2)(v).

[142] 26 C.F.R. § 1.170A-9(d)(2)(i).

[143] 26 C.F.R. § 1.170A-9(d)(2)(v)(B). There is a four-year computation period for this. 26 C.F.R. § 1.170A-9(c)(2)(vi)(a).

[144] 26 C.F.R. § 1.170A-9(d)(2)(v)(B). There is also a four-year computation period for this. 26 C.F.R. § 1.170A-9(d)(2)(vi)(A).

Chapter 11

ARTS ORGANIZATIONS

§ 11.01 INTRODUCTION

The term "art" or "arts organization" does not appear in IRC Section 501(c)(3), nor is it mentioned in Section 170 on charitable gifts. But organizations that promote the arts can, in fact, qualify for tax exempt status, either as charitable organizations, in the "generally accepted legal sense" of that term for purposes of Section 501(c)(3) or as educational organizations.[1] Defining "promotion of the arts" through the eyes of the IRC has not been an easy task. The IRS has attempted to do so through two well-known Revenue Rulings. In the first, Revenue Ruling 64-174,[2] a foundation was formed for "charitable, educational and literary purposes," and in furtherance of these purposes, it created "interest in the development of the American theater in areas other than New York City, by aiding local communities to establish their own charitable and educational repertory theaters."[3] Although the foundation did not itself operate a theater or direct or produce plays, it encouraged communities to do so. The IRS concluded that cultural organizations devoted to the promotion of the arts and that meet the other tests of Section 501(c)(3) qualify as exempt educational or charitable organizations.[4]

In Revenue Ruling 64-175,[5] an organization whose purpose was to promote and develop the interest of the American public in the dramatic arts and that also operated a permanent repertory theater was held to be exempt under Section 501(c)(3). The main activity of the organization was to produce classic plays and make them available on tour throughout the United States. Its receipts were mainly from donations and sales of tickets. In this Ruling, the IRS stated that "it has long been the position of the Internal Revenue Service that so called 'cultural' type organizations may be exempt from Federal income tax as educational or charitable."[6] "For example . . . an association organized and operated exclusively for the purposes of giving musical concerts of an educational character is exempt."[7]

---

[1] *See* 26 C.F.R. § 1.501(c)(3)-1(d)(2); RESTATEMENT (THIRD) OF TRUSTS § 28 (2003).

[2] 1964-1 C.B. 183.

[3] *Id.*

[4] *Id.*

[5] 1964-1 C.B. 185.

[6] *Id.*

[7] *Id.* See also S.M. 1176, C.B. 1, 147 (1919), and I.T. 1475, C.B. 1–2, 184 (1922), which holds that a corporation organized to maintain a band to give free public concerts and promote musical art is exempt as an educational organization.

Cultural organizations such as museums, symphony orchestras, ballet, opera, repertory, modern dance, theater, and other similar organizations may qualify for tax exempt status as educational organizations and/or as charitable organizations.[8] These organizations are viewed as charitable and educational because they promote public appreciation of the arts, which is considered useful to the individual and beneficial to the community, as well as providing instruction and training to individuals for the purposes of improving or developing their capabilities.[9] The Regulations state that such organizations that promote culture and the arts qualify for exempt status as long as they otherwise meet the requirements of Section 501(c)(3).[10]

§ 11.02 SCOPE OF ARTS ORGANIZATIONS

While an organization may be promoting the arts or providing a cultural charitable activity, it may also be providing an educational exempt activity as well. For this reason, the exempt status of organizations that promote the arts is often described as charitable or educational or a combination of both. Therefore, the scope of what can be considered an "arts organization" is quite broad. An example of this is Revenue Ruling 64-175, which held that an organization formed to promote group harmony singing fell into the same category as organizations formed to increase public appreciation of the arts.[11] To advance group harmony singing, the group educated the general public through meetings where training and instruction in vocal harmony was provided by qualified instructors.[12] The IRS stated that this organization, which promoted the art of harmony singing, qualified as an educational organization under Section 501(c)(3).[13]

[A] Art Schools

In Revenue Ruling 65-270,[14] a nonprofit organization was formed to operate and maintain a school to teach the art of dancing. The school maintained a regular faculty, a regular curriculum, and had a regularly enrolled body of students.[15] The organization's income was from tuition and contributions. The IRS stated that "[t]he teaching of the dance by a nonprofit organization as described herein clearly constitutes the promotion of the arts and is educational"[16] in accordance with Section 501(c)(3).[17]

---

[8] 26 C.F.R. § 1.501(c)(3)-1(d)(3)(ii), Ex. (4).

[9] 26 C.F.R. § 1.501(c)(3)-1(d)(2), (3).

[10] 26 C.F.R. 1.501(c)(3)-1(d)(3)(ii) Ex. (4).

[11] Rev. Rul. 64-175, 1964-1 C.B. 185.

[12] *Id.*

[13] Rev. Rul. 66-46, 1966-1 C.B. 133.

[14] 1965-2 C.B. 160.

[15] *Id.*

[16] *Id.*

[17] *Id.*; *see also* 26 C.F.R. § 1.501(c)(3)-1(d)(3)(ii), Ex. (1).

[B]   Music

In Revenue Ruling 65-271,[18] the IRS found that a nonprofit organization created to develop and promote the appreciation of jazz music as an American art form through presentation of public jazz festivals and concerts was exempt under Section 501(c)(3). At some of the jazz festivals, students were given the opportunity to perform with outstanding professional jazz musicians and new and experimental works were often performed. The IRS stated that the organization was truly developing and promoting an appreciation of jazz music, which was both a charitable and an educational activity.[19]

[C]   Galleries

While nonprofit art galleries that are properly structured can qualify as tax exempt organizations that promote the arts, a cooperative art gallery that was formed and operated by a group of artists for the purpose of exhibiting and selling their works was denied exemption by the IRS in Revenue Ruling 71-395.[20] The gallery was formed and operated by a group of about 50 artists. Other artists were admitted by approval of the existing members. The gallery was open to the public six days a week and no admission was charged. A panel chosen by the members selected the works to be exhibited. The gallery retained a commission from sales. The IRS refused tax exemption because the gallery served the private purpose of the members, and was, therefore, not organized and operated for exempt purposes.[21]

A nonprofit organization formed to promote community understanding of modern art trends by exhibiting and selling art by local artists and that retained a commission on sales below what was customary was denied exemption by the IRS in Revenue Ruling 76-152.[22] The organization did not qualify as operating as an educational organization under Section 501(c)(3) of the IRC and could not qualify as a "museum." Ninety percent of all art sales proceeds were turned over to the individual artists. The fact that the artists had no control over the selection of the works to be displayed did not make a difference.[23] There was still a clear private benefit to the artists that was substantial, and not incidental, in nature that prevented exempt status.

In *Goldsboro Art League Inc. v. Commissioner*,[24] the issue was whether the League was operated exclusively for one or more exempt purposes as set forth in IRC Section 501(c)(3). The League operated two public galleries, one called the Art Market and the other the Art Gallery. They both exhibited and sold artwork. The Art Market showed many artists while the Art Gallery featured one artist per

---

[18]   1965-2 C.B. 161.

[19]   *Id.*

[20]   1971-2 C.B. 228.

[21]   *Id.*

[22]   1976-1 C.B. 151.

[23]   *Id.*

[24]   75 T.C. 337 (1980).

month. Out of these gallery sales, the artists received 20 percent of the proceeds. The League had a 12-member board of non-artist professionals from the community. Among its other activities, it also sponsored art demonstrations, and it displayed parts of its 52-piece permanent art collection around the community at hospitals, libraries, and other public venues.[25]

Based on its commercial sales of artwork, the IRS determined that the League operated in furtherance of a substantial commercial purpose and that it served private rather than public interests. "[S]ince [the League's] activities are indistinguishable from activities required in operating a commercial art gallery for profit,"[26] it held that it was operated for a substantial commercial purpose.[27] The organization, on the other hand, argued that its purposes were to promote the appreciation of the visual arts and to promote education in the fine arts, which were valid IRC Section 501(c)(3) purposes.[28] The Tax Court found that the art sales, when seen in light of the League's other exempt activities, were secondary and incidental to furthering the League's exempt purposes. As a result, the Tax Court determined that the League was entitled to exemption because it was organized and operated for an exempt purpose without furthering a substantial commercial purpose, and served public rather than private interests.[29]

[D] Museums

In *Bob Jones University Museum and Gallery, Inc. v. Commissioner,*[30] the petitioner was incorporated as a nonprofit museum and art gallery, located on the campus of Bob Jones University in Greeneville, South Carolina. The art gallery had been a part of the university from 1951 until its separate incorporation in 1992. The museum and art gallery established their present location on campus in 1965. The museum claims "one of the greatest collections of religious paintings and works of art in the western hemisphere."[31] Although the University was at one time exempt, its tax exempt status was revoked in 1983 in accordance with a United States Supreme Court decision.[32] The Bob Jones University Museum and Gallery, Inc. (Museum) took over the operations of the museum that was once run by the University. It entered into a three-year lease with the University at below-market rates, and its board consisted of representatives of the University Board as well as individuals from the local community. The number of visitors to the museum exceeded 20,000 persons annually, with approximately 80 percent having no connection with the University. The IRS denied the museum's tax exempt status,

---

[25] *Id.*

[26] *Id.* at 342.

[27] *Id.; see also* Better Bus. Bureau v. United States, 326 U.S. 279 (1945); Hancock Acad. of Savannah, Inc. v. Comm'r, 69 T.C. 488 (1977); Tax Ct. R. Prac. & P. 217(c)(2)(i) (stating that petitioner has the burden of proving that respondent's determination is wrong).

[28] *Goldsboro,* 75 T.C. at 339.

[29] *Id.* at 343.

[30] 71 T.C.M. (CCH) 3120 (1996).

[31] *Id.*

[32] Bob Jones Univ. v. United States, 461 U.S. 574 (1983). For further information on *Bob Jones University,* see § 9.02[A][4].

stating that the organization was not operated for exempt purposes but rather provided substantial private benefits to Bob Jones University, a non-exempt organization. The IRS gave these reasons for its contention that the University derived an impermissible benefit: (1) The Museum's payment of rent to the University; (2) the Museum's payment of salaries to employees formerly employed by the University; (3) the Museum's exhibition of artwork on loan from the University; (4) the University's influence on the Museum's board; (5) the Museum's location on the campus of the University; and (6) the reputational benefit that the University will derive from its association with the Museum.[33]

The Tax Court determined, based on a review of the record, that the Museum did satisfy the requirements of Section 501(c)(3). Upon examination, the court found the financial dealings to be at arm's length and the other alleged private benefits to be insubstantial. The court stated that any other decision would lead to the conclusion that "a taxable corporation could never split off a tax-exempt organization and conduct subsequent financial dealings with it."[34]

[E]   Theaters

A theater league brought suit to recover income taxes that it alleged were erroneously assessed and collected by the IRS in *Broadway Theatre League of Lynchburg v. United States.*[35]

> The basis of the claim is that the defendant wrongfully refused to grant the League exemption from federal income taxes under Section 501(a) of the Internal Revenue Code . . . as an organization described in Section 501(c)(3).[36]

The League was a membership or subscription organization whose primary purpose was the production of plays in the town of Lynchburg. In furtherance of its exempt activities, the League engaged various persons and organizations to provide services on a contractual basis. These included legal services, secretarial services, publishing, and play booking services. The contract with the booking agent, United Performing Arts, Inc. (United), became the center of the controversy. The contract provided that "the League shall annually conduct a membership campaign of at least a week's duration to sell seasonal tickets to a theater series of not less than four attractions . . . the League shall deal exclusively with United for the term of the contract . . . the League shall pay United, as compensation for its services, fifteen percent (15 percent) of the aggregate membership dues."[37] The contract also allowed United to reorganize the League should the League's existence ever be jeopardized.

The court originally approached the issue by saying that it would focus on whether the organization met the organizational and operational tests of Section

---

[33] *Bob Jones Univ. Museum and Gallery, Inc.*, 71 T.C.M. (CCH) 3120.

[34] *Id.*

[35] 293 F. Supp. 346 (W.D. Va. 1968).

[36] *Id.* at 347; *see also* 26 U.S.C.A. § 501 (1954).

[37] *Broadway Theatre League*, 293 F. Supp. at 355.

501(c)(3); finding the two tests intertwined as a condition precedent (organizational) and a condition subsequent (operational) to a finding of exempt status.[38] As a practical matter, however, the court primarily discussed the operational aspects of the League. The IRS argued that provisions of the United contract allowed so much control of the League by United that it was not exclusively operated for exempt purposes, but rather was operated for the benefit of United. The court disagreed. It pointed out that the contract's length had been reduced from three years to one year, and that United could incur no expense on behalf of the League without prior League approval. The reorganization power was an ultimate power, highly unlikely ever to be used. As a result, the court did not find such control of the League by United as the IRS claimed and held the organization qualified for exemption.[39]

In Revenue Ruling 73-45,[40] a nonprofit organization was "created to foster the development in a community of an appreciation for drama and musical arts by sponsoring professional presentations."[41] The productions were procured through an annually renewable contract with a commercial booking agent. The organization received donations and collected fees through membership dues, subscription fees, and ticket sales. The contract did not indicate that any private interest was being served, was negotiated at arm's length, and permitted the organization to book with other agencies. The organization qualified for exemption under Section 501(c)(3).[42]

Another important case involving a nonprofit theater company is *Plumstead Theatre Society, Inc. v. Commissioner.*[43] Plumstead planned to fulfill "its purpose by presenting professional dramatic theater productions of the classical nature, ancient and contemporary; by forming a workshop in the Los Angeles area for new American playwrights."[44] The members of the board were a diversified group, and no director received a salary. Several advanced the organization non-interest-bearing loans to cover the cost of incorporation.[45] Plays were produced in Pasadena, California, using professional actors and technicians. Admission was through normal ticket sales.

Plumstead got into trouble with the IRS when it agreed with the Kennedy Center in Washington, D.C., another exempt organization, to co-produce a play, "First Monday in October," starring Henry Fonda, and opening at the Kennedy Center. When Plumstead had difficulty coming up with its share of the production costs under its agreement with the Kennedy Center, it sold a portion of its rights in "First Monday" to a for-profit limited partnership, of which Plumstead was the general partner, and private parties were the limited partners. This partnership would then produce "First Monday" in Washington, D.C. and New York. The IRS took the position that this arrangement meant that Plumstead was no longer being

---

[38] See § 6.02 for further information on the organizational test.

[39] *Broadway Theater League,* 293 F. Supp. at 355.

[40] 1973-1 C.B. 220.

[41] *Id.*

[42] *Id.*

[43] 74 T.C. 1324 (1980).

[44] *Id.* at 1327.

[45] *Id.* at 1325.

operated exclusively for charitable and educational purposes because it now had a substantial commercial purpose and was being operated for the benefit of a private rather than a public interest.[46]

Plumstead is the first major case to consider what is becoming more and more common in the tax exempt area, namely partnerships or joint ventures between exempt organizations and for-profit or private entities.[47] In its analysis, the court stated that it has long been recognized that "the promotion and encouragement of the arts can be both charitable and educational."[48] On this basis, Plumstead certainly qualified for exempt status, even though it sold tickets and charged admission to its productions. The court did not find this to be a commercial purpose. It stated that it is in this field in particular that nonprofit and for profit enterprises coexist (theater, symphony, ballet), and even when an organization depends on ticket sales to maintain its existence, it may still qualify for exempt status. On the thornier issue of the partnership with the for-profits, the court found that the contractual arrangement was a one-time deal for one play and did not give control over the exempt organization or its activities to the for-profit parties. As a result, Plumstead was still operating for a public, rather than a private benefit.[49]

Plumstead stands for two propositions: (1) a tax exempt organization can engage in what would otherwise be commercial activities (here the production of plays and charging admissions) if the activities are in furtherance of its exempt purposes; and (2) tax exempt organizations can enter partnerships with for-profit organizations as long as the activities of the partnership are in furtherance of the tax exempt organization's exempt purposes and the tax exempt organization has control of the partnership's activities.

[F]   Performing Arts Groups

In Revenue Ruling 67-392,[50] an organization that encouraged and promoted the "advancement of young musical artists by conducting weekly workshops, sponsoring public concerts by the artists, and securing paid engagements for the artists to improve their professional standing"[51] was held exempt under Section 501(c)(3) of the IRC. The organization's primary activities were considered educational, and the organization's placement activities were considered no different from those of other educational organizations that offer placement services (colleges and universities) to their students.[52]

---

[46] *Id.*; *see also Broadway Theatre League*, 293 F. Supp. 346; 9 J. Mertens, Law of Federal Income Taxation § 34.09 (2007); B. Hopkins, Law of Tax Exempt Organizations § 20.11(b), pp. 601–05 (9th ed. 2007 & Supp. 2010).

[47] See §§ 4.04, 9.03[A], and 10.05 for further information on joint ventures and how tax exempt organizations can enter into such arrangements and still maintain their tax exempt status.

[48] *Plumstead*, 74 T.C. at 1329.

[49] *Id.* at 1331.

[50] 1967-2 C.B. 191.

[51] *Id.*

[52] *Id.*

An organization that was created to "develop and promote an appreciation of contemporary symphonic and chamber music by recording and selling, primarily to educational institutions, new works of unrecognized composers as well as neglected works of more established composers" was found to be exempt in Revenue Ruling 79-369.[53] The organization sold its recordings mostly to libraries and educational organizations. It also provided free copies to radio stations operated by educational organizations. It did not advertise, and the board was made up of recognized experts in the field.[54]

§ 11.03   CULTURAL ARTS DISTRICTS

In a number of cities, public organizations have been established to support the arts. These organizations accomplish this by creating venues in which the arts can thrive. When these efforts involve the ownership and development of real estate for the promotion of the arts, what is created is a Cultural Arts District.[55] The IRS has said that a Cultural Arts District created by a city, pursuant to state law, is a political subdivision of the state in Private Letter Ruling 200151015.[56] As such, charitable contributions to it are eligible for the maximum charitable contribution deduction.[57]

Section 170(c)(1) of the IRC states that "charitable contribution" includes a contribution of gift to or for the use of "a State, a possession of the United States, any political subdivision of a State or a possession of the United States . . . but only if the contribution is made for exclusively public purposes."[58] To determine whether an entity is a division of a state or local governmental unit, it must be determined to what extent the entity is: (1) controlled by the state or local governmental unit, and (2) motivated by a wholly public purpose.[59]

The tax exempt status of cultural districts is derived from the doctrine of intergovernmental immunity. The doctrine that the federal government will not tax the states is implicit in the Constitution, stating that "the United States may not tax instrumentalities which a state may employ in the discharge of her essential

---

[53] 1979-2 C.B. 226.

[54] *Id.*

[55] *See* Nicholas Cafardi & Jaclyn Cherry, Tax Exempt Organizations: Cases and Materials (2d ed. 2008).

[56] P.L.R. 200151015 (Sept. 17, 2001). Legislatures have determined that cultural districts serve a public purpose by encouraging economic development and tourism; by reducing unemployment; and by bringing needed capital into an area.

[57] *Id.*

[58] *Id. See also* Rev. Rul. 79-323, 1979-2 C.B. 106, holding that gifts to an industrial commission established by a state legislature for exclusively public purposes are deductible under 170(c)(1); Rev. Rul. 78-276, 1978-2 C.B. 256, stating that "political subdivision" has been defined as either (1) a division of a state or local government that is a municipal corporation, or (2) a division of a state or local government delegated sovereign power; and Shamberg v. Comm'r, 3 T.C. 131, *acq.* 1945 C.B. 6, *aff'd*, 144 F.2d 998 (2d Cir.), *cert. denied*, 323 U.S. 792 (1944).

[59] Rev. Rul. 83-131, 1983-2 C.B. 184. *See also* P.L.R. 200151015 (Sept. 17, 2001); Rev. Rul. 78-276, 1978-2 C.B. 256.

governmental duties."[60]

---

[60] Helvering v. Therrell, 303 U.S. 218, 223 (1938).

Chapter 12

OTHER IRC SECTION 501(c)(3) ORGANIZATIONS

§ 12.01 INTRODUCTION

As previously discussed, Section 501(c)(3) organizations are defined as corporations and any community chest, fund, or foundation, organized or operated as described in the IRC as exclusively for religious, charitable, scientific, testing for public safety, literacy or educational purposes, or to foster national or international amateur sports competition (but only if no part of its activities involve the provision of athletic facilities or equipment), or for the prevention of cruelty to children or animals.[1]

The major types of Section 501(c)(3) organizations include: religious organizations and churches; formal and informal educational organizations; various types of healthcare organizations; and arts organizations.[2] As encompassing as these organizations are in the realm of Section 501(c)(3) organizations not covered in previous chapters, they are not the entire story, as a quick check of the statutory language quoted above indicates.

The organizations reviewed in this chapter will include other 501(c)(3) organizations: scientific organizations, public safety testing organizations, literary organizations, organizations that foster national or international amateur sports, and organizations for the prevention of cruelty to children or animals.

§ 12.02 OTHER TAX EXEMPT CATEGORIES

Beyond the broad interpretation of "charity," the IRC Regulations expand the term to include other tax-exempt purposes that fall within the broad outlines of charity as developed by the IRS and judicial decisions. Such terms include: relieving the poor and distressed or the underprivileged; lessening the burdens of government; and promoting social welfare by organizations designed to accomplish any of the above purposes or to lessen neighborhood tensions, eliminating prejudice and discrimination, defending human and civil rights secured by law, or combating community deterioration and juvenile delinquency.[3]

---

[1] I.R.C. § 501(c)(3).

[2] See §§ 8.01 *et seq.*, 9.01 *et seq.*, 10.01 *et seq.*, 11.01 *et seq.*, and 12.01 *et seq.* for further information on the major type of tax exempt organizations.

[3] 26 C.F.R. § 1.501(c)(3)-1(d)(2).

§ 12.03   RELIEF OF POOR & DISTRESSED OR UNDERPRIVILEGED

Historically, relief of the poor has always been considered a charitable activity. The term *charitable* has a broad definition emanating from the law of charitable trusts, describing activities that promote the general welfare. One such activity that promotes the general welfare is providing relief for the poor, distressed, and underprivileged. This takes on many forms, as seen below.

[A]   Relief of the Poor

In Revenue Ruling 78-428,[4] a nonprofit organization, formed to provide legal services to indigent persons at a fee based upon the indigent clients' ability to pay, qualified for tax exemption under Section 501(c)(3). The nonprofit was supported by contributions from the general public and by fees from the clients. For each hour of legal assistance, the clients were expected to pay a nominal hourly fee based on their ability to pay. The organization provided economic relief to poor and distressed clients even though it charged a small fee. The fee did not negate the effect on the needy, and the organization qualified for exempt status.[5]

In Revenue Ruling 77-246,[6] an organization that provided low-cost, but not free, transportation to senior citizens and handicapped persons of a particular community, but that also depended on contributions, government and institutional grants in order to meet operating expenses, was considered to meet the requirements of Section 501(c)(3) status. The elderly and the handicapped qualifies as a charitable class of beneficiaries and the provision of transportation services at low cost to them served to relieve many of the forms of distress that justify considering the elderly and the handicapped as charitable classes.[7]

In Revenue Ruling 72-559,[8] an organization formed to provide substantial free legal services to low-income residents of economically distressed communities through subsidization of recently licensed law graduates qualified for exemption under Section 501(c)(3). The organization selected recent law school graduates to participate as interns in the program. In the first year, the intern was given intensive training under the supervision of experienced lawyers. After the first year, the intern set up his or her own practice in an economically depressed neighborhood with a shortage of legal services. The organization provided the intern with a yearly subsidy for three years for the intern to provide legal services to the needy while establishing a viable practice. The IRS stated that the fact that the recipients of the financial assistance were not themselves members of a charitable class did not mean that the organization was not operating for charitable purposes.[9] The term "charitable" is defined as including the promotion of social

---

[4]   1978-2 C.B. 177.

[5]   *Id.*

[6]   1977-2 C.B. 190.

[7]   *Id.*

[8]   1972-2 C.B. 247.

[9]   *Id.*

welfare by organizations designed to provide relief to the poor, distressed or underprivileged.[10]

In Revenue Ruling 2006-27,[11] the Internal Revenue Service presents three hypothetical situations involving different types of down payment assistance organizations that provide relief to the poor.

In Situation 1, the beneficiaries are low-income individuals and families with the employment and financial history necessary to qualify for a mortgage, and who would qualify but for the lack of a down payment. The organization also runs financial counseling seminars and other educational activities to prepare low-income home buyers for the responsibilities of home ownership. The organization's source of funds is a broad-based fundraising program and it awards its down payment grants without knowing the seller, agent, or other parties who might benefit from the sale. The way this organization conducts its down payment assistance program establishes that its primary purpose is to address the needs of its low-income grantees, who constitute a clear charitable class. This organization qualifies as a 501(c)(3) organization that provides relief to the poor, distressed, or underprivileged.[12]

In Situation 2, the organization functions much like the organization in Situation 1, except that it knows the seller of the home and may also know the real estate agent and the developer benefitting from the sale. The organization gets a kickback from the home seller, and most of its financial support comes from home sellers and real-estate businesses that could benefit from the sale of the homes to the organization's low-income beneficiaries. This organization does not qualify as a 501(c)(3) organization because there are clear private benefits.[13]

In Situation 3, the organization was formed to combat community deterioration. It cooperates with government agencies and community groups to develop a plan for a depressed community that has lost population and jobs to attract new businesses and to provide stable sources of decent housing for area residents. Z receives government funding to build affordable housing units for sale to low- and moderate-income families. A substantial part of its activities is to make down payment assistance available to eligible home buyers who want to buy the units that the organization has built. The organization also provides seminars and other educational help for low- and moderate-income home buyers. It gets its funds from a broad-based fundraising program. Even though its beneficiaries are not all low-income, this organization still qualifies as a 501(c)(3) organization because its primary purpose is combating community deterioration, a valid exempt activity.[14]

---

[10] 26 C.F.R. § 1.501(c)(3)-1(d)(2).

[11] 2006-1 C.B. 915.

[12] *Id.* at Situation 1.

[13] *Id.* at Situation 2.

[14] *Id.* at Situation 3.

[B]   Public Interest Law Firms

The question of whether public interest law firms are exempt has been far more controversial than the organizations assisting the poor, as described above. Law firms saw the granting of tax exemption for these organizations as a threat to their existence. Several revenue rulings and procedures followed, as seen below.[15]

In Revenue Ruling 75-74,[16] the IRS granted 501(c)(3) status to public interest law firms. The IRS based its decision on the fact that these organizations provide legal representation on issues of broad public importance. It stated that these services were not ordinarily provided by traditional private law firms.

In Revenue Ruling 75-74,[17] an organization operating as a public interest law firm, which provided representation in cases of public importance that were not economically feasible for private firms, qualified as a Section 501(c)(3) organization. The organization engaged in areas of public interest such as environmental protection, urban renewal, prison reform, freedom of information, suits challenging governmental and private action, and "test" cases of significance to the public.[18] The IRS found these activities "charitable" because the public interest firms offered services to the public that were not available commercially.[19]

Public interest law firms can receive fees for their services but only with restrictions. Initially not allowed,[20] these fees are now acceptable. According to Revenue Ruling 75-76,[21] public interest law firms can accept fees from opposing parties when the fees are awarded or approved by a court or administrative agency.

Procedures and guidelines for public interest law firms, including procedures under which a public interest law firm can accept fees for service, are outlined in Revenue Procedure 92-59.[22]

The United States District Court for the District of Columbia addressed the issue of whether to grant exemption to public interest law firms in *Center on Corporate Responsibility, Inc. v. Shultz*.[23] The Center focused on corporate involvement in social problems and conditions, and the social impact of various corporate policies. It did this by sponsoring and performing research, conducting educational programs, issuing publications, and conducting public interest

---

[15] *See also* Susan R. Jones, *Representing the Poor and Homeless: Innovations in Advocacy Tackling Homelessness Through Economic Self-Sufficiency*, 19 St. Louis U. Pub. L. Rev. 385 (2000).

[16] 1975-1 C.B. 152.

[17] 1975-1 C.B. 152.

[18] *Id.*

[19] *Id.*

[20] *See* Rev. Rul. 75-75, 1975-1 C.B. 154.

[21] 1975-1 C.B. 154.

[22] 1992-2 C.B. 411.

[23] 368 F. Supp. 863 (D.D.C. 1973). In addition to addressing the exemption of public interest law firms, considerable portions of the opinion were spent addressing the question of political influence intruding into the IRS's consideration of this exemption application. The Center's activities raised some concerns at the White House during the Nixon administration. Discussion of how to curb specific activities or remove White House enemies through taxing mechanisms was caught on tape.

litigation, among other things.[24] During its application process, communications between the Center and the IRS resulted in it ceasing any activity it had involving proxy contests (it allowed for this activity to be taken over by a related for-profit because this activity was troublesome to the IRS). Also, during the application process, the Center was given reason to believe that its application would be approved by the IRS; however, it was later denied. The decision was based to a great extent on political pressures on the IRS by the Nixon administration.[25] The court entered an injunction to prevent the IRS from denying the Center's tax exempt status for as long as its operations did not conflict with its amended exemption application.

§ 12.04   LESSENING GOVERNMENT'S BURDEN

The term "charitable" is used in Section 501(c)(3) in its generally accepted legal sense, and includes lessening the burdens of government.[26] Whether an organization's activities lessen the government's burden depends on whether there is an "objective manifestation" by the government that it considers certain activities to be part of its burden. For example, organizations such as fire and rescue organizations are easily characterized as charitable by the IRS because they provide a necessary service to the community, thereby lessening the burdens of government.

In Revenue Ruling 85-2,[27] a program providing legal assistance for guardians ad litem representing abused and neglected children in juvenile court was considered to be lessening the burdens of government and was therefore tax exempt under Section 501(c)(3). The organization employed attorneys to provide legal advice to lay volunteers who represented the children in court. The court initiated this program because it was having difficulty with the appointment of attorneys. In its analysis, the IRS stated:

> To determine whether an activity is a burden of government, the question to be answered is whether there is an object manifestation by the government that it considers such activity to be part of its burden. The fact that an organization is engaged in an activity that is sometimes undertaken by the government is insufficient to establish a burden of government. Similarly, the fact that the government or an official of the government expresses approval of an organization and its activities is also not sufficient to establish that the organization is lessening the burdens of government. The interrelationship between the organization and the government may provide evidence that the government considers the organization's activities to be its burden.[28]

---

[24] *Id.* at 866.

[25] *Id.* at 866–67. This court also found that any "interference" from the White House in this process was inappropriate. This case highlights the great influence that the charitable sector has on society and the concern that many governmental agencies and corporate have for these organization's activities. This case was no different.

[26] 26 C.F.R. § 1.501(c)(3)-1(d)(2).

[27] 1985-1 C.B. 178.

[28] *Id.*

To make this determination, all of the facts and circumstances must be considered. Here, the organization was lessening the burdens of government because the court had attempted to run the program previously with little success and therefore initiated this program.[29]

§ 12.05 PROMOTION OF SOCIAL WELFARE

An organization is considered to be operated exclusively for the promotion of social welfare if it is primarily engaged in promoting the general welfare of the people of a community and promoting the common good. The organizations usually bring about civic betterment or social improvement. The Regulations set out four examples of promoting social welfare designed to accomplish any of the following charitable purposes:

- Lessen neighborhood tensions.

- Eliminate prejudice and discrimination.

- Defend human and civil rights secured by law.

- Combat community deterioration and juvenile delinquency.[30]

In Revenue Ruling 68-655,[31] an organization formed to promote racial integration in housing, to lessen neighborhood tensions, and to prevent deterioration of neighborhoods qualified for exemption under Section 501(c)(3). The organization's activities included educating the public regarding integrated housing to prevent panic selling in formerly all-white neighborhoods. It also assisted families in purchasing homes in integrated neighborhoods. The IRS stated that these activities, along with the organization's other activities, lessened neighborhood tensions and combated potential community deterioration.[32]

Another example of social welfare can be seen in Revenue Ruling 68-70,[33] where a nonprofit organization sought to eliminate discrimination in employment. The IRS stated that this organization could qualify for exemption under Section 501(c)(3). The organization was formed to create equal opportunities for qualified workers discriminated against because of race or creed by bringing resumes of qualified individuals to the attention of employers. The IRS stated that the term charitable includes the promotion of social welfare by organizations designed to eliminate prejudice and discrimination.[34] Further, it stated that the term "education" includes

---

[29] See Oliver Houck, *"Lessening the Burdens of Government": Formulating a Test for Uniformity and Rational Federal Income Tax Subsidies*, 45 U. KAN. L. REV. 787 (1997); see also Kellen McClendon, *Do Hospitals in Pennsylvania Relieve the Government of Some of Its Burden?* 67 TEMP. L. REV. 518 (1994), for a discussion of the standard for "lessening the burden of government" as it applies to property tax exemption in Pennsylvania.

[30] 26 C.F.R. § 1.501(c)(3)-1(d)(2).

[31] 1968-2 C.B. 213.

[32] *Id.*

[33] 1968-1 C.B. 248.

[34] 26 C.F.R. § 1.501(c)(3)-1(d)(2).

the instruction of the public on subjects useful to the individual and beneficial to the community.[35]

Finally, in *National Right to Work Legal Defense and Education Foundation, Inc. v. United States*,[36] the court determined that the "right to work" was a human and civil right and that an organization that was formed to protect these rights for individuals was a charitable "social welfare" organization that qualified for 501(c)(3) status.[37]

In this case, the Foundation's primary activity was to provide legal aid to workers who suffered discrimination through compulsory unionism arrangements. The court differentiated the activities of the Foundation from the NLRB and EEOC grievance mechanisms. Relying on United States Supreme Court precedent, it stated that: "[T]he right to work for a living in the common occupations of the community is of the very essence of the personal freedom and opportunity that it was the purpose of the (Fourteenth) Amendment to secure."[38]

§ 12.06   SCIENTIFIC ORGANIZATIONS

Section 501(c)(3) provides that an organization may be exempt from federal income tax under Section 501(a) if it is organized and operated exclusively for scientific purposes.[39] The following cases and Revenue Rulings outline the requirements for a scientific organization to claim tax exemption.

In *IIT Research Institute v. United States*,[40] a suit for the refund of taxes, the issue was whether "the income from some of the plaintiff's research contracts for government and business was derived from trade or business unrelated to plaintiff's exemption as a corporation organized and operated exclusively for scientific purposes."[41] The Research Institute was "established to stimulate industrial growth and technological development by making research services available to industry on a contract basis."[42] The court found that the terms "science" and "scientific" were not defined by the IRC. It looked to the common meaning of the word, assuming that this was the intention of Congress. It then turned to Regulation Section 1.501(c)(3)-1(d)(5), which states that:

- For research to be "scientific," within the meaning of Section 501(c)(3), it must be carried on in furtherance of a "scientific" purpose. The determination as to whether such research is "scientific" does not depend on whether such research is classified as "fundamental" or "basic" as contrasted with

---

[35] 26 C.F.R. § 1.501(c)(3)-1(d)(3)(i)(b).

[36] 487 F. Supp. 801 (E.D.N.C. 1979).

[37] *Id.* at 805.

[38] *Id.* (quoting Truax v. Raich, 239 U.S. 33 (1915)).

[39] *See* 26 C.F.R. § 1.501(c)(3)-1(d)(1)(i)(c).

[40] 9 Cl. Ct. 13 (1985).

[41] *Id.* at 15.

[42] *Id.* at 16.

"applied" or "practical."[43]

- Scientific research does not include activities of a type ordinarily carried on as incident to commercial or industrial operations, as, for example, the ordinary testing or inspection of materials or products or the designing or constructing of equipment, buildings, etc.[44]

Under these definitions, the court concluded that the challenged contracts met the criteria for "scientific" research. The court also found that the contracts at issue met the requirement under Section 501(c)(3) that a "scientific" organization serve a public rather than a private interest. Regulation Section 1.501(c)(3)-1(2)(5) provides that scientific research will be carried on in the public interests if any of the following applies:

- If the results of such research (including any patents, copyrights, processes, or formulae resulting from such research) are made available to the public on a nondiscriminatory basis.

- If such research is performed for the United States, or any of its agencies or instrumentalities, or for a State or political subdivision thereof.

- If such research is directed toward benefiting the public.[45]

In Revenue Ruling 76-296,[46] the IRS reviewed two situations to determine whether commercially sponsored research that included all relevant information, which otherwise qualified as scientific research under Section 501(c)(3), was timely published in "such form as to be available to the interested public, constitute[d] scientific research carried on in the public interest."[47] If publication of research is withheld or delayed significantly beyond the time reasonably necessary to establish ownership rights, it will be considered an unrelated trade or business under Section 513. In Situation 1, the results of the commercially sponsored projects, with all the relevant information, were generally published in an appropriate time. Situation 1 qualified for tax exemption and had no unrelated trade or business activity. In Situation 2, the research was not carried out for the public interest but was kept secret for various business reasons, therefore the organization was responsible for unrelated trade or business tax.[48]

The court found that the activity in *American Kennel Club v. Hoey*[49] was not scientific and denied exempt status to the organization. The organization's primary function was the maintenance of the sport of dog shows. It attempted to assure that these shows were staffed by qualified judges and that these were fair trials. The court found that "although the non-research activity resulted in useful information"

---

[43] *Id.* at 20 (quoting 26 C.F.R. § 1.501(c)(3)-1(2)(5)).

[44] *Id.*

[45] *Id.* at 25 (quoting 26 C.F.R. § 1.501(c)(3)-1(2)(5)).

[46] 1976-2 C.B. 141.

[47] *Id.*

[48] *Id.*

[49] 148 F.2d 920 (2d Cir. 1945).

the organization did not take on the activities to generate the information.[50]

In the case of *Washington Research Foundation v. Commissioner*,[51] an organization that sought to assist and facilitate the transfer of technology from the laboratories of tax exempt colleges and universities to public use by licensing their intellectual property for commercial purposes was denied exemption because its proposed activities, even though in part educational, were primarily commercial in nature. To help exempt colleges and universities market their intellectual property through tax exempt middlemen, in effect overturning *Washington Research Foundation* by statute, Congress passed Public Law 99-514, exempting such organizations from taxation as long as they were incorporated on July 20, 1981 — a form of special interest tax exemption if there ever was one.[52]

§ 12.07 TESTING FOR PUBLIC SAFETY

Organizations that engage in "testing for public safety" can qualify as Section 501(c)(3) organizations. Their activities include the testing of consumer products, such as electrical products, to determine whether they are safe for use by the general public.[53]

In Revenue Ruling 65-61,[54] a nonprofit membership corporation was organized to test for public safety and establish safety standards for products used aboard pleasure boats. It cooperated with and assisted the Commandant of the United States Coast Guard. The activities included the testing of various items, including galley stoves, metallic fuel tanks, flame arresters, and other products used aboard pleasure craft. The organization's label of approval was placed on all products that met the minimum requirements for safety.[55] The organization was held exempt from federal income tax under 501(c)(3), although because it was not organized for any of the purposes specified in Section 170(c), contributions to it were not eligible for tax deduction.[56]

In Revenue Ruling 68-373,[57] a nonprofit engaged in testing drugs for commercial pharmaceutical companies did not qualify for exemption under 501(c)(3). The IRS stated that "scientific research does not include activities of a type ordinarily carried on as an incident to commercial or industrial operations, as, for example, the ordinary testing or inspection of materials or products."[58] Clinical testing is generally carried on as incident to a pharmaceutical company's operations. It is in

---

[50] *Id.; see also* Wash. Research Found. v. Comm'r, 50 T.C.M. (CCH) 1457 (1985); Midwest Research Inst. v. United States, 554 F. Supp. 1379 (W.D. Mo. 1983); Rev. Rul. 76-296, 1976-2 C.B. 141.

[51] 50 T.C.M. (CCH) 1457.

[52] Tax Reform Act of 1986, Pub. L. No. 99-514, § 1605, 100 Stat. 1085 (1986).

[53] 26 C.F.R. § 1.501(c)(3)-1(d)(4), -1(d)(1)(i)(d).

[54] 1965-1 C.B. 234.

[55] *Id.*

[56] *Id.*

[57] 1968-2 C.B. 206.

[58] *Id.*

the private interest of the manufacturer and not in the public interest.[59]

§ 12.08   LITERARY ORGANIZATIONS

Section 501(c)(3) of the IRC includes the word "literary" as a type of organization that qualifies for federal tax exemption. However, there is no law on the subject. Most organizations that qualify as literary organizations (literary guilds) are classified as charitable and educational. Theater groups are classified as charitable, *literary*, and educational.

In a spoof on this topic, Walter Trenerry, in his article *A Literary Pilgrim's Progress*,[60] laments the fact that the IRS does not accept applications for 501(c)(3) tax exemption by the IRS under the literary category (though there are many literary organizations). In the article, Mr. Ambler, the lawyer, learns the hard way that when incorporating an organization and seeking tax exempt status for literary organizations, or organizations publishing books, magazines, etc., it is important that there also be a charitable or educational purpose.[61] Even in Revenue Ruling 60-351,[62] the Commissioner refused tax exempt status for a nonprofit organization that published a foreign language magazine. The editors had accepted all kinds of writing to help writers who had emigrated to the United States. The Commissioner thought the magazine operated too much like a commercial enterprise and, therefore, was not tax exempt as a literary organization.[63]

Not much has changed in this area. There is still no case law on the matter, and literary organizations that qualify for tax exemption do so by designating themselves as charitable, literary, and educational organizations.

§ 12.09   NATIONAL & INTERNATIONAL AMATEUR SPORTS ORGANIZATIONS

Tax exemption for amateur athletic organizations was established in 1976 by the addition of this category to Section 501(c)(3). A restriction was placed on the exemption, however, that no part of its activities involve the provision of athletic facilities or equipment.[64] Congress stated in the legislative history that "[t]his restriction . . . is intended to prevent the allowance of these benefits for organizations which, like social clubs, provide facilities and equipment for their members."[65]

---

[59] *Id.* Rev. Rul. 68-373 is evidently not applicable to an exempt organization that produces and/or tests scientific prototypes prior to commercialization. 1986 I.R.S. EO CPE Technical Instruction Program Textbook.

[60] Walter N. Trenerry, *A Literary Pilgrim's Progress Along § 501(c)(3)*, 51 A.B.A.J. 252 (1965).

[61] *Id.*

[62] 1960-2 C.B. 169.

[63] *Id.*

[64] I.R.C. § 501(c)(3).

[65] Joint Committee on Taxation, *General Explanation of the Tax Reform Act of 1976*, 94th Cong., 2d Sess. 423–424 (1976).

This law was modified in 1982,[66] and now states that for a "qualified amateur sports organization," the requirement that no part of the organization's activities may involve the provision of athletic facilities or equipment no longer applies.[67] A qualified amateur sports organization is one that is "organized and operated primarily to conduct national or international competition in sports or to support and develop amateur athletes for national or international competition in sports."[68] In other words, an organization like the National Olympic Committee may now provide facilities and equipment to athletes and remain tax exempt. Another change in the law in 1982 specified that qualified amateur sports organizations could have a local or regional membership and still meet the requirements of Section 501(c)(3).[69]

A question regarding the definition of athletic equipment was at issue in *International E22 Class Association v. Commissioner.*[70] The issue was "whether petitioner's use of a 'master plug' and 'measurement templates' in enforcing amateur racing rules constituted the provision of athletic facilities or equipment contrary to the proscription of Section 501(c)(3) and 170(c)(2)."[71] The court found that the items at issue were not athletic facilities or equipment, but tools used in formulating and enforcing extensive measurement rules. It stated further that the term "athletic facilities" applies to physical structures like clubhouses, swimming pools, or gymnasiums, and "athletic equipment" applies to property used directly in athletic endeavors.[72] Petitioner was held tax exempt.

In *Hutchinson Baseball Enterprises, Inc. v. Commissioner,*[73] the court held, after reviewing all of the organization's activities, which included furthering the development and sportsmanship of children and young men, that the organization qualified for 501(c)(3) tax exemption. Even the organization's support of the Broncos, a privately owned team, was seen as advancing the organization's charitable mission, by providing opportunities for the children involved, thereby serving a charitable purpose.[74]

---

[66] I.R.C. § 501(j).

[67] I.R.C. § 501(j)(1)(A).

[68] *See* Richard Moot, Jr., *Tax Exempt Status of Amateur Sports Organizations*, 40 WASH. L. REV. 4 (1983).

[69] I.R.C. § 501(j)(1)(B).

[70] 78 T.C. 93 (1982); *see also* 26 C.F.R. 1.501(c)(3)-1(d)(1)(i)(g).

[71] *Id.* at 94.

[72] *Id.* at 98.

[73] 696 F.2d 757 (10th Cir. 1982).

[74] *Id.*

§ 12.10 PREVENTION OF CRUELTY TO CHILDREN & ANIMALS

An organization formed "for the purpose of preventing children from working in hazardous trades and occupations in violation of state law" was considered exempt in Revenue Ruling 67-151,[75] as being organized and operated for the prevention of cruelty to children. In Revenue Ruling 74-194,[76] an organization formed to prevent the overbreeding of cats and dogs by providing pet owners with funds to have their pets spayed or neutered, was considered tax exempt for preventing cruelty to animals. And in Revenue Ruling 66-359,[77] an organization formed to promote humane treatment of laboratory animals by carrying on a program for accreditation of animal care facilities used by medical and scientific researchers qualified for tax exemption.[78]

§ 12.11 PROTECTION OF ENVIRONMENT

An organization formed by scientists, educators, conservationists, and representatives of the community to preserve the natural environment qualified for exemption in Revenue Ruling 76-204.[79] The IRS stated that efforts to preserve and protect the natural environment for the benefit of the public serve a charitable purpose.[80] Further, the promotion of conservation and the protection of natural resources has been recognized by Congress as serving a public purpose. Here, the organization acquired and preserved ecologically significant undeveloped land and, therefore, qualified for exemption.[81] In Revenue Ruling 78-384,[82] the organization did not qualify for tax exemption. The organization, which owned a farm and restricted its use to ecologically suitable uses, stated that this benefited the public and therefore qualified for exemption. The IRS disagreed and stated that there was no ecological significance as in Revenue Ruling 76-204, and there was no real benefit to the public.[83]

---

[75] 1967-1 C.B. 134.

[76] 1974-1 C.B. 129.

[77] 1966-2 C.B. 219.

[78] Id.

[79] 1976-1 C.B. 152.

[80] See RESTATEMENT (SECOND) TRUSTS § 375 (1959).

[81] Rev. Rul 76-204, 1976-1 C.B. 152.

[82] 1978-2 C.B. 174.

[83] See LAND TRUST ALLIANCE, STARTING A LAND TRUST: A GUIDE TO FORMING A LAND CONSERVATION ORGANIZATION (1990); JANET DIEHL ET AL., THE CONSERVATION EASEMENT HANDBOOK (1988) for an overview of land trusts and conservation easements.

§ 12.12   ECONOMIC & COMMUNITY DEVELOPMENT & LOW INCOME HOUSING

Organizations involved in economic and community development and providing affordable housing for the poor have long sought tax exemption under Section 501(c)(3) as charitable organizations. These organizations operate for the relief of the poor and distressed or of the underprivileged.[84]

In Revenue Ruling 74-587,[85] an organization was formed for the relief of poverty, the elimination of prejudice, the lessening of neighborhood tensions, and the combating of community deterioration through a program of financial assistance. Although some of the recipients of the financial assistance under the program were not themselves underprivileged, they were the instruments by which charitable purposes could be accomplished (building in low-income areas, providing loans for poor individuals). The organization qualified for exemption.

In Revenue Ruling 70-585,[86] organizations created to provide housing for low- or moderate-income families under federal and state programs sought tax exemption under Section 501(c)(3). The fact that an organization received public funds did not determine whether the organization qualified as exempt. The IRS stated that the facts and circumstances of each case are looked at in keeping with Regulation Section 1.501(c)(3)-1(d)(2), which defines the term *charitable* as including the relief of the poor and distressed or of the underprivileged.[87] The IRS analyzed each of the programs in accordance with these rules. In Situation 1, the organization was held exempt from federal income tax under Section 501(c)(3) because it provided homes for low-income families who could not otherwise afford them. In Situation 2, the organization was held exempt from federal income tax under Section 501(c)(3) because it constructed new housing and made it available to members of minority groups with low and moderate income who were unable to obtain housing because of local discrimination. In Situation 3, the organization was held to be charitable within the meaning of Section 501(c)(3) and therefore, was exempt from federal income tax. The organization's purpose was to combat community deterioration by assisting in the rehabilitation of an old and run-down residential area. In Situation 4, the organization was not entitled to exemption from federal income tax under Section 501(c)(3). Its purpose was to provide housing for moderate-income families in the community and not to provide relief to the poor or to carry on a charitable purpose.[88]

In Revenue Procedure 96-32,[89] the IRS clarified standards for low-income housing organizations seeking tax exemption under Section 501(c)(3). It states that an organization will qualify for exemption if at least 75 percent of the units are occupied by low-income families, and at least 20 percent by very-low-income

---

[84] I.R.C. § 501(c)(3).

[85] 1974-2 C.B. 162.

[86] 1970-2 C.B. 115.

[87] *Id.*

[88] *Id.*

[89] 1996-1 C.B. 717.

families. The "safe harbor" requires that the housing be affordable but allows landlords to evict tenants who do not pay.[90]

Organizations that offer credit counseling to individuals with debt issues have been held to qualify either as exempt 501(c)(3) educational organizations[91] or as exempt 501(c)(4) social welfare organizations.[92] This area quickly attracted persons who took advantage of the availability of tax exemption to scam unsuspecting consumers in need of credit help.

In the case of *Polacsek v. Debticated Consumer Counseling*,[93] for example, the operators of an exempt credit counseling organization spun off their back-office operations (advertising, marketing, executive salaries, and all other non-counseling services) to a for-profit operation owned by them. The income that supported these operations were the fees collected from counselees who believed that they were dealing with a bona fide nonprofit, tax exempt organization. One counselee sued for fraud and the issue was whether the 1996 Credit Repair Organizations Act[94] applied to credit counseling organizations. The court held that it did.

As consumer credit counseling moved more and more away from purely educational and counseling activities and began to focus on debt management plans and services or debt consolidation services, with commercial aspects to them, Congress felt a need to place restrictions on exempt 501(c)(3) and (c)(4) credit counseling organizations. In the Pension Protection Act of 2006, Congress added Section 501(q) to the Internal Revenue Code. This new section creates additional requirements that a credit counseling organization (no matter whether a section 501(c)(3) or 501(c)(4) organization) must meet to qualify for tax exemption.

Section 501(q) specifies that a bona fide tax exempt credit counseling organization must: (1) provide credit counseling service tailored to the specific needs of the consumer; (2) cannot make loans; (3) can only provide incidental services to improve consumer credit ratings and cannot charge a fee for such services; (4) cannot refuse its services to a consumer based on inability to pay or ineligibility/unwillingness of the consumer to enroll in a debt management plan; (5) can only charge reasonable fees, and must waive them if the consumer is unable to pay; (6) must have a governing board, the majority of whom represent broad public interests, and no more than 49 percent of the board can be organization employees or beneficiaries; (7) cannot own more than 35 percent of an entity that is involved in credit counseling or similar businesses; and (8) cannot pay for referrals or receive payments itself for referrals to debt management plans.

---

[90] *Id.*

[91] Rev. Rul. 69-441, 1962-2 C.B. 115. For 501(c)(3) status, IRS had required that the beneficiaries had to be low-income and could not be charged fees, but gave up on both of these requirements after the courts rejected them. In fact, there is nothing wrong with a bona fide exempt educational organization charging fees or serving more than low-income persons. *See* Consumer Credit Counseling Serv. of Ala., Inc. v. United States, 44 A.F.T.R.2d (RIA) 5122 (D.D.C. 1978).

[92] Rev. Rul. 65-299, 1965-2 C.B. 165.

[93] 413 F. Supp. 2d 539 (D. Md. 2005).

[94] 15 U.S.C. § 1679 *et seq.*

Chapter 13

IRC SECTION 501(c)(4): SOCIAL WELFARE ORGANIZATIONS

§ 13.01 INTRODUCTION

Section 501(c)(4) exempts two types of organizations from the federal income tax: (1) civic leagues or organizations not organized for profit but operated exclusively for the promotion of social welfare; and (2) local associations of employees, the membership of which is limited to the employees of a designated person or persons in a particular municipality, and the net earnings of which are devoted exclusively to charitable, educational, or recreational purposes.[1] The first of these is by far the largest group of Section 501(c)(4) organizations and they are often referred to as social welfare organizations.

Social welfare organizations are defined as organizations that are primarily engaged in promoting in some way the common good and general welfare of the community.[2] There is obviously a strong similarity here with Section 501(c)(3) organizations that, by definition, provide a public benefit. There is, however, a difference between 501(c)(3) public benefit organizations and Section 501(c)(4) social welfare organizations.

In many ways, Section 501(c)(4) status is the default form for Section 501(c)(3) status. Organizations that want to be Section 501(c)(3) with the benefits that accompany that status, primarily the ability to attract tax deductible gifts, but do not meet the requirements of Section 501(c)(3) because they are politically active, must settle for Section 501(c)(4) status.[3] Section 501 (c)(4) organizations, while still exempt from the federal income tax, cannot attract tax deductible gifts.[4]

On the other side of the equation, Section 501(c)(4) organizations are able to be much more politically active than Section 501(c)(3) organizations. While the political activities test for Section 501(c)(3) organizations prevents them from lobbying substantially and from electioneering at all, the political restrictions on Section 501(c)(4) organizations are very different. Lobbying for legislation that is relevant to the organization's programs is a permissible way for a Section 501(c)(4) organization to pursue its social welfare agenda. As a result, Section 501(c)(4)

---

[1] I.R.C. § 501(c)(4).

[2] 26 C.F.R. § 1.501(c)(4)-1(a)(2)(i).

[3] 26 C.F.R. § 1.501(c)(3)-1(c)(3)(v).

[4] *See* I.R.C. § 501(c)(3), (4); Elizabeth T. Boris, *Nonprofit Organizations in a Democracy: Varied Roles and Responsibilities, in* NONPROFITS AND GOVERNMENT 4 (Boris & Steuerle, eds., 1999).

organizations can, and usually do, lobby more than insubstantially.[5] Section 501(c)(4) organizations can also electioneer as long as electioneering is not a primary activity.[6] It will not take much for the IRS to so determine.[7]

Because of their ability to be more politically active, some Section 501(c)(4) organizations fall into the category of "action organizations" as defined by the Regulations. A substantial part of an action organization's activities include attempts to influence legislation; it participates or intervenes, directly or indirectly in campaigns for public office; and its primary objective, for which it actively campaigns, can only be achieved through the legislative process.[8] Note, however, that while Section 501(c)(4) organizations are often referred to as Section 501(c)(3) defaults[9] because they pursue a community benefit and could qualify as Section 501(c)(3) organizations except for their political activity, this choice must be made at the outset, when the organization is choosing which type of exempt status to pursue. A Section 501(c)(3) organization that loses its exempt status due to impermissible political activity may not become a Section 501(c)(4) organization.[10]

§ 13.02   APPLYING TESTS FOR TAX EXEMPTION

While there is no organizational test, per se, for Section 501(c)(4) organizations, the statute requires that they be organized as non-profit organizations, subject to the non-distribution constraint.[11]

The operational test for Section 501(c)(4) organizations requires that they be operated exclusively for 501(c)(4) purposes, but the IRS interprets "exclusively" to mean "primarily," which means that non-501(c)(4) activities are permissible as long as they are not substantial.[12]

The private inurement test for Section 501(c)(4) organizations requires that no part of the net earnings of such entity inure to the benefit of any private shareholder or individual.[13] It also prohibits "excess benefit" transactions as well.[14]

The political activities test for Section 501(c)(4) organizations only prohibits substantial electioneering. Lobbying and insubstantial electioneering are permis-

---

[5] 26 C.F.R. §§ 1.501(c)(4)-1(a)(2)(ii), 1.501(c)(3)-1(c)(3)(v). *See also* Rev. Rul. 67-293, 1967-2 C.B. 185, where 501(c)(4) status was approved for an organization whose only activity was lobbying; and Rev. Rul. 68-656, 1968-2 C.B. 216.

[6] 26 C.F.R. § 1.501(c)(4)-1(a)(2)(ii); Rev. Rul. 81-95, 1981-1 C.B. 332. Electioneering expenditures made by 501(c)(4) organizations may be subject to taxation under I.R.C. § 527(f).

[7] See Rev. Rul. 67-368, 1967-2 C.B. 185, where a group that published non-partisan ratings of political candidates was denied 501(c)(4) status.

[8] 26 C.F.R. § 1.501(c)(3)-1(c)(3)(ii), (iii), (iv).

[9] I.R.C. § 501(c)(4) is often viewed as the default § 501(c)(3) status for organizations that are too politically active to qualify for exemption under § 501(c)(3). *See also* 26 C.F.R. § 1.501(c)(3)-1(c)(3)(v).

[10] I.R.C. § 504(a).

[11] *Id.* ("Civic leagues and organizations organized not for profit . . .").

[12] 26 C.F.R. § 1.501(c)(4)-1(a)(2)(i). See § 6.03 for further information on the operational test.

[13] I.R.C. § 501(c)(4)(B).

[14] I.R.C. § 4958(e)(1).

sible.[15]

§ 13.03 DEFINING SOCIAL WELFARE

The examination of whether an organization is being operated for Section 501(c)(4) purposes must start with the concept of "social welfare." This is a difficult concept to define accurately, because it is so broad. The IRS refers to Webster's New World Dictionary to define the term. Webster's defines "social welfare" as "a service or activity designed to promote the welfare of the community and the individual, as through counseling services, health clinics, recreation halls and playgrounds. . . ."[16] It then notes that the dictionary definition is a lot like its own, in the Regulations, where a social welfare organization is defined as operated exclusively for the promotion of social welfare if it is primarily engaged in promoting in some way the common good and the general welfare of the community.[17]

Because the term "social welfare" is so broad, it has become easier to refer to the types of activities the IRS has already determined to be social welfare activities. They include (but are not limited to):

* providing water and sewer service for low-income housing;[18]

* rehabilitating and finding employment for older workers;[19]

* constructing a stadium for a public school district;[20]

* providing advice on casualty insurance to students, teachers, and employees of a public school district;[21]

* providing antenna service for television reception in a community;[22]

* loaning money for the purchase and improvement of land in a designated "redevelopment area" in order to fight unemployment;[23]

* studying and educating the public, in a non-commercial manner, on simple, dignified funerals, and keeping a record of its members' wishes as to the same;[24]

---

[15] Rev. Rul. 68-656, 1968-2 C.B. 216; 26 C.F.R. § 1.501(c)(4)-1(a)(2)(ii); Rev. Rul. 2004-6, 2004-4 I.R.B. 328.

[16] I.R.S., Exempt Organizations Continuing Professional Education Technical Instruction Program Textbook Chapter G (1981).

[17] 26 C.F.R. § 1.501(c)(4)-1(a)(2)(i).

[18] Rev. Rul. 55-439, 1955-2 C.B. 257.

[19] Rev. Rul. 57-297, 1957-2 C.B. 307.

[20] Rev. Rul. 57-493, 1957-2 C.B. 314.

[21] Rev. Rul. 61-153, 1961-2 C.B. 114.

[22] Rev. Rul. 62-167, 1962-2 C.B. 142.

[23] Rev. Rul. 64-187, 1964-1 C.B. 187.

[24] Rev. Rul. 64-313, 1964-2 C.B. 146.

- operating community benefit training and youth programs as a "junior chamber of commerce;"[25]

- providing a credit counseling service;[26]

- beautifying and maintaining a public area, adjoining members' homes and businesses;[27] and

- providing crime fighting, public safety services, housing, community development, recreational, and other community services to both members and non-members, including contracting with a security patrol service.[28]

This is a rather broad list of activities that the IRS has determined are valid "social welfare" activities under IRC Section 501(c)(4). It is impossible to derive a common theme from them in terms of the activities performed. But one element that each of the above activities has in common with the others is that it provides some form of "community benefit." By definition, Section 501(c)(4) social welfare organizations must provide a community benefit.[29]

---

[25] Rev. Rul. 65-195, 1965-2 C.B. 164. Regular chambers of commerce are exempt under I.R.C. § 501(c)(6).

[26] Rev. Rul. 65-299, 1965-2 C.B. 165.

[27] Rev. Rul. 75-286, 1975-2 C.B. 210.

[28] Rev. Rul. 75-386, 1975-2 C.B. 211. *But see* Rev. Rul. 77-273, 1977-2 C.B. 194, where an organization that provided security services but charged its members for them did not qualify for 501(c)(4) status. This is not a complete list of "social welfare" organizations; it is merely a sampling. Other "social welfare" organizations include: Organizations that operate a water storage and distribution system for a community, Rev. Rul. 66-148, 1966-1 C.B. 143; provide a shooting range and firearms instruction to a community, Rev. Rul. 66-273, 1966-2 C.B. 222; operate a roller rink, in a publicly owned building, open to the public that charges only nominal dues and admission fees, Rev. Rul. 67-109, 1967-1 C.B. 136; loan money to businesses which agree to locate in a depressed area in order to combat unemployment, Rev. Rul. 67-294, 1967-2 C.B. 193; encourage young people to attend athletic events, including providing free admission, Rev. Rul. 68-118, 1968-1 C.B. 261; provide a community with recreation and ways to demonstrate interest in its customs and traditions by staging a festival that focuses on these themes, Rev. Rul. 68-224, 1968-1 C.B. 262; process consumer complaints on products and services and attempting to work out solutions with the parties involved, Rev. Rul. 78-50, 1978-1 C.B. 155; provide bus services to enable workers from a major population center to reach employment in a suburban area which was not served by public transportation, Rev. Rul. 78-69, 1978-1 C.B. 156; encourage interest in art by holding community art shows, in a non-commercial fashion, Rev. Rul. 78-131, 1978-1 C.B. 156; operate a rural airport, in an area not otherwise served, to benefit the area's economy, Rev. Rul. 78-429, 1978-2 C.B. 178; prevent and cleaning up oil spills in a port, on an equal charge basis, whether the spill was caused by a member or nonmember, Rev. Rul. 79-316, 1979-2 C.B. 228; and organize and operating a beauty pageant, including awarding cash prizes or scholarships to participants, Miss Georgia Scholarship Fund v. Commissioner, 72 T.C. 267 (1979); Rev Rul. 56-403, 1956-2 C.B. 307. The pageant's entrance requirements must be such that a broad enough class is benefited. *See also* Rev. Rul. 81-116, 1981-1 C.B. 333 where an "organization that provides and maintains free off-street parking to anyone visiting the city's downtown business district qualifies for exemption under" I.R.C. § 501(c)(4); and Rev. Rul. 87-126, 1987-48 I.R.B. 4, 1987-2 C.B. 150, where a nonprofit firefighters' association that provided firefighters with retirement benefits funded by government sources as the exclusive retirement benefits provided to these firefighters qualified for exemption as a social welfare organization under I.R.C. § 501 (c)(4). It was key to the IRS in its decision that the retirement fund was funded and operated by the local government and not the police department itself, distinguishing it from Rev. Rul. 81-58.

[29] *See* 26 C.F.R. § 1.501(c)(4)-1(a)(2).

§ 13.04   COMMUNITY BENEFIT

In determining whether an organization is promoting the welfare of the community, the issue is always: who benefits? If the beneficiary class is too small, as for example, where organizations benefit only their members, it will be difficult, if not impossible, to find the required community benefit.[30]

On the other hand, when benefits are available to the general public, a community benefit is present.[31]

[A]   Generally

In the case of *Eden Hall Farm v. United States*,[32] the IRS argued that a guest home for working girls and women did not provide a community benefit because invitations to use the home were extended by the trustees to a very limited group of women, practically all of whom were employees of the H.J. Heinz Company. The trustees in so doing were following the instructions of the testator, a former executive of the Heinz Company, who had bequeathed the property for this use. While in its early years, the sole guests were Heinz employees on vacation or convalescing, the home was opened up to other female employees of nearby hospitals and school districts and to their female guests. The court found that when one segment of the community is served, namely the thousands of working women who qualified to use the home, the community as a whole benefits. The court dismissed the IRS's emphasis on the restrictive nature of who could be invited to the home as simply a matter of honoring the testator's intent.[33]

The IRS has announced that it will not follow this case.[34] It acknowledged that organizations that provide a particular type of recreational activity, by definition, only serve those who prefer that kind of activity. Though by definition, the IRS stated that such a limitation did not prevent the activity from providing a community benefit. But a limitation on who could use a recreational facility based on where they were employed meant that the activity benefited a private group and not the common good and general welfare of the community.[35] If the restrictions placed on the property's use had been the result of the property's legitimate size constrictions rather than limiting the type of people who use the property, the IRS would have looked at the issue differently. For instance, if the property were too small to invite or accommodate more than a certain number of people, the issue could have been considered differently.

---

[30] See, for example, Police Benevolent Ass'n of Richmond v. United States, 661 F. Supp. 765 (E.D. Va. 1987), where a police benevolent society whose main activity was to provide pensions to retired police from their own contributions to the fund and from outside donations was found not to be operated for the promotion of social welfare because it was essentially a mutual self interest organization operated for the benefit of its members.

[31] *See* Comm'r v. Lake Forest, Inc., 305 F.2d 814 (4th Cir. 1962), *overruled by*, 36 T.C. 510 (1961).

[32] 389 F. Supp. 858 (W.D. Pa. 1975).

[33] *Id.*

[34] Rev. Rul. 80-25, 1980-1 C.B. 65.

[35] *Id.*

[B]   Homeowners' Associations

[1]   Generally

A large portion of the law on the determination of "community benefit" has developed in regard to homeowner's associations. In the case of *Commissioner v. Lake Forest, Inc.*,[36] the Fourth Circuit agreed with the IRS that a nonprofit housing cooperative organized by and for World War II veterans that provided low-cost housing to its members did not qualify as a social welfare organization. Applying the words of the statute, the court said that the organization was an "aggregation of homeowners bound together in a structured unit formed as an integral part of a plan for the development of a real estate subdivision and the sale and purchase of homes therein."[37] As a result, it was not a social welfare organization benefiting a community, but merely a private business enterprise.[38]

In Revenue Ruling 69-280,[39] the homeowners' association provided exterior maintenance of the roofs and walls of the members' homes. The IRS determined that this provision of a private benefit meant that the organization was not a social welfare organization benefiting a defined community, but rather a form of self-help enterprise, much like the homeowners cooperative in Lake Forest, benefiting primarily its members. As the ruling stated, "[T]he organization here described is performing services that its members would otherwise have to provide for themselves. It is a private cooperative enterprise for the economic benefit or convenience of its members."[40]

In Revenue Ruling 72-102,[41] the IRS determined that, "[f]or purposes of Section 501(c)(4) of the IRC, a neighborhood, precinct, subdivision, or housing development may constitute a community. For example, exempt civic leagues in urban areas have traditionally represented neighborhoods or other subparts of much larger political units."[42] In the facts of the ruling, a housing developer formed a homeowners' association of residents within a development that administered and enforced covenants in the housing development and owned and maintained common areas, such as green areas, sidewalks, and streets for the use of all residents in the development. The IRS found that, "[b]y administering and enforcing covenants, and owning and maintaining certain non-residential, non-commercial properties of the type normally owned and maintained by municipal governments, this organization is serving the common good and the general welfare of the people of the entire development."[43]

---

[36]   305 F.2d 814.

[37]   *Id.* at 820.

[38]   *Id.*

[39]   1969-1 C.B. 152.

[40]   *Id.*

[41]   1972-1 C.B. 149.

[42]   *Id.*

[43]   *Id.*

Within two years, the IRS realized that it had perhaps spoken too broadly in Revenue Ruling 72-102, because it gave the impression that a single housing development could qualify as a "community." In Revenue Ruling 74-99,[44] the IRS re-defined "community." In that ruling, the IRS said that, for a homeowners' association to qualify under Section 501(c)(4), "it must serve a 'community' which bears a reasonable recognizable relationship to an area ordinarily identified as governmental."[45] In that same Ruling, the IRS also clarified that exempt home-owners associations could not maintain the private property of the owners, because that would be a private benefit, and, for the same reason, that common areas maintained by the association must be open to the general public.[46] The IRS also held that, by their nature, condominium associations, although structured like homeowners' associations, were private benefit organizations.[47]

In Revenue Ruling 80-63,[48] the IRS posed and answered four questions to clarify Revenue Ruling 74-99. On whether a community had to be a certain minimum area or number of homes, the IRS said the determination of community was fact specific. It did state, however, that if common areas and facilities were open for the use and enjoyment of the general public, it would not matter if the homeowners' association qualified as its own community or not, because it was providing a public benefit.[49]

On whether a homeowners' association, which itself did not represent a commu-nity, could restrict the use of its recreational facilities to members, the IRS said that such facilities had to be open to the general public.[50] The other side of this issue, whether a homeowners' association that does represent a sufficiently large group to qualify as its own community could limit use of common and recreational areas to its members only was not answered in the ruling, however.[51]

On whether a separate organization formed to own and maintain recreational facilities, whose use was limited to members of a homeowners' association, could qualify for its own exemption, the IRS replied that it could, not as a Section 501(c)(4) organization, but as a Section 501(c)(7) social club.[52] Finally, on whether a homeowners' association that does not represent a community can own and maintain parking facilities for its members, the IRS's answer was the obvious: that it would be a private and not a public benefit.[53]

In the case of *Rancho Santa Fe Association v. United States*,[54] the court was presented with the issue of whether a homeowners' association provided a commu-

---

[44] 1974-1 C.B. 131.

[45] *Id.*

[46] *Id.*

[47] Rev. Rul. 74-17, 1974-1 C.B. 130.

[48] 1980-1 C.B. 116.

[49] *Id.*

[50] *Id.*

[51] *Id.*

[52] *Id.* (citing Rev. Rul. 69-281, 1969-1 C.B. 155).

[53] Rev. Rul. 80-63.

[54] 589 F. Supp. 54 (S.D. Cal. 1984).

nity benefit. Rancho Santa Fe was a large, self-contained housing development incorporated as a nonprofit cooperative in 1927, and granted exempt status as a social welfare organization in 1942, under a predecessor statute to Section 501(c)(4). It consisted of about 3,000 members, all of whom owned a home within the 6,100 acre Rancho Santa Fe development. In 1979, the IRS revoked its exempt status on the grounds that the homeowners association was not operated exclusively for social welfare because not all of its common areas were open to the general public.[55]

In fact, that was not exactly true. Most of Rancho Santa Fe's common areas, which consisted of more than 460 acres, including open spaces, parkland, playgrounds, athletic fields, a parking lot, a community clubhouse, hiking and bridal trails, streets, sidewalk, and the commercial area of Rancho Santa Fe, were open to the general public. What was not open to the public was the association's 18-hole golf course and its eight tennis courts. These were restricted to members and their guests.[56]

The court found that Rancho Santa Fe benefited the community in two ways. First, there was the obvious community benefit of the open space and parkland being available to members of the general public. Second, the court found that Rancho Santa Fe qualified as its own community. It was not a run-of-the-mill residential development, but "an independent community separated geographically . . . which has its own post office and zip code."[57] Because it was its own community, the benefits which it restricted to its members actually benefited the community! *Rancho Santa Fe* is most notable for this last part of the holding, and stands for the fact that a zip code constitutes a community.[58]

In *Flat Top Lake Association v. United States*,[59] an association of homeowners in a development constructed around an artificial lake sought tax exempt status as a Section 501(c)(4) social welfare organization. Although the association had the requisite number of homeowners to incorporate as a class four municipality under West Virginia law, it chose not to do so, remaining a privately held corporation. Within the development, the association performed quasi-governmental functions. It built and maintained roads and a bridge. It maintained common areas, including a park and the lake itself. It provided waste disposal and contracted for a police service. The problem was that none of these common areas was open to the public. Even road use was limited to property owners. On that basis, the court upheld the IRS's denial of exemption, saying, "Although it is unquestionably their right to do so, when a group of citizens elects, as have the inhabitants of Flat Top Lake, to separate themselves from society and establish an entity that solely advances their own private interests, no potential for general social advancement is implicated."[60] In retrospect, Flat Top Lake should have made itself its own municipality. Then, it would have qualified as a community bearing a recognizable relationship to a

---

[55] *Id.* at 55.

[56] *Id.* at 55–56.

[57] *Id.*

[58] *Id.* at 57.

[59] 868 F.2d 108 (4th Cir. 1989).

[60] *Id.* at 112.

governmental unit.[61] But then it would have had to let other people in to use the lake, park, and roads.[62]

[2]   IRC Section 528

The litigation over the exempt status of homeowners' associations under Section 501(c)(4) greatly decreased after Congress added Section 528 to the IRC in the Tax Reform Act of 1976.[63] Under Section 528, the exempt function income (membership dues, fees or assessments) of homeowners' associations, condominium management associations, residential real estate management associations, and timeshare associations is not taxed as long as the following conditions are met: the organization is organized and operated to provide for the acquisition, construction, management, maintenance, and care of association property; 60 percent or more of the association's income is exempt function income; 90 percent or more of expenditures in a tax year are for the acquisition, construction, management, maintenance, and care of association property; there is no private inurement; and the association elects to be covered by Section 528.[64] With the addition of Section 528, homeowners' associations have a safe harbor, if they choose to use it. They are, of course, still free to seek 501(c)(4) status.

In the legislative history of the Tax Reform Act of 1976,[65] Congress assessed the Section 501(c)(4) social welfare status of homeowners' associations:

> Under present law, generally a homeowner association may qualify as an organization exempt from federal income tax . . . only if it meets three requirements. First, the homeowners' association must serve a "community" that bears a reasonably recognizable relationship to an area ordinarily identified as a governmental subdivision or unit. Second, it must not conduct activities directed to the exterior maintenance of any private residence. Third, common areas or facilities that the homeowners' association owns and maintains must be for the use and enjoyment of the general public.[66]

The statute may be viewed as a "double-taxation" statute of which McGovern spoke of in his article, *The Exemption Provisions of Subchapter F.*[67] Because the income was taxed once in the hands of the association members, Congress saw no point in taxing it again in the hands of the association. Note, though, what does not escape the tax. The passive income of a Section 528 organization is taxed, because it is not exempt function income.[68] This is not the case for Section 501(c)(4)

---

[61]   Rev. Rul. 74-99, 1974-1 C.B. 131.

[62]   *Id. See also Homeowners' Association's Tax Exempt Status Revoked*, 106 J. Tax'n 251 (2007).

[63]   Pub. Law No. 94-455, 90 Stat. 1520.

[64]   See § 16.01 *et seq.* on unrelated business income tax.

[65]   Pub. L. No. 94-455, 90 Stat. 1520.

[66]   H.R. Rep. No. 94-658, at 326–32, *as reprinted in* 1976 U.S.C.C.A.N. 2897, 3222–29; S. Rep. No. 94-938, pt. 1. at 393, *as reprinted in* 1976 U.S.C.C.A.N. 2897, 3438, 3822 (citing Rev. Rul. 74-99, 1974-1 C.B. 131).

[67]   James J. McGovern, *The Exemption Provisions of Subchapter F*, 29 Tax Law. 523 (1976).

[68]   The tax is 30% of such income, minus allowable deductions for homeowners' associations, 32

organizations, whose passive income (unless debt-financed) is not taxed.[69]

§ 13.05 RELATIONSHIP BETWEEN SECTION 501(c)(4) & SECTION 501(c)(3)

In *Regan v. Taxation with Representation*,[70] the organization was originally two separate, but related organizations: one a 501(c)(3) organization and the other a 501(c)(4) organization. When the merged organization sought exempt status under Section 501(c)(3), but wished to continue its lobbying activities as if it were still a Section 501(c)(4) organization, it challenged the validity of the lobbying restrictions on Section 501(c)(3) organizations on First Amendment and equal protection grounds. The First Amendment argument did not go anywhere. There are numerous cases that say that the government has no obligation to subsidize constitutional rights.[71] The D.C. Circuit did hold, however, that the lobbying restrictions on 501(c)(3) organizations violated the equal protection clause because other 501(c) organizations, namely Section 501(c)(19) veterans' organizations were allowed to lobby, and could still attract tax-deductible donations.[72]

Reversal from the United States Supreme Court came rather quickly.[73] The First Amendment analysis was basically the same as in the lower courts. The First Amendment does not require that government subsidize a Section 501(c)(3)'s lobbying activities with tax deductible gifts.[74] Congress has made a valid judgment that tax-deductible dollars are charitable dollars, and must be used for charitable activities, which excludes, by definition, any political activities. On the equal protection argument, the United States Supreme Court said that there was a long-standing government policy of compensating veterans for their contributions to the country by providing them with certain advantages, and this policy has always been found legitimate. It reversed the circuit court.[75]

This case is actually referenced more for Justice Blackmun's concurrence.[76] He says that he would be inclined to find the lobbying restrictions on Section 501(c)(3) organizations unconstitutional on First Amendment grounds, were it not for the fact that Section 501(c)(3) organizations can have captive Section 501(c)(4) organizations that can lobby on their behalf. Lobbying, Blackmun says, is a protected First Amendment activity, and when Congress denies exempt status and eligibility to receive tax deductible gifts to an organization because of its substantial lobbying activities, it is denying a significant benefit to an organization for choosing to

---

percent for timeshare associations. I.R.C. § 528(b), (d).

[69] McGovern, *supra* note 67, at 526.

[70] 461 U.S. 540 (1983), *overruled by*, 676 F.2d 715 (D.C. Cir. 1982).

[71] *See* Buckley v. Valeo, 424 U.S. 1 (1976); Maher v. Roe, 432 U.S. 464 (1977); Harris v. McRae, 448 U.S. 297 (1980).

[72] *Taxation with Representation*, 461 U.S. at 547.

[73] *Id.*

[74] *Id.* at 546; *see also* Cammarano v. United States, 358 U.S. 498 (1959).

[75] *Id.*

[76] *Id.*

exercise its constitutional rights. This constitutional defect is cured, Blackmun says, by the ability of Section 501(c)(3) organizations to have Section 501(c)(4) affiliates through whom they can pursue their charitable goals by lobbying.[77]

As long as the IRS permits this relationship between Section 501(c)(3) organizations and Section 501(c)(4) organizations, and requires only that they be separately incorporated and keep records to show that no tax deductible contributions are used to pay for lobbying, and goes no further, Blackmun endorses this scheme. "A Section 501(c)(3) organization's right to speak is not infringed because it is free to make known its views on legislation through its Section 501(c)(4) affiliate without losing tax benefits for its nonlobbying activities."[78]

In fact, the relationship that Justice Blackmun described between Section 501(c)(3) organizations and affiliated Section 501(c)(4) organizations is quite common, although it might be said that Blackmun has it in reverse.[79] Instead of a Section 501(c)(3) charitable organization controlling an affiliated Section 501(c)(4) social welfare organization, it is more often the case that the Section 501(c)(4) predominates in the relationship, and uses the affiliated Section 501(c)(3) organization to attract tax deductible gifts for its nonlobbying activities. For example, the National Organization for Women (NOW) is a Section 501(c)(4) organization because of its political activities, but it controls a related NOW Foundation, which is a Section 501(c)(3) organization that can attract tax-deductible donations for NOW's bona fide charitable activities.[80]

Because the activities of Section 501(c)(4) social welfare organizations and those of Section 501(c)(3) public benefit organizations can overlap outside of the political arena, it can happen that donors make gifts to Section 501(c)(4) organizations thinking that they are tax deductible. Such confusion is not limited just to Section 501(c)(4) organizations, of course, but is simply more common in the 501(c)(3)-501(c)(4) overlap. To deal with this confusion, Congress has added Section 6113 to the IRC which requires non-501(c)(3) exempt organizations to disclose in their fundraising materials that gifts to them are not tax deductible.[81]

Another option available to section 501(c)(3) organizations that wish to lobby without fear of IRS action, and that would rather not rely on the "insubstantial part test" of section 501(c)(3),[82] is to elect IRC section 501(h) and file IRS form 5768.[83] IRC § 501(h) allows section 501(c)(3) charitable organizations (except for churches and auxiliaries of churches) to elect to lobby and to set a dollar limit on lobbying expenditures equal to a percentage of "exempt purpose expenditures." "Exempt purpose expenditures" include:

1.   Lobbying expenses;

---

[77] *Id.*

[78] *Id.* at 553.

[79] *Id.*

[80] *See* About Now, *available at* http://www.now.org/about.html (last visited Nov. 8, 2010).

[81] I.R.C. § 6113(a). Failure to comply can result in substantial penalties. *See* I.R.C. § 6710.

[82] I.R.C. § 501(c)(3).

[83] I.R.C. § 501(h); *see* I.R.C. § 501(c)(3).

2.   Grants to other organizations;

3.   Most in-house fundraising costs; and

4.   Funds from government grants and private foundations.

For most organizations, the list of exempt purpose expenditures is the organization's budget.[84] Expenses for separate fundraising units and outside fundraising
consultants are not included.

For this equation, the following applies. Direct lobbying includes communication
with a legislator expressing a view about specific legislation. Nonpartisan analysis,
requests for technical advice, and self-defense measures are not considered
"lobbying."[85] Grassroots lobbying includes communication with the general public
expressing a view about specific legislation with a "call to action."[86] Grassroots
lobbying may account for up to one-fourth of the total lobbying limit, and direct
lobbying may make up the rest.

§ 13.06   SECTION 501(c)(4) & FEDERAL ELECTION CAMPAIGN ACT

Section 501(c)(4) organizations may electioneer to an insubstantial degree.
Federal electioneering activities are governed by the Federal Election Campaign
Act (FECA).[87] That Act states that corporations and labor unions are prohibited
from making any political contributions or expenditures unless they establish a
separate, segregated fund for that purpose.[88] In other words, they cannot use their
general funds to electioneer, but must use these separate segregated funds, which
are solicited and used for political purposes.

In the case of *FEC v. Massachusetts Citizens for Life, Inc.*,[89] the United States
Supreme Court carved out a narrow exception from this prohibition on the use of
general funds to electioneer for political advocacy associations that are incorporated
but present no risk to the political process by their direct participation in it.[90] These
organizations are non-profit, tax exempt 501(c)(4) organizations, with no shareholders or other claims on its assets or earnings, which do not themselves accept
corporate donations, but rather get their funds from the donations and fundraising
activities of their members. Such organizations are, in effect, simply the unified
voice of their members. In such situations, the United States Supreme Court ruled
that FECA's prohibition on corporate expenditures for political purposes violated
the First Amendment.

---

[84] Nicholas P. Cafardi & Jaclyn Fabean Cherry, Tax Exempt Organizations: Cases and Materials 711
(2d ed. 2008).

[85] *Id.* at 711–12.

[86] *Id.*

[87] 2 U.S.C. §§ 431–455.

[88] *Id.* See also § 15.01 *et seq.* on § 527 Organizations.

[89] 479 U.S. 238 (1986).

[90] *Id.*

In *Beaumont v. Federal Election Commission*,[91] the Fourth Circuit also found that FECA's prohibition on corporate contributions violated the First Amendment as to such member-driven and financed advocacy organizations. Of course, all of this litigation could have been successfully avoided by the establishment of a Section 527 organization with separate, segregated funds to carry on the 501(c)(4)'s political activities.[92]

§ 13.07   LOCAL ASSOCIATIONS OF EMPLOYEES

These are the forgotten (c)(4)'s. They are local associations of employees, and as the statute states, their membership is limited to the employees of a designated person or persons in a particular municipality, and their net earnings are devoted exclusively to charitable, educational, or recreational purposes.[93]

There is not very much legal activity, cases, or revenue rulings that help to define this area. "Local" in the definition means "confined to a particular community, place or district, irrespective . . . of political subdivisions."[94] It has nothing to do with where the employees live, but rather where the employer is located. Should the employer have locations in more than one area, then an employees' association representing all the employer's locations would not be a local employees' association.[95] Retired employees remain as members of these associations if they were members when they retired.[96]

Organizations that provide certain services to employees, such as bus service, retirement or death benefits, or joint purchasing discounts do not qualify under this section, because they do not operate for charitable, educational, or religious purposes.[97] An organization that operated a gas station for members only and that used the proceeds to fund recreational activities, however, did qualify for 501(c)(4) status.[98]

---

[91] 278 F.3d 261 (4th Cir. 2002).

[92] Note that in *FEC v. Massachusetts Citizens for Life*, 479 U.S. 238 (1986), the United States Supreme Court found the statutory requirements for such separate organizations to be unduly burdensome as to member-driven and financed advocacy organizations. *And see* Citizens United v. Federal Election Comm'n, 130 S. Ct. 876 (2010), where the United States Supreme Court held that the government may not suppress political speech on the basis of the speaker's corporate identity in accordance with the First Amendment.

[93] I.R.C. § 501(c)(4).

[94] John Francis Reilly, Carter C. Hull & Barbara A. Braig Allen, *I.R.C. § 501(c)(4) Organizations*, p. I-34 (2003 EO CPE Text), *available at* http://www.irs.gov/pub/irs-tege/eotopici03.pdf.

[95] *Id.*

[96] Rev. Rul. 74-281, 1974-1 C.B. 133.

[97] Rev. Rul. 55-311, 1955-1 C.B. 72; Rev. Rul. 66-59, 1966-1 C.B. 142; Rev. Rul 79-128, 1979-1 C.B. 197 (cited in 2003 EO CPE Text).

[98] Rev. Rul. 66-180, 1966-1 C.B. 144.

§ 13.08   CREDIT COUNSELING GROUPS

Credit counseling groups have come under fire recently for alleged abuses in the way they operate their organizations. Questions about whether these groups are remaining loyal to their charitable missions continue to rise.[99] The concern is that organizations claiming to be nonprofits are actually commercial operators taking advantage of the tax exempt system.[100]

An example of such a situation can be seen in *Polacsek v. Debticated Consumer Counseling*,[101] where the defendant, Debticated Consumer Counseling, a nonprofit consumer counseling organization, claimed that it was excluded from the provisions of the Credit Repair Organizations Act (CROA) and therefore that plaintiffs had no cause of action. The question for the court was whether Debticated operated a *de facto* for-profit corporation, making it subject to CROA.

Here, the defendant was a nonprofit Credit Counseling Association and its back-office for-profit counterparts. The plaintiff was a consumer who contacted, and eventually used, the nonprofit to address her troubling financial situation.

In an effort to discern whether Debticated was a nonprofit, the court provided some background into how nonprofit credit counseling agencies began as community-based, nonprofit organizations offering a full range of counseling services with trained counselors advising consumers about how to deal with their financial situations. A popular option was for credit counseling agencies to offer debt management plans where credit counselors would contact a consumer's unsecured creditors and negotiate lower monthly payments and lower interest rates, among other things. The consumer's lower payments would then be consolidated into single payments distributed to creditors through the counseling agency. Over time, the nonprofit credit counseling agencies started contracting with for-profit affiliates to take over the "back office" types of duties (i.e., advertising, marketing, executive salaries), which is what occurred in this case.

The court denied summary judgment and remanded the case for the trier of fact to determine whether the defendant was operating as a for-profit organization.[102]

Later, I.R.C. § 501(q) was enacted,[103] which provides that a credit counseling service must be a section 501(c)(3) or a section 501(c)(4) organization. Further, it provides additional requirements that these agencies must meet in an effort to address and curtail the abuse occurring in this area of the sector.

The courts are looking beyond credit counseling groups, in their efforts to stem abuse by organizations claiming tax exemption as a cover for their commercial

---

[99] CAFARDI, *supra* note 84, at 735.

[100] *Id.* at 735–48. For further reading on the IRS scrutiny of Credit Counseling Agencies, see *IRS Takes New Steps on Credit Counseling Groups Following Widespread Abuse*, STATE NEWS SERVICE (May 15, 2006), and Sabatini, *IRS Slams Credit Counseling Agencies, Probe Finds Rampant Abuse, Dozens Losing Tax-Exempt Status*, PITTSBURGH POST-GAZETTE, May 16, 2006, at A-8.

[101] 413 F. Supp. 2d 539 (D. Md. 2005).

[102] *Id.*; *and see* Rev. Rul. 65-299, 1965-2 C.B. 165).

[103] I.R.C. § 501(q).

entities. In *Vision Service Plan v. United States*,[104] the court determined that an organization providing eye care services in medically needy or underserved neighborhoods did not operate for a community benefit, but was operated as a business in a manner similar to organizations operated for-profit. The Plan provided eye care services through small business subscribers, and through them individual enrollees. The Plan claimed it was organized as a § 501(c)(4) organization because it served broad segments of the community through direct services as well as through charity work. The court found that the Plan's operation did not equate to promoting social welfare because it competitively bid for profitable Medicaid and Medicare contracts; its reduced fees were costs absorbed by the individual doctors, not the Plan; the charitable work the Plan participated in was not substantial; and the organization engaged in cost-cutting measures common to for-profit businesses. The executive salaries were also high and consistent with for-profit businesses. After the District Court found that VSP was not a 501(c)(4), several VSP organizations filed an appeal in circuit court hoping for a better result. The court concluded that VSP did not operate primarily for the promotion of social welfare and therefore concluded that the organization did not qualify for tax exemption as a 501(c)(4).[105]

---

[104] 2005 U.S. Dist. LEXIS 38812 (E.D. Cal. Dec. 12, 2005).

[105] Vision Services Plan, Inc. v. United States, 101 A.F.T.R.2d (RIA) 656 (9th Cir. 2008); *See* 26 C.F.R. § 1.501(c)(4)-1(a)(2)(i).

Chapter 14

OTHER TAX EXEMPT ORGANIZATIONS

§ 14.01 INTRODUCTION

This chapter will focus on the more common forms of Section 501(c) tax exempt organizations beyond the Section 501(c)(3) and Section 501(c)(4) organizations discussed in earlier chapters. These organizations include Section 501(c)(2) Title Holding Companies, Section 501(c)(5) Labor Unions, Agriculture and Horticulture Organizations, Section 501(c)(6) Business Leagues, Section 501(c)(7) Social Clubs, Section 501(c)(8) Fraternal Benefit Societies, and a range of other Section 501(c) specialty organizations.

One element that all of these organizations have in common is that they are a type of mutual benefit organization, which exist to further the common goals of the organization's members rather than the public at large. While they are exempt from the federal income tax, these organizations do not normally qualify to receive tax deductible contributions or other tax exempt benefits enjoyed by 501(c)(3) organizations.[1]

§ 14.02 RATIONALES

Because these organizations are formed mainly to provide goods and services to their members at cost and only provide an incidental public benefit, one might ask why these organizations are granted tax exempt status to begin with. The answer lies in McGovern's immorality argument.[2] In general terms, members of these organizations pay membership dues to gain a mutual benefit with their co-members and any overcharge paid by the members will be refunded or used to provide future services to its members.[3] A year-end surplus, then, is more properly classified as an overage and not as income. To classify the surplus as income would result in punishing its members, through taxation, for being clever shoppers or because they performed unpaid services to society.

---

[1] Veterans organizations, fraternal societies (if the gift is used for charitable purposes), and cemetery companies may receive tax deductible contributions, pursuant to I.R.C. § 170(c)(3)(5).

[2] James J. McGovern, *The Exemption Provisions of Subchapter F*, 29 TAX LAW. 523 (1976). See §§ 5.09 and 13.04[B][2] for further information on McGovern's article.

[3] Boris Bitker & George Rahdert, *The Exemption of Nonprofit Organizations from Federal Income Taxation*, 85 YALE L.J. 299, 348–57 (1976).

§ 14.03 SECTION 501(c)(2) ORGANIZATIONS: TITLE HOLDING COMPANIES

Section 501(c)(2) allows exempt organizations to form a separate tax exempt entity called a title holding company, which is used to hold real and personal property for the benefit of one exempt parent organization. Section 501(c)(25) allows for smaller tax exempt organizations to form the same type of entity as Section 501(c)(2) by pooling their funds together in order to purchase investment property, thereby affording these smaller organizations the same benefit that larger exempt organizations receive from Section 501(c)(2).[4] These organizations are formed to collect income, pay expenses, distribute earnings to the exempt organization, overcome state laws that prevent exempt organizations from holding property, protect the nonprofit from liability, enhance the organization's ability to borrow against property and simplify management and accounting. Congress limited the benefit of these companies by permitting title holding companies to receive only up to 10 percent of gross income from unrelated business activities.[5]

§ 14.04 SECTION 501(c)(5) ORGANIZATIONS: LABOR, AGRICULTURE & HORTICULTURE ORGANIZATIONS

[A] Generally

Section 501(c)(5) provides tax exemption for labor, agriculture, and horticulture organizations that have as their objects the betterment of the conditions of those engaged in such pursuits, the improvement of the grade of their products and the development of a higher degree of efficiency in their occupation.[6] Additionally, these organizations may educate members, process grievances, negotiate working conditions, and engage in litigation and lobbying activities.[7] They can also publish tax exempt labor newspapers for their members and others,[8] operate a hiring hall,[9] provide legal defense for their members,[10] and maintain strike funds[11] all as part of their exempt function activities. The members of these organizations are allowed to receive secondary benefits, including the payment of death, sickness, accident, and other similar benefits; however, the organization will be denied tax exemption if the main benefit is geared towards the group's members and not towards the improvement of their occupation.[12]

---

[4] Staff of Joint Comm. on Taxation, 99th Cong., 2d Sess., General Explanation of The Tax Reform Act of 1986 at 1328 (Comm. Print 1987).

[5] I.R.C. § 501(c)(25)(G).

[6] 26 C.F.R. § 1.501(c)(5)-1(a)(2) (1960).

[7] Rev. Rul. 76-31, 1976-1 C.B. 157.

[8] Rev. Rul. 68-534, 1968-2 C.B. 217.

[9] Rev. Rul. 75-473, 1975-2 C.B. 213.

[10] Rev. Rul. 75-288, 1975-2 C.B. 212.

[11] Rev. Rul 67-7, 1967-1 C.B. 137.

[12] See Rev. Rul. 62-17, 1962-1 C.B. 87, for an example of secondary benefits. *See* Rev. Rul. 66-105,

The more common legal issues involving Section 501(c)(5) have arisen in the area of labor organizations. The legal issues generally revolve around determinations of which type of organizations qualify and what member benefits and activities these organizations can maintain without risking their tax exempt status.

[B]   Labor Organizations

In *Portland Co-operative Labor Temple Association v. Commissioner*,[13] the issue was whether a "labor temple" qualified for Section 501(c)(5) status as a labor organization. Because the statute does not use the term "labor unions," but rather "labor organizations," the implication is that the exemption applies to a broader category than simply labor unions. The question in this case was how broad that category could be.[14]

The temple's sole function was to maintain an office building for use by Portland area labor unions for meetings and for recreational activities. There was some incidental use of the building by non-union members. Stock in the temple was held by these labor unions and by a limited number of individual members on a cooperative basis.[15] This issue arose because neither the IRC nor case law defines what constitutes a "labor organization."[16] The Tax Appeals Court interpreted the term "labor organization" broadly, stating that it "bespeaks a liberal construction . . . including [groups] which are ordinarily organized to protect and promote the interests of labor."[17] The court then found that Portland Co-operative Labor Temple Association would qualify for tax exempt status as long as the labor unions owned all of the capital stock and the building was wholly devoted to the unions' purposes and uses. In general, the court held, an organization that is engaged exclusively in activities appropriate for an exempt organization may itself qualify for exemption under I.R.C. § 501(c)(5). On the non-member use, the court stated that exempt organizations may have incidental non-exempt activity without impairing their exempt status.[18] Given the age of this case, and the fact that it interprets the exemption broadly, rather than narrowly, its precedential value is dubious.

1966-1 C.B. 145, for an example of an organization that was denied tax exempt status when it was deemed that the organization was being used as a marketing device for its cattle ranch members rather than to improve agricultural products and techniques.

  [13] 39 B.T.A. 450 (1939).

  [14] *Id.*

  [15] *Id.* at 451–52. The organization's stock was exclusively owned and used by unions and their members. The office building housed offices, meeting halls, an auditorium, a recreation hall, two bars, cigar store, barber shop, pool room and a restaurant. The organization charged rental fees for the spaces but its operations were not geared to make a profit. *Id.* at 451–53.

  [16] I.R.S. Gen. Couns. Mem. 37942 provides that an indication of a labor organization is that it is formed as a result of a union or organization that is connected with, supplements or supports organizations that perform the role of a union. I.R.S. Gen. Couns. Mem. 37942 (Apr. 27, 1979).

  [17] Portland Co-operative Labor Temple Ass'n, 39 B.T.A. at 455.

  [18] *Id.* at 454 (citing Trinidad v. Sagrada Orden de Predicadores, 263 U.S. 578 (1924)).

[1] Savings Plans

Revenue Ruling 77-46[19] addresses whether an organization created by a collective bargaining agreement to enable union members to save money through withholding a portion of union members' pay and depositing it into a bank account qualifies for exemption when the interest on the account will be used to pay administrative expenses with the excess interest being paid to the members annually on a fixed date. The Regulations provide that labor organizations entitled to exemption from federal income tax are those that have no net earnings inuring to the benefit of any members and are engaged in the pursuit to improve their industry.[20] Traditionally, labor organizations have been created to negotiate wage, hours, and working conditions, along with providing death, sickness, and accidental benefits to employees. While the IRC has no clear definition of what constitutes a labor organization, an organization that seeks to be exempt under Section 501(c)(5) should principally perform those activities for which these organizations have traditionally been granted exemption. A savings plan is neither closely related to, nor necessary for, the exempt purposes of a labor union. As a result, the savings plan organization of Revenue Ruling 77-46 did not qualify for exemption under Section 501(c)(5) of the IRC.

[2] Pension Plans

There is an ongoing debate over whether a pension plan funded by both employers and employees qualifies as a "labor organization" under Section 501(c)(5) of the IRC. In *Morganbesser v. United States*,[21] the Second Circuit considered whether an entity whose principal purpose was managing employer- and employee-sponsored retirement plans so qualified.[22] In its analysis, the court cited General Counsel Memorandum 37942, which states that a reliable indicator of whether an organization qualifies as a labor organization is whether it is "formed as a result of . . . representation [of a union], or is connected with or supplements or supports in some way organizations which do perform that role."[23] Since the plan met that criterion, the court found that it could be classified as a labor organization.[24]

On the issue of whether the fact that the pension plan was also employer funded was fatal to the conclusion that it was a labor organization, the court cited General Counsel Memorandum 35862, which states that a pension plan is an integral part of a union's activities and an appropriate labor organization undertaking.[25] The court again referred to General Counsel Memorandum 37942, which states that "many of today's labor organizations are very heavily funded by employers, particularly as concerns their beneficiary associations."[26] Furthermore, the court pointed out,

---

[19] 1977-1 C.B. 147.

[20] 26 C.F.R. § 1.501(c)(5)-1 (1960).

[21] 984 F.2d 560 (2d Cir. 1993).

[22] *Id.*

[23] *Id.* at 563 (quoting I.R.S. Gen. Couns. Mem. 37942).

[24] *Id.*

[25] *Id.* (citing I.R.S. Gen. Couns. Mem. 35862 (June 20, 1974)).

[26] *Morganbesser*, 984 F.2d at 563 (quoting I.R.S. Gen. Couns. Mem. 37942).

General Counsel Memorandum 37942 does not cite any reason why outside funding would be inappropriate unless the funding would be provided by persons whose interests would not be connected to the purposes of the "labor organization."[27] The court also pointed out Revenue Rulings 59-6[28] and 75-473,[29] which allow entities that carry out the function of a "labor organization" to be jointly administered by employers and employees to qualify as a labor organization under Section 501(c)(5) of the IRC.

On the basis of this analysis, the court had no difficulty reaching the conclusion that the employer-employee funded pension plan at issue did qualify as a tax exempt Section 501(c)(5) labor organization.

The *Morganbesser* holding, along with its rationale, is highly contested by the IRS. The IRS announced its "nonacquiescence" in the *Morganbesser* decision by revoking Gen. Couns. Mem. 35862 and issuing a new regulation.[30] This regulation states that the Treasury Department and the IRS continue to believe an entity whose principal purpose is managing employer/employee-sponsored retirement plans does not qualify as a labor organization under Section 501(c)(5).[31] Furthermore, the regulation states that an entity is not described in Section 501(c)(5) if its principal activity is to receive, hold, invest, disburse, or manage funds associated with investment, retirement, and/or savings plans. Accordingly, the regulation provides that an entity may only qualify as an organization described in Section 501(c)(5) if it meets the following requirements:

- The entity is established and maintained by another labor organization as defined in Section 501(c)(5);

- The entity is not directly or indirectly established or maintained by any employer or government agency in whole or in part;

- The entity is funded by membership dues and interest thereon paid to the labor organization to establish and maintain the organization; and

- After the enactment of ERISA (Sept. 2, 1974), the entity's governing documents have not permitted or provided for nor did the organization accept, any contribution directly or indirectly from an employer or government agency.[32]

Shortly after the IRS's enactment of these provisions, the IRS's position received judicial support from the District of Columbia's Circuit Court in *Stichting Pen-*

---

[27] *Id.* (quoting I.R.S. Gen. Couns. Mem. 37942).

[28] 1959-1 C.B. 121.

[29] 1975-2 C.B. 213.

[30] In re Morganbesser, A.O.D. CC-1995-016 (Dec. 26, 1995), I.R.S. Gen. Couns. Mem. 39889 (Dec. 8, 1995).

[31] These plans may qualify for exemption under § 501(a), as an ERISA qualified pension plan, if they meet the requirements of § 401(a). *Morganbesser*, 984 F.2d 560; In re Morganbesser, A.O.D. CC-1995-016.

[32] 62 Fed. Reg. 40448 (July 29, 1997).

sioenfonds Voor De Gezondheid v. United States.[33] That case involved a Dutch pension-management company, funded by both employer and employee contributions, which sought to have its stock market earnings pass to it untaxed as a Section 501(c)(5) organization. Contrary to the broad interpretation of the criteria used for exemption in *Portland Co-operative Labor Temple Association,*[34] the court stated that a taxpayer must "unambiguously" prove entitlement to an exemption.[35] In addition to distinguishing the revenue rulings relied on by the court in *Morganbesser,* the court in *Stichting* pointed out that General Counsel Memoranda have no precedential value. The court could find no basis for support that a foreign pension management organization that was dually controlled by employers and employees should qualify for tax exemption in the United States simply because the IRS had ruled that dually controlled American plans could qualify for exemption, particularly because exempting foreign pension plans meant that their earnings would escape all taxation. Earnings of exempt domestic funds, by comparison, are taxed when benefits are paid to recipients.[36]

Although it cited the new regulation promulgated after *Morganbesser,* the court said that it was not applying it prospectively, but it did so to point out that *Morganbesser* had a short life.

[3] Political Activities

Section 501(c)(5) labor organizations can be active in political campaigns for or against a candidate for electoral office as long as their political activities are not so extensive as to become the organization's primary purposes. Lobbying on behalf of union goals, as opposed to electoral activity, is considered to be a bona fide 501(c)(5) activity and can be engaged in without limits. Because the portion of union dues paid for lobbying or political campaign activity is not tax deductible by the union member,[37] unions that do lobby or engage in political campaigns have to notify their members regarding the percentage of union dues paid that go for lobbying activities or pay a proxy tax.[38]

Direct expenditures from a union's general treasury funds for or in opposition to a candidate in an election will subject a Section 501(c)(5) organization to the Section 527(f) tax at the highest corporate rates on the lesser of its investment income or the amount of the electioneering expenditure. To avoid this tax, labor organizations that wish to participate in election campaigns are best advised to do so through a related

---

[33] 950 F. Supp 373 (D.D.C. 1996), *aff'd,* 129 F.3d 195 (D.C. Cir. 1997).

[34] 39 B.T.A. 450 (1939). *See* § 15.02[A].

[35] *Stichting,* 950 F. Supp. at 374.

[36] *Id.*

[37] I.R.C. § 162(e)(3).

[38] The IRC, in section 6033(e) imposes reporting and notice requirements on certain tax exempt organizations described in sections 501(c)(4), 501(c)(5), and 501(c)(6) that incur nondeductible lobbying and political expenses. Organizations that do not provide notices of amounts of membership dues allocable to nondeductible lobbying expenditures are subject to tax (commonly called a proxy tax) under IRC section 6033(e)(2) on the amount of the expenditures.

Section 527 (PAC) organization.[39] After *Citizens United v. FEC*[40] these 527 organizations can make unlimited direct expenditures (but not campaign contributions) on the union PAC's behalf for or against electoral candidates. The ability of the union to do so itself, while protected by the First Amendment, is still subject to the laws affecting tax exempt organizations, namely Sections 527 (f) and 6033(e)(2) of the IRC.

When labor organizations have become involved in political campaigns, dissenting union members have complained that their constitutional rights are being violated through the use of their union dues to finance political campaigns that the members do not support. The United States Supreme Court has recognized the rights of dissenting union members to be free of the political use of their dues.[41] In this line of cases, the Court found that a union member can enjoin the collection of dues that are not used for collective bargaining or be reimbursed the dues paid that were used for political activities that the member advised the union he or she opposed.[42] It should be stressed that the remedy is limited to restitution and injunction directed at specific union activity, because to broaden the relief would infringe on the rights of the majority members of the union. Furthermore, the courts may not create a blanket restriction on the use of union dues to fund political activities because a union's claim of a constitutional right to engage in political activity could not be terminated without raising "the gravest doubt" as to the constitutionality[43] and "issues not less than basic to a democratic society."[44]

On the broader question of whether labor unions should lose their tax exempt status for their political activities, the District of Columbia Circuit Court in *Marker v. Shultz* declined to so rule.[45] The plaintiffs, who were dissenting union members, argued that by exempting politically active labor unions from federal income taxation, the government had established a government-financed political movement in violation of the First Amendment. The court said that the tax exemption for labor unions did not involve the government in the support of their political activities, but rather was granted simply because Congress had decided that the pooled income of union members ought not to be taxed.[46]

[C] Agricultural & Horticultural Organizations

In addition to labor organizations, Section 501(c)(5) also includes an exemption for nonprofit agricultural and horticultural organizations. Agricultural organizations are those that foster "the art or science of cultivating land,

---

[39] See § 15.01 *et seq.* for further information on Section 527 organizations.

[40] 175 L. Ed. 2d 753 (2010).

[41] Int'l Ass'n of Machinists v. Street, 367 U.S. 740 (1961); Bhd. of Ry. Clerks v. Allen, 373 U.S. 113 (1963).

[42] Marker v. Shultz, 485 F.2d 1003 (D.C. Cir. 1973); *Machinists*, 367 U.S. at 774–75.

[43] United States v. CIO, 335 U.S. 106, 121 (1948).

[44] United States v. Int'l. Union, U.A.W., 352 U.S. 567, 570 (1957). Congress has put limits on what unions may do with union dues. *See* Pipefitters Local Union No. 562 v. United States, 407 U.S. 385 (1972).

[45] 485 F.2d 1003 (D.C. Cir. 1973).

[46] See § 5.09[B] for an analysis of double taxation.

harvesting crops or aquatic resources, or raising livestock."[47] Horticultural organizations foster "the art or science of cultivating fruits, flowers or vegetables."[48] The apparent distinction is that, at least by statute, agriculture can take place on land or sea, but horticulture is land-bound. Agriculture is broadly defined in the statute to answer the question of whether fish-farming was really agriculture.[49] Congress decided that it was.

These organizations must be organized to advance the science of or better the conditions of agriculture or horticulture. As such, their benefits cannot be limited to their members. Secondary benefits to members are permissible, but should providing benefits to individual members ever become the organization's primary activity, it will no longer qualify for Section 501(c)(5) tax exempt status.[50]

§ 14.05   SECTION 501(c)(6) ORGANIZATIONS: BUSINESS LEAGUES & TRADE ASSOCIATIONS

Section 501(c)(6) exempts nonprofit business leagues and trade associations from federal income taxation.[51] A business league is defined as an association of business groups organized to promote a common interest of a trade, business, or profession and exchange information on industry problems provided that the organization does not engage in regular business of a kind ordinarily carried on for profit. The organization's activities must be directed to the improvement of business conditions of one or more lines of business as distinguished from the performance of particular services for individuals and no part of the net earnings of the organization may benefit a private individual.[52] Furthermore, these organizations must provide benefits to an entire industry; however, they may limit the benefits to a component geographical branch and limit membership if there is a common business interest.[53]

The Tax Court in *American Automobile Association v. Commissioner*[54] provided a list of requirements that entities must meet to qualify as a Section 501(c)(6) organization.[55]

---

[47] I.R.C. § 501(g).

[48] Guerrero v. U.S. Fid. & Guar. Co., 98 S.W.2d 796 (Tex. 1936).

[49] *See* Rev. Rul. 74-488, 1974-2 C.B. 166.

[50] See Rev. Rul. 66-105, 1966-1 C.B. 145, denying exempt status to an agricultural organization on the grounds that its primary activity was to market individual member's livestock.

[51] These organizations include nonprofit business leagues, chambers of commerce, real estate boards, boards of trade, better business bureaus and professional football leagues. These groups include influential organizations such as the American Bar Association, the American Medical Association and the National Association of Manufacturers. The specific exemption for the National Football League is an example of McGovern's "lobbying" category of tax exempt organizations. Those with enough political clout can lobby their own tax exempt status. The primary effect of the N.F.L. exemption was to exempt from taxation the N.F.L. players' pension fund. Its licensing income, which is generated by a captive for-profit organization, is fully taxable.

[52] 26 C.F.R. § 1.506(c)(6)-1.

[53] *See* Rev. Rul. 76-400, 1976-2 C.B. 153, Rev. Rul. 77-112, 1977-1 C.B. 149.

[54] 19 T.C. 1146 (1953).

[55] *Id.*

The requirements are:

- It must be an association of persons having a common business interest;

- Its purpose must be to promote that common business interest;

- It must not be organized for profit;

- It should not be engaged in a regular business of a kind ordinarily conducted for a profit;

- Its activities should be directed toward the improvement of business conditions of one or more lines of business as opposed to the performance of particular services for individual persons; and

- Its net earnings, if any, must not inure to the benefit of any private shareholder or individual.[56]

The organization must meet each of these requirements in order to qualify as a Section 501(c)(6) business league or trade association. Of the above requirements, the two that have received the most attention from the IRS and the courts are whether the organization is conducting a business for profit and whether it truly benefits a line of business, as opposed to simply its members.

[A]   Requirement Not to Conduct a Business for Profit

Section 501(c)(6) organizations are not permitted to engage in a regular business of the kind ordinarily conducted for profit.[57] The courts look to see whether the organization's "activities advance [the] members' interests generally, by virtue of their membership in the industry, or whether they assist members in the pursuit of individual businesses."[58] When an organization primarily provides goods and services to its members in exchange for their payment of dues or other consideration, this provision of goods and services will be characterized as a business activity.[59] In determining whether a substantial part of the organization's activities are of the kind ordinarily conducted for-profit, courts will look at both time invested in the for-profit segment and the financial data regarding the for profit segment in comparison to the nonprofit segment.[60] An organization whose principal purpose and activity does qualify it as a 501(c)(6) organization, however, does not lose its exemption by merely engaging in incidental activities that would normally be subject to taxation.[61]

---

[56] *Id.* at 1158.

[57] *Id.*

[58] M.I.B., Inc. v. Comm'r, 734 F.2d 71, 78 (1st Cir. 1984) (M.I.B. collected and exchanged confidential underwriting information about applicants among its members in order to deter fraud and misrepresentation in life insurance claims; the court in *M.I.B.* ruled that the modus operandi of the organization was to perform direct services for its members rather than improve business conditions as a whole).

[59] *Id.*

[60] Associated Master Barbers & Beauticians of Am. v. Comm'r, 69 T.C. 53, 68–69 (1977).

[61] *Id.* at 67.

In *American Master Barbers & Beauticians*, the Tax Court examined whether the multiple insurance plans administered by a Section 501(c)(6) organization for its members constituted the conducting of business for a profit.[62] The IRS had determined that it did and had revoked the organization's tax exempt status. The Tax Court found that the organization devoted a substantial amount of time to its insurance activities and derived a substantial amount of its income therefrom. On this basis it concluded that the organization was conducting a for-profit business and that the IRS had correctly revoked its Section 501(c)(6) status. It also found that there was little evidence of activity by the organization to benefit the profession as a whole, which was another ground for the denial of exemption.[63]

In *Bluetooth SIG Inc. v. United States*[64] the court examined whether an association formed to own and market the Bluetooth networking protocol and trademark qualified as a Section 501(c)(6) trade association. In determining whether the association was engaging in a business ordinarily carried on for profit, the court relied on Revenue Ruling 58-294, where business league status was denied to an organization "operated for the purpose of promoting uniform business, advertising and fair trade practices in connection with the manufacture and sale of a certain patented product."[65] Finding that SIG was aiming "to promote uniform practices in connection with a certain patented technology, directly owns the relevant trademark and patent, and grants licenses to its members,"[66] and that the Bluetooth trademark was "a valuable commodity which was for sale," the court held that SIG was engaging in a business ordinarily carried on for a profit.[67]

[B]   Line of Business Requirement

Regulation Section 1.501(c)(6)-1 states that the activities of a tax exempt business league should be directed to the improvement of business conditions of one or more lines of businesses.[68] Congress set forth the "line of business" requirement to assure "that an organization's efforts do indeed benefit a sufficiently broad segment of the business community" and to support the view that an organization that is not tied to a particular community and is not industry wide should not be exempt.[69] The Commissioner has consistently denied exemption to business groups whose membership is narrower than a line of business.[70] Those groups that have failed to meet the line of business test include groups who

---

[62]   *Id.* at 69–69.

[63]   *Id.* 69–70.

[64]   611 F.3d 617 (9th Cir. 2010).

[65]   Rev. Rul. 58-294, 1958-1 C.B. 244.

[66]   *Bluetooth SIG Inc.*, 611 F.3d at 622.

[67]   The Court distinguished American Plywood Ass'n v. United States, 267 F. Supp. 830 (W.D. Wash. 1967) on the grounds that while SIG was formed to create a common interest among its members, the Plywood Association was a vehicle to advance a common and pre-existing interest among its members.

[68]   26 C.F.R. § 1.501(c)(6)-1.

[69]   Nat'l Muffler Dealers Ass'n v. United States, 440 U.S. 472 (1979).

[70]   *Id.* at 483.

marketed a single brand of automobile,[71] who were licensed to use a single patented product,[72] who benefited one type of franchise,[73] who advanced the use of computers produced by a single manufacturer,[74] and who advanced the use of "Bluetooth" wireless applications.[75] These groups have been denied exemption because they were not designed to better conditions in an entire industry, but instead, were devoted to the promotion of a particular brand of product at the expense of others in the same industry. In sum, the "line of business requirement" limitation is well-grounded in Section 501(c)(6) of the IRC and it has been stringently enforced since its inception.

[C] Membership

Many Section 501(c)(6) organizations exercise effective control over entire lines of business. Sometimes membership in the organization is required even to be active in a line of business, as for example, when the Section 501(c)(6) organization is also the certifying body for a profession or line of business. Membership in such organizations can therefore be critical to an individual business's success in the field, leading to litigation over both rejection for membership and expulsion from membership. "Ordinarily a dispute between a voluntary association and one of its members is governed by the law of contracts, the parties' contractual obligations being defined by the charter, bylaws, and any other rules or regulations of the association that were intended to create legally enforceable obligations."[76] Most states have conferred additional rights on members who can show that the organization's action, of which he or she complains, substantially impaired an "important economic interest" of his or hers. In these situations, a member can bring suit on the denial of due process or bad faith as well as contractual grounds.[77] Where membership is optional, expulsion, suspension or denial of admission is not deemed an invasion of an "important economic interest."[78] The courts have found that a drop of 35 percent in salary ($220,000 to $143,000)[79] did not impair an "important economic interest," but an "important economic interest" impairment was found in expulsion from a retail grocer's association, which denied the grocer access to trade discounts (placing him at a catastrophic competitive disadvantage)[80]

---

[71] Rev. Rul. 67-77, 1967-1 C.B. 138. *Cf.* Rev. Rul. 55-444, 1955-2 C.B. 258.

[72] Rev. Rul. 58-294, 1958-1 C.B. 244.

[73] *Nat'l Muffler Dealers Ass'n*, 440 U.S. 472.

[74] Rev. Rul. 83-164, 1983-2 C.B. 95. In *Guide Int'l Corp. v. United States*, 948 F.2d 360 (7th Cir. 1991), the court found that an organization formed to benefit one brand of computer that represented 70-75 percent of the market did not qualify as an exempt business league as defined by § 501(c)(6) of the IRC. *Id.* at 362.

[75] Bluetooth SIG Inc. v. United States, 611 F.3d 617 (9th Cir. 2010).

[76] Austin v. Am. Ass'n of Neur. Surgeons, 253 F.3d 967, 968 (7th Cir. 2001).

[77] *Id.* at 969.

[78] *Id.* at 972 (citing Treister v. Am. Acad. of Orthopaedic Surgeons, 396 N.E.2d 1225 (Ill. Ct. App. 1979) (citations omitted)).

[79] *Id.* at 971–72.

[80] Van Daele v. Vinci, 282 N.E.2d 728 (Ill. 1972).

and in the refusal to admit a duly licensed physician into a local medical society (preventing him from practicing).[81]

[D] Trade Shows

A major activity of many trade associations is the annual convention, where vendor booths exhibiting products for the trade and related demonstrations or lectures form a major part of the convention. Generally, the admission to convention activities is on a paid admission basis and is open to the general public. A question arose as to whether the money from admissions would generate unrelated business income for the trade association. The short answer is no. IRC Section 513(d) provides that the qualified convention and trade show activities of a business league or trade association are not unrelated trade or business activities.

IRC Section 513(d) defines tradeshow activities to include any activity with the purpose of: (1) attracting persons in an industry (without regard to membership in the sponsoring organization); (2) educating persons engaged in the industry in the development of new products, services, or rules and regulations affecting the industry. Even if the tradeshow attracts members of the public, it will not generate unrelated business income as long as the purpose of the show is to display industry products or stimulate interest in, and demand for, industry products or services.[82]

To ensure admission fees are not subject to the unrelated business income tax, the tradeshow must be held in association with the annual convention of an organization whose purposes include stimulating interest in, or demand for, the products and services of a particular industry.[83]

The "held in association" with a convention standard is critical to the analysis. The IRS has held that virtual trade show type activities held over the Internet generate exempt income only if the Internet activities are in association with an actual, physical convention.[84]

[E] Political Activities

Section 501(c)(6) trade associations can be active in political campaigns for or against a candidate for electoral office as long as their political activities are not so extensive as to become the organization's primary purpose. Lobbying on behalf of legislative goals to advance the trade organization's exempt purposes, on the other hand, is considered to be a bona fide 501(c)(6) activity and can be engaged in without limits.[85]

The extent of the organization's lobbying and or political activities may affect the ability of the organization's for-profit members to deduct their dues as business expenses under IRC Section 162. Congress has passed legislation that forbids

---

[81] Falcone v. Middlesex Cnty. Med. Soc'y, 170 A.2d 791 (N.J. 1961).

[82] I.R.C. § 513(d)(3)(A).

[83] I.R.C. § 513(d)(3)(B).

[84] Rev. Rul. 2004-112, 2004-2 C.B. 985.

[85] Rev. Rul. 61-177, 1961-2 C.B. 117.

businesses from deducting any business expense, in whole or in part, that was paid in connection with influencing legislation.[86] Influencing legislation is defined as any attempt to influence any legislation through communicating with any member or employee of a legislative body or any government official or employer who may participate in the formulation of legislation.[87] The rule excludes from the definition of influencing legislation any attempt to influence local bodies, such as county or city councils.[88]

Section 501(c)(6) organizations that do lobby or electioneer must notify their members of the amount of their dues that went for political purposes,[89] and the members then cannot deduct that portion of their dues or political campaign as a business expense. Notification to members is not required in three specific situations: (1) when the organization's members are not entitled to deduct their dues as business expenses, (2) when the only lobbying was in-house expenditures that did not exceed $2,000,[90] and (2) when the 501(c)(6) organization itself elects to pay a 35 percent "proxy tax" on its political expenditures instead of notifying its members of the non-deductible portion of their dues.[91]

This lobbying tax was challenged in *American Society of Association Executives v. United States*[92] as unduly burdening free speech rights. The circuit court relied on the *Regan v. Taxation with Representation* case,[93] where the United States Supreme Court upheld the lobbying restrictions on Section 501(c)(3) organizations, with specific reference to the fact that free speech rights were not violated because 501(c)(3)s could do their lobbying activity through related 501(c)(4)s as long as no (c)(3) money flowed to the (c)(4) for this purpose.[94] The circuit court said that a similar option was open to the Section 501(c)(6) — that is, it could divide into a (c)(6) that lobbied and one that did not. Because this option was available to plaintiffs, and because the general legislative scheme that refused to subsidize lobbying by Section 501(c)(6) organizations with tax deductible dollars was constitutional, the court dismissed the organization's challenge to the lobbying tax.[95]

Electioneering to an insubstantial degree, while permitted to a Section 501(c)(6) organization, will trigger the Section 527(f) tax on the organization's electoral

---

[86] I.R.C. § 162(e)(1). Trade Associations must annually disclose the estimated portion of members dues that will be allocated to political activities. I.R.C. § 6033(e).

[87] I.R.C. § 162(e)(4)(A); *see also* I.R.C. § 162(e)(5)(C); 26 C.F.R. § 1.162-29(b)(3); I.R.C. § 162(e)(4)(B); 26 C.F.R. § 1.162-29(b)(4).

[88] I.R.C. § 162(e)(2).

[89] I.R.C. § 6033(e).

[90] I.R.C. § 162(e)(5)(B)(i). "In house expenditures" are lobbying expenditures other than the payments to professional lobbyists or dues that are allocated to political activities. I.R.C. § 162(e)(5)(B)(ii).

[91] I.R.C. § 6033(e)(2).

[92] 195 F.3d 47 (D.C. Cir. 1999).

[93] 461 U.S. 540 (1983).

[94] *Am. Soc'y of Ass'n Execs.*, 195 F.3d at 50–51.

[95] *Id.* at 51.

expenses. As with Section 501(c)(5) labor unions, the way around this is for the trade association to establish a Section 527 PAC and follow its rules on political expenditures. Members cannot deduct as a business expense that portion of their dues that the Section 501(c)(6) organization uses for electioneering.[96]

[F] Antitrust Regulations

Nonprofit organizations are not exempt from the anti-trust laws. In their trade promoting activities, it has happened that Section 501(c)(6) organizations have run afoul of the prohibitions of the Sherman Act.[97] In *Goldfarb v. Virginia State Bar*,[98] a Section 501(c)(6) bar association was found guilty of violating the Sherman Act for fixing minimum service prices. In *National Collegiate Athletic Association v. University of Oklahoma*,[99] the exempt organization restrained trade in violation of the Sherman Act by preventing individual colleges from bargaining for their own television contracts.

§ 14.06 SECTION 501(c)(7) ORGANIZATIONS: SOCIAL CLUBS

IRC Section 501(c)(7) creates the "social club" exemption. It provides income tax exemption to clubs organized for pleasure, recreation, and other nonprofitable purposes, as long as substantially all of its activities are for exempt purposes and no part of its earnings inures to the benefit of any private shareholder. The purpose of a social club is to permit individuals to join together, to provide recreational or social facilities, and/or to furnish goods and services to its members. To qualify for exemption, personal interaction must exist among members. In general, this exemption extends to social and recreational clubs that are supported solely by membership fees, dues, and assessments.[100] The basis for their exemption from federal income taxes lies in the double taxation argument. Social club income is really only the pooled income of its members.[101] Section 501(c)(7) organizations include athletic clubs, golf clubs (including country clubs), garden clubs, fraternities, sororities, diving clubs, travel clubs, book clubs, chess clubs and so on, almost ad infinitum.

[A] Organizational & Operational Requirements

To be tax exempt, a social club must establish that: (1) it is a club both organized and operated exclusively for pleasure, recreation, and other nonprofit purposes; and (2) that no part of its net earnings inures to the benefit of any private individual.

---

[96] I.R.C. § 162(e)(1)(B).

[97] *See* 15 U.S.C. §§ 7, 15.

[98] 421 U.S. 773 (1975).

[99] 468 U.S. 85 (1984).

[100] 26 C.F.R. § 1.501(c)(7)-1.

[101] McGlotten v. Connally, 338 F. Supp. 448 (D.D.C. 1972); *see also* S. Rep. 91-552, at 71 (1969).

To meet the first requirement there must be "personal contacts," "fellowship" or a "commingling" amongst the club's members.[102] "Fellowship" does not need to be present among every member as long as commingling is a material part of the organization.[103] Members of the organization should be tied together by some common objective directed toward pleasure, recreation, and other nonprofit purpose. The organization's primary objective should not be to provide a service to its members or to save money for its members.[104] An organization in which the only personal contact among the members consisted of an online forum failed to meet the "commingling" requirement.[105]

The membership of the club must be limited, and not extend to the general public, but membership restrictions based on race, color, or religion are not acceptable.[106] Social clubs that issue corporate membership are, in effect, dealing with the general public. Corporate members of a club are not the kind of members contemplated by the statute.

A social club that is engaged in business is considered not to be operating for pleasure, recreation, and other nonprofit purposes. A club that engages in business, by making services and recreational facilities open to the general public or by selling real estate, timber, or other products, is not organized and operated exclusively for exempt purposes.[107]

Solicitation by advertisement or otherwise for public patronage of its facilities will be considered *prima facie* evidence that the club is engaged in business and is not operating for tax exempt purposes.[108]

This does not mean that a social club will lose its exemption if it has dealings with the general public. A social club may gain a minimal portion of its gross receipts from the general public's participation in the club's affairs provided that the participation is incidental to and in furtherance of the organization's purpose and that the outside income does not inure to the members' benefit.[109] This allowance of outside income is especially true when the receipts from the general public are to pay for their share of the expense or when the transactions are

---

[102] *See* Rev. Rul. 69-635, 1969-2 C.B. 126.

[103] I.R.S. Gen. Couns. Mem. 23688; Rev. Rul. 58-589, 1958-2 C.B. 266. Statewide and nationwide organizations that are made up of local groups and chapters satisfy the fellowship requirement, as long as "fellowship" constitutes a material part of the local groups and chapters.

[104] *See* Rev. Rul. 70-32, 1970-1 C.B. 132.

[105] I.R.S. Priv. Ltr. Rul. 201043042 (Oct. 29, 2010).

[106] An organization that limits its membership to people of a particular religion will not be considered as discriminating if the organization's purpose is to further the teachings or principles of that religion.

[107] The term "general public" does not include a member's family or dependents.

[108] 26 C.F.R. § 1.501(c)(7)-1(b).

[109] An organization may receive 35 percent of its gross receipts from something other than membership fees, dues and assessments. Of that 35 percent, not more than 15 percent may be derived from the general public's use of the clubs facilities or services or from other activities not furthering the organizations purpose. I.R.S. Tech. Adv. Mem. 199912033 (June 25, 1998). This other income (clubs' investment income and net revenue from non-members) is not extended tax exemption under § 501(c)(7) of the IRC. *See* I.R.C. § 512(a)(3).

incidental, trivial, non-recurrent activities.[110] When a substantial part of a Section 501(c)(7) organization's income is from the general public, however, it will not qualify for exemption because this means it has a substantial non-exempt purpose, namely serving the general public.[111]

In order to police non-member usage of social clubs, the IRS issued Revenue Procedure 71-17,[112] which establishes record-keeping requirements for general public usage. A significant factor reflecting a non-exempt purpose is gross receipts from the general public.[113] The IRS considers annual gross receipts of more than $2,500 or more than five percent of total receipts, whichever is greater, as triggering the presumption of a non-exempt purpose. When a group of eight or fewer individuals, one of whom is a member who pays the tab, uses a club, the presumption is that they are all guests of the member, and not members of the general public. When 75 percent or more of a group using club facilities are members, who pay for club services, it is presumed that the entire group are guests of the members, and not the general public. Adequate records must be kept for this last situation.

With respect to all other situations involving use by non-members, the club must maintain detailed records on the date, the total number in the party, the total number of non-members, the total charges, the charges attributable to non-members and the charges paid by members.[114] If a member pays for non-members, a statement signed by the member is required, indicating whether and how much the member will be reimbursed. Where the member's employer reimburses the member or makes a direct payment to the organization for charges attributable to nonmembers, a statement signed by the member indicating the name of the employer, the amount of payment attributable to the employer for nonmember's use, the nonmember's name and business or other relationship to the member and the business, personal, or social purpose of the member served by nonmember's use is required.[115] These provisions ensure that the business use of the social club reflects "personal contacts," "fellowship" or a "commingling" amongst the business entity or its employee or guests and the other members.

The second part of the test is a private inurement test.[116] While individual members of social clubs obviously derive benefits from their membership, these benefits are a permissible result of the dues and assessments that they have paid to the club. Private inurement occurs when non-dues-generated benefits accrue to members, as for example when a social club engages in a business activity for profit (such as the provision of goods and services to non-members) that is designed to

---

[110] *See* Barstow Rodeo and Riding Club, Inc. v. Comm'r, 12 T.C.M. (CCH) 1351 (1953); Santee Club v. White, 87 F.2d 5 (1st Cir. 1936).

[111] Rev. Rul. 66-149, 1966-1 C.B. 146. However, the IRS allowed an exception where income is derived from investment of the proceeds of the organization's former clubhouse, pending the acquisition of new premises.

[112] 1971-1 C.B. 683.

[113] *Id.*

[114] *Id.*

[115] *Id.*

[116] See § 6.04 for further information on a similar private inurement test.

benefit the members through lower dues or enhanced facilities. The only way the club's net earnings may inure to members of the organization is in the form of additional services offered by the club without an increase in dues or fees. The pro rata distribution of assets to members upon dissolution of a social club is not considered private inurement, although it may be a taxable event to the recipient.[117]

[B]   Taxation

Social clubs are really a disfavored form of tax exempt organization. The only income on which social clubs do not pay federal income taxes is their member-generated income. Member-generated income is income from dues, fees, charges, or similar amounts paid by members as consideration for providing them, their dependents or guests, goods, facilities, or services in furtherance of the organization's exempt purposes.[118] All other income is taxed — as for example, investment income or income for goods and services paid for by non-members.

Recalling that the rationale for the exemption of social clubs is the double-taxation rationale, it makes sense that a social club is only exempt from tax on receipts by its members because exemption is provided in order to permit individuals to come together to provide social and recreational facilities and services on a pooled income basis, without tax consequences. In other words, the tax exemption is granted to place members in the same position as if the member had purchased the goods or services. If non-member income were not taxed, the organization could reduce costs and increase services, which would create an untaxed benefit for the members of the organization. As a result, all outside income, including investment income and receipts from the general public, is taxed.

In the Tax Reform Act of 1969, a provision was added to the IRC that exempted from taxation the investment income of social clubs that was set aside for charitable or educational purposes.[119]

Because Section 501(c)(7) organizations are taxed on their outside income, a significant amount of litigation has occurred on how this tax is computed. In *Portland Golf Club v. Commissioner*,[120] a Section 501(c)(7) golf club had taxable investment income against which it tried to take as a deduction the losses it had suffered in its other taxable activity, the sale of food and drink to non-members. These losses would have completely offset the investment income. The United States Supreme Court held that losses from these sales could be taken as a deduction against investment income only if those sales were motivated by an intent to profit. Because of its method of cost allocation of fixed club expenses to its sales to non-members, the club was found not to be operating on a profit motive, and the deduction was not allowed.[121]

---

[117] Rev. Rul. 58-501, 1958-2 C.B. 262.

[118] I.R.C. § 512(a)(3)(B).

[119] I.R.C. § 512(a)(3)(B)(i).

[120] 497 U.S. 154 (1990).

[121] *Id.*

In *Ye Mystic Krewe of Gasparilla v. Commissioner*,[122] a social club staged an annual "pirate invasion" of Tampa, Florida, and a parade, from which it derived concession and souvenir income. The issue was whether the expenses of the "invasion" and parade could be deducted against this income, and this in turn depended on whether these expenses were directly connected with the production of the income. In a fact-specific holding, the court said that expenses for providing seating, refreshments, and an event logbook were related to the production of concession income and could be deducted, but the expenses of the invasion and parade itself were not related to the concession income and could not be deducted. On a side issue involving the taxation of investment income from a special fund used to maintain the organization's pirate ship during the year, which was on public view, but not accessible to the public, the court did not accept the Krewe's position that viewing the ship was an educational activity that would have exempted fund income from taxation.

[C] Rights of Association & Anti-Discrimination Requirements

Membership in social clubs is protected by the First Amendment's freedom of association guarantee. Members in a social club have a constitutional right to associate with others of their choice in the pursuit of a common activity.[123] With the First Amendment rights comes the right to deny membership to individuals whom the members of the organization choose not to associate with. Membership can be denied for any reason, or no reason, but it cannot be denied for certain discriminatory reasons. The courts and the IRS have ruled that gender, race, and religion cannot be used as the exclusive reason to exclude members.[124] IRC Section 501(i) states that for an organization to qualify as tax exempt under Section 501(c)(7), it must not have any written policy to discriminate on race, color, or religion. The statute does, however, create an exception for a club that in good faith limits its membership to the members of a particular religion in order to further the teachings of that particular religion, and not to exclude individuals of a particular race or color.[125]

In *Roberts*,[126] and in *Board of Directors, Rotary International v. Rotary Club of Duarte*,[127] the United States Supreme Court refused to rule that business clubs that did not allow female members were entitled to discriminate on First Amendment freedom of association grounds. Both cases were based on the clubs' large size, non-selectivity, inclusive rather than exclusive purpose, and practice of inviting or allowing non-members to attend meetings, which, according to the

---

[122] 80 T.C. 755 (1983).

[123] Roberts v. U.S. Jaycees, 468 U.S. 609 (1984).

[124] *See* I.R.C. § 501(i); McGlotten v. Connally, 338 F. Supp. 448 (D.D.C. 1972); Bd. of Dirs., Rotary Int'l v. Rotary Club of Duarte, 481 U.S. 537 (1987); N.Y. St. Club Ass'n v. City of New York, 487 U.S. 1 (1988).

[125] I.R.C. § 501(i)(2).

[126] 468 U.S. 609.

[127] 481 U.S. 537.

Court, established that the organizations were not sufficiently personal or private to warrant constitutional protection under the freedom of association. Evidently the rules are different for what the Court determines to be an "expressive association." When these groups are forced by governmental action to include those whose inclusion would distort or subvert their message, then freedom of expression (which is different from freedom of association) trumps the government's interests.[128]

§ 14.07   SECTION 501(c)(8) ORGANIZATIONS: FRATERNAL BENEFIT ASSOCIATIONS

A fraternal beneficiary society has been defined as "one whose members have adopted the same, or very similar calling, avocation, or profession, or who are working in unison to accomplish some worthy object, and who for that reason have banded themselves together as an association or society to aid and assist one another, and to promote [a] common cause."[129] Section 501(c)(8) creates the exemption from federal income taxation for "fraternal beneficiary societies," also known as fraternal benefit organizations.

[A]   Organizational & Operational Requirements

Under Section 501(c)(8), a fraternal benefit organization must: (1) be a fraternal organization, (2) operate under the lodge system or operate for the exclusive benefit of the members of a fraternal organization itself operating under the lodge system,[130] and (3) provide for payment of life, sick, accident, or other benefits to the members of such society, order, or association or their dependents. Operating under a lodge system means carrying on its activities under a form of organization that comprises local branches, chartered by a parent organization and largely self-governing, called lodges, chapters, or the like.[131]

All members must be eligible to receive benefits and these benefits must not be limited to any particular class of members.[132] The benefits must be limited to members and their dependents, and if the benefits can be conferred outside this class of people, exemption will not be recognized. In Revenue Ruling 64-194,[133] the IRS examined a situation in which members of a fraternal organization who joined after age 50 formed a different class of "social" members who did not receive the sick, accident, or death benefits that other "beneficial" members did. The benefits were paid from funds contributed only by the beneficial members. On that basis,

---

[128] *See* Boy Scouts of Am. v. Dale, 530 U.S. 640 (2000); I.R.C. § 501(i).

[129] Nat'l Union v. Marlow, 74 F. 775, 778 (8th Cir. 1896).

[130] "Operating under a lodge system" means carrying on activities under a form of organization that comprises local branches and/or chapters that are largely self-governing and that are chartered by a parent organization. 26 C.F.R. § 1.501(c)(8)-1; *see also* W. Funeral Benefit Ass'n v. Hellmich, 2 F.2d 367, 369 (E.D. Mo. 1924).

[131] Rev. Rul. 64-194, 1964-2 C.B. 149; 26 C.F.R. § 1.501(c)(8)-1.

[132] *See* Rev. Rul. 64-194, 1964-2 C.B. 149. It is not essential that every member actually be covered by the fraternal organization's programs.

[133] *Id.*

and despite the evident limitation on benefits, the IRS agreed that the organization qualified for Section 501(c)(8) status.[134]

[B] Taxation

Fraternal organizations receive more favorable tax treatment than social clubs. Fraternal organizations receive exemption from both their exempt function and investment income. The only item these organizations are taxed on is "unrelated business income."[135] Furthermore, a contribution from individuals to a fraternal benefit society under the lodge system is tax-deductible if the donation is used exclusively for religious, charitable, scientific, literary, or educational purposes, or for the prevention of cruelty to children and animals.[136]

[C] Discrimination

In *McGlotten v. Connally*,[137] the District Court for the District of Columbia dealt with a constitutional challenge to the tax exempt status of a Section 501(c)(8) organization brought by a member of a minority group who had been rejected for membership. The court determined that it violated the public policy of the United States to allow a Section 501(c)(8) organization that discriminated on the basis of race to receive tax deductible gifts. The court further ruled that exempting 501(c)(8)'s investment income from taxation was enough of a governmental benefit to make the Fifth Amendment applicable. They therefore could not discriminate on racial grounds and maintain their exempt status.[138]

§ 14.08 SECTION 501(c)(10) ORGANIZATIONS: DOMESTIC FRATERNAL ORGANIZATIONS

A second type of fraternal organization is a "Domestic Fraternal Society" and is provided for in Section 501(c)(10) of the IRC. A Section 501(c)(10) organization must: (1) be a domestic fraternal society; (2) operate under a lodge system; (3) dedicate all of their net earnings exclusively to religious, charitable, scientific, literary, education, and or fraternal purposes; and (4) not provide life, sickness, accident, or other benefits to its members.[139] These organizations may arrange for third-party insurance options for its members without jeopardizing their exempt status. They may not provide such insurance themselves, however, and this is the critical distinction that differentiates them from Section 501(c)(8) fraternal benefit organizations.

---

[134] *Id.*

[135] McGlotten v. Connally, 338 F. Supp. 448 (D.D.C. 1972).

[136] I.R.C. § 170(c)(4).

[137] 338 F. Supp. 448 (D.D.C. 1972).

[138] *Id.*

[139] Regulations relating to § 501(c)(10) expressly exclude national college fraternities. *See* 26 C.F.R. § 1.501(c)(10)-1; Zeta Beta Tau Fraternity, Inc. v. Comm'r, 87 T.C. 421 (1986). Fraternities and sororities are typically considered Section 501(c)(7) social clubs.

In the case of *Hip Sing Association, Inc. v. Commissioner*,[140] the issue was whether an organization, organized and operated more according to Chinese ethnic customs than American corporate or federal tax law, could qualify as a Section 501(c)(10) organization. With a bit of shoe-horning, the court decided that all of the requirements were present: it was a fraternal society, it operated for mutual benefit fraternal purposes, and it did not provide insurance. The only real question was the existence of a lodge system. The court decided that, even though it was the local organizations that formed the parent, as opposed to the normal course of events where the locals are the creation of the parent, it was operated under a lodge system.[141]

§ 14.09   SECTION 501(c)(19) ORGANIZATIONS: VETERANS ORGANIZATIONS

Veterans' organizations qualify for exemption under Section 501(c)(19). Their exempt purpose includes assisting disabled veterans and current members of the armed forces and their dependents; entertaining and caring for hospitalized veterans; perpetuating the memory of deceased veterans and comforting their survivors; carrying on traditionally charitable and educational programs; sponsoring patriotic activities; providing insurance benefits; and providing social and recreational activities for members.[142]

These organizations have also been permitted to lobby in furtherance of these exempt purposes without limitation.[143]

A veterans' organization qualifies for Section 501(c)(19) exemption if: (1) it is organized in the United States or its possessions; (2) at least 75 percent of its members are past or present members of the armed forces and substantially all other members are cadets, spouses, or widowers of members of the armed forces or of cadets; and (3) there is no private inurement.[144]

Congress created Section 501(c)(19) in 1972 to provide better tax benefits for veterans' organizations. Until then, veterans groups had to qualify under Section 501(c)(4) or Section 501(c)(7) in order to be tax exempt. Veterans' organizations are exempt not only on their exempt function income, but Congress has also granted them exemption from the unrelated business income tax.[145] Veterans' organizations are also eligible to receive tax-deductible gifts.[146]

Under Section 501(c)(23), any association organized before 1880, more than 75 percent of whose members are present or past members of the armed forces, a

---

[140] 43 T.C.M (CCH) 1092 (1982).

[141] *Id.*

[142] 26 C.F.R. § 1.501(c)(19)-1(c).

[143] This preferential treatment has been upheld by the Supreme Court in *Taxation with Representation*, 461 U.S. 540.

[144] I.R.C. § 501(c)(19); *see also* 26 C.F.R. § 1.501(c)(19)-1(b).

[145] I.R.C. § 512(a)(4).

[146] I.R.C. § 170(c)(3).

principal purpose of which is to provide insurance and other benefits to veterans or their dependents, is exempt from federal income taxation.

§ 14.10 SECTION 501(m) ORGANIZATIONS: COMMERCIAL TYPE INSURERS

In 1986, Congress enacted Section 501(m), which denies tax exemption to an organization that would otherwise be exempt under Section 501(c)(3) or (c)(4), but that provides "commercial type insurance" as a substantial part of its activities.[147] This change in the law was evidently aimed at Blue Cross and Blue Shield-type organizations, which were very active in the health insurance market. Section 501(m) casts a very wide net, but it does have some exceptions that have engendered most of the litigation in this area. The statute does not define "commercial type insurance" but it does say that "insurance provided at substantially below cost to a class of charitable recipients" is not commercial type insurance.[148]

In *Paratransit Insurance Corporation v. Commissioner*,[149] although the insured parties were all 501(c)(3) social service agencies that provided transit to the poor, the elderly, and the handicapped and evidently qualified as "charitable recipients," their pooled insurance fund did not charge them "substantially below cost rates."[150] As a result, the Tax Court found that the pooled insurance fund was a taxable organization. A similar result was reached by the Claims Court in *Nonprofits' Insurance Alliance of California v. United States*.[151] To correct these results, Congress added Section 501(n) to the IRC. Under Section 501(n), a qualified charitable risk pool composed solely of Section 501(c)(3) organizations may qualify for tax exemption without the need to provide its services "substantially below cost." The statute, however, does not allow the pooling of medical malpractice risks.[152] Recall that Blue Cross-Blue Shield type organizations were the original target of this "commercial type insurance" legislation to begin with.

§ 14.11 OTHER MUTUAL BENEFIT ORGANIZATIONS

There are other tax exempt mutual benefit organizations that are highly specialized and complicated. A sample of these groups would include: employee benefit organizations (I.R.C. § 501(c)(9)), local teachers retirement funds (I.R.C. § 501(c)(11)), nonprofit cemetery companies (I.R.C. § 501(c)(13)), trusts to provide supplemental unemployment compensation benefits (I.R.C. § 501(c)(17)), and trusts to provide group legal services (I.R.C. § 501(c)(20)).

---

[147] Commercial type insurance does not include insurance provided at substantially below cost to a class of charitable recipients. I.R.C. § 501(m)(3)(A).

[148] I.R.C. § 501(m)(3)(A).

[149] 102 T.C. 745 (1994).

[150] *Id.*

[151] 32 Fed. Cl. 277 (1994).

[152] I.R.C. § 501(n)(2)(A).

§ 14.12 ISSUES INVOLVING VOLUNTARY MEMBERSHIP ASSOCIATIONS

Membership in a voluntary, nonprofit association confers legal rights in the member in regard to the association. These rights are contractual, property, and due process rights. When a member believes that these rights have been violated, they can be expected to seek relief in the courts.[153] The association also has rights vis-á-vis members or prospective members. In terms of deciding who can qualify for membership, voluntary associations have a First Amendment right of association that insulates their membership decisions, unless they are made for a discriminatory reason.[154] This section will consider a member's rights in a voluntary organization, how courts have adjudicated those rights, and the limits on a voluntary organization's right to associate.

[A] Membership as a Contractual Right

When a member joins an association, the basic documents of the association — articles and bylaws — as they exist at the time the member joined, form a contract between the member and the association. Should those documents be changed at a later date to vary the rights of the member, the member can insist on his or her rights as they existed when he or she joined the organization. This is the case even when the association has reserved a right to amend these documents. As the New Jersey Supreme Court said in *Lambert v. Fisherman's Dock Cooperative*:[155]

> [i]t is the law generally that a reserved right to amend the by-laws of an association, whether to be exercised by the majority or, in some cases, a larger proportion of stockholders, members or directors, is a limited rather than an absolute right, even though the reservation is expressed in broad and general terms. It is often said that such a right to amend may not be extended so as to impair or destroy a contract or vested right.[156]

[B] Membership as a Property Right

Payment is often required when members join voluntary associations, especially mutual benefit associations. This buy-in creates a property right in the organization, entitling the member to the services of the organization, and also some form of payout upon withdrawal from the organization or upon the organization's dissolution. As with the contract rights discussed above, the courts have held that, upon withdrawal, a member is due the compensation that was provided for in the organization's basic documents at the time the member paid in, regardless of any subsequent changes.[157]

---

[153] *See* Zechariah Chafee, *The Internal Affairs of Associations Not for Profit*, 43 Harv. L. Rev. 993, 1007 (1930); *Roberts*, 468 U.S. at 623.

[154] *Roberts*, 468 U.S. at 623.

[155] 297 A.2d 566 (N.J. 1972).

[156] *Id.* at 568.

[157] *See* Lambert v. Fishermen's Dock Co-op., Inc., 297 A.2d 566 (N.J. 1972); Loch v. Paola Farmers' Union Co-op. Creamery & Store Ass'n, 285 P. 523 (Kan. 1930); Whitney v. Farmers' Co-op. Grain Co., 193

The general rule regarding a member's property rights upon the dissolution of the organization is that those rights too are fixed when the member joins; however, a member who has withdrawn prior to dissolution has no claim on the organization's assets upon dissolution.[158]

[C]   Court Examination of Membership Decisions

In cases involving the expulsion of a member from a voluntary association, the role of the court is to determine whether the organization has acted in good faith, in accordance with its own basic documents and in accordance with the law of the land.[159] Because voluntary associations are not governmental entities, a member's due process rights in an expulsion situation are standards of fundamental fairness[160] and the contract rights he or she has with the organization.[161] These contract rights are the source of the good faith and procedural correctness requirements when a member is expelled and, of course, in any such situation, rights conferred on a member by law must also be honored.

The court's analysis begins with the organization's own established procedures. Procedural fairness requires that notice of charges be given and that the member has a right to state his or her side of the case. If the breaches of the organization's procedures are minimal, the court may waive the breach if there was substantial compliance with the rules. If the organization followed its own rules in good faith and these rules were fair, in the sense that there was notice and an opportunity to be heard, then the court will not intervene. Only when a member's property or contractual rights were violated, or the action was in patent bad faith, or the expulsion was on a basis that itself violates the law, e.g., the member refused to perform an illegal act, do the courts normally agree to hear expulsion cases.[162]

The situation is a bit different with expulsion from Section 501(c)(5) and 501(c)(6) professional associations, however. Very often, membership in a labor union or professional organization may be required for the member to practice a particular trade or profession. Beyond that, loss of membership in a labor union or professional association conveys to the public that the expelled member may not be fit to engage in a particular trade or profession. As a result, court scrutiny of such expulsion decisions differ in degree from an examination of expulsion from a purely

---

N.W. 103 (Neb. 1923); 8 Fletcher, Cyclopedia Corporations § 4177 (Perm. ed.); 1 Hornstein, Corporation Law and Practice § 269 (1959).

[158] *See* Raulston v. Everett, 561 S.W.2d 635 (Tex. Civ. App. 1978); De Bruyn v. Golden Age Club of Cheyenne, 399 P.2d 390 (Wyo. 1965); Attinson v. Consumer-Farmer Milk Coop., 94 N.Y.S.2d 891 (Sup. Ct. 1950).

[159] *See* Bernstein v. Alameda-Contra Costa Med. Asso., 293 P.2d 862 (Cal. Ct. App. 1956); Smith v. Kern County Med. Ass'n, 19 Cal. 2d 263, 265 (1942).

[160] Blodgett v. Univ. Club, 930 A.2d 210 (D.C. 2007).

[161] Some states have adopted provisions that a member of a social club may not be expelled except pursuant to a fair and reasonable procedure that is carried out in good faith. *See* Cal. Corp. Code § 7341; Minn. Stat. § 317A.411 (2004); Miss. Code Ann. § 79-11-189; Aluisi v. Fort Wash. Golf and Country Club, 42 Cal. Rptr. 2d 761 (Ct. App. 1995).

[162] *See* Chafee, *supra* note 153, at 1023–36; *Developments in the Law-Judicial Control of Actions of Private Associations*, 76 Harv. L. Rev. 983, 1006–1111 (1963).

social organization such as Section 501(c)(7) social clubs or Section 501(c)(8) fraternal benefit organizations,[163] although the basic analysis is still the same: did the organization act in good faith, absent any illegal actions, observing the member's contractual due process and property rights?[164]

In the case of *Falcone v. Middlesex County Medical Society*,[165] the New Jersey Superior Court eschewed a property or contracts analysis in a case involving an osteopath who was denied membership in a Section 501(c)(6) professional medical society, as a result of which he lost staff privileges at a local hospital. The court cited with favor the analysis of Professor Chafee, which criticized both the contract and property theories as inadequate to protect the rights of individuals.[166] The court then proceeded to a policy analysis in which it looked at: (1) the nature of the defendant society and (2) whether the injury complained of was substantial. The court stated that if the findings in: (1) and (2) justified judicial scrutiny of defendant's action, then it would proceed to determine whether the defendant society applied proper procedural safeguards, acted in accordance with its own law; and, if so, whether it was reasonable and consistent with public policy.[167]

In the area of professional association membership, *Falcone* is obviously a move away from a strict property or contracts analysis toward a broader standard of court review based on public policy.

[D]   Voluntary Associations & Freedom of Association

A voluntary organization's First Amendment right of freedom of association is not absolute. Infringements on an organization's right to associate may be justified by laws or governmental regulations that serve compelling state interests, unrelated to the suppression of ideas, that cannot be achieved by less restrictive means.[168] The United States Supreme Court has reasoned that a court should look at the attributes of "relative smallness," "a high degree of selectivity in decisions to begin and maintain affiliation," "seclusion from others in critical aspects of the relationship," and the organization's purpose to determine if an organization should be afforded the freedom of association as an intrinsic element of the personal liberty of its members.[169] Any association lacking these qualities is too remote from the concerns giving rise to the constitutional protection of freedom of

---

[163]   *See* Waugaman v. Skyline Country Club, 172 So. 2d 381 (Ala. 1965).

[164]   *See Bernstein*, 293 P.2d 862.

[165]   162 A.2d 324 (N.J. Super. Ct. Law Div. 1960).

[166]   Chafee, *supra* note 153.

[167]   *Falcone*, 162 A.2d at 331.

[168]   See *Roberts*, 468 U.S. 609, enforcing a Minnesota statute that required women to be admitted as voting members to the U.S. Jaycees; see also Curran v. Mount Diablo Council of the Boy Scouts of America, 17 Cal. 4th 670 (1998), which provides an example of an organization that meets the requirement of constitutional protection. In this case the court ruled that a homosexual could be excluded as a member of the organization because the scouts met regularly in small groups to foster close friendship, trust and loyalties, and the members had to participate in a variety of activities, ceremonies, and rituals that were designed to teach the moral principals to which the organization subscribed.

[169]   *See Roberts*, 468 U.S. at 620; *Bd. of Dirs. of Rotary Int'l*, 481 U.S. 537.

association to merit First Amendment protection.[170] Beyond this analysis, the courts will also look to see if the exclusion of a class of member will impede on the organization's civic, charitable, lobbying, fundraising, and other activities that merit constitutional protection.[171] When the analysis reveals that the organization is so large or indiscriminate in its membership that personal rights of freedom of association do not attach and that no expressive purpose of the association is threatened, it will not uphold membership restrictions that are contrary to the law.[172]

It is important to note that voluntary associations that qualify as Section 501(c)(7) or (c)(8) organizations may not engage in the exclusion of members based on discriminatory standards set forth in Section 501(i) of the IRC. These anti-discrimination policies, as related to mutual benefit organizations, are discussed in the previous sections of this chapter. Section 501(c)(5) labor unions and Section 501(c)(6) professional and trade associations may not discriminate either, but the source of this prohibition is the Civil Rights Act of 1964.[173]

[E]   Exercising State-Like Powers

Voluntary associations that exercise state-like powers or act with authority delegated to them by the state are subject to constitutional limitations on their actions.[174] The courts have applied these constitutional limitations to voluntary associations, such as condominium or homeowners associations, that exercise government-like powers over those who live within the association.[175] An example of such a limitation is seen in *City of Ladue v. Gilleo*,[176] where the United States Supreme Court invalidated on First Amendment free speech grounds an ordinance adopted by a homeowners' association that prohibited, with very few exceptions, any type of residential signs within the association's territory.[177]

[F]   Judicial Intervention into Church Disputes

The constitutional guarantee of free exercise of religion affords religious organizations substantial autonomy in conducting their internal affairs.[178] Courts will not become engaged in doctrinal disputes unless a party is seeking a determination of rights to use the church property.[179] The general rule for

---

[170]   *Roberts*, 468 U.S. at 620.

[171]   *See id.* at 626; *Curran*, 17 Cal. 4th 670.

[172]   *See Roberts*, 468 U.S. 609.

[173]   Civil Rights Act of 1964, 42 U.S.C. § 2000 *et. seq.*

[174]   *See* Marsh v. Alabama, 326 U.S. 501 (1946).

[175]   Stewart E. Sterk, *Minority Protection in Residential Private Governments*, 77 B.U.L. Rev. 273 (1997).

[176]   512 U.S. 43 (1994).

[177]   *Id.*

[178]   Owen v. Bd. of Dirs. of Rosicrucian Fellowship, 342 P.2d 424 (Cal. Ct. App. 1959).

[179]   *Developments in the Law-Judicial Control of Actions of Private Associations*, 76 Harv. L. Rev. 983, 1006–1111 (1963).

religious organizations is that courts will not interfere with or disregard church tribunals whenever there is a question of discipline, faith, or ecclesiastical rule, custom, or law and when the decision has been decided by the highest of church judicatories.[180]

However, there are some exceptions when the courts will become involved in religious disputes. One example is if one or both factions ask the court to get involved as a referee. In this instance, the stakes must be secular, as where property is concerned, and involve the kind of dispute that the court would normally decide in context of a secular nonprofit and involve rights under corporate, contract or trust law.[181]

---

[180] *See Owen*, 342 P.2d 424.

[181] Ira Mark Ellman, *Driven from the Tribunal: Judicial Resolution of Internal Church Disputes*, 69 CAL. L. REV. 1378, 1382–89, 1397–1400 (1981).

Chapter 15

IRC SECTION 527: POLITICAL ORGANIZATIONS

§ 15.01 INTRODUCTION

Section 527 Political Organizations are a peculiar type of tax exempt organization.[1] Unlike those organizations exempt from federal income taxation under the various subsections of IRC Section 501(c), Section 527 Political Organizations provide no community benefit or mutual benefit to their members. Their entire purpose is to advance the political careers of the politicians whom they support, a clear private benefit. The argument could be made that the federal income tax exemption of Section 527 organizations by Congress is an example of Congress creating a separate category of tax exempt organizations simply because it could,[2] although another argument could be made that the basis for the exemption of Section 527s is the double taxation argument. The income was taxed once in the hands of those who donated their money to Section 527 organizations, so it should not be taxed again when it is received by the Section 527 organization.[3]

Before 1973, all of the income of political organizations was considered to consist of non-taxable gift income.[4] In 1973, the IRS announced that the investment income of a political organization was subject to income taxation.[5] In 1974, the IRS followed this announcement with a ruling that the non-gift income of an unincorporated political organization; that is, its passive investment income, was taxable.[6] This led Congress to add Section 527 to the IRC in 1975. As originally adopted, the statute taxed political organizations on all of their income, except for contributions, dues, and other fundraising income expended for political purposes.[7] The statute also provided that Section 501(c) organizations were to be taxed on their political expenditures.[8] In 1981, the statute was amended to include lower tax rates on the

---

[1] *See* I.R.C. § 527; 26 C.F.R. § 1.527-6.

[2] Congress' stated rationale was that political activity was not a trade or business that should be taxed. S. Rep. No. 93-1357 (1974), *reprinted in* U.S.C.C.A.N. 7478. See § 5.01 *et seq.* for further information on rationales for tax exemption.

[3] *See* James J. McGovern, *The Exemption Provisions of Subchapter F*, 29 TAX LAW. 523, 526 (1976).

[4] There was also a specific revenue procedure stating that dollars expended by a political organization on behalf of a political candidate were not income as to the candidate. Rev. Proc. 68-19, 1968-1 C.B. 810.

[5] I.R.S. Announcement 73-84, 1973-2 C.B. 461.

[6] Rev. Rul. 74-21, 1974-1 C.B. 14.

[7] Act of Jan. 21, 1974, Pub. L. No. 93-625, § 10(a), 88 Stat. 2018 (1974), added I.R.C. § 527, effective for tax years beginning after December 31, 1974.

[8] I.R.C. § 527(f).

principal campaign committee of candidates for Congress.[9]

In 1988, Congress broadened the definition of political activities on which exempt funds could be expended.[10] In 2000, the IRS closed a loophole that had allowed some 527 organizations to avoid the Federal Election Campaign Act (FECA) reporting requirements.[11]

§ 15.02   DEFINING A POLITICAL ORGANIZATION

Most Section 527 Political Organizations are known to the world, informally, as PACs, or political action committees. Earlier in this book, the difference between electioneering and lobbying was explained.[12] One way to think of Section 527 political organizations is as electioneering organizations. They exist to participate in campaigns for political office. The statute defines them as a party, committee, association, fund, or other organization (whether or not incorporated) organized and operated primarily for the purpose of directly or indirectly accepting contributions or making expenditures, or both,[13] in order to influence the selection, nomination, election, or appointment of any individual to any Federal, State, or local public office or office in a political organization, or the election of Presidential or Vice-Presidential electors, whether or not such individual or electors are selected, nominated, elected, or appointed.[14]

§ 15.03   ORGANIZATIONAL & OPERATIONAL TESTS

Political organizations need not have any specific legal structure, but they must meet the organizational and operational tests as defined in the Regulations. A political organization meets the organizational test if it can show that it was organized primarily for the purpose of carrying on the political activity specified in the statute.[15] If its articles of organization provide that its primary purpose is to carry on these political activities, then the organizational test is met. But an

---

[9] I.R.C. § 527(h).

[10] I.R.C. § 527(e)(2). In 1988, Congress broadened the definition of political activities to include expenditures for a public office if they would have been deductible by the officeholder under I.R.C. § 162(a).

[11] The problem was that FECA only required reporting of "express advocacy" expenditures, and it was not clear whether 527 organization expenditures for political activities were all express advocacy expenditures, leading to some 527's not reporting under FECA, 2 U.S.C. §§ 431–455. The 2000 amendment added a mandatory reporting requirement for 527's. I.R.C. § 527(j). The constitutionality of the 2000 amendment was immediately challenged. See Nat'l Fed'n of Republican Assemblies v. United States, 218 F. Supp. 2d 1300 (S.D. Ala. 2002), which upheld the constitutionality of the disclosure requirement of the names of organizers and donors, but not of expenditures, for federal elections, and which found the disclosure requirement for donors and expenditures in non-federal elections to be unconstitutional.

[12] See § 6.05 for further information on the political activities test for tax exemption.

[13] I.R.C. § 527(e)(1).

[14] I.R.C. § 527(e)(2). In 1988, Congress broadened the definition of political activities to include expenditures for a public office if they would have been deductible by the officeholder under I.R.C. § 162(a).

[15] 26 C.F.R. § 1.527-2(a)(2).

organization need not be incorporated or established as a formal trust or even a formal association in order to qualify as a Section 527 political organization.[16] Something as informal as a segregated bank account can qualify as a political organization.[17] When the organization has no formal articles of organization, then the IRS looks to the statements of the members of the organization at the time the organization is established to determine whether the organization was formed to act as a political organization.[18] In comparison to the very formal organizational test required of other exempt organizations, this test is extremely generous.[19]

A political organization meets the operational test if its primary activities are performed to influence the selection, nomination, election, or appointment of persons to federal, state, or local public office, whether or not such persons are selected, nominated, elected, or appointed.[20] These campaign activities are the exempt function activities of a Section 527 organization. The Regulations also allow a political organization to conduct nonpartisan educational workshops that are not meant to influence the political process, to pay an incumbent's office expenses, and to carry on social activities unrelated to its political purposes, as long as these activities do not become the primary activities of the organization.[21] The IRS has provided, in a number of rulings, what it considers to be permissible Section 527 exempt function political activities. For example, election night celebrations are considered political activities, as are after-election bonuses to campaign workers.[22] A legislator's expenses as a delegate to the national convention of his or her political party are political activities,[23] as are payments for polls, voter canvassing, and research on behalf of the holder of one elective office who is considering running for another elective office.[24]

Exempt function political activities also include such things as distributing voter guides or distributing a candidate's voting record, a grass-roots mailing in favor of a referendum, where the mailing features a particular candidate, or paying a salary to a candidate while he or she campaigns for office.[25] Election expenditures to train campaign staff members for the next election, work on party rules or party reform proposals, or to plan the party's convention are also exempt function expenditures.[26] Payment of the candidate's spouse's expenses, if the spouse is involved in campaign-

---

[16] Id.

[17] Rev. Rul. 79-11, 1979-1 C.B. 207.

[18] Id.

[19] See § 6.02 for further information on the organizational test for tax exemption.

[20] I.R.C. § 527(e)(2).

[21] 26 C.F.R. § 1.527-2(a)(3).

[22] Rev. Rul. 87-119, 1987-2 C.B. 151. The bonuses must, of course, be "reasonable," and are taxable to the campaign worker.

[23] Rev. Rul. 79-12, 1979-1 C.B. 208.

[24] Rev. Rul. 79-13, 1979-1 C.B. 208.

[25] P.L.R. 9652026 (Dec. 27, 1996); I.R.S. Tech. Adv. Mem. 9130008 (Apr. 16, 1991); I.R.S. Tech. Adv. Mem. 95-16-006 (Jan. 10, 1995). But see I.R.S. Tech. Adv. Mem. 92-44-003 (Apr. 15, 1992), where an organization which lobbied in favor of a municipal tax bill was considered not to be a 527 organization, since lobbying (as opposed to electioneering) activities are not exempt activities under § 527.

[26] 26 C.F.R. § 1.527-2(c)(5)(vii).

ing, are also considered exempt function expenditures.[27] Campaign termination activities, such as paying off campaign debts, and closing out the records, are also considered to be exempt functions.[28]

§ 15.04   DETERMINING TAXATION

Section 527 political organizations must pay the federal income tax on their political organization taxable income.[29] This is defined by the statute as their gross income, minus deductions directly connected with the production of gross income, and minus their exempt function income.[30] Exempt function income is all income from contributions of money or property, membership dues, fees or assessments, proceeds from a political fundraising or entertainment event, proceeds from the sale of campaign materials (unless the sales are so regular as to constitute a trade or business), and proceeds from bingo games, as long as these amounts are segregated for use only in exempt function political activities.[31] There is also a flat $100 exemption.[32]

As mentioned above, what is left of organizational income, minus the statutory deductions, will be the organization's passive investment income, namely its interest income, dividend income and capital gains income. This passive investment income is taxed at the highest corporate rates,[33] except for the passive income of principal campaign committees of candidates for Congress, which are taxed at graduated corporate rates.[34]

§ 15.05   NEWSLETTER FUNDS

There had been a question as to whether funds used by candidates for public office to publish newsletters on their behalf created a form of benefit that was taxable to the candidate. Section 527(g) provides that newsletter funds qualify, by themselves, as exempt political organizations.[35] These funds must be established and maintained by an individual who has publicly announced his or her candidacy for public office, and who meets the legal qualifications for the office.[36] Newsletter funds can only be used for the preparation and circulation of the newsletter. Such expenses can include secretarial services, printing, addressing, and mailing costs.[37] Newsletter funds cannot be used for other political activities or transferred to other

---

[27] 26 C.F.R. § 1.527-2(c)(5)(ii); I.R.S. Tech. Adv. Mem. 93-20-002 (Jan. 14, 1993).

[28] 26 C.F.R. § 1.527-2(c)(3).

[29] I.R.C. § 527(b).

[30] I.R.C. § 527(c)(1).

[31] I.R.C. § 527(c)(3).

[32] I.R.C. § 527(c)(2)(A). This deduction cannot be taken by "newsletter funds."

[33] I.R.C. § 527(b)(1).

[34] I.R.C. § 527(h)(1).

[35] I.R.C. § 527(g)(1).

[36] I.R.C. § 527(g)(3).

[37] 26 C.F.R. § 1.527-7(c).

political organizations.[38] If newsletter funds are used for other than newsletter purposes, the amount so used is treated as expended for the personal use of the person establishing and maintaining the fund.[39] In addition, once this non-newsletter use of funds occurs, all future contributions to the fund will also be treated as income to the person who established and maintained the fund.[40]

§ 15.06   SEGREGATED FUNDS

Because all that a Section 527 organization needs to do to meet the organizational requirement is to exist as a separate, segregated fund, any 501(c) organization, except for those prohibited by the statute from electioneering, can operate a Section 527 political organization as a separate, segregated fund.[41] Section 501 (c)(3) organizations are prohibited from electioneering,[42] but so too are Section 501(c)(2) title holding companies and Section 501(c)(20) group legal service plans because the language of the statute in their respective sections limits them to an "exclusive" purpose. All other Section 501(c) organizations can take advantage of Section 527. They may use affiliated Section 527 organizations, such as a separate, segregated fund, to make expenditures for political campaign or electioneering purposes as long as these expenditures do not rise to such a level that the electioneering becomes a primary purpose of the organization.[43]

Such funds must be clearly identified and kept separate and segregated from the organization's other funds. They must have their own treasurer, who is responsible for record keeping.[44] Records must be kept of receipts and disbursements, identifying the political activity of each expenditure.[45] Failure to keep adequate records will result in an expenditure being classified as a non-exempt expenditure.[46] A Section 501(c) organization can transfer the political contributions that it solicits to this fund. It can also transfer dues income, as long as the dues are not deductible as a business expense by the dues payor.[47] These transfers must be promptly made by the Section 501(c) organization directly to the separate fund.[48] The Section 501(c) organization cannot transfer investment income to the separate fund.[49] The Regulations provide that the purpose of such funds must be to receive and

---

[38] 26 C.F.R. § 1.527-7(d).

[39] 26 C.F.R. § 1.527-7(a).

[40] *Id.*

[41] *See* I.R.C. § 501; 26 C.F.R. § 1.501(c)(3)-1(b)(3).

[42] I.R.C. § 501(c)(3) organizations may, however, establish a separate § 527 fund to avoid the § 527(f) tax on political expenditures for activities that attempt to influence the appointment of persons to non-elective office (e.g., federal judgeships). Tax deductible dollars received by the § 501(c)(3) organization cannot be placed in this fund.

[43] *See* I.R.C. § 527; 26 C.F.R. § 1.527-7(a).

[44] 2 U.S.C. § 432(a).

[45] 26 C.F.R. § 1.527-2(b)(2).

[46] I.R.S. Tech. Adv. Mem. 94-09-003 (Feb. 26, 1993).

[47] I.R.C. § 162(e)(2)(A); 26 C.F.R. § 1.162-20(c)(3).

[48] 26 C.F.R. § 1.527-6(e).

[49] *Id.*

segregate election campaign income (and earnings on such income) from the organization's other income.[50] Expenditures for the establishment and administration of a political organization or the solicitation of political contributions may be made from the segregated fund.[51] For tax purposes, such funds are treated as separate organizations.[52] As the Senate Finance Committee reported when it advised the adoption of Section 527:

> [A] Section 501(c) organization that is permitted to engage in political activities would establish a separate organization that would operate primarily as a political organization, and directly receive and disburse all funds related to nomination, etc. activities. In this way, the campaign-type activities would be taken entirely out of the Section 501(c) organization to the benefit of both the organization and the administration of the tax laws.[53]

In the case of *Alaska Public Service Employees Local 71 v. Commissioner*,[54] a Section 501(c)(5) labor union maintained a segregated fund for electioneering purposes. The problem was that the union transferred $25,000 from its general fund, which included dues and investment income, to the segregated fund. The IRS sought to tax the union on this transfer under IRC Section 527(b) and (f). While the union tried to argue that the transfer was permissible under the Regulations, the court pointed to the clear language in Regulation Section 1.527-6(e), which prohibited the transfer of investment income, and specifically interest income, on dues, to a separate, segregated fund for use in political activities.[55] Because the dollars in the fund were undesignated, the labor union could not meet its burden of demonstrating that it had not used dues investment income when it made the transfer. Because the labor union had transferred $25,000 back from the separate, segregated fund to its general fund in a subsequent tax year, it tried to argue that it had undone the improper transfer, and that there should be no adverse tax consequences. The IRS pointed out, and the court agreed, that the rules apply tax year by tax year, and that a transfer in a subsequent tax year cannot reverse that tax consequences incurred in a prior year. As a result, the union was liable for the tax, on the lesser of its investment income in the relevant tax year or the amount of the improper transfer.[56] Because its investment income for the tax year was $59,127, it was taxed, at corporate rates, on the lesser amount of $25,000.[57]

---

[50] 26 C.F.R. § 1.527-2(b)(1).

[51] *Id.*

[52] I.R.C. § 527(f)(3).

[53] S. Rep. No. 93-1357, at 25, 30 (1974), *reprinted in* 1974 U.S.C.C.A.N. 7478, 7502, 7507.

[54] 62 T.C.M. (CCH) 1664 (1991).

[55] *Id.*; 26 C.F.R. § 1.527-6(e)(2), (3).

[56] *Alaska Pub. Serv. Emps.*, 62 T.C.M. (CCH) 1664. This is the tax imposed by I.R.C. § 527(f)(1).

[57] *Alaska Pub. Serv. Emps.*, 62 T.C.M. (CCH) 1664.

§ 15.07   THE SECTION 527(f) TAX

The 501(c) organizations that cannot participate in political campaign activities using a Section 527 organization are taxed on their political campaign expenditures under Section 527(f). These organizations, such as Section 501(c)(3) organizations, are taxed at the highest corporate rates on the lesser of the organization's net investment income for the taxable year when the political expenditures were made or its total political campaign expenditures for that year.[58]

The creation of this tax on the political campaign activities of a Section 501(c)(3) organizations is not meant to upset the general statutory scheme under which 501(c)(3) organizations may not electioneer at all. Section 501(c)(3) organizations that do intervene in political campaigns are in violation of the political activities test and can lose their exempt status because of such activities.[59]

In addition to the Section 527(f) tax, Section 501(c)(3) organizations and their managers are specifically subject to tax under IRC Section 4955 for their political campaign expenditures. All of these penalties, the 527(f) tax, the 4955 tax, and loss of exempt status can occur concurrently.

The Section 527(f) tax also falls on Section 527 organizations if they use non-exempt income, such as investment income, for political purposes. This was the case with the Alaska Public Service Employees Union, referred to above, which transferred investment income to a separate, segregated 527 fund for use in political activity.[60]

§ 15.08   FILING & REPORTING REQUIREMENTS

A Section 527 organization need not apply for recognition of its exempt status, but in order to be treated as Section 527 organizations, some organizations are required to give Form 8871 notice to the IRS that they are seeking tax exemption under Section 527.[61] Exempt from filing this notice are Section 501(c) organizations taxed on their political campaign expenditures under Section 527(f), organizations that reasonably anticipate that their gross annual receipts will be under $25,000 in a taxable year, a political committee of a state or local candidate, a state or local committee of a political party, and organizations already subject to reporting under the Federal Election Campaign Act.[62] All other 527 organizations must file the Form 8871 with the IRS.[63]

---

[58]   The level of taxation is established in I.R.C. § 527(b), referring to I.R.C. § 11(b).

[59]   Christian Echoes Nat'l Ministry v. United States, 470 F.2d 849 (10th Cir. 1972), *cert. denied*, 414 U.S. 864 (1973); Branch Ministries, Inc. v. Rossotti, 40 F. Supp. 2d 15 (D.D.C. 1999), *aff'd*, 211 F.3d 137 (D.C. Cir. 2000).

[60]   *Alaska Pub. Serv. Emps.*, 62 T.C.M. (CCH) 1664.

[61]   It is possible, of course, to file a request for a private letter ruling that an organization so qualifies.

[62]   I.R.C. § 527(i)(5), (6).

[63]   *See* I.R.S. Form 8871 (Rev. July 2003). The organization must file electronically as provided in I.R.C. § 527(i)(1)(A). To file electronically, go to www.irs.gov/polorgs (last visited May 10, 2011). I.R.S. Form 8871 *Instructions* (Rev. July 2003).

This notice is to be transmitted electronically to the IRS within 24 hours of the organization's formation, to be followed up in writing.[64] The notice must include the organization's name, address, including its electronic address, its purposes, names and addresses of officers, highly compensated employees, contact person, custodian of records, and members of its Board of Directors.[65] Because Section 527 organizations are not required to have highly developed organizational structures in order to qualify as Section 527 organizations, some of this information may not even exist. The notice must also identify all related entities.[66]

Failure to file the Form 8871 notice in a timely fashion will result in the taxation of what otherwise would have been exempt income, i.e., contributions, membership dues, fundraising (including bingo) proceeds.[67] Nor can an organization that fails to file Form 8871 take a deduction for its political expenditures because IRC Section 162(e) does not allow deductions for political activities. In effect, the only allowable deductions that an organization can take are those associated with the production of its taxable income.[68]

In any calendar year in which a Section 527 organization either accepts contributions or makes expenditures, it must make periodic reports to the IRS on Form 8872.[69] Political organizations that are exempt from filing Form 8871 are also exempt from filing Form 8872.[70] These reports may be filed either on a monthly basis or, in a non-election year on a semi-annual basis, and in an election year on a quarterly basis.[71] In an election year, separate pre- and post-election reports are also required.[72]

The Form 8872 reports the amount, date, and purpose of each expenditure made by the Section 527 organization to a person when the total payments to the person exceed $500 in a calendar year, and it also reports the name, address, occupation, and employer of all contributors who, in a calendar year, gave $200 or more to the organization.[73] There is a safe harbor exception for failure to file the Form 8872 for reasonable cause.[74]

Section 527 organizations are also required to file Form 1120-POL for years in which they have taxable income in excess of $100 or gross receipts in excess of $25,000.[75] As noted above, Section 527 organizations pay the highest corporate rates

---

[64] I.R.C. § 527(i)(1)(A); *see also* Rev. Rul. 2004-49, 2004-1 C.B. 939.

[65] I.R.C. § 527(i)(3).

[66] I.R.C. § 168(h)(4) defines related entities.

[67] I.R.C. § 527(c)(3), (i)(4).

[68] I.R.C. § 527(i)(4).

[69] I.R.C. § 527(j).

[70] It is possible, of course, to file a request for a private letter ruling that an organization so qualifies.

[71] I.R.C. § 527(j)(2); Rev. Rul. 2000-49, 2000-2 C.B. 430.

[72] I.R.C. § 527(j)(2)(A)(i).

[73] *See* I.R.S. Form 8871 (Rev. July 2003).

[74] Rev. Proc. 2007-27, 2007-1 C.B. 887.

[75] I.R.C. § 6012(a)(6); *see also* I.R.S. Form 1120-POL (2004).

on their taxable income.[76] As do most other tax exempt organizations, Section 527 organizations must also file the Form 990.[77]

§ 15.09   RECENT LITIGATION

In recent years, there has been a spate of litigation on the First Amendment rights of tax exempt organizations and PACs (Section 527 organizations) that contribute to political campaigns or that make independent expenditures on behalf of candidates for political office. This litigation has not been in the area of tax exemption law, but rather in the area of campaign finance, and the applicability of congressionally imposed limits on campaign spending and campaign contributions. Section 527 organizations are subject to federal regulation under federal election laws.[78]

In *FEC v. Massachusetts Citizens for Life*,[79] the U.S. Supreme Court held that the federal election law (2 U.S.C. § 441b), which required that corporate expenditures on behalf of political candidates be financed through a political committee (i.e., a Section 527 organization) expressly established to engage in campaign spending, as opposed to expenditures from its general corporate treasury, was unconstitutional as applied to a Section 501(c)(4) pro-life advocacy organization that accepted no business corporation or union contributions. The law, the Court said, infringed on protected speech without a compelling justification for such infringement.

In *FEC v. Beaumont*,[80] the U.S. Supreme Court considered the issue of whether the same statute's (441b) prohibition on direct corporate donations to a political candidate, as opposed to contributions to such campaigns through a PAC that the statute permitted, was unconstitutional as applied to another 501(c)(4), North Carolina Right to Life, Inc., an organization very similar to Massachusetts Citizens for Life. The Court held that it was not, distinguishing between the restrictions on independent corporate expenditures that it had disallowed in *Massachusetts Citizens for Life*, and restrictions on the right to make direct corporate contributions to a political candidate that it continued to hold constitutional in the North Carolina case.

---

[76] I.R.C. § 527(b)(1).

[77] I.R.C. § 6033(g). See § 20.01 *et seq.* for further information on the filing requirements for tax exempt organizations.

[78] The Federal Election Campaign Act of 1971, 2 U.S.C. §§ 431–455, which was amended by Bipartisan Campaign Reform Act of 2002 (McCain Feingold), Pub. L. No. 107–155, 116 Stat. 81 (2002).

[79] 479 U.S. 238 (1986).

[80] 539 U.S. 146 (2003).

In *FEC v. Wisconsin Right to Life, Inc.*,[81] the U.S. Supreme Court had overturned that part of the Bipartisan Campaign Reform Act of 2002 (called "McCain-Feingold") that prohibited corporations from paying for political ads 60 days before a general election, or 30 days before a primary, when the ad was an "issue ad" that did not clearly endorse or oppose a candidate. The Court said that "issue ads," which were not susceptible of interpretation as an ad urging the election or defeat of a candidate, qualified for an "as applied" exception to the McCain-Feingold limits on 'issue ads" close to an election. The Court, however, failed to overturn *McConnell v. FEC*,[82] where it had upheld McCain-Feingold's regulations against "express advocacy" ads just before an election, drawing a distinction between these types of ads, which did urge the election or defeat of a particular candidate, and "issue ads."

In *Citizens United v. FEC*,[83] which involved a Section 501(c)(4) organization's challenge to McCain-Feingold's restrictions on "express advocacy" ads just before an election, the Court overturned that part of McCain-Feingold, which prohibited organizations, not just 501(c)(4)s, but also including corporations and unions, from using their general treasury funds to pay for express advocacy ads just before an election. In the case of *EMILY's List v. FEC*,[84] the D.C. Circuit, in addition to ruling that new FEC regulations on soliciting and spending political contributions by a 527 exceeded statutory authority (441), also ruled that 527s have a First Amendment right to solicit and spend without limit on electoral campaigns provided that they do so independently, i.e., not in concert with a candidate or a party. "[I]ndividual citizens may spend money without limit (apart from the limit on their own contributions to candidates or parties) in support of the election of particular candidates."[85] The challenged rules had placed a limit of $5,000 limit on contributions from individual donors that 527s could spend on an election. In the case of *SpeechNow.org v. FEC*,[86] the D.C. Circuit held 441's contribution limits unconstitutional "as applied to individuals' contributions to SpeechNow, [an expenditure only group]."[87] As a result of all of this litigation, the Federal Election Commission has issued a draft advisory opinion that states, as to an independent expenditure organization, "there is no basis to limit the amount of contributions . . . from individuals, political committees, corporations and labor organizations."[88] While this litigation has had the effect of lifting some of the restrictions imposed by federal election law on 527 spending, it must be remembered that as to 501(c) organizations, the restrictions on their electoral activity comes, not from the federal election laws, but from the federal tax exemption law, in which, as to 501(c)(4)s, 501(c)(5)s and 501(c)(6)s, the restriction on "electioneering" is that "no substantial part" of their activities may consist of intervening in a political campaign on behalf of or in

---

[81]   551 U.S. 449 (2007).

[82]   540 U.S. 93 (2003).

[83]   175 L. Ed. 2d 753 (2010).

[84]   581 F.3d 1 (D.C. Cir. 2009).

[85]   *Id.* at 10.

[86]   599 F.3d 686 (D.C. Cir. 2010).

[87]   *Id.* at 689.

[88]   A.O. 2010-11 (F.E.C.) (July 22, 2010).

opposition to a particular candidate. The way around this, for these organizations, is to found their own, related 527 organizations. But also recall that Section 501(c)(3)s cannot normally have related 527 organizations.[89]

---

[89] *See supra* note 42.

Chapter 16

UNRELATED BUSINESS INCOME TAX

§ 16.01 INTRODUCTION

The tax on the unrelated business income of tax exempt organizations was added to the IRC in 1950. Before this, the law was quite generous to tax exempt organizations and allowed all of their income, from whatever source, to be tax exempt, as long as it met the "destination" test.[1] This test was first described in *Trinidad v. Sagrada Orden de Predicadores* (The Sacred Order of Preachers).[2] The Sacred Order of Preachers, otherwise known as the Dominicans, a Roman Catholic religious order, owned multiple interests in the Philippines, including rental properties, a chocolate confectionery and a winery.[3] The income from all of these activities was found to be tax exempt as long as the profits were destined to support the exempt activities of the organization.[4] One prominent law school achieved its national status in part through the wise use of the dollars thrown off by its ownership of a noodle factory that, because they were used for the school's exempt educational purposes, were tax exempt under *Trinidad*'s destination test.[5]

This changed in 1950 when Congress amended the IRC to levy a tax on the unrelated business activities of all IRC Section 501(c)(3) tax exempt organizations except for churches, Section 501(c)(5) labor organizations and Section 501(c)(6) business leagues and chambers of commerce.[6] For these organizations, the destination test was no more. Now, in order to be tax exempt, income had to come from activities that were "substantially related" to the organization's exempt purposes.[7] This type of income is called "exempt function income."[8] Income from these related activities passes without tax to the organization, even in the case of Section 501(c)(3), when those activities are commercial in nature, as long as they are in furtherance of the organization's exempt purposes.[9] A business or activity that

---

[1] *See* J. Brooks, *The Marts of Trade: The Law School and the Noodle Factory*, THE NEW YORKER, Dec. 26, 1977, at 48.

[2] 263 U.S. 578 (1924); *see also* Roche's Beach v. Comm'r, 96 F.2d 776 (2d Cir. 1938) (applying the destination test to income from a commercial beach operation); Sand Springs Home v. Comm'r, 6 B.T.A. 198 (1927).

[3] *Trinidad*, 263 U.S. at 579.

[4] *Id.* at 581.

[5] *See* Brooks, *supra* note 1; *see also* C. F. Mueller Co. v. Comm'r, 190 F.2d 120 (3d Cir. 1951).

[6] I.R.C. §§ 511–513.

[7] I.R.C. § 513(a).

[8] I.R.C. § 512(a)(3)(B).

[9] 26 C.F.R. § 1.501(c)(3)-1(e)(1).

simply raises money for an exempt organization, however, is not considered to be "substantially related," even when all of the money goes to pay for exempt function activities.[10] The 1950 amendments also cover "feeder" organizations. An example of a feeder organization would be the noodle factory and the law school where the noodle factory had a separate legal existence from the tax exempt law school, but fed, or paid, all of its profits to the school. Under the 1950 amendments, feeder organizations no longer qualify as tax exempt.[11]

The unrelated business activities of a tax exempt organization can cause other problems for an exempt organization beyond the need to pay income taxes on these activities.[12] If unrelated business activities become too large a part of the organization's overall activities, they will jeopardize the organization's exempt status under the operational test. An exempt organization, a substantial part of whose activities is for non-exempt purposes, fails the operational test.[13] If a tax exempt organization's unrelated business activities grow to be too large a part of the organization's total operations, the organization will be in violation of the operational test and no longer qualify for tax exempt status.[14] It is clear from the legislative history of the unrelated business income tax that a major purpose of the tax on the unrelated business activities of otherwise exempt organizations was to deal with the problem of unfair competition between untaxed businesses operated by tax exempt organizations and similar businesses operated by for-profit corporations that were fully taxable.[15] The courts have not been uniform in endorsing the prevention of unfair competition as the only basis of the unrelated business income tax, however, citing the need for revenue as a corollary reason.[16]

In 1969, Congress revisited the tax on the unrelated business activities of tax exempt organizations. The prior exception for churches, social clubs, and fraternal benefit organizations and other 501(c) organizations not covered by the 1950 act was done away with. Now, for all intents and purposes, all Section 501(c) organizations

---

[10] That, of course, would be the destination of income rule from Trinidad v. Sagrada Orden, 263 U.S. 578 (1924), which has long since been rejected.

[11] I.R.C. § 502 denies exemption to "feeder" organizations-organizations that carry on a trade or business and then pay all of their profits to exempt organizations. Feeder organizations have a separate legal existence from the exempt organization that they "feed," so strictly speaking the tax imposed on the unrelated business activities of tax exempt organizations by I.R.C. § 511 did not cover them.

[12] Unrelated business income can cause problems for an organization under the IRS tests for tax exemption. For further information on the tests for tax exemption, see § 6.01 et seq.

[13] See People's Educ. Camp v. Comm'r, 331 F.2d 923 (2d Cir. 1964).

[14] See Orange Cnty. Agric. Soc'y, Inc. v. Comm'r, 55 T.C.M. (CCH) 1602 (1988), aff'd, 893 F.2d 529 (2d Cir. 1990) (exemption denied based on the fact that one-third of the organization's income came from unrelated business activities); see also United States v. Cmty. Servs., 189 F.2d 421 (4th Cir. 1951); Scripture Press Found. v. United States, 285 F.2d 800 (Ct. Cl. 1961); Fides Publishers Ass'n v. United States, 263 F. Supp. 924 (N.D. Ind. 1967).

[15] H.R. REP. No. 2319, at 36–37 (1950); S. REP. No. 2375, at 28–29 (1950). See also Hope Sch. v. U.S., 612 F.2d 298 (7th Cir. 1980); 26 C.F.R. § 1.513-1(b). This rationale was re-iterated in 1976. See S. REP. No. 94-938, pt. 1, at 601 (1976), reprinted in 1976 U.S.C.C.A.N. 3438, 4025.

[16] Clarence La Belle Post No. 217, Veterans of Foreign Wars v. United States, 580 F.2d 270 (8th Cir. 1978); La. Credit Union League v. United States, 693 F.2d 525 (5th Cir. 1982); American Med. Ass'n v. United States, 887 F.2d 760 (7th Cir. 1989).

are subject to this tax.[17] The 1969 amendments also stopped abuses in "sale and lease back" transactions by exempt organizations by making almost all debt-financed income subject to the tax on unrelated business.[18]

§ 16.02   DEFINING UNRELATED BUSINESS INCOME

The unrelated business income tax, or UBIT for short, taxes the unrelated business taxable income of an otherwise exempt organization.[19] Unrelated business taxable income is in turn defined as the gross income derived by any organization from any unrelated trade or business regularly carried on by it, less allowable deductions.[20]

Three elements can be pulled from this definition and the accompanying Regulations to determine where UBIT falls. Under the IRC, UBIT is payable by tax exempt organizations on its net income when it is:

- From a trade or business

- Regularly carried on

- Substantially unrelated to the organization's exempt purposes[21]

[A]   Trade or Business

"Trade or business" includes any activity that is carried on for the production of income from the sale of goods or the performance of services.[22] An activity does not lose identity as a trade or business merely because it is carried on within a larger aggregate of similar activities that may or may not be related to the exempt purposes of the organization.[23] For example, an educational organization publishes a journal of learned articles in furtherance of its exempt educational purposes, but it also sells advertisements in the journal. The selling of advertising still qualifies as a trade or business, even though carried on in the context of a larger exempt activity — publishing the journal. This is called the "fragmentation" rule, because it allows the IRS to fragment, that is, break up, an exempt organization's activities into its exempt and non-exempt parts, and consider the non-exempt parts as a taxable trade or business.[24]

The Regulations provide further clarity of what constitutes a trade or business. They state that, in general, any activity that is carried on for the production of income and that otherwise possesses the characteristics required to constitute a

---

[17] Still not covered are § 501(c)(1) U.S. government entities created and granted tax exemption by Congress. I.R.C. § 511(a)(2)(A).

[18] I.R.C. §§ 514, 512(b)(4); see also § 16.06.

[19] I.R.C. § 511(a).

[20] I.R.C. § 512(a)(1).

[21] 26 C.F.R. § 1.513-1 et seq.

[22] I.R.C. § 513(c).

[23] Id.

[24] See § 16.02[B] for further information on the fragmentation rule.

'trade or business' within the meaning of Section 162 constitutes a trade or business as those terms are used in IRC Section 511.[25] IRC Section 162 details allowable trade or business deductions, premised on the fact that a trade or business is operated to generate a profit, and that expenses used to generate that profit are deductible.[26] As the Second Circuit said in applying Section 162, "It is well established that the existence of a genuine profit motive is the most important criterion for the finding that a given course of activity constitutes a trade or business."[27] In addition to the presence of a profit motive, it has been held that Section 162's definition of a "trade or business" requires "extensive activity over a substantial period of time during which the taxpayer holds himself out as a provider of goods and services."[28]

In *United States v. American Bar Endowment*,[29] the issue was whether the insurance program of the American Bar Endowment, a Section 501(c)(3) organization, constituted a trade or business. The American Bar Endowment provided life, health, accident, and disability insurance policies, underwritten by commercial insurers, to about 20 percent of its members. Because of the groups' favorable risk rating, the cost of these policies was lower than other commercially available policies, but the Endowment billed its members at commercial rates, and used the difference paid by the members (which it characterized as dividends) to fund its charitable activities. The Endowment required its members to assign these "dividends" to the Endowment as a condition for their participation in the insurance program. The Endowment solicited members for this program, collected premiums, maintained policy holders' files, and answered members' questions and screened claims for benefits.[30]

The Claims Court had previously held that, because the Endowment did not operate its insurance program in a competitive, commercial manner, it did not constitute a trade or business.[31]

The United States Supreme Court criticized the Claims Court holding, saying that the Claims Court had improperly bifurcated the Endowment's activities into the provision of insurance and the acceptance of contributions (the "dividends") for its charitable activities. This characterization effectively removed any profit-seeking activities from the mix.[32]

The United States Supreme Court did not agree that the "dividends" were a true charitable contribution for, among other reasons, the lack of a truly voluntary

---

[25] 26 C.F.R. § 1.513-1(b).

[26] I.R.C. § 162.

[27] Lamont v. Comm'r, 339 F.2d 377, 380 (2d Cir. 1964); *see also* St. Joseph Farms of Ind. v. Comm'r, 85 T.C. 9 (1985). In another version of the "profit motive" requirement, the Tax Court has said that an activity must be carried on in a commercial and competitive manner in order to qualify as a trade or business. *Id.* at 19–20.

[28] McDowell v. Ribicoff, 292 F.2d 174, 178 (3d Cir. 1961).

[29] 477 U.S. 105 (1986).

[30] *Id.* at 107.

[31] American Bar Endowment v. United States, 4 Cl. Ct. 404 (1984).

[32] *Am. Bar Endowment*, 477 U.S. 105.

aspect to these "contributions." Rather, it saw these dividends generated by the Endowment's insurance program as a form of profit. This determination and the Endowment's heavy involvement in the plan's promotion, marketing, and management easily allowed the Court to characterize this activity as a trade or business, saying that the Endowment's insurance activity "is both 'the sale of goods' and the 'performance of services,' and possesses the general characteristics of a trade or business."[33]

In another insurance case, the *American Academy of Family Physicians v. United States*,[34] a Section 501(c)(6) business league, owned and sponsored group disability, medical, and life insurance policies that were available to Academy members and their employees. The reserves in this insurance program were to be turned over to the Academy as individual policies terminated. These reserves generated annual investment income. The insurance program was underwritten by a for-profit insurance company, which annually paid this investment income to the Academy. The IRS sought to tax these payments as a form of unrelated business income. Again the issue was whether the Academy's insurance activities constituted a trade or business.[35] The Eighth Circuit found that the payment of investment income to the Academy on the reserves that it would eventually own were "the way the parties decided to acknowledge the Academy's eventual claim to the reserves while the [commercial carrier] was still holding and using these reserves."[36] As a result, they were not compensation for services performed by the Academy and did not constitute a profit. The court also held that because the Academy's participation in the insurance program was purely passive inasmuch as others did all of the promotion, marketing, and administration of the program, it did not possess the general characteristics of a trade or business.[37]

In yet another insurance case, *Professional Insurance Agents of Michigan v. Commissioner*,[38] a Section 501(c)(6) business league provided various forms of insurance to its members in their professional and personal capacities by placing these policies with commercial carriers. The Professional Insurance Agents (PIA) marketed these policies to its members and helped to administer them, for which services it was paid by the commercial carriers.[39] The court had no trouble finding that a profit motive was present, especially after PIA's president testified that PIA selected these commercial carriers based on the level of remuneration it received. As a result, the income that PIA received from the commercial carriers qualified as unrelated business income.[40]

---

[33] *Id.* at 110–11.

[34] 91 F.3d 1155 (8th Cir. 1996).

[35] *Id.* at 1157.

[36] *Id.* at 1159.

[37] *Id.*

[38] 726 F.2d 1097 (6th Cir. 1984).

[39] *Id.* at 1098.

[40] *Id.* at 1102.

[B]   Fragmentation Rule

In *United States v. American College of Physicians*,[41] a Section 501(c)(3) organization published a monthly journal on internal medicine that contained scholarly articles related to its exempt purposes. The journal also carried advertisements for pharmaceuticals, medical supplies, medical equipment, and notices for openings in the field of internal medicine. It was the organization's policy only to carry advertisements that presented information relevant to the field of internal medicine. The issue was whether the advertisement income constituted unrelated business income.[42] Citing the language of IRC Section 513(c), an activity does not lose its identity as a trade or business merely because it is carried on within a larger complex of other endeavors that may, or may not, be related to the exempt purposes of the organization, the United States Supreme Court held that the sale of advertisements clearly constituted a trade or business, thus meeting the first prong of the three-pronged test for unrelated business income.[43]

This case is probably the best example of the fragmentation rule, originally promulgated by the IRS in 1967,[44] and adopted by Congress in the 1969 amendments to the unrelated business tax law with the language of Section 513(c). The fragmentation rule allows the IRS to reach into an exempt organization's activities, separate out what is related and what is not, and characterize the income from unrelated activities as a taxable unrelated trade or business income. Advertising is perhaps the easiest example of the fragmentation rule at work, but there are many other examples. The income from a hospital pharmacy that serves both hospital patients and off-the-street clients can be fragmented so that sales to non-patients qualify as unrelated business income.[45]

[C]   Regularly Carried On

A trade or business is regularly carried on if it manifests a frequency and continuity and is pursued in a manner generally similar to comparable commercial activities of nonexempt organizations.[46] In applying the "regularly carried on" prong of the three-pronged test, the Regulations specifically direct that this part of the test must be applied in light of the purpose of the unrelated business income tax to place exempt organization business activities upon the same tax basis as the nonexempt business endeavors with which they compete.[47]

What this means is that, if the nonexempt business activity with which the unrelated business activity competes is normally conducted on a year-round basis, then the unrelated business activity must be conducted on a year-round basis to be

---

[41] 475 U.S. 834 (1986).

[42] *Id.* at 835–36.

[43] *Id.* at 840.

[44] *Id.*; 26 C.F.R. § 1.513-1(b); 32 Fed. Reg. 17,657 (Dec. 12, 1967); *see also* Hi-Plains Hosp. v. United States, 670 F.2d 528 (5th Cir. 1982).

[45] 26 C.F.R. § 1.513-1(b).

[46] 26 C.F.R. § 1.513-1(c)(1).

[47] *Id.*

considered to be "regularly carried on." On the other hand, if the competing nonexempt business is only seasonal, then the competing unrelated business activity need only be conducted on a seasonal basis in order to be considered to be "regularly carried on."[48]

The Regulations give some examples to flesh out the rules.[49] A sandwich stand operated by a hospital auxiliary at a state fair for two weeks out of the year does not qualify as "regularly carried on." But if the same sandwich stand were open one day a week, every week of the year, on a sidewalk outside the hospital, that would be "regularly carried on." The operation of an outdoor track for horse racing only several weeks of a year would be considered "regularly carried on" because it is usual to conduct such a business only for a short season.[50]

The Regulations also speak of "intermittent activities."[51] If the competing activities of nonexempt organizations are carried on only intermittently, then the unrelated business activity of the exempt organization need only to be conducted intermittently in order to be "regularly carried on." Common sense suggests that such comparisons will be rare, however, because any nonexempt business that wishes to turn a profit must be conducted more than simply now and then. As an example of an intermittent activity that would not qualify as "regularly carried on," the Regulations state that the publication of advertising in programs for individual sports events or music or drama performances will not ordinarily be deemed to be the regular carrying on of business.[52]

This was exactly the case in *Suffolk County Patrolmen's Benevolent Association, Inc. v. Commissioner.*[53] The Patrolmen's Benevolent Association, a Section 501(c)(5) labor organization, sponsored annual vaudeville shows as a form of fund-raiser. To put on these shows, they contracted with for-profit organizations that, in exchange for a fixed share in the proceeds, provided the performers and sold advertising in the programs that were distributed at the shows. In any year, the show gave three or four performances. The IRS sought to tax the Patrolmen's Benevolent Association's share of the advertising proceeds. There was no doubt that the sale of advertising qualified as a trade or business unrelated to the Patrolmen's exempt purposes.[54] The issue was whether the activity was regularly carried on. The IRS argued that the relevant period on which to base this determination was the entire time during which the ads were sold, which was 8 to 16 weeks prior to the time of the show, or the six-year period during which the Patrolmen had a contract with the for-profit promoter.[55] The court rejected both of these arguments and found the advertising income to be non-taxable. It cited the Regulations, which specifically state that the annually recurrent nature of an

---

[48] *Id.*

[49] 26 C.F.R. § 1.513-1(c)(2)(i).

[50] *Id.*

[51] 26 C.F.R. § 1.513-1(c)(2)(ii).

[52] *Id.*

[53] 77 T.C. 1314 (1981).

[54] *Id.* at 1314.

[55] *Id.* at 1322–24.

intermittent activity will not cause it to be regarded as regularly carried on.[56] It also said that it could find nowhere in the legislative history or the Regulations themselves where any period was relevant apart from the actual duration of the event, which in this case was three or four days a year. To buttress its decision, the court further cited the Regulations, which describe publication of advertising in programs for sports events or music or drama performances as not being a business "regularly carried on."[57]

A very similar situation occurred in *National Collegiate Athletic Association v. Commissioner*,[58] where the IRS sought to tax the NCAA on the advertising income it received from for-profit companies for ads published in programs for the 1982 NCAA championship tournament. Again the question was what time period would be used to determine whether the activity was regularly carried on. The IRS argued it was the time spent soliciting and preparing the ads, which was a substantial period. The NCAA argued that it was only the eight-day period over three weeks during which the tournament games were played.[59] The Tenth Circuit agreed with the NCAA, relying on the *Suffolk County Patrolmen's* case and on the language in the Regulations that specified that certain intermittent activity occurs so infrequently that neither its recurrence nor the manner of its conduct will cause it to be regarded as a trade or business regularly carried on.[60] The court found the NCAA's sale of advertising was just such an infrequent activity. The court went on to consider the impact that the NCAA's sale of advertising would have on its competition, such as sports magazines that sold the same type of advertising. Because the NCAA's ads were only a once-a-year event, the court found there to be no unfair competition, so that application of the unrelated business income tax in this case would not serve the statutory purpose.[61]

In *State Police Association of Massachusetts v. Commissioner*,[62] the issue was the sale of advertising by a Section 501(c)(5) labor organization in an annual yearbook. The Police tried to rely on the *Suffolk Patrolmen's* case and the *NCAA* case to say that their ad sales were not carried on regularly, but the trouble was that its yearbook did not come attached to an event. It was simply a yearbook with ads in it that were sold 46 weeks a year. The court had no trouble finding the sale of ads to be regularly carried on. On the Police's argument that they did not regularly engage in a business because they did not carry on the sale of ads with the entrepreneurial zeal that characterized a commercial concern, the court said that the Regulations did not require that actual competition or competitive equality be shown.[63]

---

[56] *Id.* at 1323; *see also* 26 C.F.R. § 1.513-1(c)(2)(iii).

[57] *Id.* at 1320–21; *see also* 26 C.F.R. § 1.513-1(c)(2)(ii).

[58] 914 F.2d 1417 (10th Cir. 1990).

[59] *Id.* at 1422.

[60] *Id.*; *see also* 26 C.F.R. § 1.513-1(c)(2)(iii).

[61] *Id.* at 1424–25.

[62] 125 F.3d 1 (1st Cir. 1997).

[63] *Id.*

There are also contrasting Revenue Rulings on this issue. Revenue Ruling 73-424[64] held that the sale of advertising for an exempt organization's annual yearbook over a three-month period by a commercial firm under contract to the exempt organization produced unrelated business taxable income.[65] But Revenue Ruling 75-201[66] held that advertising income from an annual concert book distributed at an annual ball was not unrelated business income to the sponsoring exempt organization.[67] The difference between the two rulings is that the first had no event attached to it, but was simply a three-month sales campaign, while the second involved ad sales for a once-a-year event.[68]

[D]   Substantially Unrelated

The determination of whether a business activity is or is not related to an organization's exempt purposes requires an examination of the relationship between the business activities and the accomplishment of the organization's exempt purposes.[69] A business is related to an organization's exempt purposes only where the conduct of the business activities has a substantial causal relationship to the achievement of exempt purposes.[70] A business activity that simply produces income for the exempt organization is not considered to be in furtherance of exempt purposes.[71]

In order to determine whether a substantial causal relationship exists between a business activity and an organization's exempt purposes, the performance of the business activity, such as the production or distribution of goods, or the performance of services, must contribute in an important way to the organization's exempt purposes.[72] This determination will always turn on the facts and circumstances of each case. For example, income to an exempt inter-collegiate athletic association from the sale of broadcast rights to the athletic events it sponsored was held not to be subject to the unrelated business income tax. The IRS's reasoning was that an athletic program furthered an exempt member university's educational purposes, and that income from these events, whether it be ticket sales or broadcast rights, was related income.[73]

The gift shop of an exempt museum that sells greeting cards that carry reproductions of artworks either in the museum or in other museums does not throw off any unrelated business taxable income from this activity.[74] Because these

---

[64]   1973-2 C.B. 190.

[65]   *Id.*

[66]   1975-1 C.B. 164.

[67]   *Id.*

[68]   *See* Rev. Ruls. 73-424, 75-201.

[69]   26 C.F.R. § 1.513-1(d)(1).

[70]   26 C.F.R. § 1.513-1(d)(2).

[71]   *Id.*; *see also* Indep. Ins. Agents of Huntsville, Inc. v. Comm'r, 998 F.2d 898 (11th Cir. 1993).

[72]   26 C.F.R. § 1.513-1(d)(2).

[73]   Rev. Rul. 80-296, 1980-2 C.B. 195.

[74]   Rev. Rul. 73-104, 1973-1 C.B. 263.

sales are related to the museum's exempt purpose of increasing art appreciation, the income is related and untaxed. But the gift shop of an exempt museum that sells not only reproductions from its collection and those of other museums, but also sells scientific books and souvenir items of the city where the museum is located does throw off unrelated business income as to the scientific books and the souvenirs because they are unrelated to the museum's exempt purposes. This, of course, is the fragmentation rule.[75]

In determining whether business activities contribute in an important way to an organization's exempt purposes, the size and extent of the activities involved must be considered in relationship to the nature and extent of the exempt function they purport to serve.[76] For example, where business activities are in furtherance of exempt purposes, but are conducted on a much larger scale than is necessary to accomplish those purposes, the income from the excess portion will be considered to be for commercial, and not for related purposes, and will be subject to the unrelated business income tax.[77]

In the case of *St. Luke's Hospital of Kansas City v. United States*,[78] a teaching hospital performed pathology tests for the patients of staff physicians who were not patients in the hospital. Teaching its intern physicians how to perform and read pathology tests was one of its exempt functions. The IRS claimed that the income generated by the pathology tests on non-patients was unrelated business taxable income.[79] The IRS fragmented the income on pathology tests of non-patients from the income on pathology tests of those who were patients and sought to tax the former. There was no question that income from pathology tests performed on hospital patients was related, non-taxable income. Because the volume of in-house pathology tests would not have been sufficient for the hospital's physician training program, the court found the entire program, including the non-patient tests, to be substantially related to the hospital's exempt educational purposes.[80]

On the question of whether the size or extent of the non-patient pathology tests indicated a commercial, non-exempt purpose, the court found the hospital's outside pathology revenue to be insignificant.[81]

Shortly after the *St. Luke's Hospital* case, the IRS issued Revenue Ruling 85-110[82] in which the IRS persisted in its view that the "performance of diagnostic laboratory testing, otherwise available in the community, by a tax-exempt hospital, upon specimens from private office patients of a hospital's staff physicians, generally constitutes an "unrelated" taxable business. The Revenue Ruling relied,

---

[75] Rev. Rul. 73-105, 1973-1 C.B. 264.

[76] 26 C.F.R. § 1.513-1(d)(3).

[77] *Id.*

[78] 494 F. Supp. 85 (W.D. Mo. 1980).

[79] *Id.* at 90. This is an operation of the fragmentation rule. See § 16.02[B] for further information on the fragmentation rule.

[80] *St. Luke's Hosp.*, 494 F. Supp. at 90.

[81] *Id.* at 91.

[82] 1985-2 C.B. 166.

as did the IRS's prior argument in St. Luke's, on the fragmentation rule.[83]

In the case of the *San Antonio Bar Association v. United States*,[84] the San Antonio Bar Association, a Section 501(c)(6) business league, sold forms for real estate transactions. These forms had been drawn up by volunteer members of the bar association and were accompanied by an instruction manual. They were meant to replace standard forms created and used by title companies. The San Antonio Bar Association's standard forms program was so successful that it was soon selling forms state-wide in conjunction with the State Bar of Texas. The IRS sought to tax the income from the sale of these forms as an unrelated business activity. The district court did not agree. It found that the sale of these forms was substantially related to the bar association's exempt purposes, "as an integral part of an overall project to design, maintain, provide and encourage the use of a basic real estate practice system, [which] primarily promoted the common business interests of the legal profession, advanced the professional interests of persons licensed to practice law, and improved relations between the bench, bar, and public."[85]

In a case discussed earlier, *Professional Insurance Agents of Michigan v. Commissioner*,[86] a Section 501(c)(6) business league was providing insurance to its members. On the question of whether the insurance program was substantially related to the organization's exempt purposes, the court distinguished between benefits that the organization provided its members as a group and those that it provided to them as individuals. When Section 501(c)(6) organizations provide benefits to the members as members of the group, they are advancing the interests of the entire business, and there exists a substantial relationship between the benefit program and the organization's exempt purposes. But where the benefits are provided to members, not as a group benefit, but in their individual capacity, as the individual insurance benefits of the program in question, then there is no substantial relation between the benefit-providing program and the organization's exempt purposes.[87]

In *United States v. American College of Physicians*,[88] discussed earlier, a Section 501(c)(3) organization's monthly scholarly journal carried advertisements that the organization claimed conveyed information relevant to its exempt purposes. The issue was whether these advertisements were substantially related to achieving the organization's exempt purposes. On a factual analysis of the ads, it was clear that they were repetitive, not informative, and sometimes dealt with matters that had no clear relationship to the organization's exempt purposes. Saying that it would not adopt a *per se* rule holding that the sale of advertisements

---

[83] *Id.*

[84] 80-2 U.S. Tax Cas. (CCH) ¶ 9594 (W.D. Tex. 1980).

[85] *Id. But see* Rev. Rul. 78-51, 1978-1 C.B. 165, where the IRS stated that the sale of standard legal forms by a bar association is a commercial activity, not in furtherance of exempt purposes.

[86] 726 F.2d 1097.

[87] *Id. See also* Nat'l Water Well Ass'n v. Comm'r, 92 T.C. 75 (1989), where another insurance program for the individual members of a § 501(c)(6) organization was held to be unrelated to the organization's exempt purposes.

[88] 475 U.S. 834.

could never be related to an organization's exempt purposes, the United States Supreme Court held that, in this case, these ads did not contribute in an important way to the organization's educational purposes, and were therefore substantially unrelated.[89]

Another fragmentation case involved a tax exempt 501(c)(3) university that used its fieldhouse for both related student uses and also for commercial uses, such as ice shows. There was no doubt that the income from the commercial use was unrelated, but in the case of *Rensselaer Polytechnic Institute v. Commissioner*,[90] the question before the court was how to fragment the university's expenses for the fieldhouse between exempt and commercial uses, for purposes of computing deductions against unrelated business income. IRC § 512(a)(1) allows deductions for business expenses, losses, depreciation, and other costs "directly connected" with the business. The university had certain fixed costs for the fieldhouse, whether it was used for non-related activities or not. The question was how to apportion these fixed costs to both exempt and non-exempt activities. The university thought that they should be apportioned over actual use time — giving it a higher level of deduction. IRS argued that "idle time" should figure into the computation, resulting in a lower level of deduction. The Treasury Regulations required an allocation on a "reasonable" basis, and the Second Circuit found the university's approach on expense allocation to be reasonable.[91]

§ 16.03   TAX IMPACT OF UNRELATED BUSINESS INCOME

One court has appropriately summed up the tax impact of the unrelated business income statute and accompanying Regulations by describing three levels of possible tax impact. The first is that when a trade or business is sufficiently causally related, both in type and volume, to the exempt functions of an organization, it neither jeopardizes the organization's exemption nor justifies the imposition of the unrelated business tax under Sections 511 through 515. In this context, the fact that the trade or business involved is commercial in nature is immaterial.[92] The second is that when a trade or business, although sufficiently causally related in type to an organization's exempt function, is conducted at such a level that it exposes the organization to the unrelated business tax but not so as to justify the denial of the organization's exemption.[93] Third, when a trade or business that, although ostensibly causally related in type to an organization's exempt function, is carried on in such a volume that it constitutes the primary purpose of the organization, the organization should not be accorded exempt status.[94]

---

[89] *Id.*

[90] 732 F.2d 1058 (2d Cir. 1984).

[91] *Id.* at 1061–62.

[92] 26 C.F.R. § 1.513-1(d)(4)(iv), Ex. (5); *see also* Squire v. Students Book Corp., 191 F.2d 1018, 1020 (9th Cir. 1951).

[93] Iowa St. Univ. of Sci. and Tech. v. U.S., 500 F.2d 508 (Ct. Cl. 1974).

[94] *See* Am. Inst. for Econ. Research v. United States, 302 F.2d 934 (Ct. Cl. 1962). This text, including footnotes, is from Afro-Am. Purchasing Ctr., Inc. v. Comm'r, 37 T.C.M. (CCH) 184 (1978).

The court missed a fourth category, however, perhaps because it is the most obvious. It is a trade or business that is not causally related to the exempt functions of an organization, but that is so insubstantial in the organization's overall activities as not to constitute a primary purpose of the organization; this trade or business does not jeopardize the organization's exempt status but does incur the unrelated business income tax.

§ 16.04   PASSIVE INCOME MODIFICATIONS

In IRC Section 512(b), Congress created what the statute calls "modifications."[95] The effect of these "modifications" is basically to exempt certain forms of passive income from the unrelated business income tax. When it created the unrelated business income tax in 1950, Congress realized that certain forms of income were traditional in the tax exempt sector and posed no competitive advantage. The report of the House Finance Committee said,

> [t]he tax applied to unrelated business income does not apply to dividends, interest, royalties (including, of course, overriding royalties), rents (other than certain rents on property acquired with borrowed funds), and gains from sales of property. Your committee believes that such "passive" income should not be taxed where it is used for exempt purposes because investments producing incomes of these types have long been recognized as proper for educational and charitable organizations.[96]

As a result, the statute creates exceptions to the unrelated business income tax income from the following sources:

- Dividends, interest, payments with respect to securities loans, payments received as consideration for entering into an agreement to make a loan, and annuity payments.[97] Dividends on stock, interest on loans, payments that brokers make when they borrow securities from an exempt organization,[98] consideration that exempt organizations receive when they enter into an agreement to make a loan, and income from annuities[99] are all clearly forms of passive income and are not taxed, unless the income-producing property, the stock and so forth, was acquired by the exempt organization with borrowed funds. If it is so acquired, it is referred to as debt-financed

---

[95]   I.R.C. § 512(b).

[96]   H.R. Rep. No. 2319, at 36, 38 (1950). The Senate Finance Committee also said:

> Dividends, interest, royalties, most rents, capital gains and losses and similar items are excluded from the base of the tax on unrelated income because your committee believes that they are 'passive' in character and are not likely to result in serious competition for taxable businesses having similar income. Moreover, income producing investments of these types have long been recognized as a proper source of income for educational and charitable organizations and trusts.

S. Rep. No. 2375, at 30–31 (1950).

[97]   I.R.C. § 512(b)(1). Note that dividends from controlled foreign insurance companies are taxable. I.R.C. § 512(b)(17).

[98]   The conditions for such loans are described in I.R.C. § 512(a)(5).

[99]   Interest and annuity payments by "controlled organizations" may be taxable. I.R.C. § 512(b)(13); 26 C.F.R. § 1.512(b)-1(a)(1).

property.[100] Congress did not want exempt organizations to be able to generate passive income with borrowed funds, primarily because of past abuses in this area.[101]

• Royalties, including overriding royalties.[102] This is a very broad exception for exempt organizations. Basically, they can receive payments for the right to use their name, their mailing lists, their membership lists, and other intangible property such as patents, trademarks or copyrights, free of the unrelated business income tax, because all of these payments can, legitimately, be characterized as royalty payments.[103] Perhaps because of its breadth, this is one area that has seen substantial litigation by the IRS.

[A] Mailing Lists

One major area of litigation has been over the marketing of mailing lists by exempt organizations. There was extensive litigation with the Disabled American Veterans on this issue.[104] The rule that has developed is that the income that an exempt organization receives from renting out its mailing list will be considered a royalty payment as long as the rental of the list is not accompanied by more than insubstantial services performed by the exempt organization.[105] So, for example, where the exempt organization performs substantial services by preparing the mailing labels, or sorting or rating the list in connection with its rental, the provision of these services will mean that the rental income for the mailing list is not exempt royalty income.

In the case of *Sierra Club, Inc. v. Commissioner*,[106] the Sierra Club, a Section 501(c)(4) organization, rented its mailing list, but it performed no services in connection with the rental. Rather it contracted with one commercial concern, Triplex, to maintain a computerized database of the list and with another, Names and Chilcut, to administer the actual rentals, including sorting the list and providing mailing labels. The Sierra Club did not market the list, provide labels or provide any other services to list renters, nor did it pay Triplex to do so. Triplex,

---

[100] I.R.C. § 514.

[101] *See* H.R. Rep. No. 91-413, pt. 1, at 45 (1969); *see also* Univ. Hill Found. v. Comm'r, 51 T.C. 548 (1969), *rev'd*, 446 F.2d 701 (9th Cir. 1971), *cert. denied*, 405 U.S. 965 (1972).

[102] I.R.C. § 512(b)(2).

[103] Mineral royalties, whether measured by production or gross or taxable income derived from the property are also excluded from UBIT, except where the exempt organization owns a working interest in a mineral property and shares in the development costs of the operation. 26 C.F.R. § 1.512(b)-1(b).

[104] *See* Disabled Am. Veterans v. United States, 650 F.2d 1178 (Ct. Cl. 1981), *aff'd and remanded*, 704 F.2d 1570 (Fed. Cir. 1983) (*DAV I*); Disabled Am.Veterans v. Commissioner, 94 T.C. 60 (1990) (*DAV II*), *rev'd on other grounds*, 942 F.2d 309 (6th Cir. 1991) (*DAV III*). *See also* Rev. Rul. 81-178, 1981-2 C.B. 135, which said that "payments for the use of trademarks, trade names, service marks, or copyrights, whether or not payment is based on the use made of such property, are ordinarily classified as royalties for federal tax purposes," but that by definition, "royalties do not include payments for personal services."

[105] This was *DAV I*. *See also* Fraternal Order of Police III, Ill. St. Troopers Lodge No. 41 v. Comm'r, 833 F.2d 717 (7th Cir. 1987); Tex. Farm Bureau v. United States, 53 F.3d 120 (5th Cir. 1995) (provision of services by the exempt organization made otherwise exempt income taxable).

[106] 86 F.3d 1526 (9th Cir. 1996).

rather, was paid for these services by Names and Chilcut, who billed the list renter. Nor did the Sierra Club pay Names and Chilcut to market the list; rather Names and Chilcut received a commission on each rental. The Ninth Circuit found that this separation of tasks left the Sierra Club only with income from actual list rentals and none from the provision of services. As a result, the list rental income constituted exempt royalty income.[107]

[B] Affinity Cards

Another highly litigated royalty income issue involves affinity cards. Tax exempt organizations contract with financial concerns, banks, or credit card companies, for the use of the exempt organization's name and logo on a credit card that is marketed to the exempt organization's members or others with an affinity for the organization, such as the alumni of a college or university. The exempt organization then receives a monthly fee, designated as a "royalty payment" of usually one-half percent of total cardholder sales for that month. The exempt organization may agree with the financial concern to assist in the solicitation or encouragement of their members to sign up for and utilize the credit card.[108]

The *Sierra Club* case discussed above also had an affinity card-royalty income issue. The Sierra Club had agreed to help market the card, and again the issue was whether the provision of services converted exempt royalty income into non-exempt unrelated business income. The Ninth Circuit remanded this issue to the Tax Court, which held that, because the Sierra Club did not control the marketing of the affinity card, and because the amount it received was tied to monthly sales and not to any services provided by the Sierra Club, the Club's income from the affinity card program was properly considered royalty, and not unrelated business, income.[109]

After litigating and losing the affinity card-royalty income issue,[110] the IRS appears to have finally accepted the proposition that unless more than insubstantial services are provided by the exempt organization in the affinity card program, the courts will consider this type of income to be exempt royalty income. This, of course, is the same balance that was struck in regard to income from the rental of mailing lists.[111]

As with so many areas of tax law, the right legal structure in the royalties area can result in what would otherwise be a taxable event not being taxed at all. The structure that the Sierra Club gave to its mailing list rental business resulted in

---

[107] *Id.*

[108] *See* Miss. St. Univ. Alumni v. Comm'r, 74 T.C.M. (CCH) 458 (1997); Alumni Ass'n of the Univ. of Or. v. Comm'r, 71 T.C.M. (CCH) 2093 (1996), *aff'd*, 193 F.3d 1098 (9th Cir. 1999); Kevin M. Yamamoto, *Taxing Income from Mailing List and Affinity Card Arrangements: A Proposal*, 38 SAN DIEGO L. REV. 221 (2001).

[109] Sierra Club, Inc. v. Comm'r, 77 T.C.M. (CCH) 1569 (1999).

[110] *Alumni Ass'n of the Univ. of Or.*, 71 T.C.M. (CCH) 2093, *Miss. St. Univ. Alumni*, 74 T.C.M. (CCH) 458.

[111] *See Sierra Club, Inc.*, 86 F.3d 1526.

the income passing to it as exempt royalty income. Revenue Ruling 69-430[112] is a classic example of the right structure in the royalties area. If an exempt organization itself arranges for the printing, distribution, advertisement, and retail sale of a book, the publication of which is not in furtherance of its exempt purposes, the income it receives will be unrelated business taxable income. On the other hand, if the exempt organization had transferred its rights in the book to a commercial publisher in return for royalties, the royalty income it received would have passed to it untaxed.[113]

[C] Rental Income

The rental income of an exempt organization is not normally taxed,[114] but there are some exceptions.

Rental income that also includes payment for personal services to the tenant is fully taxable as unrelated business income. For example, a university that rents its stadium to a professional football team, but also provides field maintenance, laundry, and security services to the team cannot exclude the income that it receives from the team as rent.[115] For the same reason, boarding house and hotel income is not covered by the rental exclusion, but is unrelated business taxable income.[116] Rental income where more than 50 percent of the rental amount is attributable to the rental of personal property is fully taxable as unrelated business income.[117] Rental income where only an incidental amount (no more than 10 percent) of the rental amount is attributable to the rental of personal property, however, is not taxed at all.[118] In situations where the amount of rental attributable to personal property is higher than 10 percent but not more than 50 percent, then the amount attributable to the rental of personal property is taxable as unrelated business income.[119]

Rental income where the amount of the rent depends in whole or in part on the income or profit derived by the tenant from the leased property is fully taxable as unrelated business income, except that rental income based on a fixed percentage of sales or receipts is not taxed.[120]

---

[112] 1969-2 C.B. 129.

[113] *Id.*

[114] I.R.C. § 512(b).

[115] Rev. Rul. 80-298, 1980-2 C.B. 197.

[116] 26 C.F.R. § 1.512(b)-1(c)(5).

[117] I.R.C. § 512 (b)(3)(B)(i).

[118] I.R.C. § 512(b)(3)(A)(ii); 26 C.F.R. § 1.512(b)-1(c)(2)(ii)(b).

[119] 26 C.F.R. § 1.512(b)-1(c)(2)(ii)(b).

[120] I.R.C. § 512(b)(3)(B)(ii).

[D]   Capital Gains or Losses

Gains received or losses incurred by an exempt organization from the sale, exchange, or other disposition of capital gains property are excluded from the unrelated business income tax.[121] This exception, however, does not apply to gains or losses from the sale, exchange, or disposition of stock in trade or other inventory-type property or property held primarily for sale to customers in the ordinary course of business.[122] Income from the sales of inventory or of property held for sale to customers in the ordinary course of business is not excludable.[123]

[E]   Research Income

Payments for research that an exempt organization receives from a governmental unit, the research income of colleges, universities, and hospitals, and the research income of a research organization organized primarily to carry on fundamental research, the results of which are freely available to the general public, are not subject to the unrelated business income tax.[124]

[F]   Revenue from Controlled Organizations

In its original version, Section 512(b)(13) of the Code did not allow tax exempt organizations to convert the taxable business income of a controlled (50% or more) organization into non-taxable unrelated business income in the hands of the exempt organization by having the controlled organization pay this income to the exempt organization in the form of interest, royalties, rents, or other payments that would reduce the tax liability of the controlled organization.[125] Dividends paid by controlled organizations were not unrelated business taxable income in the hands of the exempt organization because they were not a business deduction (as were interest, royalties, and rents) that reduced the tax liability of the controlled organization.[126]

All of this changed with the Pension Protection Act of 2006,[127] which amended Section 512(b)(13) to say that only "excess qualifying specified payments" from the controlled organization are unrelated business taxable income in the hands of the exempt parent. A qualifying specified payment is one made to the parent by the controlled organization pursuant to a written, enforceable contract in place as of August 17, 2006. The "excess payment" that is taxed is the amount over the qualifying payment as determined by I.R.C. § 482.[128] Originally, this exception was

---

[121]   I.R.C. § 512(b)(5).

[122]   I.R.C. § 512(b)(5)(A), (B).

[123]   I.R.C. § 512(b)(5).

[124]   I.R.C. § 512(b)(7), (8), (9). *See also* Rev. Rul. 76-296, 1976-2 C.B. 141, for an explanation of whether commercially sponsored research income is subject to UBIT.

[125]   *See* H. L. Gutman, *Taxing Transactions Between Exempt Parents and Their Affiliates*, 84 TAX NOTES 1081 (1999).

[126]   I.R.C. § 512(b)(13).

[127]   Pension Protection Act of 2006, Pub. L. No. 109-280, § 1205, 120 Stat. 780 (2006).

[128]   I.R.C. § 512(b)(13)(E)(i).

to last from tax years 2006 through 2008, but has now been extended through tax year 2011.[129]

[G]   A Special Exception

Revenues from services provided under a license issued by a federal regulatory agency, (i.e., television stations under FCC regulation) owned and operated by religious orders, or an educational organization maintained by such a religious order, are exempt from unrelated business income tax, as long as they abide by the restrictions of IRC Section 512(b)(15)(A) through (C).[130]

[H]   Commercial Insurance Activity

Although it is not a Section 512(b) "modification," the income to Section 501(c)(3) and 501(c)(4) organizations from "commercial-type insurance," even when it might be considered in furtherance of an exempt purpose (promoting the health of the community), is subject to the unrelated business income tax.[131]

[I]   Membership Dues

The rules on unrelated business income divide the dues income of Section 501(c)(5) and 501(c)(6) organizations into two types: dues income from full, voting members of the organization, and dues income from associate members, i.e., members who have less than full voting rights.[132] Membership income from full voting members is related, exempt function income for 501(c)(5) and 501(c)(6) organizations.[133] Membership income from associate members, where the associate member category has been formed or availed for the principal purpose of producing unrelated business income, by, for example, providing to these unrelated parties some of the benefits that full members enjoy, such as insurance, newsletters, group discounts, etc. is unrelated business taxable income. Dues income from associate members whose dues are not a purchase of benefits, but are simply dues, is not unrelated business income.[134]

Although it is not a Section 512(b) modification, the dues paid by either category of members, full or associate, of Section 501(c)(5) agricultural and horticultural (but not labor) organizations do not constitute unrelated business income under Section 512(d), even when such memberships entitle the member to specific benefits and privileges, as long as the annual dues amount is not more than $100 (in 1995 dollars indexed for inflation).[135] If annual dues exceed $100 per member, then

---

[129] Tax Relief, Unemployment Insurance Reauthorization, and Job Creation Act of 2010, Pub. L. No. 111-312, § 747, 124 Stat. 3296 (2010).

[130] I.R.C. § 512(b)(15); 26 C.F.R. § 1.512(b)-1(j). *Cf.* Iowa St. Univ. of Sci. and Tech. v. U.S., 500 F.2d 508 (Ct. Cl. 1974).

[131] I.R.C. § 501(m).

[132] I.R.C. § 512(d).

[133] I.R.C. § 512(a)(3)(B).

[134] *See* Rev. Proc. 95-21, 1995-1 C.B. 686; Rev. Proc. 97-12, 1997-1 C.B. 631.

[135] I.R.C. § 512(d).

the dues paid by associate (as opposed to full) members will be taxable as unrelated business income.[136] Apart from the statutory exception for Section 501(c)(5) horticultural and agricultural organizations, none of whose membership income is taxable if it is under the $100 annual limit, the membership income of other Section 501(c)(5) organizations (i.e., primarily labor unions), is exempt function income as long as it comes from full, voting members.[137]

The same is true of the dues income of Section 501(c)(6). Dues paid by full voting members is exempt function income. Dues paid by associate members, whose dues are really a purchase of benefits from the organization, is unrelated business income.[138]

In the case of *National League of Postmasters of the United States v. Commissioner*,[139] the issue was whether the dues income of "League Benefit Members," a form of associate member of a Section 501(c)(5) labor organization, was unrelated taxable income to the labor union. Through their membership, LBM members had access to the League's health insurance plan, newsletter, group legal services, travel, credit card, eyewear, and long-term care insurance program. Despite some generalized language in the League's corporate articles that attempted to classify benefits to these associate members as a bona fide exempt purpose, the courts were not buying. This was clearly an example of an associate member category formed for the principal purpose of producing income by providing to these unrelated parties some of the benefits that full members enjoy, such as insurance, newsletters, and group discounts. As such, the dues income from the LBM members was unrelated business taxable income to the union.[140]

§ 16.05 PARTNERSHIP INCOME

Because the statute did exclude interest, rents, and royalties as a form of passive income, some exempt organizations tried to stretch this exception to include the income from limited partnership interests, because that, also, was a form of passive income. In the case of *Service Bolt & Nut Co. v. Commissioner*,[141] a tax exempt profit-sharing trust argued that a limited partnership interest was a passive investment that did not, unlike a general partnership interest, produce unrelated business income. The trust's argument was contrary to the clear meaning of the statute, which specified that partnership income was unrelated business income.[142] The court did not agree that there was some kind of implicit distinction between general partnership income (active and taxable) and limited partnership income (passive and not taxable). Rather, it interpreted the statute to make any partnership

---

[136] Rev. Proc. 95-21, 1995-1 C.B. 686.

[137] *See* I.R.C. § 512(d), (a)(3)(B); Rev. Proc. 95-21, 1995-1 C.B. 686.

[138] Rev. Proc. 97-12, 1997-1 C.B. 631.

[139] 86 F.3d 59 (4th Cir. 1996).

[140] *Id.*

[141] 78 T.C. 812 (1982).

[142] *Id.* at 816–18; I.R.C. §§ 512(c), 513(b).

interests of an exempt organization taxable as unrelated business income.[143] Partnership income would, of course, not be taxable where the partnership was formed to advance the exempt organization's exempt purposes as in *Plumstead Theatre Society Inc. v. Commissioner.*[144]

§ 16.06   DEBT-FINANCED INCOME

While most passive investment income of exempt organizations is not taxable as unrelated business income, there is an exception if the income-producing investment property is debt-financed.[145] As with the general provisions of the law on unrelated business taxable income, Congress established the debt-financing exception to combat abuses that had arisen. One particular case, *Commissioner v. Brown*,[146] was cited in the House report on the debt-financing legislation, as follows:

> A sells an incorporated business to B, a charitable foundation, which makes a small (or no) down payment and agrees to pay the balance of the purchase price only out of profits to be derived from the property. B liquidates the corporation and then leases the business assets to C, a new corporation formed to operate the business. A (collectively, the stockholders of the original business) manages the business for C and frequently holds a substantial minority interest in C. C pays 80 percent of its business profits as "rent" to B, who then passes on 90 percent of those receipts to A until the original purchase price is paid in full. B has no obligation to pay A out of any funds other than the "rent" paid by C.[147]

With some minor variations (C was owned by the attorneys for A, but it employed all of A's principals; the scheme fell apart before full payment was made to A), this is based on the case of *Commissioner v. Brown.*[148]

What the owners of the business corporation did here was to trade the ordinary income they received from a for-profit concern, which would have been taxed at normal rates, for "sales income" for the concern, taxable at lower capital gains rates. Another advantage was that B's income, its lease payments from C, would not be taxed because they were passive investment income to a charity, but C would be able to deduct these lease payments as a business expense. This meant that the owners of A would get their payments free of corporate tax, and subject only to

---

[143] *Serv. Bolt & Nut Co.*, 78 T.C. at 818.

[144] 74 T.C. 1324 (1980).

[145] I.R.C. § 514.

[146] 380 U.S. 563 (1965).

[147] H.R. Rep. No. 91-413, pt. 1, at 45 (1969).

[148] 380 U.S. 563. The factual situation discussed by the House of Representatives, H.R. Rep. No. 91-413, pt. 1, at 45 (1969), is very similar to Univ. Hills Found. v. Comm'r, 51 T.C. 548 (1969), *rev'd*, 446 F.2d 701 (9th Cir. 1971), *cert. denied*, 405 U.S. 965 (1972), where an exempt foundation supporting Loyola University of Los Angeles had extensive sale and lease back arrangements with commercial concerns, including the largest hotel in San Diego. The IRS revoked its exempt status, concluding that its extensive leases constituted a substantial non-exempt activity, and it also sought to tax the rental from the lease backs. The Tax Court sided with the Foundation on both counts. The Ninth Circuit reversed, but by that time § 514 of the 1969 amendments to the IRC had become effective.

personal taxation at capital gains rates.[149]

The United States Supreme Court upheld this rather convoluted arrangement as a valid business deal, and refused to agree with the IRS that it was not a true sale. The Court said that if a remedy were needed to make such transactions taxable, Congress should supply it.[150]

Congress did. The 1969 Tax Reform Act added Section 514 on debt-financed income to the Sections on the unrelated business income tax. The effect of IRC Section 514 is to tax as unrelated business income the revenue produced by the investments of exempt organizations if they were acquired with borrowed dollars. This means that all of the forms of passive investment income made exempt from taxation by IRC Section 512(d), dividends, interest, royalties, rents, and capital gains, are taxable if the property that produces them was debt-financed.[151] In the *Brown* case, this would have meant that the charitable donee would have had to pay tax on those lease payments, thus destroying a substantial part of the benefit of that transaction.[152]

This tax falls in proportion to the debt on the property. For example, if an exempt organization has a $50,000 mortgage on a rental property for which it paid $100,000, then 50 percent of the rent is taxable, debt-financed income.[153] As the mortgage is paid down, the percentage of taxable, debt-financed rental income will also go down.[154] The same would be true of capital gains on the property. The tax would go down as the debt-financed portion of the property was paid down.[155] Similarly, deductions can be taken on the income from the property in proportion to the debt-financed amount. On the $100,000 rental property, with its $50,000 mortgage, half of the regular business deductions for the property could be deducted in determining the exempt organization's unrelated business taxable amount.[156]

There are, of course, some exceptions. If 85 percent of the debt-financed property is used for exempt purposes, e.g., an office building 85 percent occupied by the exempt organization with the rest rented out to third parties, then it is not treated as debt-financed. The third-party rent payments are untaxed.[157] If the gross income from the property is already being taxed as unrelated business

---

[149] *Brown*, 380 U.S. at 567–68.

[150] *Id.* at 579.

[151] *See* I.R.C. § 514; H.R. Rep. No. 91-413, pt. 1, at 45 (1969).

[152] *See Brown*, 380 U.S. 563. These types of sales and lease-backs had generated taxable rental income under an earlier version of § 514, but there was an exemption for leases of five years or less, which made the statute practically worthless. *See Univ. Hills Found.*, 51 T.C. 548 (1969), *rev'd*, 446 F.2d 701 (9th Cir. 1971), *cert. denied*, 405 U.S. 965 (1972).

[153] The mortgage can be on the acquisition of the property, or it can be an after-acquisition loan to improve the property. Both forms of mortgage result in "acquisition indebtedness." *See* I.R.C. § 514(c).

[154] I.R.C. § 514(a)(1). The formula is the average acquisition indebtedness for the taxable year divided by the average adjusted basis of the property during the taxable year. *See* 26 C.F.R. § 1.514(a)-1(a)(1)(ii).

[155] I.R.C. § 514(a)(1). *See* 26 C.F.R. § 1.514(a)-1(a)(1)(v) for basis calculations.

[156] I.R.C. § 514(a)(2).

[157] I.R.C. § 514(b)(1)(A); 26 C.F.R. § 1.514(b)-1(b)(ii).

income, then as to such income, the property is not treated as debt-financed.[158] If the income from the property is exempt as research income, then as to such income, the property is not treated as debt-financed.[159] If the property is used by the exempt organization to house a business staffed substantially by volunteers, or a business is carried on primarily for the convenience of the employees or of those served by the exempt organization, or a business selling donated merchandise, then to the extent of such use, the property is not treated as debt-financed.[160]

In *Southwest Texas Electrical Cooperative, Inc. v. Commissioner*,[161] the issue was whether the investment property purchased by the exempt electrical cooperative, namely Treasury Notes paying nine percent interest, had been debt-financed. The dollars used by the cooperative to purchase the Treasury Notes had been borrowed at five percent for a construction project. Because the construction loan was a reimbursement loan — that is, the cooperative used its own dollars for construction and was then reimbursed by the lender, the cooperative argued that it had used its own dollars for the purchase of the Treasury Notes, and not borrowed funds. The court looked at the definition of debt-financed property in the statute.[162] Property is debt-financed if it is held to produce income and if, at any time during the taxable year or the 12 months prior to its sale, there is acquisition indebtedness attributable to it. Acquisition indebtedness is defined as the unpaid amount of the indebtedness incurred by the organization in acquiring or improving the property; the indebtedness incurred before the acquisition or improvement of such property if such indebtedness would not have been incurred but for such acquisition or improvement; and the indebtedness incurred after the acquisition or improvement of such property if such indebtedness would not have been incurred but for such acquisition or improvement and the incurrence of such indebtedness was reasonably foreseeable at the time of such acquisition or improvement.[163]

The court found that the indebtedness incurred before the acquisition or improvement of the property and that the indebtedness would not have been incurred but for the acquisition or improvement. The cooperative conceded that it drew on the construction loan only after deciding to invest in Treasury Notes. The indebtedness would not have been incurred but for the acquisition of the Treasury Notes. The interest on the Treasury Notes was taxable, debt-financed income.[164]

The Regulations point out that "acquisition indebtedness" can occur on an ongoing or continuous basis.[165] They give the example of an exempt organization that purchases an office building for its own use with $600,000 of its own funds and a $400,000 mortgage. Although purchased with borrowed funds, the office building is not treated as debt-financed because of the exceptions in the statute discussed

---

[158]　I.R.C. § 514(b)(1)(B).

[159]　I.R.C. § 514(b)(1)(C).

[160]　I.R.C. § 514(b)(1)(D).

[161]　67 F.3d 87 (5th Cir. 1995).

[162]　*Id.* at 89; I.R.C. § 514(b)(1).

[163]　I.R.C. § 514(c)(1)(A), (B), (C).

[164]　*Sw. Tex. Elec.*, 67 F.3d at 89–90.

[165]　26 C.F.R. § 1.514(c)-1(a)(4), -1(c)(1).

above.[166] The exempt organization sells the office building, but does not pay off the mortgage. Instead, it uses the proceeds from the sale to purchase another rental property, one that it does not use for its exempt activities. The second property is considered to be debt-financed, because the acquisition indebtedness of the first property carries over to it.[167] There is another important point to note in this example from the Regulations. Property purchased with borrowed funds is not automatically classified as debt-financed. That will depend on the property's use. The next case is a good example of that principle.[168]

In the case of *Gundersen Medical Foundation, Ltd. v. United States*,[169] the issue was whether rental income to the Foundation, a Section 501(c)(3) organization, from a mortgaged building housing a for-profit medical practice (the Clinic) was taxable debt-financed income to the Foundation.[170] There is wording in the statute that is almost directly on point. IRC Section 514(b) states that real property subject to a lease to a medical clinic entered into primarily for purposes that are substantially related to the exempt functions of an educational or charitable organization, is not considered debt-financed property. There is also an example in the Regulations of an exempt hospital leasing an office building to physicians and surgeons, who provide services to the hospital and that hospital's rental income is not treated as debt-financed.[171] The court cited both of these references. The court here found that the rental income was not debt-financed income, though it expressed concern that the Foundation was not itself a hospital, but rather a medical school. But the court, in its findings of fact that precede its opinion, found that the exempt educational program of the Foundation was carried on at the Clinic and that the general practice of medicine by the Clinic improved the education provided by the Foundation.[172] Those findings were enough. Under the statute, the rental income, although from mortgaged property, is not considered debt-financed income. The use controls, not the source of the funds.[173]

In *Bartels Trust v. United States*,[174] the issue was whether the income from securities purchased on margin by a tax exempt charitable trust was taxable debt-financed income to the trust. The trust first tried to argue that trading on margin was not a trade or business. The Court said that did not matter. The statute itself defined debt-financed income as unrelated business income.[175] The Court also brushed aside the trust's assertion that its trading on margin did not constitute unfair competition. Although unfair competition may have been a reason for the statute, a showing of unfair competition was not required by the statute. The trust's

---

[166] I.R.C. § 514(b)(1)(A).

[167] 26 C.F.R. § 1.514(c)-1(a)(4).

[168] *Id.*

[169] 536 F. Supp. 556 (W.D. Wis. 1982).

[170] *Id.* at 556–57.

[171] *Id.* at 564–65; 26 C.F.R. § 1.514(b)-1(c)(1).

[172] *Gunderson*, 536 F. Supp. at 567.

[173] I.R.C. § 514(b); 26 C.F.R. § 1.514(b)-1(c)(1).

[174] 209 F.3d 147 (2d Cir.), *cert. denied*, 531 U.S. 978 (2000).

[175] *Id.* at 150–51 (citing I.R.C. §§ 512(b)(4) and 514(a)(1)).

argument that its margin trading income was not debt-financed income under the statute because it was not periodic in nature was easily rejected. The statute clearly taxes both capital gains and recurring income. Finally, the trust argued that its margin trading income was exempt under IRC Section 514(c)(4), which states that acquisition indebtedness does not cover indebtedness inherent in the organization's exempt purpose. The trust's exempt purpose was to support the University of New Haven as a Section 509(a)(3) organization.[176] Aside from the need to raise money, which is never a related purpose, the Court found that there was nothing inherent in the trust's exempt functions that required it to borrow money or trade on margin to do so. The trust lost on all counts. Its margin-trading income was taxable as debt-financed income.[177]

In *Mose and Garrison Siskin Memorial Foundation v. United States*,[178] an exempt foundation was the owner of a number of insurance policies on individuals, which it had solicited as a form of charitable giving, and on which the contributors continued to pay premiums. The foundation withdrew the accumulated cash value of these policies and invested it in marketable securities and other income-producing property. The issue was whether these investments were debt-financed. There was no doubt that the foundation was responsible for paying interest to the insurance companies on the withdrawn cash value, but its investment income on the invested cash value exceeded this interest amount. Perhaps the best argument that the foundation had was the peculiar nature of life insurance policy loans, where the borrower assumed no liability, but where the insurer looked to cash surrender values for repayment.[179] Nonetheless, there were a number of cases that had already found life insurance policy loans to be a form of indebtedness.[180] What seemed like a good idea to the foundation ended up producing debt-financed taxable income.[181]

There are two statutory exceptions to the rule that debt-financed passive income is to be treated as unrelated taxable income to the exempt organization. The first exception deals with "neighborhood land."[182] When an exempt organization purchases, via debt-financing, property in its neighborhood[183] that it plans to use for its exempt purposes, by tearing down any structure on it, or in the case of a purchase of bare land, by using the land for its exempt purposes, then any income it receives from the property for the first five years of ownership, which can in certain

---

[176] *Id.* at 156.

[177] *Id.* A similar case, *Henry E. and Nancy Horton Bartels Trust ex rel. Cornell Univ. v. United States*, 88 Fed. Cl. 105 (2009), *aff'd*, 617 F.3d 1357 (Fed. Cir. 2010), involving another Bartels Trust for Cornell University, was similarly decided.

[178] 790 F.2d 480 (6th Cir. 1986).

[179] *Id.* at 483.

[180] *Id.; see also* Minnis v. Comm'r, 71 T.C. 1049 (1979).

[181] *Mose and Garrison*, 790 F.2d at 483.

[182] I.R.C. § 514(b)(3)(A).

[183] Property is in the "neighborhood" when it is contiguous, or separated only by a street, stream or railroad tracks or is within one mile, when other contiguous property was not available. 26 C.F.R. § 1.514(b)-1(d)(1)(ii).

circumstances be extended to 10 years,[184] prior to its conversion to exempt purposes uses, is not debt-financed income. The second statutory exception to the debt-financing rules is for income produced by debt-financed property acquired by a Section 501(c)(3) formal educational organization, its Section 509(a)(3) supporting organizations, a Section 401 pension or profit sharing trust or a Section 501(c)(25) title holding company.[185] Despite its debt-financing, this income is not subject to the unrelated business income tax, as long as it meets certain requirements, i.e., the purchase price was for a certain sum, it was not based on the income to be obtained from the property, there was no leaseback to the seller of more than 25 percent of the property, and there was no seller-financing of the purchase.[186]

§ 16.07   ADDITIONAL EXCEPTIONS

In addition to the "modifications" of IRC Section 512(b), Section 513 also creates some exceptions to the application of the tax on the unrelated business income of exempt organizations.[187]

[A]   Businesses Operated by Volunteer Labor

A trade or business in which substantially all the work in carrying on such trade or business is performed for the organization without compensation is not subject to the unrelated business income tax. The Regulations give as an example of this exception an exempt orphanage operating a retail store and selling goods to the general public, where substantially all of the work in carrying on such business is performed for the organization by volunteers without compensation.[188]

[B]   Convenience Businesses

A trade or business carried on by a Section 501(c)(3) organization or a state college or university "primarily for the convenience of its members, students, patients, officers or employees . . ." is not subject to the unrelated business income tax.[189] The Regulations give, as an example of this exception, a college laundry operated for the convenience of its students.[190] Other good examples would be college and hospital cafeterias and college bookstores.

---

[184] The organization gets the benefit of the second five years "only if the organization establishes to the satisfaction of the Secretary that it is reasonably certain that the land will be used" for exempt purposes. I.R.C. § 514(b)(3)(A). Churches can have up to fifteen years. I.R.C. § 514(b)(3)(E).

[185] I.R.C. § 514(c)(9).

[186] I.R.C. § 514(c)(9)(B).

[187] I.R.C. § 513.

[188] 26 C.F.R. § 1.513-1(e). *See also* the Volunteer Protection Act of 1997, Pub. L. No. 105-19, 111 Stat. 26, (codified at 42 U.S.C. §§ 14501–14505), which protects volunteers from individual liability for ordinary negligence.

[189] I.R.C. § 513(a)(2).

[190] 26 C.F.R. § 1.513-1(e).

In a very strange reading of the "convenience of members" exception, the court in *St. Luke's Hospital of Kansas City v. United States*[191] found that pathology tests performed by the hospital for patients of its medical staff constituted a business carried on for the convenience of the "members" of the medical staff and therefore did not generate unrelated business taxable income.[192] This was surely an incorrect reading of this exception.[193]

[C] Businesses Selling Donated Merchandise

A trade or business that consists of the selling of merchandise, substantially all of which has been received by the organization as gifts or contributions is not subject to the unrelated business income tax.[194] The Regulations give as an example of this exception thrift shops operated by a tax exempt organization where those desiring to benefit such organization contribute old clothes, furniture, etc., to be sold to the general public with the proceeds going to the exempt organization.[195]

[D] Qualified Public Entertainment Activities

An entertainment or recreational activity of Section 501(c)(3), (4) or (5) organizations traditionally conducted at fairs or expositions promoting agricultural and educational purposes, in conjunction with an international, national, state, regional or local fair or exposition, in accordance with state law permitting such activities, is not subject to the unrelated business income tax.[196]

[E] Qualified Convention & Trade Show Activities

The convention and trade show activity of a Section 501(c)(3), (4), (5) or (6) organization that regularly conducts as one of its substantial exempt purposes a show that stimulates interest in, and demand for, the products of a particular industry or segment of such industry or that educates persons in attendance regarding new developments or products and services related to the exempt activities of the organization, is not subject to the unrelated business income tax.[197] This means that the income from the exhibitors' booths at these conventions is exempt income, even when the exhibitors are themselves doing business at their booths.[198]

---

[191] 494 F. Supp. 85 (W.D. Mo. 1980).

[192] *Id.* at 89.

[193] *See* I.R.S. Priv. Ltr. Rul. 9739043 (Sept. 26, 1997); and Rev. Rul. 85-109, 1985-2 C.B. 165, stating that the IRS will not follow that portion of the *St. Luke's Hospital of Kansas City* decision holding that private patient specimen testing is for the convenience of the hospital's members. The IRS's position is that hospital staff physicians are neither "members" nor "employees" of the hospital. However, since the laboratory testing services provide a supply of specimens needed in the hospital's teaching program, they are substantially related to the hospital's exempt purpose.

[194] I.R.C. § 513(a)(3).

[195] 26 C.F.R. § 1.513-1(e).

[196] I.R.C. § 513(d)(2).

[197] I.R.C. § 513(d)(3).

[198] 26 C.F.R. § 1.513-3(d)(1). See also Rev. Rul. 2004-112, 2004-51 I.R.B. 985, for examples of how

[F] Hospital Cooperative Services

Services provided at cost to a tax exempt hospital with no more than 100 patient beds by another exempt hospital, which if performed on its own behalf by the recipient hospital would constitute exempt function activities, are not subject to the tax on unrelated business income. A tax exempt hospital can do the laundry, pharmacy, billing, computer services, etc. for another (100 beds or less) exempt hospital, bill for it at cost and not be taxed on the income.[199]

[G] Bingo

Churches and veterans organizations operate bingos. Churches and veterans organizations have substantial lobbying clout. IRC Section 513(f) exempts the bingo income of all exempt organizations (not just Section 501(c)(3) churches and Section 501(c)(19) veterans organizations) from the unrelated business income tax in states and localities where bingo is legal. But bingo means bingo; this exception does not extend to other games of chance.[200]

[H] Distribution of Low-Cost Articles

The distribution of low cost articles incidental to the solicitation of charitable contributions does not generate unrelated business taxable income.[201] The value of low cost articles is indexed for inflation, which in 2011 is $9.70, per individual distributee, aggregated by calendar year when more than one article is sent out.[202] These articles are incidental to a charitable solicitation where the individual did not request the distribution, did not consent to it, and the distribution was accompanied by a request for a donation and a disclaimer that there was no need to pay for the article.[203] This means that the income that an exempt organization, which is able to receive tax deductible gifts, receives when it mails out items like those little return address labels, is not subject to the unrelated business income tax.

[I] Qualified Sponsorship Payments

In 1991, the IRS, in a Technical Advice Memorandum, concluded that Mobil Oil's payment to an exempt organization to sponsor the Mobil Oil Cotton Bowl was subject to the unrelated business income tax under IRC Section 511.[204]

Internet activities conducted by trade associations may result in UBIT liability.

[199] I.R.C. § 513(e).

[200] *See* Educ. Ass'n v. Comm'r, 77 T.C.M. (CCH) 1525 (1999), where an exempt organization's sale of pickle cards (a small game of chance) was an unrelated, taxable business activity. *But see* Vigilant Hose Co. of Emmitsburg v. United States, 87 A.F.T.R.2d (RIA) 2398 (D. Md. 2001), where the sales of tip jars (another small game of chance) by a tavern which were turned over to the exempt organization did not constitute a taxable trade or business of the exempt organization.

[201] I.R.C. § 513(h)(1)(A).

[202] I.R.C. § 513(h)(2); Rev. Proc. 2010-40, 2010-46 I.R.B. 663.

[203] I.R.C. § 513(h)(3).

[204] I.R.S. Tech. Adv. Mem. 9147007 (Aug. 16, 1991).

This type of payment is a sponsorship payment.[205] Mobil Oil paid the exempt organization that put on the Cotton Bowl in order to have the bowl named after it. This is a form of advertising, and advertising income is specifically designated as unrelated business income in the statute.[206] Many charitable organizations, however, depended on such sponsorship payments for their existence. Sponsorship income to the 2002 Olympics, for example, totaled almost $840 million dollars.

In the debate that followed, the IRC was amended with the addition of IRC Section 513(i) in 1997.[207] This section of the IRC exempts certain qualified sponsorship payments from the tax on unrelated business income. It defines a qualified sponsorship payment as a payment made by a person engaged in a trade or business with respect to which there is no arrangement or expectation that such person will receive any substantial return benefit other than the use or acknowledgment of the name or logo of the person's trade or business in connection with the exempt organization's activities. Such payments pass untaxed to the exempt organization unless there is a substantial return benefit. Substantial return benefits consist of any benefit other than the use or acknowledgment of the sponsor's name or logo or a disregarded benefit.[208]

A disregarded benefit is any benefit provided to the payor that is worth more than two percent of the sponsorship payment.[209] In determining whether the two percent limit has been exceeded, all return benefits, other than the use or acknowledgment of the sponsor's name or logo, are included. When return benefits exceed the two percent limit, only the amount by which the sponsorship payment exceeds the fair market value of the entire return benefit is a qualified, untaxed sponsorship payment. The amount of the payment attributable to the entire return benefit (and not just the part in excess of the two percent) is taxed as unrelated business income tax.[210]

For example, a Section 501(c)(3) art museum organizes an exhibit. A corporate sponsor makes a sponsorship payment to the museum in return for which its name and logo appear on all of the advertisements for the exhibit, such as banners, brochures, and public service announcements. Thus far, there is no unrelated business tax issue. These are all permissible benefits for the sponsorship payment because they are all simply uses of the sponsor's name in advertising the exhibit. But then, the museum hosts a dinner for the officers of the sponsoring corporation. The dinner is a return benefit. If the cost of the dinner exceeds two percent of the sponsorship payment, then the sponsorship payment is untaxed only to the extent it exceeds the total cost of the dinner. The cost of the dinner is unrelated business taxable income to the museum because the sponsor "paid" for it.[211]

---

[205] *See* Frances R. Hill, *Corporate Sponsorship in Transactional Perspective: General Principles and Special Cases in the Law of Tax Exempt Organizations*, 13 U. Miami Ent. & Sports L. Rev. 5 (1995).

[206] I.R.C. § 513(c).

[207] *See* I.R.C. § 513(i).

[208] *Id.*

[209] 26 C.F.R. § 1.513-4(c)(2)(ii).

[210] *Id.*

[211] 26 C.F.R. § 1.513-4(f), Ex. 2.

Sponsorship arrangements in which the exempt organization agrees to provide services to the sponsor create the same kind of problem. Where, for example, a university enters into a multi-year contract with a sports drink company under which the company will provide sports drinks to the university's athletic teams in exchange for an acknowledgment of this arrangement in banners at the university's athletic facility, but the contract also calls for the university's coaches to make appearances for the sponsor and to assist in the sponsor's promotional activities, these services are a substantial return benefit that will result in unrelated taxable business income if they exceed the two percent limit.[212]

Mere posting of the sponsor's name and a hyperlink to its web site on the exempt organization's web site creates no return benefit. When the hyperlink on the exempt organization's website is accompanied by an endorsement of the sponsor's products or services, however, a substantial return benefit has occurred.[213]

The use of the sponsor's name in event advertising by the exempt organization cannot include advertising for the sponsor's services or products, such as messages containing qualitative or comparative language, price information, or other indications of savings or value, or an endorsement or an inducement to purchase the sponsor's products or services.[214] Nor can the sponsorship payment be based on the level of event attendance, broadcast ratings, or other factors indicating the degree of public exposure to the event.[215] Nor can it include the use or acknowledgment of the sponsor's name or logo in regularly scheduled and printed material published by or on behalf of the payee organization that is not related to and primarily distributed in connection with the event.[216] All of these would constitute unrelated taxable business income because they have crossed the boundary from qualified sponsorship payment to payment for advertising.[217]

Exclusive sponsorship arrangements do not, in themselves, result in unrelated business taxable income. An arrangement that acknowledges an exclusive sponsor of an exempt organization's activity and that does not provide any advertising or substantial return benefit to the sponsor is permissible.[218] But an exclusive provider arrangement that limits the sale, distribution, availability, or use of competing products, services, or facilities in connection with an exempt organization's activity does create a substantial return benefit, and thus, unrelated business taxable income.[219] For example, an "All Pepsi Campus" publicly so designated where competing soft drinks are not sold creates a substantial return benefit to Pepsi.[220]

---

[212] Rev. Rul. 81-178, 1981-2 C.B. 135.

[213] 26 C.F.R. § 1.513-4(f), Exs. 11, 12.

[214] I.R.C. § 513(i)(2)(A).

[215] I.R.C. § 513(i)(2)(B)(i).

[216] I.R.C. § 513(i)(2)(B)(ii)(I).

[217] I.R.C. § 513(i)(2)(A), (i)(2)(B)(i), (i)(2)(B)(ii)(I).

[218] 26 C.F.R. § 1.513-4(c)(2)(vi)(A).

[219] 26 C.F.R. § 1.513-4(c)(2)(vi)(B).

[220] 26 C.F.R. § 1.513-4(f) Ex. 6.

§ 16.08 SPECIAL SITUATION FOR SOCIAL CLUBS

The unrelated taxable income of Section 501(c)(7) social clubs is defined as all income except exempt function income.[221] In other words, income need not be generated by a trade or business regularly carried on, substantially unrelated to its exempt purposes, for a social club to incur the unrelated business income tax. It simply has to be non-exempt function income, and it is taxed as unrelated business income. Exempt function income is income from dues, fees, charges, or similar amounts paid by the organization's members in consideration for goods, facilities, or services provided to them, their dependents, or their guests, in furtherance of the organization's exempt purposes. Everything else is non-exempt function income, and is taxable.[222]

Congress imposed the unrelated business income tax on all the non-membership income of social clubs because of a perceived unfairness. "[W]here the organization receives income from sources outside the membership . . . upon which no tax is paid, the membership receives a benefit not contemplated by the exemption in that untaxed dollars can be used by the organization to provide pleasure or recreation (or other benefits) to its membership. . . . [I]n such a case, the exemption is no longer simply allowing individuals to join together for recreation or pleasure without tax consequences. Rather, it is bestowing a substantial additional advantage to the members of the club by allowing tax-free dollars to be used for their personal recreational or pleasure purposes."[223]

Applying the statutory definition to the example of a Section 501(c)(7) golf club would mean that the dues and assessments paid by members generate non-taxable exempt function income. It also means that greens fees paid by members for themselves, their family members, or their guests are non-taxable exempt function income. If the golf course is open to members of the public, however, the greens fees paid by non-members would be unrelated taxable income. In the same vein, if there were a clubhouse on the golf course that served both members and non-members, the income from the food and drink sold to members would be non-taxable exempt function income, but the income from food and drink served to non-members would be unrelated taxable income. When it provides goods or services to non-members, thereby generating taxable income, the social club may deduct the expenses connected with the generation of that income as long as the activity is run with a profit motive.[224]

The passive income of Section 501(c)(7) organizations is not exempt function income. This means that its interest and investment income is taxed as unrelated business income under IRC Section 512(a). A Section 501(c)(7) organization can deduct expenses related to income-producing activities. This poses an interesting issue: whether losses incurred in an income-producing activity can be used as

---

[221] I.R.C. § 512(a)(3)(A).

[222] I.R.C. § 512(a)(3)(B).

[223] S. Rep. No. 91-552, at 71 (1969).

[224] I.R.C. §§ 512(a)(3)(A), 162.

deductions against passive income.[225] For example, can the social club that serves non-members in its clubhouse, but that loses money on the activity, deduct these losses against its investment income?

The IRS's position is that these losses can be used to offset passive income as long as the activity that generated the losses is carried on in an attempt to make a profit. Thus, where a social club provides food and drink to non-members at prices that do not cover costs, there is no profit motive and no deduction for losses allowable against other income.[226] In the case of *Portland Golf Club v. Commissioner*,[227] the United States Supreme Court took up this issue because of an apparent split in the Circuits.

The Portland Golf Club had investment income, which it duly reported on its Form 990, but took as a deduction against its interest income losses that it said it suffered in selling food and drink to non-members. The United States Supreme Court upheld the IRS's position, saying that "petitioner may use losses incurred in sales to non-members to offset investment income only if those sales were motivated by an intent to profit."[228] The problem was with the methods that the Golf Club had used to determine losses on one hand and demonstrate a profit motive on the other.[229]

The Golf Club had used a gross-to-gross formula in allocating fixed expenses to the non-member sales in order to determine net income (or losses) from the sales. Under this formula, the deduction of fixed expenses resulted in the sales showing a loss, which was then a deduction against the Club's investment income. But then the Club attempted to show that it had a profit motive in these sales, not by using the gross-to-gross formula in allocating expenses, which would have shown a consistent loss and lack of a profit motive, but by looking at the actual economic cost of the activity.[230]

The United States Supreme Court said that they could not have it both ways. They had to use the same formula in demonstrating a profit motive as they did in computing losses. Having used the gross-to-gross formula in computing losses, they were stuck with it in demonstrating a profit motive. And because, under the gross-to-gross expense formula, non-member sales activity consistently lost money, there was no profit motive, and therefore losses from this activity could not be used as a deduction against investment income.[231]

---

[225] I.R.C. §§ 512(a)(3)(A), 162.

[226] Rev. Rul. 81-69, 1981-1 C.B. 351; The Brook, Inc. v. Comm'r, 799 F.2d 833 (2d Cir. 1986); N. Ridge Country Club v. Comm'r, 877 F.2d 750 (9th Cir. 1989). *But see* The Cleveland Athletic Club, Inc. v. United States, 779 F.2d 1160 (6th Cir. 1985), which did not require proof of a profit motive, but only a "basic purpose of economic gain" for losses to be deductible. *Id.* at 1165.

[227] 497 U.S. 154 (1990).

[228] *Id.* at 163–64.

[229] *Id.* at 168.

[230] *Id.* at 169.

[231] *Id.* at 171.

Another problem area with social clubs occurs in regard to their sales of property.[232] Normally, income from the sale of property will qualify as passive, untaxed income to an exempt organization. But because the unrelated business income tax falls differently on social clubs, such sales income, because it does not come from members, is unrelated business taxable income. Congress, in IRC Section 512(3)(D), allowed social clubs to sell property used directly in the performance of exempt functions, and not pay any tax on the sales income as long as in a period beginning one year before the sale and ending three years after it, the organization had used the proceeds to purchase other property used directly in performance of its exempt functions.[233]

In *Atlanta Athletic Club*,[234] the issue was whether the property that was sold had been used directly in performance of the club's exempt functions. If it did not qualify as having been used directly in the performance of the Club's exempt functions, tax was due on the sale proceeds. The Tax Court had determined that the tax was due, because the Club's uses of the property, which was vacant land, across the road from Club facilities, was too sporadic to qualify the land as "directly used" for the Club's exempt purposes. In what was basically a re-reading of the facts, the Eleventh Circuit found that holding "Turkey Trots," kite-flying contests, pasture parties, hot air balloon rides, fishing contests, and operating jogging trails on the property qualified it as directly used for the Club's exempt recreational purposes. Because the sale proceeds were used to construct a new tennis facility and renovate the clubhouse (which passed unremarked, even though such use appears not to meet the terms of the statute, which speaks in terms of a subsequent purchase), the court found the terms of Section 512(a)(3)(D) were met and no tax was due.[235]

While this section has focused on Section 501(c)(7) social clubs, the same statutory definition of unrelated business income as basically all non-membership income applies equally to Section 501(c)(9) Voluntary Employees' Beneficiary Associations, Section 501(c)(17) Supplemental Unemployment Benefit Trusts and Section 501(c)(20) Group Legal Services Plans.[236]

---

[232] *See* Atl. Athletic Club v. Comm'r, 980 F.2d 1409 (11th Cir. 1993).

[233] I.R.C. § 512(3)(D).

[234] 980 F.2d 1409.

[235] *Id.*

[236] I.R.C. § 512(a)(3)(A), (B).

Chapter 17

CHARITABLE CONTRIBUTIONS

§ 17.01 INTRODUCTION

Charitable contributions and gifts are governed by Section 170 of the IRC:

Section 170. Charitable, etc., contributions and gifts.

(a) Allowance of deduction.

(1) General Rule. There shall be allowed as a deduction any charitable contribution (as defined in subsection (c)) payment of which is made within the taxable year. A charitable contribution shall be allowable as a deduction only if verified under regulations prescribed by the Secretary.[1]

The tax laws governing tax exempt charitable organizations and deductible gifts are closely intertwined. The IRC frequently cross references many of the sections on organizations that are considered charitable with the income tax charitable contribution deduction rules.[2]

Not all donations to all tax exempt organizations are deductible. While contributions to 501(c)(3) organizations are generally deductible (which is why organizations seek (c)(3) status), contributions to other 501 organizations are usually not deductible or there are limitations imposed on what does qualify for a deduction. For example, contributions to 501(c)(1) organizations are only deductible if made for exclusively public purposes,[3] and deductions to 501(c)(4) organizations are not generally deductible; however, (c)(4)s may establish a charitable fund, to which contributions are deductible. These funds must meet the requirements of 501(c)(3) and the notice requirements of Section 508(a).[4]

For purposes of Section 170, a gift will qualify as a "charitable contribution" if it is donated to or for the use of the following types of organizations:[5]

(1) a state or possession of the United States, or a political subdivision of any of the foregoing, or the United States or the District of Columbia, but only if the contribution or gift is made for exclusively public purposes;

---

[1] I.R.C. § 170(a)(1).

[2] *See* I.R.C. §§ 501(c), 170.

[3] I.R.C. § 170(c)(1).

[4] *See* I.R.C. §§ 501(c)(3), (4), 508(a).

[5] *See* I.R.C. § 170(c).

(2) a corporation, trust, or community chest, fund, or foundation;[6]

(3) organizations organized and operated exclusively for religious, charitable, scientific, or literary purposes, or to foster national or international amateur sports competition or for preventing cruelty to children or animals; (4) organizations where no part of their net earnings inures to the benefit of any private shareholder or individual; and (5) organizations not disqualified for tax exemption under Section 501(c)(3) by reason of attempting to influence legislation and that does not participate in, or intervene in, any political campaign on behalf of or in opposition to any candidate for public office.

Other types of organizations that qualify to receive charitable gifts include certain war veterans' organizations; certain domestic fraternal societies operating under the lodge system, where the contribution is to be used exclusively for a proper charitable purpose; and certain cemetery companies owned and operated exclusively for the benefit of their members.[7]

The first charitable income tax deductions were enacted as part of a tax bill that raised federal tax rates to help finance the costs of World War I.[8] The deduction became available to corporations in 1935. Since that time, the charitable deduction has been a feature of the income tax system. Congress has justified the charitable deduction as an efficient alternative to government support for nonprofit organizations providing a public benefit.[9]

The Commission on Private Philanthropy and Public Needs explained that the charitable contribution deduction was instituted to sustain the level of giving in the face of new steep tax rates. The deduction protected the individual giver when donating personal income because the amount given does not enrich the giver specifically; rather, it is for the good of the charity and the general public.[10] High tax bracket contributors have a greater incentive to give than those at the other end of the income scale because their deductions may be greater and can affect their taxable income in a more positive way. The estate and gift tax charitable deduction (providing an unlimited deduction for charitable bequests) was added to the IRC in 1918. The justification for such a deduction was that wealth transferred for public purposes should not be taxed.[11]

---

[6] The corporation, trust, or community chest, fund or foundation must be created or organized in the U.S. or in any possession thereof (but not in a foreign country), or under the laws of the U.S., any state, the District of Columbia, or any possession of the U.S. *See* I.R.C. § 170.

[7] *See* I.R.C. § 170(c)(1)–(5).

[8] *See* Joan A. Wallace & Robert W. Fisher, *The Charitable Deduction Under § 170 of the IRC, in* RESEARCH PAPERS SPONSORED BY THE [FILER] COMMISSION ON PRIVATE PHILANTHROPY AND PUBLIC NEEDS § IV, p. 2131 (1977).

[9] *See* H. R. Rep. No. 1860, 75th Cong., 3d Sess. 19 (1938).

[10] THE COMMISSION ON PRIVATE PHILANTHROPY & PUBLIC NEEDS (THE FILER COMMISSION), GIVING IN AMERICA — TOWARDS A STRONGER VOLUNTARY SECTOR 6 (Report of the Commission 1975).

[11] John Holt Myers, *Estate Tax Deduction for Charitable Benefits: Proposed Limitations*, RESEARCH PAPERS SPONSORED BY THE [FILER] COMMISSION ON PRIVATE PHILANTHROPY AND PUBLIC NEEDS § IV, p. 2299 (1977).

§ 17.02 POLICY CONSIDERATIONS

Just as there has been debate over the rationale for tax exemption, there has also been debate over whether tax deductions for charitable gifts are justified. Several scholars and government-sponsored commissions have researched and written about the justification for this deduction. One author, William Andrews, in an article for the *Harvard Law Review*,[12] proposed the following theory. Mr. Andrews disagreed with the idea that the charitable contribution deduction is a type of subsidy. He believes that there are better explanations for why this tax deduction has developed. One such explanation is that charitable giving is like alms to the poor, in that "the benefits produced by charitable contributions have certain shared characteristics which provide the basis for principled arguments in favor of deduction. Almost all charitable organizations other than those that distribute alms to the poor produce something in the nature of common or social goods or services."[13] The only controversy becomes whether contributions to organizations such as churches, museums, etc., which produce common goods, should be reflected in the consumption component (personal income) of any of the individuals associated with them.[14] Mr. Andrews does not believe this to be necessary or beneficial.

In a 1988 *Virginia Law Review* article, Mark Gergen discusses the argument that there should be no income tax deduction for charitable contributions.[15] He defines the subsidy theory, the joy of giving theory and the pluralism theory. He discusses Andrews' arguments for the charitable contribution deduction but disagrees with it and points out several of the problems that he sees with those theories.

Teresa Odendahl, in CHARITY BEGINS AT HOME: GENEROSITY AND SELF INTEREST AMONG THE PHILANTHROPIC ELITE,[16] believes that philanthropy of the wealthy does nothing to relieve the plight of the poor, disadvantaged or disabled. She contends that the wealthy have elite interests and therefore support their own interests through giving. Wealthy philanthropists are more likely to support ballet, opera, symphony and theatre, which are all tax exempt organizations, than to support soup kitchens, homeless shelters, and after-school programs for disadvantaged communities. In her studies she has found that there is a "culture of philanthropy" where those who have inherited "old money" and those who have become wealthy through "new money" are most involved in voluntary activities. They contribute disproportionately to arts and culture rather than to the needs of the poor.[17]

She believes that to remedy this situation, public policy and the tax system need to be reformed. Regarding the philosophy of providing exemption for certain organizations, Odendahl believes that some contributions are more altruistic than

---

[12] William D. Andrews, *Personal Deductions in an Ideal Income Tax*, 86 HARV. L. REV. 309 (1972).

[13] *Id.* at 357.

[14] *Id.* at 331–37.

[15] Mark P. Gergen, *The Case for a Charitable Contributions Deduction*, 74 VA. L. REV. 1393 (1988).

[16] TERESA ODENDAHL, CHARITY BEGINS AT HOME: GENEROSITY AND SELF INTEREST AMONG THE PHILANTHROPIC ELITE 3–5, 232–40 (1990).

[17] *Id.*

others and more effectively provide for the public good.[18] In her opinion, the IRC should be revised to reflect this reality so that not all organizations that currently qualify for exemption would do so in the future. She states that both the income and estate tax system favor the wealthy. Some changes to the IRC could affect which organizations are supported and to what extent. Although worthy of thought, Odendahl's theories would affect charitable giving inequitably and could create a more negative atmosphere than she believes is already present.[19]

§ 17.03 DEFINING CHARITABLE GIFT

[A] Overview

A charitable contribution is deductible by an individual or corporate taxpayer if it is made with donative intent, to or for the use of a qualified donee, with no expectation of a return benefit.[20] The deductible amount is subject to some limitations, which include a limitation on who is a donee and the valuation of gifts and services. A qualified donee or organization includes groups that are religious, charitable, educational, scientific, or literary in purpose or that prevent cruelty to children or animals or that foster national or international amateur sports competition.[21] The burden to show that there was an intent to make a gift and to prove the value of the gift is on the taxpayer.[22]

The United States Supreme Court defined "gift" in *Comm'r v. Duberstein.*[23] The Court stated that a gift is a transfer without consideration and no expectation of a return benefit. The standard applied by the Court for determining donative intent is that a gift must be made with "detached and disinterested generosity."[24]

[B] Dual Payments

In *United States v. American Bar Endowment,*[25] the United States Supreme Court was again faced with the question of what constituted a charitable gift. The American Bar Endowment (ABE), a 501(c)(3) organization, provided its members with opportunities to purchase life, health, accident, and disability insurance policies. The ABE negotiated premium rates with insurers, solicited its members, collected their premiums, transmitted the premiums to the insurer, maintained files on the policies, and screened claims for benefits.[26]

---

[18] *Id.*

[19] *Id.*

[20] 26 C.F.R. § 1.170A-1(h).

[21] I.R.C. § 501(c)(3).

[22] 26 C.F.R. § 1.170A-1(h).

[23] 363 U.S. 278 (1960).

[24] *Id.* at 285.

[25] 477 U.S. 105 (1986).

[26] *Id.* at 108.

The issue for the Supreme Court was whether the ABE's members could claim a charitable deduction for the portion of their premium payments that exceeded the actual cost to the organization of providing insurance.[27] In its analysis, the Court stated that "a payment of money generally cannot constitute a charitable contribution if the contributor expects a substantial benefit in return."[28] However, it continued, a taxpayer may receive a nominal benefit in return for a contribution. When the size of the payment is out of proportion to the benefit received, it would not serve the purpose of IRC Section 170 to deny a deduction altogether. A taxpayer may therefore claim "a deduction for the difference between a payment to a charitable organization and the market value of the benefit received in return, on the theory that the payment has the "dual character of a purchase and a contribution."[29] Members of the ABE were not permitted to deduct their premiums as charitable deductions because they failed to demonstrate that they intentionally paid more than market value because they wished to make a gift. There was no intent to give a gift, but an expectation to receive a service for their payment.

The Tax Court reviewed Revenue Ruling 67-246,[30] where the IRS set forth a two-pronged test for determining when part of a "dual payment" is deductible. "First, the payment is deductible only if and to the extent it exceeds the market value of the benefit received. Second, the excess payment must be 'made with the intention of making a gift.' "[31]

The Claims Court in *American Bar Endowment* held that respondent failed to show that he had intentionally paid more than the market value for ABE's insurance because he wished to make a gift, failing the second prong of the test. The United States Supreme Court in *American Bar Endowment* agreed, stating that the "sine qua non of a charitable contribution is a transfer of money or property without adequate consideration."[32]

---

[27] *Id.* at 106.

[28] *Id. See also* S. Rep. No. 1622, 83d Cong., 2d Sess., 196 (1954); Singer Co. v. United States, 449 F.2d 413, 196 Ct. Cl. 90 (1971).

[29] *American Bar Endowment*, 477 U.S. at 117; *see also* Rev. Rul. 67-246, 1967-2 C.B. 104 (price of ticket to charity ball deductible to the extent it exceeds the fair market value of admission); Rev. Rul. 68-432, 1968-2 C.B. 104, 105 (noting the possibility that a payment to a charitable organization may have "dual character").

[30] 1967-2 C.B. 104.

[31] *American Bar Endowment*, 477 U.S. at 117; *see also* Rev. Rul. 67-246, 1967-2 C.B. 104, 105; Murphy v. Comm'r, 54 T.C. 249, 254 (1970); Arceneaux v. Comm'r, 36 T.C.M. (CCH) 1461 (1977).

[32] *See Arceneaux*, 36 T.C.M. (CCH) at 1464 (1977). *Compare* Oppewal v. Comm'r, 468 F.2d 1000, 1002 (1st Cir. 1972), expressing "dissatisfaction with such subjective tests as the taxpayer's motives in making a purported charitable contribution" and relying solely on differential between amount of payment and value of benefit.

[C]   Charitable Contributions of Property

The charitable contribution of a gift of property is treated differently from a cash gift, especially when the property is encumbered.[33] This issue was discussed in *Ebben v. Commissioner of Internal Revenue*,[34] where the court held that the transfer by gift of encumbered property to a charity is a "sale" under Section 1011(b). In the case, the taxpayer gave property to Pitzer College subject to a note and deed of trust in the amount of $544,584. Taxpayer conceded that the amount of an encumbrance on property contributed to charity is an "amount realized by the tax payer."[35] The court defined the transaction as a sale in keeping with this logic. The court referred to Regulation Section 1.1011-2(a)(3), which states that if property is transferred subject to an indebtedness, the amount of indebtedness must be treated as an amount realized to the taxpayer for purposes of determining whether there is a sale or exchange to which Section 1011(b) and this section apply, even though the transferee does not agree to assume or pay the indebtedness.[36]

[D]   Determining Gifts Qualified for Deduction

The IRS gives a number of examples in Revenue Ruling 67-246[37] defining what qualifies as a gift. In response to a taxpayer's request for advice concerning fundraising practices that involved the deductibility of payments in connection with admission to charity balls, bazaars, banquets, shows, and athletic events, the IRS stated that funds are raised in two different ways through these types of events. One is through the sale of admissions or other privileges or benefits connected with the event, and the other is through the use of the affair as an occasion for solicitation of gifts in combination with the sale of admissions or other privileges or benefits.[38]

Revenue Ruling 67-246 provides guidelines and examples regarding the deductibility of such payments to charitable organizations. To be deductible as a charitable contribution under IRC Section 170, a gift must be to or for the use of a qualified donee with no consideration. The IRS explains that, as a general rule, where a transaction involves a payment in the form of a purchase of an item of value, the presumption arises that no gift has been made for charitable contribution purposes. The presumption is that the payment is the purchase price.[39]

Thus, where consideration is in the form of admissions, or other privileges or benefits are received in connection with payments by patrons of fundraising affairs, the presumption is that the payments are not gifts. If a charitable contribution

---

[33] *See* I.R.S. Publication 526, *Charitable Contributions* (Rev. Dec. 2009).

[34] 783 F.2d 906 (9th Cir. 1986).

[35] *Id.* at 912; *see also* I.R.S. Publication 526.

[36] *Ebben*, 783 F.2d at 912.

[37] 1967-2 C.B. 104; *see also* Estate of Levine v. Comm'r, 72 T.C. 780, 789–91 (1979), *aff'd*, 634 F.2d 12, 15 (2d Cir. 1980); Crane v. Comm'r, 331 U.S. 1 (1947); Comm'r v. Tufts, 461 U.S. 300, 307–10 (1983).

[38] Rev. Rul. 67-246, 1967-2 C.B. 104.

[39] *Id.*

deduction is claimed, the burden is on the taxpayer to establish that the amount paid is not the purchase price of the privilege or benefit, and that part of the payment does qualify as a gift.[40]

[E]　Determining When a Gift Has Been Made

To show that a gift has been made, there must be proof that the portion of the payment claimed as a gift represents the excess of the total amount paid over the value of the consideration received. This can be established by evidence that the payment exceeds the fair market value of the privileges or benefits received by the amount claimed to have been paid as a gift. A letter from the charity explaining the value of the gift will meet this requirement.[41]

Another important element in establishing that a gift has been made is evidence that the excess of the value received was made with the intention to make a gift. A payment can qualify as a deductible gift only to the extent that it is shown to exceed the fair market value of any consideration received in the form of privileges or other benefits.[42]

In cases where a fundraising activity is designed to solicit payments intended to be in part a gift and in part the purchase price of admission to or participation in an event, the organization conducting the activity must employ procedures that make it clear that not only is a gift being solicited in connection with the sale of admission or other privileges, but also the amount of the gift being solicited.[43] The amount attributable to the purchase of admissions or other privileges and the amount solicited as a gift should be determined in advance. The respective amounts should be stated in making the solicitation and clearly indicated on any ticket, receipt, or other evidence issued in connection with the payment. In making such a determination, the full fair market value of the admission and other benefits or privileges must be taken into account. If there are comparable events, these should be used to fix fair market value. Where there is no counterpart, a reasonable estimate of the fair market value can be used.[44]

The fact that the full amount or a portion of the payment is used exclusively for charitable purposes has no bearing on the determination as to the value of admission or other privileges. Also, the fact that the tickets or other privileges are not utilized does not entitle the patron to any greater charitable contribution deduction than otherwise allowable. The test is not whether the right to admission or privileges is exercised, but whether the right was accepted or rejected by the taxpayer. If a patron desires to support an affair, but does not intend to use the tickets or exercise the privileges, he can make an outright gift and not accept or keep any tickets or evidence of privileges related to the event.[45] The IRS provides

---

[40] *Id.*

[41] *Id.*

[42] *Id.*

[43] *Id.*

[44] *Id.*

[45] *Id.*

12 examples to illustrate these principles following the explanation in this Revenue Ruling.[46]

[F]   Determining Validity of Gifts

Additional cases highlight the analysis used by the courts and by the IRS when determining whether a contribution has been made for charitable purposes. However, the courts and the IRS do not always agree.

In *Hernandez v. Commissioner of Internal Revenue*,[47] the United States Supreme Court granted certiorari to determine whether taxpayers could deduct payments made to branch churches of the Church of Scientology in order to receive services known as "auditing" and "training." The Court held that the payments were not deductible. It explained that the petitioners' payments to the Church did not qualify as contributions or gifts.[48] The Court believed these payments to be part of a "quintessential quid pro quo exchange: in return for their money, petitioners received an identifiable benefit, namely, auditing and training sessions."[49] The Court found an inherently reciprocal nature to the exchange. Petitioners also made a selective prosecution claim that failed, and then argued that these services were no different from pew rents, building fund assessments, etc., which are deductible for other churches, but the Court refused once again to allow a deduction. Justices O'Connor and Scalia dissented, stating that the IRS had misapplied its long-time rules for allowing charitable contribution deductions for fixed payments to other religions.[50]

The IRS changed its position in 1993 and entered into a settlement agreement with the Church of Scientology. Years later, the Court of Appeals for the Ninth Circuit was faced with a similar issue in *Sklar v. Commissioner*.[51] The petitioners in this case challenged the IRS's disallowance of their deductions, as charitable contributions, of part of the tuition payments made to their children's religious schools.[52] The IRS claimed that the costs were personal tuition expenses and were not deductible. The petitioners sought to deduct 55 percent of the tuition, on the basis that this represented the portion of the school day allocated to religious education. They contended that the costs were deductible under IRC Section 170, as payments for which they had received "solely intangible religious benefits."[53] They also argued that the IRS permitted a similar deduction to the Church of Scientology, and that it would be "a violation of administrative consistency and of

---

[46] *Id.*

[47] 490 U.S. 680 (1989).

[48] *Id.* at 684; *see also* I.R.C. § 170.

[49] *Hernandez*, 490 U.S. at 691.

[50] *Id.* at 703. *See also* Lary v. United States, 787 F.2d 1538 (11th Cir. 1986) where the court determined that donating blood to an organization is not considered a charitable contribution; and therefore the value cannot be deducted. Instead, the court considered the contribution a sale or performance of a service.

[51] 282 F.3d 610 (9th Cir. 2002).

[52] *Id.* at 612.

[53] *Id.*

the Establishment Clause to deny them, as Orthodox Jews, the same deduction."[54]

In *Sklar*, the Ninth Circuit Court cited *DeJong v. Commissioner*,[55] where the Tax Court had found that tuition that is paid for educating a taxpayer's children is a personal expense that is not deductible under IRC Section 170.[56] They also clarified that *Hernandez* was still controlling case law.[57] The taxpayers argued that the decision was changed when the IRS entered into a settlement agreement with the Church of Scientology.[58] The Ninth Circuit Court considered the IRS's refusal to disclose the terms of its settlement agreement, the constitutionality of the agreement, and the tuition payments as "dual payments" under the IRC in making their determination.[59]

The Ninth Circuit Court determined that the Sklars received the education of their children in return for their tuition payments. They were not entitled to a charitable deduction for these payments, and the decision of the Tax Court was affirmed.

Justice Silverman concurred with the decision, but stated that any decision in the Church of Scientology case was not relevant.[60] He stated that the decision was based on IRC Section 170, *Hernandez v. Commissioner*,[61] and *United States v. American Bar Endowment*,[62] and not on the *Church of Scientology* closing agreement. In 2008, the Circuit Court affirmed the IRS's determination that the tuition and fees paid by them to the Orthodox Jewish day school that their children attended were not charitable deductions.[63]

In Revenue Procedure 90-12,[64] the IRS established guidelines for charitable organizations to help in advising patrons about the deductible amount of contributions when something of value is received in return by the donor.[65] The IRS briefly reviewed Revenue Ruling 67-246,[66] which asked charities to determine the fair market value of benefits in advance of solicitation so that they can inform the donor of the deductible amount of their gift. Because certain charities had

---

[54] *Id.*

[55] *Id.* (*citing* De Jong v. Comm'r, 309 F.2d 373, 376 (9th Cir. 1962)).

[56] *Id.*

[57] *Id.* at 612; *see also Hernandez, supra*, 490 U.S. 680.

[58] *Id. See also* Rev. Rul. 93-73, 1993-2 C.B. 75, which declared "obsolete" the *Church of Scientology*, Rev. Rul. 78-189, 1978-1 C.B. 68, explicitly prohibiting the deduction of the costs of auditing, training, and other courses in the Church as charitable contribution deductions under I.R.C. § 170. *See also* Douglas Frantz, *$12.5 Million Deal With I.R.S. Lifted Cloud Over Scientologists*, N.Y. TIMES, Dec. 31, 1997; and IRS, *Closing Agreement between IRS and Church of Scientology*, 19 EXEMPT ORG. TAX REV. 227 (1998), where the entire settlement agreement is reprinted.

[59] *Sklar*, 282 F.3d at 620.

[60] *Id.* at 620.

[61] *Id.*; 490 U.S. 680 (1989).

[62] 477 U.S. 105 (1986).

[63] Sklar v. Comm'r, 549 F.3d 1252 (9th Cir. 2008).

[64] 1990-1 C.B. 471.

[65] *Id.; see also* I.R.C. § 170.

[66] 1967-2 C.B. 104.

stated the difficulty in making this determination, especially when small items are involved, the IRS set forth several guidelines in this regard.

The IRS stated that benefits received in connection with a payment to a charity will be considered to have insubstantial value if two requirements are met: (1) a payment occurs in the context of a fund raising campaign and the charity informs the patrons of how much of their gift is deductible; and (2) either (a) the fair market value of all the benefits received is not more than two percent of the gift, or $91, whichever is less (indexed for inflation), or (b) the payment is $45.50 (adjusted for inflation) or more and the only benefits are token items (mugs, t-shirts, etc.) bearing the name or logo of the organization.[67]

The Revenue Procedure also provided that newsletters or program guides are not treated as if they have a measurable fair market value or cost if their primary purpose is to inform members of the activities of an organization and if not available to nonmembers by paid subscription or through newsstand sales.[68] Whether a publication is a commercial quality publication depends on all the facts and circumstances. Publications that contain articles written for compensation and that accept advertising will be treated as commercial quality, having a fair market value or cost. Professional journals are usually considered commercial quality. The cost of commercial quality publications includes the cost of production and distribution and must be computed without regard to income from advertising, newsstand, or subscription sales.[69]

§ 17.04   DEDUCTION LIMITATIONS FOR TAXPAYERS

Congress never intended for the charitable tax deduction to be unlimited. The deduction was initially limited to 15 percent of the donor's "net income," and has continued to increase through the years to become ever more complicated. The limitations have remained to assure that no taxpayer completely avoids paying taxes by making charitable contributions. Mostly, the limitations affect the wealthiest and most generous philanthropists.[70]

The deductibility of charitable contributions within a tax year is confined by certain percentage limitations. In the case of individuals, the limitations are governed by the donor's contribution base, which is essentially the same as his adjusted gross income (AGI). An individual who itemizes deductions may deduct charitable contributions of up to 50 percent, 30 percent or 20 percent of his AGI, depending on the type of property that is contributed and the type of organization to which the property is being donated. These percentage limitations generally apply to gifts of cash and ordinary income property.[71]

---

[67] Rev. Proc. 2007-66, 2007-45 I.R.B. 970, *modifying* Rev. Proc. 90-12, 1990-1 C.B. 471. Cost (as opposed to fair market value) of all benefits received by a donor must, in the aggregate, be within the limits established for "low cost articles" ($9.10 or less) under I.R.C. § 513(h)(2).

[68] Rev. Proc. 90-12, 1990-1 C.B. 471.

[69] *Id.*

[70] *See* I.R.C. § 170.

[71] *See* I.R.C. § 170; 26 C.F.R. §§ 1.170-1–1.170-3; *see also* Nicholas P. Cafardi & Jaclyn Fabean

Typically, the deductible value of a contribution is the fair market value of the property on the date of the gift, but there are several exceptions to this rule. If ordinary income property is gifted, the deduction is limited to the donor's base or AGI. If a sale of the property by the donor would result in ordinary income or short-term capital gains, the property is ordinary income property. Examples of ordinary income property include: inventory held for sale to customers; capital assets held for less than one year; property used in the donor's trade or business; and property created by the taxpayer (i.e., paintings, manuscripts, etc.).[72]

As noted above, the allowable tax deduction for a charitable contribution depends on many different factors. Limitations that influence the deductible amount include: varying percentages of the donor's income; type of property donated; classification of the recipient organization as a public charity or private foundation; character of the property given as a capital versus an ordinary income property; and type of transfer (i.e., whether the gift is made outright or in trust and whether the donation is of a taxpayer's entire interest or a partial interest).[73]

The percentage limitations that apply are as follows:[74]

- an individual may annually deduct up to 50 percent of his adjusted gross income for gifts of cash and ordinary income property to public charities and private operating foundations;

- up to 30 percent of an individual's income may be offset by donations of long-term capital gain property to public charities and private operating foundations and for gifts of cash to a private foundation;

- gifts to a private foundation of property other than cash, as a rule, are deductible only up to the taxpayer's cost basis. A fair market value deduction for gifts of certain appreciated securities, limited to 20 percent of an individual's income, is also allowed;

- corporate donations are deductible up to 10 percent of the company's pretax income; and

- no percentage limitation applies for gift and estate tax charitable deductions.[75]

If total donations made in one year exceed the above limits, the excess amount can be carried over and claimed for up to five subsequent years. This is subject to the applicable percentage limitations.[76]

CHERRY, TAX EXEMPT ORGANIZATIONS: CASES AND MATERIALS 680 (2d ed. 2008).

[72] Id.

[73] STEVEN D. SIMPSON, TAX COMPLIANCE FOR TAX-EXEMPT ORGANIZATIONS, Ch. 10 (2009).

[74] See I.R.C. § 170(b).

[75] I.R.C. §§ 2055, 2522.

[76] I.R.C. § 170(d).

§ 17.05 FORM AND TIMING

A gift (as discussed above) must be made to or for the use of a qualified donee to be tax deductible. The definition of qualified donee includes gifts made in trust for an organization. It does not include gifts to individuals, but only the types of organizations defined by the IRC.[77]

In *Davis v. United States*,[78] the issue before the United States Supreme Court was "whether the funds petitioners transferred to their two sons while they served as full-time, unpaid missionaries for the Church of Jesus Christ of Latter-day Saints (Church)" were deductible as charitable contributions "to or for the use of" the Church.[79]

The petitioners were members of the Mormon Church. They claimed a charitable deduction for the money they transferred to their sons' personal checking accounts. Their sons were serving as missionaries of the Church. It was customary for parents of missionaries to provide this type of support during the child's time of service. The missionaries were encouraged to use the money carefully and only at a minimum.[80]

The petitioners claimed that the payments were charitable contributions "for the use of" the Church or deductible as unreimbursed expenditures incident to the rendering of services to a charitable organization.[81]

In its decision, the United States Supreme Court stated that a taxpayer may claim a deduction for a charitable contribution only if the contribution is made "to or for the use of" a qualified organization.[82] In its analysis, the Supreme Court stated that "[C]ongress sought to provide tax benefits to charitable organizations, to encourage the development of private institutions that serve a useful public purpose or supplement or take the place of public institutions of the same kind."[83] The Commissioner's interpretation assured that contributions would be used to foster such development because it required the contributions to be made in trust or some similar legal arrangement. A problem arose here because a characteristic of a trust is that the beneficiary has the legal power to enforce the trustees duty to comply with the terms of the trust. Petitioners did not create a trust but transferred money into their sons' personal accounts, and the sons had no legal obligation to use the funds as specified by the petitioners.[84] There was no one legally obligated to assure that the fund would be used for the appropriate purpose.

---

[77] I.R.C. § 501(c)(3).

[78] 495 U.S. 472 (1990).

[79] *Id.; see also* 26 U.S.C. § 170; 26 C.F.R. § 1.170A-1(a), (b), (g).

[80] *Davis*, 495 U.S. at 473–74.

[81] *Id.; see also* 26 C.F.R. § 1.170A-1(g).

[82] *See* I.R.C. § 170.

[83] *Davis*, 495 U.S. at 482–83.

[84] *Id.* at 486.

The petitioners' alternative argument was that the transfer of funds into their sons' account was a contribution "to" the Church.[85] They argued that Regulation Section 1.170A-1(g)[86] allowed them to claim deductions for their sons' unreimbursed expenditures incident to their sons' contribution of services. The United States Supreme Court disagreed, stating that the Regulation allowed for a deduction for expenses for their own contribution of services but not for their sons'.[87] The Court held that petitioners' transfer of funds into their sons' accounts was not a contribution "to or for the use of" the Church for purposes of IRC Section 170.[88]

[A]   Un-reimbursed Expenses

Un-reimbursed expenses of board members and volunteers of tax exempt charitable organizations are deductible. These expenditures are treated as contributions "to" a charity and are subject to the 50 percent limitation on cash contributions.[89] Individual taxpayers may deduct charitable contributions in the year in which they are paid.[90]

[B]   Contributions by Check

Contributions paid by check are deductible when the check is mailed or unconditionally delivered to the charity, as long as it clears in due course.[91] Contributions charged to a credit card are deductible as of the date the charge is made to the account.[92] Pledges and promissory notes are viewed as an unenforceable promise to pay and thus are not deductible until payment is actually made to the charity.[93]

[C]   Contributions of Stock

Gifts of stock are considered complete when a properly endorsed stock certificate is delivered to the donee or its agent. If stock is held at the donor's bank or broker, the date of the gift is the date the stock is transferred on the books of

---

[85] *Id.* at 484.

[86] *See* 26 C.F.R. § 1.170A-1(g) (contributions of services). "No deduction is allowable under IRC § 170 for a contribution of services. However, unreimbursed expenditures made incident to the rendition of services to an organization contributions to which are deductible may constitute a deductible contribution. For example, the cost of a uniform without general utility which is required to be worn in performing donated services is deductible. Similarly, out-of-pocket transportation expenses necessarily incurred in performing donated services are deductible."

[87] *Davis*, 495 U.S. at 470.

[88] *Id.* at 489.

[89] I.R.C. § 170(b)(1)(A); *see also* Rockefeller v. Comm'r, 676 F.2d 35 (2d Cir. 1982); Rev. Rul. 84-61, 1984-1 C.B. 39.

[90] 26 C.F.R. § 1.170A-1(a).

[91] 26 C.F.R. § 1.170A-1(b).

[92] Rev. Rul. 78-38, 1978-1 C.B. 67.

[93] Rev. Rul. 68-174, 1968-1 C.B. 81; *see also* 26 C.F.R. § 1.170A-1(a); MARY FRANCES BUDIG ET AL., PLEDGES TO NON-PROFIT ORGANIZATIONS: ARE THEY ENFORCEABLE AND MUST THEY BE ENFORCED? (1993).

the corporation. Gifts of stock are valued at the average of the high and low market prices on the day of the gift.[94]

[D]   Pledge as Payment

The act of making a pledge or delivering a promissory note does not constitute a "payment" as a charitable deduction and is therefore not deductible. Once the pledge is satisfied or the note is paid, then the charitable donation qualifies for deduction.[95]

[E]   Corporate Donations

Corporations may not deduct more than 10 percent of their taxable income (as adjusted) in any given tax year. When a corporation reports its income on the accrual basis, the payment of the contribution can be made on or before the fifteenth day of the third month following the close of the taxable year, provided that the board of directors authorized the contribution during the taxable year.[96]

§ 17.06   SUBSTANTIATION & DISCLOSURE REQUIREMENTS

There are two rules to meet the substantiation and disclosure requirements for federal income tax reporting purposes:

- a donor is responsible for obtaining a written acknowledgement from a charity for any single contribution of $250 or more before the donor can claim a charitable contribution deduction on his federal income tax return; and

- a charitable organization is required to provide a written disclosure to a donor who receives goods or services in exchange for a single payment in excess of $75. . . .[97]

The written acknowledgement from the organization should include the following: name of organization; amount of cash contribution; description (but not value) of non-cash contribution; statement that no goods or services were provided by the organization in return for the contribution, if that was the case; description and good faith estimate of the value of goods or services, if any, that an organization provided in return for the contribution, and a statement that goods or services, if any, that an organization provided in return for the contribution consisted entirely of intangible religious benefits, if that was the case.[98]

---

[94]   26 C.F.R. § 1.170A-1(b).

[95]   26 C.F.R. § 1.170A-1(a); *see also* Rev. Rul. 68-174, 1968-1 C.B. 81.

[96]   I.R.C. § 170(a)(2).

[97]   I.R.S. Publication 1771, *Charitable Contributions-Substantiation Requirements* (Rev. 3 2008); *see also* I.R.C. §§ 170(f)(8)(A), 6115(a).

[98]   *Id.*

For a written acknowledgement to be contemporaneous, a donor must receive the acknowledgement by the earlier of: the date on which the donor actually files his individual federal income tax return for the year of the contribution; or the due date (including extensions) of the return.[99]

Insubstantial goods or services that a charitable organization provides in exchange for contributions do not have to be described in an acknowledgement. Goods and services are considered to be insubstantial if the payment occurs in the context of a fundraising campaign in which a charitable organization informs the donor of the amount of the contribution that is a deductible contribution, and:

- the fair market value of the benefit received does not exceed the lesser of two percent of the payment or $91; or

- the payment is at least $45.50, the only items provided bear the organization's name or logo (calendars, mugs, posters), and the cost of these items is within the limits for "low-cost articles," which is $9.10.[100]

Annual membership benefits are also considered insubstantial if provided in exchange for an annual payment of $75 or less and consist of annual recurring rights or privileges.[101]

The IRC sections and regulations also exempt from the written acknowledgement requirement such things as intangible religious benefits, and some unreimbursed expenses, and also sets forth other written disclosure and acknowledgement requirements.[102] IRS Announcement 2000-84,[103] states that e-mail acknowledgements and disclosures of "quid pro quo" return benefits do satisfy the substantiation and disclosure requirements if the acknowledgement can be printed out and contains the required information of IRC Sections 170(f)(8) and 6115.[104]

§ 17.07 CONTRIBUTIONS OF PROPERTY

If contributing property to a qualified organization, the amount of the charitable contribution is generally the fair market value of the property at the time of the contribution.[105] Fair Market Value is the price at which the property would change hands between a willing seller and a willing buyer.[106] A Form 8283 must be filed (as an attachment to the donor's tax return) and must be acknowledged by the recipient organization and the independent appraiser. There is a penalty if a taxpayer

---

[99] *Id.*

[100] *Id.* These dollar amounts are adjusted for inflation.

[101] I.R.S. Publication 1771, *Charitable Contributions-Substantiation Requirements* (Rev. 3 2008); *see also* I.R.C. §§ 170(f)(8)(A), 6115(a).

[102] *See also* IRS Publication 526, *Charitable Contributions* (Rev. Dec. 2009); Rev. Proc. 90-12, 1990-1 C.B. 471.

[103] 2000-42 I.R.B. 385.

[104] *Id.*

[105] I.R.S. Publication 526.

[106] 26 C.F.R. § 1.170A-1(c)(2).

overstates the value or adjusted basis of donated property.[107]

[A] Types of Property Donated

There are specific rules that apply to the donation of particular types of property. The following is a summary of some of these.

[1] Capital Gain Property

A gift of capital gain property (appreciated stock or real estate held by the taxpayer for more than one year) provides attractive tax benefits. Capital gain property is property eligible for special tax rates because of its holding period and investment nature.[108] A donor avoids tax on a gain that would have been recognized if the donated property would have been sold and may deduct the fair market value of the property subject to applicable percentage limitations.[109]

This fair market deduction is not available if the gift of appreciated capital gain property is to a private foundation. To determine the charitable deduction, the donor's gift is reduced by the amount of long-term capital gain that would have been recognized if the property had been sold for fair market value and had not been contributed.[110] Capital gain property worth less than its basis is usually not contributed as the donor cannot deduct the loss.[111]

In *Blake v. Commissioner*,[112] the court was faced with the tax law involving step transaction analysis. This is where the taxpayer "contributes" a substantially appreciated asset to a charitable organization, which then liquidates the contribution and purchases another asset from the taxpayer.[113] The issue in the case was whether the taxpayer was entitled to treat the transfer of the first asset (corporate stock) as a contribution and treat the transfer of the second asset (a yacht) as a sale or "whether, as the Tax Court held, the transaction here must be re-characterized for tax purposes as a sale of the stock by the taxpayer followed by a contribution to the charity of the vessel."[114] The vessel was sold by the charity shortly after it was purchased for a little less than half of what the charity paid the taxpayer out of the proceeds of the stock.[115]

The court held that the gain realized on the sale of the stock was attributable to the taxpayer and the market value of the yacht (although not challenged in this case) was deductible as a contribution. It stated that where there is an expectation on the part of the donor that is reasonable, "with an advance understanding that the

---

[107] I.R.S. Publication 526.

[108] I.R.C. § 170(b)(1)(C).

[109] I.R.C. § 170(b)(1)(C).

[110] I.R.C. § 170(e)(1)(A), (B)(ii); *see also* Rev. Rul. 78-197, 1978-1 C.B. 83.

[111] *Id.*

[112] 697 F.2d 473 (2d Cir. 1982).

[113] *Id.*

[114] *Id.* at 474.

[115] *Id.*

donee charity will purchase the asset with the proceeds of the donated stock, the transaction will be looked at as a unitary one."[116]

[2] Ordinary Income Property

Ordinary income property is property that, if sold, results in ordinary income or short term capital gain for the taxpayer. Ordinary income property includes inventory, "dealer property" (property held for sale to customers), works of art, and intellectual property created by a donor.[117]

Taxpayers who donate ordinary income property can only deduct their basis in that property. The purpose is to place these donors in the same position they would be in had they sold the property and then contributed the proceeds to charity. The ordinary income rules reduce the tax benefit for contributions of inventory and other "dealer" property.[118]

In Revenue Ruling 79-256,[119] the question for the IRS was whether IRC Section 170(e) applied and required that the amount of taxpayers' charitable contributions be reduced by any gain that would not have been long-term capital gain if the property had been sold by the taxpayer at its fair market value. The first taxpayer donated ornamental plants, while the second taxpayer donated limited edition lithograph prints. The IRS decided that the amount of each taxpayer's contribution had to be reduced by the excess of the fair market value of the contributed property over each taxpayer's cost as of the dates of contribution.[120]

[3] Tangible Personal Property

IRC Section 170 allows a donor to take a full fair market value deduction for gifts of tangible personal property. These are items such as jewelry, antiques, art objects, books, or yachts. If the donated tangible personal property is not used by the donee for its exempt purposes, the gift must be reduced by the amount of long-term capital gain that the donor would have recognized if the property were sold rather than contributed.[121]

A specific section that addresses contributions of clothing and household goods was added to the IRC by the Pension Protection Act of 2006, requiring that such items be in good condition or better for an individual, partnership, or corporation to be allowed a deduction for such a contribution. "The term 'household items' includes furniture, furnishings, electronics, appliances, linens, and other similar items."

---

[116] *Id.* at 480. *See also* Palmer v. Comm'r, 62 T.C. 684 (1974), *aff'd on other grounds*, 523 F.2d 1308 (8th Cir. 1975), holding that even an expectation of a stock redemption would not warrant denying charitable contribution status; and Rev. Rul. 78-197, 1978-1 C.B. 83, stating that the IRS will treat redemption proceeds as income to the donor "only if the donee is legally bound, or can be compelled by the corporation, to surrender the shares for redemption."

[117] I.R.C. § 170(e)(1).

[118] I.R.C. § 170(e)(1)(A); I.R.S. Publication 526.

[119] 1979-2 C.B. 105.

[120] *Id.*

[121] I.R.C. § 170(e)(1)(B).

Contributions of single items including a qualified appraisal are treated differently.[122] To evaluate whether contributed property is used for exempt purposes, regulations provide that it must be "reasonable to anticipate" that the organization will use the property for an exempt purpose.[123]

[4] Bargain Sales

A sale of property for less than its fair market value is a "bargain sale." Bargain sales offer two benefits: (1) a charitable deduction for the bargain element (fair market value of the property); and (2) a reduction of the tax that the donor would pay if the property had been sold for its full fair market value.[124]

A bargain sale is bifurcated into a sale and a gift. Under a special rule, the donor's basis in the property must be allocated between the sale and gift transaction in proportion to the fair market value of each.[125]

[5] Partial Interests (Not in Trust)

IRC Section 170(a)(3) states that a contribution of a remainder interest in tangible personal property is deductible only when all intervening noncharitable interests have expired. There are three major exceptions to the limitations on deductions for partial interests not in trust. They are: contributions of qualified conservation easements; gifts of remainder interests in a personal residence or farm; and gifts of an undivided portion of a donor's entire interest in property.[126]

The Tax Court addressed the issue of a partial interest not in trust in *Winokur v. Commissioner.*[127] There, the taxpayer (an art collector who served on the board of the Carnegie Institute Museum of Art in Pittsburgh, Pennsylvania), donated a 10 percent undivided interest in a collection of 44 works of art. A second 10 percent interest was donated the following year. In each case, the gift provided that the Institute had the right to possession of the art for a specified number of days for a year following the donation. The Institute did not take physical possession of any of the art during the 12 months following each gift. The taxpayer then donated the remaining 80 percent interest in five of the works of art and the Institute took possession of these.[128]

In its analysis, the court stated that the relevant statutory and regulatory language suggested that it was the right or entitlement to possession, not actual physical possession, that controls whether a present interest would be regarded as

---

[122] I.R.C. § 170(f)(16); Pension Protection Act of 2006, Pub. L. No. 109-280, § 1226, 120 Stat. 780, 1226 (2006).

[123] 26 C.F.R. § 1.170A-4(b)(3)(ii).

[124] I.R.C. § 1011(b).

[125] *Id.; see also* Guest v. Comm'r, 77 T.C. 9 (1981) (gift of encumbered property was treated as a bargain sale).

[126] I.R.C. § 170(f)(3)(B); 26 C.F.R. § 1.170A-7(b)(1).

[127] 90 T.C. 733 (1988).

[128] *Id.*

a future interest.[129] Because the Institutes' failure to take physical possession was voluntary and not caused by the acts of petitioner, the court held that petitioner and the Institute shared the works of art as tenants in common. Therefore, the donations of 10 percent undivided interest in art qualified for a charitable contribution deduction under Section 170.[130]

[6] Qualified Conservation Contributions

A charitable deduction for gifts of "qualified conservation contributions" is permitted under IRC Section 170(f)(3)(B)(iii).[131] This is to encourage the preservation of open space land, including agricultural property. There are three requirements for a "qualified conservation contribution" as follows:

- the gift must be a "qualified property interest," defined as the donor's entire interest in the property, a remainder interest, or a perpetual restriction on the use that can be made of the property;[132]

- the contribution must be made to a governmental unit, public charity, or organization that is controlled by and supports a public charity or governmental unit;[133] and

- the contribution must be exclusively for one or more specified "conservation purposes. . . ."[134]

The value of a conservation easement is based on an appraisal to determine the difference between the fair market value of the property without the restriction and the fair market value after it is encumbered with an easement.[135]

[B] Valuation and Appraisals

A charitable contribution deduction for a donation of long-term capital gain property can be taken for the fair market value on the date of the gift. Any taxpayer who contributes property with a claimed value of more than $5,000 is required to have the property appraised (a "qualified appraisal") prior to donating it to charity.[136] IRS Revenue Procedure 66-49 sets forth the procedure to be used by taxpayers, individual appraisers, and valuation groups for federal income tax purposes.[137] In Revenue Procedure 96-15,[138] the IRS provides the procedure for obtaining a "statement of value" for donated works of art before the taxpayer files a federal income tax return claiming a charitable deduction. The "statement of

---

[129] I.R.C. § 170(a)(3); 26 C.F.R. § 1.170(A)-7(b)(1).

[130] *Winokur*, 90 T.C. at 738.

[131] *See* I.R.C. § 170(h).

[132] I.R.C. § 170(h)(2).

[133] I.R.C. § 170(h)(3).

[134] I.R.C. §170(h)(4)(A).

[135] 26 C.F.R. § 1.170A-14(h)(3)(i).

[136] 26 C.F.R. § 170A-13(c)(2)(i)(A).

[137] 1966-2 C.B. 1257.

[138] 1996-1 C.B. 627.

value" can be used for income, estate, or gift tax purposes.[139]

§ 17.08   CHARITABLE CONTRIBUTION VEHICLES

Aside from outright gifts to charity, as discussed above, there are other giving techniques using specific formats and charitable giving vehicles to donate cash and property to charity. Many of these contribution vehicles are established to become operable upon the donor's death, while others are partial gifts in the present with the remainder of the gift occurring in the future upon the occurrence of some event (in many cases, the donor's death). Funds set up to distribute gifts to charity have also become common.

[A]   Donor Advised Funds

A Donor Advised Fund (DAF) was defined for the first time in the Pension Protection Act of 2006 (PPA)[140] as a "fund or account (i) which is separately identified by reference to contributions of a donor or donors, (ii) which is owned and controlled by a sponsoring organization, and (iii) with respect to which a donor (or any person appointed or designated by such donor) has, or reasonably expects to have, advisory privileges with respect to the distribution or investment of amounts held in such fund or account by reason of the donor's status as a donor."[141]

Though in use for years previous to the enactment of the Act, it was the purported abuses that prompted the Senate to direct the Treasury Department to conduct a study and recommend action. The concern was that donor advised funds were being used for some taxpayers' personal benefit.[142]

Out of this study came the Pension Protection Act,[143] which not only defined donor advised funds, but also imposed excise taxes in an effort to curb abuse. The definition in the Act includes two exceptions. First, a fund that is established to benefit a single charitable organization is not a donor advised fund. Second, a fund established to provide grants to individuals for "travel, study, or similar purposes" if certain requirements are met is not a donor advised fund.[144]

A DAF will generally bear the name of the donor or the name of someone the donor chooses.[145]

---

[139] *Id.*

[140] Pension Protection Act of 2006, Pub. L. No. 109-280, § 1226, 120 Stat. 780, 1226 (2006).

[141] I.R.C. § 4966(d)(2)(A).

[142] *Enforcement Problems, Accomplishments, and Future Direction: Hearing Before the S. Comm. on Finance on Exempt Organizations*, 109th Cong. 5–6 (2005) (written statement of Mark W. Everson, Commissioner, Internal Revenue Service).

[143] Pension Protection Act of 2006, Pub. L. No. 109-280, § 1226, 120 Stat. 780, 1226 (2006).

[144] Joint Comm. On Taxation, JCX-38-06, Technical Explanation of H.R. 4, the "Pension Protection Act of 2006," as passed by the House on July 28, 2006, and as considered by the Senate on August 3, 2006, at 345 (2006), *available at* http://www.house.gov/jct/x-38-06.pdf.

[145] *See* Victoria B. Bjorklund, Current Developments for Charitable Giving to Donor-Advised Funds, Supporting Organizations and Donor-Managed Investment Accounts (2005).

The Sponsoring Charity of a DAF can be organized as either a nonprofit corporation or a trust. It owns and operates the DAF. Each DAF is a separate account to which one or more donor-advisers may advise the Sponsoring Charity as to investments and grants. A donor-adviser can make nonbinding recommendations as to recipients and investments. The Sponsoring Charity can deny the recommendation, as its board has fiduciary responsibility for management of the fund.[146]

Contributions to a DAF are deductible under IRC Section 170. DAFs offer a deduction at the most favorable rate in the year in which the gift is made. Payouts are permitted over a period of years. Because most DAFs are classified as public charities by the IRS, donors can claim deductions at the higher public charity levels. These funds "are less costly to create and maintain than a private foundation, while having many of the grantmaking advantages of a private foundation."[147]

The PPA imposed two new excise taxes.[148]

The first is an excise tax on taxable distributions and the second is an excise tax on prohibited benefits.[149] A taxable distribution is one where: (1) the distribution is to an individual, or (2) the distribution is not used for charitable purposes by an organization, or (3) when the sponsoring organization does not exercise "expenditure responsibility"[150] over the distribution. The tax imposed is 20 percent.[151] The excise tax on prohibited benefits is 125 percent on the donor or donor advisor and 10 percent on any fund manager who knowingly makes such a distribution.[152] This applies when "a donor or donor advisor recommends a grant from a donor advised fund that results in such person receiving, directly or indirectly, a more than incidental benefit."[153] PPA also made the excise tax on private foundations with excess business holdings and the foundation excise tax on excess benefit transactions applicable to donor advised funds.[154]

---

[146] *Id.*

[147] *Id; see also* I.R.C. § 170(f)(18); Eugene R. Steurele, *Will Donor-Advised Funds Revolutionize Philanthropy?*, CHARTING A CIVIL SOCIETY, No. 5, Sept. 1999, *available at* http://www.urban.org/UploadedPDF/cnp_5.pdf; Pension Protection Act of 2006, Pub. L. No. 109-280, § 1226, 120 Stat. 780, 1226 (2006).

[148] I.R.C. § 4966; I.R.C. § 4967 (2009).

[149] *Id.*

[150] I.R.C. § 4945(h) (2009).

[151] *Id.*

[152] I.R.C. § 4967(a)(1) and (2).

[153] Michael J. Hussey, *Avoiding Misuse of Donor Advised Funds*, 58 CLEV. ST. L. REV. 59 (2010); I.R.C. § 4967(a)(1).

[154] *Id.*

[B] Community Foundations

A community foundation is an organization established to receive gifts or bequests from the public and to administer them for charitable purposes in the community in which the foundation is located.[155]

The community foundation can be organized as either a nonprofit corporation, a trust, or as a combination of the two forms. The governing body (board of directors) of this organization must be made up of a broad cross section of the community. Community foundations are treated as public charities (as a publicly supported organization under IRC Section 170(b)(A)(6)). Community foundations seek funds from private sources to build capital for local charitable purposes and allocate and distribute the funds to meet public needs.[156]

[C] Pooled Common Funds

A Pooled Common Fund is a charitable giving vehicle that pools charitable contributions into a common fund, allowing a donor to retain the right to designate annually the charities to which his funds should be given. The fund qualifies as a private foundation, although the more liberal charitable income tax deduction is allowed.[157]

[D] Planned Giving

The term "planned giving" was developed by fundraisers to describe types of charitable giving that are structured (through giving vehicles) so as to be realized according to specific documents (trusts), with funding arrangements shared by the donor and donee or structured to take effect only upon the donor's death. Planned gifts can be as simple as a donor providing for a charity in his will. Many times the donor informs the charity of this future gift so that it can plan for this donation. Other times, a charity is surprised by a gift designated in a donor's will, although the donor planned for this much earlier.[158]

Although a very complex area, there are several vehicles that are more common, as discussed below. These vehicles offer tax advantages to the donor and a benefit to the charities that are named in the vehicle.

[1] Charitable Remainder Trusts

A charitable remainder trust is created to allow a donor to make a gift of property in trust and retain an interest for himself for life or for a term of years.[159] There are two types of charitable remainder trusts, an annuity trust and a unitrust.

---

[155] *See* Paul Treusch, Tax-Exempt Charitable Organizations, Ch. 12-D1 (3d ed. 1988).

[156] John A. Edie, First Steps in Starting a Foundation 35–38 (4th ed. 1997).

[157] *See* I.R.C. § 170(b)(1)(E)(iii); *see also* Malvin E. Bank, *Community Foundations: Are Donor-Directed Funds New Vehicles for Utilizing Community Foundations*, 7 Exempt Org. Tax. Rev. 42 (1993).

[158] *See generally* James Edward Harris, *Level Five Philanthropy: Designing a Plan for Strategic, Effective, Efficient Giving*, 26 U. Ark. Little Rock L. Rev. 19 (2003).

[159] I.R.C. § 664; *see also* Paul D. Callister, *Charitable Remainder Trusts: An Overview*, 51 Tax Law.

An annuity trust pays out a fixed annual dollar amount to the income beneficiary. In a unitrust the income beneficiary receives annual payments based on a fixed percentage of the trust assets valued each year.[160]

[2]   Charitable Lead Trust

A charitable lead trust is the opposite of the remainder trust in that it pays a defined percentage of its principal for a specific period of time to a charity. At the end of the trust's life, the property is returned to the donor or to another designated beneficiary. This trust must be a qualifying annuity or unitrust. Here, the donor receives an immediate tax deduction equal to the present value of the charity income stream. However, the donor is considered the "grantor" of the trust and must report the trust income annually.[161]

[3]   Remainder Interests

A remainder interest in a personal residence (it need not be a principal residence and can be a vacation home) or farm (including land and buildings used for the production of crops, livestock, etc.) qualifies for charitable income, gift, and estate tax deductions.[162] Typically, the donor continues to live in the residence or on the farm during his life with the property passing to charity upon his death.[163]

[4]   Charitable Gift Annuities

In a charitable gift annuity, the donor transfers property to a charity in return for the commitment from the charity that it will pay an annual sum to the donor for the donor's life or for the life of the donor and his spouse. The annual amount received by the donor is taxed in accordance with regular annuity tax laws. A portion of each annuity payment is a tax free return on capital and a portion is taxable as ordinary income.[164] A donation of appreciated property is afforded different tax treatment.[165]

---

549 (1998); Barry L. Kohler, *Doing Well by Doing Good: The Many Uses of the Charitable Remainder Trust*, 12 MAINE BAR J. 240 (1997).

[160] I.R.C. § 664(d); *see also* Lindquist v. Mack (In re Mack), 269 B.R. 392 (Bankr. D. Minn. 2001), and Rev. Proc. 90-30, 1990-1 C.B. 534, for examples of charitable remainder trusts. For other samples, see Rev. Proc. 2005-54, which supersedes sections 4 of Rev. Proc. 90-30; Rev. Proc. 2005-55, which supersedes sections; Rev. Proc. 2005-56, which supersedes sections 6; Rev. Proc. 2005-58, which supersedes sections 7; and Rev. Proc. 2005-59, which supersedes sections 8.

[161] I.R.C. § 671 (donor is treated as the owner of the trust property because he retains a reversionary interest in the principal).

[162] I.R.C. § 170(f)(3)(B)(i).

[163] 26 C.F.R. § 1.170A-12.

[164] I.R.C. § 72.

[165] 26 C.F.R. §§ 1.170A-1(d), 1.1011-2(b).

[E] Estate Tax Exclusions

In *St. Louis Union Trust Company v. United States*,[166] Judge Frank Landwehr bequeathed his law books to the Bar Association of Saint Louis, and after his sister's death the assets in trust were to be used to "provide a suitable building and facilities to serve as a headquarters, office and meeting place for all lawyers and association of lawyers in the St. Louis area. . . ."[167] At issue in this case was the federal estate tax return filed for the decedent's estate claiming, as a deduction under IRC Section 2055(a)(2), the value of the residuary gift to the Association.[168]

IRC Section 2055(a)(2) requires that four conditions be satisfied for a bequest or devise to be deductible: the donee corporation must be organized exclusively for religious, charitable, scientific, literary, or educational purposes; the donee corporation must be operated exclusively for those purposes; no part of its net earnings may inure to the benefit of any private individual; and no substantial part of its activities may be the carrying on of propaganda or otherwise attempting to influence legislation.[169]

Only one of the four conditions of Section 2055(a)(2) was at issue here, and that was whether the Association was "operated exclusively for . . . charitable, scientific . . . or educational purposes."[170] After reviewing the facts of the case at length and reviewing the activities of the Association, the court held that the activity was clearly charitable, and that deductions under Section 2055(a)(2) were appropriately taken.[171]

§ 17.09   DISASTER RELIEF & INTERNATIONAL GIVING

Disaster relief and international charitable giving have become of increasing importance since September 11, 2001. Although organizations and vehicles for giving to disaster relief efforts existed long before the many disasters of recent years, today there is much more attention being given to how these charitable funds are being managed. Donors are more concerned because of reports of mismanagement and fraudulent behavior in some instances.

[A] Disaster Relief

After September 2001, rules were established by the IRS to govern charitable giving to charities in response to the terrorist attacks of 9/11. The "Victims of Terrorism Tax Relief Act of 2001" applies to individuals interested in using a charitable organization to provide help to victims of disasters or other emergency hardship situations. The Act defines "disasters" as being caused by floods, fires, riots, storms or similar large-scale events. "Emergency hardship" is defined as

---

[166] 374 F.2d 427 (8th Cir. 1967).

[167] *Id.* at 429.

[168] *Id.*

[169] *See* I.R.C. § 2055(a)(2).

[170] I.R.C. § 2055(a)(2).

[171] *St. Louis Union Trust Co.*, 374 F.2d at 435.

illness, death, accident, violent crime, or other personal events.[172]

The rules allow individuals to help by providing charitable donations to existing charitable organizations that can establish assistance programs for a particular disaster or emergency hardship situations. New charitable organizations can be established with the specific intent to provide disaster relief. The group of individuals that may receive assistance from a charitable organization is called a charitable class. A charitable class must be large or indefinite enough that providing aid to members of the class benefits the community as a whole.[173]

Charitable organizations are now permitted to disburse aid to victims of terrorism attacks and their families without making a special assessment of need, which was previously required. One of the most recent disasters, the Indian Ocean Tsunami, was determined by the IRS to be a "qualified disaster" under IRC Section 139, which defines the term as:

1.   A disaster which results from a terroristic or military action,

2.   Federally declared disaster,

3.   A disaster which results from an accident involving a common carrier, or from any other event, which is determined by the Secretary to be of a catastrophic nature, or

4.   With respect to amounts described in subsection (b)(4), a disaster which is determined by an applicable Federal, State, or local authority (as determined by the Secretary) to warrant assistance from the Federal, State, or local government or agency or instrumentality thereof.[174]

[B]   International Giving

The "Principles of International Charity," developed by the Treasury Guidelines Working Group of Charitable Sector Organizations and Advisors in March 2005, states in its preamble:

> Many U.S-based charitable organizations promote international charity: private foundations, public charities, corporate foundations, corporate grantmaking programs, donor-advised funds, friends organizations, churches and religious organizations. In general, the charitable activities of these groups can be divided into two types: the provision of resources through grants to domestic or foreign organizations for use in international

---

[172]   Victims of Terrorism Tax Relief Act of 2001. *See also* I.R.S. Notice 2005-23, and I.R.S. Publication 3833, *Disaster Relief (Be Part of the Program)* (Rev. July 2009), which provides guidance on how to administer disaster relief programs consistent with the applicable federal tax rules for charities.

[173]   *Id.*

[174]   *Id. See also* I.R.S. Notice 2010-16, which declared the Haiti earthquake a I.R.C. § 139 "qualified disasters" and IRS Notice 2010-36 which declared the Chilean earthquake as a I.R.C. § 139 "qualified disasters"; I.R.C. § 139; I.R.C. § 692(c)(2) for the definition of terroristic or military action; I.R.C.§165(h)(3)(C)(i) for a definition of a federally declared disaster.

work, and the provision of services through program operations abroad carried out directly or in partnership with indigenous organizations.[175]

[1] Global Terrorism

In November 2002, the United States Treasury Department issued "Anti-Terrorist Financing Guidelines: Voluntary Best Practices For U.S.-Based Charities," indicating that charities could reduce the possibility that charitable funds would be diverted to terrorist purposes by following the Guidelines.[176]

In November 2003, the Military Family Tax Relief Act was enacted to provide tax breaks for military personnel and their families. Included in this Act is a provision that suspends the tax exempt status of any organization identified as a "terrorist organization."[177]

The courts faced this issue in *Holy Land Foundation for Relief and Development v. Ashcroft*,[178] where, in December 2001, the Office of Foreign Asset Control designated Holy Land Foundation as a "Specially Designated Global Terrorist"[179] pursuant to Executive Order issued under the International Emergency Economic Powers Act.[180] The designation was accompanied by an order to block all of the organization's assets. An appeal was brought from the district court.

Here, the court rejected the Holy Land Foundation's claim that the designation exceeded Treasury's authority. It stated that the district court properly disposed of the Foundation's due process claims under Rule 12(b)(6). The court found that the Foundation's First Amendment rights of freedom of association and freedom of speech were not violated, and supported the grant of summary judgment for the government on Holy Land Foundation's claim that the designation and blocking order substantially burdened its exercise of religion in violation of the Religious Freedom Restoration Act (RFRA), 42 U.S.C. § 2000bb-1.[181]

The court stated that the government had not exceeded its power because RFRA only bars the government from placing a "substantial burden" on a person's exercise of religion if there is no "compelling governmental interest." Further, the

---

[175] Treasury Guidelines Working Group of Charitable Sector Organizations and Advisors, *Principles of International Charity* (March 2005), *available at* www.independentsector.org/uploads/Policy_PDFs/CharityPrinciples.pdf (last visited Nov. 9, 2010).

[176] *See* I.R.S. Publication 78, *Cumulative List of Charities* (July 8, 2010); I.R.S. Announcement 2003-74, 2003-48 I.R.B. 1171 (pursuant to I.R.C. § 501(p), certain organizations designated as supporting or engaging in terrorist activities or supporting terrorism are no longer recognized as tax exempt or eligible to receive deductible charitable contributions); I.R.C. § 501(p); *see also* Benevolence Int'l Found., Inc. v. Ashcroft, 200 F. Supp. 2d 935 (N.D. Ill. 2002); Global Relief Found., Inc. v. O'Neill, 315 F.3d 748 (7th Cir. 2002), *cert. denied*, 540 U.S. 1003 (2003).

[177] *Id.; see also* I.R.C. § 501(p); Jacqueline Benson, *Send Me Your Money: Controlling International Terrorism by Restricting Fundraising in the United States*, 21 Hous. J. Int'L L. 321 (1999).

[178] 333 F.3d 156 (D.C. Cir. 2003).

[179] *Id.*

[180] International Emergency Economic Powers Act, 50 U.S.C. § 1701, *et seq.*

[181] *Id.*

government must use the "least restrictive means" to further the interest.[182] The court found that no one in the Holy Land Foundation advanced the position that spreading terrorism is mandated by the religion of Islam. The district court's decision was upheld.[183]

[2] Gifts to Corporations Operating in Foreign Countries

The IRS generally requires that United States charitable 501(c)(3) organizations operating overseas or distributing aid in foreign countries maintain control over the distribution of funds and discretion over the use of the funds in order for contributions to be tax deductible.

In *Bilingual Montessori School of Paris v. Commissioner*,[184] the issue before the court was whether the School was an organization described in Section 170(c)(2)(A) so that contributions were deductible under Section 170(a). The school was a nonprofit corporation incorporated under the laws of Delaware. Its purpose (as stated in its Articles of Incorporation) was to operate a private school to teach children between the ages of two and six methods developed by Dr. Montessori. The methods included integrating physically and mentally handicapped children with normal children.[185]

Petitioner did not conduct any activities and did not have any employees in the United States. All officers and directors of the organization resided in France. All contributions were disbursed to cover expenses incurred in operating the school in Paris. Yet the court found that petitioner was not a sham but a legal entity existing pursuant to the laws of the State of Delaware.[186]

It stated that petitioner was exempt under IRC Section 501(c)(3) and that gifts and bequests were deductible under Sections 2055 and 2522. The court based its decision on the fact that the organization was organized in the United States, and that the incorporator and director of the school expended contributions received by it for costs incurred in operating the school.[187]

Revenue Ruling 63-252 takes a slightly different view of this issue,[188] stating that contributions to certain domestic charitable organizations are deductible if it can be shown that the gift is to, or for, the use of the domestic corporation and that the domestic corporation is not serving as an agent or channel for a foreign charitable

---

[182] *Id.; see also* 42 U.S.C. § 2000bb-1(a)(b).

[183] *Holy Land*, 333 F.3d at 167. For further cases, see Islamic American Relief Agency v. Gonzales, 477 F.3d 728 (D.C. Cir. 2007); Humanitarian Law Project v. U.S. Treasury, 578 F.3d 1133 (9th Cir. 2009); Kindhearts for Charitable Humanitarian Development v. Geithner, 647 F. Supp. 2d 857 (N.D. Ohio 2009); People's Mojahedin Organization of Iran v. U.S. Dept. of State, 613 F.3d 220 (D.C. Cir. 2010); Al Haramain Islamic Foundation v. U.S. Dept. of Treasury, 585 F. Supp. 2d 1233 (D. Or. 2008); U.S. v. Mubayyid, 476 F. Supp. 2d 46, 47 (D. Mass. 2007).

[184] 75 T.C. 480 (1980).

[185] *Id.*

[186] *Id.*

[187] *Id.* at 181.

[188] 1963-2 C.B. 101; *see also* Harvey P. Dale, *Foreign Charities*, 48 TAX LAW. 657 (1995); Penina Kessler Lieber, *1601-2001: An Anniversary of Note*, 62 U. PITT. L. REV. 731 (2001).

organization. Further, the requirements of Section 170(c)(2)(A) would be nullified if contributions inevitably committed to a foreign organization were held deductible solely because in the course of transmittal they came to rest momentarily in a domestic organization.[189]

Charitable contributions that are made directly to foreign organizations are generally not tax deductible, unless permitted by a tax treaty. The United States currently has tax treaties with Canada, Mexico, and Israel. The treaties set forth limits for charitable giving to these countries.[190]

[3]   Private Foundation Grants to Foreign Grantees

In Revenue Procedure 92-94,[191] the IRS provides a procedure to assure that foundation grants to foreign grantees are treated as "qualifying distributions" under Section 4942 (foundation payout requirements) and are not treated as "taxable expenditures" under Section 4945. Although many foreign grantees do not have exempt classification rulings from the IRS, a foreign charity can comply with private foundation rules if it obtains an affidavit of the grantee or an opinion of counsel from the grantor or grantee certifying that the organization's operations and sources of support qualify it as a public charity. An affidavit meeting very specific requirements must be produced.[192]

In the United States, foreign governments and international organizations qualify for federal tax exemption under IRC Section 892. However, as stated above, donors cannot always receive a tax deduction for donations to organizations made to organizations outside the United States.[193]

---

[189] *Id.*

[190] I.R.S. Publication 526, *Charitable Contributions* (Rev. Dec. 2009).

[191] 1992-2 C.B. 507.

[192] *Id.; see also* Rev. Proc. 75-50, 1975-2 C.B. 587; *Italian Legislative Decree 460* (Italy reorganized the fiscal legal principles of nonprofit organizations in 1997, by creating ONLUS (Organizzazione non lucrative di utilita or Non-profit organization of social utility); the entities which qualify under this decree can accept donations from the state, individuals and corporations (with individuals and corporations allowed to claim tax deductions)).

[193] *Id.; see also* I.R.C. § 170(c)(2)(A).

Chapter 18

FUNDRAISING

§ 18.01 INTRODUCTION

By definition, IRC Section 501(c)(3) organizations, which qualify as public charities under Section 509(a) and Section 170(b)(1)(A)(vi), must solicit contributions from the general public to retain public charity status.[1] Cases concerning the charitable status of an organization are often decided based on the charity's efforts to raise money. Charities must raise money because the IRC requires that, among other things, they receive substantial support from the general public, or in some cases, more than a third of their support from gifts, grants, or contributions.[2] Charitable organizations depend on these charitable gifts for financial reasons. These funds are often a crucial part of their operating budget.

Because fundraising has become such an important part of a charity's existence, many organizations hire professional fundraisers or solicitors to assist them with these efforts.

Along with the growth in this area has come regulation. The concern has been that fundraising professionals take advantage of charities and donors by retaining too great a percentage of the funds that are collected and by obtaining too much control over the organization.[3]

§ 18.02 STATE INVOLVEMENT

Charitable giving is a more than $303 billion-a-year business.[4] With such large amounts of money involved, competition has increased and instances of misuse of charitable funds have become more frequent. Policing charitable solicitation is primarily a matter of state law, but when the state regulations of solicitations affects

---

[1] *See* I.R.C. § 509(a) *et seq.*; I.R.C. § 170(b)(1)(A)(vi).

[2] See § 19.05[A][6][b][iii] for further information on the facts and circumstances test.

[3] *See generally Fundraising: Rule Revised on Seeking Donations*, 9 City Law 73 (2003); Hans Famularo, *Cyberspace Charities: Fundraising Tax Issues for Nonprofit Organizations in an Internet World*, 22 Hastings Comm. & Ent. L.J. 301 (2000); Pamela M. Dubov, *Municipal Authority: Charitable Solicitations Regulation:* American Charities for Reasonable Fundraising Regulation v. Pinellas County, 32 F. Supp. 2d 1308 (M.D. Fla. 1998), 29 Stetson L. Rev. 906 (2000). And see Illinois *ex rel.* Madigan v. Telemarketing Associates, Inc., 538 U.S. 600, 624 (2003) where the court determined that "states may maintain fraud actions when fundraisers make false or misleading representations designed to deceive."

[4] *See* Holly Hall, *Charitable Giving Fell 3.2% Last Year, Report Finds*, Chron. Philanthropy (June 8, 2010); The Center on Philanthropy at Indiana University, *Giving USA 2010, The Annual Report on Philanthropy for the Year 2009, Executive Summary*, Giving Usa Foundation, *available at* www.pursuantmedia.com/givingusa/0510/.

free speech, federal constitutional issues arise.

A majority of states have developed elaborate registration and filing systems requiring charities and fundraising solicitors to register, file annual reports, and notify the state of any change in status.[5] Solicitation of donors provides a charity with an opportunity to not only raise funds, but also to communicate a message or provide education.[6] Attempts at regulation by the states have been challenged by charities, which argue that the regulation is unconstitutional and burdensome.[7]

State regulatory schemes usually have three common elements: (1) they require mandatory disclosure through state and local registration and licensing, making financial and operational information available to the public; (2) they make it unlawful for any fraudulent solicitation activities to be carried on by professional solicitors or anyone raising money on the organization's behalf; and (3) they require contractual provisions that control the cost of solicitation and administration so that the amount available for the charitable purpose is increased.[8]

The federal courts become involved when solicitation efforts cause the organization to violate one of the four tests for tax exemption, usually the operational test or the private inurement test. In *United Cancer Council Inc. v. Commissioner*,[9] the appeals court reviewed a decision of the Tax Court that upheld an IRS decision to revoke the tax exempt status of United Cancer Council (UCC). The revocation was based on a finding that the organization had breached the private inurement requirement of Section 501(c)(3). The issue before the appeals court was to determine if the Tax Court erred in finding that a part of United Cancer Council's net earnings inured to the benefit of a private shareholder or individual.[10]

The United Cancer Council was a charity that sought to encourage preventive and ameliorative approaches to cancer. It was once a part of the American Cancer Society but had become a splinter organization. The Council began as a very small organization (annual budget of $35,000) when it hired a professional fundraiser. The fundraising company, Watson & Hughey Company ("W & H"), fronted the cost of the fundraising effort and entered into a five-year contract with the charity. The contract gave W & H co-ownership over the prospective donor list, denied UCC the right to ever sell or lease the list, and gave W & H the right to use the list in any way it wished.[11]

---

[5] *See* Ellen Harris et al., N.Y.U. Program on Philanthropy and the Law, *Fundraising into the 1990's: State Regulation of Charitable Solicitation After Riley*, 24 U.S.F. L. REV. 571, 572 (1990); *see also* Loren Prescott, Jr., *Pennsylvania Charities, Tax Exemption, and the Institutions of Purely Public Charity Act*, 73 TEMP. L. REV. 951 (2000); American Charities for Reasonable Fundraising Regulation v. Pinellas County, 189 F. Supp. 2d 1319 (M.D. Fla. 2001); American Target Advertising, Inc. v. Giani, 199 F.3d 1241 (10th Cir. 2000).

[6] Harris, *supra* note 5; Prescott, Jr. *supra* note 5.

[7] Harris, *supra* note 5; Prescott, Jr. *supra* note 5.

[8] Karen S. Quandt, *The Regulation of Charitable Fundraising and Spending Activities*, 1975 WIS. L. REV. 1158, 1160.

[9] 165 F.3d 1173 (7th Cir. 1999).

[10] *Id.*

[11] *Id.*

As a result of the fundraising, UCC raised $28.8 million with $26.5 million owed to W & H. The balance ($2.3 million) was spent by UCC for services to cancer patients and on research.[12]

The term "any private shareholder or individual" in the inurement clause of Section 501(c)(3) has been interpreted to mean an insider of the charity.[13] It looks to the issue of control. The court found nothing to support the IRS's theory and the Tax Court's finding that W & H had seized control and had become an insider triggering the inurement provision. The court found "no diversion of charitable revenues to an insider here, nothing that smacks of self-dealing, disloyalty, breach of fiduciary obligation or other misconduct. . . ."[14] Therefore, the case was reversed and remanded, although the court did not address the private benefit issue, which it believed was the more relevant issue because that issue had not been preserved for appeal.

§ 18.03   CONSTITUTIONAL RESTRICTIONS

There are several cases that deal with the constitutional rights inherent in the solicitation of funds. An overview of these cases and their holdings follows.

In *Schaumburg v. Citizens for a Better Environment*,[15] the Village of Schaumberg enacted an ordinance that prohibited the door-to-door or on-street charitable solicitation by organizations not using at least 75 percent of their receipts for "charitable purposes."[16] The purposes defined excluded solicitation expenses, salaries, overhead, and other administrative expenses. Citizens for a Better Environment was denied a permit and challenged the ordinance on constitutional grounds. The United States Supreme Court held that the ordinance was unconstitutionally overbroad, in violation of the First and Fourteenth Amendments.[17]

The Court reviewed a series of cases that through the years have dealt with the issue of door-to-door solicitation.[18]

It stated that prior authorities "clearly establish that charitable appeals for funds, on the street or door to door, involve a variety of speech interests-communication of information, the dissemination and propagation of views and ideas, and the advocacy of causes that are within the protection of the First Amendment. Soliciting financial support is undoubtedly subject to reasonable regulation but the latter must be undertaken with due regard. . . ."[19]

---

[12] *Id.* at 1175.

[13] *Id.* at 1176.

[14] *Id.* at 1179.

[15] 444 U.S. 620 (1980).

[16] *Id.*

[17] *Id.*

[18] Schneider v. State, 308 U.S. 147 (1939); Cantwell v. Connecticut, 310 U.S. 296 (1940); Valentine v. Chrestensen, 316 U.S. 52 (1942); Jamison v. Texas, 318 U.S. 413 (1943); Murdock v. Pennsylvania, 319 U.S. 105 (1943); Thomas v. Collins, 323 U.S. 516 (1945); Breard v. Alexandria, 341 U.S. 622 (1951); Hynes v. Mayor of Oradell, 425 U.S. 610 (1976).

[19] *Schaumburg,* 444 U.S. at 632.

In *Riley v. National Federation of the Blind*,[20] the United States Supreme Court held that specific aspects of the North Carolina Charitable Solicitations Act unconstitutionally infringed upon freedom of speech. The Act governed the solicitation of charitable contributions by professional fund-raisers. The aspects of the Act found unconstitutional were: it defined the prima facie "reasonable fee" that a professional fundraiser could charge as a percentage of the gross revenues solicited; required professional fund-raisers to disclose to potential donors the gross percentage of revenues retained in prior solicitations; and required professional fundraisers to obtain a license before engaging in solicitation.[21]

The North Carolina Charitable Solicitation Act defined an "unreasonable" or "excessive fee" by a three-tiered schedule. A fee of up to 20 percent of the collected gross receipts was considered reasonable. If the fee was between 20 and 30 percent, the Act considered it unreasonable if the solicitation did not involve the dissemination of information, or advocate upon the issues that were to benefit from the solicitation. A fee exceeding 30 percent was considered unreasonable, unless the fundraiser could rebut the presumption by showing that the solicitation involved the dissemination of information and the charity could not raise money or disseminate this information without his or her assistance.[22]

The Court believed the three-tiered, percentage-based definition of "unreasonable" did not pass constitutional muster.[23] The Court considered the second requirement of disclosure to be content-based regulation of speech and, therefore, unconstitutional. It stated that mandating speech "that a speaker would not otherwise make necessarily alters the content of the speech."[24] The Court found that the regulation included in the Act, which required the licensing of fundraisers, could not stand. The Court stated that this power to require a license carries with it the power to "directly and substantially . . . affect the speech they utter."[25]

Although percentage limitations on fundraising costs have been deemed impermissible by the United States Supreme Court, courts continue to struggle with balancing the interests of the states to regulate charitable solicitation with the mandates of the Constitution. In *Telco Communications v. Carbaugh*,[26] the Fourth Circuit upheld a section of a Virginia solicitation statute requiring professional solicitors to disclose to the public that the previous year's financial statements were available. The court upheld this section as promoting the state's interest. In *Independent Charities of America v. Minnesota*,[27] the Eighth Circuit found no violation of free speech where the solicitation statute restricted participation in the state's employees annual fund drive to charities organized in the state.[28]

---

[20] 487 U.S. 781 (1988).

[21] *Id.* at 788.

[22] *Id.*

[23] *See Schaumburg*, 444 U.S. 620; Sec'y of State of Md. v. Joseph H. Munson Co., 467 U.S. 947 (1984).

[24] *Riley*, 487 U.S. at 795.

[25] *Id.* at 801.

[26] 885 F.2d 1225 (4th Cir. 1989).

[27] 82 F.3d 791 (8th Cir.), *cert. denied*, 519 U.S. 993 (1996).

[28] *Id.* at 801.

The United States Supreme Court again looked at these issues in *Watchtower Bible & Tract Society v. Village of Stratton*[29] and *Illinois ex rel. Madigan v. Telemarketing Associates.*[30] In *Watchtower,* the Court struck down a local ordinance that made it a misdemeanor for canvassers to promote any cause without first obtaining a permit. The Court held the regulation overbroad and a violation of the First Amendment.[31] In *Madigan,* the Court held that fraudulent charitable solicitation is unprotected speech, where a fundraiser misrepresented the percentage of money raised that would be used for charitable purposes.[32]

A different type of fundraising was questioned in *Young v. New York City Transit Authority,*[33] where the issue was whether "the prohibition of begging and panhandling in the New York City subway system violated the First Amendment."[34] The New York City regulations prohibited solicitations for any purposes except for certain non-commercial activities like "public speaking, distribution of written materials; solicitation for charitable, religious or political causes; and artistic performances including the acceptance of donations."[35] The United States Supreme Court held that this section of the statute did not violate the First Amendment, noting Judge Rehnquist's dissent in *Schaumburg,*[36] that "[N]othing in the United States constitution should prevent residents of a community from making the collective judgment that certain worthy charities may solicit . . . while at the same time insulating themselves against panhandlers, profiteers, and peddlers."[37]

Charities and fundraisers continue to be regulated by the states. Some states regulate more stringently than others in order to protect their citizens, although as the United States Supreme Court has noted, donors are generally aware that there are costs incurred relating to fundraising and they know that they are free to inquire about them at any time.[38] More than 30 states that require charities to register before beginning their fundraising have adopted a common form titled the "Uniform Registration Statement."[39]

---

[29] 536 U.S. 150 (2002).

[30] 538 U.S. 600 (2003).

[31] *Watchtower,* 536 U.S. at 169.

[32] *Madigan,* 538 U.S. at 623.

[33] 903 F.2d 146 (2d Cir.), *cert. denied,* 489 U.S. 984 (1990).

[34] *Id.* at 147.

[35] *Id.* (citing N.Y. COMP. CODES R. & REGS. tit. 21 § 1050.6(c)).

[36] *Schaumburg,* 444 U.S. at 644.

[37] *Id.*

[38] *Riley,* 487 U.S. at 799.

[39] Form developed by a partnership of the National Association of State Charities Officials, the National Association of Attorneys General and the Multi-State Filer Program.

§ 18.04　INTERNET SOLICITATION

Today, a large percentage of nonprofit organizations solicit funds over the Internet or provide information on their web pages about how to donate money to their charity.[40] The jurisdictional and constitutional issues are great and are being addressed by states and courts alike. To simplify compliance with charitable solicitation registration laws in the various states, the National Association of State Charity Officials (NASCO) and the National Association of Attorneys General have developed the Unified Registration Statement (URS), as discussed above.[41]

> When charities include a request for donations on their website, the request can be seen in any state by anyone who accesses the charities' websites, raising the question whether they might be considered to be soliciting residents of every state, and, thus, be required to register in every state.[42]

In response, after meeting with representatives of the charitable community, NASCO issued nonbinding Advisory Guidelines to its members, known as the Charleston Principles. These Principles state that out-of-state web sites should be required to register in a state only if they affirmatively target residents in that state.[43]

§ 18.05　PROPOSALS FOR REFORM

Because of the growth in this area and the inconsistent treatment of solicitations from state to state, some argue for the federalization of the oversight of fundraising practices.[44] Several bills have been introduced in Congress addressing contingent fee fundraising practices, though no bills have been enacted. The starting point for federal oversight has been the IRS requirement that exempt organizations list on their annual Form 990s the amount of professional fundraising fees paid to outside fundraisers. Yet Internet fundraising remains a state issue.[45] It remains to be seen whether there can ever be a complete federalized regulation of charitable fundraising.

---

[40] *See* Bruce R. McBrearty, *Are Nonprofit Fundraisers Ready for the Internet?*, 29 FUNDRAISING MGMT. 28 (Oct. 1998); *And see* Obermaier v. Kenneth Copeland Evangelistic Ass'n, Inc., 208 F. Supp. 2d 1288 (M.D. Fla. 2002) involving a Texas organization which frequently solicited donations through the internet from residents of Florida where the court found that the district court in Florida had jurisdiction.

[41] Suzanne Ross McDowell, *Exempt Organizations and the Internet*, REPRESENTING AND MANAGING TAX EXEMPT ORGANIZATIONS (2005).

[42] *Id.*

[43] See www.nasconet.org for further information on NASCO and their Advisory Guidelines (last accessed May 27, 2005).

[44] *See Developments in the Law: Nonprofit Corporations*, 105 HARV. L. REV. 1578 (1992).

[45] *See* Famularo, *supra* note 3.

Chapter 19

PRIVATE FOUNDATIONS

§ 19.01 INTRODUCTION

The law on private foundations comprises perhaps the most complicated part of the entire IRC.[1] Private foundations are a peculiar type of Section 501(c)(3) organization. Unlike the Section 501(c)(3) organizations covered in this book, such as religious, educational, or healthcare organizations, private foundations do not generally do any charity. What they do, mostly, is give away money to organizations that then do charity. Private foundations, then, are basically funding organizations.[2]

Unlike the Section 501(c)(3) organizations that actually perform charity, and as a result, attract a large contributor base that wants to support their charitable efforts, private foundations do not have large bases of public support. In most cases, private foundations owe their existence to one major donor, such as a philanthropist or a business corporation, who started the private foundation with one large endowment, and who may still have lines of control to the private foundation. Because private foundations are bona fide 501(c)(3) organizations, they may attract additional tax deductible gifts, but their major source of income is the investment income produced by their endowment. One private foundation, the Bill and Melinda Gates Foundation, funded by a gift of Microsoft stock, has an endowment in the tens of billions of dollars.[3]

In 1969, Congress, after some splashy public hearings detailing the abuses of charitable endowments narrowly controlled by one family or by one business corporation, wrote the law on private foundations.[4] Congress created two separate classes of Section 501(c)(3) organizations: those that were private foundations and those that were not. It then wrote a very special set of rules for private foundations into the IRC, to prevent the abuses that they had seen.[5]

After these restrictive rules for private foundations were imposed by the Tax Reform Act of 1969, creative accountants, lawyers, and tax-preparers found ways for wealthy people to use Section 509(a)(3) supporting organizations — which are

---

[1] *See* I.R.C. § 509.

[2] *See* Robert DeGaudenzi, *Tax-Exempt Public Charities: Increasing Accountability and Compliance*, 36 Cath. Law. 203, 215 (1995); Mark Rambler, *Best Supporting Actor: Refining the 509(A)(3)Type 3 Charitable Organization*, 51 Duke L.J. 1367, 1368 (2002).

[3] For further information on the Bill and Melinda Gates Foundation, visit www.gatesfoundation.org (last visited May 31, 2011).

[4] Tax Reform Act of 1969, Pub. L. No. 91-172, 83 Stat. 487 (1969).

[5] *Id.; see also* I.R.C. § 509.

nonprivate foundations, and so exempt from the private foundation restrictions — to continue the abuses that the 1969 Act was meant to stop. As a result, Congress in the Pension Protection Act of 2006[6] split 509(a)(3) organizations into two types: those that were functionally integrated with the supported public charity and those that were not. It then went on to impose additional requirements on these 509(a)(3) non-functionally integrated supporting organizations.

§ 19.02 DEFINING PRIVATE FOUNDATIONS

Sections 509(a)(1) through (4) were inserted into the IRC to define private foundations. Rather than define these organizations directly, however, these sections specify what types of Section 501(c)(3) organizations are *not* private foundations.

Section 509(a)(1) organizations, sometime referred to as the traditional public charities, are comprised of churches and their integrated auxiliaries, formal educational organizations, hospitals and medical research organizations, organizations that support state universities, units of government, and charitable organizations with a broad base of public support, determined by an income test.[7]

Section 509(a)(2) organizations are referred to as "gross receipts" or "service provider" organizations. They must receive more than one-third of their support from gifts, grants, contributions, membership fees and "gross receipts" from admissions, sales of goods or services, where the fee generating activity is related to the performance of the organization's exempt purposes, and can receive no more than one-third of their support from gross investment income and net unrelated business income. Organizations in this group include, for example, museums or symphony orchestras that charge admission.[8]

Section 509(a)(3) organizations are "supporting" organizations. These organizations do not require public support, but they must support other Section 501(c)(3) organizations, and they must do so through some formal relationship with the supported charity. This requires that they be operated, supervised, or controlled by, or that they be supervised or controlled in connection with, or that they be operated in connection with, the supported organization. In practical terms, this means that, in addition to the formal relationship, the supporting organization either turns its income over to the supported organization or that it runs programs that benefit the supported organization.[9]

Section 509(a)(4) organizations test for public safety. This is a specialized category, which is also listed in the language of Section 501(c)(3).[10]

---

[6] Pub. L. No. 109-280, 120 Stat. 780 (2006).

[7] § 509(a)(1) organizations are actually defined in I.R.C. § 170(b)(1)(A)(i)-(vi), the section of the I.R.C. which identifies those charities capable of receiving tax deductible gifts. *See also* 26 C.F.R. § 1.509(a)-2.

[8] *See* I.R.C. § 509(a)(2); 26 C.F.R. § 1.509(a)-3.

[9] *See* I.R.C. § 509(a)(3); 26 C.F.R. § 1.509(a)-4.

[10] *See* I.R.C. § 509(a)(4).

Any Section 501(c)(3) organization that does not fit into one of the above four categories is a "private foundation," and is subject to the restrictive rules that govern private foundations. Organizations that are listed in Sections 509(a)(1), 509(a)(2), 509(a)(3) and 509(a)(4) are technically "non-private foundations." This is how they are identified in the IRC, but they are almost never called that. Section 501(c)(3) organizations that are not private foundations are generally referred to as "public charities."[11]

§ 19.03 AVOIDING PRIVATE FOUNDATION STATUS

Section 501(c)(3) organizations prefer not to be characterized as "private foundations" if possible, but the IRC presumes that all 501(c)(3) organizations are private foundations unless the organization can prove otherwise.[12] Proving otherwise means demonstrating to the IRS that the organization fits into one of the four types of organizations described in Section 509(a)(1)-(4), and is therefore a non-private foundation, or a public charity.

There are significant advantages to being a public charity instead of a private foundation. The main reason is that private foundations are subject to the provisions of IRC Sections 4940–4945, while public charities are not. Under these provisions, private foundations:

- Must pay a two percent excise tax on their net investment income (IRC Section 4940).

- Must not engage in self-dealing (IRC Section 4941).

- Must give away annually five percent of their net investment assets (IRC Section 4942).

- Must not have excess business holdings in any business enterprise (IRC Section 4943).

- Must not make any jeopardizing investments (IRC Section 4944).

- Must not make any expenditures for political activities or grants prohibited (IRC Section 4945).

Additionally, private foundations are subject to more burdensome reporting requirements than public charities. The Form 990-PF required of private foundations is more detailed and complex than the Form 990 or 990-EZ required of public charities.[13] Another major advantage for public charities over private foundations lies in their ability to attract tax deductible gifts. While public charities are "50 percent charities," private foundations are only "30 percent charities."[14] This means that an individual can deduct up to 50 percent of adjusted gross income as gifts to

---

[11] This can be very confusing for those just learning about the tax-exempt sector. This concept is developed further in § 19.05.

[12] I.R.C. § 509(a); *see also* Change-All Souls Hous. Corp. v. United States, 671 F.2d 463, 465 (Ct. Cl. 1982).

[13] See § 20.01 *et seq.* for further information on the filing requirements for tax exempt organizations.

[14] I.R.C. § 170(b)(1)(A), (B)(i).

a public charity, but can only deduct up to 30 percent of adjusted gross income for gifts to private foundations. In donating capital gains property to a public charity, a donor can take a charitable deduction for the fair market value of the gift,[15] but gifts of capital gains property to a private foundation are normally at basis.[16]

§ 19.04 RULES FOR PRIVATE FOUNDATIONS

[A] The Federal Excise Tax — IRC Section 4940

Although they qualify as tax exempt 501(c)(3) organizations, and therefore do not pay federal income taxes, private foundations pay something that is an awful lot like an income tax. The tax is not called an income tax, however, it is called an "excise tax." The IRS explains the difference by saying that it is a tax on the investment activity of private foundations. But the fact of the matter is that this "excise tax" taxes the net investment income of the private foundation.

Net investment income is the amount by which the sum of gross investment income and capital gain net income exceed allowable deductions.[17] Gross investment income includes dividends, rents, royalties, and payments with respect to loans of securities and similar sources, but not tax exempt bond interest.[18] It also includes any unrelated business income.[19] Capital gain net income is the excess of capital gains over losses[20] from the disposition of property used to produce dividends, rents, royalties, or property used to produce unrelated business income, unless the capital gain was already taxed as unrelated business income.[21] Allowable deductions are all the ordinary and necessary expenses paid for the production or collection of gross investment income or for the management, conservation, or maintenance of income-producing property.[22] The private foundation can allocate a percentage of its overall administrative expenses as a deduction to the extent those administrative activities were attributable to investment income.[23]

This excise tax is currently a two percent tax on net investment income. Some private foundations qualify for a one percent rate if their annual payout amounts are high enough.[24]

---

[15] I.R.C. § 170(e).

[16] I.R.C. § 170(e)(1)(B)(ii). *But see* I.R.C. § 170(e)(5) (creating an exception for a gift of "qualified appreciated stock").

[17] I.R.C. § 4940(c)(1).

[18] I.R.C. § 4940(c)(2).

[19] I.R.C. § 4940(c)(5).

[20] Capital losses can be subtracted from capital gains for the applicable tax year, but they cannot be deducted from gross investment income, nor can they be carried over. I.R.C. § 4940(c)(4)(C).

[21] I.R.C. § 4940(c)(4)(A); *see* Greenacre Found. v. United States, 762 F.2d 965 (Fed. Cir. 1985) (sale of income-producing property shortly after its receipt as a gift was considered capital gain net income).

[22] I.R.C. § 4940(c)(3).

[23] 26 C.F.R. § 53.4940-1(e).

[24] I.R.C. § 4940(e)(2)(A).

In *Zemurray Foundation v. United States*,[25] a private foundation owned a one-half interest in timberland that it had never used to produce any income. When the foundation sold this half-interest, the IRS determined that the gain from the sale was subject to the excise tax of Section 4940 as a form of capital gains net income. While the statute levied the tax on the sale or other disposition of property used for the production of interest, dividends, rents, and royalties,[26] the Regulations added a fifth category, namely property that produces capital gains through appreciation.[27] At the district court level, the Regulation was found to be overbroad and invalid.[28] The district court held that the word "used" in Section 4940 had to be interpreted in its ordinary sense to mean "actually used," and not "susceptible to use" as the IRS argued.[29]

On appeal, the Fifth Circuit overturned the district court's interpretation of the word "used."[30] It found that the tax was proper as long as the property sold was "susceptible of use" to produce capital gains net income. This decision appeared to approve the IRS's non-statutory fifth category of taxable income, that is, the sale of property that produces capital gains through appreciation. It sent the case back to the district court for findings of fact consistent with this interpretation.[31] On remand, the district court found that the timberland was not capable of producing interest, dividends, rents, or royalties.[32] On the fifth category, the district court said that "the Fifth Circuit clearly meant to uphold the validity of the fifth category only to the extent that the category encompasses property includable in one or more of the first four categories."[33] Because the property did not fall into one of these four categories, the district court found the sale to be non-taxable under Section 4940.[34]

On appeal, the Fifth Circuit ate its unfortunate words that "used" means "susceptible of use."[35] It had never meant to broaden the reach of the statute, it said. What it really meant to say was that the statute taxed the sale of property that "generally produces" interest, dividends, rents, or royalties, which, of course, is a completely different standard from "susceptible of use" to produce those kinds of income. On this basis, it affirmed the district court and held the Regulation that added the fifth category to be invalid.[36]

---

[25] 687 F.2d 97 (5th Cir. 1982).

[26] I.R.C. § 4940(c)(4)(A).

[27] 26 C.F.R. § 53.4940-1(f)(1).

[28] Zemurray Found. v. United States, 509 F. Supp. 976 (E.D. La. 1981), *rev'd and remanded*, 687 F.2d 97 (1982).

[29] *Id.* at 979–80.

[30] *Zemurray Found.*, 687 F.2d at 102.

[31] *Id.*

[32] Zemurray Found. v. United States, 84-1 U.S. Tax Cas. (CCH) P9246 (E.D. La. 1983), *aff'd*, 755 F.2d 404 (5th Cir. 1985).

[33] *Id.* at 9.

[34] *Id.*

[35] Zemurray Found. v. United States, 755 F.2d 404 (5th Cir. 1985).

[36] *Id.*

[B] Tax on Self-Dealing — IRC Section 4941

To understand the tax on self-dealing by a private foundation, there must first be an understanding of the concept of a "disqualified person." By definition, self-dealing refers to certain prohibited transactions between a private foundation and a disqualified person.[37]

IRC Section 4946 defines "disqualified persons" as the directors, officers, and trustees of the private foundation, the manager or executive director of the private foundation,[38] substantial contributors to the private foundation, and all of their parents, spouses, children, children's spouses, grandchildren, and grandchildren's spouses. A substantial contributor is someone who has given more than $5,000 in the applicable tax year, provided that the gift exceeds two percent of total gifts that year; or a person who owns more than a 20 percent interest in a business that is a substantial contributor.[39] A corporation or business entity that is controlled (at least a 35 percent ownership interest) by a disqualified person or a group of disqualified persons is also, itself, a disqualified person.[40]

There are several types of transactions that a private foundation may not engage in with a disqualified person. First, a private foundation may not enter into a sale or exchange, or the leasing of property with a disqualified person.[41] Sales, exchanges, and leases between a private foundation and a disqualified person are not permitted, even at fair market value, and even if the private foundation is getting a bargain. The transfer of gift property, for which the private foundation does not pay the disqualified person, but on which it assumes an indebtedness, is also prohibited.[42] The sale by a private foundation of stock in a corporation that is a disqualified person is permissible in a corporate liquidation, merger, redemption of stock, recapitalization or similar situation, as long as the private foundation is getting the same terms as others similarly situated and those terms are at market or above.[43]

Second, a private foundation may not lend money or other extension of credit[44] to a disqualified person. Loans between private foundations and disqualified persons are not permitted, except that a disqualified person may make an interest-free loan to the private foundation, as long as the loan is used exclusively for the private foundation's exempt purposes.[45]

---

[37] I.R.C. § 4941.

[38] Once officers, directors or managers resign, they are no longer disqualified persons, unless, in a facts and circumstances analysis, they maintain some level of control in the organization. Rev. Rul. 76-448, 1976 -2 C.B. 368; *see also* I.R.S. Priv. Ltr. Rul. 8711001 (Oct. 31, 1986).

[39] *See* I.R.C. § 4940(d)(3)(C) ("substantial contributor" defined).

[40] *See* I.R.C. § 4946(a) ("disqualified person" defined).

[41] I.R.C. § 4941(d)(1)(A).

[42] If the indebtedness was placed on the property more than ten years before the transfer, the transfer without consideration, but subject to the indebtedness, is not prohibited. I.R.C. § 4941(d)(2)(A).

[43] I.R.C. § 4941(d)(2)(F).

[44] I.R.C. § 4941(d)(1)(B).

[45] I.R.C. § 4941(d)(1)(B), (2)(B).

Third, the private foundation may not furnish goods, services, or facilities to a disqualified person.[46] The furnishing of goods, services, or facilities between private foundations and disqualified persons are not permitted, except that the disqualified person may supply goods, services, or facilities to the private foundation without charge, as long as the goods, services, or facilities are used exclusively by the private foundation for its exempt purposes.[47] When the private foundation normally furnishes goods, services, or facilities to the general public, it may also furnish them to a disqualified person on similar, but not discounted, terms.[48]

Fourth, the private foundation may not make payments of compensation[49] to a disqualified person. Actually, some payments of compensation are permissible. After all, the private foundation has to pay its manager, even though the manager is a disqualified person. But that payment can only be for services rendered to the private foundation that are reasonable and necessary for carrying out the private foundation's exempt purposes; and it cannot be excessive, which means it should be negotiated at arm's length by the foundation's board and the manager and must be at market rates.[50] Obviously, payments to parties who are not working for the foundation are not permitted. Although they were not mentioned in the definition of who was a "disqualified person," government officials are disqualified from receiving any compensation from a private foundation.[51] A government official is anyone from the President of the United States down to congressional staffers who are paid $15,000 or more annually, to local officials who are paid at least $20,000 annually, to the personal assistants or secretaries of any of the above.[52] There are some exceptions to this very broad prohibition for certain types of prizes, awards, scholarships, retirement benefits, travel reimbursement, and gifts of nominal value.[53] And payments for services or grants that become effective after government service are allowable, as long as they were not arranged with the public official more than 90 days before government service ended.[54]

Fifth, a private foundation may not transfer income or assets to, or for use by or for the benefit of, a disqualified person.[55] This last type of "self-dealing" was Congress's way of closing the circle. Any type of self-dealing that was not covered in the specific enumerations above was meant to be covered by this very general prohibition.[56] The wide net cast by this prohibition caught a private foundation that

---

[46] I.R.C. § 4941(d)(1)(C).

[47] I.R.C. § 4941(d)(1)(C), (2)(C).

[48] I.R.C. § 4941(d)(2)(D).

[49] I.R.C. § 4941(d)(1)(D).

[50] I.R.C. § 4941(d)(1)(D), (2)(E).

[51] I.R.C. § 4941(d)(1)(F).

[52] I.R.C. § 4946(c).

[53] I.R.C. § 4941(d)(2)(G); 26 C.F.R. § 53.4941(d)-3(e).

[54] 26 C.F.R. § 53.4941(d)-3(e)(8).

[55] I.R.C. § 4941(d)(1)(E).

[56] *Id.*

placed some paintings that it owned in the home of a major contributor, who, of course, was a disqualified person.[57]

The penalty tax on self-dealing is 10 percent of the value of the transaction on the self-dealer (i.e., the disqualified person)[58] and five percent, but not more than $20,000 on the foundation manager who knowingly participated in the self-dealing transaction.[59] If the self-dealing is not corrected within the taxable period, then additional taxes of 200 percent of the value of the transaction can be imposed on the self-dealer and 50 percent on the participating foundation manager, again with a limit of $20,000.[60]

The case of *Estate of Bernard J. Reis v. Commissioner*[61] involved the estate of one of the executors of the estate of the famous American artist, Mark Rothko. The Rothko estate benefited, in part, a private foundation — the Mark Rothko Foundation — created by the artist three years before his death in 1970. Besides being an executor of the Rothko estate, Reis was also an officer and employee of the Marlborough Gallery, the art gallery that was given exclusive sales rights over Rothko's works in a contract signed by Rothko's executors, including Reis. An audit of the Rothko Foundation determined that Reis was liable for the Section 4941 self-dealing excise tax. Reis's estate fought these taxes on three grounds: (1) the unconstitutional vagueness of 4941(d)(1)(E); the assets of the estate were separate from the assets of the Foundation and the self-dealing rules do not apply to them; and (3) no self-dealing tax should apply to Reis because any benefit to him was, at best, non-pecuniary.[62] As to the vagueness-unconstitutionality argument, the court pointed to a long line of cases that had upheld the constitutionality of the challenged section of 4941. On the taxpayer's argument that the assets of the Rothko estate were separate from the assets of the Rothko Foundation, the court pointed to the Treasury Regulations that clearly state that the interest of a private foundation in the property of an estate, as a beneficiary thereof, will be treated as an asset of the Foundation under IRC §4941(d)(1)(E). On the argument that Reis had received no pecuniary benefits from the alleged self-dealing, the court said that the statute did not require pecuniary benefits; it did, however, require significant, as opposed to insignificant or tenuous benefits. Because this was on a motion for summary judgment, the level of benefit had to be established at trial.

In *Madden v. Commissioner*,[63] a private foundation controlled by the Madden family (father, mother, and daughter) operated an outdoor sculpture museum. The private foundation received and paid for janitorial services that were performed by a company controlled by the father, John Madden, one of the foundation's managers. Because a foundation manager, who was a disqualified person, controlled the janitorial company, the janitorial company was also a disqualified

---

[57]   Rev. Rul. 74-600, 1974-2 C.B. 385.

[58]   I.R.C. § 4941(a)(1).

[59]   I.R.C. § 4941(a)(2).

[60]   I.R.C. § 4491(b)(1), (b)(2), (c)(2).

[61]   87 T.C. 1016 (1986).

[62]   *Id.* at 1019.

[63]   74 T.C.M. (CCH) 440 (1997).

person. The IRS levied the IRC Section 4941 self-dealing tax on the disqualified persons for this transaction and also levied a self-dealing tax on all three foundation managers. The private foundation and its managers argued that this transaction was covered by the exception in Section 4941(d)(2)(E), which allowed a private foundation to pay reasonable compensation to a disqualified person for personal services necessary to carrying out its exempt purposes. Interpreting this exception narrowly, the Tax Court found that janitorial services did not qualify as personal services. The personal services exception, the court thought, was limited to professional and managerial services. The self-dealing tax on the disqualified persons was upheld.[64]

Relying on the tax Regulations' requirements for knowing participation,[65] the Tax Court found that all three foundation managers knew of these payments, knew that the furnishing of services between a private foundation and a disqualified person was self-dealing, and made the payments willfully. As a result, the court held that the self-dealing tax on all three foundation managers was also proper.[66]

There were some additional payments made by the private foundation for work that was done to artwork owned by John Madden. The Tax Court upheld the self-dealing tax on him, which he conceded. The court did not uphold the self-dealing tax on the other foundation's managers for these payments, however, because they did not have the requisite knowledge and they corrected the transaction when they discovered it. On a third payment by the foundation to satisfy an obligation of another company controlled by John Madden, the Tax Court found the facts on this issue too murky to assess against the foundation managers.[67]

In *Deluxe Check Printers v. United States*,[68] a private foundation had received 75,000 shares in a business corporation that was also a substantial contributor to the foundation, and therefore a "disqualified person" as to the foundation. Over a period of two years, the foundation redeemed these shares for the mean between the over-the-counter bid and asked prices as of the close of the previous day's business. The IRS taxed these redemptions as acts of self-dealing under IRC Section 4941(d)(1)(A). The foundation pled the exception in IRC Section 4941(d)(2)(F), which excludes from self-dealing certain securities transactions between private foundations and disqualified person corporations if "all of the securities of the same class as that held by the foundation are subject to the same terms and such terms provide for receipt by the foundation of no less than market value."[69]

Because the redemption plan pursuant to which the private foundation had redeemed its shares excluded by its terms any redemption of shares by corporate officers and directors, the Court of Claims held that not all shares were subject to

---

[64] *Id.*

[65] *Id.; see also* 26 C.F.R. § 53.4941(a)-1(b)(3).

[66] *Madden*, 74 T.C.M. (CCH) 440.

[67] *Id.*

[68] 14 Cl. Ct. 782 (1988), *aff'd in part, rev'd in part sub nom.*, Deluxe Corp. v. United States, 885 F.2d 848 (Fed. Cir. 1989).

[69] *Deluxe Corp.*, 885 F.2d at 850.

the same terms, and that therefore the exception did not apply, and the private foundation's redemption of shares was taxable as self-dealing.[70]

The Federal Circuit Court decided otherwise. It found that the reason for the redemption restriction on the shares of officers and directors was to deal with insider trading concerns. It found that the redemption restriction was not on the shares as shares, but only on them as the property of officers and directors, and applied only while they were officers and directors. As a result, all shares were subject to the same redemption terms.[71]

This was also the reading that the circuit court (and the Court of Claims) gave to the Regulation's requirement that the corporation had to make a bona fide offer on a uniform basis to all shareholders.[72] The restriction on officers' and directors' redemption did not violate this Regulation either. Finally, the circuit court reversed the Court of Claims' finding that the corporation had not demonstrated that the redemption program paid the private foundation "no less than fair market value" as the statute required. The Circuit found the program's pricing method to be reasonable and in accord with law.[73]

[C]   Tax on Failure to Distribute Income — IRC Section 4942

In order to prevent private foundations from hoarding their charitable assets, Congress has decreed that they must make an annual distribution of what the IRS calls the "distributable amount."[74] Failure to distribute the entire "distributable amount" will result in an excise tax of 30 percent of the undistributed amount to the foundation, and a 100 percent confiscatory tax if the foundation fails to correct it (i.e., make the required distribution) by the end of the taxable period.[75] The taxable period is the close of the following tax year.[76]

The distributable amount is determined by looking at the foundation's net investment assets. Net investment assets are those assets held to produce income; in other words, the foundation's endowment, such as stocks, bonds, income-producing real estate, and not its computers, office equipment, or office building.[77] The private foundation must give away to other charities, annually, "approximately" five percent of these net investment assets, which is the "distributable amount."[78]

---

[70] *Deluxe Check Printers*, 14 Cl. Ct. at 792.

[71] *Deluxe Corp.*, 885 F.2d, at 852–53.

[72] 26 C.F.R. § 53.4941(d)-3(d)(1).

[73] *Deluxe Corp.*, 885 F.2d at 853.

[74] I.R.C. § 4942(d). Just to make things more confusing, the IRC further defines the "distributable amount" in I.R.C. § 4942(e) as the "minimum investment return." They are basically the same thing.

[75] I.R.C. § 4942(a), (b).

[76] I.R.C. § 4942(a).

[77] Also excluded as related-function assets are artworks loaned to schools and museums, an island held as a conservation site, and the assets of a business staffed almost entirely by volunteers. *See* Rev. Rul. 75-207, 1975-1 C.B. 361, Rev. Rul. 76-85, 1976-1 C.B. 357.

[78] I.R.C. § 4942(a).

The term "approximately" is used because the IRS allows the foundation to count towards this five percent not just actual grants to other charities,[79] but also the two percent excise tax on private foundations;[80] acquisition indebtedness on investment assets;[81] grant administrative expenses;[82] direct charitable activities (most private foundations will do little of this);[83] assets acquired to carry out the foundation's exempt purposes;[84] set-asides for special projects approved by the IRS;[85] and program-related investments.[86] Against these deductions, the private foundation must add back in any money it gets from repayments of previous distributions,[87] any money it gets from the sale or other disposition of assets previously treated as qualifying distributions,[88] and any money it had set aside for an approved project that it did not use for the project.[89] So the five percent must be approximated.

The amount distributed by a private foundation must be "qualifying distributions."[90] A qualifying distribution is a distribution to a public charity, governmental unit, or to a private operating foundation to accomplish a religious, charitable, educational, scientific, literary, or other public charitable purpose. Distributions to a non-operating private foundation can also qualify if the granting foundation maintains expenditure responsibility (the right to obtain records or other sufficient evidence that the grant has been used for charitable purposes).[91] The recipient of a qualified distribution cannot be an organization controlled directly or indirectly by the foundation itself or by a disqualified person.[92] Non-qualifying distributions do not count toward the annual distribution amount.[93]

---

[79] I.R.C. § 4942(g)(3).

[80] I.R.C. § 4942(d)(2).

[81] I.R.C. § 4942(e)(1)(B).

[82] I.R.C. § 4942(g)(1)(A), (4).

[83] I.R.C. § 4942(g)(1)(A).

[84] I.R.C. § 4942(g)(1)(B).

[85] I.R.C. § 4942(g)(2). The set-aside can simply be a book-keeping entry. Rev. Rul. 78-148, 1978-1 C.B. 380. A set-aside that allowed a private foundation to control the funds during a three year building project, and earn income therefrom was not allowed. Rev. Rul. 79-319, 1979-2 C.B. 388. A set-aside to cover a four year park conversion project, however, was permitted. *See* Rev. Rul. 74-450, 1974-2 C.B. 388.

[86] I.R.C. § 4942(g)(1)(B), (j)(4); *see* I.R.S. Priv. Ltr. Rul. 9340002 (Oct. 8, 1993) (purchase and operation of a local for-profit hotel corporation by a private foundation, whose purpose was to preserve architectural heritage and assist community development, was found not to be program related).

[87] I.R.C. § 4942(f)(2)(C)(i).

[88] I.R.C. § 4942(f)(2)(C)(ii).

[89] I.R.C. § 4942(f)(2)(C)(iii).

[90] I.R.C. § 4942(g).

[91] I.R.C. § 4942(g)(3).

[92] I.R.C. § 4942(g)(1)(a).

[93] For an interesting state court case on this issue see *In re* Estate of John A. Hermann, 312 A.2d 16 (Pa. 1973).

[B]   Tax on Excess Business Holdings — IRC Section 4943

Congress did not want private foundations exercising a controlling interest in business enterprises, especially business enterprises that were also owned by persons associated with the foundation, because the risk was too high that the foundation's business interests would be exercised, not in favor of the foundation, but for the interests of these other parties. As a result, private foundations are assessed a tax on any controlling interest they own in a business enterprise that does not perform an exempt function of the foundation.[94]

In the language of the IRC, a controlling interest is referred to as an "excess business holding."[95] To determine "excess business holdings," the ownership interests of any disqualified persons must be added together with the ownership interest of the private foundation.[96] Private foundations, adding in the ownership interests of any disqualified persons, who own more than a 20 percent interest in a business enterprise are subject to the excess business holdings tax.[97] In situations where effective control of the business enterprise rests in hands other than those of disqualified persons, the amount of the business holdings of the private foundation and disqualified persons can rise to 35 percent without incurring the excess business holdings tax.[98]

In Revenue Ruling 81-111,[99] the IRS posits two situations. In the first, the private foundation and a disqualified person together own 35 percent of the voting stock of Corporation N, but another person, unrelated to the private foundation, owns the remaining 65 percent. Obviously, this second person has "effective control" of the corporation, and the 35 percent owned by the private foundation and the disqualified person is not an "excess business holding." In the second situation, the private foundation and a disqualified person together own 35 percent of the voting stock of Corporation M, but the ownership of the remaining 65 percent of voting shares is scattered, in small amounts, among numerous parties, none of whom is in a position to exercise control of the corporation. In this second situation, the private foundation and the disqualified person's 35 percent ownership is an "excess business holding." In this second situation, since there is no other party in effective control of the corporation, the interests of the private foundation and any disqualified persons cannot exceed the 20 percent limitation.[100]

Once the private foundation knows or has reason to know of the event that has caused it to have an excess business holding, the private foundation has 90 days to

---

[94] I.R.C. § 4943(a)(1), (d)(3)(A); I.R.S. Priv. Ltr. Rul. 9340002 (Oct. 8, 1993) (private foundation's ownership of 100 percent of the stock in a for-profit hotel corporation, since it was not program related, was an excess business holding).

[95] I.R.C. § 4943(c)(1).

[96] I.R.C. § 4943(c)(2)(A)(ii).

[97] I.R.C. § 4943(c)(2)(A).

[98] I.R.C. § 4943(c)(2)(B).

[99] 1981-1 C.B. 509.

[100] *Id.*

dispose of it before the penalty tax accrues.[101] The tax on excess business holdings is 10 percent of the value of the holdings, assessed for the tax year in which it occurred.[102] There is a punitive 200 percent tax if the private foundation does not divest the excess holdings within the taxable period.[103]

There are some types of business enterprise ownership that are not subject to the excess business holdings tax. It also does not apply to a trade or business where at least 95 percent of the income is from passive sources.[104] A passive income source is dividends, interest, royalties, rents, or capital gains income.[105]

As mentioned above, it also does not apply to business enterprises that are "functionally related" to the private foundation.[106] A functionally related business is one that does not qualify as an unrelated trade or business as defined in Section 513 on the unrelated business activities of tax exempt organizations.[107] Finally, it does not apply to program-related investments.[108]

Because they are capable of receiving tax deductible gifts and bequests, it can happen that a private foundation receives donations of voting stock or other forms of ownership in a business enterprise. The IRC Sections on excess business holdings makes an allowance for this. Anytime a private foundation finds itself in an excess business holdings situation that was not caused by its, or a disqualified person's, purchase of the ownership interest, it has up to five years to reduce its holdings before it is subject to the tax.[109] In the case of an exceptionally large gift, where the private foundation has made diligent efforts to sell, but could not except at prices substantially below market, this period is extendable for an additional five years.[110]

[E]   Tax on Jeopardizing Investments — IRC Section 4944

Because the ability of private foundations to fund charitable activities depends on the soundness of the investments it makes with its endowment, Congress wished to discourage what it considered to be risky investments by private foundations. It has done so by placing a tax on what it called "jeopardizing investments" by private foundations.[111]

A jeopardizing investment is one in which the foundation managers "failed to exercise ordinary business care and prudence, under the facts and circumstances

---

[101]   26 C.F.R. § 53.4943-2(a)(1)(ii) (except in gift or bequest situations, for which, see below).

[102]   I.R.C. § 4943(a)(1), (2).

[103]   I.R.C. § 4943(b).

[104]   I.R.C. § 4943(d)(3)(B).

[105]   I.R.C. § 512(b)(1), (2), (3), (5).

[106]   I.R.C. § 4943(d)(3)(A).

[107]   I.R.C. § 4942(j)(4).

[108]   26 C.F.R. § 53.4943-10(b).

[109]   I.R.C. § 4943(c)(6).

[110]   I.R.C. § 4943(c)(7).

[111]   I.R.C. § 4944.

prevailing at the time of making the investment, in providing for the long- and short-term financial needs of the foundation to carry out its exempt purposes."[112]

The IRS does not treat any category of investment as per se being a jeopardizing investment. The Regulations do give examples, however, of the type of investment to which the IRS will give heightened scrutiny. These are "[t]rading in securities on margin, trading in commodity futures, investments in working interests in oil and gas wells, the purchase of 'puts' and 'calls,' and 'straddles,' the purchase of warrants, and selling short."[113] In addition to this list, investment in junk bonds, risk arbitrage, hedge funds, derivatives, distressed real estate, and international equities in third-world countries would, in most instances, qualify as the type of high-risk investments that would jeopardize a private foundation's endowment. Loans by a private foundation to third parties at below market rates and for a lengthy period of time are jeopardizing investments.[114]

Investments by private foundations in program-related activities are not considered jeopardizing investments.[115] A program-related investment is an investment whose primary purpose is to accomplish religious, charitable, scientific, literary, or educational purposes, or to foster national or international sports competitions or for the prevention of cruelty to children or animals;[116] and no significant purpose of which is the production of income, the appreciation of property, substantial lobbying, or any electioneering.[117] An investment is considered to be made for these charitable purposes if "it significantly furthers the accomplishment of the private foundation's exempt activities and if the investment would not have been made but for such relationship between the investment and the accomplishment of the foundation's exempt activities."[118] In the examples of what a program-related investment might be, the Regulations posit a private foundation, dedicated to the relief of the poor and distressed, which makes below-market loans to minority businesses to keep them in business.[119] Although this is a risky investment, because it is program-related it does not fall into the category of "jeopardizing investments."[120]

In Revenue Ruling 80-133,[121] a private foundation paid the premiums for a whole life insurance policy on a donor. The private foundation was the owner of the policy. Given the age of the insured donor and the cost of premiums, there was no way the eventual payout would be greater than the sum of the premiums. Because the amount of the premiums paid was in excess of any recoverable amount, the

---

[112] 26 C.F.R. § 53.4944-1(a)(2)(i).

[113] *Id.*

[114] I.R.S. Priv. Ltr. Rul. 8711001 (Oct. 31, 1986).

[115] 26 C.F.R. § 53.4944-3(a)(1).

[116] 26 C.F.R. § 53.4944-3(a)(1)(i). This is the list from I.R.C. § 170(c)(2)(B), which is the same list as I.R.C. § 501(c)(3), minus "testing for public safety" organizations.

[117] 26 C.F.R. § 53.4944-3(a)(1)(ii), (iii).

[118] 26 C.F.R. § 53.4944-3(a)(2)(i).

[119] 26 C.F.R. § 53.4944-3(b)(1).

[120] 26 C.F.R. § 53.4944-3(a)(1).

[121] 1980-1 C.B. 258.

purchase of the insurance policy and the payment of premiums was considered a jeopardizing investment by the IRS.[122]

The first tier of taxes on jeopardizing investments is 10 percent of the amount of the investment, payable by the private foundation and a similar 10 percent, but not more than $10,000, payable by the foundation managers who participated in the decision to make the investment.[123] If there is a failure to exit the investment within the taxable period, there is a second tier tax on the private foundation of 25 percent of the amount of the investment, and, if the foundation manager refuses to agree to make the correction, the $10,000 limit on the tax on the five percent tax on participating managers goes up to $20,000.[124] If the foundation managers, after full disclosure, acted on the written opinion of legal or investment counsel that the investment was not jeopardizing, however, the tax will not be levied on them.[125] Where more than one manager participated in the decision to make a jeopardizing investment, the tax is per transaction, not per manager.[126]

In *Thorne v. Commissioner*,[127] a private foundation invested all of its money in an offshore interest-bearing account in the Aruba Bonaire Curacao Trust Company (ABC), a Bahamian corporation, on the informal, unwritten advice of a lawyer. The foundation manager did not make any personal inquiries into the integrity of ABC and therefore did not know that its business license had been revoked and that it had been stricken from the register of Bahamian corporations prior to the time when the foundation made its deposits. The Tax Court had no trouble finding this to be a jeopardizing investment and upholding the imposition of first tier taxes on the foundation and its manager. Because the foundation had failed to exit the investment after notice from the IRS, the court also upheld second tier taxes on the foundation, but, in an odd turn, did not uphold them on the foundation manager on the grounds that he had not "refused to agree" to the correction because he had never been asked! The notice by the IRS of the imposition of first tier taxes was not, in itself, a request to correct in the view of the court.[128]

[F]   Tax on Taxable Expenditures — IRC Section 4945

This is a catch-all provision that Congress added at the end of the restrictions on private foundations. It describes a number of activities, primarily political, that Congress thought were improper for private foundations, and it taxes them in order to discourage them. The first tier tax on a private foundation for engaging in these activities is 20 percent of the amount expended.[129] There is also a first tier tax of five percent of the amount expended, but not to exceed $10,000, on the

---

[122] *Id.*

[123] I.R.C. § 4944(a)(1), (a)(2), (d)(2).

[124] I.R.C. § 4944(b)(1), (b)(2), (d)(2).

[125] 26 C.F.R. § 53.4944-1(b)(2)(v).

[126] I.R.C. § 4944(d).

[127] 99 T.C. 67 (1992).

[128] *Id.*

[129] I.R.C. § 4945(a)(1).

foundation managers who authorized these activities.[130] Should the private foundation fail to recover the amount expended within the taxable period, the second tier tax on the private foundation skyrockets to a confiscatory 100 percent of the amount expended,[131] and, for foundation managers who refused to make the correction, to 50 percent of the amount expended, but not to exceed $20,000.[132] Where more than one manager participated in the decision, the tax is per transaction, not per manager.[133]

[1] Carrying on Propaganda or Attempting to Influence Legislation

Under the Political Activities Test,[134] Section 501(c)(3) organizations can lobby insubstantially or elect the lobbying expenditure limits of Section 501(h). Private foundations do not have this luxury. The prohibition on lobbying for them is absolute, and they must pay the tax on taxable expenditures on the first dollar that they expend in lobbying activity.[135] If a private foundation funds another organization, and that organization carries on lobbying activity, this is not considered lobbying by the private foundation as long as the grant was not earmarked for lobbying.[136]

There are some lobbying-like activities, however, that are permitted for private foundations and that will not subject them to this tax. For example, private foundations may provide nonpartisan analysis, study, or research to lawmakers.[137] This research may even advocate a point of view, and may be presented to the public as well as to legislators, as long as it includes a full and fair exposition of the facts.[138] Private foundations can also provide technical advice or assistance, based on their knowledge or skill in a given area, to governmental bodies when invited to do so in writing.[139]

---

[130] I.R.C. § 4945(a)(2), (c)(2).

[131] I.R.C. § 4945(b)(1).

[132] I.R.C. § 4945(b)(2). The private foundation in Thorne v. Comm'r, 99 T.C. 67, was subject to second tier taxes for improper grants to individuals and organizations under I.R.C. § 4945(b)(1); but Thorne escaped second tier taxes on the grounds that he had not refused to make the correction because he was never asked; I.R.C. § 4945(c)(2).

[133] I.R.C. § 4945(c)(1).

[134] See § 6.05.

[135] I.R.C. § 4945(d)(1).

[136] See I.R.C. § 4945(d)(1); 26 C.F.R. § 53.4945-2(a)(6).

[137] 26 C.F.R. § 53.4945-2(d)(1).

[138] 26 C.F.R. § 53.4945-2(d)(1)(ii).

[139] 26 C.F.R. § 53.4945-2(d)(2)(i), (ii).

[2]   Influencing Elections & Carrying on Voter Registration Drives

The restriction on electioneering for private foundations is absolute.[140] As with lobbying, the private foundation is subject to a tax on taxable expenditures for every dollar that it spends electioneering. Voter registration drives are normally a prohibited form of electioneering, but there is an exception for drives that are nonpartisan, are not confined to one election period and are carried on in five or more states.[141] This exception applies as long as the private foundation expends substantially all of its income for exempt purposes, i.e., not on the voter registration drive, has broad public support, and does not accept gifts for voter registration drives limited to one state or one election period.[142]

[3]   Travel & Study Grants to Individuals

It is a taxable expenditure for a private foundation to make a grant to an individual for travel, study, or similar purposes unless the grant is awarded on an objective, nondiscriminatory basis, pursuant to a procedure approved in advance by the IRS.[143] The Regulations give the IRS 45 days to respond to a private foundation's request to approve their grant-making process.[144] If the IRS does not respond within this period, the grant-making process is treated as approved from the date of submission until receipt of notice from the IRS to the contrary.[145] Grants that are made before the IRS's approval is sought are treated as taxable expenditures.[146]

A grant to an individual is objective and non-discriminatory where the group from which the grantee was selected was itself chosen on the basis of criteria related to the purposes of the grant and where the group is sufficiently broad as to constitute a charitable class.[147] As an additional condition, the grant must qualify as either: (1) a scholarship or fellowship grant excludable from the grantee's gross income under IRC Section 117(a)[148] and be used to study at a formal educational institution,[149] or (2) as a prize or award that is excludable from the awardee's gross income under IRC Section 74(b) and where the awardee is selected from the general public,[150] or (3) as a grant whose purpose is to achieve a specific objective, produce a report or similar product by the grantee, or improve or enhance a

---

[140]   I.R.C. § 4945(d)(2). It is, of course, absolute for public charities as well. I.R.C. § 501(c)(3).

[141]   I.R.C. § 4945(f)(2).

[142]   26 C.F.R. § 53.4945-3(b)(1).

[143]   I.R.C. § 4945(g).

[144]   26 C.F.R. § 53.4945-4(d)(3).

[145]   *Id.; see also* Rev. Rul. 81-46, 1981-1 C.B. 514.

[146]   German Soc'y of Md. v. Comm'r, 80 T.C. 741 (1983).

[147]   26 C.F.R. § 53.4945-4(b)(2).

[148]   IRS approval of a private foundation scholarship program does not, in itself, guarantee that the scholarship meets the § 117 exclusion from income. *See* Rev. Rul. 77-44, 1977-1 C.B. 355.

[149]   I.R.C. § 4945(g)(1).

[150]   I.R.C. § 4945(g)(2).

literary, artistic, musical, scientific, or other similar capacity, skill, or talent of the grantee.[151]

The IRS has established procedures for scholarship programs operated by private foundations to make sure that the program is not functioning as a disguised benefit for those who control the foundation. This had been a problem in the past with private foundation scholarships established by business corporations that primarily benefited the children of those who worked at the corporation. In Revenue Procedure 76-47,[152] the IRS required a showing that a scholarship program is truly charitable — that it serves a public and not a private interest. The selection process for scholarship recipients must be reasonable and objective. It should award scholarships to no more than 25 percent of applicants. In a private foundation that is primarily funded by a business corporation, scholarships to children of corporate employees cannot exceed 10 percent of eligible applicants.[153]

[4] Grants to Organizations

It is a taxable expenditure for a private foundation to make grants to an organization that is not a public charity[154] or a private operating foundation[155] unless it maintains "expenditure responsibility" for the grant. First of all, what kind of an organization is not a public charity or a private operating foundation? The first, and most obvious, answer is other private foundations. Private foundations may make grants to other private foundations as long as the grant is for Section 501(c)(3) charitable purposes and the grantor private foundation has maintained "expenditure responsibility." Such grants are not taxable expenditures.[156]

Another category of possible grantee organizations would be other 501(c) tax exempt organizations, as, for example, Section 501(c)(4) social welfare organizations, or Section 501(c)(8) fraternal benefit organizations. Any of these could be recipients of grants from a private foundation as long as the grant is to be used by them for 501(c)(3) charitable purposes[157] and as long as the grantor private foundation has maintained "expenditure responsibility." Such grants are not taxable expenditures.[158]

Expenditure responsibility involves a three-step process. First, before a grant is made to an organization, the private foundation grantor must make a pre-grant inquiry into the identity, prior history, and experience of the grantee organization

---

[151] I.R.C. § 4945(g)(3).

[152] 1976-2 C.B. 670.

[153] *Id.; see also* Rev. Proc. 80-39, 1980-2 C.B. 772 (loan programs by employer controlled private foundations).

[154] That is, is not an organization described in I.R.C. § 509(a)(1)-(3).

[155] Private operating foundations are defined in I.R.C. § 4942(j)(3). They are a type of private foundation that performs or "operates" (as opposed to simply funding) charitable activities.

[156] *See* Sanders, *Final Regs of § 4945: Working with the New Rules Restricting Foundations' Activities*, 38 J. Tax'n 130 (1973); Bandy, *Planning Techniques to Avoid the Taxes on Private Foundations and Related Entities*, 40 J. tax'n 244 (1974).

[157] 26 C.F.R. § 53.4945-6(c)(1)(ii).

[158] I.R.S. Priv. Ltr. Rul. 9340002 (Oct. 8, 1993).

and its managers.[159] Second, in making the grant, the private foundation must have an agreement in writing with the grantee organization, committing the grantee to repay any portion of the grant not used for the purposes of the grant, to submit full and complete annual reports on the manner in which the funds are spent and the progress made in accomplishing the purposes of the grant, to maintain records of receipts and expenditures and to make its books and records available to the grantor and, finally, not to use the grant for any non-exempt purpose.[160] Third, once a grant is made, the private foundation grantor must exert all reasonable efforts and establish adequate procedures: (1) to see that the grant is spent solely for the charitable purposes for which it was made, (2) to obtain full and complete reports from the grantee on how grant funds are spent, and (3) to make full and detailed reports to the IRS with respect to the expenditure, if required.[161]

In *Mannheimer Charitable Trust v. Commissioner*,[162] the IRS assessed the first tier tax (then 10 percent) on a private foundation for failure to exercise expenditure responsibility in grants it made to two other private foundations that were related to it. The three foundations (one grantor, two grantees) had all been established by a common founder, and there were three persons who were interlocking directors. This had the practical effect of keeping the donor foundation aware of how the grantee foundations were using its grants to them. But the grantor foundation had not made pre-grant inquiries, did not have written grant agreements, and had not sought to receive full and complete reports from the grantees on how the grant funds were spent. In other words, the private foundation grantor had complied with none of the three requirements of expenditure responsibility explained above. It tried to argue that it had complied with the law simply by listing the grants and grantees on its own 990-PF filing. The Tax Court found this superficially appealing, but still not in compliance with "full and complete" reports required by IRC Section 4945(h)(3). The Tax Court upheld the 10 percent tax, admitting that perhaps the grantor foundation and its related grantee foundations had not engaged in any diversion of charitable assets from charitable purposes. But, the Tax Court said, the law is the law, and it covers all.[163]

[5] Expenditures for Non-Charitable Purposes

In a catch-all phrase at the end of IRC Section 4945(d), Congress imposes the tax on taxable expenditures on any amount paid or incurred by a private foundation for "any purpose other than one specified in section 170(c)(2)(B)."[164] That section defines a charitable organization as one organized and operated exclusively for religious, charitable, scientific, literary, or educational purposes, or to foster national and international sports competitions or to prevent cruelty to children and animals. This, of course, is the entire Section 501(c)(3) list with the exception of

---

[159] 26 C.F.R. § 53.4945-5(b)(2)(i).

[160] 26 C.F.R. § 53.4945-5(b)(3).

[161] I.R.C. § 4945(h).

[162] 93 T.C. 35 (1989).

[163] *Id.*

[164] I.R.C. § 4945(d)(5).

public safety testing organizations, and it denotes those organizations capable of attracting tax deductible gifts.[165]

Any expenditure that a private foundation makes for a purpose outside of this list is considered a non-charitable expenditure, and is taxed as a Section 4945(d) taxable expenditure. As examples of this type of expenditure, the Regulations cite unreasonable administrative expenses, including compensation, consultant fees, and other fees for services rendered, unless the private foundation can demonstrate that they were paid in the good faith belief that they were reasonable and were consistent with ordinary business care and prudence.[166]

§ 19.05   FOUR CATEGORIES OF NON-PRIVATE FOUNDATIONS (PUBLIC CHARITIES)

[A]   Section 509(a)(1): Traditional Public Charities

There are six different kinds of Section 509(a)(1) organizations, and they are defined in the IRC by reference to Section 170(b)(1)(A)(i)-(vi), which is the section that deals with tax deductible charitable gifts.[167]

[1]   Sections 509(a)(1) & 170(b)(1)(A)(i) Organizations

These are churches or conventions, or associations of churches.[168] Tax exempt churches, conventions, and associations of churches are always public charities.[169]

[2]   Sections 509(a)(1) & 170(b)(1)(A)(ii) Organizations

These are formal educational organizations (regular faculty, regular curriculum, regularly enrolled student body, regular place of instruction).[170] Tax exempt formal educational organizations are always public charities.[171]

[3]   Sections 509(a)(1) & 170(b)(1)(A)(iii) Organizations

These are hospitals and medical research organizations.[172] Tax exempt hospitals and medical research organizations are always public charities.[173]

---

[165] I.R.C. § 170(c)(2)(B).

[166] 26 C.F.R. § 53.4945-6(b)(2).

[167] *See* I.R.C. §§ 509(a)(1), 170(b)(1)(A)(i)-(vi).

[168] See § 8.01 *et seq.* for further information on churches or conventions or associations of churches.

[169] *See* I.R.C. § 170(b)(1)(A)(i).

[170] See § 9.01 *et seq.* for further information on educational organizations.

[171] *See* I.R.C. § 170(b)(1)(A)(ii).

[172] See § 10.08 for further information on medical research organizations.

[173] *See* I.R.C. § 170(b)(1)(A)(ii).

[4]   Sections 509(a)(1) & 170(b)(1)(A)(iv) Organizations

Endowment funds organized and operated in connection with state and municipal colleges and universities are public charities. These funds exist because many public colleges and universities are prohibited by state law from receiving gifts or bequests. As an alternative, 170(b)(1)(A)(iv) organizations can receive these gifts, can allow their donors a deduction, and can use the gifts or bequests for the benefit of a state college or university. Expenditures for the benefit of a state college or university include expenditures for their normal functions, such as acquiring or maintaining campus property and buildings, erecting campus buildings, acquiring and maintaining college equipment or furnishings, scholarships, libraries, and student loans.[174]

In order to qualify under IRC Section 170(b)(1)(A)(iv), an organization must also receive a substantial part of its support from the public. Public support is explained more fully in the discussion below about Section 170(b)(1)(A)(vi) organizations. The definitions are very similar, except that public support for state and municipal college and university endowment funds does not include support from certain government agencies that do qualify as support for Section 170(b)(1)(A)(vi) organizations.[175]

[5]   Sections 509(a)(1) & 170(b)(1)(A)(v) Organizations

These are governmental units described in IRC Section 170(c)(1) — that is, states, possessions of the United States, or any political subdivision thereof; the District of Columbia; and Indian tribal governments.[176] A political subdivision is defined as "any division of any state or local governmental unit which is a municipal corporation or which has been delegated that right to exercise part of the sovereign power of the unit."[177]

Most governmental units are exempt from federal income taxes under IRC Section 115, and not under Section 501(c)(3). Because private foundations and non-private foundations, or public charities, are both subsets of Section 501(c)(3), the private foundation status of Section 115 governmental units would seem not to be an issue, inasmuch as they are not Section 501(c)(3) organizations to begin with.

In any event, governmental units exercising sovereign authority are tax exempt public charities.

---

[174]   *See* I.R.C. § 170(b)(1)(A)(iv); 26 C.F.R. § 1.170A-9(c)(2)(i).

[175]   Rev. Rul. 82-132, 1982-2 C.B. 107; 26 C.F.R. § 1.170A-9(c)(2)(ii).

[176]   The exclusion of tribal governments from private foundation status is pursuant to I.R.C. § 7871(a)(7)(B).

[177]   *See* 26 C.F.R. § 1.103-1(b); I.R.C. § 170(b)(1)(A)(v). The definition is not in the Regulations for § 170. In Rev. Rul. 75-359, 1975-2 C.B. 79, a voluntary association of counties created for joint research and training purposes did not qualify, because it had not been delegated sovereign powers. *See also* Tex. Learning Tech. Group v. Comm'r, 96 T.C. 686 (1991) (organization formed to develop and administer programs for its member public school districts did not qualify, since it had not been delegated sovereign power).

[6]   Sections 509(a)(1) & 170(b)(1)(A)(vi) Organizations

[a]   Introduction

These are known as "publicly supported organizations." They get most of their support either from contributions from the general public or from the government. The Regulations give, as examples of this kind of organization, "publicly or governmentally supported museums of history, art or science, libraries, community centers to promote the arts, organizations providing facilities for the support of an opera, symphony orchestra, ballet, or repertory drama . . . and organizations such as the American Red Cross or the United Givers Fund."[178]

[b]   Tests for Public Support

[i]   Generally

An organization is publicly supported if it can normally meet the one-third support test, also called the "mechanical" test, or if it can normally meet the 10 percent support test, also called the "facts and circumstances" test.[179] Publicly supported organizations are exempted from private foundation status on the grounds that their dependence upon the support of the public or the government will prevent them from the financial abuses that private foundation status was meant to curb.

In determining whether an organization meets either the one-third mechanical test or the 10 percent facts and circumstances test, the process starts with ascertaining the total support of the organization. If public support is one-third of total support, the one-third mechanical test is met. If public support is 10 percent of total support, the first part of the 10 percent facts and circumstances test is met. There is a second part of the facts and circumstances test that requires the organization to demonstrate that it is working to attract new and additional public or governmental support on a regular basis.[180]

[ii]   Determining Amount of Public Support & One-Third Mechanical Test

Total support of an organization includes: gifts and grants, including governmental grants; contributions (but not the contribution of services, which is not deductible);[181] membership fees, as long as they are meant to support the organization, and not to pay for admissions, merchandise, services, or the use of facilities; net unrelated business income; gross investment income, excluding

---

[178]   26 C.F.R. § 1.170 A-9(e)(1)(ii); *see also* I.R.C. § 170(b)(1)(A)(vi).

[179]   I.R.C. § 170(b)(1)(A)(vi), (c)(2); 26 C.F.R. § 1.170A-9(f)(2), (3), (4).

[180]   *See* Nicholas Cafardi & Jaclyn Cherry, Tax Exempt Organizations: Cases and Materials 914–15 (2d ed. 2008).

[181]   A qualified sponsorship payment, except for a payment in the form of services, counts as a contribution. *See* 26 C.F.R. § 1.513-4(c) (definition of a qualified sponsorship payment).

capital gains;[182] tax revenues levied for the benefit of an organization and paid to or expended on behalf of the organization; and value of services or facilities furnished by a governmental unit to the organization without charge, unless the services or facilities are furnished to the general public without charge.[183]

The total of all of the above will be the number under the line (the denominator) of the fraction that needs to be figured to determine whether the organization meets the one-third test or the first part of the 10 percent facts and circumstances test. Note that the above list does not include any income from the organization's exempt functions, such as tuition, income from the sale of related items or museum or theater admissions.[184] The value of donated services such as might be supplied by volunteers to the organization is explicitly excluded.[185]

Public support of an organization is determined by winnowing the above list, and removing items from "Total Support" that are not attributable to "Public Support."

In determining the "Public Support" part of the fraction, the following items from "Total Support" are not considered: net unrelated business income; gross investment income, excluding capital gains;[186] and any gift or grant, not from the government or a public charity, to the extent it exceeds two percent of the organization's total support for the tax period.[187]

Of the entire "Total Support" list, it is easy to see that unrelated business income and investment income do not come either from the public or from the government, and so should not be considered as a form of public support. As for the two percent limitation on gifts and grants, they generally will come from individuals, business entities, or private foundations. The IRC does not want just one donor of this type to be able to confer "public support" status, and therefore, public charity status, on what would otherwise be a private foundation.[188]

Note that gifts or grants from the government or from public charities are not subject to the two percent limitation, again because these kinds of gifts do manifest public support. But if gifts from a governmental unit or a public charity are "earmarked gifts," that is to say, they have been given to them by a donor with the express or implied understanding that they will be passed on by the governmental unit or public charity to another donee organization, then they are subject to the two percent limitation even though they come from (actually, through) a governmental unit or public charity.[189]

---

[182] *See* I.R.C. § 509(e).

[183] I.R.C. § 509(d)(5), (6).

[184] 26 C.F.R. § 1.170A-9(f)(7)(i)(A). In *Williams Home, Inc. v. United States*, 540 F. Supp. 310 (W.D. Va. 1982), the transfer of assets by the aged to a nursing home upon their admission was exempt function income, not public support.

[185] 26 C.F.R. § 1.107A-9(f)(7)(i)(B).

[186] *See* St. John's Orphanage, Inc. v. United States, 16 Cl. Ct. 299 (1989) (investment income of a foundation was held not to be a form of public support).

[187] 26 C.F.R. § 1.170A-9(f)(6). *See generally* 26 C.F.R. § 1.170A-9(f)(6), (7), (8).

[188] 26 C.F.R. § 1.170A-9(f)(6)(v).

[189] *Id.*

[iii]   Ten Percent Facts & Circumstances Test

In applying the 10 percent "Facts and Circumstances" test, the fraction is put together in the same way, except that in the resulting fraction, public support need only be 10 percent of total support as long as the organization can show that it is organized and operated to attract new and additional public or governmental support on a continuous basis. An organization will be considered to meet this requirement if it maintains a continuous and bona fide governmental or public fundraising program that is reasonable in light of its charitable activities;[190] and as long as there are other factors that establish its public support, such as:

- Its actual level of public support exceeds 10 percent and approaches 33⅓ percent; the higher the actual level of public support, the less the organization will have to rely on the following facts.[191]

- It has a broad level of public support; this is a numbers game (determining the number of actual donors). The higher, the better. The smaller, especially when support comes from just one family or the employees of one business entity, the worse.[192]

- It has a governing board that is broadly representative of the public, and not of just the personal or private interests of a limited number of donors; these might include public officials, clergy, educators, civic leaders, and persons with special knowledge or expertise in the organization's field.[193]

- It generally provides facilities or services directly for the benefit of the general public on a continuing basis, like a museum or library that opens its building to the public, a symphony orchestra that gives public performances, a conservation organization that provides educational services to the public, or an old age home that provides domiciliary or nursing services for the general public.[194]

- Other factors, such as participation in or sponsorship by the civic community; a definite program serving the community; a significant level of government support and corresponding accountability; and broad rules and opportunities for persons to become members of the organization and for enlargement of the membership.[195]

In the case of the *Trustees for the Home of Aged Women v. United States*,[196] the private foundation did not meet the one-third support test due to the exclusion of its investment income from the public support total. Without its investment income, it would have met the one-tenth support test, except that in examining the "facts and circumstances," the Home was found not to have a continuous and bona fide

---

[190] 26 C.F.R. § 1.170A-9(f)(3)(ii).

[191] 26 C.F.R. § 1.170A-9(f)(3)(iii).

[192] 26 C.F.R. § 1.170A-9(f)(3)(iv).

[193] 26 C.F.R. § 1.170A-9(f)(3)(v).

[194] 26 C.F.R. § 1.170A-9(f)(3)(vi)(A).

[195] 26 C.F.R. § 1.170A-9(f)(3)(vi)(C).

[196] 86-1 U.S.T.C. ¶ 9290 (D. Mass. 1986).

program for the solicitation of funds. As a result, the Home was denied public charity status as a publicly supported Section 170(b)(1)(A)(vi) organization. It remained a private operating foundation.[197]

[c]   Exception for Organizations Dependent Primarily on Related Activities (Exempt Function) Income

There are some exceptions to the above formula for determining if an organization is publicly supported, either by the one-third support mechanical test, or the one-tenth support facts and circumstances test.

The first exception is for organizations whose income is mostly from its exempt functions.[198] Exempt function income is totally excluded from the support tests. It figures neither in the numerator nor the denominator. It can happen, then, that such an organization can receive rather minor gifts, yet still qualify under either of the public support tests. For example, an organization has exempt function income of $500,000 and receives a number of small gifts totaling $5,000 in the tax period. That is the sum total of its income. If these numbers are plugged into the support tests described above, the fraction will be $5,000 over $5,000, or a public support percentage of 100 percent. It should qualify as publicly supported. But the Regulations say that an organization that gets most of its income from exempt functions, and only an insignificant amount from public support, does not meet either of the public support tests.[199] On the question of what level of public support is "insignificant," there is no bright-line rule. In the example given in the Regulations, which is exactly the example cited above, public support was slightly less than one percent of total income, including exempt function income.[200]

[d]   Exception for Unusual Grants

The second exception is for "Unusual Grants." Unusual grants are those that come from out of the blue, typically from a party that is not related to the organization and has no prior history with it. The Regulations define unusual grants as grants that are: (1) attracted by the publicly supported nature of the foundation, (2) unusual or unexpected in amount, and (3) adversely affecting the organization's publicly supported status.[201] The Regulations also say that the following questions are to be considered in determining whether a gift is "unusual": (1) was it made by a disqualified person? (2) was it inter vivos or a bequest? (3) was it cash or a tangible asset that furthers the organization's exempt purposes? (4) does the organization rely on unusual grants, or does it attract a significant amount of public support? (5) is the organization governed by a body representative of the larger community? and (6) have conditions or restrictions been placed on the

---

[197] *Id.*

[198] 26 C.F.R. § 1.170A-9(f)(7)(ii). In the Regulations, such organizations are referred to as "Organizations dependent primarily on gross receipts from related activities."

[199] 26 C.F.R. § 1.170A-9(f)(7)(ii).

[200] *Id.*

[201] 26 C.F.R. § 1.170A-9(f)(6)(ii).

gift?[202] These same factors are contained in Revenue Procedure 81-7,[203] but the Procedure also asks, if the gift is for operating expenses, whether the terms and amount of the gift are expressly limited to underwriting no more than one year's operating expenses.[204]

In performing the public support test for Section 509(a)(1)-Section 170(b)(1)(A)(vi) organizations, "unusual grants" are excluded from both the numerator and the denominator of the fraction. In the normal process for determining levels of public support, gifts and grants are included in the denominator (i.e., total support). But no more than two percent of any gift can be included in the numerator for public support. As a result, an unexpectedly large gift could inflate the denominator, while not doing much for the numerator, causing the organization to flunk either the one-third or one-tenth public support test. The Regulations, therefore, allow the exclusion of "unusual grants" entirely from the public support tests.[205]

[e]   Normally & Relevant Taxable Period

The tests for public support are "normally" tests. Both the one-third support test and the one-tenth support test are to be based on the organization's normal sources of support.[206] An organization will be considered as "normally" receiving the required levels of public support (one-third or one-tenth) for the current tax year and the following tax year if, for the four tax years immediately preceding the current taxable year, the aggregate amount of the support received meets either public support test.[207] For example, if an organization's support in years 2002, 2003, 2004 and 2005 (as an aggregate, and not year by year) meets either the one-third support test or the one-tenth support test, plus, for one-tenth organizations, the organization has the necessary program to attract additional public support, then the organization will be considered to meet the test in 2006 and 2007 as well.[208]

[f]   Substantial & Material Changes

It can happen that substantial and material changes occur in an organization's levels of public support that are not covered by the unusual grant exception. An unusually large gift from a disqualified person is one example. In these circumstances, the Regulations require an organization to take an extra year to determine their "normal" level of public support.[209] For example, if substantial and material changes occur in an organization's sources of support for tax year 2006,

---

[202] 26 C.F.R. § 1.509(a)-3(c)(4).

[203] 1981-1 C.B. 621.

[204] *Id.*

[205] 26 C.F.R. § 1.170A-9(f)(6)(ii); *see also* Rev. Proc. 81-7.

[206] 26 C.F.R. § 1.170A-9(f)(4)(i), (ii).

[207] 26 C.F.R. § 1.170A-9(f)(4)(i), (ii).

[208] For an illustration of how this works, see the calculations in *Trustees for the Home for Aged Women,* 86-1 U.S.T.C. ¶ 9290.

[209] 26 C.F.R. § 1.170A-9(f)(4)(v).

even though it may have met the requirements for support in 2001-2005, it will not meet the requirements of Regulation Section 170(b)(1)(A)(vi) unless it meets the requirements for support for a computation period consisting of the taxable years 2002-2006.[210]

A new organization that has been in existence for at least eight months or more can get an advance ruling from the IRS that covers the first five years of its existence.[211] The IRS will issue this advance ruling, meaning the organization can be treated as meeting the requirements of Section 170(b)(1)(A)(vi) if the organization, based on the data from Form 1023 filing, can be reasonably expected to meet the public support requirements of a non-private foundation. If the support levels during the five-year advance ruling period do not meet the required public support levels, then the organization is subject to the two percent private foundation excise tax from the first year of its existence.[212] Donors during the advance ruling period can take the public charity 50 percent of adjusted gross income deduction, even if, at the end of the advance ruling period, there is a determination that the organization does not actually qualify as a public charity, unless they were responsible for or had reason to know of the facts that led to denial of public charity status.[213]

[g]   Community Trusts

[i]   Generally

A community trust, sometimes also called a community foundation, is an organization that receives gifts and bequests from the public and then uses them for charitable purposes in the community that it serves. Many of America's major cities have such foundations. The oldest of them, the Cleveland Foundation, was started in 1914. Even though these organizations are referred to as "trusts" in the Regulations, they can also be corporations or associations or some combination of all three-trusts, corporations, and unincorporated associations.[214]

These community trusts are created in order to attract gifts of a capital or endowment nature from many donors that are meant to benefit a specific community or area. They are usually governed by a board composed of representatives of the community or area they serve. Individual contributions can be held as separate trusts or funds, often named after the donors, within the overall entity of the community trust.

Community trusts can qualify as public charities, i.e., non-private foundations in the same way that other Section 170(b)(1)(A)(vi) organizations do, by meeting the

---

[210] *Id.; see* 26 C.F.R. § 1.509(a)-3(c)(6).

[211] 26 C.F.R. § 1.170A-9(f)(5)(i). The Regulations identify the advance ruling period as 2 or 3 years; it is, in fact, 5 years. *See* I.R.S. Publication 557 *Tax Exempt Status for Your Organization* (Rev. Oct., 2010).

[212] 26 C.F.R. § 1.170(A)-9(f)(5)(iii)(B).

[213] 26 C.F.R. § 1.170(A)-9(f)(5)(iii)(C).

[214] 26 C.F.R. § 1.170(A)-9(f)(11)(i).

one-third mechanical test or the one-tenth facts and circumstances test.[215] Community trusts can meet the requirement of the facts and circumstances test that they have a continuous and bona fide governmental or public fund raising program if they solicit gifts and bequests from a large spectrum of donors in their community. They can make these requests for gifts through banks or trust companies, through lawyers, estate-planners, accountants and other professionals, or in any way that alerts donors to the community trust as a potential donee of gifts to benefit the community.[216] A community trust is not required to engage in periodic, community-wide fundraising like a community chest or United Way.[217]

The Regulations treat community trusts as if they are one entity as opposed to a related group of private foundations as long as they meet the "single entity test." Once the community trust qualifies as a single entity, and meets one of the public support tests, the trusts or funds transferred to it will be treated as gifts to a public charity, and not to a private foundation, if they qualify as "component parts" of the single entity.[218]

[ii]   Single Entity Test

In order to meet the "single entity" test, a community trust must be commonly known as a community trust, fund or foundation, or similar name conveying the idea of a capital or endowment fund that supports charitable activities in the community.[219] It must have a common governing instrument to which all the funds it holds are subject.[220] It must have a common governing body that directs the gifts of the trust or, where a fund designates a particular charitable beneficiary, monitors the distribution to that beneficiary.[221] The governing body must have the ability to modify any restriction or condition on the distribution of gifts for charitable purposes if, in its sole judgment, the restriction becomes unnecessary, incapable of fulfillment, or inconsistent with the community's charitable needs.[222] The governing body must have the ability to replace any trustee, custodian, or agent of a fund that it holds for breach of fiduciary duty or for failure to produce a reasonable return.[223] The governing body must, by resolution or otherwise, commit itself to exercise its powers in the best interests of the community,[224] and must also commit itself to obtain information and take appropriate steps to ensure that each trustee or custodian of a component part follows the terms of the common

---

[215]   26 C.F.R. § 1.170A-9(f)(10).

[216]   *Id.*

[217]   *Id.*

[218]   26 C.F.R. § 1.170A-9(f)(11)(ii)(B).

[219]   26 C.F.R. § 1.170A-9(f)(11)(iii).

[220]   26 C.F.R. § 1.170A-9(f)(11)(iv).

[221]   26 C.F.R. § 1.170A-9(f)(11)(v).

[222]   26 C.F.R. § 1.170A-9(f)(11)(v)(B)(1). The community foundation meets this requirement if it uses the master trust agreement language of Rev. Rul. 77-333, 1977-2 C.B. 75. Other sample language is found in Rev. Rul. 77-334, 1977-2 C.B. 77.

[223]   26 C.F.R. § 1.170A-9(f)(11)(v)(B)(2), (3).

[224]   26 C.F.R. § 1.170A-9(f)(11)(v)(E).

governing instrument and obtains a reasonable rate of return.[225] The community trust must prepare periodic financial reports treating all of the funds that it holds as components of the trust.[226]

[iii]   Component Part Test

Once this rather complex "single entity" test is met for the community trust itself, the "component part" test is applied to determine whether the individual funds that the community trust holds qualify as component parts of the community trust.

To qualify as a component part of a community trust, a trust or fund must be created by a gift, bequest or transfer to the community trust, and it may not be subject to any material restriction or condition with respect to the transferred assets.[227] Material restrictions refer to lines of control that a donor may attempt to retain on the gift.[228] Issues of donor control are factually determined. The following do not constitute elements of control: naming the gift or fund after the donor;[229] using the gift for charitable purposes designated by the donor in the transfer instrument;[230] and maintaining the gift in a separate fund, with a delayed distribution period as long as the community trust is the legal owner of the fund and its governing body exercises ultimate control.[231]

In summary, a community trust can qualify as a Section 170(b)(1)(A)(vi) public charity if it meets one of the public support tests: the one-third "mechanical" test or the one-tenth "facts and circumstances" test. Once it so qualifies, and once both the "single entity" test and the "component part" tests are met, the trusts or funds transferred to a community trust will be treated as gifts to a public charity, and not to a private foundation.[232]

---

[225] 26 C.F.R. § 1.170A-9(f)(11)(v)(F).

[226] 26 C.F.R. § 1.170A-9(f)(11)(vi).

[227] 26 C.F.R. § 1.170A-9(f)(11)(ii)(A), (B). Material restrictions are defined by reference to 26 C.F.R. § 1.507-2(a)(8).

[228] 26 C.F.R. § 1.507-2(a)(8)(i), (iv). Issues of donor control are factually determined by looking at such items as (1) whether the assets transferred are transferred in fee or subject to some obligation of the donor, i.e., a mortgage, or some obligation to the donor, i.e., right of first refusal; (2) whether they are to be used in a manner consistent with exempt purposes; (3) whether the governing body of the transferee has been given ultimate control of the gift; (4) whether the governing body is independent from the donor; and (5) whether the donor's advice on the distribution of the fund is always, or even frequently followed by the community trust.

[229] 26 C.F.R. § 1.507-2(a)(8)(iii)(A).

[230] 26 C.F.R. § 1.507-2(a)(8)(iii)(B). The designation of a charitable donee at the time the transfer is made is permissible, whereas the donor maintaining a right to direct the gift to a charity after the transfer to the community trust is an element of control.

[231] 26 C.F.R. § 1.507-2(a)(8)(iii)(C).

[232] 26 C.F.R. § 1.170A-9(f)(11)(ii)(B).

[B]   Section 509(a)(2): Gross Receipt or Service Provider Organizations

Section 509(a)(2) non-private foundations or public charities are referred to as "gross receipts" or "service provider" organizations. While they are similar to Section 509(a)(1)-Section 170(b)(1)(A)(vi) "publicly-supported" organizations in a number of ways, there are some important differences between them. The non-private foundation status of a Section 509(a)(1)-Section 170(b)(1)(A)(vi) is based on the fact that it receives public support. The non-private foundation status of a Section 509(a)(2) organization is based on the fact that it provides services to the public.[233]

In order to qualify for non-private foundation, or public charity, status, a Section 509(a)(2) organization must meet two tests: a positive test and a negative test. First, on the positive side, it must normally receive more than one-third of its total support from public support. This sounds a lot like the public support test for Section 509(a)(1)-Section 170(b)(1)(A)(vi) organizations that was described in the previous section, but there are some critical differences. While public support for Section 509(a)(1) organizations had to be *at least* one-third of total support, public support for Section 509(a)(2) organizations must be *more than* one-third of total support. While gross receipts from exempt (or related) activities was *excluded* in figuring both public support and total support for Section 509(a)(1) organizations, it is *included* in figuring both public support and total support for Section 509(a)(2) organizations; in other words it goes in both the numerator and the denominator of the public support equation. This is why Section 509(a)(2) organizations are sometimes referred to as "gross receipts" organizations, because it is the inclusion of gross receipts in figuring their public support equation that distinguishes them from Section 509(a)(1) organizations.[234]

There are two important limitations here, however. First, in figuring its public support equation, a Section 509(a)(2) organization includes all gross receipts in the denominator of the equation, but in the numerator, gross receipts from any one person or from any bureau or agency of a governmental unit are excluded to the extent they exceed the greater of $5,000 or one percent of the organization's total support in any taxable year. Second, gifts, grants, contributions, and gross receipts from related activities are includable in the numerator only to the extent that they are received from non-disqualified persons, governmental units, and public charities.[235]

In other words, support from disqualified persons are a part of total support for a Section 509(a)(2) organization, but they are not a part of public support. Gifts and grants (as opposed to gross receipts) from governmental units and public charities are part of both total support and public support.[236]

---

[233] *See* I.R.C. § 509(a)(2); 26 C.F.R. § 1.509(a)-2.

[234] *See* 26 C.F.R. §§ 1.170-2, 1.509(a)-3.

[235] I.R.C. § 509(a)(2)(A); 26 C.F.R. § 1.509(a)-3(a)(1).

[236] *See* 26 C.F.R. §§ 1.509(a)-2, 1.170A-9.

For Section 509(a)(2) organizations, total support includes: gifts and grants, including governmental grants; contributions (but not the contribution of services, which is not deductible);[237] membership fees, even if they are payment for admissions or services; gross receipts from admissions, sales of merchandise, performance of services or the furnishing of facilities in any activity that is related to the organization's exempt function; net unrelated business income; gross investment income, excluding capital gains;[238] tax revenues levied for the benefit of an organization and paid to or expended on behalf of the organization; and value of services or facilities furnished by a governmental unit to the organization without charge, unless the services or facilities are furnished to the general public without charge.[239]

Public support of a Section 509(a)(2) organization is determined by winnowing the above list, and removing items from "Total Support" that are not attributable to "Public Support." In determining the "Public Support" part of the fraction, the following items from "Total Support" are not considered: gifts, grants, contributions, membership fees and gross receipts paid by a "disqualified person;"[240] gross receipts from admissions, sales of merchandise, performance of services or the furnishing of facilities in any activity that is related to the organization's exempt function, but not including receipts from any person or governmental unit to the extent that such receipts exceed the greater of $5,000 or one percent of the organization's total support for the tax period;[241] net unrelated business income; and gross investment income, excluding capital gains.[242]

It is obviously important in creating the public support equation of a Section 509(a)(2) organization to distinguish between gross receipts and gifts and grants. This is because gross receipts from any one person or any one governmental unit are includable in the numerator only to the extent they do not exceed the greater of $5,000 or 1 percent of total support. There is no such limitation on gifts and grants. The simple difference between gifts and grants and gross receipts is that gross receipts involve an exchange of some kind between the payor and the Section 509(a)(2) organization that benefits the payor and not the general public. Payments for services, facilities or products that are provided to serve the direct and immediate needs of the payor, rather than to confer a direct benefit upon the

---

[237] A qualified sponsorship payment, except for a payment in the form of services, counts as a contribution. For a definition of a "qualified sponsorship payment," see 26 C.F.R. § 1.513-4(c).

[238] See I.R.C. § 509(e). Gain from the sale or exchange of a capital asset, whether long term or short term, is not included per I.R.C. § 509(d).

[239] I.R.C. § 509(d)(6).

[240] "Disqualified persons" are defined in I.R.C. § 4946 and include foundation managers, substantial contributors and governmental officials. When disqualified persons try to sanitize their gift to a § 509(a)(2) organization by giving it to a public charity but earmarking it for the § 509(a)(2) organization, it is still subject to the exclusion of gifts whose source is a disqualified person, even though, normally, gifts from public charities are fully includable in the numerator of the recipient's support equation. 26 C.F.R. § 1.509(a)-3(j)(1).

[241] I.R.C. § 509(a)(2)(A)(ii).

[242] See St. John's Orphanage, 16 Cl. Ct. 299, where the investment income of a foundation was held not to be a form of public support.

general public, are "gross receipts."[243] In a gift or a grant, the donor has not received anything, except items of minimal value, from the Section 509(a)(2) organization.

After it meets the more than one third public support test, in order to qualify as a Section 509(a)(2) organization, the organization must meet a second, negative test. This second test is a factor of the organization's investment and unrelated business income. To meet this test, the Section 509(a)(2) organization must not normally receive one third or more of its total support from gross investment income and the excess of any unrelated business income over any income tax paid on the unrelated business income, i.e., net unrelated business income.

To create this equation, the total support calculation is as explained above. That is the denominator of the equation. The numerator is: gross investment income, excluding capital gains; and net unrelated business income. If this equation yields a fraction greater than one-third, then the organization does not qualify as a Section 509(a)(2) organization, even if it meets the positive test of receiving more than one-third of its support from the public.

In *Education Athletic Association, Inc. v. Commissioner*,[244] an organization sought to qualify as a Section 509(a)(2) organization. Its sole source of income was from the sale of games of chance to bars, which the organization tried to classify as "gross receipts" income. Once the IRS determined that these sales were actually an unrelated business activity, the organization flunked the negative test because 100 percent (far more than one-third) of its support was net unrelated business income.[245]

In determining whether a Section 509(a)(2) organization "normally" meets both the positive and negative tests, the time calculation is performed in the same way as for Section 509(a)(1)-170(b)(1)(A)(vi) organizations.[246] Section 509 (a)(2) organizations get the benefit of the special rules on unusual grants and substantial and material changes in calculating normal levels of support.[247]

[C] Section 509(a)(3): Supporting Organizations

These are supporting organizations. They support other public charities or governmental units. An organization qualifies as a Section 509(a)(3) organization if:

- It is organized and at all times thereafter is operated exclusively for the benefit of, to perform the functions of, or to carry out the purposes of one or more Section 509(a)(1) or 509(a)(2) organizations; and

- It is operated, supervised, or controlled by one or more Section 509(a)(1) or 509(a)(2) organizations, or it is supervised or controlled in connection with one or more Section 509(a)(1) or 509(a)(2) organizations, or it is operated in

---

[243] 26 C.F.R. § 1.509(a)-3(g)(2). Consult 26 C.F.R. § 1.509(a)-3(g)(3) for examples.

[244] 77 T.C.M. (CCH) 1525 (1999).

[245] *Id.*

[246] 26 C.F.R. § 1.509(a)-3(c)(1)(i).

[247] 26 C.F.R. § 1.509(a)-3(c)(1)(ii), (3).

connection with one or more Section 509(a)(1) or 509(a)(2) organizations; and

- It is not controlled, directly or indirectly, by a disqualified person other than a foundation manager or a Section 509(a)(1) or 509(a)(2) organization.[248]

[1] Relationships

The first relationship, that of being organized and operated exclusively for the benefit of a supported charity, is very similar to the organizational test that all Section 501(c)(3) organizations must meet. The governing instruments of the supporting organization must limit its purposes to those set forth in IRC Section 509(a)(3)(A), must limit its activities to these same purposes, must identify the supported organization, and must prohibit the organization from benefiting any other organization.[249]

The second relationship, that of being operated, supervised, or controlled by one or more Section 509(a)(1) or 509(a)(2) organizations, or supervised or controlled in connection with one or more Section 509(a)(1) or 509(a)(2) organizations, or operated in connection with one or more Section 509(a)(1) or 509(a)(2) organizations is much more complex. It really breaks out into three possible relationships, or three different types of supporting organizations:

- "operated, supervised or controlled by" — This is a Type I supporting organization in which the relationship between the supported organization and the supporting organization is a parent-subsidiary relationship.[250] The parent supported organization will exercise a large degree of control over the supporting organization, usually by appointing its board of directors.[251]

- "supervised or controlled in connection with" — This is a Type II supporting organization in which the relationship is not parent-subsidiary, but more subsidiary-subsidiary reporting to a joint parent. This relationship requires that the control or management of the supporting organization be vested in the same persons that control or manage the supported organization.[252]

---

[248] *See* 26 C.F.R. § 1.509(a)-4. A § 509(a)(1) or 509(a)(2) organization can be a "disqualified person" because it is often a "major donor."

[249] 26 C.F.R. § 1.509(a)-4(c). *See* Rev. Rul. 75-437, 1975-2 C.B. 218 (charitable trust for scholarships did not meet the organizational test because it did not contain the requisite statement of purpose; the fact that the educational purposes of the trust were consistent with those of the public school system was also not enough to satisfy the organizational test); *see also* Windsor Found. v. United States, 40 A.F.T.R.2d (RIA) 6004 (1977) (organizational test was not met because there was no substantial identity of interest between the Foundation and the charitable organizations it supported, and the operational test was not met because the Foundation's operations were not limited to supporting public charities). *Cf.* Goodspeed Scholarship Fund v. Comm'r, 70 T.C. 515 (1978); Nellie Callahan Scholarship Fund v. Comm'r, 73 T.C. 626 (1980) (Tax Court accepted language defining a beneficiary class, instead of language designating a beneficiary charity, as meeting the organizational test).

[250] 26 C.F.R. § 1.509(a)-4(g)(1)(i).

[251] *Id.*

[252] 26 C.F.R. § 1.509(a)-4(h)(1). See Rev. Rul. 75-437, 1975-2 C.B. 218, where the trustee of a scholarship trust to benefit public school students was a commercial bank and where the IRS held that

- "operated in connection with" — This is a Type III supporting organization, and this relationship is the most difficult to define. The IRS uses two separate tests: the Responsiveness Test and the Integral Part Test to determine whether it exists between a supporting organization and a supported public charity. The supporting organization can meet either test to qualify as being "operated in connection with" the supported public charity. After the Pension Protection Act of 2006, Type III supporting organizations are further broken down into favored "functionally integrated" and disfavored "non-functionally integrated" varieties.[253]

The third relationship that defines Section 509(a)(3) supporting organizations is really the lack of a relationship. A Section 509(a)(3) organization cannot be controlled, directly or indirectly, by a disqualified person other than a foundation manager or a Section 509(a)(1) or 509(a)(2) organization.[254]

In Revenue Ruling 80-207,[255] an organization made distributions to a university, and might otherwise have qualified for Section 509(a)(3) status as a supporting organization except for the structure of its board of directors. The board had four members. One director was a substantial contributor to the organization, and, therefore, a disqualified person.[256] Two other directors were employees of a corporation, more than 35 percent of which was owned by the director who was a substantial contributor. While the director-employees themselves were not disqualified persons, the corporation that they worked for was a disqualified person.[257] The fourth director was chosen by the university. No director had any veto power over the others.[258]

Because only one of the directors was a disqualified person who did not have any veto power over the other directors, there was no direct control of the organization by a disqualified person. But when those two director-employees of a disqualified person were taken into account, that meant that three out of four directors were either disqualified persons or worked for one and were able to be easily influenced by it. That, the IRS held, constituted indirect control of the organization by disqualified persons. As a result, the organization did not qualify for Section 509(a)(3) status.

[2] Responsiveness Test

The Responsiveness Test for Type III supporting organizations originally had two different versions. The supporting organization only needed to meet one of them. The first, or the "Interlocking Organizations-Significant Voice" version of the

---

the complete independence of the trustee meant that the trust was neither "operated, supervised or controlled by" nor "supervised or controlled in connection with" the public school system.

[253] I.R.C. § 4943(f)(5)(B).

[254] I.R.C. § 509(a)(1) or § 509(a)(2) organizations can be "disqualified persons because they are often times "major donors."

[255] 1980-2 C.B. 193.

[256] *Id.; see also* I.R.C. § 4946(a)(1)(A).

[257] Rev. Rul. 80-207; *see also* I.R.C. § 4946(a)(1)(E).

[258] Rev. Rul. 80-207.

Responsiveness Test is met if:

- one or more of the officers, directors, or trustees of the supporting organization are elected or appointed by the officers, directors, trustees, or membership of the supported organization;[259] or

- one or more of the members of the governing bodies of the supported organization are also officers, directors, or trustees of, or hold other important offices in, the supporting organization;[260] or

- the officers, directors, or trustees of the supporting organization maintain a close and continuous working relationship with the officers, directors, and trustees of the supported organization;[261] and

- by reason of one of the above, the officers, directors, or trustees of the supported organization have a significant voice in the investment policies of the supporting organization, the timing of grants, the manner of making them, and the selection of recipients, and in directing the use of the income or assets of the supporting organization.[262]

Prior to the revisions of the Pension Protection Act of 2006, there was a second version of the "Responsiveness Test" called the "Charitable Trust" test. That test was met if:

- the supporting organization is a charitable trust under state law;[263] and

- the supported organization is named as a beneficiary of the trust in the trust's governing document;[264] and

- The named beneficiary supported organization has the power to enforce the trust and compel an accounting under state law.[265]

There was a line of cases applying the "charitable trust" test that are now no longer relevant.[266] For a charitable trust to meet the Responsiveness Test now, it must meet the Interlocking Organizations-Significant Voice Test.[267] In fact, after

---

[259] 26 C.F.R. § 1.509(a)-4(i)(2)(ii)(a).

[260] 26 C.F.R. § 1.509(a)-4(i)(2)(ii)(b).

[261] 26 C.F.R. § 1.509(a)-4(i)(2)(ii)(c).

[262] 26 C.F.R. § 1.509(a)-4(i)(2)(ii)(d). See Rev. Rul. 75-437, where the use of a commercial bank as trustee meant that the supported organizations did not have a significant voice in directing the investment policies of the trust or the timing and making of grants, thereby failing the first version of the Responsiveness Test. *See also Windsor Found.*, 40 A.F.T.R.2d (RIA) 6004.

[263] 26 C.F.R. § 1.509(a)-4(i)(2)(iii)(a).

[264] 26 C.F.R. § 1.509(a)-4(i)(2)(iii)(b).

[265] 26 C.F.R. § 1.509(a)-4(i)(2)(iii)(c). See Rev. Rul. 75-437, 1975-2 C.B. 218, where the failure of the trust document to name a supported organization beneficiary and the lack of enforcement power in the trust meant that it also failed the second version of the Responsiveness Test.

[266] Nellie Callahan Scholarship Fund v. Comm'r, 73 T.C. 626 (1980); Goodspeed Scholarship Fund v. Comm'r, 70 T.C. 515 (1978).

[267] Pension Protection Act of 2006, Pub L. No. 109-280, § 1241(c), 120 Stat. 780 (2006). I.R.S. Announcement 2010-19 explains the steps a charitable trust must take to maintain its status as a supporting organization.

the reforms of the Pension Protection Act of 2006, all Type III supporting organizations must meet the Interlocking Organizations-Significant Voice version of the Responsiveness Test.

The Pension Protection Act of 2006 eliminated the "charitable trust" version of the Responsiveness Test as of August 2007.[268] As a result, all that is left is the "Interlocking Organizations-Significant Voice" version, as considered by the following cases.

In *Change-All Souls Housing Corporation v. United States*,[269] the organization had been established by a church and a private foundation, who were the members of the organization. The organization's purpose was to provide low- and moderate-income housing in Washington, D.C. The organization was recognized as a Section 501(c)(3) organization, but not as a public charity. The IRS's position was that the organization's relationship with its private foundation member meant that it supported a private foundation, and therefore did not qualify itself as a public charity. The Court of Claims disagreed. It held that the organization met the "Interlocking Organizations-Significant Voice" version of the Responsiveness Test as to the church-member, and that its responsiveness to the church was not diminished by its relationship with its private foundation-member.[270]

In *Cockerline Memorial Fund v. Commissioner*,[271] the IRS had denied non-private foundation status under Section 509(a)(3) to a college scholarship fund that benefited students from Oregon, with a preference, but not a requirement, that the trustees of the fund favor students attending Northwest Christian College in Eugene, Oregon. The fund had seven trustees and the President of Northwest was, ex officio, one of the seven under the terms of the trust. On the issue of whether the fund met the Responsiveness Test, the IRS argued that one of seven trustees linked to the supported organization was not enough to meet the first version of the Responsiveness Test. The Tax Court referred them to their own regulations, which required that *one* or more of the members of the governing body of the publicly supported organization also be officers, directors or trustees of, or hold other important offices in, the supporting organizations."[272] The Tax Court found that the "one" person requirement had been met. It also found, on the facts, that Northwest did exercise a significant voice in the fund's affairs, and held that the "Charitable Trust" version of the "Responsiveness Test" (now no longer applicable) had been met.[273]

In *Roe Foundation Charitable Trust*,[274] the trust failed to meet either version of the Responsiveness Test. The trust failed to name any Section 509(a)(1) or Section 509(a)(2) organization as a beneficiary, and lacked any enforcement mechanism, except that allowed by state law to the state's attorney general. As a result, the

---

[268] Pub. L. No. 109-280, § 1241(e)(1), 120 Stat. 780 (2006).

[269] 671 F.2d 463 (Ct. Cl. 1982).

[270] *Id.*

[271] 86 T.C. 53 (1986).

[272] *Id.; see also* 26 C.F.R. § 1.509(a)-4(i)(2)(ii)(b).

[273] *Cockerline Mem'l Fund*, 86 T.C. 53.

[274] 58 T.C.M. (CCH) 402 (1989).

"Charitable Trust" version of the Responsiveness Test was not met. The supported organization only appointed one out of four members of the supporting organization's governing board. The Tax Court did not find that to be a significant voice in the operations of the supporting organization. On this basis, the Tax Court found that the trust failed the "Interlocking Organizations-Significant Voice" version of the Responsiveness Test as well.[275]

[3]   Integral Parts Test

The Integral Part Test is met if the supporting organization maintains a significant involvement in the operations of the supported organization and if the supported organization is, in turn, dependent on the supporting organization.[276] The Integral Part Test also has two versions. In the first version of the Integral Part Test, usually referred to as the "But For" Test, there are two requirements:

- The activities that the supporting organization engages in, for or on behalf of the supported organization, are activities that perform the functions of, or carry out the purposes of, the supported organization; and

- But for the involvement of the supporting organization, these activities would normally be engaged in by the supported organization itself.[277]

In the second version of the Integral Part Test, usually referred to as the "Attentiveness" Test, there are three parts:

- The supporting organization makes payments of substantially all of its income to or for the use of one or more publicly supported organizations;[278] and

- The amount of support received by one or more of the publicly supported organizations is sufficient to insure the attentiveness of those supported organizations to the affairs of the supporting organization;[279] and

- A substantial amount of the total support of the supporting organization must go to those publicly supported organizations that meet this "attentiveness" requirement.[280]

Type III supporting organizations that meet the "But For" test or that are the parent of each of the supported organizations qualify as "functionally integrated." Those that do not meet either of these requirements are considered "non-functionally integrated" Type III supporting organizations.

---

[275] *Id.*

[276] 26 C.F.R. § 1.509(a)-4(i)(3)(i).

[277] 26 C.F.R. § 1.509(a)-4(i)(3)(ii). See Rev. Rul. 75-437, where a charitable trust that provided scholarships for students in a school district did not meet the "But For" Test because the school district would not normally be engaged in a scholarship program, and its cessation would not make the school district start one.

[278] 26 C.F.R. § 1.509(a)-4(i)(3)(iii)(a). See Rev. Rul. 76-208, 1976-1 C.B. 161, where "substantially all" was found to be at least 85 percent of the supporting organization's income.

[279] 26 C.F.R. § 1.509(a)-4(i)(3)(iii)(a).

[280] *Id.*

In *Lapham Foundation v. Commissioner*,[281] the issue was whether the Foundation qualified as a Section 509(a)(3) supporting organization by meeting the Integral Part Test as to its supported organization, the American Endowment Foundation (AEF), a public charity that operated a donor-advised fund program.[282] The Lapham Foundation was one such fund. Because the Lapham Foundation intended to recommend to AEF that it use the Lapham Foundation's funds to benefit public charities in Northville, Michigan, it claimed that it met the "But For" Test. But for the Lapham Foundation's support, AEF would not be supporting any charities in Northville. That did not fly. The court pointed out that recommendations to donor-advised funds are not binding, and AEF was dedicated to nationwide grant-making activities, not just to a small corner of Michigan, and those nationwide activities would continue whether or not AEF got any funds from Lapham. The "But For" Test was not met. As to the "Attentiveness" Test, while the Lapham Foundation was giving "substantially all" of its income to AEF, it only amounted to $7,600 in AEF's budget of over $7 million. This amount was not sufficient to insure attentiveness, and therefore the requirements of the "Attentiveness" Test were not met. Because the Lapham Foundation met neither the "But For" Test nor the "Attentiveness" Test as to AEF, it was not an Integral Part of AEF and was not a Section 509(a)(3) supporting organization.[283]

In *Cuddeback v. Commissioner*,[284] a charitable trust was created to support two churches, each getting 10 percent of trust income, and a public charity that operated a multi-care facility getting the remaining 80 percent. In deciding its status as a Section 509(a)(3) supporting organization, the Tax Court held that the organization had not shown that the support it provided to the three supported organizations was sufficient to insure their attentiveness, nor that, without its support, the three organizations' programs would suffer. As a result, the organization did not meet the Integral Part Test, and was not a Section 509(a)(3) non-private foundation.[285]

In *Roe Foundation v. Commissioner*,[286] the organization was held not to meet the "But For" Test because it did not demonstrate that it was engaged in any activities or was performing any functions that, but for its involvement, the supported organization would have to perform on its own. The organization was to be funded with a testamentary gift, but the testators were still alive and well. Without any funds, the court found that the organization was incapable of performing any activities or functions that benefited anyone. Without any funds to expend, there was nothing for the supported organization to be attentive to either, and so the "Attentiveness" Test was not met. Failing both versions of the Integral Part Test ("But For" and "Attentiveness"), the organization could not qualify as an

---

[281] 82 T.C.M. (CCH) 586 (2002).

[282] See § 17.08[A] for further information on donor-advised funds.

[283] *Id.*

[284] 84 T.C.M. (CCH) 623 (2002).

[285] *Id.*

[286] 58 T.C.M. (CCH) 402 (1989).

Integral Part of the allegedly supported organization.[287]

[4]   Functionally and Non-Functionally Integrated Type III Supporting Organizations

The Pension Protection Act of 2006, in creating this distinction between functionally and non-functionally integrated Type III supporting organizations, also placed significant disabilities on the non-functionally integrated organizations. Non-functionally integrated Type III supporting organizations, even though they are still non-private foundations, by virtue of being Section 509(a)(3) organizations, are subject to the same excess business holdings restrictions under IRC Section 4943 as are private foundations (i.e., no more than 20% ownership of a business entity).[288] This means that wealthy donors can no longer use these organizations as a place to park the stock of closely held business corporations, get a tax break for a deductible gift, and through their control of the supporting organization, still have corporate control. Type III non-functionally integrated supporting organizations are also subject to the annual payout requirements of Section 4942, but without the set-asides allowed by Section 4942(g).[289] Finally, grants to a non-functionally integrated Type III supporting organization by another private foundation are not considered qualifying distributions under IRC 4942.

[5]   Other Pension Protection Act Restrictions on Section 509(a)(3) Supporting Organizations

In addition to creating the distinction between functionally integrated and non-functionally integrated Type III supporting organizations, the Pension Protection Act of 2006 also placed some limitations on the activities of all Type III supporting organizations, regardless of type. It provides that a Type III supporting organization must annually provide to each of its supported organizations such information as the IRS may require to ensure that the supporting organization is responsive to the needs of its supported organization. It prohibits a Type III supporting organization from supporting any supported organization not organized in the United States. The Pension Protection Act also restricts Type I and Type III supporting organizations from accepting contributions from a person who, alone or with other related persons, directly or indirectly controls the governing body of a supported organization of the Type I or Type III supporting organization.[290]

[D]   Section 509(a)(4): Public Safety Testing Organizations

Section 509(a)(4) excludes from classification as non-private foundations those organizations that qualify under Section 501(c)(3) as public safety testing organizations.[291] These organizations test consumer products for safety in their

---

[287] *Id.*

[288] I.R.C. 4943(f).

[289] 26 C.F.R. § 1.509(a)-4.

[290] *See* Pension Protection Act of 2006, Pub. L. No. 109-280, 120 Stat. 780 (2006).

[291] See § 12.07 further information on public safety testing organizations.

use by the general public. Their presence here, as a statutory exception to private foundation status, is a testament to the effectiveness of their professional lobbyists.

§ 19.06 PRIVATE OPERATING FOUNDATIONS

Private operating foundations do just what their name suggests: they operate their own programs of Section 501(c)(3) activities as opposed to simply funding such activities. These private operating foundations are still subject to most of the same rules that govern all the other private foundations, the "non-operating" private foundations, but there are some exceptions. In certain areas, private operating foundations are treated as "public charities" and not as private foundations.

Private operating foundations are treated as public charities for purposes of the charitable contribution deduction. A donor to a private operating foundation gets the same deduction rates as those for Section 509(a)(1), (2) and (3) public charities on his or her tax return,[292] and not the lesser rates for private foundations.[293] Private operating foundations are also treated like public charities for purposes of the estate tax and the gift tax.[294]

Private operating foundations do not have to make the required annual minimum distribution (five percent of net investment assets) that private non-operating foundations must make.[295] The trade-off, though, is that private operating foundations must regularly spend their adjusted net income in the performance of their exempt activities.[296]

Private operating foundations can receive gifts and grants from other private foundations as a "qualifying distribution" under Section 4942's income distribution requirements. Normally, private foundations can only make gifts and grants to public charities, although grants to private non-operating foundations are possible under certain limited circumstances.[297]

Gifts and grants to private operating foundations identified as "exempt operating foundations"[298] do not require the same "expenditure responsibility" that gifts to private non-operating foundations require.[299] Exempt operating foundations are not subject to the Section 4940 excise tax.[300]

---

[292] I.R.C. § 170(b)(1)(A)(vii), (E)(i), (e)(1)(B)(ii), (3)(A), (5)(C)(i).

[293] I.R.C. § 170(b)(1)(B).

[294] I.R.C. §§ 2055(e)(4), 2503(g).

[295] I.R.C. § 4942(a)(1).

[296] I.R.C. § 4942(j)(3)(A).

[297] See I.R.C. § 4942(g)(1)(A)(ii), (3). Basically the non-operating private foundation must itself then give the grant away for charitable purposes and keep adequate records demonstrating this fact.

[298] I.R.C. § 4940(d)(2) defines an "exempt operating foundation" as a private operating foundation that has been publicly supported for at least ten taxable years (using either the § 509(a)(1)-§ 170(b)(1)(A)(vi) or § 509(a)(2) public support tests); that has a governing body made up of individuals of whom 75 percent are not disqualified persons and which is broadly representative of the general public; and that does not have a disqualified person as an officer.

[299] I.R.C. § 4945(d)(4)(B), (h).

[300] I.R.C. § 4940(d).

Private operating foundations are defined in IRC Section 4942(j)(3). To be considered a private operating foundation, an organization must meet an "income" test and, in addition, one of either an "assets" test, an "endowment" test or a "support" test.

In order to meet the income test, a private operating foundation must make qualifying distributions equal to substantially all of its adjusted net income[301] or substantially all of its minimum investment return (five percent of its net asset value) whichever is lesser, directly for the conduct of its charitable activities.[302] The Regulations define "substantially all" as 85 percent or more.[303]

Qualifying distributions are defined in IRC Section 4942(g)(1). They include amounts paid or set aside to accomplish charitable purposes or paid to a governmental unit for exclusively public purposes, together with necessary administrative expenses.[304]

In order to meet the assets test, a private operating foundation must demonstrate that at least 65 percent of its total assets are (1) devoted to exempt function activities, (2) devoted to functionally related businesses, (3) in the stock of a controlled corporation, substantially all of whose assets are devoted to the foundation's exempt activities, or (4) devoted to some combination of these three.[305]

In order to meet the endowment test (sometimes also called the "expenditures" test), a private operating foundation must normally expend at least two-thirds of its minimum investment return for the performance of its exempt function activities. Because the minimum investment return is equal to five percent of the foundation's net investment assets, this test works out to an annual expenditure of 3.3 percent of the foundation's endowment, i.e., its net investment asset base.[306]

In order to meet the support test, the private foundation must meet three requirements: (1) it must receive substantially all (85 percent or more) of its support (excluding gross investment income) from the general public and from five or more unrelated exempt non-private foundations; (2) no single unrelated exempt organization accounts for more than 25 percent of its support; and (3) not more than half of its support is normally received from gross investment income.[307]

---

[301] Adjusted net income is defined in I.R.C. § 4942(f).

[302] If the private operating foundation's qualifying distributions exceed the minimum investment return, but not adjusted net income, then substantially all of its qualifying distributions must be made directly for the active conduct of the private operating foundation's charitable activities. But, if the private operating foundation's minimum investment return is less than its adjusted net income, then only that portion of the qualifying distributions equal to substantially all of the foundation's adjusted net income must be made directly for the active conduct of its charitable activities. 26 C.F.R. § 53.4942(b)-1(a)(1)(ii).

[303] 26 C.F.R. § 53.4942(b)-1(c).

[304] 26 C.F.R. § 53.4942(a)-3(a)(8).

[305] I.R.C. § 4942(j)(3)(B)(i); 26 C.F.R. § 53.4942(b)-2(a)(1)(i). The 65 percent rule is in 26 C.F.R. § 53.4942(b)-2(a)(5), where "substantially more than half" is defined.

[306] I.R.C. § 4942(j)(3)(B)(ii).

[307] I.R.C. § 4942(j)(3)(B)(iii); 26 C.F.R. § 53.4942(b)-2(c)(2)(ii), (b)-1.

In the case of *The "Miss Elizabeth" D. Leckie Scholarship Fund v. Commissioner*,[308] the Tax Court faced the question of whether a private foundation that awarded scholarships qualified as an operating foundation. The court found that, due to the foundation's "significant involvement"[309] in the grants process it met the "qualifying distributions" income test. Further, because these grants consumed more than two-thirds of the foundation's minimum investment return, it also met the endowment test.

§ 19.07   TERMINATING A PRIVATE FOUNDATION

IRC Section 507 deals with the termination of private foundation status. Termination of a private foundation can occur either voluntarily by action of the private foundation itself, or involuntarily by action of the IRS. An involuntary termination can occur under IRC Section 507(a)(2) for willful repeated acts or failures to act in violation of the statute or regulations governing private foundations. Willful and repeated acts or failure to act means at least two acts or failures, both of which are voluntary, conscious, and intentional.[310] Involuntary termination can also occur under IRC Section 507(a)(2) for one willful and flagrant act or failure to act in violation of the statute or the regulations. A willful and flagrant act or failure to act is one that is voluntarily, consciously, and knowingly committed and that would appear to be a "gross" violation to a reasonable person.[311] In the case of an involuntary termination, the IRS can impose a tax equal to the lower of the total tax benefits that the private foundation received from its Section 501(c)(3) status, or the value of the net assets of the foundation.[312]

A voluntary termination of a private foundation can happen in five different ways: (1) it can transfer all of its assets to a 501(c)(3) public charity (nonprivate foundation); (2) it can transfer all of its assets to a 501(c)(3) private foundation; (3) it can transform itself into a public charity; (4) it can transfer its assets to non-charitable parties; (5) it can just stop functioning. Termination of a private foundation requires IRS notification.[313] Transfer of a foundations assets can also trigger an excise tax.[314]

When termination occurs through a transfer of assets to a public charity, the transfer must be to a public charity that has been in existence and has qualified as a public charity for the preceding five years.[315] The private foundation must also

---

[308] 87 T.C. 251 (1986).

[309] "Significant involvement" is defined in 26 C.F.R. § 53.4942(b)-1(b)(2)(ii).

[310] 26 C.F.R. § 1.507-1(c)(1).

[311] 26 C.F.R. § 1.507-1(c)(2).

[312] I.R.C. § 507(c). The IRS can abate the tax if the private foundation distributes its assets to a public charity that has been in existence for at least 5 years, or takes other corrective action under state law preserving its assets for charitable purposes. I.R.C. § 507(g).

[313] I.R.C. § 507(a)(1).

[314] I.R.C. § 4945(d).

[315] I.R.C. § 507(b)(1)(A).

submit a statement to the IRS that it is terminating and pay any tax due.[316] This process of private foundation to public charity transfer is also outlined in Revenue Ruling 2003-13.[317] The transfer of a private foundation's assets to another private foundation constitutes a significant disposition under Section 507(b)(2). Such a transfer to another private foundation is not an automatic termination, but it can be if all assets are transferred and the proper notice is given to the IRS.[318] Such a transfer is also covered by the Section 507(c) tax. Private foundation to private foundation transfers are covered in Revenue Ruling 2002-28.[319] The transfer of a private foundation to public charity status is achieved by the private foundation refiling for status as a Section 509(a)(1) - (4) organization.

A terminating transfer of private foundation assets to private parties is problematical, for the obvious reasons. Yet this is just what happened in the case of *Gladney v. Commissioner.*[320] As a result of the state court's interpretation of the terms of a will, the assets of a private foundation that had been operating a home for elderly men, but which was now barely functioning, were turned over to the decedent's heirs. The question in that case was whether the IRC § 507 statutory notice of termination had been appropriately given to the IRS. The Tax Court had held that the federal statutory notice requirements were met by the foundation's board of trustees filings with IRS after the distribution of the assets.[321] The Fifth Circuit disagreed. The Tax Court had also held that the heirs who received the foundation's assets were not liable for the excise tax levied in such situations by IRC § 4945, and that this fact had also relieved the foundation of the § 507 notice requirement. The Fifth Circuit, while agreeing that no excise tax was due, held that this fact still did not relieve the foundation of the § 507 notice requirement.

There is, of course, one final way for private foundations to terminate themselves, and that is to do nothing, simply notify the IRS, and cease operations. The Regulations provide for payment of any tax due,[322] which in this case would be the Section 507(c) termination tax, which in effect confiscates the private foundation's remaining assets, if there are any to seize. But this tax is subject to abatement if the private foundation distributes its assets to a public charity that is more than five years old or if it takes action, under state law, to preserve its assets for charitable purposes.[323]

---

[316] I.R.C. § 507(a)(1), (c).

[317] 2003-1 C.B. 305.

[318] I.R.C. § 507(a)(1); 26 C.F.R. §§ 1.507-1(b)(6), 1.507-3(d).

[319] 2002-1 C.B. 941.

[320] 745 F.2d 955 (5th Cir. 1984).

[321] Gladney v. Comm'r, 45 T.C.M. (CCH) 280 (1982).

[322] 26 C.F.R. § 1.507-1(b)(1).

[323] I.R.C. § 507(g).

§ 19.08 PRIVATE FOUNDATION FORMS

The IRS has recently issued a new Form 8940 that private foundations are to use for a "Request for Miscellaneous Determination." The types of requests covered by this form are: (1) advance IRS approval of Section 4942(g)(2) set-asides; (2) advance IRS approval of voter registration activities covered by Section 4945(F); (3) advance IRS approval of scholarship procedures under Section 4945(g); (4) exemption from Form 990 filing requirements; (5) advance IRS approval that a potential grant or contribution constitutes an "Unusual Grant"; (6) change in Type of a Section 509(a)(3) organization; (7) reclassification of foundation status, including a voluntary request from a public charity for private foundation status; (8) termination of private foundation status under Section 507(b)(1)(B) — advance ruling request; (9) termination of private foundation status under Section 507(b)(1)(B) — 60–month period ended.[325]

---

[325] *See* Rev. Proc. 2011-4, 2011-1 I.RB. 123; Instructions to Form 8940 (Rev. June, 2011).

Chapter 20

SECURING & MAINTAINING TAX EXEMPT STATUS

§ 20.01 INTRODUCTION

Section 501 of the IRC recognizes the existence of tax exempt organizations.[1] As long as an organization fits into one of the categories described in subsections (c) or (d) of Section 501, it may qualify as tax exempt, provided it does not fail any substantive requirements[2] or fall under the provisions of IRC Section 502 or Section 503.[3]

Generally, organizations seeking exemption from taxation must notify the IRS and file annual information returns. The requirements for notification by Section 501(c)(3) organizations are codified under IRC Section 508. Filing and public disclosure requirements are codified under Sections 6033, 6103, 6104, and 6652. Based upon these filings, the IRS is charged with determining whether an organization is in compliance with the substantive requirements for exempt organizations under the IRC. The IRS's determination that an organization is exempt is made objectively based on the information provided by the organization.[4]

§ 20.02 APPLYING FOR TAX EXEMPT STATUS

For most qualified organizations, it is not enough to simply declare themselves "tax exempt." With a few exceptions,[5] Section 501(c)(3) organizations seeking exemption must submit a Form 1023 application, which provides information to the IRS specifying their qualifications for tax exemption.[6] The information provided in the application must be sufficient for the IRS to determine that the organization

---

[1] See Appendix E for a detailed list of organizations exempt from federal income taxation.

[2] Substantive requirements for tax exempt organizations include the following: organizational and operational requirements, lack of private inurement, limitations on lobbying and political activities etc. See § 6.01 *et seq.* for further information on the substantive requirements for tax exempt organizations.

[3] I.R.C. § 502 provides generally that "feeder organizations" are not tax exempt. I.R.C. § 503 provides additional requirements for exemption to certain tax exempt organizations such as § 501(c)(17) and § 501(c)(18) organizations.

[4] References in cases and literature to the IRS "granting tax exempt status to an organization" is a bit of a misnomer. The IRS does not grant tax exempt status; it recognizes that an organization qualifies for that status.

[5] *See* I.R.C. § 508(a), (c)(1); 26 C.F.R. § 1.508-1(a)(3), (3)(i)(C); *see also* § 20.02[A].

[6] *See* I.R.C. § 508(a). The notification requirement for § 508 should not be confused with the notification requirement under § 509(a). I.R.C. § 509(a) requires that a 501(c)(3) organization notify the

meets the requirements of exemption as outlined in the IRC. If the information provided is not sufficient to determine that an organization meets the substantive requirements for exemption, the IRS will not recognize the organization as exempt; and donations to the organization will not be deductible.

The IRS summarized the informational requirements under Section 508 in Revenue Procedure 2011-9.[7] The IRS will provide a letter to the organization determining that it does indeed qualify as tax exempt if its application and supporting documents establish that it meets the particular requirements of the section under which exemption is claimed. Revenue Procedure 2011-9 states, "A mere restatement of exempt purposes or a statement that proposed activities will be in furtherance of such purposes will not satisfy this requirement. . . . The organization must fully describe all of the activities in which it expects to engage, including the standards, criteria, procedures or other means adopted or planned for carrying out the activities, the anticipated sources of receipts, and the nature of contemplated expenditures."[8]

A Section 501(c) organization must provide sufficient information to the IRS by completing a Form 1023 or a Form 1024.[9] The purpose of Forms 1023 and 1024 is to elicit necessary information (as summarized in Revenue Procedure 2011-9), so that the IRS can determine whether an organization meets the substantive requirements to qualify as tax exempt.[10] Form 1023 is for organizations seeking exemption as 501(c)(3) religious, charitable, or educational organizations.[11] Form 1024 is used for other exempt organizations.[12]

IRS that it is not a private foundation. For further information on the I.R.C. § 509(a) requirement, see § 19.05.

[7] 2011-2 I.R.B. 283 (This revenue procedure is updated annually).

[8] *Id.*

[9] While the majority of exempt organizations do file either IRS Form 1023 or 1024, there are some exempt organizations that may provide notification by other means, i.e., § 501(c)(11), (14), (16), (18), (21), (22), (23), (26) and (27) organizations may apply for exemption by letter signed by an officer of the organization with accompanying documentation. Section 521(a) Farmers' Cooperative Associations are required to complete Form 1028; Section 527 Political organizations are required to complete Form 8871. *See* I.R.S. Publication 557 *Tax Exempt Status for Your Organization* 60, 61 (Rev. Oct. 2010).

[10] See § 6.01 *et seq.* for the substantive requirements of tax exempt organizations. If the organization does not meet the substantive requirements for tax exemption, the IRS will not recognize the organization as exempt, and the organization will be unable to accept tax-deductible donations.

[11] Other organizations may use Form 1023, but they are not discussed here. Other organizations that use Form 1023 include: § 501(e) Cooperative Hospital Services Organizations; § 501(f) Cooperative Services Organizations of Operating Educational Organizations; § 501(k) Child Care Organizations; and § 501(n) Charitable Risk Pools. *See* I.R.S. Publication 557 *Tax Exempt Status for Your Organization* 60, 61 (Rev. Oct. 2010).

[12] Organizations required to complete IRS Form 1024 include: § 501(c)(2) Title Holding Corporations for Exempt Organizations; § 501(c)(4) Civic Leagues, Social Welfare Organizations, and Local Associations of Employees; § 501(c)(5) Labor, Agricultural, and Horticultural Organizations; § 501(c)(6) Business Leagues, Chambers of Commerce, and Real Estate Boards; § 501(c)(7) Social and Recreational Clubs; § 501(c)(8) Fraternal Beneficiary Societies and Associations; § 501(c)(9) Voluntary Employees Beneficiary Associations; § 501(c)(10) Domestic Fraternal Societies and Associations; § 501(c)(12) Benevolent Life Insurance Associations, Mutual Ditch or Irrigation Companies, Mutual or Cooperative Telephone Companies; § 501(c)(13) Cemetery Companies; § 501(c)(15) Mutual Insurance Companies or Associations; § 501(c)(17) Supplemental Unemployment Benefit Trusts; § 501(c)(19) Black Lung Benefit

[A] Organizations Exempt From Filing Form 1023

Several types of organizations are exempt from the Section 508 notice requirement. That is, these organizations do not have to file Form 1023 (or any other form for that matter) to be considered tax exempt and therefore become eligible to receive tax deductible gifts.[13] The organizations exempt from the notice requirement include: churches, their integrated auxiliaries, and conventions or associations of churches;[14] any Section 501(d); apostolic organizations; or public charities (i.e. not private foundations as defined in Section 509(a)) whose gross receipts for each taxable year are normally not more than $5,000.[15]

Many organizations not required to file with the IRS choose to do so because this serves as a stamp of approval, in the nature of a determination letter, that the organization is a bona fide exempt organization. Proof of tax exemption becomes important when donors need verification for claiming charitable tax deductions on their personal income tax returns. Once the IRS accepts the organization's application and determines its validity, it is listed in IRS Publication 78.[16]

This same principle applies to those organizations covered by Form 1024. Although non-501(c)(3) organizations do not, strictly speaking, have to seek IRS recognition, most of them do go through the Form 1024 process so that there is a record of IRS recognition of their status.

[B] Form 1023

This section focuses on those charitable, religious, educational, and other organizations covered by Section 501(c)(3) securing IRS recognition of tax exempt status by filing an "Application for Recognition of Exemption" Form 1023 with the IRS.[17] To qualify, an organization must be a nonprofit corporation, a charitable trust, or an unincorporated association.[18] Individuals and partnerships cannot qualify.[19]

Trusts; § 501(c)(25) Title Holding Corporations or Trusts with Multiple Parents; 501(c)(6) State-Sponsored High Risk Health Coverage Organizations; 501(c)(7) Qualified State Sponsored Workers' Compensation Organizations. *See* I.R.S. Publication 557 *Tax Exempt Status for Your Organization* 60, 61 (Rev. Oct. 2010).

[13] I.R.C. § 508(c).

[14] I.R.C. § 508(c)(1)(A).

[15] I.R.C. § 508(c)(1)(B). The IRS determines whether an organization has annual gross receipts greater than $5,000 using an objective set of rules outlined in 26 C.F.R. § 1.508-1(a)(3)(e)(ii). Rev. Rul. 80-259 illustrates the application of the rules in 26 C.F.R. § 1.508-1(a)(3)(e)(ii).

[16] I.R.S. Publication 78 *Cumulative List of Organizations described in* § 170(C) of the IRC of 1986 (Jan. 14, 2011). Online searches are possible at www.irs.gov.

[17] IRS Form 1023 seems to be in a constant process of revision. It was revised in October, 2004 and in June, 2006. It is currently being revised to deal with the elimination of the advance ruling process.

[18] Form 1023, Part II, Question 2, asks if the organization is a "limited liability" company (LLC); however, LLCs are treated as a corporation rather than a partnership for purposes of their exemption application. *See* IRS Form 8832 *Entity Classification Election* (Rev. Jan., 2011).

[19] I.R.S. Publication 557 *Tax Exempt Status for Your Organization* 16 (Rev. Oct. 2010).

The purpose of Form 1023 is to assist the IRS in determining first, if the organization has complied with the substantive requirements for tax exempt organizations; and second, if the organization is a private or non-private foundation. To determine if the organization has complied with the substantive requirements for tax exempt organizations, the IRS asks for information in Form 1023 that allows it to determine if the organization is organized and operated exclusively for exempt purposes; if the organization violates the private benefit prohibition; if the organization engages in private inurement or excess benefit prohibitions; and if the organization engages in prohibited political activities.[20]

In the technical language of the IRS there are two major categories of Section 501(c)(3) organizations: private foundations and non-private foundations (i.e., public charities).[21] The IRC presumes that all Section 501(c)(3) organizations are private foundations, and thus subject to tighter regulation, than public charities, unless the organization can show otherwise.[22] This is reflected in the questions of Form 1023. A number of the inquiries in Form 1023 are there to help the IRS separate the private foundations from the public charities.[23]

Providing the information requested in Form 1023 can be a time-consuming task. The Form requires the organization to provide a narrative description of its past, present, and future activities; detailed financial data, including a budget and fundraising information; and answers to a long list of questions relating to the organization's governing body, their relationship to the organization, and their compensation.[24]

When submitting Form 1023, only the applicable schedules and related attachments should be submitted; however, sample Form 1023 in Appendix A includes all Schedules for purposes of review. For instance, a formal educational organization (which is the category of the fictional organization described in Appendix A) would file Form 1023 and attach: (1) organizational documents, (articles and bylaws); (2) Schedule B and documentation of a nondiscriminatory policy; and (3) all other required attachments.[25] A hospital, however, would file Form 1023 with organizational documents, Schedule C, and any other required attachments.

---

[20] See §§ 6.01 et seq. and 7.01 et seq. for detailed discussions of these tests and limits on tax exempt organizations.

[21] See I.R.C. § 509.

[22] An organization proves to the IRS that it is not a private foundation by providing information that qualifies it for one of the exceptions to private foundation status as outlined in I.R.C. § 509(a)(1)-(4).

[23] For example, Form 1023, Section II, Schedule D, asks questions regarding the relationship with supported organizations to determine if the organization fits into the § 509(a)(3) exception to private foundation status.

[24] IRS Form 1023 Application for Recognition of Exemption Under § 501(c)(3) of the IRC (Rev. June, 2006).

[25] Id. at 15; see also § 20.02[C].

[C] Schedules & Attachments

In addition to Form 1023 and its applicable schedules, the organization will need to provide further information, such as: employer identification numbers (EIN), articles of organization; bylaws or rules of operation; and Form 2848 Power of Attorney. In addition, the applicant will, as necessary, need to include attachments containing information or explanations of answers to questions on the Form. Attachments may include such things as financial data, information on the Board of Directors, and printed materials or publications. The EIN is used by the IRS as an account number and is required regardless of whether the organization has employees. Organizations can apply for an EIN by filling out Form SS-4 and calling the IRS, following instructions on the IRS web site, or submitting a Form SS-4 by fax or mail to the appropriate office.[26]

A copy of the founding documents of an organization must also be included. These documents include articles of incorporation (and the certificate of incorporation, if available) or articles of association or a trust document or other enabling document.[27] Without some kind of founding document, an organization cannot qualify as tax exempt. Bylaws are not, strictly speaking, founding documents, but if an organization has adopted bylaws, then they should be included with the application. If the founding documents do not state a charitable purpose or fail to discuss final distribution and private inurement issues, the application will fail.[28]

If the organization has an attorney who will be the contact person on the application, then Form 2848 Power of Attorney, naming this individual, should accompany Form 1023. This Power of Attorney allows the IRS to speak with the Attorney about any issues or concerns that arise with the application. Without the Power of Attorney Form, there can be no discussion. A sample Power of Attorney Form has been provided in Appendix B. The "Power of Attorney Form 2848" should not be confused with the "Tax Information Authorization Form 8821." The Tax Information Authorization Form gives any individual, corporation, firm, organization or partnership the authority to inspect and receive any confidential information in any office of the IRS. The Form requires that the scope of authorization be outlined by describing the type of tax information to be shared and period for which information is to be shared.

[D] Submitting Form 1023

Once Form 1023 is completed by the organization, it should be submitted to the IRS at the address indicated on the Form, along with the applicable attachments and the appropriate user fee.[29] Upon receiving the application, the IRS will

---

[26] The EIN is required on Form 1023; however, obtaining an EIN is fairly easy and most organizations receive an EIN electronically via the internet, phone or fax. *See* Form 1023 "Instructions" 6 (Rev. June, 2006). A sample Form SS-4 is provided in Appendix C.

[27] Form 1023 "Instructions" 4 (Rev. June, 2006).

[28] Form 1023 "Instructions" 7 (Rev. June, 2006).

[29] *See* Form 1023 Part XI.

determine if it is complete before reviewing it. When an application is determined to be incomplete (i.e., missing necessary information such as founding documents), the IRS will notify the organization and ask that additional information be provided. In the case of an application under IRC Section 501(c)(3) that is returned incomplete, the 270-day period referred to in IRC Section 7428(b)(2) will not be considered as starting until the date a substantially completed Form 1023 is refilled or remailed to the IRS.[30]

In rare instances, when an application raises unusual issues of law, it will be referred by EO Determinations to EO Technical for advice. The applicant organization can also request a referral to the Exempt Organization Technical Division when it believes that the application raises issues that are unusual, complex, or without uniform governing precedent.[31]

An organization may withdraw its application in writing at any time prior to a determination (adverse or otherwise) by the IRS. The IRS will not consider the withdrawal of an application under section 501(c)(3) as either a failure to make a determination or an exhaustion of administrative remedies.[32] A withdrawal will not prevent the information contained in the application form from being used by IRS in any subsequent examination of the organization.[33]

[E]   Form 1024

Form 1024 is used for other types of 501(c) organizations, including the Section 501(c)(4), (6), (7), and (8) organizations.[34] Form 1024 seeks to elicit the same type of information that Form 1023 does. That is, information that demonstrates to the IRS that the organization qualifies as exempt from taxation. However, because there are differences between Section 501(c)(3) organizations and other Section 501(c) organizations, there are several important differences in the forms. Form 1024 asks for information on the type of organization, how it is governed, and what its finances are.[35] As with Form 1023, copies of the founding documents must be supplied. Because non-Section 501(c)(3) organizations are not subject to the same limitations in terms of organization and operation (political activity) that Section 501(c)(3) organizations are, the founding document need not contain the limitations on these activities.[36]

Because most of the organizations covered by Form 1024 tend to be membership or sometimes shareholder-type organizations, the Form 1024 does ask for detailed information on the membership or shareholders and what benefits they

---

[30] Rev. Proc. 2011-9, 2011-2 I.R.B. 283.

[31] *Id.*

[32] Rev. Proc. 2011-9; I.R.C. § 7428(a)(2), (b)(2).

[33] I.R.S. Publication 557 *Tax Exempt Status for Your Organization* 4 (Rev. Oct. 2010); Rev. Proc. 2011-9.

[34] See § 14.01 *et seq.* for further information on these exempt organizations.

[35] IRS FORM 1024 APPLICATION FOR RECOGNITION OF EXEMPTION UNDER § 501(A) (Rev. Sept. 1998).

[36] *Id.*

will derive from the organization and how those benefits will be determined.[37]

§ 20.03   DETERMINING TAX EXEMPT STATUS

Once the IRS receives an application and determines that it is complete, it will proceed to examine the Form (1023 or 1024) and its attachments to determine if the organization qualifies for exemption.

[A]   Date of Exemption

A determination by the IRS that an organization does meet the qualifications for exemption will generally be effective as of the date the organization was formed (as long as the application was received by the IRS within 27 months of the organization's formation).[38] When the IRS determines that some modification needs to be made by the organization in order to qualify for exemption (i.e., amendments to corporate articles, changes in the scope or type of activities), the effective date on which the organization became tax exempt will be specified by the IRS in the letter acknowledging these modifications as effective.[39]

As long as the Form 1023 is filed within 27 months of the organization's formation, and as long as no subsequent substantive amendments are required by the IRS, then gifts made during this period to the organization are deductible under Section 170(c). If substantive amendments are required, gifts may only be deductible from the date of amendment. If Form 1023 is filed more than 27 months after the organization's formation, gifts are deductible only from the date of filing.[40]

[B]   Advance Ruling

A ruling or determination letter will be issued to the exempt organization applicant in advance of its beginning operations if its application and supporting documents clearly establish that it meets the requirements of the IRC section under which it is seeking tax exempt status.[41] IRS will not normally issue determination letters if litigation on the organization's exempt status is pending.[42] This advance ruling requires that the organization describe its proposed operations in enough detail to permit IRS to conclude that it will meet the exemption requirements. A restatement of the organization's exempt purpose or a statement that it will be operated in furtherance of exempt purposes will not satisfy this requirement. The organization must fully describe the activities in which it expects to engage. This includes standards, procedures, or other means adopted or planned

---

[37] *Id.*

[38] Rev. Proc. 92-85, 1992-2 C.B. 490, provides for an automatic 27-month retroactive exemption rule. *See also* IRS Form 1023 "Instructions" 4 (Rev. June, 2010).

[39] I.R.S. Publication 557 *Tax Exempt Status for Your Organization* 5 (Rev. Oct. 2010).

[40] *Id.*

[41] Rev. Proc. 2011-9, 2011-2 I.R.B. 283; I.R.S. Publication 557 *Tax Exempt Status for Your Organization* 5 (Rev. Oct. 2010).

[42] *See* sources cited *supra* note 41.

by the organization to carry out its activities, expected sources of funds, and the nature of its contemplated expenses.[43]

On September 9, 2008, the IRS issued temporary Income Tax Regulations, which eliminate the advance ruling process for a section 501(c)(3) organization's foundation status.[44] Under the new regulations, effective immediately, the IRS will automatically classify a new section 501(c)(3) organization as a public charity for its first five years if it can show in its application that it can reasonably be expected to be publicly supported. After the first five years, the IRS will monitor the organization's public charity status using the public support information it reports annually on the Schedule A of its Form 990, Return of Organization Exempt From Income Tax. Its public support test is based on a five-year computation period that consists of the current year and the four years immediately preceding the current year.[45]

[C] Determination Letter

The IRS will issue a determination letter if an organization has established that it meets the particular requirements of the IRC section pursuant to which it is claiming exemption.[46] A proposed adverse ruling or determination letter will be issued to an organization that has not provided sufficiently detailed information to establish that it qualifies for exemption or if the information provided establishes that it does not qualify for exemption.[47] An organization can appeal a proposed adverse ruling or determination letter.[48]

Determination letters can be issued either by EO Determinations or EO Technical.[49] EO Determinations does the run-of-the-mill determinations. EO Technical does determinations that present issues that are not specifically covered by statute, or the regulations, or by an IRS ruling, opinion, or court decision. EO Determinations will refer those applications that have been specifically reserved by revenue procedure or by other official Service instructions for handling by EO Technical for purposes of establishing uniformity or centralized control of designated categories of cases.[50] EO Technical will notify the applicant organization upon receipt of a referred application, and will consider each such application and issue a ruling directly to the organization.[51]

---

[43] *See* sources cited *supra* note 41.

[44] Implementation of Form 990, 73 Fed. Reg. 52528 (Sept. 9, 2008).

[45] *Frequently Asked Questions About the Elimination of the Advance Ruling Process*, IRS, http://www.irs.gov/charities/charitable/article/0,,id=184578,00.html (last updated August 19, 2010).

[46] *See* sources cited *supra* note 41.

[47] *See* sources cited *supra* note 41.

[48] *See* sources cited *supra* note 41.

[49] Rev. Proc. 2011-4, 2011-1 I.R.B. 123.

[50] *Id.*

[51] *Id.*

[D] The Appeals Process

A proposed adverse determination letter issued by EO Determinations will advise the organization of its opportunity to appeal the determination by requesting Appeals Office consideration.[52] To do this, the organization must submit a statement of the facts, law, and arguments in support of its position within 30 days from the date of the adverse determination letter. The organization must also state whether it wishes an Appeals Office conference. Any determination letter issued on the basis of technical advice from EO Technical may not be appealed to the Appeals Office on issues that were the subject of the technical advice. A proposed adverse ruling issued by EO Technical will advise the organization of its opportunity to file a protest statement within 30 days and to request a conference. If a conference is requested, the conference procedures outlined in Rev. Proc. 2011-4, section 12, are applicable.[53]

If an organization does not submit a timely appeal of a proposed adverse determination letter issued by EO Determinations, or a timely protest of a proposed adverse ruling issued by EO Technical, a final adverse determination letter or ruling will be issued to the organization.[54] If an organization submits an appeal of the proposed adverse determination letter, EO Determinations will first review the appeal, and if it determines that the organization qualifies for tax-exempt status, issue a favorable exempt status determination letter. If EO Determinations maintains its adverse position after reviewing the appeal, it will forward the appeal and the exemption application.[55]

The Appeals Office will consider the organization's appeal.[56] If the Appeals Office agrees with the proposed adverse determination, it will either issue a final adverse determination or, if a conference was requested, contact the organization to schedule a conference.[57] At the end of the conference process, which may involve the submission of additional information, the Appeals Office will either issue a final adverse determination letter or a favorable determination letter. If the Appeals Office believes that an exemption or private foundation status issue is not covered by published precedent or that there is non-uniformity, the Appeals Office must request technical advice from EO Technical in accordance with Rev. Proc. 2011-5, section 4.04.[58]

If an organization submits a protest of a proposed adverse exempt status ruling, EO Technical will review the protest statement. If the protest convinces EO

---

[52] Rev. Proc. 2011-9, 2011-2 I.R.B. 283.

[53] *Id.*

[54] *Id.*

[55] *Id.*

[56] At any level of the appeals process, a principle officer or trustee of the organization may speak on its behalf. If a representative (e.g., attorney or CPA) attends an appeals conference without a principal officer or trustee, the representative must file a proper power of attorney or a tax information authorization before the IRS will allow them to receive or inspect confidential information. *See* Appendix B for Sample Forms 2848.

[57] Rev. Proc. 2011-9, 2011-2 I.R.B. 283.

[58] *Id.*

Technical that the organization qualifies for tax-exempt status, a favorable ruling will be issued.[59] If EO Technical maintains its adverse position after reviewing the protest, it will either issue a final adverse ruling or, if a conference was requested, contact the organization to schedule a conference. At the end of the conference process, which may involve the submission of additional information, EO Technical will either issue a final adverse ruling or a favorable exempt status ruling.[60]

An organization may withdraw its appeal or protest before the Service issues a final adverse determination letter or ruling. Upon receipt of the withdrawal request, the Service will complete the processing of the case in the same manner as if no appeal or protest was received.[61]

[E] Section 7428 Declaratory Judgment Provisions

Generally, a declaratory judgment proceeding under § 7428 of the Tax Code[62] can be filed in the United States Tax Court, the United States Court of Federal Claims, or the district court of the United States for the District of Columbia with respect to an adverse determination by the Service, or a failure of the Service to make a determination, with respect to the initial or continuing qualification or classification of an organization under § 501(c)(3), the deductibility of contributions under § 170(c)(2); § 509(a) private foundation status; or operating foundation status under §4942 (j) (3).[63]

Before filing a declaratory judgment action to gain exempt status, an organization must exhaust its administrative remedies by taking, in a timely manner, all reasonable steps to secure a determination from the Service. These include:

1. the filing of a substantially completed application Form 1023 or group exemption request under § 501(c)(3);

2. the timely submission of all additional information requested by the Service to perfect an exemption application or request for determination of private foundation status; and

3. the exhaustion of all administrative appeals available within the Service.[64]

An organization will in no event be deemed to have exhausted its administrative remedies prior to the earlier of the completion of the above steps, and the sending by the Service by certified or registered mail of a final determination letter or ruling; or the expiration of the 270-day period described in § 7428(b)(2) in a case where the Service has not issued a final determination letter or ruling within 270 days and the organization has taken, in a timely manner, all reasonable steps to

---

[59] *Id.*

[60] *Id.*

[61] *Id.*

[62] 26 U.S.C. § 7428.

[63] 26 U.S.C. § 7428(a)(1).

[64] Rev. Proc. 2011-9, 2011-2 I.R.B. 283.

secure a determination letter or ruling.[65]

These declaratory judgment proceedings are all conducted on the administrative record.

[F] Group Rulings

A group exemption letter is issued by the IRS when a central organization applies for exemption on behalf of a group of organizations. A central organization is an organization that has one or more subordinates under its general supervision or control. Subordinate organizations are chapters, locals, posts, or units of the central organization.

Group rulings are the IRS's way of simplifying the recognition process for local branches of national or centrally managed organizations that have already been recognized by the IRS as exempt. A central organization requests a group ruling by certifying to the IRS that the subsidiary organizations are operated by or in conjunction with it. A central organization is an organization that has one or more subordinates under its general supervision or control. A subordinate organization is a chapter, local post, or unit of a central organization. A central organization may be subordinate itself, such as a state organization that has subordinate units and is itself affiliated with a central national organization. A subordinate organization may or may not be incorporated, but it must have an organizing document. A subordinate that is organized and operated in a foreign country cannot be included in a group exemption letter. A subordinate described in IRC Section 501(c)(3) cannot be included in a group exemption letter if it is a private foundation.[66]

There is no form to request a Group Ruling from the IRS.[67] Rather, the central organization sends in a letter, signed by a principal officer of the central organization, indicating the date of its own recognition of exempt status letter, and its EIN number. It must also submit a list of all of its subordinate organizations with their individual EIN numbers and information verifying that the listed subordinate organizations are affiliated with the central organization; are subject to its general supervision or control; are themselves eligible to qualify for exempt status under the same section of 501(c) as the central organization; are not private foundations (if the group application is for 501(c)(3) organizations); are all on the same accounting period; a detailed description of the purposes and activities of the subordinate organizations, including the source of receipts and nature of expenditures; a sample copy of a uniform governing instrument; and a statement of each subordinate organization's consent.[68]

---

[65] 26 U.S.C. § 7428(b)(2).

[66] I.R.S. Publication 557 *Tax Exempt Status for Your Organization* 7 (Rev. Oct. 2010); Rev. Proc. 80-27, 1980-1 C.B. 677; 26 C.F.R. § 601.201(n)(8).

[67] There is no form for the group application, but all of the information needed can be submitted to the IRS by letter from the central organization. I.R.S. Publication 557 *Tax Exempt Status for Your Organization* 6–7 (Rev. Oct. 2010).

[68] *See* sources cited *supra* note 66.

A group ruling can be maintained in effect from year to year based on the following conditions: the continued existence of the central organization, the continued exemption of the central organization, the submission by the central organization of changes in existing subordinates, subordinates no longer to be included, and the addition of new subordinates, together with the information described in the prior paragraph about these new subordinates.[69]

Every tax year, the central organization must re-certify to the IRS that its subsidiary organizations continue to be related to it, that they are non-profit organizations, that no part of the net earnings of these organizations inures to the benefit of any individual, that no substantial part of their activities is for the promotion of legislation, and that none are private foundations.[70]

§ 20.04 MAINTAINING TAX EXEMPT STATUS

The IRS not only requires that an organization demonstrate its qualification for tax exemption in the application process, but also the organization demonstrate its qualification throughout its entire life. Every minute of its existence, a tax exempt organization must comply with the substantive requirements of exemption, and if it does not, it faces the loss or revocation of its tax exempt status by the IRS or the imposition of a penalizing tax. The IRS polices the ongoing compliance of these requirements through the reporting requirements imposed by the IRC.[71]

[A] Reporting Requirements

There are four types of annual informational returns that exempt organizations must file with the IRS depending on their income levels. These are Form 990N, Form 990EZ, Form 990 and Form 990PF.

[1] Form 990N

Most small tax-exempt organizations whose annual gross receipts are normally $50,000 or less are required to electronically submit Form 990-N, also known as the e-Postcard, unless they choose to file a complete Form 990 or Form 990-EZ instead.[72] This e-Postcard contains eight basic questions: (1) Employer identification number (EIN), also known as a Taxpayer Identification Number (TIN); (2) Indication of the tax year; (3) Legal name and mailing address; (4) Any other names the organization uses; (5) Name and address of a principal officer; (6) Web site address if the organization has one; (7) Confirmation that the organization's annual gross receipts are normally $50,000 or less; (8) If applicable, a statement that the organization has terminated or is terminating (going out of business).[73]

---

[69] I.R.S. Publication 557 *Tax Exempt Status for Your Organization* 7 (Rev. Oct. 2010).

[70] *Id.*

[71] I.R.S. Publication 557 *Tax Exempt Status for Your Organization* 8 (Rev. Oct. 2010).

[72] Unless it is a church, their integrated auxiliaries, or a convention or association of churches, or the exclusively religious activities of a religious order. 26 U.S.C. § 6033(a)(3)(A)(i), (iii).

[73] 26 U.S.C. § 6033(i); 26 C.F.R. Part 1, [TD 9454] RIN 1545-BG37 (July, 2009).

If an organization does not file its Form 990N e-Postcard on time, the IRS will send a reminder notice. There is no penalty assessment for late filing of the e-Postcard, but an organization that fails to file required e-Postcards (or information returns — Forms 990 or 990-EZ if those are due) for three consecutive years will automatically lose its tax-exempt status under the provisions of the Pension Protection Act of 2006.[74] The revocation of the organization's tax-exempt status will not take place until the filing due date of the third year.

The e-Postcard is due every year by the fifteenth day of the fifth month after the close of the organization's tax year. For example, if its tax year ended on December 31, the e-Postcard is due May 15 of the following year. If the due date falls on a Saturday, Sunday, or legal holiday, the due date is the next business day. An e-Postcard cannot be filed until after the organization's tax year ends.[75]

[2] Form 990EZ

Exempt organizations with gross receipts normally above $50,000 but less than $200,000 or whose total assets do not exceed $500,000 can file Form 999 EZ. This is a two-page form that is due every year by the fifteenth day of the fifth month after the close of the organization's tax year. Organizations that file Form 990-EZ can ask for up to two 90-day extensions of time to file, using Form 8868. Failure to make a timely annual filing will result in penalties.[76]

[3] Form 990

Exempt organizations with gross receipts equal to or more than $200,000, or who have total assets at or worth more than $500,000 must file Form 990. This form was revised in 2008 and now asks for much more information, including questions on how the exempt organization is governed. The basic form, not including schedules, is 12 pages long, with a front page that is meant to give the viewer a quick summary statement of mission and activities, contributions and grants, program service revenue, investment income, grants, salaries, fundraising expenses, revenue less expenses, total assets and total liabilities. The Form 990 is due every year by the fifteenth day of the fifth month after the close of the organization's tax year. Organizations that file Form 990 can ask for up to two 90-day extensions of time to file, using Form 8868. Failure to make a timely annual filing will result in penalties.[77]

[4] Form 990PF

All private foundations must file Form 990PF. This form is used to figure the excise tax based on the private foundation's investment income and to report charitable distributions by the private foundation.[78] The Form 990PF is due every

---

[74] 26 U.S.C. § 6033(j).

[75] 26 C.F.R. Part 1, [TD 9454] RIN 1545-BG37 (July, 2009).

[76] IRS Form 990 Instructions; 26 C.F.R. § 1.6033-2.

[77] IRS Form 990 Instructions; 26 C.F.R. § 1.6033-2.

[78] I.R.C. § 4940; IRS Form 990PF Instructions.

year by the fifteenth day of the fifth month after the close of the organization's tax year. Organizations that file Form 990 can ask for up to two 90-day extensions of time to file, using Form 8868. Failure to make a timely annual filing will result in penalties.[79]

[5] Electronic Filing

For tax years ending on or after December 31, 2006, exempt organizations with $10 million or more in total assets may be required to e-file if the organization files at least 250 returns in a calendar year, including income, excise, employment tax, and information returns. Private foundations and non-exempt charitable trusts are required to file Forms 990-PF electronically regardless of their asset size, if they file at least 250 returns annually. The electronic filing requirement does not apply to Form 8868. Part 1 of Form 8868 for the automatic three month extension can be filed electronically or by paper.[80]

[6] Public Availability of Form 990s and Form 990T (Unrelated Business Income)

In addition to filing a Form 990 with the IRS, Section 6104 requires that Section 501(c) and Section 501(d) organizations have a copy of the organization's exemption application documents and the current year's Form 990 (and those of the prior two years) available at their principal office (and at any regional or district office with three or more employees) available for public inspection.[81] The organization may, however, black-out or omit the names of donors and their gift amounts.[82]

IRC Section 6104 was enacted by Congress in 1987 in an effort to allow the public to monitor the activities of exempt organizations as the IRS does not have the manpower to do so. The public, however, does not have a private right of action against the organization that refuses to disclose information.[83] If an organization refuses to disclose information pursuant to Section 6104, the individual requesting the information must complain to the government (i.e., IRS). The IRS has the discretion to seek enforcement of disclosure or impose fines.[84]

Section 6104(d) also requires organizations, upon request, to provide photocopies of this information (charging only reasonable fees for this service) to the public or otherwise make the information widely available. One way of making the information "widely available" is through the Internet.[85] It is important to note, however, that making a document widely available to avoid the hassle of making and sending

---

[79] IRS Form 990PF Instructions; 26 C.F.R. § 1.6033-2.

[80] I.R.C. § 6011(e); Returns Required on Magnetic Media, 72 Fed. Reg. 63807-01 (Nov. 13, 2007); I.R.S. Notice 2010-13 (Jan. 2010).

[81] I.R.C. § 6104.

[82] I.R.S. Publication 557 *Tax Exempt Status for Your Organization* 12 (Rev. Oct. 2010).

[83] Tax Analysts v. IRS and Christian Broad. Network (CBN), Inc., 214 F.3d 179 (D.C. Cir. 2000).

[84] *Id.; see also* Schuloff v. Queens Coll. Found., 994 F. Supp. 425 (E.D.N.Y. 1998) (relied on Congress' intent to deny a private right of action).

[85] www.guidestar.com is a popular web-site listing many exempt organizations' informational returns (last visited March 13, 2005).

copies, does not mean that an organization may prevent a member of the public from personally inspecting the documents at the organization's national or regional office.[86]

Recently, the IRS and several courts have brought into question the scope of the disclosure requirements of Section 6104. The issues have arisen when discussing "closing agreements," which are documents generated by organizations and the IRS during the application process for tax exemption. In 2000, the IRS announced that it considered closing agreements as "Pre-filing agreements" under Section 7121, and as such, they are not subject to the disclosure requirements of Section 6104, but confidential under the provisions of Section 6103(b)(2)(A).[87] However, in *Tax Analysts*,[88] an exempt organization, CBN, allegedly engaged in prohibited political activities prompting the IRS to audit it. The IRS and CBN came to an agreement during this audit that preserved CBN's exempt status. Tax Analysts requested a copy of the closing agreement from the IRS, citing Section 6104.[89] The IRS refused to disclose the information based on its reasoning in IRS Notice 2000-12 that closing agreements are pre-filing agreements and subject to confidentiality under Section 6103. The United States Court of Appeals for the District of Columbia determined that Section 6104's reference to "all documents" should not be taken literally. Instead, they determined that the contents of each document determines if it is confidential under Section 6103 or subject to disclosure under Section 6104. In this case, the court remanded the case to district court for an *in camera* hearing regarding the contents of the requested documents.[90]

In *Sklar v. Commissioner*,[91] the Court of Appeals for the Ninth Circuit agreed with the court in *Tax Analysts* that the contents of closing agreements determines whether it is or is not subject to disclosure. In this case, Sklar sought a deduction for religious tuition payments, which the IRS denied. Sklar sought the closing agreement between the IRS and the Church of Scientology to show similar deductions were being allowed in that instance. The court determined that while the IRS should have disclosed the information in the closing agreement, the deduction sought by Sklar was clearly not allowed; therefore the court did not require this information to be disclosed to Sklar.[92]

The Pension Protection Act of 2006 revised IRC § 6104 to say that "any annual return filed under section 6011 which relates to any tax imposed by section 511 (relating to imposition of tax on unrelated business income of charitable, etc. organizations) by such organization, but only if such organization is described in section 501(c)(3) . . . shall be made available by such organization for inspection

---

[86] *See* 26 C.F.R. § 301.6104(d)-2(b).

[87] I.R.S. 2000-1 C.B. 727, Notice 2000-12.

[88] 214 F.3d 179.

[89] Tax Analysts also requested a copy of the document from CBN, however, the court held that no private right of action exists against the organization. Instead the party requesting disclosure must complain to the IRS.

[90] *Id.*

[91] 282 F.3d 610 (9th Cir. 2002).

[92] *Id.*

during regular business hours by any individual at the principal office of such organization." And that "upon request of an individual . . . a copy of such annual return, reports, and exempt status application materials or such notice materials shall be provided to such individual without charge other than a reasonable fee for any reproduction and mailing costs." This availability of the Form 990T on a section 501(c)(3) organization's unrelated business income return applies to the current year and the two prior year's returns.[93]

[B] Loss of Tax Exempt Status

The IRS may, at any time, determine that an organization fails to meet the substantive requirements of its exempt status through an audit process.[94] During an audit, agents of the IRS will examine information about the organization such as its application for exemption (e.g., Form 1023); their reporting documents (e.g., Form 990); and any organizational documents (e.g., bylaws and articles). Depending on the type of audit, the IRS agents may also conduct site tours and interviews with directors of the board, executives, and/or employees.[95]

When the IRS determines that exemption should be revoked, it can wreak havoc on an organization, its donors, and its employees. Not only must an organization explain its eligibility for exemption in Forms 1023 or 1024, but it must be ever-vigilant throughout its lifespan in the maintenance of its tax exempt status to avoid revocation. It does this by continuing to operate as stated in its founding documents; being aware of private inurement, pubic benefit and conflict of interest issues; maintaining appropriate records; keeping forms on file and available to the public; and filing timely tax and other returns. As with the appeals process, in the initial application process, an organization may appeal revocation of its exemption through the federal courts, but only after the IRS has revoked the exemption.

The *New Community Senior Citizen Housing v. Commissioner*[96] and *AHW Corporation v. Commissioner*[97] cases highlight a practical issue faced by organizations who disagree with the IRS on whether a proposed transaction is an exempt transaction. *New Community* holds that an organization already recognized as tax exempt may not obtain judicial review of an adverse ruling on a proposed transaction other than by actually performing the proposed transaction.[98] When the organization in *AHW Corp.* sought to engage in a proposed transaction that the IRS would not consider an exempt activity,[99] it had to either yield to the request by the IRS not to engage in that activity or engage in

---

[93] I.R.C. § 6104(d)(2).

[94] See Internal Revenue Manual (IRM) § 4.75 for further information on the Audit Procedure for tax exempt organizations.

[95] See IRM § 4.75.27.1, regarding Correspondence Examinations; IRM § 4.75.11, regarding On-Site Examinations; and IRM § 4.75.29, regarding Team Examination procedures.

[96] 72 T.C. 372 (1979).

[97] 79 T.C. 390 (1982).

[98] *New Cmty. Senior Citizen Hous.*, 72 T.C. 372.

[99] In its application process, AHW described one of activities as providing at cost managerial and consulting services (the proposed transaction). The commissioner issued a proposed adverse ruling,

that activity and have its exemption revoked. AHW decided to concede to the IRS and not engage in the activity. The IRS, therefore, recognized AHW as an exempt organization as long as it did not engage in the prohibited proposed transaction. When AHW sought judicial review over the proposed transaction, the case was dismissed because AHW's request for Section 501(c)(3) status had been granted and there was no "actual controversy."[100] Therefore, an organization that disagrees with the IRS on whether a particular activity is exempt, must engage in that activity, have its exemption revoked or be subject to an excise tax before it can seek judicial relief.[101]

AHW removed the proposed transaction from its description of its activities and the commissioner granted the exemption. *AHW Corp.*, 79 T.C. 390.

[100] *AHW Corp.*, 79 T.C. at 397.

[101] The development and use of excise taxes and Intermediate Sanctions have lessened this burden. Now when organizations engage in certain non-exempt activity, it no longer results in immediate revocation of exemption. Rather, excise taxes are imposed and the organization can appeal the imposition of that tax. See § 6.06 for further information on excise taxes and intermediate sanctions.

APPENDIX A

Department of the Treasury
Internal Revenue Service

Notice 1382

(Rev. November 2010)

Changes for Form 1023:

- Mailing address
- Parts IX, X and XI

Changes for Form 1023, Application for Recognition of Exemption Under Section 501(c)(3) of the Internal Revenue Code

Change of Mailing Address

The mailing address shown on Form 1023 Checklist, page 28, the first address under the last checkbox; and in the Instructions for Form 1023, page 4 under *Where to File,* has been changed to:

> Internal Revenue Service
> P.O. Box 12192
> Covington, KY 41012-0192

Changes for Parts IX and X

Changes to Parts IX and X are necessary to comply with new regulations that eliminated the advance ruling process. Until Form 1023 is revised to reflect this change, please follow the directions on this notice when completing Part IX and Part X of Form 1023. For more information about the elimination of the advance ruling process, visit us at *www.IRS.gov* and click on *Charities & Non-Profits.*

Part IX. Financial Data

The instructions at the top of Part IX on page 9 of Form 1023 are now as follows. For purposes of this schedule, years in existence refer to completed tax years.

1. If in existence less than 5 years, complete the statement for each year in existence and provide projections of your likely revenues and expenses based on a reasonable and good faith estimate of your future finances for a total of:

a. Three years of financial information if you have not completed one tax year, or

b. Four years of financial information if you have completed one tax year.

2. If in existence 5 or more years, complete the schedule for the most recent 5 tax years. You will need to provide a separate statement that includes information about the most recent 5 tax years because the data table in Part IX, has not been updated to provide for a 5th year.

Part X. Public Charity Status

Do not complete line 6a on page 11 of Form 1023, and **do not sign** the form under the heading "Consent Fixing Period of Limitations Upon Assessment of Tax Under Section 4940 of the Internal Revenue Code."

Only complete line 6b and line 7 on page 11 of Form 1023, if in existence 5 or more tax years.

---

www.IRS.gov

Notice **1382** (Rev. 11-2010)
Cat. No. 52336F

Part XI. Increase in User Fees

User fee increases are effective for all applications postmarked after January 3, 2010.

1. $400 for organizations whose gross receipts do not exceed $10,000 or less annually over a 4-year period.

2. $850 for organizations whose gross receipts exceed $10,000 annually over a 4-year period.

See *www.IRS.gov* web page link on Form 1023, page 12, Part XI, User Fee Information, for the current user fees.

Cyber Assistant is a web-based software program designed to help organizations prepare a complete and accurate Form 1023 application. Once the IRS announces the availability of Cyber Assistant, the user fees will change again.

1. $200 for organizations using Cyber Assistant (regardless of size) to prepare their Form 1023, or

2. $850 for all other organizations not using Cyber Assistant (regardless of size) to prepare their Form 1023.

The IRS will announce when Cyber Assistant is available and the effective date of the user fee change. Sign up for the *Exempt Organization (EO) Update,* EO's subscription newsletter, at *www.irs.gov/charities,* to automatically receive an alert that Cyber Assistant is available.

Form 1023
(Rev. June 2006)
Department of the Treasury
Internal Revenue Service

Application for Recognition of Exemption
Under Section 501(c)(3) of the Internal Revenue Code

OMB No. 1545-0056

Note: *If exempt status is approved, this application will be open for public inspection.*

Use the instructions to complete this application and for a definition of all **bold** items. For additional help, call IRS Exempt Organizations Customer Account Services toll-free at 1-877-829-5500. Visit our website at **www.irs.gov** for forms and publications. If the required information and documents are not submitted with payment of the appropriate user fee, the application may be returned to you.

Attach additional sheets to this application if you need more space to answer fully. Put your name and EIN on each sheet and identify each answer by Part and line number. Complete Parts I - XI of Form 1023 and submit only those Schedules (A through H) that apply to you.

Part I Identification of Applicant

1 Full name of organization (exactly as it appears in your **organizing document**)

ABC Initiative for Childhood Education

2 c/o Name (if applicable)

Sam Smith

3 **Mailing address** (Number and street) (see instructions) | Room/Suite

111 1st Avenue

4 Employer Identification Number (EIN)

#######

City or town, state or country, and ZIP + 4

Anytown, XY 00001-0001

5 Month the annual accounting period ends (01 – 12)

07 - July

6 Primary contact (officer, director, trustee, or **authorized representative**)

a Name: **Attorney Janet jones**

b Phone: **111-111-1111**

c Fax: (optional)

7 Are you represented by an authorized representative, such as an attorney or accountant? If "Yes," provide the authorized representative's name, and the name and address of the authorized representative's firm. Include a completed Form 2848, *Power of Attorney and Declaration of Representative,* with your application if you would like us to communicate with your representative.   ☑ Yes   ☐ No

8 Was a person who is not one of your officers, directors, trustees, employees, or an authorized representative listed in line 7, paid, or promised payment, to help plan, manage, or advise you about the structure or activities of your organization, or about your financial or tax matters? If "Yes," provide the person's name, the name and address of the person's firm, the amounts paid or promised to be paid, and describe that person's role.   ☐ Yes   ☑ No

9a Organization's website: **www.websiteaddress.org**

b Organization's email: (optional) **abice@netmail**

10 Certain organizations are not required to file an information return (Form 990 or Form 990-EZ). If you are granted tax-exemption, are you claiming to be excused from filing Form 990 or Form 990-EZ? If "Yes," explain. See the instructions for a description of organizations not required to file Form 990 or Form 990-EZ.   ☐ Yes   ☑ No

11 Date incorporated if a corporation, or formed, if other than a corporation. (MM/DD/YYYY)   **07** / **15** / **2008**

12 Were you formed under the laws of a **foreign country?**
If "Yes," state the country.   ☐ Yes   ☑ No

For Paperwork Reduction Act Notice, see page 24 of the instructions.   Cat. No. 17133K   Form **1023** (Rev. 6-2006)

Form 1023 (Rev. 6-2006)   Name: EIN: —   Page **2**

Part II   Organizational Structure

You must be a corporation (including a limited liability company), an unincorporated association, or a trust to be tax exempt. (See instructions.) **DO NOT file this form unless you can check "Yes" on lines 1, 2, 3, or 4.**

1 Are you a **corporation**? If "Yes," attach a copy of your articles of incorporation showing **certification**   ☑ **Yes**   ☐ **No**
of filing with the appropriate state agency. Include copies of any amendments to your articles and
be sure they also show state filing certification.

2 Are you a **limited liability company (LLC)**? If "Yes," attach a copy of your articles of organization showing   ☐ **Yes**   ☑ **No**
certification of filing with the appropriate state agency. Also, if you adopted an operating agreement, attach
a copy. Include copies of any amendments to your articles and be sure they show state filing certification.
Refer to the instructions for circumstances when an LLC should not file its own exemption application.

3 Are you an **unincorporated association**? If "Yes," attach a copy of your articles of association,   ☐ **Yes**   ☑ **No**
constitution, or other similar organizing document that is dated and includes at least two signatures.
Include signed and dated copies of any amendments.

4a Are you a **trust**? If "Yes," attach a signed and dated copy of your trust agreement. Include signed   ☐ **Yes**   ☑ **No**
and dated copies of any amendments.
b Have you been funded? If "No," explain how you are formed without anything of value placed in trust.   ☐ **Yes**   ☑ **No**

5 Have you adopted **bylaws**? If "Yes," attach a current copy showing date of adoption. If "No," explain   ☑ **Yes**   ☐ **No**
how your officers, directors, or trustees are selected.

Part III   Required Provisions in Your Organizing Document

The following questions are designed to ensure that when you file this application, your organizing document contains the required provisions to meet the organizational test under section 501(c)(3). Unless you can check the boxes in both lines 1 and 2, your organizing document does not meet the organizational test. **DO NOT file this application until you have amended your organizing document.** Submit your original and amended organizing documents (showing state filing certification if you are a corporation or an LLC) with your application.

1 Section 501(c)(3) requires that your organizing document state your exempt purpose(s), such as charitable,   ☑
religious, educational, and/or scientific purposes. Check the box to confirm that your organizing document
meets this requirement. Describe specifically where your organizing document meets this requirement, such as
a reference to a particular article or section in your organizing document. Refer to the instructions for exempt
purpose language. Location of Purpose Clause (Page, Article, and Paragraph):   **pages 4-5, Attachment #3**

2a Section 501(c)(3) requires that upon dissolution of your organization, your remaining assets must be used exclusively   ☑
for exempt purposes, such as charitable, religious, educational, and/or scientific purposes. Check the box on line 2a to
confirm that your organizing document meets this requirement by express provision for the distribution of assets upon
dissolution. If you rely on state law for your dissolution provision, do not check the box on line 2a and go to line 2c.

2b If you checked the box on line 2a, specify the location of your dissolution clause (Page, Article, and Paragraph).
Do not complete line 2c if you checked box 2a.   **page 6 -Attachment #3**

2c See the instructions for information about the operation of state law in your particular state. Check this box if   ☐
you rely on operation of state law for your dissolution provision and indicate the state:

Part IV   Narrative Description of Your Activities

Using an attachment, describe your *past, present,* and *planned* activities in a narrative. If you believe that you have already provided some of this information in response to other parts of this application, you may summarize that information here and refer to the specific parts of the application for supporting details. You may also attach representative copies of newsletters, brochures, or similar documents for supporting details to this narrative. Remember that if this application is approved, it will be open for public inspection. Therefore, your narrative description of activities should be thorough and accurate. Refer to the instructions for information that must be included in your description.

Part V   Compensation and Other Financial Arrangements With Your Officers, Directors, Trustees, Employees, and Independent Contractors

1a List the names, titles, and mailing addresses of all of your officers, directors, and trustees. For each person listed, state their
total annual **compensation**, or proposed compensation, for all services to the organization, whether as an officer, employee, or
other position. Use actual figures, if available. Enter "none" if no compensation is or will be paid. If additional space is needed,
attach a separate sheet. Refer to the instructions for information on what to include as compensation.

Name	Title	Mailing address	Compensation amount (annual actual or estimated)
Sam Smith	President	111 1st Avenue Anytown, XY 00001-0001	none
Barbara Brown	Vice President	111 1st Avenue Anytown, XY 00001-0001	none
Jeffery James	Secretary	1111 1st Avenue Anytown, XY 00001-0001	none
Henrietta Higgins	Treasurer	1111 1st Avenue Anytown, XY 00001-0001	

Form **1023** (Rev. 6-2006)

Form 1023 (Rev. 6-2006)　　Name:　　　　　　　　　　　　　　EIN:　　　　–　　　　　　Page **3**

Part V　**Compensation and Other Financial Arrangements With Your Officers, Directors, Trustees, Employees, and Independent Contractors** *(Continued)*

b List the names, titles, and mailing addresses of each of your five highest compensated employees who receive or will receive compensation of more than $50,000 per year. Use the actual figure, if available. Refer to the instructions for information on what to include as compensation. Do not include officers, directors, or trustees listed in line 1a.

Name	Title	Mailing address	Compensation amount (annual actual or estimated)
none			**none**

c List the names, names of businesses, and mailing addresses of your five highest compensated **independent contractors** that receive or will receive compensation of more than $50,000 per year. Use the actual figure, if available. Refer to the instructions for information on what to include as compensation.

Name	Title	Mailing address	Compensation amount (annual actual or estimated)
none			**none**

The following "Yes" or "No" questions relate to *past, present, or planned* relationships, transactions, or agreements with your officers, directors, trustees, highest compensated employees, and highest compensated independent contractors listed in lines 1a, 1b, and 1c.

2a Are any of your officers, directors, or trustees **related** to each other through **family** or **business relationships**? If "Yes," identify the individuals and explain the relationship.　☐ Yes　☑ No

b Do you have a business relationship with any of your officers, directors, or trustees other than through their position as an officer, director, or trustee? If "Yes," identify the individuals and describe the business relationship with each of your officers, directors, or trustees.　☐ Yes　☑ No

c Are any of your officers, directors, or trustees related to your highest compensated employees or highest compensated independent contractors listed on lines 1b or 1c through family or business relationships? If "Yes," identify the individuals and explain the relationship.　☐ Yes　☑ No

3a For each of your officers, directors, trustees, highest compensated employees, and highest compensated independent contractors listed on lines 1a, 1b, or 1c, attach a list showing their name, qualifications, average hours worked, and duties.

b Do any of your officers, directors, trustees, highest compensated employees, and highest compensated independent contractors listed on lines 1a, 1b, or 1c receive compensation from any other organizations, whether tax exempt or taxable, that are related to you through **common control**? If "Yes," identify the individuals, explain the relationship between you and the other organization, and describe the compensation arrangement.　☐ Yes　☑ No

4 In establishing the compensation for your officers, directors, trustees, highest compensated employees, and highest compensated independent contractors listed on lines 1a, 1b, and 1c, the following practices are recommended, although they are not required to obtain exemption. Answer "Yes" to all the practices you use.

a Do you or will the individuals that approve compensation arrangements follow a conflict of interest policy?　☑ Yes　☐ No

b Do you or will you approve compensation arrangements in advance of paying compensation?　☑ Yes　☐ No

c Do you or will you document in writing the date and terms of approved compensation arrangements?　☑ Yes　☐ No

Form **1023** (Rev. 6-2006)

Form 1023 (Rev. 6-2006)   Name: EIN: —   Page **4**

Part V **Compensation and Other Financial Arrangements With Your Officers, Directors, Trustees, Employees, and Independent Contractors** *(Continued)*

d Do you or will you record in writing the decision made by each individual who decided or voted on compensation arrangements? ☑ Yes   ☐ No

e Do you or will you approve compensation arrangements based on information about compensation paid by **similarly situated** taxable or tax-exempt organizations for similar services, current compensation surveys compiled by independent firms, or actual written offers from similarly situated organizations? Refer to the instructions for Part V, lines 1a, 1b, and 1c, for information on what to include as compensation. ☑ Yes   ☐ No

f Do you or will you record in writing both the information on which you relied to base your decision and its source? ☑ Yes   ☐ No

g If you answered "No" to any item on lines 4a through 4f, describe how you set compensation that is **reasonable** for your officers, directors, trustees, highest compensated employees, and highest compensated independent contractors listed in Part V, lines 1a, 1b, and 1c.

5a Have you adopted a **conflict of interest policy** consistent with the sample conflict of interest policy in Appendix A to the instructions? If "Yes," provide a copy of the policy and explain how the policy has been adopted, such as by resolution of your governing board. If "No," answer lines 5b and 5c. ☑ Yes   ☐ No

b What procedures will you follow to assure that persons who have a conflict of interest will not have influence over you for setting their own compensation?

c What procedures will you follow to assure that persons who have a conflict of interest will not have influence over you regarding business deals with themselves?

Note: A conflict of interest policy is recommended though it is not required to obtain exemption. Hospitals, see Schedule C, Section I, line 14.

6a Do you or will you compensate any of your officers, directors, trustees, highest compensated employees, and highest compensated independent contractors listed in lines 1a, 1b, or 1c through **non-fixed payments**, such as discretionary bonuses or revenue-based payments? If "Yes," describe all non-fixed compensation arrangements, including how the amounts are determined, who is eligible for such arrangements, whether you place a limitation on total compensation, and how you determine or will determine that you pay no more than reasonable compensation for services. Refer to the instructions for Part V, lines 1a, 1b, and 1c, for information on what to include as compensation. ☐ Yes   ☑ No

b Do you or will you compensate any of your employees, other than your officers, directors, trustees, or your five highest compensated employees who receive or will receive compensation of more than $50,000 per year, through non-fixed payments, such as discretionary bonuses or revenue-based payments? If "Yes," describe all non-fixed compensation arrangements, including how the amounts are or will be determined, who is or will be eligible for such arrangements, whether you place or will place a limitation on total compensation, and how you determine or will determine that you pay no more than reasonable compensation for services. Refer to the instructions for Part V, lines 1a, 1b, and 1c, for information on what to include as compensation. ☐ Yes   ☑ No

7a Do you or will you purchase any goods, services, or assets from any of your officers, directors, trustees, highest compensated employees, or highest compensated independent contractors listed in lines 1a, 1b, or 1c? If "Yes," describe any such purchase that you made or intend to make, from whom you make or will make such purchases, how the terms are or will be negotiated at **arm's length**, and explain how you determine or will determine that you pay no more than **fair market value**. Attach copies of any written contracts or other agreements relating to such purchases. ☐ Yes   ☑ No

b Do you or will you sell any goods, services, or assets to any of your officers, directors, trustees, highest compensated employees, or highest compensated independent contractors listed in lines 1a, 1b, or 1c? If "Yes," describe any such sales that you made or intend to make, to whom you make or will make such sales, how the terms are or will be negotiated at arm's length, and explain how you determine or will determine you are or will be paid at least fair market value. Attach copies of any written contracts or other agreements relating to such sales. ☐ Yes   ☑ No

8a Do you or will you have any leases, contracts, loans, or other agreements with your officers, directors, trustees, highest compensated employees, or highest compensated independent contractors listed in lines 1a, 1b, or 1c? If "Yes," provide the information requested in lines 8b through 8f. ☐ Yes   ☑ No

b Describe any written or oral arrangements that you made or intend to make.

c Identify with whom you have or will have such arrangements.

d Explain how the terms are or will be negotiated at arm's length.

e Explain how you determine you pay no more than fair market value or you are paid at least fair market value.

f Attach copies of any signed leases, contracts, loans, or other agreements relating to such arrangements.

9a Do you or will you have any leases, contracts, loans, or other agreements with any organization in which any of your officers, directors, or trustees are also officers, directors, or trustees, or in which any individual officer, director, or trustee owns more than a 35% interest? If "Yes," provide the information requested in lines 9b through 9f. ☐ Yes   ☑ No

Form **1023** (Rev. 6-2006)

Form 1023 (Rev. 6-2006)   Name: EIN: –   Page **5**

Part V   **Compensation and Other Financial Arrangements With Your Officers, Directors, Trustees, Employees, and Independent Contractors** *(Continued)*

 b Describe any written or oral arrangements you made or intend to make.

 c Identify with whom you have or will have such arrangements.

 d Explain how the terms are or will be negotiated at arm's length.

 e Explain how you determine or will determine you pay no more than fair market value or that you are paid at least fair market value.

 f Attach a copy of any signed leases, contracts, loans, or other agreements relating to such arrangements.

Part VI   **Your Members and Other Individuals and Organizations That Receive Benefits From You**

The following "Yes" or "No" questions relate to goods, services, and funds you provide to individuals and organizations as part of your activities. Your answers should pertain to *past, present,* and *planned* activities. (See instructions.)

1a In carrying out your exempt purposes, do you provide goods, services, or funds to individuals? If "Yes," describe each program that provides goods, services, or funds to individuals. ☐ **Yes** ☑ **No**

 b In carrying out your exempt purposes, do you provide goods, services, or funds to organizations? If "Yes," describe each program that provides goods, services, or funds to organizations. ☐ **Yes** ☑ **No**

2 Do any of your programs limit the provision of goods, services, or funds to a specific individual or group of specific individuals? For example, answer "Yes," if goods, services, or funds are provided only for a particular individual, your members, individuals who work for a particular employer, or graduates of a particular school. If "Yes," explain the limitation and how recipients are selected for each program. ☑ **Yes** ☐ **No**

3 Do any individuals who receive goods, services, or funds through your programs have a family or business relationship with any officer, director, trustee, or with any of your highest compensated employees or highest compensated independent contractors listed in Part V, lines 1a, 1b, and 1c? If "Yes," explain how these related individuals are eligible for goods, services, or funds. ☐ **Yes** ☑ **No**

Part VII   **Your History**

The following "Yes" or "No" questions relate to your history. (See instructions.)

1 Are you a **successor** to another organization? Answer "Yes," if you have taken or will take over the activities of another organization; you took over 25% or more of the fair market value of the net assets of another organization; or you were established upon the conversion of an organization from for-profit to non-profit status. If "Yes," complete Schedule G. ☐ **Yes** ☑ **No**

2 Are you submitting this application more than 27 months after the end of the month in which you were legally formed? If "Yes," complete Schedule E. ☐ **Yes** ☑ **No**

Part VIII   **Your Specific Activities**

The following "Yes" or "No" questions relate to specific activities that you may conduct. Check the appropriate box. Your answers should pertain to *past, present,* and *planned* activities. (See instructions.)

1 Do you support or oppose candidates in **political campaigns** in any way? If "Yes," explain. ☐ **Yes** ☑ **No**

2a Do you attempt to **influence legislation**? If "Yes," explain how you attempt to influence legislation and complete line 2b. If "No," go to line 3a. ☐ **Yes** ☑ **No**

 b Have you made or are you making an **election** to have your legislative activities measured by expenditures by filing Form 5768? If "Yes," attach a copy of the Form 5768 that was already filed or attach a completed Form 5768 that you are filing with this application. If "No," describe whether your attempts to influence legislation are a substantial part of your activities. Include the time and money spent on your attempts to influence legislation as compared to your total activities. ☐ **Yes** ☑ **No**

3a Do you or will you operate bingo or **gaming** activities? If "Yes," describe who conducts them, and list all revenue received or expected to be received and expenses paid or expected to be paid in operating these activities. **Revenue and expenses** should be provided for the time periods specified in Part IX, Financial Data. ☐ **Yes** ☑ **No**

 b Do you or will you enter into contracts or other agreements with individuals or organizations to conduct bingo or gaming for you? If "Yes," describe any written or oral arrangements that you made or intend to make, identify with whom you have or will have such arrangements, explain how the terms are or will be negotiated at arm's length, and explain how you determine or will determine you pay no more than fair market value or you will be paid at least fair market value. Attach copies or any written contracts or other agreements relating to such arrangements. ☐ **Yes** ☑ **No**

 c List the states and local jurisdictions, including Indian Reservations, in which you conduct or will conduct gaming or bingo.

Form **1023** (Rev. 6-2006)

Form 1023 (Rev. 6-2006)   Name: EIN: −   Page **6**

Part VIII   Your Specific Activities *(Continued)*

4a Do you or will you undertake **fundraising**? If "Yes," check all the fundraising programs you do or will   ☐ **Yes**   ☐ **No**
conduct. (See instructions.)

☑ mail solicitations   ☐ phone solicitations
☑ email solicitations   ☑ accept donations on your website
☐ personal solicitations   ☑ receive donations from another organization's website
☐ vehicle, boat, plane, or similar donations   ☐ government grant solicitations
☑ foundation grant solicitations   ☑ Other

Attach a description of each fundraising program.

b Do you or will you have written or oral contracts with any individuals or organizations to raise funds   ☐ Yes   ☑ No
for you? If "Yes," describe these activities. Include all revenue and expenses from these activities
and state who conducts them. Revenue and expenses should be provided for the time periods
specified in Part IX, Financial Data. Also, attach a copy of any contracts or agreements.

c Do you or will you engage in fundraising activities for other organizations? If "Yes," describe these   ☐ Yes   ☑ No
arrangements. Include a description of the organizations for which you raise funds and attach copies
of all contracts or agreements.

d List all states and local jurisdictions in which you conduct fundraising. For each state or local
jurisdiction listed, specify whether you fundraise for your own organization, you fundraise for another
organization, or another organization fundraises for you.

e Do you or will you maintain separate accounts for any contributor under which the contributor has   ☐ Yes   ☑ No
the right to advise on the use or distribution of funds? Answer "Yes" if the donor may provide advice
on the types of investments, distributions from the types of investments, or the distribution from the
donor's contribution account. If "Yes," describe this program, including the type of advice that may
be provided and submit copies of any written materials provided to donors.

5 Are you **affiliated** with a governmental unit? If "Yes," explain.   ☐ Yes   ☑ No

6a Do you or will you engage in **economic development**? If "Yes," describe your program.   ☐ Yes   ☑ No
b Describe in full who benefits from your economic development activities and how the activities
promote exempt purposes.

7a Do or will persons other than your employees or volunteers **develop** your facilities? If "Yes," describe   ☐ Yes   ☑ No
each facility, the role of the developer, and any business or family relationship(s) between the
developer and your officers, directors, or trustees.

b Do or will persons other than your employees or volunteers **manage** your activities or facilities? If   ☐ Yes   ☑ No
"Yes," describe each activity and facility, the role of the manager, and any business or family
relationship(s) between the manager and your officers, directors, or trustees.

c If there is a business or family relationship between any manager or developer and your officers,
directors, or trustees, identify the individuals, explain the relationship, describe how contracts are
negotiated at arm's length so that you pay no more than fair market value, and submit a copy of any
contracts or other agreements.

8 Do you or will you enter into **joint ventures**, including partnerships or **limited liability companies**   ☐ Yes   ☑ No
treated as partnerships, in which you share profits and losses with partners other than section
501(c)(3) organizations? If "Yes," describe the activities of these joint ventures in which you
participate.

9a Are you applying for exemption as a childcare organization under section 501(k)? If "Yes," answer   ☐ Yes   ☑ No
lines 9b through 9d. If "No," go to line 10.

b Do you provide child care so that parents or caretakers of children you care for can be **gainfully**   ☐ Yes   ☐ No
employed (see instructions)? If "No," explain how you qualify as a childcare organization described
in section 501(k).

c Of the children for whom you provide child care, are 85% or more of them cared for by you to   ☐ Yes   ☐ No
enable their parents or caretakers to be gainfully employed (see instructions)? If "No," explain how
you qualify as a childcare organization described in section 501(k).

d Are your services available to the general public? If "No," describe the specific group of people for   ☐ Yes   ☐ No
whom your activities are available. Also, see the instructions and explain how you qualify as a
childcare organization described in section 501(k).

10 Do you or will you publish, own, or have rights in music, literature, tapes, artworks, choreography,   ☑ **Yes**   ☐ No
scientific discoveries, or other **intellectual property**? If "Yes," explain. Describe who owns or will
own any copyrights, patents, or trademarks, whether fees are or will be charged, how the fees are
determined, and how any items are or will be produced, distributed, and marketed.

Form 1023 (Rev. 6-2006)   Name: EIN: —   Page **7**

Part VIII Your Specific Activities *(Continued)*

11   Do you or will you accept contributions of: real property; conservation easements; closely held   ☐ **Yes**   ☑ **No**
securities; intellectual property such as patents, trademarks, and copyrights; works of music or art;
licenses; royalties; automobiles, boats, planes, or other vehicles; or collectibles of any type? If "Yes,"
describe each type of contribution, any conditions imposed by the donor on the contribution, and
any agreements with the donor regarding the contribution.

12a Do you or will you operate in a **foreign country** or **countries?** If "Yes," answer lines 12b through   ☐ **Yes**   ☑ **No**
    12d. If "No," go to line 13a.
  b Name the foreign countries and regions within the countries in which you operate.
  c Describe your operations in each country and region in which you operate.
  d Describe how your operations in each country and region further your exempt purposes.

13a Do you or will you make grants, loans, or other distributions to organization(s)? If "Yes," answer lines   ☐ **Yes**   ☑ **No**
    13b through 13g. If "No," go to line 14a.
  b Describe how your grants, loans, or other distributions to organizations further your exempt purposes.
  c Do you have written contracts with each of these organizations? If "Yes," attach a copy of each contract.   ☐ **Yes**   ☐ **No**
  d Identify each recipient organization and any **relationship** between you and the recipient organization.
  e Describe the records you keep with respect to the grants, loans, or other distributions you make.
  f Describe your selection process, including whether you do any of the following:
    (i) Do you require an application form? If "Yes," attach a copy of the form.   ☐ **Yes**   ☐ **No**
    (ii) Do you require a grant proposal? If "Yes," describe whether the grant proposal specifies your   ☐ **Yes**   ☐ **No**
      responsibilities and those of the grantee, obligates the grantee to use the grant funds only for the
      purposes for which the grant was made, provides for periodic written reports concerning the use
      of grant funds, requires a final written report and an accounting of how grant funds were used,
      and acknowledges your authority to withhold and/or recover grant funds in case such funds are,
      or appear to be, misused.
  g Describe your procedures for oversight of distributions that assure you the resources are used to
    further your exempt purposes, including whether you require periodic and final reports on the use of
    resources.

14a Do you or will you make grants, loans, or other distributions to foreign organizations? If "Yes,"   ☐ **Yes**   ☑ **No**
    answer lines 14b through 14f. If "No," go to line 15.
  b Provide the name of each foreign organization, the country and regions within a country in which
    each foreign organization operates, and describe any relationship you have with each foreign
    organization.
  c Does any foreign organization listed in line 14b accept contributions earmarked for a specific country   ☐ **Yes**   ☐ **No**
    or specific organization? If "Yes," list all earmarked organizations or countries.
  d Do your contributors know that you have ultimate authority to use contributions made to you at your   ☐ **Yes**   ☐ **No**
    discretion for purposes consistent with your exempt purposes? If "Yes," describe how you relay this
    information to contributors.
  e Do you or will you make pre-grant inquiries about the recipient organization? If "Yes," describe these   ☐ **Yes**   ☐ **No**
    inquiries, including whether you inquire about the recipient's financial status, its tax-exempt status
    under the Internal Revenue Code, its ability to accomplish the purpose for which the resources are
    provided, and other relevant information.
  f Do you or will you use any additional procedures to ensure that your distributions to foreign   ☐ **Yes**   ☐ **No**
    organizations are used in furtherance of your exempt purposes? If "Yes," describe these procedures,
    including site visits by your employees or compliance checks by impartial experts, to verify that grant
    funds are being used appropriately.

Form **1023** (Rev. 6-2006)

Form 1023 (Rev. 6-2006)	Name:	EIN: –	Page **8**

Part VIII Your Specific Activities *(Continued)*

		Yes	No
15	Do you have a **close connection** with any organizations? If "Yes," explain.	☐ Yes	☑ No
16	Are you applying for exemption as a **cooperative hospital service organization** under section 501(e)? If "Yes," explain.	☐ Yes	☑ No
17	Are you applying for exemption as a **cooperative service organization of operating educational organizations** under section 501(f)? If "Yes," explain.	☐ Yes	☑ No
18	Are you applying for exemption as a **charitable risk pool** under section 501(n)? If "Yes," explain.	☐ Yes	☑ No
19	Do you or will you operate a **school**? If "Yes," complete Schedule B. Answer "Yes," whether you operate a school as your main function or as a secondary activity.	☑ Yes	☐ No
20	Is your main function to provide **hospital** or **medical care**? If "Yes," complete Schedule C.	☐ Yes	☑ No
21	Do you or will you provide **low-income housing** or housing for the **elderly** or **handicapped**? If "Yes," complete Schedule F.	☐ Yes	☑ No
22	Do you or will you provide scholarships, fellowships, educational loans, or other educational grants to individuals, including grants for travel, study, or other similar purposes? If "Yes," complete Schedule H.	☐ Yes	☑ No

Note: Private foundations may use Schedule H to request advance approval of individual grant procedures.

Form **1023** (Rev. 6-2006)

Form 1023 (Rev. 6-2006)   Name: EIN: –   Page **9**

Part IX   Financial Data

For purposes of this schedule, years in existence refer to completed tax years. If in existence 4 or more years, complete the schedule for the most recent 4 tax years. If in existence more than 1 year but less than 4 years, complete the statements for each year in existence and provide projections of your likely revenues and expenses based on a reasonable and good faith estimate of your future finances for a total of 3 years of financial information. If in existence less than 1 year, provide projections of your likely revenues and expenses for the current year and the 2 following years, based on a reasonable and good faith estimate of your future finances for a total of 3 years of financial information. (See instructions.)

A. Statement of Revenues and Expenses

		Type of revenue or expense	Current tax year (a) From 7/15/08 To 7/14/09	3 prior tax years or 2 succeeding tax years (b) From 7/15/09 To 7/14/10	(c) From 7/15/10 To 7/14/11	(d) From To	(e) Provide Total for (a) through (d)
Revenues	1	Gifts, grants, and contributions received (do not include unusual grants)	450,000	500,000	500,000		1,4450,000
	2	Membership fees received	0	0	0		0
	3	Gross investment income	0	0			0
	4	Net unrelated business income	0	0	0		0
	5	Taxes levied for your benefit	0	0	0		0
	6	Value of services or facilities furnished by a governmental unit without charge (not including the value of services generally furnished to the public without charge)	0	0	0		0
	7	Any revenue not otherwise listed above or in lines 9–12 below (attach an itemized list)	0	0	0		0
	8	Total of lines 1 through 7	450,000	500,000	500,000		1,450,000
	9	Gross receipts from admissions, merchandise sold or services performed, or furnishing of facilities in any activity that is related to your exempt purposes (attach itemized list)	0	0	0		0
	10	Total of lines 8 and 9	450,000	500,000	500,000		1,450,000
	11	Net gain or loss on sale of capital assets (attach schedule and see instructions)	0	0	0		0
	12	**Unusual grants**	0	0	0		
	13	Total Revenue Add lines 10 through 12	450,000	500,000	500,000		1,450,000
Expenses	14	Fundraising expenses	10,000	10,000	10,000		
	15	Contributions, gifts, grants, and similar amounts paid out (attach an itemized list)	0	0	0		
	16	Disbursements to or for the benefit of members (attach an itemized list)	0	0	0		
	17	Compensation of officers, directors, and trustees	0	0	0		
	18	Other salaries and wages	100,000	120,000	130,000		
	19	Interest expense	0	0	0		
	20	Occupancy (rent, utilities, etc.)	10,000	10,000	15,000		
	21	Depreciation and depletion	0	0	0		
	22	Professional fees	0	0	0		
	23	Any expense not otherwise classified, such as program services (attach itemized list)	280,000	290,000	295,000		
	24	Total Expenses Add lines 14 through 23	400,000	430,000	440,000		

Form **1023** (Rev. 6-2006)

Form 1023 (Rev. 6-2006)   Name: EIN: —   Page **10**

Part IX Financial Data *(Continued)*

B. Balance Sheet (for your most recently completed tax year)

			Year End:
			(Whole dollars)
Assets			
1	Cash	1	150,000
2	Accounts receivable, net	2	0
3	Inventories	3	0
4	Bonds and notes receivable (attach an itemized list)	4	0
5	Corporate stocks (attach an itemized list)	5	0
6	Loans receivable (attach an itemized list)	6	0
7	Other investments (attach an itemized list)	7	0
8	Depreciable and depletable assets (attach an itemized list)	8	0
9	Land	9	0
10	Other assets (attach an itemized list)	10	0
11	Total Assets (add lines 1 through 10)	11	150,000
Liabilities			
12	Accounts payable	12	0
13	Contributions, gifts, grants, etc. payable	13	0
14	Mortgages and notes payable (attach an itemized list)	14	0
15	Other liabilities (attach an itemized list)	15	0
16	Total Liabilities (add lines 12 through 15)	16	0
Fund Balances or Net Assets			
17	Total fund balances or net assets	17	150,000
18	Total Liabilities and Fund Balances or Net Assets (add lines 16 and 17)	18	150,000

19 Have there been any substantial changes in your assets or liabilities since the end of the period shown above? If "Yes," explain.   ☐ Yes   ☐ No

Part X Public Charity Status

Part X is designed to classify you as an organization that is either a **private foundation** or a **public charity**. Public charity status is a more favorable tax status than private foundation status. If you are a private foundation, Part X is designed to further determine whether you are a **private operating foundation**. (See instructions.)

1a Are you a private foundation? If "Yes," go to line 1b. If "No," go to line 5 and proceed as instructed. If you are unsure, see the instructions.   ☐ Yes   ☑ **No**

b As a private foundation, section 508(e) requires special provisions in your organizing document in addition to those that apply to all organizations described in section 501(c)(3). Check the box to confirm that your organizing document meets this requirement, whether by express provision or by reliance on operation of state law. Attach a statement that describes specifically where your organizing document meets this requirement, such as a reference to a particular article or section in your organizing document or by operation of state law. See the instructions, including Appendix B, for information about the special provisions that need to be contained in your organizing document. Go to line 2.   ☐

2 Are you a private operating foundation? To be a private operating foundation you must engage directly in the active conduct of charitable, religious, educational, and similar activities, as opposed to indirectly carrying out these activities by providing grants to individuals or other organizations. If "Yes," go to line 3. If "No," go to the signature section of Part XI.   ☐ Yes   ☐ No

3 Have you existed for one or more years? If "Yes," attach financial information showing that you are a private operating foundation; go to the signature section of Part XI. If "No," continue to line 4.   ☐ Yes   ☐ No

4 Have you attached either (1) an affidavit or opinion of counsel, (including a written affidavit or opinion from a certified public accountant or accounting firm with expertise regarding this tax law matter), that sets forth facts concerning your operations and support to demonstrate that you are likely to satisfy the requirements to be classified as a private operating foundation; or (2) a statement describing your proposed operations as a private operating foundation?   ☐ Yes   ☐ No

5 If you answered "No" to line 1a, indicate the type of public charity status you are requesting by checking one of the choices below. You may check only one box.

The organization is not a private foundation because it is:

a 509(a)(1) and 170(b)(1)(A)(i)—a church or a convention or association of churches. Complete and attach Schedule A.   ☐

b 509(a)(1) and 170(b)(1)(A)(ii)—a **school**. Complete and attach Schedule B.   ☑

c 509(a)(1) and 170(b)(1)(A)(iii)—a **hospital**, a cooperative hospital service organization, or a medical research organization operated in conjunction with a hospital. Complete and attach Schedule C.   ☐

d 509(a)(3)—an organization supporting either one or more organizations described in line 5a through c, f, g, or h or a publicly supported section 501(c)(4), (5), or (6) organization. Complete and attach Schedule D.   ☐

Form **1023** (Rev. 6-2006)

Form 1023 (Rev. 6-2006)   Name: EIN: –   Page **11**

Part X	**Public Charity Status** *(Continued)*

e 509(a)(4)—an organization organized and operated exclusively for testing for public safety. ☐

f 509(a)(1) and 170(b)(1)(A)(iv)—an organization operated for the benefit of a college or university that is owned or operated by a governmental unit. ☐

g 509(a)(1) and 170(b)(1)(A)(vi)—an organization that receives a substantial part of its financial support in the form of contributions from publicly supported organizations, from a governmental unit, or from the general public. ☐

h 509(a)(2)—an organization that normally receives not more than one-third of its financial support from gross **investment income** and receives more than one-third of its financial support from contributions, membership fees, and gross receipts from activities related to its exempt functions (subject to certain exceptions). ☐

i A publicly supported organization, but unsure if it is described in 5g or 5h. The organization would like the IRS to decide the correct status. ☐

6 If you checked box g, h, or i in question 5 above, you must request either an **advance** or a **definitive ruling** by selecting one of the boxes below. Refer to the instructions to determine which type of ruling you are eligible to receive.

a **Request for Advance Ruling:** By checking this box and signing the consent, pursuant to section 6501(c)(4) of the Code you request an advance ruling and agree to extend the statute of limitations on the assessment of excise tax under section 4940 of the Code. The tax will apply only if you do not establish public support status at the end of the 5-year advance ruling period. The assessment period will be extended for the 5 advance ruling years to 8 years, 4 months, and 15 days beyond the end of the first year. You have the right to refuse or limit the extension to a mutually agreed-upon period of time or issue(s). Publication 1035, *Extending the Tax Assessment Period*, provides a more detailed explanation of your rights and the consequences of the choices you make. You may obtain Publication 1035 free of charge from the IRS web site at *www.irs.gov* or by calling toll-free 1-800-829-3676. Signing this consent will not deprive you of any appeal rights to which you would otherwise be entitled. If you decide not to extend the statute of limitations, you are not eligible for an advance ruling. ☐

Consent Fixing Period of Limitations Upon Assessment of Tax Under Section 4940 of the Internal Revenue Code

For Organization

---   ------------------------------------   --------------------------
(Signature of Officer, Director, Trustee, or other   (Type or print name of signer)   (Date)
authorized official)

                                                  (Type or print title or authority of signer)

For IRS Use Only

---   --------------------------
IRS Director, Exempt Organizations   (Date)

b **Request for Definitive Ruling:** Check this box if you have completed one tax year of at least 8 full months and you are requesting a definitive ruling. To confirm your public support status, answer line 6b(i) if you checked box g in line 5 above. Answer line 6b(ii) if you checked box h in line 5 above. If you checked box i in line 5 above, answer both lines 6b(i) and (ii). ☐

(i) **(a)** Enter 2% of line 8, column (e) on Part IX-A. Statement of Revenues and Expenses. _____

    (b) Attach a list showing the name and amount contributed by each person, company, or organization whose gifts totaled more than the 2% amount. If the answer is "None," check this box. ☐

(ii) **(a)** For each year amounts are included on lines 1, 2, and 9 of Part IX-A. Statement of Revenues and Expenses, attach a list showing the name of and amount received from each **disqualified person.** If the answer is "None," check this box. ☐

    (b) For each year amounts are included on line 9 of Part IX-A. Statement of Revenues and Expenses, attach a list showing the name of and amount received from a disqualified person, whose payments were more than the larger of (1) 1% of line 10, Part IX-A. Statement of Revenues and Expenses, or (2) $5,000. If the answer is "None," check this box. ☐

7 Did you receive any unusual grants during any of the years shown on Part IX-A. Statement of Revenues and Expenses? If "Yes," attach a list including the name of the contributor, the date and amount of the grant, a brief description of the grant, and explain why it is unusual.   ☐ **Yes**   ☐ **No**

Form **1023** (Rev. 6-2006)

Form 1023 (Rev. 6-2006)   Name: EIN: —   Page **12**

Part XI   User Fee Information

You must include a user fee payment with this application. It will not be processed without your paid user fee. If your average annual gross receipts have exceeded or will exceed $10,000 annually over a 4-year period, you must submit payment of $750. If your gross receipts have not exceeded or will not exceed $10,000 annually over a 4-year period, the required user fee payment is $300. See instructions for Part XI, for a definition of **gross receipts** over a 4-year period. Your check or money order must be made payable to the United States Treasury. *User fees are subject to change. Check our website at www.irs.gov and type "User Fee" in the keyword box, or call Customer Account Services at 1-877-829-5500 for current information.*

1	Have your annual gross receipts averaged or are they expected to average not more than $10,000?		☑ **Yes**	☐ **No**
	If "Yes," check the box on line 2 and enclose a user fee payment of $300 (Subject to change—see above).			
	If "No," check the box on line 3 and enclose a user fee payment of $750 (Subject to change—see above).			
2	Check the box if you have enclosed the reduced user fee payment of $300 (Subject to change).			☐
3	Check the box if you have enclosed the user fee payment of $750 (Subject to change).			☑

I declare under the penalties of perjury that I am authorized to sign this application on behalf of the above organization and that I have examined this application, including the accompanying schedules and attachments, and to the best of my knowledge it is true, correct, and complete.

Please Sign Here ▶

_____   **Sam Smith**   ##/ ##/ ##
(Signature of Officer, Director, Trustee, or other   (Type or print name of signer)   (Date)
authorized official)

                                   President, ABC Initiative
                                   _____
                                   (Type or print title or authority of signer)

Reminder: Send the completed Form 1023 Checklist with your filled-in-application.   Form **1023** (Rev. 6-2006)

EXAMPLES OF ATTACHMENTS TO ACCOMPANY SAMPLE FORM 1023[*]

Form 1023 requests that organizations attach certain organizational documents with its application. In The ABC Initiative for Childhood Education example, as a corporation, it should include its articles of incorporation and its bylaws. The following is an excerpt from IRS Instructions for Form 1023 p. 7-8 (Rev. Oct. 2004) which discusses the requirements for such documents:

> A corporation's organizing document is its "articles of incorporation."
> . . . If formed under state statute, your articles of incorporation must show certification of filing. This means your articles show evidence that on a specific date they were filed with and approved by an appropriate state authority [e.g. Secretary of State for the State of Incorporation]. . . .
> "Bylaws" are generally the internal rules and regulations of an organization. If you have bylaws, you should submit a current copy. . ."

PART IV: NARATIVE DESCRIPTION OF YOUR ACTIVITIES

Example: The ABC Initiative for Childhood Education Example:

The ABC Initiative is a pre-school providing quality education to children ages two years through kindergarten. The school is dedicated to the total development of the child. Each child is looked upon as a unique individual, capable of developing self-discipline, independence, and a love and respect for self, others and all of creation.

The goal of ABC Initiative for Childhood Education is to cultivate the child's own natural desire to learn. This objective is approached in two ways. First, by allowing the child to experience the excitement of learning by his/her own choice rather than by being forced; and second, by helping the child to perfect all his/her natural tools for learning, so that his/her ability will be at a maximum in future learning situations.

Equipment is available in the classroom that invites the child to read, write and calculate during his/her own periods of interest and readiness. The school takes advantage of these periods of fascination for learning allowing the child freedom to select individual activities which correspond to his or her periods of interest.

A child enters the School between the age of two and three and a half years of age. He/she will begin with simple exercises. The exercises and equipment which is used will help to develop concentration, coordination and working habits necessary for the more advanced exercises he or she will perform at later ages.

The School is a unique cycle of learning designed to take advantage of a child's sensitive years between two and six when he or she can absorb information from an enriched environment. By pursuing his or her individual interests in a classroom, he

---

[*] The Forms and Attachments in this book have been filled-in with fictitious names and information to give a sense of the information the IRS seeks. For our fictitious educational organization, Schedule B is the only schedule the would normally be included with the materials sent with Form 1023, however, all schedules have been included for review.

or she gains an early enthusiasm for learning, which is the key to him/her becoming a truly educated person.

PART V Question 3(a).

ABC Initiative does not have any compensated employees (greater than $50,00/year compensation), so it would only list the officers from PART V Question 1(a). The attachment answering this question would include the following type of information: resume, average hours worked for the organization, and duties conducted for the organization.

PART V Question 5(a).

Form 1023 asks for information regarding a Conflict of Interest Policy. The following is an example of such a Policy taken from Instructions for Form 1023 p. 25 (Rev. Oct. 2004). Actual Conflict of Interest Policies should be created to fit the organization and its operation.

Sample Conflict of Interest Policy

Article I

Purpose

The purpose of the conflict of interest policy is to protect this tax-exempt organization's (Organization) interest when it is contemplating entering into a transaction or arrangement that might benefit the private interest of an officer or director of the Organization or might result in a possible excess benefit transaction. This policy is intended to supplement but not replace any applicable state and federal laws governing conflict of interest applicable to nonprofit and charitable organizations.

Article II

Definitions

1. Interested Person

Any director, principal officer, or member of a committee with governing board delegated powers, who has a direct or indirect financial interest, as defined below, is an interested person.

2. Financial Interest

A person has a financial interest if the person has, directly or indirectly, through business, investment, or family: (a) An ownership or investment interest in any entity with which the Organization has a transaction or arrangement, (b) A compensation arrangement with the Organization or with any entity or individual with which the Organization has a transaction or arrangement, or (c)A potential ownership or investment interest in, or compensation arrangement with, any entity or individual with which the Organization is negotiating a transaction or arrangement.

Compensation includes direct and indirect remuneration as well as gifts or favors that are not insubstantial. A financial interest is not necessarily a conflict of interest. Under Article III, Section 2, a person who has a financial interest may have a conflict of interest only if the appropriate governing board or committee decides that a conflict of interest exists.

Article III

Procedures

1. Duty to Disclose

In connection with any actual or possible conflict of interest, an interested person must disclose the existence of the financial interest and be given the opportunity to disclose all material facts to the directors and members of committees with governing board delegated powers considering the proposed transaction or arrangement.

2. Determining Whether a Conflict of Interest Exists

After disclosure of the financial interest and all material facts, and after any discussion with the interested person, he/she shall leave the governing board or committee meeting while the determination of a conflict of interest is discussed and voted upon. The remaining board or committee members shall decide if a conflict of interest exists.

3. Procedures for Addressing the Conflict of Interest

(a) An interested person may make a presentation at the governing board or committee meeting, but after the presentation, he/she shall leave the meeting during the discussion of, and the vote on, the transaction or arrangement involving the possible conflict of interest. (b) The chairperson of the governing board or committee shall, if appropriate, appoint a disinterested person or committee to investigate alternatives to the proposed transaction or arrangement. (c) After exercising due diligence, the governing board or committee shall determine whether the Organization can obtain with reasonable efforts a more advantageous transaction or arrangement from a person or entity that would not give rise to a conflict of interest. (d) If a more advantageous transaction or arrangement is not reasonably possible under circumstances not producing a conflict of interest, the governing board or committee shall determine by a majority vote of the disinterested directors whether the transaction or arrangement is in the Organization's best interest, for its own benefit, and whether it is fair and reasonable. In conformity with the above determination it shall make its decision as to whether to enter into the transaction or arrangement.

4. Violations of the Conflicts of Interest Policy

(a)If the governing board or committee has reasonable cause to believe a member has failed to disclose actual or possible conflicts of interest, it shall inform the member of the basis for such belief and afford the member an opportunity to explain the alleged failure to disclose. (b) If, after hearing the member's response and after making further investigation as warranted by the circumstances, the governing board or committee determines the member has failed to disclose an actual or possible conflict of interest, it shall take appropriate disciplinary and corrective action.

Article IV

Records of Proceedings

The minutes of the governing board and all committees with board delegated powers shall contain: (a) The names of the persons who disclosed or otherwise were found to have a financial interest in connection with an actual or possible conflict of interest, the nature of the financial interest, any action taken to determine whether a conflict of interest was present, and the governing board's or committee's decision as to whether a conflict of interest in fact existed. (b) The names of the persons who were present for discussions and votes relating to the transaction or arrangement, the content of the discussion, including any alternatives to the proposed transaction or arrangement, and a record of any votes taken in connection with the proceedings.

Article V

Compensation

(a) A voting member of the governing board who receives compensation, directly or indirectly, from the Organization for services is precluded from voting on matters pertaining to that member's compensation. (b) A voting member of any committee whose jurisdiction includes compensation matters and who receives compensation, directly or indirectly, from the Organization for services is precluded from voting on matters pertaining to that member's compensation. (c) No voting member of the governing board or any committee whose jurisdiction includes compensation matters and who receives compensation, directly or indirectly, from the Organization, either individually or collectively, is prohibited from providing information to any committee regarding compensation.

Article VI
Annual Statements

Each director, principal officer and member of a committee with governing board delegated powers shall annually sign a statement which affirms such person: (a) Has received a copy of the conflicts of interest policy, (b) Has read and understands the policy, (c) Has agreed to comply with the policy, and (d) Understands the Organization is charitable and in order to maintain its federal tax exemption it must engage primarily in activities which accomplish one or more of its tax-exempt purposes.

Article VII

Periodic Reviews

To ensure the Organization operates in a manner consistent with charitable purposes and does not engage in activities that could jeopardize its tax-exempt status, periodic reviews shall be conducted. The periodic reviews shall, at a minimum, include the following subjects: (a) Whether compensation arrangements and benefits are reasonable, based on competent survey information, and the result of arm's length bargaining. (b) Whether partnerships, joint ventures, and arrangements with management organizations conform to the Organization's written policies, are properly recorded, reflect reasonable investment or payments for goods and services, further charitable purposes and do not result in inurement, impermissible private benefit or in an excess benefit transaction.

Article VIII

Use of Outside Experts

When conducting the periodic reviews as provided for in Article VII, the Organization may, but need not, use outside advisors. If outside experts are used, their use shall not relieve the governing board of its responsibility for ensuring periodic reviews are conducted.

PART VIII Question 4(a).

ABC Initiative engages in several types of fundraising activities and must provide a description of each fundraising program.

PART X Question 5(b).

ABC Initiative is a school so it must complete Schedule B. For completeness, all Schedules have been attached to this appendix.

SCHEDULE B Section II, Question 2.

As a school, ABC Initiative must comply with the requirements of nondiscrimination (as discussed in Section 9.02. Such a policy may consist of the following:

Example Nondiscrimination Policy: ABC Initiative for Childhood Education, Inc. admits students of any race, color, national and ethnic origin to all the rights, privileges, programs and activities generally accorded or made available to students at the school. It does not discriminate on the basis of race, color, national and ethnic origin in administration of its educational policies and school-administered programs.

SCHEDULE B Section II, Question 7(a) requests a list incorporators, founders, board members, and donors of land or buildings.

Form 1023 (Rev. 6-2006)   Name: EIN: –   Page **13**

Schedule A. Churches

1a Do you have a written creed, statement of faith, or summary of beliefs? If "Yes," attach copies of relevant documents.   ☐ **Yes**   ☐ **No**

b Do you have a form of worship? If "Yes," describe your form of worship.   ☐ **Yes**   ☐ **No**

2a Do you have a formal code of doctrine and discipline? If "Yes," describe your code of doctrine and discipline.   ☐ **Yes**   ☐ **No**

b Do you have a distinct religious history? If "Yes," describe your religious history.   ☐ **Yes**   ☐ **No**

c Do you have a literature of your own? If "Yes," describe your literature.   ☐ **Yes**   ☐ **No**

3 Describe the organization's religious hierarchy or ecclesiastical government.

4a Do you have regularly scheduled religious services? If "Yes," describe the nature of the services and provide representative copies of relevant literature such as church bulletins.   ☐ **Yes**   ☐ **No**

b What is the average attendance at your regularly scheduled religious services?   _____

5a Do you have an established place of worship? If "Yes," refer to the instructions for the information required.   ☐ **Yes**   ☐ **No**

b Do you own the property where you have an established place of worship?   ☐ **Yes**   ☐ **No**

6 Do you have an established congregation or other regular membership group? If "No," refer to the instructions.   ☐ **Yes**   ☐ **No**

7 How many members do you have?   _____

8a Do you have a process by which an individual becomes a member? If "Yes," describe the process and complete lines 8b–8d, below.   ☐ **Yes**   ☐ **No**

b If you have members, do your members have voting rights, rights to participate in religious functions, or other rights? If "Yes," describe the rights your members have.   ☐ **Yes**   ☐ **No**

c May your members be associated with another denomination or church?   ☐ **Yes**   ☐ **No**

d Are all of your members part of the same **family**?   ☐ **Yes**   ☐ **No**

9 Do you conduct baptisms, weddings, funerals, etc.?   ☐ **Yes**   ☐ **No**

10 Do you have a school for the religious instruction of the young?   ☐ **Yes**   ☐ **No**

11a Do you have a minister or religious leader? If "Yes," describe this person's role and explain whether the minister or religious leader was ordained, commissioned, or licensed after a prescribed course of study.   ☐ **Yes**   ☐ **No**

b Do you have schools for the preparation of your ordained ministers or religious leaders?   ☐ **Yes**   ☐ **No**

12 Is your minister or religious leader also one of your officers, directors, or trustees?   ☐ **Yes**   ☐ **No**

13 Do you ordain, commission, or license ministers or religious leaders? If "Yes," describe the requirements for ordination, commission, or licensure.   ☐ **Yes**   ☐ **No**

14 Are you part of a group of churches with similar beliefs and structures? If "Yes," explain. Include the name of the group of churches.   ☐ **Yes**   ☐ **No**

15 Do you issue church charters? If "Yes," describe the requirements for issuing a charter.   ☐ **Yes**   ☐ **No**

16 Did you pay a fee for a church charter? If "Yes," attach a copy of the charter.   ☐ **Yes**   ☐ **No**

17 Do you have other information you believe should be considered regarding your status as a church? If "Yes," explain.   ☐ **Yes**   ☐ **No**

Form **1023** (Rev. 6-2006)

Form 1023 (Rev. 6-2006)   Name: EIN: —   Page **14**

Schedule B. Schools, Colleges, and Universities

If you operate a school as an activity, complete Schedule B

1a Do you normally have a regularly scheduled curriculum, a regular faculty of qualified teachers, a regularly enrolled student body, and facilities where your educational activities are regularly carried on? If "No," do not complete the remainder of Schedule B.   ☑ **Yes**   ☐ **No**

b Is the primary function of your school the presentation of formal instruction? If "Yes," describe your school in terms of whether it is an elementary, secondary, college, technical, or other type of school. If "No," do not complete the remainder of Schedule B.   ☑ **Yes**   ☐ **No**

2a Are you a public school because you are operated by a state or subdivision of a state? If "Yes," explain how you are operated by a state or subdivision of a state. Do not complete the remainder of Schedule B.   ☐ **Yes**   ☑ **No**

b Are you a public school because you are operated wholly or predominantly from government funds or property? If "Yes," explain how you are operated wholly or predominantly from government funds or property. Submit a copy of your funding agreement regarding government funding. Do not complete the remainder of Schedule B.   ☐ **Yes**   ☑ **No**

3 In what public school district, county, and state are you located?
Anytown School District, Anytown County, XY

4 Were you formed or substantially expanded at the time of public school desegregation in the above school district or county?   ☐ **Yes**   ☑ **No**

5 Has a state or federal administrative agency or judicial body ever determined that you are racially discriminatory? If "Yes," explain.   ☐ **Yes**   ☑ **No**

6 Has your right to receive financial aid or assistance from a governmental agency ever been revoked or suspended? If "Yes," explain.   ☐ **Yes**   ☑ **No**

7 Do you or will you contract with another organization to develop, build, market, or finance your facilities? If "Yes," explain how that entity is selected, explain how the terms of any contracts or other agreements are negotiated at arm's length, and explain how you determine that you will pay no more than fair market value for services.   ☐ **Yes**   ☑ **No**

Note. Make sure your answer is consistent with the information provided in Part VIII, line 7a.

8 Do you or will you manage your activities or facilities through your own employees or volunteers? If "No," attach a statement describing the activities that will be managed by others, the names of the persons or organizations that manage or will manage your activities or facilities, and how these managers were or will be selected. Also, submit copies of any contracts, proposed contracts, or other agreements regarding the provision of management services for your activities or facilities. Explain how the terms of any contracts or other agreements were or will be negotiated, and explain how you determine you will pay no more than fair market value for services.   ☑ **Yes**   ☐ **No**

Note. Answer "Yes" if you manage or intend to manage your programs through your own employees or by using volunteers. Answer "No" if you engage or intend to engage a separate organization or independent contractor. Make sure your answer is consistent with the information provided in Part VIII, line 7b.

Information required by **Revenue Procedure 75-50.**

1 Have you adopted a racially nondiscriminatory policy as to students in your organizing document, bylaws, or by resolution of your governing body? If "Yes," state where the policy can be found or supply a copy of the policy. If "No," you must adopt a nondiscriminatory policy as to students before submitting this application. See Publication 557.   ☑ **Yes**   ☐ **No**

2 Do your brochures, application forms, advertisements, and catalogues dealing with student admissions, programs, and scholarships contain a statement of your racially nondiscriminatory policy?   ☑ **Yes**   ☐ **No**

a If "Yes," attach a representative sample of each document.
b If "No," by checking the box to the right you agree that all future printed materials, including website content, will contain the required nondiscriminatory policy statement.   ► ☐

3 Have you published a notice of your nondiscriminatory policy in a newspaper of general circulation that serves all racial segments of the community? (See the instructions for specific requirements.) If "No," explain.   ☑ **Yes**   ☐ **No**

4 Does or will the organization (or any department or division within it) discriminate in any way on the basis of race with respect to admissions; use of facilities or exercise of student privileges; faculty or administrative staff; or scholarship or loan programs? If "Yes," for any of the above, explain fully.   ☑ **Yes**   ☐ **No**

Form **1023** (Rev. 6-2006)

Form 1023 (Rev. 6-2006)   Name: EIN: –   Page **15**

Schedule B. Schools, Colleges, and Universities *(Continued)*

5 Complete the table below to show the racial composition for the current academic year and projected for the next academic year, of: (a) the student body, (b) the faculty, and (c) the administrative staff. Provide actual numbers rather than percentages for each racial category.

If you are not operational, submit an estimate based on the best information available (such as the racial composition of the community served).

Racial Category	(a) Student Body		(b) Faculty		(c) Administrative Staff	
	Current Year	Next Year	Current Year	Next Year	Current Year	Next Year
African-Americ	20	20	1	1	1	1
Asian-America	20	20	1	1	1	1
Caucasian	20	20	1	1	1	1
Hispanic-Ameri	20	20	1	1	1	1
Total	**80**	**80**	**4**	**4**	**4**	**4**

6 In the table below, provide the number and amount of loans and scholarships awarded to students enrolled by racial categories.

Racial Category	Number of Loans		Amount of Loans		Number of Scholarships		Amount of Scholarships	
	Current Year	Next Year	Current Year	Next Year	Current Year	Next Year	Current Year	Next Year
n/a								
Total								

7a Attach a list of your incorporators, founders, board members, and donors of land or buildings, whether individuals or organizations.

b Do any of these individuals or organizations have an objective to maintain segregated public or private school education? If "Yes," explain.   ☐ Yes   ☑ **No**

8 Will you maintain records according to the non-discrimination provisions contained in Revenue Procedure 75-50? If "No," explain. (See instructions.)   ☑ **Yes**   ☐ No

Form **1023** (Rev. 6-2006)

Form 1023 (Rev. 6-2006)   Name: EIN: −   Page **16**

Schedule C. Hospitals and Medical Research Organizations

Check the box if you are a **hospital**. See the instructions for a definition of the term "hospital," which includes an organization whose principal purpose or function is providing **hospital** or **medical care**. Complete Section I below.   ☐

Check the box if you are a **medical research organization** operated in conjunction with a hospital. See the instructions for a definition of the term "medical research organization," which refers to an organization whose principal purpose or function is medical research and which is directly engaged in the continuous active conduct of medical research in conjunction with a hospital. Complete Section II.   ☐

Section I   Hospitals

1a	Are all the doctors in the community eligible for staff privileges? If "No," give the reasons why and explain how the medical staff is selected.	☐ **Yes**	☐ **No**
2a	Do you or will you provide medical services to all individuals in your community who can pay for themselves or have private health insurance? If "No," explain.	☐ **Yes**	☐ **No**
b	Do you or will you provide medical services to all individuals in your community who participate in Medicare? If "No," explain.	☐ **Yes**	☐ **No**
c	Do you or will you provide medical services to all individuals in your community who participate in Medicaid? If "No," explain.	☐ **Yes**	☐ **No**
3a	Do you or will you require persons covered by Medicare or Medicaid to pay a deposit before receiving services? If "Yes," explain.	☐ **Yes**	☐ **No**
b	Does the same deposit requirement, if any, apply to all other patients? If "No," explain.	☐ **Yes**	☐ **No**
4a	Do you or will you maintain a full-time emergency room? If "No," explain why you do not maintain a full-time emergency room. Also, describe any emergency services that you provide.	☐ **Yes**	☐ **No**
b	Do you have a policy on providing emergency services to persons without apparent means to pay? If "Yes," provide a copy of the policy.	☐ **Yes**	☐ **No**
c	Do you have any arrangements with police, fire, and voluntary ambulance services for the delivery or admission of emergency cases? If "Yes," describe the arrangements, including whether they are written or oral agreements. If written, submit copies of all such agreements.	☐ **Yes**	☐ **No**
5a	Do you provide for a portion of your services and facilities to be used for charity patients? If "Yes," answer 5b through 5e.	☐ **Yes**	☐ **No**
b	Explain your policy regarding charity cases, including how you distinguish between charity care and bad debts. Submit a copy of your written policy.		
c	Provide data on your past experience in admitting charity patients, including amounts you expend for treating charity care patients and types of services you provide to charity care patients.		
d	Describe any arrangements you have with federal, state, or local governments or government agencies for paying for the cost of treating charity care patients. Submit copies of any written agreements.		
e	Do you provide services on a sliding fee schedule depending on financial ability to pay? If "Yes," submit your sliding fee schedule.	☐ **Yes**	☐ **No**
6a	Do you or will you carry on a formal program of medical training or medical research? If "Yes," describe such programs, including the type of programs offered, the scope of such programs, and affiliations with other hospitals or medical care providers with which you carry on the medical training or research programs.	☐ **Yes**	☐ **No**
b	Do you or will you carry on a formal program of community education? If "Yes," describe such programs, including the type of programs offered, the scope of such programs, and affiliation with other hospitals or medical care providers with which you offer community education programs.	☐ **Yes**	☐ **No**
7	Do you or will you provide office space to physicians carrying on their own medical practices? If "Yes," describe the criteria for who may use the space, explain the means used to determine that you are paid at least fair market value, and submit representative lease agreements.	☐ **Yes**	☐ **No**
8	Is your board of directors comprised of a majority of individuals who are representative of the community you serve? Include a list of each board member's name and business, financial, or professional relationship with the hospital. Also, identify each board member who is representative of the community and describe how that individual is a community representative.	☐ **Yes**	☐ **No**
9	Do you participate in any joint ventures? If "Yes," state your ownership percentage in each joint venture, list your investment in each joint venture, describe the tax status of other participants in each joint venture (including whether they are section 501(c)(3) organizations), describe the activities of each joint venture, describe how you exercise control over the activities of each joint venture, and describe how each joint venture furthers your exempt purposes. Also, submit copies of all agreements. **Note.** Make sure your answer is consistent with the information provided in Part VIII, line 8.	☐ **Yes**	☐ **No**

Form **1023** (Rev. 6-2006)

Form 1023 (Rev. 6-2006)   Name: EIN: –   Page **17**

Schedule C. Hospitals and Medical Research Organizations *(Continued)*

Section I   **Hospitals** *(Continued)*

10 Do you or will you manage your activities or facilities through your own employees or volunteers? If   ☐ **Yes**   ☐ **No**
"No," attach a statement describing the activities that will be managed by others, the names of the
persons or organizations that manage or will manage your activities or facilities, and how these
managers were or will be selected. Also, submit copies of any contracts, proposed contracts, or
other agreements regarding the provision of management services for your activities or facilities.
Explain how the terms of any contracts or other agreements were or will be negotiated, and explain
how you determine you will pay no more than fair market value for services.

Note. Answer "Yes" if you do manage or intend to manage your programs through your own
employees or by using volunteers. Answer "No" if you engage or intend to engage a separate
organization or independent contractor. Make sure your answer is consistent with the information
provided in Part VIII, line 7b.

11 Do you or will you offer recruitment incentives to physicians? If "Yes," describe your recruitment   ☐ **Yes**   ☐ **No**
incentives and attach copies of all written recruitment incentive policies.

12 Do you or will you lease equipment, assets, or office space from physicians who have a financial or   ☐ **Yes**   ☐ **No**
professional relationship with you? If "Yes," explain how you establish a fair market value for the
lease.

13 Have you purchased medical practices, ambulatory surgery centers, or other business assets from   ☐ **Yes**   ☐ **No**
physicians or other persons with whom you have a business relationship, aside from the purchase? If
"Yes," submit a copy of each purchase and sales contract and describe how you arrived at fair
market value, including copies of appraisals.

14 Have you adopted a **conflict of interest policy** consistent with the sample health care organization   ☐ **Yes**   ☐ **No**
conflict of interest policy in Appendix A of the instructions? If "Yes," submit a copy of the policy and
explain how the policy has been adopted, such as by resolution of your governing board. If "No,"
explain how you will avoid any conflicts of interest in your business dealings.

Section II   **Medical Research Organizations**

1 Name the hospitals with which you have a relationship and describe the relationship. Attach copies
of written agreements with each hospital that demonstrate continuing relationships between you and
the hospital(s).

2 Attach a schedule describing your present and proposed activities for the direct conduct of medical
research; describe the nature of the activities, and the amount of money that has been or will be
spent in carrying them out.

3 Attach a schedule of assets showing their fair market value and the portion of your assets directly
devoted to medical research.

Form **1023** (Rev. 6-2006)

Form 1023 (Rev. 6-2006)   Name: EIN: –   Page **18**

Schedule D. Section 509(a)(3) Supporting Organizations

Section I   Identifying Information About the Supported Organization(s)

1   State the names, addresses, and EINs of the supported organizations. If additional space is needed, attach a separate sheet.

Name	Address	EIN
	....	–
	....	–

2   Are all supported organizations listed in line 1 public charities under section 509(a)(1) or (2)? If "Yes," go to Section II. If "No," go to line 3.   ☐ **Yes**   ☐ **No**

3   Do the supported organizations have tax-exempt status under section 501(c)(4), 501(c)(5), or 501(c)(6)?   ☐ **Yes**   ☐ **No**

If "Yes," for each 501(c)(4), (5), or (6) organization supported, provide the following financial information:

- Part IX-A. Statement of Revenues and Expenses, lines 1–13 and
- Part X, lines 6b(ii)(a), 6b(ii)(b), and 7.

If "No," attach a statement describing how each organization you support is a public charity under section 509(a)(1) or (2).

Section II   Relationship with Supported Organization(s)—Three Tests

To be classified as a supporting organization, an organization must meet one of three relationship tests:

Test 1: "Operated, supervised, or controlled by" one or more publicly supported organizations, or
Test 2: "Supervised or controlled in connection with" one or more publicly supported organizations, or
Test 3: "Operated in connection with" one or more publicly supported organizations.

1   Information to establish the "operated, supervised, or controlled by" relationship (Test 1)
Is a majority of your governing board or officers elected or appointed by the supported organization(s)? If "Yes," describe the process by which your governing board is appointed and elected; go to Section III. If "No," continue to line 2.   ☐ **Yes**   ☐ **No**

2   Information to establish the "supervised or controlled in connection with" relationship (Test 2)
Does a majority of your governing board consist of individuals who also serve on the governing board of the supported organization(s)? If "Yes," describe the process by which your governing board is appointed and elected; go to Section III. If "No," go to line 3.   ☐ **Yes**   ☐ **No**

3   Information to establish the "operated in connection with" responsiveness test (Test 3)
Are you a trust from which the named supported organization(s) can enforce and compel an accounting under state law? If "Yes," explain whether you advised the supported organization(s) in writing of these rights and provide a copy of the written communication documenting this; go to Section II, line 5. If "No," go to line 4a.   ☐ **Yes**   ☐ **No**

4   Information to establish the alternative "operated in connection with" responsiveness test (Test 3)

a   Do the officers, directors, trustees, or members of the supported organization(s) elect or appoint one or more of your officers, directors, or trustees? If "Yes," explain and provide documentation; go to line 4d, below. If "No," go to line 4b.   ☐ **Yes**   ☐ **No**

b   Do one or more members of the governing body of the supported organization(s) also serve as your officers, directors, or trustees or hold other important offices with respect to you? If "Yes," explain and provide documentation; go to line 4d, below. If "No," go to line 4c.   ☐ **Yes**   ☐ **No**

c   Do your officers, directors, or trustees maintain a close and continuous working relationship with the officers, directors, or trustees of the supported organization(s)? If "Yes," explain and provide documentation.   ☐ **Yes**   ☐ **No**

d   Do the supported organization(s) have a significant voice in your investment policies, in the making and timing of grants, and in otherwise directing the use of your income or assets? If "Yes," explain and provide documentation.   ☐ **Yes**   ☐ **No**

e   Describe and provide copies of written communications documenting how you made the supported organization(s) aware of your supporting activities.

Form **1023** (Rev. 6-2006)

Form 1023 (Rev. 6-2006)   Name: EIN: −   Page **19**

Schedule D. Section 509(a)(3) Supporting Organizations *(Continued)*

Section II	**Relationship with Supported Organization(s)—Three Tests** *(Continued)*

5 Information to establish the "operated in connection with" integral part test (Test 3)

Do you conduct activities that would otherwise be carried out by the supported organization(s)? If "Yes," explain and go to Section III. If "No," continue to line 6a. ☐ **Yes** ☐ **No**

6 Information to establish the alternative "operated in connection with" integral part test (Test 3)

a Do you distribute at least 85% of your annual **net income** to the supported organization(s)? If "Yes," go to line 6b. (See instructions.) ☐ **Yes** ☐ **No**

If "No," state the percentage of your income that you distribute to each supported organization. Also explain how you ensure that the supported organization(s) are attentive to your operations.

b How much do you contribute annually to each supported organization? Attach a schedule.

c What is the total annual revenue of each supported organization? If you need additional space, attach a list.

d Do you or the supported organization(s) **earmark** your funds for support of a particular program or activity? If "Yes," explain. ☐ **Yes** ☐ **No**

7a Does your organizing document specify the supported organization(s) by name? If "Yes," state the article and paragraph number and go to Section III. If "No," answer line 7b. ☐ **Yes** ☐ **No**

b Attach a statement describing whether there has been an historic and continuing relationship between you and the supported organization(s).

Section III	**Organizational Test**

1a If you met relationship Test 1 or Test 2 in Section II, your organizing document must specify the supported organization(s) by name, or by naming a similar purpose or charitable class of beneficiaries. If your organizing document complies with this requirement, answer "Yes." If your organizing document does not comply with this requirement, answer "No," and see the instructions. ☐ **Yes** ☐ **No**

b If you met relationship Test 3 in Section II, your organizing document must generally specify the supported organization(s) by name. If your organizing document complies with this requirement, answer "Yes," and go to Section IV. If your organizing document does not comply with this requirement, answer "No," and see the instructions. ☐ **Yes** ☐ **No**

Section IV	**Disqualified Person Test**

You do not qualify as a supporting organization if you are **controlled** directly or indirectly by one or more **disqualified persons** (as defined in section 4946) other than **foundation managers** or one or more organizations that you support. Foundation managers who are also disqualified persons for another reason are disqualified persons with respect to you.

1a Do any persons who are disqualified persons with respect to you, (except individuals who are disqualified persons only because they are foundation managers), appoint any of your foundation managers? If "Yes," (1) describe the process by which disqualified persons appoint any of your foundation managers, and (2) provide the names of these disqualified persons and the foundation managers they appoint, and (3) explain how control is vested over your operations (including assets and activities) by persons other than disqualified persons. ☐ **Yes** ☐ **No**

b Do any persons who have a family or business relationship with any disqualified persons with respect to you, (except individuals who are disqualified persons only because they are foundation managers), appoint any of your foundation managers? If "Yes," (1) describe the process by which individuals with a family or business relationship with disqualified persons appoint any of your foundation managers, (2) provide the names of these disqualified persons, the individuals with a family or business relationship with disqualified persons, and the foundation managers appointed, and (3) explain how control is vested over your operations (including assets and activities) in individuals other than disqualified persons. ☐ **Yes** ☐ **No**

c Do any persons who are disqualified persons, (except individuals who are disqualified persons only because they are foundation managers), have any influence regarding your operations, including your assets or activities? If "Yes," (1) provide the names of these disqualified persons, (2) explain how influence is exerted over your operations (including assets and activities), and (3) explain how control is vested over your operations (including assets and activities) by individuals other than disqualified persons. ☐ **Yes** ☐ **No**

Form **1023** (Rev. 6-2006)

Form 1023 (Rev. 6-2006)   Name: EIN: –   Page **20**

Schedule E. Organizations Not Filing Form 1023 Within 27 Months of Formation

Schedule E is intended to determine whether you are eligible for tax exemption under section 501(c)(3) from the postmark date of your application or from your date of incorporation or formation, whichever is earlier. If you are not eligible for tax exemption under section 501(c)(3) from your date of incorporation or formation, Schedule E is also intended to determine whether you are eligible for tax exemption under section 501(c)(4) for the period between your date of incorporation or formation and the postmark date of your application.

1   Are you a church, association of churches, or integrated auxiliary of a church? If "Yes," complete Schedule A and stop here. Do not complete the remainder of Schedule E.   ☐ **Yes**   ☐ **No**

2a   Are you a public charity with annual **gross receipts** that are normally $5,000 or less? If "Yes," stop here. Answer "No" if you are a private foundation, regardless of your gross receipts.   ☐ **Yes**   ☐ **No**

  b   If your gross receipts were normally more than $5,000, are you filing this application within 90 days from the end of the tax year in which your gross receipts were normally more than $5,000? If "Yes," stop here.   ☐ **Yes**   ☐ **No**

3a   Were you included as a subordinate in a group exemption application or letter? If "No," go to line 4.   ☐ **Yes**   ☐ **No**

  b   If you were included as a subordinate in a group exemption letter, are you filing this application within 27 months from the date you were notified by the organization holding the group exemption letter or the Internal Revenue Service that you cease to be covered by the group exemption letter? If "Yes," stop here.   ☐ **Yes**   ☐ **No**

  c   If you were included as a subordinate in a timely filed group exemption request that was denied, are you filing this application within 27 months from the postmark date of the Internal Revenue Service final adverse ruling letter? If "Yes," stop here.   ☐ **Yes**   ☐ **No**

4   Were you created on or before October 9, 1969? If "Yes," stop here. Do not complete the remainder of this schedule.   ☐ **Yes**   ☐ **No**

5   If you answered "No" to lines 1 through 4, we cannot recognize you as tax exempt from your date of formation unless you qualify for an extension of time to apply for exemption. Do you wish to request an extension of time to apply to be recognized as exempt from the date you were formed? If "Yes," attach a statement explaining why you did not file this application within the 27-month period. Do not answer lines 6, 7, or 8. If "No," go to line 6a.   ☐ **Yes**   ☐ **No**

6a   If you answered "No" to line 5, you can only be exempt under section 501(c)(3) from the postmark date of this application. Therefore, do you want us to treat this application as a request for tax exemption from the postmark date? If "Yes," you are eligible for an advance ruling. Complete Part X, line 6a. If "No," you will be treated as a private foundation.   ☐ **Yes**   ☐ **No**

  Note. Be sure your ruling eligibility agrees with your answer to Part X, line 6.

  b   Do you anticipate significant changes in your sources of support in the future? If "Yes," complete line 7 below.   ☐ **Yes**   ☐ **No**

Form **1023** (Rev. 6-2006)

Form 1023 (Rev. 6-2006)   Name: EIN: –   Page **21**

Schedule E. Organizations Not Filing Form 1023 Within 27 Months of Formation *(Continued)*

7 Complete this item only if you answered "Yes" to line 6b. Include projected revenue for the first two full years following the current tax year.

Type of Revenue	Projected revenue for 2 years following current tax year		
	(a) From .... To	**(b)** From .... To	**(c)** Total
1 Gifts, grants, and contributions received (do not include unusual grants)			
2 Membership fees received			
3 Gross investment income			
4 Net unrelated business income			
5 Taxes levied for your benefit			
6 Value of services or facilities furnished by a governmental unit without charge (not including the value of services generally furnished to the public without charge)			
7 Any revenue not otherwise listed above or in lines 9–12 below (attach an itemized list)			
8 Total of lines 1 through 7			
9 Gross receipts from admissions, merchandise sold, or services performed, or furnishing of facilities in any activity that is related to your exempt purposes (attach itemized list)			
10 Total of lines 8 and 9			
11 Net gain or loss on sale of capital assets (attach an itemized list)			
12 Unusual grants			
13 Total revenue. Add lines 10 through 12			

8 According to your answers, you are only eligible for tax exemption under section 501(c)(3) from the postmark date of your application. However, you may be eligible for tax exemption under section 501(c)(4) from your date of formation to the postmark date of the Form 1023. Tax exemption under section 501(c)(4) allows exemption from federal income tax, but generally not deductibility of contributions under Code section 170. Check the box at right if you want us to treat this as a request for exemption under 501(c)(4) from your date of formation to the postmark date.   ▶ ☐

Attach a completed Page 1 of Form 1024, Application for Recognition of Exemption Under Section 501(a), to this application.

Form **1023** (Rev. 6-2006)

Schedule F. Homes for the Elderly or Handicapped and Low-Income Housing

Section I	General Information About Your Housing

1 Describe the type of housing you provide.

2 Provide copies of any application forms you use for admission.

3 Explain how the public is made aware of your facility.

4a Provide a description of each facility.
  b What is the total number of residents each facility can accommodate?
  c What is your current number of residents in each facility?
  d Describe each facility in terms of whether residents rent or purchase housing from you.

5 Attach a sample copy of your residency or homeownership contract or agreement.

6 Do you participate in any joint ventures? If "Yes," state your ownership percentage in each joint venture, list your investment in each joint venture, describe the tax status of other participants in each joint venture (including whether they are section 501(c)(3) organizations), describe the activities of each joint venture, describe how you exercise control over the activities of each joint venture, and describe how each joint venture furthers your exempt purposes. Also, submit copies of all joint venture agreements.   ☐ **Yes**   ☐ **No**

  Note. Make sure your answer is consistent with the information provided in Part VIII, line 8.

7 Do you or will you contract with another organization to develop, build, market, or finance your housing? If "Yes," explain how that entity is selected, explain how the terms of any contract(s) are negotiated at arm's length, and explain how you determine you will pay no more than fair market value for services.   ☐ **Yes**   ☐ **No**

  Note. Make sure your answer is consistent with the information provided in Part VIII, line 7a.

8 Do you or will you manage your activities or facilities through your own employees or volunteers? If "No," attach a statement describing the activities that will be managed by others, the names of the persons or organizations that manage or will manage your activities or facilities, and how these managers were or will be selected. Also, submit copies of any contracts, proposed contracts, or other agreements regarding the provision of management services for your activities or facilities. Explain how the terms of any contracts or other agreements were or will be negotiated, and explain how you determine you will pay no more than fair market value for services.   ☐ **Yes**   ☐ **No**

  Note. Answer "Yes" if you do manage or intend to manage your programs through your own employees or by using volunteers. Answer "No" if you engage or intend to engage a separate organization or independent contractor. Make sure your answer is consistent with the information provided in Part VIII, line 7b.

9 Do you participate in any government housing programs? If "Yes," describe these programs.   ☐ **Yes**   ☐ **No**

10a Do you own the facility? If "No," describe any enforceable rights you possess to purchase the facility in the future; go to line 10c. If "Yes," answer line 10b.   ☐ **Yes**   ☐ **No**

  b How did you acquire the facility? For example, did you develop it yourself, purchase a project, etc. Attach all contracts, transfer agreements, or other documents connected with the acquisition of the facility.

  c Do you lease the facility or the land on which it is located? If "Yes," describe the parties to the lease(s) and provide copies of all leases.   ☐ **Yes**   ☐ **No**

Form 1023 (Rev. 6-2006)   Name: EIN: –   Page **23**

Schedule F. Homes for the Elderly or Handicapped and Low-Income Housing *(Continued)*

Section II	**Homes for the Elderly or Handicapped**		

1a Do you provide housing for the elderly? If "Yes," describe who qualifies for your housing in terms of age, infirmity, or other criteria and explain how you select persons for your housing. ☐ **Yes** ☐ **No**

b Do you provide housing for the handicapped? If "Yes," describe who qualifies for your housing in terms of disability, income levels, or other criteria and explain how you select persons for your housing. ☐ **Yes** ☐ **No**

2a Do you charge an entrance or founder's fee? If "Yes," describe what this charge covers, whether it is a one-time fee, how the fee is determined, whether it is payable in a lump sum or on an installment basis, whether it is refundable, and the circumstances, if any, under which it may be waived. ☐ **Yes** ☐ **No**

b Do you charge periodic fees or maintenance charges? If "Yes," describe what these charges cover and how they are determined. ☐ **Yes** ☐ **No**

c Is your housing affordable to a significant segment of the elderly or handicapped persons in the community? Identify your **community**. Also, if "Yes," explain how you determine your housing is affordable. ☐ **Yes** ☐ **No**

3a Do you have an established policy concerning residents who become unable to pay their regular charges? If "Yes," describe your established policy. ☐ **Yes** ☐ **No**

b Do you have any arrangements with government welfare agencies or others to absorb all or part of the cost of maintaining residents who become unable to pay their regular charges? If "Yes," describe these arrangements. ☐ **Yes** ☐ **No**

4 Do you have arrangements for the healthcare needs of your residents? If "Yes," describe these arrangements. ☐ **Yes** ☐ **No**

5 Are your facilities designed to meet the physical, emotional, recreational, social, religious, and/or other similar needs of the elderly or handicapped? If "Yes," describe these design features. ☐ **Yes** ☐ **No**

Section III	**Low-Income Housing**		

1 Do you provide low-income housing? If "Yes," describe who qualifies for your housing in terms of income levels or other criteria, and describe how you select persons for your housing. ☐ **Yes** ☐ **No**

2 In addition to rent or mortgage payments, do residents pay periodic fees or maintenance charges? If "Yes," describe what these charges cover and how they are determined. ☐ **Yes** ☐ **No**

3a Is your housing affordable to low income residents? If "Yes," describe how your housing is made affordable to low-income residents. ☐ **Yes** ☐ **No**

Note. Revenue Procedure 96-32, 1996-1 C.B. 717, provides guidelines for providing low-income housing that will be treated as charitable. (At least 75% of the units are occupied by low-income tenants or 40% are occupied by tenants earning not more than 120% of the very low-income levels for the area.)

b Do you impose any restrictions to make sure that your housing remains affordable to low-income residents? If "Yes," describe these restrictions. ☐ **Yes** ☐ **No**

4 Do you provide social services to residents? If "Yes," describe these services. ☐ **Yes** ☐ **No**

Form **1023** (Rev. 6-2006)

Form 1023 (Rev. 6-2006) Name: _____ EIN: ____ – ____ Page **24**

Schedule G. Successors to Other Organizations

1a Are you a **successor** to a **for-profit organization**? If "Yes," explain the relationship with the **predecessor** organization that resulted in your creation and complete line 1b. ☐ Yes ☐ No

b Explain why you took over the activities or assets of a for-profit organization or converted from for-profit to nonprofit status.

2a Are you a successor to an organization other than a for-profit organization? Answer "Yes" if you have taken or will take over the activities of another organization; or you have taken or will take over 25% or more of the fair market value of the net assets of another organization. If "Yes," explain the relationship with the other organization that resulted in your creation. ☐ Yes ☐ No

b Provide the tax status of the predecessor organization.

c Did you or did an organization to which you are a successor previously apply for tax exemption under section 501(c)(3) or any other section of the Code? If "Yes," explain how the application was resolved. ☐ Yes ☐ No

d Was your prior tax exemption or the tax exemption of an organization to which you are a successor revoked or suspended? If "Yes," explain. Include a description of the corrections you made to re-establish tax exemption. ☐ Yes ☐ No

e Explain why you took over the activities or assets of another organization.

3 Provide the name, last address, and EIN of the predecessor organization and describe its activities.
Name: _____ **EIN:** ____ – ____
Address: _____

4 List the owners, partners, principal stockholders, officers, and governing board members of the predecessor organization. Attach a separate sheet if additional space is needed.

Name	Address	Share/Interest (If a for-profit)

5 Do or will any of the persons listed in line 4, maintain a working relationship with you? If "Yes," describe the relationship in detail and include copies of any agreements with any of these persons or with any for-profit organizations in which these persons own more than a 35% interest. ☐ Yes ☐ No

6a Were any assets transferred, whether by gift or sale, from the predecessor organization to you? ☐ Yes ☐ No
If "Yes," provide a list of assets, indicate the value of each asset, explain how the value was determined, and attach an appraisal, if available. For each asset listed, also explain if the transfer was by gift, sale, or combination thereof.

b Were any restrictions placed on the use or sale of the assets? If "Yes," explain the restrictions. ☐ Yes ☐ No

c Provide a copy of the agreement(s) of sale or transfer.

7 Were any debts or liabilities transferred from the predecessor for-profit organization to you? ☐ Yes ☐ No
If "Yes," provide a list of the debts or liabilities that were transferred to you, indicating the amount of each, how the amount was determined, and the name of the person to whom the debt or liability is owed.

8 Will you lease or rent any property or equipment previously owned or used by the predecessor for-profit organization, or from persons listed in line 4, or from for-profit organizations in which these persons own more than a 35% interest? If "Yes," submit a copy of the lease or rental agreement(s). Indicate how the lease or rental value of the property or equipment was determined. ☐ Yes ☐ No

9 Will you lease or rent property or equipment to persons listed in line 4, or to for-profit organizations in which these persons own more than a 35% interest? If "Yes," attach a list of the property or equipment, provide a copy of the lease or rental agreement(s), and indicate how the lease or rental value of the property or equipment was determined. ☐ Yes ☐ No

Form **1023** (Rev. 6-2006)

Form 1023 (Rev. 6-2006)   Name: EIN: –   Page **25**

Schedule H. Organizations Providing Scholarships, Fellowships, Educational Loans, or Other Educational Grants to Individuals and Private Foundations Requesting Advance Approval of Individual Grant Procedures

Section I	*Names of individual recipients are not required to be listed in Schedule H.* Public charities and private foundations complete lines 1a through 7 of this section. See the instructions to Part X if you are not sure whether you are a public charity or a private foundation.

1a Describe the types of educational grants you provide to individuals, such as scholarships, fellowships, loans, etc.

  b Describe the purpose and amount of your scholarships, fellowships, and other educational grants and loans that you award.

  c If you award educational loans, explain the terms of the loans (interest rate, length, forgiveness, etc.).

  d Specify how your program is publicized.

  e Provide copies of any solicitation or announcement materials.

  f Provide a sample copy of the application used.

2 Do you maintain case histories showing recipients of your scholarships, fellowships, educational loans, or other educational grants, including names, addresses, purposes of awards, amount of each grant, manner of selection, and relationship (if any) to officers, trustees, or donors of funds to you? If "No," refer to the instructions.   ☐ **Yes**   ☐ **No**

3 Describe the specific criteria you use to determine who is eligible for your program. (For example, eligibility selection criteria could consist of graduating high school students from a particular high school who will attend college, writers of scholarly works about American history, etc.)

4a Describe the specific criteria you use to select recipients. (For example, specific selection criteria could consist of prior academic performance, financial need, etc.)

  b Describe how you determine the number of grants that will be made annually.

  c Describe how you determine the amount of each of your grants.

  d Describe any requirement or condition that you impose on recipients to obtain, maintain, or qualify for renewal of a grant. (For example, specific requirements or conditions could consist of attendance at a four-year college, maintaining a certain grade point average, teaching in public school after graduation from college, etc.)

5 Describe your procedures for supervising the scholarships, fellowships, educational loans, or other educational grants. Describe whether you obtain reports and grade transcripts from recipients, or you pay grants directly to a school under an arrangement whereby the school will apply the grant funds only for enrolled students who are in good standing. Also, describe your procedures for taking action if the terms of the award are violated.

6 Who is on the selection committee for the awards made under your program, including names of current committee members, criteria for committee membership, and the method of replacing committee members?

7 Are relatives of members of the selection committee, or of your officers, directors, or **substantial contributors** eligible for awards made under your program? If "Yes," what measures are taken to ensure unbiased selections?   ☐ **Yes**   ☐ **No**

  Note. If you are a private foundation, you are not permitted to provide educational grants to **disqualified persons**. Disqualified persons include your substantial contributors and foundation managers and certain family members of disqualified persons.

Section II	**Private foundations complete lines 1a through 4f of this section. Public charities do not complete this section.**

1a If we determine that you are a private foundation, do you want this application to be considered as a request for advance approval of grant making procedures?   ☐ **Yes**   ☐ **No**   ☐ **N/A**

  b For which section(s) do you wish to be considered?
  - 4945(g)(1)—Scholarship or fellowship grant to an individual for study at an educational institution   ☐
  - 4945(g)(3)—Other grants, including loans, to an individual for travel, study, or other similar purposes, to enhance a particular skill of the grantee or to produce a specific product   ☐

2 Do you represent that you will (1) arrange to receive and review grantee reports annually and upon completion of the purpose for which the grant was awarded, (2) investigate diversions of funds from their intended purposes, and (3) take all reasonable and appropriate steps to recover diverted funds, ensure other grant funds held by a grantee are used for their intended purposes, and withhold further payments to grantees until you obtain grantees' assurances that future diversions will not occur and that grantees will take extraordinary precautions to prevent future diversions from occurring?   ☐ **Yes**   ☐ **No**

3 Do you represent that you will maintain all records relating to individual grants, including information obtained to evaluate grantees, identify whether a grantee is a disqualified person, establish the amount and purpose of each grant, and establish that you undertook the supervision and investigation of grants described in line 2?   ☐ **Yes**   ☐ **No**

Form **1023** (Rev. 6-2006)

Schedule H. Organizations Providing Scholarships, Fellowships, Educational Loans, or Other Educational Grants to Individuals and Private Foundations Requesting Advance Approval of Individual Grant Procedures *(Continued)*

Section II	Private foundations complete lines 1a through 4f of this section. Public charities do not complete this section. *(Continued)*

4a Do you or will you award scholarships, fellowships, and educational loans to attend an educational institution based on the status of an individual being an *employee of a particular employer?* If "Yes," complete lines 4b through 4f. ☐ **Yes** ☐ **No**

b Will you comply with the seven conditions and either the percentage tests or facts and circumstances test for scholarships, fellowships, and educational loans to attend an educational institution as set forth in Revenue Procedures 76-47, 1976-2 C.B. 670, and 80-39, 1980-2 C.B. 772, which apply to inducement, selection committee, eligibility requirements, objective basis of selection, employment, course of study, and other objectives? (See lines 4c, 4d, and 4e, regarding the percentage tests.) ☐ **Yes** ☐ **No**

c Do you or will you provide scholarships, fellowships, or educational loans to attend an educational institution to employees of a particular employer? ☐ **Yes** ☐ **No** ☐ **N/A**

If "Yes," will you award grants to 10% or fewer of the eligible applicants who were actually considered by the selection committee in selecting recipients of grants in that year as provided by Revenue Procedures 76-47 and 80-39? ☐ **Yes** ☐ **No**

d Do you provide scholarships, fellowships, or educational loans to attend an educational institution to children of employees of a particular employer? ☐ **Yes** ☐ **No** ☐ **N/A**

If "Yes," will you award grants to 25% or fewer of the eligible applicants who were actually considered by the selection committee in selecting recipients of grants in that year as provided by Revenue Procedures 76-47 and 80-39? If "No," go to line 4e. ☐ **Yes** ☐ **No**

e If you provide scholarships, fellowships, or educational loans to attend an educational institution to children of employees of a particular employer, will you award grants to 10% or fewer of the number of employees' children who can be shown to be eligible for grants (whether or not they submitted an application) in that year, as provided by Revenue Procedures 76-47 and 80-39? ☐ **Yes** ☐ **No** ☐ **N/A**

If "Yes," describe how you will determine who can be shown to be eligible for grants without submitting an application, such as by obtaining written statements or other information about the expectations of employees' children to attend an educational institution. If "No," go to line 4f.

Note. Statistical or sampling techniques are not acceptable. See Revenue Procedure 85-51, 1985-2 C.B. 717, for additional information.

f If you provide scholarships, fellowships, or educational loans to attend an educational institution to *children of employees of a particular employer* without regard to either the 25% limitation described in line 4d, or the 10% limitation described in line 4e, will you award grants based on facts and circumstances that demonstrate that the grants will not be considered compensation for past, present, or future services or otherwise provide a significant benefit to the particular employer? If "Yes," describe the facts and circumstances that you believe will demonstrate that the grants are neither compensatory nor a significant benefit to the particular employer. In your explanation, describe why you cannot satisfy either the 25% test described in line 4d or the 10% test described in line 4e. ☐ **Yes** ☐ **No**

Form 1023 Checklist
(Revised June 2006)
Application for Recognition of Exemption under Section 501(c)(3) of the Internal Revenue Code

Note. *Retain a copy of the completed Form 1023 in your permanent records. Refer to the* General Instructions *regarding Public Inspection of approved applications.*

Check each box to finish your application (Form 1023). Send this completed Checklist with your filled-in application. If you have not answered all the items below, your application may be returned to you as incomplete.

☑ Assemble the application and materials in this order:
- Form 1023 Checklist
- Form 2848, *Power of Attorney and Declaration of Representative* (if filing)
- Form 8821, *Tax Information Authorization* (if filing)
- Expedite request (if requesting)
- Application (Form 1023 and Schedules A through H, as required)
- Articles of organization
- Amendments to articles of organization in chronological order
- Bylaws or other rules of operation and amendments
- Documentation of nondiscriminatory policy for schools, as required by Schedule B
- Form 5768, Election/Revocation of Election by an Eligible Section 501(c)(3) Organization To Make Expenditures To Influence Legislation (if filing)
- All other attachments, including explanations, financial data, and printed materials or publications. Label each page with name and EIN.

☑ User fee payment placed in envelope on top of checklist. DO NOT STAPLE or otherwise attach your check or money order to your application. Instead, just place it in the envelope.

☑ Employer Identification Number (EIN)

☑ Completed Parts I through XI of the application, including any requested information and any required Schedules A through H.
- You must provide specific details about your past, present, and planned activities.
- Generalizations or failure to answer questions in the Form 1023 application will prevent us from recognizing you as tax exempt.
- Describe your purposes and proposed activities in specific easily understood terms.
- Financial information should correspond with proposed activities.

☑ Schedules. Submit only those schedules that apply to you and check either "Yes" or "No" below.

Schedule A Yes ___ No ___	Schedule E Yes ___ No ___
Schedule B Yes ✓ No ___	Schedule F Yes ___ No ___
Schedule C Yes ___ No ___	Schedule G Yes ___ No ___
Schedule D Yes ___ No ___	Schedule H Yes ___ No ___

☑ An exact copy of your complete articles of organization (creating document). Absence of the proper purpose and dissolution clauses is the number one reason for delays in the issuance of determination letters.

- Location of Purpose Clause from Part III, line 1 (Page, Article and Paragraph Number)_____
- Location of Dissolution Clause from Part III, line 2b or 2c (Page, Article and Paragraph Number) or by operation of state law _____

☑ Signature of an officer, director, trustee, or other official who is authorized to sign the application.
- Signature at Part XI of Form 1023.

☑ Your name on the application must be the same as your legal name as it appears in your articles of organization.

Send completed Form 1023, user fee payment, and all other required information, to:

Internal Revenue Service
P.O. Box 192
Covington, KY 41012-0192

If you are using express mail or a delivery service, send Form 1023, user fee payment, and attachments to:

Internal Revenue Service
201 West Rivercenter Blvd.
Attn: Extracting Stop 312
Covington, KY 41011

Printed on recycled paper

APPENDIX B

Form **2848** (Rev. June 2008) Department of the Treasury Internal Revenue Service	**Power of Attorney and Declaration of Representative** ▶ Type or print. ▶ See the separate instructions.	OMB No. 1545-0150

For IRS Use Only
Received by:
Name _____
Telephone _____
Function _____
Date __ / __ / __

Part I   Power of Attorney

Caution: Form 2848 will not be honored for any purpose other than representation before the IRS.

1   Taxpayer information. Taxpayer(s) must sign and date this form on page 2, line 9.

Taxpayer name(s) and address	Social security number(s)	Employer identification number
ABC Initiative for Childhood Education, Inc 111 1st Avenue Anytown, XY 00001-0001		## ########
	Daytime telephone number (111) 111-1111	Plan number (if applicable)

hereby appoint(s) the following representative(s) as attorney(s)-in-fact:

2   Representative(s) must sign and date this form on page 2, Part II.

Name and address	
Janet Jones, Attorney 2222 2nd Street Anytown, XY 00002-0002	CAF No. ------------------------------------ Telephone No. _____ **222-222-2222** Fax No. ------ **222-222-2222** Check if new: Address ☐ Telephone No. ☐ Fax No. ☐
Name and address	CAF No. ------------------------------------ Telephone No. ------------------------------------ Fax No. ------------------------------------ Check if new: Address ☐ Telephone No. ☐ Fax No. ☐
Name and address	CAF No. ------------------------------------ Telephone No. ------------------------------------ Fax No. ------------------------------------ Check if new: Address ☐ Telephone No. ☐ Fax No. ☐

to represent the taxpayer(s) before the Internal Revenue Service for the following tax matters:

3   Tax matters

Type of Tax (Income, Employment, Excise, etc.) or Civil Penalty (see the instructions for line 3)	Tax Form Number (1040, 941, 720, etc.)	Year(s) or Period(s) (see the instructions for line 3)
Exemption from Federal Income tax	**1023**	**July 2008 - present**

4   Specific use not recorded on Centralized Authorization File (CAF). If the power of attorney is for a specific use not recorded on CAF, check this box. See the instructions for **Line 4. Specific Uses Not Recorded on CAF** . . . . ▶ ☑

5   Acts authorized. The representatives are authorized to receive and inspect confidential tax information and to perform any and all acts that I (we) can perform with respect to the tax matters described on line 3, for example, the authority to sign any agreements, consents, or other documents. The authority does not include the power to receive refund checks (see line 6 below), the power to substitute another representative or add additional representatives, the power to sign certain returns, or the power to execute a request for disclosure of tax returns or return information to a third party. See the line 5 instructions for more information.

Exceptions. An unenrolled return preparer cannot sign any document for a taxpayer and may only represent taxpayers in limited situations. See **Unenrolled Return Preparer** on page 1 of the instructions. An enrolled actuary may only represent taxpayers to the extent provided in section 10.3(d) of Treasury Department Circular No. 230 (Circular 230). An enrolled retirement plan administrator may only represent taxpayers to the extent provided in section 10.3(e) of Circular 230. See the line 5 instructions for restrictions on tax matters partners. In most cases, the student practitioner's (levels k and l) authority is limited (for example, they may only practice under the supervision of another practitioner).

List any specific additions or deletions to the acts otherwise authorized in this power of attorney: **n/a** ------------------
----

----

6   Receipt of refund checks. If you want to authorize a representative named on line 2 to receive, **BUT NOT TO ENDORSE OR CASH**, refund checks, initial here _____ and list the name of that representative below.

Name of representative to receive refund check(s) ▶

For Privacy Act and Paperwork Reduction Act Notice, see page 4 of the instructions.   Cat. No. 11980J   Form **2848** (Rev. 6-2008)

Form 2848 (Rev. 6-2008)   Page **2**

7   **Notices and communications.** Original notices and other written communications will be sent to you and a copy to the first representative listed on line 2.

a   If you also want the second representative listed to receive a copy of notices and communications, check this box . . . . .   ▶ ☐

b   If you do not want any notices or communications sent to your representative(s), check this box   . . . .   ▶ ☐

8   **Retention/revocation of prior power(s) of attorney.** The filing of this power of attorney automatically revokes all earlier power(s) of attorney on file with the Internal Revenue Service for the same tax matters and years or periods covered by this document. If you **do not** want to revoke a prior power of attorney, check here.   .   .   .   .   ▶ ☐

   YOU MUST ATTACH A COPY OF ANY POWER OF ATTORNEY YOU WANT TO REMAIN IN EFFECT.

9   **Signature of taxpayer(s).** If a tax matter concerns a joint return, **both** husband and wife must sign if joint representation is requested, otherwise, see the instructions. If signed by a corporate officer, partner, guardian, tax matters partner, executor, receiver, administrator, or trustee on behalf of the taxpayer, I certify that I have the authority to execute this form on behalf of the taxpayer.

   ▶ **IF NOT SIGNED AND DATED, THIS POWER OF ATTORNEY WILL BE RETURNED.**

_____ Signature	------------ Date	------------ Title (if applicable)
Sam Smith, President ------------ Print Name	☐☐☐☐☐ PIN Number	**ABC Initiative for Childhood Education, Inc.** ------------ Print name of taxpayer from line 1 if other than individual
------------ Signature	------------ Date	------------ Title (if applicable)
------------ Print Name	☐☐☐☐☐ PIN Number	

Part II   **Declaration of Representative**

Caution: *Students with a special order to represent taxpayers in qualified Low Income Taxpayer Clinics or the Student Tax Clinic Program (levels k and l), see the instructions for Part II.*

Under penalties of perjury, I declare that:

● I am not currently under suspension or disbarment from practice before the Internal Revenue Service;

● I am aware of regulations contained in Circular 230 (31 CFR, Part 10), as amended, concerning the practice of attorneys, certified public accountants, enrolled agents, enrolled actuaries, and others;

● I am authorized to represent the taxpayer(s) identified in Part I for the tax matter(s) specified there; and

● I am one of the following:

a   Attorney—a member in good standing of the bar of the highest court of the jurisdiction shown below.

b   Certified Public Accountant—duly qualified to practice as a certified public accountant in the jurisdiction shown below.

c   Enrolled Agent—enrolled as an agent under the requirements of Circular 230.

d   Officer—a bona fide officer of the taxpayer's organization.

e   Full-Time Employee—a full-time employee of the taxpayer.

f   Family Member—a member of the taxpayer's immediate family (for example, spouse, parent, child, brother, or sister).

g   Enrolled Actuary—enrolled as an actuary by the Joint Board for the Enrollment of Actuaries under 29 U.S.C. 1242 (the authority to practice before the Internal Revenue Service is limited by section 10.3(d) of Circular 230).

h   Unenrolled Return Preparer—the authority to practice before the Internal Revenue Service is limited by Circular 230, section 10.7(c)(1)(viii). You must have prepared the return in question and the return must be under examination by the IRS. See **Unenrolled Return Preparer** on page 1 of the instructions.

k   Student Attorney—student who receives permission to practice before the IRS by virtue of their status as a law student under section 10.7(d) of Circular 230.

l   Student CPA—student who receives permission to practice before the IRS by virtue of their status as a CPA student under section 10.7(d) of Circular 230.

r   Enrolled Retirement Plan Agent—enrolled as a retirement plan agent under the requirements of Circular 230 (the authority to practice before the Internal Revenue Service is limited by section 10.3(e)).

   ▶ **IF THIS DECLARATION OF REPRESENTATIVE IS NOT SIGNED AND DATED, THE POWER OF ATTORNEY WILL BE RETURNED.** See the Part II instructions.

Designation—Insert above letter **(a–r)**	Jurisdiction (state) or identification	Signature	Date
a	**XY**		

Form **2848** (Rev. 6-2008)

APPENDIX C

Note: Form SS-4 begins on the next page of this document.

Attention

Limit of five (5) Employer Identification Number (EIN) Assignments per Business Day

Due to a high volume of requests for EINs, the IRS will begin limiting the number

of EINs assigned per day to a responsible party identified on Form SS-4.

Effective April 11, 2011, a responsible party will be limited to **five (5) EINs** in one

business day. This limit is in effect whether you apply online, by phone, fax, or

mail.

Form **SS-4** (Rev. January 2010) Department of the Treasury Internal Revenue Service	**Application for Employer Identification Number** (For use by employers, corporations, partnerships, trusts, estates, churches, government agencies, Indian tribal entities, certain individuals, and others.) ▶ See separate instructions for each line. ▶ Keep a copy for your records.	OMB No. 1545-0003 EIN

Type or print clearly.

1	Legal name of entity (or individual) for whom the EIN is being requested
	ABC Initiative for Childhood Education, Inc.

2	Trade name of business (if different from name on line 1)	3	Executor, administrator, trustee, "care of" name
			Sam Smith, President

4a	Mailing address (room, apt., suite no. and street, or P.O. box)	5a	Street address (if different) (Do not enter a P.O. box.)
	111 1st Avenue		
4b	City, state, and ZIP code (if foreign, see instructions)	5b	City, state, and ZIP code (if foreign, see instructions)
	Anytown, XY 00001-0001		

6	County and state where principal business is located
	Anytown County, XY

7a	Name of responsible party	7b	SSN, ITIN, or EIN
	Sam Smith, President		

8a	Is this application for a limited liability company (LLC) (or a foreign equivalent)? . . . . ☐ Yes ☐ No	8b	If 8a is "Yes," enter the number of LLC members . . . . ▶

8c	If 8a is "Yes," was the LLC organized in the United States? . . . . ☐ Yes ☐ No

9a Type of entity (check only one box). **Caution.** If 8a is "Yes," see the instructions for the correct box to check.

- ☐ Sole proprietor (SSN) _____
- ☐ Partnership
- ☑ Corporation (enter form number to be filed) ▶ **0000000**
- ☐ Personal service corporation
- ☐ Church or church-controlled organization
- ☐ Other nonprofit organization (specify) ▶_____
- ☐ Other (specify) ▶
- ☐ Estate (SSN of decedent) _____
- ☐ Plan administrator (TIN) _____
- ☐ Trust (TIN of grantor) _____
- ☐ National Guard ☐ State/local government
- ☐ Farmers' cooperative ☐ Federal government/military
- ☐ REMIC ☐ Indian tribal governments/enterprises
- Group Exemption Number (GEN) if any ▶

9b	If a corporation, name the state or foreign country (if applicable) where incorporated	State **xy**	Foreign country

10 **Reason for applying** (check only one box)

- ☐ Started new business (specify type) ▶ _____
- ☐ Hired employees (Check the box and see line 13.)
- ☑ Compliance with IRS withholding regulations
- ☐ Other (specify) ▶
- ☐ Banking purpose (specify purpose) ▶_____
- ☐ Changed type of organization (specify new type) ▶_____
- ☐ Purchased going business
- ☐ Created a trust (specify type) ▶_____
- ☐ Created a pension plan (specify type) ▶_____

11	Date business started or acquired (month, day, year). See instructions. **7/15/08**	12	Closing month of accounting year **07-July**
13	Highest number of employees expected in the next 12 months (enter -0- if none). If no employees expected, skip line 14.	14	If you expect your employment tax liability to be $1,000 or less in a full calendar year **and** want to file Form 944 annually instead of Forms 941 quarterly, check here. (Your employment tax liability generally will be $1,000 or less if you expect to pay $4,000 or less in total wages.) If you do not check this box, you must file Form 941 for every quarter. ☐

Agricultural	Household	Other **4**

15	First date wages or annuities were paid (month, day, year). **Note.** If applicant is a withholding agent, enter date income will first be paid to nonresident alien (month, day, year) . . . . ▶ **9/15/08**

16 Check **one** box that best describes the principal activity of your business.

- ☐ Construction ☐ Rental & leasing ☐ Transportation & warehousing
- ☐ Real estate ☐ Manufacturing ☐ Finance & insurance
- ☐ Health care & social assistance ☐ Wholesale-agent/broker
- ☐ Accommodation & food service ☐ Wholesale-other ☐ Retail
- ☑ Other (specify) **Educational - school**

17	Indicate principal line of merchandise sold, specific construction work done, products produced, or services provided. **educational services**

18	Has the applicant entity shown on line 1 ever applied for and received an EIN? ☐ Yes ☑ No If "Yes," write previous EIN here ▶

Third Party Designee	Complete this section **only** if you want to authorize the named individual to receive the entity's EIN and answer questions about the completion of this form.		
	Designee's name		Designee's telephone number (include area code) ( )
	Address and ZIP code		Designee's fax number (include area code) ( )

Under penalties of perjury, I declare that I have examined this application, and to the best of my knowledge and belief, it is true, correct, and complete.

Name and title (type or print clearly) ▶ **Sam Smith, President**	Applicant's telephone number (include area code) (**111**) **111-1111**
Signature ▶ Date ▶	Applicant's fax number (include area code) ( )

For Privacy Act and Paperwork Reduction Act Notice, see separate instructions. Cat. No. 16055N Form **SS-4** (Rev. 1-2010)

Do I Need an EIN?

File Form SS-4 if the applicant entity does not already have an EIN but is required to show an EIN on any return, statement, or other document.[1] See also the separate instructions for each line on Form SS-4.

IF the applicant...	AND...	THEN...
Started a new business	Does not currently have (nor expect to have) employees	Complete lines 1, 2, 4a–8a, 8b–c (if applicable), 9a, 9b (if applicable), and 10–14 and 16–18.
Hired (or will hire) employees, including household employees	Does not already have an EIN	Complete lines 1, 2, 4a–6, 7a–b (if applicable), 8a, 8b–c (if applicable), 9a, 9b (if applicable), 10–18.
Opened a bank account	Needs an EIN for banking purposes only	Complete lines 1–5b, 7a–b (if applicable), 8a, 8b–c (if applicable), 9a, 9b (if applicable), 10, and 18.
Changed type of organization	Either the legal character of the organization or its ownership changed (for example, you incorporate a sole proprietorship or form a partnership) [2]	Complete lines 1–18 (as applicable).
Purchased a going business [3]	Does not already have an EIN	Complete lines 1–18 (as applicable).
Created a trust	The trust is other than a grantor trust or an IRA trust [4]	Complete lines 1–18 (as applicable).
Created a pension plan as a plan administrator [5]	Needs an EIN for reporting purposes	Complete lines 1, 3, 4a–5b, 9a, 10, and 18.
Is a foreign person needing an EIN to comply with IRS withholding regulations	Needs an EIN to complete a Form W-8 (other than Form W-8ECI), avoid withholding on portfolio assets, or claim tax treaty benefits [6]	Complete lines 1–5b, 7a–b (SSN or ITIN optional), 8a, 8b–c (if applicable), 9a, 9b (if applicable), 10, and 18.
Is administering an estate	Needs an EIN to report estate income on Form 1041	Complete lines 1–6, 9a, 10–12, 13–17 (if applicable), and 18.
Is a withholding agent for taxes on non-wage income paid to an alien (i.e., individual, corporation, or partnership, etc.)	Is an agent, broker, fiduciary, manager, tenant, or spouse who is required to file Form 1042, Annual Withholding Tax Return for U.S. Source Income of Foreign Persons	Complete lines 1, 2, 3 (if applicable), 4a–5b, 7a–b (if applicable), 8a, 8b–c (if applicable), 9a, 9b (if applicable), 10, and 18.
Is a state or local agency	Serves as a tax reporting agent for public assistance recipients under Rev. Proc. 80-4, 1980-1 C.B. 581 [7]	Complete lines 1, 2, 4a–5b, 9a, 10, and 18.
Is a single-member LLC	Needs an EIN to file Form 8832, Classification Election, for filing employment tax returns and excise tax returns, or for state reporting purposes [8]	Complete lines 1–18 (as applicable).
Is an S corporation	Needs an EIN to file Form 2553, Election by a Small Business Corporation [9]	Complete lines 1–18 (as applicable).

[1] For example, a sole proprietorship or self-employed farmer who establishes a qualified retirement plan, or is required to file excise, employment, alcohol, tobacco, or firearms returns, must have an EIN. A partnership, corporation, REMIC (real estate mortgage investment conduit), nonprofit organization (church, club, etc.), or farmers' cooperative must use an EIN for any tax-related purpose even if the entity does not have employees.

[2] However, do not apply for a new EIN if the existing entity only (a) changed its business name, (b) elected on Form 8832 to change the way it is taxed (or is covered by the default rules), or (c) terminated its partnership status because at least 50% of the total interests in partnership capital and profits were sold or exchanged within a 12-month period. The EIN of the terminated partnership should continue to be used. See Regulations section 301.6109-1(d)(2)(iii).

[3] Do not use the EIN of the prior business unless you became the "owner" of a corporation by acquiring its stock.

[4] However, grantor trusts that do not file using Optional Method 1 and IRA trusts that are required to file Form 990-T, Exempt Organization Business Income Tax Return, must have an EIN. For more information on grantor trusts, see the Instructions for Form 1041.

[5] A plan administrator is the person or group of persons specified as the administrator by the instrument under which the plan is operated.

[6] Entities applying to be a Qualified Intermediary (QI) need a QI-EIN even if they already have an EIN. See Rev. Proc. 2000-12.

[7] See also *Household employer* on page 4 of the instructions. **Note.** State or local agencies may need an EIN for other reasons, for example, hired employees.

[8] See *Disregarded entities* on page 4 of the instructions for details on completing Form SS-4 for an LLC.

[9] An existing corporation that is electing or revoking S corporation status should use its previously-assigned EIN.

APPENDIX D

Form **990**	**Return of Organization Exempt From Income Tax**	OMB No. 1545-0047
	Under section 501(c), 527, or 4947(a)(1) of the Internal Revenue Code (except black lung benefit trust or private foundation)	**2010**
Department of the Treasury Internal Revenue Service	► The organization may have to use a copy of this return to satisfy state reporting requirements.	**Open to Public Inspection**

A For the 2010 calendar year, or tax year beginning _____ Month, Day _____ , 2010, and ending _____ Month, Day _____ , 20 11

B Check if applicable:	C Name of organization Jones Flower Gardens	D Employer identification number
☐ Address change	Doing Business As	##-#######
☐ Name change	Number and street (or P.O. box if mail is not delivered to street address) Room/suite	E Telephone number
☐ Initial return	**One Anytown Park Drive**	555-555-5555
☐ Terminated	City or town, state or country, and ZIP + 4	
☐ Amended return	**Anytown, XY 00001-0001**	G Gross receipts $ 11,195,275

F Name and address of principal officer: **Sandra Smith**
One Anytown Park Drive, Anytown, XY 00001-0001

H(a) Is this a group return for affiliates? ☐ Yes ☑ No
H(b) Are all affiliates included? ☐ Yes ☐ No
If "No," attach a list. (see instructions)

I Tax-exempt status: ☑ 501(c)(3)   ☐ 501(c) ( )◄ (insert no.) ☐ 4947(a)(1) or ☐ 527

J Website: ► www.jonesflowergardens.org

H(c) Group exemption number ►

K Form of organization: ☑ Corporation ☐ Trust ☐ Association ☐ Other ►   **L** Year of formation: **M** State of legal domicile:

Part I Summary

Activities & Governance	1	Briefly describe the organization's mission or most significant activities: Run and operate public flower gardens and flower conservatory to inspire and educate the general population on the importance of plants, sustainable growth and a green environment	
	2	Check this box ► ☐ if the organization discontinued its operations or disposed of more than 25% of its net assets.	
	3	Number of voting members of the governing body (Part VI, line 1a)	3	41
	4	Number of independent voting members of the governing body (Part VI, line 1b) . . .	4	41
	5	Total number of individuals employed in calendar year 2010 (Part V, line 2a)	5	139
	6	Total number of volunteers (estimate if necessary)	6	506
	7a	Total unrelated business revenue from Part VIII, column (C), line 12	7a	268,904
	b	Net unrelated business taxable income from Form 990-T, line 34	7b	-525,281

		Prior Year	Current Year
Revenue	8	Contributions and grants (Part VIII, line 1h)	10,080,862	7,735,741
	9	Program service revenue (Part VIII, line 2g)	1,738,215	1,211,955
	10	Investment income (Part VIII, column (A), lines 3, 4, and 7d)	85,344	-119,823
	11	Other revenue (Part VIII, column (A), lines 5, 6d, 8c, 9c, 10c, and 11e) . . .	636,197	677,926
	12	Total revenue—add lines 8 through 11 (must equal Part VIII, column (A), line 12)	12,540,618	9,505,799
Expenses	13	Grants and similar amounts paid (Part IX, column (A), lines 1–3)	17,438	17,897
	14	Benefits paid to or for members (Part IX, column (A), line 4)		
	15	Salaries, other compensation, employee benefits (Part IX, column (A), lines 5–10)	3,054,820	2,896,705
	16a	Professional fundraising fees (Part IX, column (A), line 11e)		0
	b	Total fundraising expenses (Part IX, column (D), line 25) ► 403,788		
	17	Other expenses (Part IX, column (A), lines 11a–11d, 11f–24f)	3,758,570	3,856,628
	18	Total expenses. Add lines 13–17 (must equal Part IX, column (A), line 25) .	6,830,828	6,771,230
	19	Revenue less expenses. Subtract line 18 from line 12	5,709,790	2,734,569

		Beginning of Current Year	End of Year
Net Assets or Fund Balances	20	Total assets (Part X, line 16)	49,125,036	52,063,113
	21	Total liabilities (Part X, line 26)	1,403,658	952,745
	22	Net assets or fund balances. Subtract line 21 from line 20	47,721,378	51,110,368

Part II Signature Block

Under penalties of perjury, I declare that I have examined this return, including accompanying schedules and statements, and to the best of my knowledge and belief, it is true, correct, and complete. Declaration of preparer (other than officer) is based on all information of which preparer has any knowledge.

Sign Here	► Signature of officer	Date
	► Type or print name and title	

Paid Preparer Use Only	Print/Type preparer's name **Silas Smith**	Preparer's signature	Date	Check ☐ if self-employed	PTIN
	Firm's name ► **AAA Accounting Inc.**			Firm's EIN ►	##-#######
	Firm's address ► **333 Third Street, Anytown, XY 00001-0001**			Phone no.	555-555-0000

May the IRS discuss this return with the preparer shown above? (see instructions) . . . . ☑ Yes ☐ No

For Paperwork Reduction Act Notice, see the separate instructions.   Cat. No. 11282Y   Form **990** (2010)

Form 990 (2010)   Page **2**

| **Part III** | **Statement of Program Service Accomplishments** |

Check if Schedule O contains a response to any question in this Part III . . . . ☐

1 Briefly describe the organization's mission:

To inspire and educate the general population on the importance of plants, sustainable growth and a clean environment

----

----

2 Did the organization undertake any significant program services during the year which were not listed on the prior Form 990 or 990-EZ? . . . . ☐ **Yes** ☑ **No**

If "Yes," describe these new services on Schedule O.

3 Did the organization cease conducting, or make significant changes in how it conducts, any program services? . . . . ☐ **Yes** ☑ **No**

If "Yes," describe these changes on Schedule O.

4 Describe the exempt purpose achievements for each of the organization's three largest program services by expenses. Section 501(c)(3) and 501(c)(4) organizations and section 4947(a)(1) trusts are required to report the amount of grants and allocations to others, the total expenses, and revenue, if any, for each program service reported.

4a (Code: _____) (Expenses $ ____2,135,310 including grants of $ _____) (Revenue $ ____2,140,161)

The Public Services Program has the most contact with the public. It trains the volunteer docents who greats guests to our

facilities and who lead the public on tours of these facilities (outdoor gardens and interior conservatory facility).

It manages the docents schedules and makes sure that someone is always available to visitors.

4b (Code: _____) (Expenses $ ____908,225 including grants of $ _____90,535) (Revenue $ _____)

The Plants and Gardens Program actually plants and maintains the flower and plant exhibits in the outside gardens and interior

conservatory. It also plans and stages special exhibits and show throughout the year: the Fall Flower Show, the Winter Festival, the

Spring Flower Show, the Summer Carnival.

4c (Code: _____) (Expenses $ ____460,828 including grants of $ _____156,607) (Revenue $ ____234,619)

The educational program puts together the scripts for docents to use when leading tours of the facilities. It has also created

powerpoint shows for use in local grade schools and high schools on our mission to educate the populace on the importance of

plants, sustainable growth and a clean environment.

4d Other program services. (Describe in Schedule O.)

(Expenses $ ____2,271,364 including grants of $ _____) (Revenue $ _____)

4e Total program service expenses ▶ _____5,775,727

Form **990** (2010)

Form 990 (2010)   Page **3**

Part IV	**Checklist of Required Schedules**		

		Yes	No
1	Is the organization described in section 501(c)(3) or 4947(a)(1) (other than a private foundation)? *If "Yes," complete Schedule A* **1**	✓	
2	Is the organization required to complete Schedule B, Schedule of Contributors? (see instructions) . . . **2**	✓	
3	Did the organization engage in direct or indirect political campaign activities on behalf of or in opposition to candidates for public office? *If "Yes," complete Schedule C, Part I* **3**		✓
4	**Section 501(c)(3) organizations.** Did the organization engage in lobbying activities, or have a section 501(h) election in effect during the tax year? *If "Yes," complete Schedule C, Part II* **4**		✓
5	Is the organization a section 501(c)(4), 501(c)(5), or 501(c)(6) organization that receives membership dues, assessments, or similar amounts as defined in Revenue Procedure 98-19? *If "Yes," complete Schedule C, Part III* **5**		
6	Did the organization maintain any donor advised funds or any similar funds or accounts where donors have the right to provide advice on the distribution or investment of amounts in such funds or accounts? *If "Yes," complete Schedule D, Part I* **6**		✓
7	Did the organization receive or hold a conservation easement, including easements to preserve open space, the environment, historic land areas, or historic structures? *If "Yes," complete Schedule D, Part II* . . . **7**		✓
8	Did the organization maintain collections of works of art, historical treasures, or other similar assets? *If "Yes," complete Schedule D, Part III* **8**	✓	
9	Did the organization report an amount in Part X, line 21; serve as a custodian for amounts not listed in Part X; or provide credit counseling, debt management, credit repair, or debt negotiation services? *If "Yes," complete Schedule D, Part IV* **9**		✓
10	Did the organization, directly or through a related organization, hold assets in term, permanent, or quasi-endowments? *If "Yes," complete Schedule D, Part V* **10**	✓	
11	If the organization's answer to any of the following questions is "Yes," then complete Schedule D, Parts VI, VII, VIII, IX, or X as applicable.		
a	Did the organization report an amount for land, buildings, and equipment in Part X, line 10? *If "Yes," complete Schedule D, Part VI* **11a**	✓	
b	Did the organization report an amount for investments—other securities in Part X, line 12 that is 5% or more of its total assets reported in Part X, line 16? *If "Yes," complete Schedule D, Part VII* **11b**		
c	Did the organization report an amount for investments—program related in Part X, line 13 that is 5% or more of its total assets reported in Part X, line 16? *If "Yes," complete Schedule D, Part VIII* **11c**		
d	Did the organization report an amount for other assets in Part X, line 15 that is 5% or more of its total assets reported in Part X, line 16? *If "Yes," complete Schedule D, Part IX* **11d**		
e	Did the organization report an amount for other liabilities in Part X, line 25? *If "Yes," complete Schedule D, Part X*	**11e**		
f	Did the organization's separate or consolidated financial statements for the tax year include a footnote that addresses the organization's liability for uncertain tax positions under FIN 48 (ASC 740)? *If "Yes," complete Schedule D, Part X* . **11f**		
12a	Did the organization obtain separate, independent audited financial statements for the tax year? *If "Yes," complete Schedule D, Parts XI, XII, and XIII* **12a**	✓	
b	Was the organization included in consolidated, independent audited financial statements for the tax year? *If "Yes," and if the organization answered "No" to line 12a, then completing Schedule D, Parts XI, XII, and XIII is optional* **12b**		✓
13	Is the organization a school described in section 170(b)(1)(A)(ii)? *If "Yes," complete Schedule E* **13**		✓
14a	Did the organization maintain an office, employees, or agents outside of the United States? **14a**		✓
b	Did the organization have aggregate revenues or expenses of more than $10,000 from grantmaking, fundraising, business, and program service activities outside the United States? *If "Yes," complete Schedule F, Parts I and IV* **14b**		✓
15	Did the organization report on Part IX, column (A), line 3, more than $5,000 of grants or assistance to any organization or entity located outside the United States? *If "Yes," complete Schedule F, Parts II and IV* . . **15**		✓
16	Did the organization report on Part IX, column (A), line 3, more than $5,000 of aggregate grants or assistance to individuals located outside the United States? *If "Yes," complete Schedule F, Parts III and IV* **16**		✓
17	Did the organization report a total of more than $15,000 of expenses for professional fundraising services on Part IX, column (A), lines 6 and 11e? *If "Yes," complete Schedule G, Part I (see instructions)* **17**		✓
18	Did the organization report more than $15,000 total of fundraising event gross income and contributions on Part VIII, lines 1c and 8a? *If "Yes," complete Schedule G, Part II* **18**	✓	
19	Did the organization report more than $15,000 of gross income from gaming activities on Part VIII, line 9a? *If "Yes," complete Schedule G, Part III* **19**		✓
20a	Did the organization operate one or more hospitals? *If "Yes," complete Schedule H* **20a**		
b	If "Yes" to line 20a, did the organization attach its audited financial statements to this return? **Note.** Some Form 990 filers that operate one or more hospitals must attach audited financial statements (see instructions) **20b**		

Form **990** (2010)

Form 990 (2010)   Page **4**

Part IV   **Checklist of Required Schedules** *(continued)*

			Yes	No
21	Did the organization report more than $5,000 of grants and other assistance to governments and organizations in the United States on Part IX, column (A), line 1? *If "Yes," complete Schedule I, Parts I and II*	21		✓
22	Did the organization report more than $5,000 of grants and other assistance to individuals in the United States on Part IX, column (A), line 2? *If "Yes," complete Schedule I, Parts I and III*	22	✓	
23	Did the organization answer "Yes" to Part VII, Section A, line 3, 4, or 5 about compensation of the organization's current and former officers, directors, trustees, key employees, and highest compensated employees? *If "Yes," complete Schedule J*	23	✓	
24a	Did the organization have a tax-exempt bond issue with an outstanding principal amount of more than $100,000 as of the last day of the year, that was issued after December 31, 2002? *If "Yes," answer lines 24b through 24d and complete Schedule K. If "No," go to line 25*	24a		✓
b	Did the organization invest any proceeds of tax-exempt bonds beyond a temporary period exception? . .	24b		
c	Did the organization maintain an escrow account other than a refunding escrow at any time during the year to defease any tax-exempt bonds?	24c		
d	Did the organization act as an "on behalf of" issuer for bonds outstanding at any time during the year? . .	24d		
25a	**Section 501(c)(3) and 501(c)(4) organizations.** Did the organization engage in an excess benefit transaction with a disqualified person during the year? *If "Yes," complete Schedule L, Part I*	25a		✓
b	Is the organization aware that it engaged in an excess benefit transaction with a disqualified person in a prior year, and that the transaction has not been reported on any of the organization's prior Forms 990 or 990-EZ? *If "Yes," complete Schedule L, Part I*	25b		✓
26	Was a loan to or by a current or former officer, director, trustee, key employee, highly compensated employee, or disqualified person outstanding as of the end of the organization's tax year? *If "Yes," complete Schedule L, Part II* . .	26		✓
27	Did the organization provide a grant or other assistance to an officer, director, trustee, key employee, substantial contributor, or a grant selection committee member, or to a person related to such an individual? *If "Yes," complete Schedule L, Part III*	27		✓
28	Was the organization a party to a business transaction with one of the following parties (see Schedule L, Part IV instructions for applicable filing thresholds, conditions, and exceptions):			
a	A current or former officer, director, trustee, or key employee? *If "Yes," complete Schedule L, Part IV* . . .	28a		✓
b	A family member of a current or former officer, director, trustee, or key employee? *If "Yes," complete Schedule L, Part IV*	28b		✓
c	An entity of which a current or former officer, director, trustee, or key employee (or a family member thereof) was an officer, director, trustee, or direct or indirect owner? *If "Yes," complete Schedule L, Part IV* . . .	28c		✓
29	Did the organization receive more than $25,000 in non-cash contributions? *If "Yes," complete Schedule M*	29		✓
30	Did the organization receive contributions of art, historical treasures, or other similar assets, or qualified conservation contributions? *If "Yes," complete Schedule M*	30		✓
31	Did the organization liquidate, terminate, or dissolve and cease operations? *If "Yes," complete Schedule N, Part I*	31		✓
32	Did the organization sell, exchange, dispose of, or transfer more than 25% of its net assets? *If "Yes," complete Schedule N, Part II*	32		✓
33	Did the organization own 100% of an entity disregarded as separate from the organization under Regulations sections 301.7701-2 and 301.7701-3? *If "Yes," complete Schedule R, Part I*	33		✓
34	Was the organization related to any tax-exempt or taxable entity? *If "Yes," complete Schedule R, Parts II, III, IV, and V, line 1*	34		✓
35	Is any related organization a controlled entity within the meaning of section 512(b)(13)?	35		✓
a	Did the organization receive any payment from or engage in any transaction with a controlled entity within the meaning of section 512(b)(13)? *If "Yes," complete Schedule R, Part V, line 2* . . . . ☐ **Yes** ☐ **No**			
36	**Section 501(c)(3) organizations.** Did the organization make any transfers to an exempt non-charitable related organization? *If "Yes," complete Schedule R, Part V, line 2*	36		✓
37	Did the organization conduct more than 5% of its activities through an entity that is not a related organization and that is treated as a partnership for federal income tax purposes? *If "Yes," complete Schedule R, Part VI*	37		✓
38	Did the organization complete Schedule O and provide explanations in Schedule O for Part VI, lines 11 and 19? **Note.** All Form 990 filers are required to complete Schedule O	38	✓	

Form **990** (2010)

Form 990 (2010)   Page **5**

Part V	**Statements Regarding Other IRS Filings and Tax Compliance**

Check if Schedule O contains a response to any question in this Part V . . . . ☐

				Yes	No
1a	Enter the number reported in Box 3 of Form 1096. Enter -0- if not applicable	**1a**	40		
b	Enter the number of Forms W-2G included in line 1a. Enter -0- if not applicable	**1b**	0		
c	Did the organization comply with backup withholding rules for reportable payments to vendors and reportable gaming (gambling) winnings to prize winners?			**1c**	✓	
2a	Enter the number of employees reported on Form W-3, Transmittal of Wage and Tax Statements, filed for the calendar year ending with or within the year covered by this return	**2a**	139		
b	If at least one is reported on line 2a, did the organization file all required federal employment tax returns? .			**2b**	✓	
	Note. If the sum of lines 1a and 2a is greater than 250, you may be required to e-file. (see instructions)					
3a	Did the organization have unrelated business gross income of $1,000 or more during the year?			**3a**	✓	
b	If "Yes," has it filed a Form 990-T for this year? If "No," provide an explanation in Schedule O			**3b**	✓	
4a	At any time during the calendar year, did the organization have an interest in, or a signature or other authority over, a financial account in a foreign country (such as a bank account, securities account, or other financial account)?			**4a**		✓
b	If "Yes," enter the name of the foreign country: ▶ ------------------------------------- See instructions for filing requirements for Form TD F 90-22.1, Report of Foreign Bank and Financial Accounts.					
5a	Was the organization a party to a prohibited tax shelter transaction at any time during the tax year? . . .			**5a**		✓
b	Did any taxable party notify the organization that it was or is a party to a prohibited tax shelter transaction?			**5b**		✓
c	If "Yes" to line 5a or 5b, did the organization file Form 8886-T?			**5c**		
6a	Does the organization have annual gross receipts that are normally greater than $100,000, and did the organization solicit any contributions that were not tax deductible?			**6a**	✓	
b	If "Yes," did the organization include with every solicitation an express statement that such contributions or gifts were not tax deductible?			**6b**	✓	
7	**Organizations that may receive deductible contributions under section 170(c).**					
a	Did the organization receive a payment in excess of $75 made partly as a contribution and partly for goods and services provided to the payor?			**7a**	✓	
b	If "Yes," did the organization notify the donor of the value of the goods or services provided?			**7b**	✓	
c	Did the organization sell, exchange, or otherwise dispose of tangible personal property for which it was required to file Form 8282?			**7c**		✓
d	If "Yes," indicate the number of Forms 8282 filed during the year	**7d**				
e	Did the organization receive any funds, directly or indirectly, to pay premiums on a personal benefit contract?			**7e**		✓
f	Did the organization, during the year, pay premiums, directly or indirectly, on a personal benefit contract? .			**7f**		✓
g	If the organization received a contribution of qualified intellectual property, did the organization file Form 8899 as required?			**7g**		
h	If the organization received a contribution of cars, boats, airplanes, or other vehicles, did the organization file a Form 1098-C?			**7h**		
8	**Sponsoring organizations maintaining donor advised funds and section 509(a)(3) supporting organizations.** Did the supporting organization, or a donor advised fund maintained by a sponsoring organization, have excess business holdings at any time during the year?			**8**		✓
9	**Sponsoring organizations maintaining donor advised funds.**					
a	Did the organization make any taxable distributions under section 4966?			**9a**		✓
b	Did the organization make a distribution to a donor, donor advisor, or related person?			**9b**		✓
10	**Section 501(c)(7) organizations.** Enter:					
a	Initiation fees and capital contributions included on Part VIII, line 12	**10a**				
b	Gross receipts, included on Form 990, Part VIII, line 12, for public use of club facilities .	**10b**				
11	**Section 501(c)(12) organizations.** Enter:					
a	Gross income from members or shareholders	**11a**				
b	Gross income from other sources (Do not net amounts due or paid to other sources against amounts due or received from them.)	**11b**				
12a	**Section 4947(a)(1) non-exempt charitable trusts.** Is the organization filing Form 990 in lieu of Form 1041?			**12a**		✓
b	If "Yes," enter the amount of tax-exempt interest received or accrued during the year . . .	**12b**				
13	**Section 501(c)(29) qualified nonprofit health insurance issuers.**					
a	Is the organization licensed to issue qualified health plans in more than one state?			**13a**		✓
	Note. See the instructions for additional information the organization must report on Schedule O.					
b	Enter the amount of reserves the organization is required to maintain by the states in which the organization is licensed to issue qualified health plans	**13b**				
c	Enter the amount of reserves on hand	**13c**				
14a	Did the organization receive any payments for indoor tanning services during the tax year?			**14a**		✓
b	If "Yes," has it filed a Form 720 to report these payments? If "No," provide an explanation in Schedule O .			**14b**		

Form **990** (2010)

Form 990 (2010)   Page **6**

| **Part VI** | **Governance, Management, and Disclosure** *For each "Yes" response to lines 2 through 7b below, and for a "No" response to line 8a, 8b, or 10b below, describe the circumstances, processes, or changes in Schedule O. See instructions.* |

Check if Schedule O contains a response to any question in this Part VI . . . . ☐

Section A. Governing Body and Management

			Yes	No
1a	Enter the number of voting members of the governing body at the end of the tax year . .	1a · 41		
b	Enter the number of voting members included in line 1a, above, who are independent .	1b · 41		
2	Did any officer, director, trustee, or key employee have a family relationship or a business relationship with any other officer, director, trustee, or key employee?	2		✓
3	Did the organization delegate control over management duties customarily performed by or under the direct supervision of officers, directors or trustees, or key employees to a management company or other person? . .	3		✓
4	Did the organization make any significant changes to its governing documents since the prior Form 990 was filed?	4		✓
5	Did the organization become aware during the year of a significant diversion of the organization's assets? .	5		✓
6	Does the organization have members or stockholders?	6		✓
7a	Does the organization have members, stockholders, or other persons who may elect one or more members of the governing body?	7a		✓
b	Are any decisions of the governing body subject to approval by members, stockholders, or other persons?	7b		✓
8	Did the organization contemporaneously document the meetings held or written actions undertaken during the year by the following:			
a	The governing body?	8a	✓	
b	Each committee with authority to act on behalf of the governing body?	8b	✓	
9	Is there any officer, director, trustee, or key employee listed in Part VII, Section A, who cannot be reached at the organization's mailing address? *If "Yes," provide the names and addresses in Schedule O.*	9		✓

Section B. Policies *(This Section B requests information about policies not required by the Internal Revenue Code.)*

			Yes	No
10a	Does the organization have local chapters, branches, or affiliates?	10a		✓
b	If "Yes," does the organization have written policies and procedures governing the activities of such chapters, affiliates, and branches to ensure their operations are consistent with those of the organization? .	10b		
11a	Has the organization provided a copy of this Form 990 to all members of its governing body before filing the form?	11a	✓	
b	Describe in Schedule O the process, if any, used by the organization to review this Form 990.			
12a	Does the organization have a written conflict of interest policy? *If "No," go to line 13*	12a	✓	
b	Are officers, directors or trustees, and key employees required to disclose annually interests that could give rise to conflicts?	12b	✓	
c	Does the organization regularly and consistently monitor and enforce compliance with the policy? *If "Yes," describe in Schedule O how this is done.*	12c	✓	
13	Does the organization have a written whistleblower policy?	13	✓	
14	Does the organization have a written document retention and destruction policy?	14	✓	
15	Did the process for determining compensation of the following persons include a review and approval by independent persons, comparability data, and contemporaneous substantiation of the deliberation and decision?			
a	The organization's CEO, Executive Director, or top management official	15a	✓	
b	Other officers or key employees of the organization	15b	✓	
	If "Yes" to line 15a or 15b, describe the process in Schedule O. (See instructions.)			
16a	Did the organization invest in, contribute assets to, or participate in a joint venture or similar arrangement with a taxable entity during the year?	16a		✓
b	If "Yes," has the organization adopted a written policy or procedure requiring the organization to evaluate its participation in joint venture arrangements under applicable federal tax law, and taken steps to safeguard the organization's exempt status with respect to such arrangements?	16b		

Section C. Disclosure

17   List the states with which a copy of this Form 990 is required to be filed ▶   XY

18   Section 6104 requires an organization to make its Forms 1023 (or 1024 if applicable), 990, and 990-T (501(c)(3)s only) available for public inspection. Indicate how you make these available. Check all that apply.

     ☐ Own website   ☐ Another's website   ☑ Upon request

19   Describe in Schedule O whether (and if so, how), the organization makes its governing documents, conflict of interest policy, and financial statements available to the public.

20   State the name, physical address, and telephone number of the person who possesses the books and records of the organization: ▶ Sandra Smith, One Anytown Park Drive, Anytown, XY 00001-0001

Form **990** (2010)

Form 990 (2010)   Page **7**

| **Part VII** | **Compensation of Officers, Directors, Trustees, Key Employees, Highest Compensated Employees, and Independent Contractors** |

Check if Schedule O contains a response to any question in this Part VII . . . . □

Section A.   Officers, Directors, Trustees, Key Employees, and Highest Compensated Employees

1a Complete this table for all persons required to be listed. Report compensation for the calendar year ending with or within the organization's tax year.

• List all of the organization's **current** officers, directors, trustees (whether individuals or organizations), regardless of amount of compensation. Enter -0- in columns (D), (E), and (F) if no compensation was paid.

• List all of the organization's **current** key employees, if any. See instructions for definition of "key employee."

• List the organization's five **current** highest compensated employees (other than an officer, director, trustee, or key employee) who received reportable compensation (Box 5 of Form W-2 and/or Box 7 of Form 1099-MISC) of more than $100,000 from the organization and any related organizations.

• List all of the organization's **former** officers, key employees, and highest compensated employees who received more than $100,000 of reportable compensation from the organization and any related organizations.

• List all of the organization's **former directors or trustees** that received, in the capacity as a former director or trustee of the organization, more than $10,000 of reportable compensation from the organization and any related organizations.

List persons in the following order: individual trustees or directors; institutional trustees; officers; key employees; highest compensated employees; and former such persons.

□ Check this box if neither the organization nor any related organization compensated any current officer, director, or trustee.

(A) Name and Title	(B) Average hours per week (describe hours for related organizations in Schedule O)	(C) Position (check all that apply)						(D) Reportable compensation from the organization (W-2/1099-MISC)	(E) Reportable compensation from related organizations (W-2/1099-MISC)	(F) Estimated amount of other compensation from the organization and related organizations
		Individual trustee or director	Institutional trustee	Officer	Key employee	Highest compensated employee	Former			
(1) Sandra Smith Executive Direcor	50			✓	✓	✓		223,807	0	49,067
(2) Anna Smithe Chair	5	✓						0	0	0
(3) Bart Smyth Vice-Chair	5	✓						0	0	0
(4) Carl Smythe Treasurer	5	✓						0	0	0
(5) Dee Smath Secretary	5	✓						0	0	0
(6) Fred Smeth Trustee	2	✓						0	0	0
(7) Gail Smoth Trustee	2	✓						0	0	0
(8) Hank Smuth Trustee	2	✓						0	0	0
(9) Et cetera for all other Trustees	2	✓						0	0	0
(10)										
(11)										
(12)										
(13)										
(14)										
(15)										
(16)										

Form **990** (2010)

Form 990 (2010)   Page **8**

| Part VII | Section A. Officers, Directors, Trustees, Key Employees, and Highest Compensated Employees *(continued)* |

(A) Name and title	(B) Average hours per week (describe hours for related organizations in Schedule O)	(C) Position (check all that apply)						(D) Reportable compensation from the organization (W-2/1099-MISC)	(E) Reportable compensation from related organizations (W-2/1099-MISC)	(F) Estimated amount of other compensation from the organization and related organizations
		Individual trustee or director	Institutional trustee	Officer	Key employee	Highest compensated employee	Former			
(17)										
(18)										
(19)										
(20)										
(21)										
(22)										
(23)										
(24)										
(25)										
(26)										
(27)										
(28)										

1b Sub-total . . . . ▶ | 223,807 | | 49,067
  c Total from continuation sheets to Part VII, Section A . . . . . ▶
  d Total (add lines 1b and 1c) . . . . ▶ | 223,807 | | 49,067

2 Total number of individuals (including but not limited to those listed above) who received more than $100,000 in reportable compensation from the organization ▶

		Yes	No
3	Did the organization list any **former** officer, director or trustee, key employee, or highest compensated employee on line 1a? *If "Yes," complete Schedule J for such individual* **3**		✓
4	For any individual listed on line 1a, is the sum of reportable compensation and other compensation from the organization and related organizations greater than $150,000? *If "Yes," complete Schedule J for such individual* **4**	✓	
5	Did any person listed on line 1a receive or accrue compensation from any unrelated organization or individual for services rendered to the organization? *If "Yes," complete Schedule J for such person* **5**		✓

Section B. Independent Contractors

1 Complete this table for your five highest compensated independent contractors that received more than $100,000 of compensation from the organization.

(A) Name and business address	(B) Description of services	(C) Compensation
IC One, address	Advertising/PR	812,173
IC Two, address	Architectural design	396,171
IC Three, address	Food Services	320,035
IC Four, address	Health Insurance	254,035
IC Five, address	HVAC Contractor	228,884

2 Total number of independent contractors (including but not limited to those listed above) who received more than $100,000 in compensation from the organization ▶ **10**

Form **990** (2010)

Form 990 (2010)   Page **9**

| Part VIII | Statement of Revenue |

				(A) Total revenue	(B) Related or exempt function revenue	(C) Unrelated business revenue	(D) Revenue excluded from tax under sections 512, 513, or 514
Contributions, gifts, grants and other similar amounts	1a	Federated campaigns	1a				
	b	Membership dues	1b	567,984			
	c	Fundraising events	1c				
	d	Related organizations	1d				
	e	Government grants (contributions)	1e	2,079,600			
	f	All other contributions, gifts, grants, and similar amounts not included above	1f				
	g	Noncash contributions included in lines 1a-1f: $					
	h	**Total.** Add lines 1a–1f ▶		7,735,741			
Program Service Revenue			Business Code				
	2a	Educational Tours/Classes	900,099	171,328	171,328		
	b	Admissions	900,099	1,040,627	1,040,627		
	c						
	d						
	e						
	f	All other program service revenue .					
	g	**Total.** Add lines 2a–2f ▶		1,21,955			
	3	Investment income (including dividends, interest, and other similar amounts) ▶		113,551			113,551
	4	Income from investment of tax-exempt bond proceeds ▶					
	5	Royalties ▶					
			(i) Real	(ii) Personal			
	6a	Gross Rents	579,718				
	b	Less: rental expenses	219,860				
	c	Rental income or (loss)	359,858				
	d	Net rental income or (loss) ▶		359,858			359,858
	7a	Gross amount from sales of assets other than inventory	(i) Securities 847,043	(ii) Other			
	b	Less: cost or other basis and sales expenses	1,080,417				
	c	Gain or (loss)	-233,374				
	d	Net gain or (loss) ▶		-233,374			-233,374
Other Revenue	8a	Gross income from fundraising events (not including $ 101,985 of contributions reported on line 1c). See Part IV, line 18	a				
	b	Less: direct expenses	b	107,802			
	c	Net income or (loss) from fundraising events ▶		-5,817			
	9a	Gross income from gaming activities. See Part IV, line 19	a				
	b	Less: direct expenses	b				
	c	Net income or (loss) from gaming activities ▶					
	10a	Gross sales of inventory, less returns and allowances	a	531,550			
	b	Less: cost of goods sold	b	281,400			
	c	Net income or (loss) from sales of inventory ▶		250,150	38,710	211,440	
		Miscellaneous Revenue	Business Code				
	11a	Misc	900, 099	73,735	16,271	57,464	
	b						
	c						
	d	All other revenue					
	e	**Total.** Add lines 11a–11d ▶		73,735			
	12	**Total revenue.** See instructions. ▶		9,505,799	1,261,119	268,904	240,035

Form **990** (2010)

Form 990 (2010)   Page **10**

Part IX   **Statement of Functional Expenses**

Section 501(c)(3) and 501(c)(4) organizations must complete all columns.
All other organizations must complete column (A) but are not required to complete columns (B), (C), and (D).

Do not include amounts reported on lines 6b, 7b, 8b, 9b, and 10b of Part VIII.	**(A)** Total expenses	**(B)** Program service expenses	**(C)** Management and general expenses	**(D)** Fundraising expenses
1 Grants and other assistance to governments and organizations in the U.S. See Part IV, line 21 . .	0	0		
2 Grants and other assistance to individuals in the U.S. See Part IV, line 22	8,897	8,897		
3 Grants and other assistance to governments, organizations, and individuals outside the U.S. See Part IV, lines 15 and 16	9,000	9,000		
4 Benefits paid to or for members	0	0		
5 Compensation of current officers, directors, trustees, and key employees	245,874	172,112	36,881	36,881
6 Compensation not included above, to disqualified persons (as defined under section 4958(f)(1)) and persons described in section 4958(c)(3)(B) . .	0	0	0	0
7 Other salaries and wages	1,986,032	1,542,000	251,452	210,580
8 Pension plan contributions (include section 401(k) and section 403(b) employer contributions) . .	116,972	87,505	14,878	14,589
9 Other employee benefits	372,930	289,764	50,669	32,497
10 Payroll taxes	174,897	128,505	23,468	22,924
11 Fees for services (non-employees):				
a Management	0	0	0	0
b Legal	25,219	1,077	24,094	48
c Accounting	32,317	1,380	30,876	61
d Lobbying	25,517	1,090	24,379	48
e Professional fundraising services. See Part IV, line 17				
f Investment management fees	28,443	28,337	106	0
g Other	763,092	656,335	42,037	64,720
12 Advertising and promotion	345,218	345,218	0	0
13 Office expenses	14,120	5,155	8,208	757
14 Information technology	61,848	46,135	12,468	3,245
15 Royalties	0	0	0	0
16 Occupancy	398,786	385,224	11,258	2,304
17 Travel	37,823	31,635	4,300	1,888
18 Payments of travel or entertainment expenses for any federal, state, or local public officials	0	0	0	0
19 Conferences, conventions, and meetings .	0	0	0	0
20 Interest	2,286	2,286	0	0
21 Payments to affiliates	0	0	0	0
22 Depreciation, depletion, and amortization .	1,097,472	1,093,846	3,626	0
23 Insurance	136,209	131,449	3,960	800
24 Other expenses. Itemize expenses not covered above (List miscellaneous expenses in line 24f. If line 24f amount exceeds 10% of line 25, column (A) amount, list line 24f expenses on Schedule O.)				
a Programs Supplies/ Costs	230,474	230,474	0	0
b Equipment Rental	285,819	230,141	44,159	11,519
c Bldgs & Ground Maintenance	353,280	353,280	0	0
d Equipment	2,775	1,077	1,300	398
e Dues	15,930	11,805	3,596	529
f All other expenses				
25 Total functional expenses. Add lines 1 through 24f	6,771,230	5,775,727	591,715	403,788
26 Joint costs. Check here ▶ ☐ if following SOP 98-2 (ASC 958-720). Complete this line only if the organization reported in column (B) joint costs from a combined educational campaign and fundraising solicitation . .				

Form **990** (2010)

Form 990 (2010)

| **Part X** | **Balance Sheet** | | | |

			(A) Beginning of year		(B) End of year
Assets	1	Cash—non-interest-bearing		1	
	2	Savings and temporary cash investments	10,426,799	2	11,595,612
	3	Pledges and grants receivable, net	1,954,248	3	2,600,519
	4	Accounts receivable, net	26,029	4	20,480
	5	Receivables from current and former officers, directors, trustees, key employees, and highest compensated employees. Complete Part II of Schedule L		5	
	6	Receivables from other disqualified persons (as defined under section 4958(f)(1)), persons described in section 4958(c)(3)(B), and contributing employers and sponsoring organizations of section 501(c)(9) voluntary employees' beneficiary organizations (see instructions)		6	
	7	Notes and loans receivable, net		7	
	8	Inventories for sale or use	180,326	8	158,530
	9	Prepaid expenses and deferred charges	99,223	9	105,433
	10a	Land, buildings, and equipment: cost or other basis. Complete Part VI of Schedule D **10a** 39,025,881			
	b	Less: accumulated depreciation **10b** 5,653,012	33,611,390	10c	33,372,869
	11	Investments—publicly traded securities		11	
	12	Investments—other securities. See Part IV, line 11		12	
	13	Investments—program-related. See Part IV, line 11		13	
	14	Intangible assets		14	
	15	Other assets. See Part IV, line 11	2,827,021	15	4,209,670
	16	**Total assets.** Add lines 1 through 15 (must equal line 34)	49,125,036	16	52,063,113
Liabilities	17	Accounts payable and accrued expenses	779,376	17	776,238
	18	Grants payable		18	
	19	Deferred revenue	124,282	19	176,507
	20	Tax-exempt bond liabilities	500,000	20	
	21	Escrow or custodial account liability. Complete Part IV of Schedule D		21	
	22	Payables to current and former officers, directors, trustees, key employees, highest compensated employees, and disqualified persons. Complete Part II of Schedule L		22	
	23	Secured mortgages and notes payable to unrelated third parties		23	
	24	Unsecured notes and loans payable to unrelated third parties		24	
	25	Other liabilities. Complete Part X of Schedule D		25	
	26	**Total liabilities.** Add lines 17 through 25	1,403,658	26	952,745
Net Assets or Fund Balances		**Organizations that follow SFAS 117, check here ▶ ☑ and complete lines 27 through 29, and lines 33 and 34.**			
	27	Unrestricted net assets	37,285,574	27	38,219,090
	28	Temporarily restricted net assets	8,639,379	28	11,094,548
	29	Permanently restricted net assets	1,796,425	29	1,796,730
		Organizations that do not follow SFAS 117, check here ▶ ☐ and complete lines 30 through 34.			
	30	Capital stock or trust principal, or current funds		30	
	31	Paid-in or capital surplus, or land, building, or equipment fund		31	
	32	Retained earnings, endowment, accumulated income, or other funds		32	
	33	Total net assets or fund balances	47,721,378	33	51,110,368
	34	Total liabilities and net assets/fund balances	49,125,036	34	52,063,113

Form **990** (2010)

Form 990 (2010)   Page **12**

Part XI	**Reconciliation of Net Assets**

Check if Schedule O contains a response to any question in this Part XI . . . . □

1	Total revenue (must equal Part VIII, column (A), line 12)	1	9,505,799
2	Total expenses (must equal Part IX, column (A), line 25)	2	6,771,230
3	Revenue less expenses. Subtract line 2 from line 1	3	2,734,569
4	Net assets or fund balances at beginning of year (must equal Part X, line 33, column (A)) . . .	4	47,721,378
5	Other changes in net assets or fund balances (explain in Schedule O)	5	3,388,990
6	Net assets or fund balances at end of year. Combine lines 3, 4, and 5 (must equal Part X, line 33, column (B))	6	51,110,368

Part XII	**Financial Statements and Reporting**

Check if Schedule O contains a response to any question in this Part XII . . . . □

			Yes	No
1	Accounting method used to prepare the Form 990: □ Cash ☑ Accrual □ Other _____ If the organization changed its method of accounting from a prior year or checked "Other," explain in Schedule O.			
2a	Were the organization's financial statements compiled or reviewed by an independent accountant? . . .	2a		✓
b	Were the organization's financial statements audited by an independent accountant?	2b	✓	
c	If "Yes" to line 2a or 2b, does the organization have a committee that assumes responsibility for oversight of the audit, review, or compilation of its financial statements and selection of an independent accountant?	2c	✓	
	If the organization changed either its oversight process or selection process during the tax year, explain in Schedule O.			
d	If "Yes" to line 2a or 2b, check a box below to indicate whether the financial statements for the year were issued on a separate basis, consolidated basis, or both: □ Separate basis □ Consolidated basis □ Both consolidated and separate basis			
3a	As a result of a federal award, was the organization required to undergo an audit or audits as set forth in the Single Audit Act and OMB Circular A-133?	3a		✓
b	If "Yes," did the organization undergo the required audit or audits? If the organization did not undergo the required audit or audits, explain why in Schedule O and describe any steps taken to undergo such audits	3b		

Form **990** (2010)

SCHEDULE A
(Form 990 or 990-EZ)

Department of the Treasury
Internal Revenue Service

Public Charity Status and Public Support

Complete if the organization is a section 501(c)(3) organization or a section
4947(a)(1) nonexempt charitable trust.

▶ Attach to Form 990 or Form 990-EZ. ▶ See separate instructions.

OMB No. 1545-0047

2010

Open to Public Inspection

Name of the organization	Employer identification number
Jones Flower Gardens	##-#######

Part I — Reason for Public Charity Status (All organizations must complete this part.) See instructions.

The organization is not a private foundation because it is: (For lines 1 through 11, check only one box.)

1 ☐ A church, convention of churches, or association of churches described in **section 170(b)(1)(A)(i).**

2 ☐ A school described in **section 170(b)(1)(A)(ii).** (Attach Schedule E.)

3 ☐ A hospital or a cooperative hospital service organization described in **section 170(b)(1)(A)(iii).**

4 ☐ A medical research organization operated in conjunction with a hospital described in **section 170(b)(1)(A)(iii).** Enter the hospital's name, city, and state:

5 ☐ An organization operated for the benefit of a college or university owned or operated by a governmental unit described in **section 170(b)(1)(A)(iv).** (Complete Part II.)

6 ☐ A federal, state, or local government or governmental unit described in **section 170(b)(1)(A)(v).**

7 ☑ An organization that normally receives a substantial part of its support from a governmental unit or from the general public described in **section 170(b)(1)(A)(vi).** (Complete Part II.)

8 ☐ A community trust described in **section 170(b)(1)(A)(vi).** (Complete Part II.)

9 ☐ An organization that normally receives: (1) more than 33⅓% of its support from contributions, membership fees, and gross receipts from activities related to its exempt functions—subject to certain exceptions, and (2) no more than 33⅓% of its support from gross investment income and unrelated business taxable income (less section 511 tax) from businesses acquired by the organization after June 30, 1975. See **section 509(a)(2).** (Complete Part III.)

10 ☐ An organization organized and operated exclusively to test for public safety. See **section 509(a)(4).**

11 ☐ An organization organized and operated exclusively for the benefit of, to perform the functions of, or to carry out the purposes of one or more publicly supported organizations described in section 509(a)(1) or section 509(a)(2). See **section 509(a)(3).** Check the box that describes the type of supporting organization and complete lines 11e through 11h.

  a ☐ Type I   b ☐ Type II   c ☐ Type III–Functionally integrated   d ☐ Type III–Other

  e ☐ By checking this box, I certify that the organization is not controlled directly or indirectly by one or more disqualified persons other than foundation managers and other than one or more publicly supported organizations described in section 509(a)(1) or section 509(a)(2).

  f If the organization received a written determination from the IRS that it is a Type I, Type II, or Type III supporting organization, check this box . . . . ☐

  g Since August 17, 2006, has the organization accepted any gift or contribution from any of the following persons?

		Yes	No
(i) A person who directly or indirectly controls, either alone or together with persons described in (ii) and (iii) below, the governing body of the supported organization?	11g(i)		
(ii) A family member of a person described in (i) above?	11g(ii)		
(iii) A 35% controlled entity of a person described in (i) or (ii) above?	11g(iii)		

  h Provide the following information about the supported organization(s).

(i) Name of supported organization	(ii) EIN	(iii) Type of organization (described on lines 1–9 above or IRC section (see instructions))	(iv) Is the organization in col. (i) listed in your governing document?		(v) Did you notify the organization in col. (i) of your support?		(vi) Is the organization in col. (i) organized in the U.S.?		(vii) Amount of support
			Yes	No	Yes	No	Yes	No	
(A)									
(B)									
(C)									
(D)									
(E)									
Total									

For Paperwork Reduction Act Notice, see the Instructions for Form 990 or 990-EZ.

Cat. No. 11285F

Schedule A (Form 990 or 990-EZ) 2010

Schedule A (Form 990 or 990-EZ) 2010   Page **2**

Part II   **Support Schedule for Organizations Described in Sections 170(b)(1)(A)(iv) and 170(b)(1)(A)(vi)**
(Complete only if you checked the box on line 5, 7, or 8 of Part I or if the organization failed to qualify under Part III. If the organization fails to qualify under the tests listed below, please complete Part III.)

Section A. Public Support

Calendar year (or fiscal year beginning in) ▶	(a) 2006	(b) 2007	(c) 2008	(d) 2009	(e) 2010	(f) Total
1 Gifts, grants, contributions, and membership fees received. (Do not include any "unusual grants.") . . .	6,889,121	12,878,739	7,770,127	10,080,862	7,735,741	45,354,590
2 Tax revenues levied for the organization's benefit and either paid to or expended on its behalf . . .						
3 The value of services or facilities furnished by a governmental unit to the organization without charge						
4 **Total.** Add lines 1 through 3	6,889,121	12,878,739	7,770,127	10,080,862	7,735,741	45,354,590
5 The portion of total contributions by each person (other than a governmental unit or publicly supported organization) included on line 1 that exceeds 2% of the amount shown on line 11, column (f)						
6 **Public support.** Subtract line 5 from line 4.						

Section B. Total Support

Calendar year (or fiscal year beginning in) ▶	(a) 2006	(b) 2007	(c) 2008	(d) 2009	(e) 2010	(f) Total
7 Amounts from line 4	6,889,121	12,878,739	7,770,127	10,080,862	7,735,741	45,354,590
8 Gross income from interest, dividends, payments received on securities loans, rents, royalties and income from similar sources	302,805	462,964	883,652	551,264	639,269	2,893,954
9 Net income from unrelated business activities, whether or not the business is regularly carried on			9,946			9,946
10 Other income. Do not include gain or loss from the sale of capital assets (Explain in Part IV.)	5,027	6,250	7,209	3,400	20,807	42,693
11 **Total support.** Add lines 7 through 10						48,301,183
12 Gross receipts from related activities, etc. (see instructions)					**12**	8,302,599

13   **First five years.** If the Form 990 is for the organization's first, second, third, fourth, or fifth tax year as a section 501(c)(3) organization, check this box and **stop here** . . . . ▶ ☐

Section C. Computation of Public Support Percentage

14   Public support percentage for 2010 (line 6, column (f) divided by line 11, column (f)) . . . .   **14**   70.7 %

15   Public support percentage from 2009 Schedule A, Part II, line 14 . . . .   **15**   65.1 %

16a   **33 1/3% support test—2010.** If the organization did not check the box on line 13, and line 14 is 33 1/3% or more, check this box and **stop here.** The organization qualifies as a publicly supported organization . . . . ▶ ☑

   b   **33 1/3% support test—2009.** If the organization did not check a box on line 13 or 16a, and line 15 is 33 1/3% or more, check this box and **stop here.** The organization qualifies as a publicly supported organization . . . . . . ▶ ☐

17a   **10%-facts-and-circumstances test—2010.** If the organization did not check a box on line 13, 16a, or 16b, and line 14 is 10% or more, and if the organization meets the "facts-and-circumstances" test, check this box and **stop here.** Explain in Part IV how the organization meets the "facts-and-circumstances" test. The organization qualifies as a publicly supported organization . . . . ▶ ☐

   b   **10%-facts-and-circumstances test—2009.** If the organization did not check a box on line 13, 16a, 16b, or 17a, and line 15 is 10% or more, and if the organization meets the "facts-and-circumstances" test, check this box and **stop here.** Explain in Part IV how the organization meets the "facts-and-circumstances" test. The organization qualifies as a publicly supported organization . . . . ▶ ☐

18   **Private foundation.** If the organization did not check a box on line 13, 16a, 16b, 17a, or 17b, check this box and see instructions . . . . ▶ ☐

Schedule A (Form 990 or 990-EZ) 2010

Schedule A (Form 990 or 990-EZ) 2010   Page **3**

| **Part III** | **Support Schedule for Organizations Described in Section 509(a)(2)** |

(Complete only if you checked the box on line 9 of Part I or if the organization failed to qualify under Part II. If the organization fails to qualify under the tests listed below, please complete Part II.)

Section A. Public Support

Calendar year (or fiscal year beginning in) ▶	**(a)** 2006	**(b)** 2007	**(c)** 2008	**(d)** 2009	**(e)** 2010	**(f)** Total
1 Gifts, grants, contributions, and membership fees received. (Do not include any "unusual grants.")						
2 Gross receipts from admissions, merchandise sold or services performed, or facilities furnished in any activity that is related to the organization's tax-exempt purpose . . .						
3 Gross receipts from activities that are not an unrelated trade or business under section 513						
4 Tax revenues levied for the organization's benefit and either paid to or expended on its behalf . . .						
5 The value of services or facilities furnished by a governmental unit to the organization without charge						
6 **Total.** Add lines 1 through 5						
7a Amounts included on lines 1, 2, and 3 received from disqualified persons .						
b Amounts included on lines 2 and 3 received from other than disqualified persons that exceed the greater of $5,000 or 1% of the amount on line 13 for the year						
c Add lines 7a and 7b						
8 **Public support** (Subtract line 7c from line 6.)						0

Section B. Total Support

Calendar year (or fiscal year beginning in) ▶	**(a)** 2006	**(b)** 2007	**(c)** 2008	**(d)** 2009	**(e)** 2010	**(f)** Total
9 Amounts from line 6						
10a Gross income from interest, dividends, payments received on securities loans, rents, royalties and income from similar sources .						
b Unrelated business taxable income (less section 511 taxes) from businesses acquired after June 30, 1975						
c Add lines 10a and 10b						
11 Net income from unrelated business activities not included in line 10b, whether or not the business is regularly carried on						
12 Other income. Do not include gain or loss from the sale of capital assets (Explain in Part IV.)						
13 **Total support.** (Add lines 9, 10c, 11, and 12.)						

14 **First five years.** If the Form 990 is for the organization's first, second, third, fourth, or fifth tax year as a section 501(c)(3) organization, check this box and **stop here** . . . . ▶ ☐

Section C. Computation of Public Support Percentage

15	Public support percentage for 2010 (line 8, column (f) divided by line 13, column (f))	15	0 %
16	Public support percentage from 2009 Schedule A, Part III, line 15	16	%

Section D. Computation of Investment Income Percentage

17	Investment income percentage for **2010** (line 10c, column (f) divided by line 13, column (f)) . . .	17	0 %
18	Investment income percentage from **2009** Schedule A, Part III, line 17	18	%

19a 33¹/₃% **support tests—2010.** If the organization did not check the box on line 14, and line 15 is more than 33¹/₃%, and line 17 is not more than 33¹/₃%, check this box and **stop here.** The organization qualifies as a publicly supported organization . ▶ ☐

b 33¹/₃% **support tests—2009.** If the organization did not check a box on line 14 or line 19a, and line 16 is more than 33¹/₃%, and line 18 is not more than 33¹/₃%, check this box and **stop here.** The organization qualifies as a publicly supported organization ▶ ☐

20 **Private foundation.** If the organization did not check a box on line 14, 19a, or 19b, check this box and see instructions ▶ ☐

Schedule A (Form 990 or 990-EZ) 2010

Schedule A (Form 990 or 990-EZ) 2010   Page **4**

Part IV   **Supplemental Information.** Complete this part to provide the explanations required by Part II, line 10; Part II, line 17a or 17b; and Part III, line 12. Also complete this part for any additional information. (See instructions).

APPENDIX E

The quick reference chart that begins on page 440 briefly describes the organizations that qualify for tax exemption and the nature and scope of their activities. For analysis of the individual sections refer to the relevant Chapter or specific IRC Sections.

Code Sections	Description	Nature Of Activities	Contributions	Private Inurement	Political Activities
501(c)(1)	Corporations Organized Under Act of Congress (including Federal Credit Unions	Instrumentalities of the U.S.	Yes, if made for exclusively public purposes	No part of the organization's net earnings may benefit any private shareholder or individual.	501(c)(1) organizations are not prohibited from engaging in some political activities however engaging in these activities may take them beyond the scope of their stated purpose.
501(c)(2)	Title-Holding Corporation For Exempt Organizations	Holding title to property of an exempt organization	No, but it may establish a charitable fund, contributions to which are deductible. Such a fund must itself meet the requirements of section 501(c)(3) and the related notice requirements of section 508(a).	No part of the organization's net earnings may benefit any private shareholder or individual.	501(c)(2) organizations are not prohibited from engaging in some political activities however engaging in these activities may take them beyond the scope of their stated purpose.
501(c)(3)	Religious, Educational, Charitable, Scientific, Literary, Testing for Public Safety, to Foster National or International Amateur Sports Competition, or Prevention of Cruelty to Children or Animals Organizations	Activities of nature implied by description of class of organization	Yes	No part of the organization's net earnings may benefit any private shareholder or individual.	A 501(c)(3) organization may not engage in attempts to influence legislation nor participate, directly or indirectly, in any political campaign on behalf of or in opposition to any candidate for public office.

Code Sections	Description	Nature Of Activities	Contributions	Private Inurement	Political Activities
501(c)(4)	Civic Leagues, Social Welfare Organizations, and Local Associations of Employees	Promotion of community welfare; charitable, educational, or recreational	No, but it may establish a charitable fund, contributions to which are deductible. Such a fund must itself meet the requirements of section 501(c)(3) and the related notice requirements of section 508(a). Contributions to volunteer fire companies and similar organizations are deductible, but only if made for exclusively public purposes	No part of the organization's net earnings may benefit any private shareholder or individual.	Social welfare organizations may participate legally in some political activity on behalf of or in opposition to candidates for public office, but there can be no direct or indirect participation or intervention in political campaigns on behalf of or in opposition to any candidate for public office.
501(c)(5)	Labor, Agricultural, and Horticultural Organizations	Educational or instructive, the purpose being to improve conditions of work, and to improve products and efficiency	No, but it may establish a charitable fund, contributions to which are deductible. Such a fund must itself meet the requirements of section 501(c)(3) and the related notice requirements of section 508(a).	No part of the organization's net earnings may benefit any member however, payments of death, sick, accident or similar benefits to individual members does not preclude exemption.	501(C)(5) organizations may engage in some political activities.

Code Sections	Description	Nature Of Activities	Contributions	Private Inurement	Political Activities
501(c)(6)	Business Leagues, Chambers of Commerce, Real Es Boards, Etc.	Improvements of business conditions of one or more lines of business	No, but it may establish a charitable fund, contributions to which are deductible. Such a fund must itself meet the requirements of section 501(c)(3) and the related notice requirements of section 508(a).	No part of me net earnings may benefit any private shareholder or individual. The organization must be devoted to improving business conditions as distinguished from performing particular services for individual persons	501(c)(6) organizations may work for the enactment of laws to advance the common business interests of the organization's members.
501(c)(7)	Social and Recreation Clubs	Pleasure, recreation, social activities	No, but it may establish a charitable fund, contributions to which are deductible. Such a fund must itself meet the requirements of section 501(c)(3) and the related notice requirements of section 508(a).	No part of the organization's net earnings may benefit any person having a personal and private interest in the activities of the organization.	501(c)(7) organizations are not prohibited from engaging in some political activities however engaging in these activities may take them beyond the scope of their stated purpose.
501(c)(8)	Fraternal Beneficiary Societies and Associations	Lodge providing for payment of life, sickness, accident, or other benefits to members	Yes, if for certain 501(c)(3) purposes. However, dues used for the general purposes of the lodge are not deductible.	Operates under lodge systems for the exclusive benefit of the members of a fraternal organization. Provides for the payment of life, sick, accident, or other benefits to the members of the society.	501(c)(8) organizations are not prohibited from engaging in some political activities however engaging in these activities may take them beyond me scope of their stated purpose.

Code Sections	Description	Nature Of Activities	Contributions	Private Inurement	Political Activities
501(c)(9)	Voluntary Employees' Beneficiary Associations	Providing for payment of life, sickness, accident, or other benefits to members	No, but it may establish a charitable fund, contributions to which are deductible. Such a fund must itself meet the requirements of section 501(c)(3) and the related notice requirements of section 508(a).	No part of the net earnings of the association may benefit any private shareholder or individual however, it may pay life, sick, accident, and similar benefits to members or their dependents, or designated beneficiaries.	501(c)(9) organizations are not prohibited from engaging in some political activities however engaging in these activities may take them beyond the scope of their stated purpose
501(c)(10)	Domestic Fraternal Societies and Associations	Lodge devoting its net earnings to charitable, fraternal, and other specified purpose. No life, sickness, or accident benefits to members	Yes, if for certain 501(c)(3) purposes	Devotes its net earnings exclusively to religious, charitable, scientific, literary, educational, and fraternal purposes and does not provide for the payment of life, sick, accident, or other benefits to its members	501(c)(10) organizations are not prohibited from engaging in some political activities however engaging in these activities may take them beyond the scope of their stated purpose.
501(c)(11)	Teachers' Retirement Fund Associations	Teachers' association for payment of retirement benefits	No, but it may establish a charitable fund, contributions to which are deductible. Such a fund must itself meet the requirements of section 501(c)(3) and the related notice requirements of section 508(a).	No part of the net earnings benefit any private shareholder or individual however providing qualified benefits to its members does not disqualify the organization.	501(c)(11) organizations are not prohibited from engaging in some political activities however engaging in these activities may take them beyond the scope of their stated purpose.

Code Sections	Description	Nature Of Activities	Contributions	Private Inurement	Political Activities
501(c)(12)	Benevolent Life Insurance Associations, Mutual Ditch or Irrigation Companies, Mutual or Cooperative Telephone Co., etc.	Activities of a mutually beneficial nature similar to those implied by the description of class of organization	No, but it may establish a charitable fund, contributions to which are deductible. Such a fund must itself meet the requirements of section 501(c)(3) and the related notice requirements of section 508(a).	Income solely to cover losses and expenses, with any excess being returned to members or retained for future losses and expenses.	501(c)(12) organizations are not prohibited from engaging in some political activities however engaging in these activities may take them beyond the scope of their stated purpose.
501(c)(13)	Cemetery Companies	Burials and incidental activities	Yes, if for general purposes of cemetery. It is not deductible if payment for member's own plot.	No part of its net earnings may benefit any private shareholder or individual however, the cemetery companies are operated exclusively for the benefit of its lot owners who hold lots for bona fide burial purposes and not merely for re-sale.	501(c)(13) organizations are not prohibited from engaging in some political activities however engaging in these activities may take them beyond the scope of their stated purpose.
501(c)(14)	State-Charted Credit Unions, Mutual Reserve Funds	Loans to members	No, but it may establish a charitable fund, contributions to which are deductible. Such a fund must itself meet the requirements of section 501(c)(3) and the related notice requirements of section 508(a).	No part of the net earnings benefit any private shareholder or individual however providing qualified benefits to its members does not disqualify the organization.	501(c)(14) organizations are not prohibited from engaging in some political activities however engaging in these activities may take them beyond the scope of their stated purpose.

Code Sections	Description	Nature Of Activities	Contributions	Private Inurement	Political Activities
501(c)(15)	Mutual Insurance Companies or Associations	Providing insurance to members substantially at cost	No, but it may establish a charitable fund, ontributions to which are deductible. Such a fund must itself meet the requirements of section 501(c)(3) and the related notice requirements of section 508(a).	No part of the net earnings benefit any private shareholder or individual however providing qualified benefits to its members does not disqualify the organization.	501(c)(15) organizations are not prohibited from engaging in some political activities however engaging in these activities may take them beyond the scope of their stated purpose.
501(c)(16)	Cooperative Organizations to Finance Crop Operations	Financing crop operations in conjunction with activities of a marketing or purchasing association	No, but it may establish a charitable fund, contributions to which are deductible. Such a fund must itself meet the requirements of section 501(c)(3) and the related notice requirements of section 508(a).	No part of the net earnings benefit any private shareholder or individual however providing qualified benefits to its members does not disqualify the organization.	501(c)(16) organizations are not prohibited from engaging in some political activities however engaging in these activities may take them beyond the scope of their stated purpose.
501(c)(17)	Supplemental Unemployment Benefit Trusts	Provides for payment of supplemental unemployment compensation benefits	No, but it may establish a charitable fund, contributions to which are deductible. Such a fund must itself meet the requirements of section 501(c)(3) and the related notice requirements of section 508(a).	Providing qualified benefits to its members does not disqualify the organization.	501(c)(17) organizations are not prohibited from engaging in some political activities however engaging in these activities may take them beyond the scope of their stated purpose.

Code Sections	Description	Nature Of Activities	Contributions	Private Inurement	Political Activities
501(c)(18)	Employee-Funded Pension Trust(created before June 25,1959)	Payment of benefits under a pension plan funded by employees	No, but it may establish a charitable fund, contributions to which are deductible. Such a fund must itself meet the requirements of section 501(c)(3) and the related notice requirements of section 508(a).	No part of the net earnings benefit any private shareholder or individual however providing qualified benefits to its members does not disqualify the organization.	501(c)(18) organizations are not prohibited from engaging in some political activities however engaging in these activities may take them beyond the scope of their stated purpose.
501(c)(19)	Post or Organization of Past or Present Members of the Armed Forces	Activities implied by nature of organization	No, unless 90% or more members are war veterans	No part of the net earnings benefit any private shareholder or individual however providing qualified benefits to its members does not disqualify the organization.	501(c)(19) organizations are not prohibited from engaging in some political activities however engaging in these activities may take them beyond the scope of their stated purpose.
501(c)(20)	Group Legal Services Plans	Activities implied by nature of organization.	No, generally	No part of the net earnings benefit any private shareholder or individual however providing qualified benefits to its members does not disqualify the organization.	501 (c)(20) organizations are not prohibited from engaging in some political activities however engaging in these activities may take them beyond the scope of their stated purpose.

Code Sections	Description	Nature Of Activities	Contributions	Private Inurement	Political Activities
501(c)(21)	Black Lung Benefit Trusts	Funded by coal mine operators to satisfy their liability for disability or death due to black lung diseases	No, but deductible as a business expense to extent allowed by section 192	No part of the net earnings benefit any private shareholder or individual however providing qualified benefits to its members does not disqualify the organization.	501 (c)(21) organizations are not prohibited from engaging in some political activities however engaging in these activities may take them beyond the scope of their stated purpose
501(c)(22)	Withdrawal Liability Payment Fund	To provide funds to meet the liability of employers withdrawing from a multi-employer pension fund	No, but deductible as a business expense to extent allowed by section 194A	No part of the net earnings benefit any private shareholder or individual however providing qualified benefits to its members does not disqualify the organization.	501 (c)(22) organizations are not prohibited from engaging in some political activities however engaging in these activities may take them beyond the scope of their stated purpose.
501(c)(23)	Veterans Organization (created before 1880)	To provide insurance and other benefits to veterans	No, unless 90% or more members are war veterans	No part of the net earnings benefit any private shareholder or individual however providing qualified benefits to its members does not disqualify the organization.	501(c)(23) organizations are not prohibited from engaging in some political activities however engaging in these activities may take them beyond the scope of their stated purpose.
501(c)(24)	Employee Retirement Income Security Act of 1974 Trust	Holding title and paying over income from property to no more than 35 beneficiaries	No	No part of the net earnings benefit any private shareholder or individual however providing qualified benefits does not disqualify die organization.	501(c)(24) organizations are not prohibited from engaging in some political activities however engaging in these activities may take them beyond the scope of their stated purpose.

Code Sections	Description	Nature Of Activities	Contributions	Private Inurement	Political Activities
501(c)(25)	Title-Holding Corporations or Trusts with Multiple Parents	Holding title and paying over income from property to 35 or fewer parents or beneficiaries	No	No part of the net earnings benefit any private shareholder or individual however providing qualified benefits does not disqualify the organization.	501(c)(25) organizations are not prohibited from engaging in some political activities however engaging in these activities may take them beyond the scope of their stated purpose.
501(c)(26)	State-Sponsored Organization Providing Health Coverage for High-Risk Individuals	Provides health care coverage to high-risk individuals	No	No part of the net earnings of the organization can benefit any private shareholder or individual.	501(c)(26) organizations are not prohibited from engaging in some political activities however engaging in these activities may take them beyond the scope of their stated purpose.
501(c)(27)	State-Sponsored Workers' Compensation Reinsurance Organization	Reimburses members for losses under workers' compensation acts	No	No part of the net earnings benefit any private shareholder or individual however providing qualified benefits does not disqualify the organization.	501(c)(27) organizations are not prohibited from engaging in some political activities however engaging in these activities may take them beyond the scope of their stated purpose.
501(c)28	National Railroad Retirement Investment Trust established under section 15(j) of the Railroad Retirement Act of 1974 [45 USCS § 231n(j)]	Investment Trust for retired railroad workers	No	No part of the net earnings benefit any private shareholder or individual, however providing qualified benefits to its members does not disqualify the organization	501(c)28 organizations are not prohibited from engaging in some political activities, however engaging in these may take them beyond the scope of their stated purpose.

Code Sections	Description	Nature Of Activities	Contributions	Private Inurement	Political Activities
501(c)29	CO-OP health insurance issuers	A qualified nonprofit health insurance issuer (within the meaning of section 1322 of the Patient Protection and Affordable Care Act [42 USCS § 18042]) which has received a loan or grant under the CO-OP program under such section	No	No, except as provided in section 1322(c)(4) of the Patient Protection and Affordable Care Act [26 USCS § 18042(c)(4)].	No substantial part of the activities of which is carrying on propaganda, or otherwise attempting, to influence legislation, and the organization does not participate in, or intervene in (including the publishing or distributing of statements), any political campaign on behalf of (or in opposition to) any candidate for public office.
501(d)	Religious and Apostolic	Regular business activities. Communal religious community	No	No part of the net earnings benefit any private shareholder or individual.	
501(e)	Cooperative Hospital Service Organizations	Performs cooperative services for hospitals	Yes	No part of the net earnings benefit any private shareholder or individual.	Some political activities allowed however engaging in these activities may take them beyond the scope of their stated purpose.
501(f)	Cooperative Service Organizations of Operating Educational Organizations	Performs cooperative services for hospitals	Yes	No part of the net earnings benefit any private shareholder or individual	501(f) organizations are not prohibited from engaging in some political activities however engaging in these activities may take them beyond the scope of then-stated purpose.

Code Sections	Description	Nature Of Activities	Contributions	Private Inurement	Political Activities
501(k)	Child Care Organizations	Provides care for children	Yes	No part of the net earnings benefit any private shareholder or individual	501 (k) organizations are not prohibited from engaging in some political activities however engaging in these activities may take them beyond the scope of their stated purpose.
501(n)	Charitable Risk Pools	Pools certain insurance risks of 501(C)(3) organizations	Yes	No part of the net earnings benefit any private shareholder or individual however providing qualified benefits does not disqualify the organization.	501(n) organizations are not prohibited from engaging in some political activities however engaging in these activities may take them beyond the scope of their stated purpose.
521(a)	Farmers' Cooperative Associations	Cooperative marketing and purchasing for agricultural producers	No	No part of the net earnings benefit any private shareholder or individual however providing qualified benefits does not disqualify the organization.	521 organizations are not prohibited from engaging in some political activities however engaging in these activities may take them beyond the scope of their stated purpose.
527	Political Organizations	A party, committee, fund, association, etc., that directly or indirectly accepts contributions or makes expenditures for political campaigns	No	No part of the net earnings benefit any private shareholder or individual however providing qualified benefits does not disqualify the organization.	By the nature of their activities they may engage in political activities.

TABLE OF CASES

[References are to pages]

[References are to pages]

[References are to pages]

N

O

P

[References are to pages]

TABLE OF STATUTES

[References are page and footnote numbers.]

[References are page and footnote numbers.]

[References are page and footnote numbers.]

[References are page and footnote numbers.]

[References are page and footnote numbers.]

Code of Federal Regulations

[References are page and footnote numbers.]

[References are page and footnote numbers.]

[References are page and footnote numbers.]

Senate Reports

Tax Court Memoranda

[References are page and footnote numbers.]

Technical Advice Memorandum

Treasury Regulations

United States Code

STATE CODES

CALIFORNIA CORPORATE CODE

FLORIDA STATUTES

GEORGIA CODE ANNOTATED

ILLINOIS CHARITABLE TRUST ACT

ILLINOIS COMPILED STATUTES ANNOTATED

MICHIGAN COMPILED LAWS

[References are page and footnote numbers.]

MISCELLANEOUS/MODEL ACTS

[References are page and footnote numbers.]

INDEX

[References are to sections.]

[References are to sections.]

[References are to sections.]

[References are to sections.]

[References are to sections.]

[References are to sections.]

[References are to sections.]

[References are to sections.]